Elements of Sociology

Sociology

John Steckley

Fifth Edition

OXFORD
UNIVERSITY PRESS

OXFORD

UNIVERSITY PRESS

Oxford University Press is a department of the University of Oxford.
It furthers the University's objective of excellence in research, scholarship,
and education by publishing worldwide. Oxford is a registered trade mark of
Oxford University Press in the UK and in certain other countries.

Published in Canada by
Oxford University Press
8 Sampson Mews, Suite 204,
Don Mills, Ontario M3C 0H5 Canada

www.oupcanada.com

First Edition published in 2007
Second Edition published in 2010
Third Edition published in 2013
Fourth Edition published in 2017

Library and Archives Canada Cataloguing in Publication

Title: Elements of sociology : a critical Canadian introduction / John Steckley.
Names: Steckley, John, 1949- author.
Description: Fifth edition. | Includes bibliographical references and index.
Identifiers: Canadiana (print) 20190165944 | Canadiana (ebook) 20190165952 | ISBN 9780199033003
(softcover) | ISBN 9780199039111 (loose leaf) | ISBN 9780199033010 (EPUB)
Subjects: LCSH: Canada—Social conditions—Textbooks. | LCSH: Sociology—Canada—Textbooks.
Classification: LCC HM586 .S84 2020 | DDC 301.0971—dc23

Cover image: Heng Yu/EyeEm/Getty Images
Cover and interior design: Laurie McGregor

Oxford University Press is committed to our environment.
Wherever possible, our books are printed on paper which comes from
responsible sources.

Printed and bound in the United States of America

1 2 3 4 — 23 22 21 20

Elements

Contents

❸ Culture   69

4 Socialization   101

5 Social Roles, Interaction, and Organization   133

6 Deviance and Crime   163

13 Health and Ability   403

Tables and Figures

Tables

Figures

Introducing ...
Elements of Sociology

In preparing this new edition of *Elements of Sociology*, we have, from the start, kept in mind one paramount goal: to produce the most dynamic, accessible, and up-to-date introduction to sociology available to Canadian students.

This revision builds on the strengths of the highly acclaimed previous editions, and incorporates new material designed to make the text even more engaging, more thought-provoking, and more relevant to students and instructors alike. We hope that as you browse through the pages that follow, you will see why we believe *Elements of Sociology* is the most exciting and innovative textbook available to Canadian sociology students today.

Six Things That Make This a One-of-a-Kind Textbook

1. A Canadian Textbook for Canadian Students

Written by a Canadian author for Canadians readers, *Elements of Sociology* highlights the stories of the figures and events at the heart of sociological inquiry in this country: John Porter and Dorothy Smith, Aileen Ross and Daniel G. Hill, the Sixties Scoop and the Quiet Revolution, Grassy Narrows and Amber Valley, Viola Desmond and much, much more.

2. An Inclusive, Narrative Approach

Sociology is the study of people, and in *Elements of Sociology*, the people tell their stories. Students will read first-hand accounts of what it's like to fast during Ramadan, to come out to your family, to experience racism on campus, to meet the expectations of Italian parents, and to raise daughters in an era of Lingerie Barbie and La Senza Girl.

3. A Visual, Thought-Provoking Presentation

Students are challenged on every page to adopt a sociological imagination and see the sociology in everyday life. Carefully chosen photos and captions, provocative critical thinking questions, and end-of-chapter review questions all invite readers to apply the theory and take a stance.

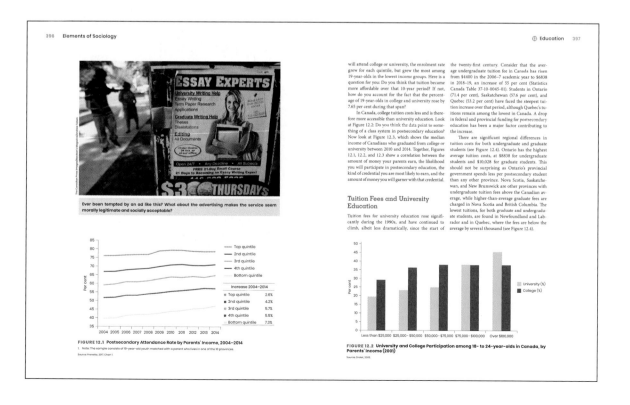

4. Coverage of Canada's Indigenous People

No sociology textbook can claim more extensive coverage of the issues that have affected and that continue to affect Canada's First Nations, Métis, and Inuit.

New! 5. Coverage of the Sociology of Dis/Ability

Reflecting the growing importance of dis/ability studies in sociology, this new edition offers wide-ranging coverage of leading dis/ability theorists and theories, from Lennard Davis and Irving Zola to Deaf culture and critical disability theory.

6. Case Studies and Compelling Viewpoints

Elements of Sociology presents three different feature boxes, scattered throughout every chapter to highlight issues, events, and ideas at the centre of sociological debate and investigation.

Telling It Like It Is

The Point Is...

Quick Hits

 Ancillary Resource Center

Student and Instructor Resources

Elements of Sociology is accompanied by a comprehensive package of online resources for students and instructors alike, all designed to enhance and complete the learning and teaching experiences. These resources are available at **www.oup.com/he/Steckley5e**.

For Instructors

- A comprehensive **instructor's manual** provides an extensive set of pedagogical tools and suggestions for every chapter, including overviews and summaries, concepts to emphasize in class, essay and research assignments, and links to relevant videos and online resources.
- Newly updated for this edition, classroom-ready **PowerPoint slides** summarize key points from each chapter and incorporate graphics and tables drawn straight from the text.
- An extensive **test generator** enables instructors to sort, edit, import, and distribute hundreds of questions in multiple-choice, true–false, and short-answer formats.
- A revised selection of carefully chosen **video clips**, matched to each chapter and available as streaming video, provide unique perspectives on themes and issues discussed in the textbook.

For Students

- *Elements of Sociology* is available in various formats, including **print**, **loose-leaf**, and—new for this edition—**enhanced ebook**, which includes all of the content as well as quizzes and reviews throughout that further enhance the learning experience.
- The **Student Study Guide** includes chapter summaries, study questions, and self-grading quizzes, as well as explore-and-discuss exercises to help you review the textbook and classroom material.

Dashboard: OUP's Learning Management System platform

Dashboard is a text-specific integrated learning system that offers quality content and tools to track student progress in an intuitive, web-based learning environment. It features a streamlined interface that connects students and lecturers with the functions used most frequently, simplifying the learning experience to save time and put student progress first.

Dashboard for *Elements of Sociology* is available through your OUP sales representative, or visit dashboard.oup.com.

 **www.oup.com/he/Steckley5e**

A Word or Two from the Author

Why Read a Sociology Text?

We live in times when it is more important than ever to be a critical consumer of social, political, medical, and environmental information. Your quality of life and the social health of your country depend on it. I know this sounds a bit extreme, but I believe it to be true. A sociology textbook (and, of course, your sociology instructor) can give you the intellectual tools that could make you such a critical consumer. Further, no matter what career you see yourself in three, ten, or eighteen years from now, you will have to be able to understand and communicate effectively with people. Again, your sociology textbook can help you here. Think of it as a literate, wise uncle/aunt, grandfather/grandmother, or elder whose opinion you value and whose advice you trust (even if you don't always take it).

Why Write a Sociology Text?

Why write a Canadian sociology textbook when there are so many out there already? I began with what I saw as an inability among introductory texts on the Canadian market to give proper voice to Indigenous and South Asian perspectives. I don't claim to have single-handedly corrected the deficiency, but by incorporating the work of authors from each group, I hope I have made a significant departure from earlier Canadian sociology textbooks.

Making "Other" Voices Heard

I realized, too, that other voices needed to be heard. While I have included the work of authors representing different ethnic backgrounds, cultures, and sexualities, I have always felt that the best way to make different voices heard is through personal narratives, which I have incorporated in each chapter. These present a variety of perspectives informed by a variety of "social locations"—trans, gay, young, old, black, Chinese, Italian, white, Muslim, Palestinian, and so on. I strongly believe that the narratives constitute one of the most important features of this textbook, and I've added more to this new edition.

> "I felt that the best way to make different voices heard was in narratives, which I have incorporated in each chapter."

Celebrating My Heroes of the Discipline

The narrative approach is not the only way in which this textbook is a little different. Some of my views are provocative, but I was tired of the dry, conservative bent of other texts, and their general failure to include much or anything about my heroes of the discipline—Dorothy Smith, Michel Foucault, Franz Fanon, Antonio Gramsci, Albert Memmi, and (apart from a perfunctory nod to his sociological imagination)

C. Wright Mills. I aimed for a more inclusive approach in covering theories and theorists, including the many women and sociologists of colour who have influenced and redirected the discipline.

"I was tired of the dry, conservative bent of other texts."

Breaking Out of the Mould

The market imperative within the broader political economy of publishing means that there is little interest in doing something different from what has already been done. It wasn't until I began the publishing process that I realized how the conservative elements within the market influenced what materialized as the final product. A low tolerance for difference and little appetite for risk mean merely reproducing what is known to have worked before. I am fortunate that Oxford, even though constrained by its own market imperative and logic, has been so supportive of my unique views and approach.

Writing for Canadian Students

A textbook is typically considered Canadian when it uses Canadian figures, Canadian data, and Canadian research—this despite the fact the text may entirely overlook the history and emergence of sociology in this country. Canadian sociology is quite different from the sociology found in Europe and the United States. For instance, the focus of early Canadian sociology was on rural life and the resource economy, which speaks to a society that is not highly urbanized or industrialized. Moreover, from the early days, the influence of the social gospel movement and social work has oriented sociology in Canada, more than its counterparts elsewhere, around issues of social justice, even today.

I am confident that this is the most Canadian introductory sociology textbook on the market. It is not an adapted American textbook with Canadian extensions; nor is it a North American textbook co-written by American and Canadian authors. I designed this book, from the ground up, as a text for Canadian students, to teach them about what I—a Canadian sociologist—have done, am doing, have failed to do, and hope others will do in the future.

"Canadian sociology is quite different from the sociology found in Europe and the US. . . . I am confident that this is the most Canadian introductory sociology textbook on the market."

Introducing New Qualitative Research Methods

While contemporary sociology still engages in foundational methods, there has been an expansion of qualitative methodological approaches that have been influenced by feminism, queer theory, poststructuralism, postcolonialism, cultural studies, and critical disability theory, many of which had been ghettoized into other disciplines, like anthropology and women's studies. These methods are not new, but they have not been part of the methodological lexicon in sociology. In order to represent contemporary sociology accurately, I went beyond a conventional discussion of quantitative and qualitative methods to include ethnographic research, case studies, and narratives, as well as content and discourse analysis, psychoanalysis, semiotics, and genealogy. I wanted to introduce students to concepts, ideas, and themes that will be recurring throughout their education, and in this way, to inspire their imagination.

Conveying the Discipline's Vitality

To give an accurate survey of sociology today means stressing what is current, what is being done, and whom is being studied. The discipline generally and the theory specifically are exciting, yet I feel this message is not conveyed to students, who often see sociology as boring or irrelevant, buried in the past. Sociological theory has shifted immensely, with influences from queer theory, feminist psychoanalysis, postcolonialism, and poststructuralism. Whether the exclusion of these influences is the result of the status quo or the belief that they are too complex for students to comprehend, it is a misrepresentation that in the end benefits no one, and one that I have tried to correct.

> "The discipline generally and the theory specifically are exciting, yet I feel this message is not conveyed to students, who often see sociology as boring or irrelevant."

Making Students Think

A casual flip through the pages of this text will reveal an abundance of photographs and other illustrations. The photos are not just pretty distractions to keep students looking at the book. They serve a purpose. I have chosen photos and have written captions that I hope will encourage students to adopt a sociological perspective. The same objective is served by the numerous critical-thinking questions scattered throughout the chapters. Inviting students to give their views is not just a critical thinking exercise; it's a recognition that our next generation of sociologists have important ideas to share—ideas well worth listening to. I hope that student readers will later in life challenge people by asking the crucial question *How do you know that?*

My Thanks

It takes a number of people to put together a book of this size and scope. First, I would like to thank the people at Oxford University Press who made major contributions to this project. David Stover I thank for suggesting (twice) that I write this book. Ian Nussbaum, who signed me on for the new edition, deserves to be acknowledged for setting things in place, as does in-house editor Eric Sinkins, who, with amazing effort and diplomatic skill, always gets the manuscript across the goal line. For this new edition, I would thank Joanne Muzak, for her careful copy editing, and Amy Gordon for her gentle nipping at my heels (she was obviously a border collie in a past life). I would like to acknowledge the following reviewers, as well as several anonymous reviewers, whose thoughtful comments and suggestions have helped to shape this edition of *Elements of Sociology*:

- **Fiona Angus**, MacEwan University
- **Sarah Beer**, Dawson College
- **Deanna Behnke-Cook**, University of Guelph
- **Taina Maki-Chahal**, Lakehead University
- **Rebecca Collins-Nelsen**, Brescia University College at Western University
- **Helene A. Cummins**, Brescia University College at Western University
- **Kristen Desjarlais-deKlerk**, Medicine Hat College
- **Laurie Forbes**, Lakehead University
- **Ryan Higgitt**, University of New Brunswick
- **Jasmin Hristov**, University of British Columbia, Okanagan
- **Kate Krug**, Cape Breton University
- **Patrick C. Lalonde**, University of Waterloo
- **Chris Martin**, Algonquin College
- **Patricia Pakvis**, King's University College at Western University
- **John Patterson**, Canadore College
- **Jen Wrye**, North Island College
- **Abdollah Zahiri**, Seneca College of Applied Arts and Technology

For helping me write the initial draft of this book, I would also like to thank several of my former colleagues at Humber. Les Takahashi, Jim Jackson, John Metcalfe, and Joey Noble all contributed to this work with their support and helpful ideas. Librarians Jennifer Rayment and Marlene Beck worked major feats of magic to make obscure articles and books appear. And I would like to thank Guy Letts for his invaluable help in earlier versions of this text.

Closer to home, there is the Steckley household menagerie: Ross our new puppy and Trudy, the dogs that are, and Wiikwaas, Egwene, and Cosmo, the beloved and terribly missed dogs that were; the parrots: Quigley, Tikkifinn, Stanee, Louis, Lime, Sam, Poccopeck, and Gus, as well as Benji, Misha, Finn, Juno, and Tika, who provided support on earlier editions. No joke—I couldn't write without their wonderful distraction. And then there is Brenda, our cat, who is always on the back of the couch to greet me at the front door when I return home.

Finally, there is my wife, Angie. She supported me through the lows and highs of this project, when I was not the easiest person to live with (either low or high). When the sands of my life shift, there is always a rock I can depend on.

John Steckley
September 2019

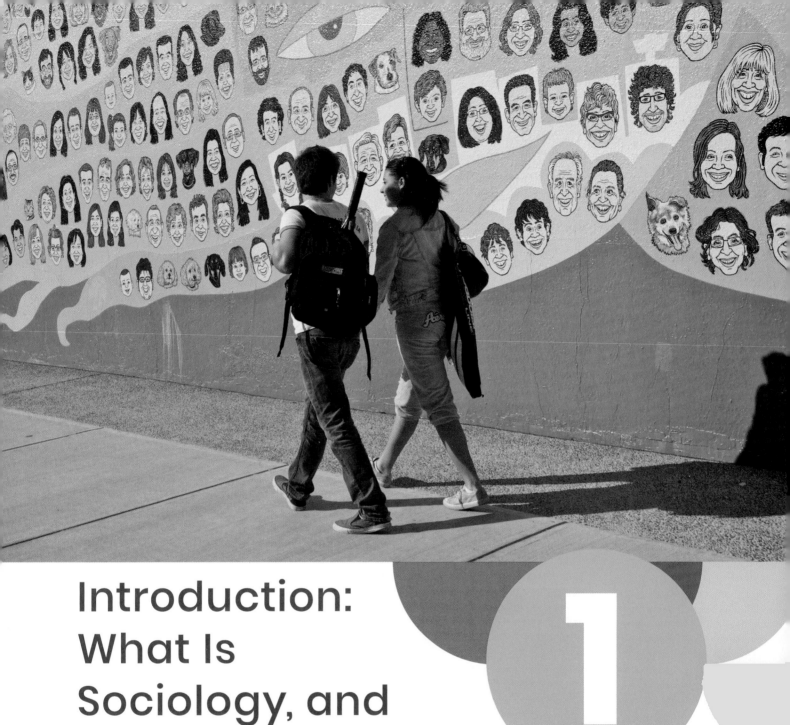

Introduction: What Is Sociology, and How Did It Begin?

Reading this chapter will help you to ...

- Know your social location and explain how it shapes your perspective on the world around you.
- Explain what the sociological imagination is and how it helps students of sociology understand society.
- State the factors that spurred the growth of sociology in Europe and North America.
- Trace the development of sociology in Canada.
- Identify and explain the five main approaches sociologists use to pursue their inquiries.
- Distinguish the four types of sociology based on audience.

For Starters

Doughnut Shops, Drive-Throughs, and the Value of Sociology

I am a big fan of coffee-and-doughnut shops. When I go to a doughnut shop, I savour the experience: I park my car, walk in, chat with the server, and enjoy the social aspect of the transaction. I have never used a drive-through (or a "drive-thru"). I believe this would limit the overall experience—the socializing with fellow patrons, the customer service, the ritual of surveying the assortment of doughnuts and choosing the perfect one. For that matter, it doesn't really save time, based on my informal observations.

I often wondered why some people use the drive-through instead of parking and coming into the shop. Who would rather interact over an intercom and receive their orders through a pickup window? I long thought it was either young men too attached to their cars to leave them

unattended in the parking lot, or else lazy, unfit, older men who drive everywhere rather than walk.

My opinion changed because of a student in one of my sociology classes. He carried out his own study, in Newmarket, north of Toronto. He spent an hour one morning in the parking lot of the local doughnut shop, taking notes on who was using the drive-through and who was walking in through the front door. Over that period, he observed 91 people walk in and 95 people drive through. And he did notice a gender difference in the two groups, but not the one I had predicted: in terms of the counter sales, 42 of the customers were women and 49 were men, but of the drive-through patrons, 70 were women and just 25 were men. The student also observed that compared with middle-aged and older women,

young women were much more likely—by a ratio of nearly 7 to 1—to use the drive-through. This was in stark contrast to the male drive-through customers, among whom there was a roughly 1 to 1 ratio of the two age-determined groups.

Another statistic enabled the student to come up with a hypothesis to account for the results of his research. He observed that compared with the parked cars of the walk-in clientele, the cars entering the drive-through were more likely to have child seats in them. Further, he often identified young children among the passengers of the drive-through vehicles.

The student's hypothesis was that at that hour and at that location, young mothers with infants and toddlers were significantly more likely to use the drive-through because it was easier than going through the complicated process of unbuckling their children and bringing them into the restaurant. To be really convincing, his hypothesis would have to be tested for other times and locations, but it presented a compelling example of how sociology can be used to challenge assumptions (mine, in this case) and better understand the social world around us.

Introduction: Why This Textbook Is a Little Different

This textbook is not like the others. It will offer candid observations, occasional humour, and lots of stories told from the perspective of the author (me), my students, and my colleagues in **sociology**. In keeping with contemporary sociological terminology, I call these stories **narratives**. Narratives make up an important branch of sociological literature, one recognizing that to properly understand someone's situation, we need to hear the person's story told in their own words, or "voice." For this reason, every chapter of this textbook will make use of narratives to illustrate key points and concepts.

Another difference between this book and others is that it will not be some mysteriously anonymous account of the discipline. I will not ask you to imagine that it tumbled out of the hands of the gods as the One True Book of Sociology. Instead, I invite you to accept it as my educated but not infallible views on the subject. So you should know some things about me before you read on. My name is John, and I will be your author for the next 15 chapters. I am a white male who has taught and written about sociology and anthropology for over 40 years. I am old enough that I was a hippie (*not* a hipster) before the word was in common use. I still have long hair and a longer beard. I was born and raised in a middle-class family in Don Mills, then a suburb of

Toronto, and have lived for the last 20 some years in the village of Bolton, a little north of the Big Smoke. I am a diabetic, but generally I am abled and healthy. Over the course of this book, you will learn several

THE CANADIAN PRESS/Adrian Wyld

Former Attorney General Jody Wilson-Raybould, testifying at a justice committee hearing into allegations of government interference in the judicial process, was given the opportunity to present what she called "my truth." She is an Indigenous person who traces her heritage to three of the member tribes of the Kwakwaka'wak nation, referred to historically (and inaccurately) as Kwakiutl. What is the difference between an abstract notion of "truth" and one person's own truth? Which truth would you expect to find in a narrative?

things about me—about my passion for preserving Indigenous languages, my love of parrots (we currently have eight), my (once fraught) relationship with my two stepsons, to cite just a few examples. These details, which inform every page of this book, are important aspects of my **social location**, which you should be aware of. After all, how else can you read this book critically, the way you're meant to? You might occasionally find yourself saying, "It is not surprising that an old, white, middle-class man (two weeks from 70 as I write this) from suburban Toronto would say that." Assessing the context in which a piece of knowledge (like a textbook) is produced is an important part of thinking like a sociologist.

There are two basic strategies that a textbook writer can take. One is to create a kind of reference book that touches on pretty much every conceivable topic within the discipline. That sort of book can be good for students who need support outside of the

The Point Is...

Your Social Location Gives You a Unique Perspective

If I were to say that television does a poor job of representing diversity, would you agree or disagree?

One of the aims in writing this textbook is to help you appreciate the importance of your social location to the way you interpret events and the experiences of others. Your social location is the set of social traits that informs your views on the world around you. Consider the following questions:

- Are you over or under the age of 20? 30?
- What is your assigned sex?
- What is your gender? (Think it's the same thing? It's not, as we'll see in Chapter 9.)
- What is your ethnic background? Where are your parents from? What about your parents' parents?
- Would you say you've grown up in an upper-class, middle-class, or lower-class neighbourhood? And is that neighbourhood in the city, the suburbs, or a small town?
- Do you have a medical condition that affects your everyday experience? It could be something visible like having to use a wheelchair or glasses, or something invisible like an anxiety disorder or ADHD.
- Do you feel like you're part of "the mainstream"?

Your answers to these questions combine to produce your social location, which gives you a unique set of experiences and outlook on the world around you. When one of these traits sets you apart from the mainstream—say, you identify as transgender, or you use a hearing aid—we can predict a pattern of social behaviour that involves discrimination against you because these traits tend to be negatively valued by society generally. We can also predict that the discrimination you face will be different if your social location involves two or more variables that set you apart from the mainstream—say, you identify as transgender and you use a hearing aid. At the same time, holding two or more traits that are generally valued by society—say, being white and being wealthy—can place you in a position of social privilege. The idea that two or more traits can combine, or "intersect," to increase your experience of discrimination or privilege is known as **intersectionality**, a topic we will consider further in Chapter 8.

Now, look around you: How many people do you think share your social location? Not too many will share your exact social location, although many of those around you will share certain aspects of it.

So, how do you think you might respond to the question above—the one about diversity and television—if you were a second-generation Iranian American? What if you were a member of a First Nations band who grew up on a reserve in Manitoba? Or an intersex person who identifies as female? Or a wheelchair athlete? See how your perspective on that question changes depending on where you're socially located?

classroom or away from the instructor. The other approach is to write a book that arouses the curiosity of the reader as a student of the discipline, even if only for one semester. That is what I'm trying to do here. In other words, I have tried to avoid writing a textbook you will lose interest in because it tries to introduce you to too much, too quickly.

Introduction to Sociology

Sociologists notice social patterns. Things tend to happen differently to you depending on your sex, age, class, ethnicity, "race," religion, sexual orientation, and ability. If you are a woman, for instance, you typically pay more in Canada for a haircut and to have your shirt dry-cleaned than you would if you were a man (Vermond, 2016). You are not paying more because the service you receive is any different: it's just that your hair and your shirt, because they are designated as "female," are subject to what

we call the "pink tax," making them more expensive to cut and to clean (respectively). You may also find it hard to take a one-handed photo with a smartphone, because as several writers have noted, smartphones are built to accommodate (typically) larger male hands (Ryan, 2013; Criado-Perez, 2019). If you are a young black man driving a car at night, you are more likely than a young white male driver to be pulled over by the police: you are guilty of the offence known facetiously as "driving while black"; that's another social pattern. South Asian students of mine have told me that they have been pulled over for "driving while brown."

What if you are a young, white, heterosexual male? If you are, you occupy a privileged social location (congratulations). You have never experienced the kind of discrimination that comes from being elderly, black, gay, or female. At the same time, you may find that in some environments—the college classroom of the twenty-first century, for instance—your experience as a white male is not always valued. And you

Joe Sohm/Visions of America/UIG via Getty Images

Would you take a $20 haircut from this barber? Or would you pay considerably more to receive the same haircut from a stylist at a salon? Women typically pay more than men do to have their hair cut: How do you account for this social pattern?

The Point Is...

If You're Reading This, You Probably Support Legal Weed

That's not just a hunch—it's based on research.

According to a poll conducted by the Canadian market research company Forum Research in October 2018—the same month that recreational marijuana became legal in this country—Canadians under the age of 35 were more likely to favour (74 per cent) than to oppose (22 per cent) legalized cannabis (Forum Research, 2018). In fact, there is a direct relationship between age and approval of legalization: the older you are, the more likely you are to disapprove of cannabis legalization (see Figure 1.1).

What does the information presented in Figure 1.1 mean? It doesn't mean that three-quarters of adults under 35 are regular pot users. In fact, only 58 per cent of those under 35 said they had tried cannabis. This means that a number of Canadians under 35 who have never even tried cannabis nevertheless approve of its legalization.

What about Canadians 65 and older, 55 per cent of whom disapprove of legalization? Can we put their negativity down to bad pot experiences? Alas, the survey found that only 22 per cent of those 65 and over had used cannabis, meaning that a good number of people in this age category disapprove of marijuana without ever having tried it. I belong to the 65-and-over category, and I can state that I smoked as a teenager but haven't in decades. I approve of its legalization, but I've long been an exception to my age group on a number of issues.

What we can take from the research, I think, is that younger people are more open to the cannabis legalization in the same way they are more liberal-minded on a number of social issues, such as same-sex marriage. They have lived in times when pot use was more open and less subject to censure than it was when the 65+ generation were teenagers. In the 1950s and 1960s, society was still under the influence of a powerful and largely misleading anti-marijuana propaganda campaign that linked cannabis with crime (see Zhang, 2017).

What else does the research tell us? Men are a little more likely than women to support the legalization of marijuana (56% versus 48%) and are more likely than women to have a somewhat or very positive view of marijuana generally (36% versus 32%) (Forum Research, 2018). Residents of Quebec and Alberta have the lowest opinion of cannabis and are the least likely to support its legalization (Figure 1.2).

Some of these findings may surprise you. If they don't, it's either because you're following Forum's Instagram feed or, more likely, because you've noticed patterns in the comments you've heard people make about marijuana legalization, in the media, among your peers, at family get-togethers, and so on. If so, congratulations: noticing these social patterns is an important part of doing sociology. If not, don't worry: we'll get you there.

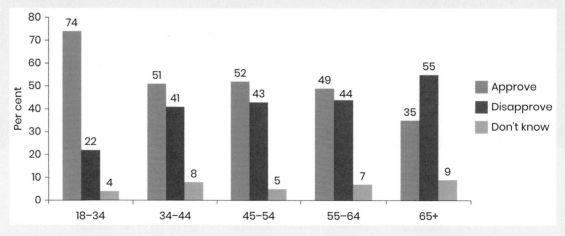

FIGURE 1.1 Canadians' Support for Legalized Cannabis by Age, October 2018

Source: Forum Research, 2018.

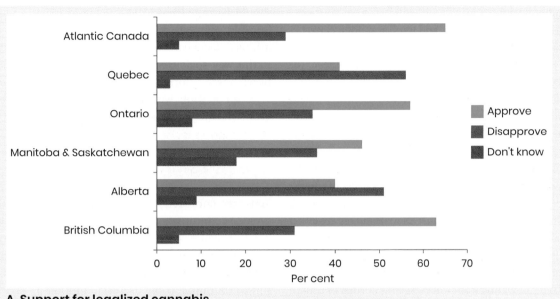

A. Support for legalized cannabis

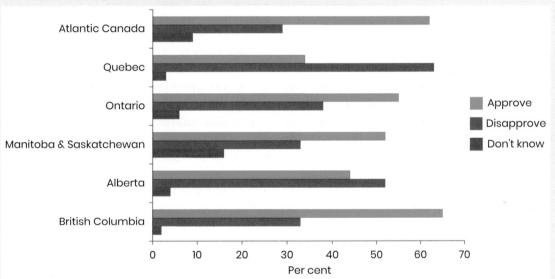

B. Support for the sale of cannabis edibles (cookies, bars, drinks, etc.)

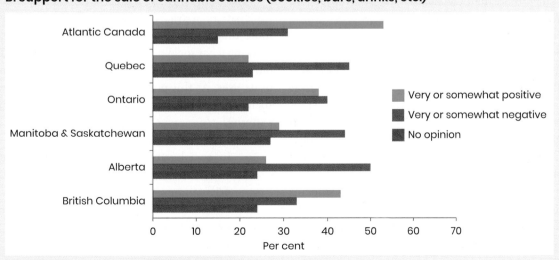

C. Feelings about cannabis generally

FIGURE 1.2 Canadians' Feelings about Cannabis by Region, October 2018

Source: Forum Research, 2018.

might be poor, finding it difficult to pay for your education, accommodation, and food, and not feel particularly "privileged." That is another social pattern.

Sociologists also investigate and challenge the social patterns that other people perceive. For example, why do so many people, even those in the medical profession, assume that male nurses are gay? This stereotype has never been demonstrated statistically, in part because it would be highly unethical to ask a male nurse about his sexual preferences. Sociologists studying the subject might investigate the effects of movies like *Meet the Parents* (2000—a little before your time), where characters declare that all male nurses are either gay or, at the very least, "sissies." Does this stereotype discourage men from entering the nursing profession for fear of being seen as *deviant* (by which we mean simply deviating from what is seen as normal or usual)?

Sociology and Issues

Sociology can help students understand issues facing society today. A divisive social issue of recent years is the legalization of marijuana for recreational use. Since October 2018, Canadians from sea to sea have been able to smoke marijuana legally. However, a poll conducted at the time of legalization suggested that many Canadians remain strongly opposed to the new law. What can sociologists tell us about this issue?

Sociology can't say what is moral, or "right," in an issue such as this. There isn't a scientific way of measuring that. But sociology *can* tell us about who tends to be in favour of Canada's new marijuana laws: younger people, those with a higher annual income, men more than women, and East and West Coast Canadians more than Canadians living between Quebec and Alberta. As well, sociology can speak about who tends to be against legalized marijuana: people 65 and older, those making between $20,000 and $40,000 annually, and people living in Quebec (Forum Research, 2018). Beyond this, sociology might also help students understand the impact that socializing influences such as parents and the media have on their own opinions about marijuana. You can have more choice in forming your own opinion when you understand what has helped to shape it in the past.

This leads to a question that sociology students often ask: How come I got a low mark when it's just an opinion and there are no right or wrong answers? Everyone has a right to an opinion; however, people should become knowledgeable about issues before forming opinions on them. Sociology gives us a means to form considered opinions on social issues. In this way, sociology helps students distinguish between a well-informed opinion and an uninformed view spouted off without careful thought (say, by peers who aren't taking sociology).

What Is Sociology?

You may have noticed that so far I have cleverly avoided defining what sociology is. That's because it's not a straightforward thing to do, and in some ways not particularly useful. Defining something is very different from understanding it. I could give you a simple (but not terribly useful) definition by saying that *sociology is the systematic or scientific study of society*. Can you imagine the multiple-choice questions that could come from that?

Sociology is:

a) the systematic study of society
b) the unsystematic study of society
c) "statistical stuff and heavy-duty theoretical bullshit" (see Mills, below)
d) all of the above.

The answer could easily be the final one, "all of the above." I could just as easily refer you to the glossary at the back of this book, where **sociology** is defined as "the social science that studies the development, structure, and functioning of human society." Does that help?

The truth is, giving a precise, all-encompassing explanation of what sociology *is* would be much more difficult (and probably less useful) than explaining what sociology *does*. This is why I've begun our introduction to sociology by highlighting some of its uses. At this point it is enough to know that sociology involves looking for and looking at social patterns

- in social variables, such as age, gender, "race," ethnicity, religion, ability, and sexual orientation;
- in social institutions, such as education, religion, and the family; and
- in social interactions.

Quick Hits

Sociology and Related Disciplines

Academic disciplines are artificial constructions. There is nothing "natural" about the borderlines that separate sociology from other established disciplines such as anthropology, economics, history, psychology, philosophy, or political science. These various fields have much in common, and there is a lot of cross-referencing in the books and articles written by specialists in each discipline.

Students who have taken courses in psychology, anthropology, or philosophy will notice that sociology regularly encroaches on their territory. At the same time, you will find that people teaching such varied subjects as Canadian studies, communication, criminology, cultural studies, education, Indigenous studies, international relations, and women's studies often have degrees in sociology.

TABLE 1.1 Sociology and Related Disciplines

Discipline	Emphasis
anthropology	The comparative study of human societies and cultures and the way they developed.
economics	The production and consumption of wealth, including the distribution of goods and services among individuals and groups.
philosophy	Major thinkers and turns of thought in particular societies, and how they have addressed the major questions of life.
political science	Systems of government and how they serve citizens.
psychology	The human mind, the social and biological influences on it, and its functions, especially those affecting behaviour.
social work	The way our understanding of society and individuals can be applied to improving people's well-being.
sociology	The development, structure, and functioning of human society, especially as seen in group interaction, social relations, social institutions, and social structures.

By the time you've reached the end of this textbook, I hope that you will have formed your own idea of what sociology really *is*.

Why Study Sociology?

Studying sociology helps you obtain a greater understanding of the *social world*, which encompasses the social practices, attitudes, and institutions that surround us. Studying sociology will also help you to better understand yourself in terms of whether you follow or do not follow patterns of social behaviour predicted by sociological variables. Imagine two first-year sociology students: one is an 18-year-old white woman from Montreal's wealthy Westmount neighbourhood, whose parents are both employed and hold post-secondary degrees; the other is a 30-year-old immigrant from Haiti, who is living in the rough-and-tumble borough of Montréal-Nord and who is the first member of his family to go to university. One situation is predicted by the sociological variables; the other is not.

Sociology, in this way, helps you develop an understanding about others around you in the multicultural and generally diverse social world that is Canada, as well as in the smaller social worlds of neighbourhoods, classrooms, social media sites, pubs, and workplaces. Thinking more globally, sociology helps you better understand the larger world of nations and their social institutions.

Telling It Like It Is   An Author's POV

Not a Sociological Phenomenon, Eh?

In August 2014, after 15-year-old Tina Fontaine's lifeless body was found wrapped in a bag in the Red River in Winnipeg, Indigenous rights groups and women's rights activists called on the government to hold an inquiry into why Indigenous women are disproportionately targeted for murder and other violent crime. In response, then Prime Minister Stephen Harper said that violent crime involving Indigenous women was not a "sociological phenomenon" but a series of more or less isolated incidents best left to the police. Sociology instructors across the nation said, "Thank you, Stephen, for helping me write my first lecture of the semester."

Sociology, as we have just seen, involves looking for patterns predicted by sociological variables—age, "race," sex, gender, class, and ability. When we consider Indigenous women living in Canada, we can say that they have at least three strikes against them: they are Indigenous, they are usually poor, and they are women, embodying three traits that mainstream society judges negatively. This makes it easier for people to treat them violently and to exploit them sexually; it makes it easier for politicians and the media to neglect their problems and for police to treat them like non-humans. It makes it easy for someone like Stephen Harper, who is white, wealthy, male, and powerful, to say that the killing of Tina Fontaine was just an isolated crime; after all, the variables that make up his social location rule. Imagine if powerful white men started to disappear and turn up dead in disproportionate numbers. Do you think these would be treated as isolated crimes?

Indigenous women are far more likely than other women, and other Canadians, to be victims of homicide, domestic violence, and violence generally; they are more likely to go missing or enter the sex trade; they are more likely to have grown up in foster care, and they are more likely to be teenage parents and lone (i.e. single) parents. That Indigenous women are represented in unusually large numbers in these statistical findings is an example of what sociologists call **disproportionate representation**. This is a sociological phenomenon. It does not take a lot of sociological imagination to realize that.

The Heart of Sociology: The Sociological Imagination

One of sociology's most useful instruments is the **sociological imagination**. The term was coined by C. Wright Mills (1916–1962), who sums it up nicely as

> the capacity to shift from one perspective to another—from the political to the psychological; from examination of a single family to comparative assessment of the national budgets of the world. . . . It is the capacity to range from the most impersonal and remote transformations to the most intimate features of the human self—and to see the relationship between the two. (1959, p. 4)

Mills argues that when we create and communicate sociological knowledge, our ideas must show "how society works" in terms of our own personal lives. If you go to buy a good pair of rubber boots (as my wife did), and the only ones you can get are yellow and relatively flimsy, then you are likely a woman, and your own frustrating shopping experience reflects the way society thinks of and treats women in general.

What happens when we fail to exercise our sociological imagination is discussed by Henry Giroux in *Beyond the Spectacle of Terrorism: Global Uncertainty and the Challenge of the New Media* (2006). Commenting on the lack of sociological imagination in the post-9/11 political posturing of George W. Bush, Giroux warned that "[d]emocracy begins to fall and political life becomes impoverished when society can no longer translate private problems into social issues" (2006, p. 1). He spelled this out in detail in a chapter called "Acts of Translation":

> As the very idea of the social collapses into the private realm of the self and its fears, it becomes more difficult for people

The Point Is...

C. Wright Mills Was a Rebel with a Cause

In my first year of university, the sociologist who fed my imagination was C. Wright Mills. He took on the rich and powerful and challenged his conservative colleagues and his country's government in the staid and stuffy 1950s. His public critique of American society caught the attention of the FBI, who started a file on him. He rode a motorcycle to work, and dressed in plaid shirts, old jeans, and work boots. Mills became my first sociologist hero.

Mills published seven books. These include two trilogies and an important stand-alone volume that gave its name to a key characteristic of the very best sociologists and sociology students: *The Sociological Imagination* (1959). His first trilogy, a study of the three main socioeconomic classes in the United States, comprises *The New Men of Power: America's Labor Leaders* (1948), *White Collar: The American Middle Classes* (1951), and *The Power Elite* (1956). The last of these found a wide and varied audience that included the then young Cuban revolutionary Fidel Castro, who, after he had overthrown the American-backed dictator Fulgencio Batista, invited Mills to visit so they could discuss his ideas. After the book was translated into Russian, Mills was asked to visit Moscow.

In the early 1950s, Mills issued a challenge to those writing sociology. Responding in a letter to a question about whether sociology writing could be improved, Mills wrote,

> It doesn't look good. I think for two reasons: First, there is no real writing tradition in sociology, as there is, for example, in history. It just doesn't exist. Second, the field is now split into statistical stuff and heavy duty theoretical bullshit. In both cases, there's no writing but only turgid polysyllabic slabs of stuff. So, because that is now the field, no men get trained, have models to look up to; there is no aspiration to write well. (2001, pp. 154–5)

While Mills himself has disproved the first point, the second critique stands. So much of sociological writing is mired in jargon and fails to resonate with a broad audience. So sociologists and sociology students, your duty is clear. Prove him wrong and aspire to write well, avoiding the "theoretical bullshit" and "polysyllabic slabs"!

Photo by Yaroslava Mills

Consider this photo of C. Wright Mills: Does he look like an educator to you? Why or why not?

to develop a vocabulary for understanding how individual insecurity, dread, and misery could be translated into concerns of an engaged and critical citizenry. Instead, they are told that their privately held misery is a fall from grace, a flaw in character that must be suffered in isolation. Poverty, for example, is now imagined to be a problem of individual failing. Racism is rationalized and represented as simply an act of individual discrimination or prejudice. Homelessness is reduced to a freely chosen decision made by lazy people. (Giroux, 2006, p. 4)

In other words, without the sociological imagination, the individual, not society, becomes the primary focus of blame. The sociological imagination enables us to see an individual's circumstances in the context of broader social forces that affect us all and warrant our attention.

The Origins of Sociology

People since ancient times have contemplated social systems and looked for patterns in human social relationships. Perhaps the earliest person whose recorded writings reflect a true sociological imagination is the Chinese philosopher **Confucius** (c. 551–479 BCE). A strong proponent of role modelling—a topic discussed often in sociology today—Confucius believed it was better for leaders to engage in moral practices that modelled the principles they wanted their citizens to follow than to overuse laws to enforce morality. In his words, "If you use laws to direct the people, and punishments to control them, they will merely try to evade the laws, and will have no sense of shame" (Kaizuka, 2002, p. 126). We can all think of politicians who would have benefitted from following the wise sociological advice of Confucius.

While Confucius's teachings touched on some important sociological themes, the first person to carry out a systematic study of sociological subjects and set his thoughts down in writing is most likely Arab scholar **Ibn Khaldûn** (1332–1406). In his *Kitâb al-'Ibâr*, or "Book of Lessons" (which is actually seven books), he examined various types of societies

What Do YOU Think?

Even if you're new to sociology, you might have heard of people like Marx, Durkheim, and Weber before picking up this textbook, yet you probably hadn't heard of Ibn Khaldûn. Why do you think that Ibn Khaldûn has only recently been recognized for his contributions to the development of sociology?

and their histories, cultures, and economies. The introductory volume, *Al Muqaddimah* (*An Introduction to History*), contains a wealth of research on, and insights into, the cyclical rise and fall of powerful tribes and nations.

The Development of Sociology in Europe

Sociology became an area of academic interest in nineteenth-century Europe, specifically in France, Germany, and Britain. It developed in response to the dramatic social changes taking place at that time: industrialization, urbanization, and significant population increases. Cities were growing rapidly, both because of natural population increases and because of the dramatic influx of people from the countryside looking for jobs in newly minted factories. Concerned scholars such as the economist **Thomas Malthus** (1766–1834), a forerunner of modern sociologists, began to wonder whether Europe's cities could cope with such tremendous population growth. The politics of the time were also favourable to the growth of sociology, with the French Revolution in particular providing evidence

What Do YOU Think?

1. Why do you think it was that sociology developed in Europe rather than Africa, the Middle East, China, or South Asia?
2. How might sociology have developed differently as a discipline if the early thinkers had been African, Middle Eastern, Chinese, or South Asian?

that citizens could bring about social change swiftly and on a massive scale.

Max Weber: A Founder of Modern Sociology

One example of the intellectual impact of early sociology is seen in the work of German sociologist **Max Weber** (pronounced VAY-ber; 1864–1920). One of his most important and well-known contributions was his identification of a set of values embodied in early Protestantism, which he called the **Protestant (work) ethic**. He believed that these values contributed significantly to the development of modern capitalism.

Weber's theory was based on a number of related ideas. One is the notion, popular among early Protestants, that there is a predestined "elect," a group of people who have been chosen to be "saved" during the Second Coming of Christ. Naturally, it was important to early Protestants to be seen as part of this exclusive group. Success through hard work was considered one proof of membership; another was the accumulation of **capital** (money and other assets used to generate money, like factories) through hard work and thriftiness. Working hard, making profitable use of one's time, and living a materially *ascetic* (self-denying) life by acquiring property and saving rather than spending lavishly are all principles of Weber's Protestant work ethic. As Weber explained,

> The span of human life is infinitely short and precious to make sure of one's own election. Loss of time through sociability, idle talk, luxury, even more sleep than is necessary for health . . . is worthy of absolute moral condemnation. . . . [Time] is infinitely valuable because every hour lost is lost to labour for the glory of God. Thus inactive contemplation is also valueless, or even directly reprehensible if it is at the expense of one's daily work. For it is less pleasing to God than the active performance of His will in a calling. (1930, pp. 157–8)

Weber later elaborated on how demonstrating these values represents proof of being one of God's chosen

few, and how these values supposedly fuelled the rise of capitalism:

> The religious valuation of restless, continuous, systematic work in a worldly calling, as the . . . surest and most evident proof of rebirth and genuine faith, must have been the most powerful conceivable lever for the expansion of . . . the spirit of capitalism. (1958, p. 172)

Although the idea of the Protestant (work) ethic took hold firmly enough that it entered popular thought and speech, it was never demonstrated sociologically that capitalism developed primarily in Protestant rather than in Catholic countries, or that the work ethic Weber associated with Protestantism was somehow missing from other religions. Latin American scholars argue that the rise of capitalism began with colonialism, a movement in which Catholic Spain and Portugal were major early players. Weber paid little attention to the role that colonialism played in the rise of capitalism as an instrument for exploiting colonized countries. Spain looted Aztec and Inca gold to become, for a time, the richest country in Europe. Weber, by attributing the development of capitalism to the strength of the Protestant will, might have been trying too hard to account for the relatively recent economic and political superiority of European Protestants.

What Do YOU Think?

Marianne Weber, the wife of Max Weber, was a sociologist in her own right. She was a public figure in German social and political circles, and was well known for her writings on marriage and divorce, women's work inside and outside the home, and the changing role of women in a patriarchal society. She outlived Max Weber by over 30 years, and edited 10 volumes of his work for posthumous publication. Why do you think her own work is only now beginning to receive critical attention in the English-speaking world?

TABLE 1.2 Some Early European Sociologists and Their Contributions

Sociologist (years, nationality)	Key Works	Contribution
Auguste Comte (1798–1857, French)	• *The Course in Positivist Philosophy* (1830–42) • *A General View of Positivism* (1848)	A proponent of positivist philosophy, he aimed to develop a social science that could be used for social reconstruction.
Harriet Martineau (1802–1876, British)	• *Illustrations of Political Economy* (1834) • *Society in America* (1837)	Widely viewed as the first woman sociologist, she wrote extensively on social, economic, and historical topics and translated several of Comte's works.
Karl Marx (1818–1883, German)	• *The German Ideology* (1846) • *The Communist Manifesto* (1848, with Friedrich Engels) • *Capital* (1867)	The founder of modern communism, he viewed social change in terms of economic factors.
Herbert Spencer (1820–1903, British)	• *Social Statistics* (1851) • *First Principles* (1862) • *The Study of Sociology* (1873)	Social evolutionist sought to apply Darwin's theory of natural selection to human societies and coined the term "survival of the fittest."
Friedrich Nietzsche (1844–1900, German)	• *Human, All Too Human* (1878) • *Beyond Good and Evil* (1886) • *On the Genealogy of Morals* (1887) • *The Will to Power* (1901)	Philosopher rejected Christianity's compassion for the weak and championed the "will to power" and the *Übermensch* ("superman"), who could rise above the restrictions of ordinary morality.
Émile Durkheim (1858–1917, French)	• *The Division of Labour in Society* (1893) • *The Rules of the Sociological Method* (1895) • *Suicide* (1897) • *The Elementary Forms of the Religious Life* (1912)	Among the first to consider society as a legitimate subject of scientific observation, he studied society in terms of "social facts" such as ethics, occupations, and suicide.
Georg Simmel (1858–1918, German)	• *On Social Differentiation* (1890) • *The Philosophy of Money* (1900) • *Sociology: Investigations on the Forms of Sociation* (1908)	Father of microsociology studied the way people experience the minutiae of daily life.
Max Weber (1864–1920, German)	• *The Protestant Ethic and the Spirit of Capitalism* (1904–5) • *Economy and Society* (1922)	Identified a set of values, the "Protestant (work) ethic," to which he attributed the rise of capitalism.
Antonio Gramsci (1891–1937, Italian)	• *Prison Notebooks* (1948)	Marxist theorist and co-founder of Italy's Communist Party developed a theory of hegemony and power while in prison for political activism.

Note: We have identified all works by their English titles, although several of these works first appeared, in the years indicated, in languages other than English.

What Do YOU Think?

Look at the list of early sociologists in Table 1.2. Why are most of them men?

The Spread of Sociology to North America

During the late nineteenth and early twentieth centuries in North America, the emergence of conditions similar to those that existed already in Europe—the arrival of millions of immigrants, the development of cities and urban life, and the growing impact of technology on the daily lives of individuals—spurred the growth of sociology. Social change happened quickly in the United States, which was undergoing a rapid transition from an essentially rural society to a nation of fast-growing urban centres revolving around industry and commerce. This development came with considerable human costs, as people were pressed into severely inadequate living and working conditions, and large cities were divided into ethnic communities or ghettos. Social scientists in the United States were inspired to study the new ways that Americans were living, working, and sharing space, and one of the country's oldest sociology departments, at the University of Chicago, arose primarily as a way of understanding the problems associated with the rapid immigration of thousands of Europeans to the American city.

Canada underwent urbanization and industrialization at a slower rate and, as we will see shortly, had a different set of social concerns that fuelled the growth of sociology in this country. But like Canadian politics, Canadian entertainment media, and Canadian culture generally, our sociology was not untouched by what was happening south of the border, and several of Canada's early sociologists had ties to the Chicago school, which had a significant influence on the development of sociology across the continent.

Chicago: The City as Training Ground for Aspiring Sociologists

In the latter half of the nineteenth century, Chicago exemplified the conditions that were conducive to the birth and growth of academic sociology. It became the second largest city in the United States, thanks to spectacular rates of immigration, which fostered the growth of ethnic communities. At the same time, working conditions, particularly in the city's notorious stockyards, were spectacularly bad.

It is little surprise, then, that Chicago was central to much of the early history of sociology not just in the United States but in North America. With its founding in 1892, the University of Chicago's Department of Sociology became the first sociology department in North America, and during the 1920s and 1930s, the "Chicago school" became synonymous with both the specialized subdiscipline of urban sociology and a number of prominent sociologists, including Robert Park, Ernest Burgess, Everett C. Hughes, George Herbert Mead, Edwin Sutherland, and Jane Addams.

The Chicago School: Park, Burgess, and Addams
Robert E. Park

The leading figure of the Chicago school of sociology, **Robert Park** (1864–1944) travelled a long road before settling down as a sociologist. He taught for a year at Harvard but left the university to work with the African American educator and activist Booker T. Washington (1856–1915) at the Tuskegee Institute in Alabama. It was not until 1914 that Park joined the faculty of the University of Chicago, where he taught until his retirement in 1933. It was there that, with Ernest Burgess, he wrote what was considered at the time the "bible" of introductory sociology textbooks, *Introduction to the Science of Sociology* (1921). It continued to exert a tremendous impact on the discipline long after the two authors had died.

Park was a pioneer in urban sociology, based largely on his work in Chicago. His research was focused on the concept of human ecology, which views the city as the main habitat for the human species, the same way that an African jungle may be home to the needle-clawed bushbaby or the Senegal parrot (my examples). The city was Park's laboratory, and he was a consummate observer. My favourite quotation about him comes from the German sociologist René König: "You must imagine Park as a tireless pedestrian, roaming through Chicago in every direction, this way and that, noting down his observations as he goes" (1978; quoted in Lindner, 1996, p. 1). König's description captures the spirit of ethnography, the main research method used by Park and the Chicago school. (There will be more on ethnography in Chapter 2.)

Ernest Burgess

A formative member of the Chicago school, Ernest Burgess (1886–1966) was, like Park, an urban sociologist. His field of study is surprising when you consider that he was born and raised in tiny Lidbury, Ontario, a village that was not even incorporated as a town until 1910. As well as co-authoring *Introduction to the Science of Sociology*, Burgess collaborated with Park and Roderick McKenzie to produce a classic study of urban sociology, *The City: Suggestions for the Study of Human Nature in the Urban Environment* (Park, Burgess, & McKenzie, [1925] 1967).

Burgess was one of those sociologists who added a physics-like statistical precision to the field, particularly when it came to making predictions (something sociologists are often hesitant to do). In his research in criminology, one of sociology's subfields, he developed a 21-point scoring system to measure the likelihood that an inmate on parole would reoffend (Burgess, 1928). Modified versions of Burgess's criminology scale are still used, but not all of his statistical measures have survived the test of time. In *Predicting Success or Failure in Marriage* (Burgess & Cottrell, 1939)—an interesting project for a man who never married—he introduced a rubric for gauging the strength of a marriage; neither love nor affection were among the variables taken into account in this system.

TABLE 1.3 Some Early American Sociologists and Their Contributions

Sociologist	Key Works	Contribution
William Graham Sumner (1840–1910)	• *Folkways: A Study of the Sociological Importance of Usages, Manners, Customs, Mores, and Morals* (1906)	Yale professor who taught the first American course in sociology and explored the social significance of manners, mores, and taboos.
Thorstein Veblen (1857–1929)	• *The Theory of the Leisure Class* (1899) • *The Theory of the Business Enterprise* (1904)	Economist and social critic who attacked American "conspicuous consumption."
Jane Addams (1860–1935)	• "The Subjective Necessity for Social Settlements" (1893) • *Hull-House Maps and Papers* (1896)	Social worker/activist, sociologist, and intellectual who established America's first settlement house, in Chicago.
George Herbert Mead (1863–1931)	• *Mind, Self, and Society* (1934)	Father of "symbolic interactionism" who looked at how the self is constructed through personal exchanges with others.
Charles Horton Cooley (1864–1929)	• *Human Nature and the Social Order* (1902) • *Social Organization: A Study of the Larger Mind* (1909)	Symbolic interactionist who advanced the idea of the looking-glass self, asserting that the self is created and reinforced through social interaction.
Robert Park (1864–1944)	• *Introduction to the Science of Sociology* (1921) • *The City: Suggestions for the Study of Human Nature in the Urban Environment* (1925)	Urban sociologist who was a founding member of the Chicago school of sociology.
W.E.B. Du Bois (1868–1963)	• *The Souls of Black Folk* (1903) • *Black Reconstruction in America* (1935)	Documented the experience of American blacks from a sociological perspective.
Edwin Sutherland (1883–1950)	• "White Collar Criminality" (1940) • *White Collar Crime* (1949)	Criminal sociologist and symbolic interactionist who introduced the idea of white-collar crime.
E. Franklin Frazier (1894–1962)	• *The Negro Family in the United States* (1939)	Baltimore-born sociologist who performed pioneering studies of African American families.
Everett C. Hughes (1897–1983)	• *French Canada in Transition* (1943) • "Dilemmas and Contractions of Status" (1945)	Chicago school sociologist who studied the ethnic division of labour in the French Canadian province of Quebec.

Jane Addams

Though she was never a member of Chicago's Department of Sociology, **Jane Addams** (1860–1935) had close and influential ties with the faculty there. But her interest in Chicago's urban neighbourhoods was beyond academic: she was a pioneering social reformer and worked tirelessly to improve the welfare of those living in poverty in the inner city.

In 1889, Addams, with Ellen Gates Starr (1859–1940), turned a run-down mansion in one of Chicago's poorest communities into North America's first **settlement house**. With help from a number of local sponsors, Addams paid for rent and repairs to the mansion, and established Hull House as an innovative outreach and research centre, offering social and educational services to people of different ethnic backgrounds and social classes. The residents of Hull House—the middle-class, university-educated women who volunteered at the centre—led courses in a range of domestic and cultural subjects for families in Hull House's predominantly working-class immigrant community. At the same time, the centre served as a training ground for social workers. The first of its kind in North America, it set the model for settlement houses established in other cities around the world.

Addams today is recognized for her accomplishments as an activist, author, community organizer, university lecturer, and public intellectual, a leading figure in what was termed the Progressive Era. However, with the establishment of Hull House, she made studying the relationship between poverty, pollution, sanitation, and diseases such as typhoid fever and tuberculosis a central pillar of the house's mission, and for this reason we can add sociologist to the list of roles in which she distinguished herself.

The Development of Canadian Sociology

While there is no distinctly Canadian approach to sociological research and practice, the way the discipline developed in this country and its focal points are unique. The relationship between French and English, the development of the Canadian West, the connection between class and ethnicity, and a close working relationship with anthropology have all been fundamental to the development of a Canadian perspective on sociology.

McGill University: Dawson, Hughes, and Miner

The first professional, institutionalized sociologist in Canada was **Carl Addington Dawson** (1887–1964). Born in Prince Edward Island, Dawson completed his MA and PHD at the University of Chicago. In 1922, shortly after joining the faculty at McGill, he founded the university's sociology department, an accomplishment not without opposition. Senior administrators worried about the left-wing political leanings of sociologists (they still do), and academics in other departments did not want their scholarly territory infringed upon. Dawson succeeded in spite of these objections. McGill's remained the only independent department of sociology until 1961.

Dawson's work reflected two elements of early Canadian sociology: (1) the **social gospel** movement and (2) hands-on social work. The social gospel movement developed as an attempt by people trained for the ministry to apply Christian principles of human welfare to the treatment of social, medical, and psychological ills brought on by industrialization and unregulated capitalism, not just in Canada but in the United States, Britain, Germany, and other European countries during the late nineteenth century. Out of the social gospel movement came the Social Service Council of Canada (1912), which, through various churches, carried out the first sociological surveys of Canadian cities.

Dawson's affinity with the social gospel movement was natural—his first degree was in divinity—but his inspiration to become involved in social work came from his time studying at the University of Chicago. The Chicago school put an emphasis on going out into communities—what Park called "living laboratories"—to observe them firsthand. Dawson took this approach and, with his students, applied it to the living laboratory of Montreal. Their research was given a jump-start in 1929, when they were awarded a $110,000 Rockefeller Foundation grant to study unemployment in the city.

That same year, Dawson and Warren E. Gettys became the first Canadians to write a sociology textbook (three cheers for sociology textbooks!). The text was an instant success, adopted by over 150 colleges and universities across North America within a year. While there was not a great deal of Canadian content, it helped legitimize the study and practice of sociology in Canada.

Another figure vital to the development of sociology at McGill was **Everett C. Hughes** (1897–1983). Like Dawson, he was a graduate of the University of Chicago, and the Ohio-born Hughes joined the sociology department at McGill in 1927. Hughes was a firm believer in community research. While at McGill, Hughes focused on the "ethnic division of labour," a situation that enabled English Canadians to rise above French Canadians in large companies, creating a disparity that he wished to correct. Out of this research came *French Canada in Transition* (1943). By the time the landmark study was published, Hughes had already returned to the States to take a position in the faculty of his alma mater.

Horace Miner (1912–1993) was another American sociologist who put the study of French Canada at the forefront of Canadian sociology. As a graduate student at (can you guess?) the University of Chicago, he came to Quebec to study the parish of St Denis. His book *St Denis: A French-Canadian Parish* (1939) shows the blurred distinction between sociology and anthropology in Canada. His work is best described as an **ethnography**, a study of a community based on extensive fieldwork, whose primary research activities include direct observation of and interaction with the people observed. Ethnography is the main research method used in social anthropology. Miner described the rural peasants and farmers of his study as a **folk society**, following the model of University of Chicago anthropologist Robert Redfield, who coined the term. The close connection between sociology and anthropology can still be seen in Canadian universities where the two disciplines are joined in the same department.

© McCord Museum

What kind of work do you think is being performed at this Montreal office *c.* 1920? Are the people you see here more likely to be anglophones or francophones?

The University of Toronto: Harold Innis and S.D. Clark

Around the same time, a different sociological tradition, that of **political economy**, was beginning at the University of Toronto. Political economy is an interdisciplinary approach involving sociology, political science, economics, law, anthropology, and history. It looks primarily at the relationship between politics and the economics of the production, distribution, and consumption of goods. It is often Marxist in nature, pointing to the tensions that arise in the extraction and distribution of goods.

A Canadian pioneer in this field was **Harold Innis** (1894–1952), who joined the University of Toronto in 1920. Innis was more economic historian than sociologist, but his work has exerted a strong influence on Canadian sociology. He argued that the availability of *staples*—resources such as fish, animal fur, minerals, and wheat—shaped the economic and social development of Canada. I wonder what he would think of the oil projects in northern Alberta today.

Innis was also a mentor to the first person hired at the university specifically as a sociologist, **Samuel Delbert Clark** (1910–2003). Born in Alberta, S.D. Clark received his first two degrees from the University of Saskatchewan before joining the Department of Political Economy at the University of Toronto in 1938. Sociology remained a branch of that department until 1963, when it became a stand-alone department, with Clark as its chair. Summarizing Clark's influence, sociologist Deborah Harrison wrote,

> The importance of S.D. Clark within the development of Canadian sociology is universally recognized. Clark's publications span more than forty prolific years, with at least the first fifteen occurring when almost no other sociologists were writing in Canada; he is generally acknowledged as the father of the Canadian approach to the discipline. . . . For reasons of both his scholarly engagement and his articulation of a "Canadian" sociology, Clark is the most important sociologist Canada has yet produced. (Harrison, 1999)

Clark can be considered a "sociological historian": consider a selection of his chapter headings in *The Developing Canadian Community* (1962):

- The Farming–Fur-Trade Society of New France
- The Rural Village Society of the Maritimes
- The Backwoods Society of Upper Canada
- The Gold-Rush Society of British Columbia and the Yukon
- The Prairie Wheat-Farming Frontier and the New Industrial City
- The Religious Influence in Canadian Society
- The Canadian Community and the American Continental System
- History and the Sociological Method

Social Class and Ethnicity: John Porter

Fundamentally missing from the work of both Innis and Clark are the themes of class and ethnicity. These themes received their definitive treatment in what is generally recognized as the best-known work of Canadian sociology, *The Vertical Mosaic: An Analysis of Social Class and Power in Canada* (1965), by **John Porter** (1921–1979). Porter joined the faculty of Carleton University in 1949, becoming the university's first full-time appointment in sociology. The title of his book plays on the term **cultural mosaic**, a metaphor frequently used to characterize Canada's multicultural society. A mosaic is a type of artwork composed of many small tiles that lend different colours to the picture. A society that is a cultural mosaic is one "in which racial, ethnic, and religious groups maintain a distinct identity, rather than being absorbed into a 'melting pot'" (Lundy & Warme, 1990, p. 583). A **melting pot** encourages the "rapid assimilation of recent immigrants into their new society" (Lundy & Warme, 1990, p. 586).

Porter coined the term **vertical mosaic** to describe the situation he observed in Canada, in which systemic discrimination produced a hierarchy of racial, ethnic, and religious groups. Keeping with the metaphor of the mosaic, we can say that the different tiles were stacked and not arranged evenly. Tiles representing white Anglo-Saxon Protestants were at the top of the hierarchy, followed by French Canadian tiles, the tiles of the more successful ethnic groups (notably Jewish, Chinese, and Italian), and

AP Photo/Matt Rourke

Melting pot or cultural mosaic?

finally those of everyone else, with the racially marginalized groups at the bottom. Porter concluded that ethnicity was the main factor determining how the tiles were ranked.

Three Early Women Sociologists and the Writing of Gender in Canada

Annie Marion MacLean

Annie Marion MacLean (*c.* 1870–1934) was the first Canadian woman to obtain a PhD in sociology. Born in Prince Edward Island, she received her first two degrees from Acadia University before earning her PhD at the University of Chicago. She also taught there, although, despite her excellent qualifications, in a very subordinate position.

MacLean pioneered the sociological study of working women, especially in *Wage-Earning Women* (1910), which was based on a survey of some 13,500 women. She conducted her research in department stores, in "sweat shop" factories, and among hop-pickers in rural Oregon. Though born in Canada, she was never hired by a Canadian university.

Aileen Ross

The first woman hired as a sociologist at a Canadian university was **Aileen Ross** (1902–1995), a Montrealer, who taught sociology at the University of

Toronto for three years before joining the faculty at McGill. She earned her first degree at the London School of Economics, and her MA (in 1941) and PhD (in 1950) from the University of Chicago.

Ross devoted her books to two of her foremost concerns: women and India. She published *The Hindu Family in an Urban Setting* (1962) after carrying out several years of research in India. *The Lost and the Lonely: Homeless Women in Montreal* (1982) was the first study of homeless women in Canada. Her research strategy for that study is discussed in the next chapter, on page 46.

Helen C. Abell

Alberta-born **Helen C. Abell** (1917–2005) has been called the founder of rural sociology in Canada. After receiving a degree in human nutrition at the University of Toronto (1941), she worked as a nutritionist for the Ontario Department of Agriculture, and then as an officer in the Canadian Women's Army Corps during the Second World War. She received her PhD in rural sociology (the first Canadian to do so) in 1951. She then established a rural sociology research unit in the federal Department of Agriculture. Her research, notes Jenny Kendrick,

> played an important role in identifying systematically the roles women played on the farm. This was an invaluable contribution to the policy arena, virtually forcing society and policymakers to lay aside their stereotypes of the marginal contributions of farm women to agriculture. (quoted in Eichler, 2001, p. 382)

The Growth of Sociology in Canada

In 1958, there were fewer than 20 sociology professors in Canada, teaching in just 9 universities (Clark, 1976, p. 120). Sociology did not become a significant area of study and teaching in Canada until the 1960s and 1970s, as baby boomers entered universities and colleges. The growth of sociology during that time is astounding. Hiller and Di Luzio, for example, report that the University of Alberta "had no sociology majors in 1956–57, but a year later had nine, followed by 24 (1957–58), 44 (1959–60), and 62 (1960–61).

The number of majors there reached a peak for the twentieth century at 776 in 1987" (Hiller & Di Luzio, 2001, p. 490).

During this era of growth in sociology, most of the sociologists hired to teach in Canadian postsecondary institutions were from the United States and Britain. Of those with doctorates teaching sociology and anthropology in Canada in 1967, 72 per cent had PhDs from the United States, 10 per cent from Britain, and only 6 per cent from Canada (Gallagher & Lambert, 1971, p. vii). In 1973–4, 45 per cent of the full-time sociology faculty in Canada was made up of non-Canadians (Hofley, 1992, p. 106). This should not be surprising given that only 22 doctorates in sociology were conferred at Canadian universities between 1924 and 1967 (Gallagher & Lambert, 1971, p. vi).

The lack of Canadian sociologists meant that sociology textbooks lacked a Canadian perspective. When John Hofley was hired to teach sociology at Carleton University in 1966, he saw "very little about Canada in the sociology texts that were available" (Hofley, 1992, p. 104). The 1970s saw a big movement to "Canadianize" sociology textbooks. Today most introductory sociology textbooks used in Canadian schools are either Canadian in origin or "Canadianized" versions of American textbooks.

Still missing from Canadian sociology textbooks is an adequate representation of Indigenous sociologists. In my doctoral dissertation, *Aboriginal Voices and the Politics of Representation in Canadian Sociology Textbooks* (2003), I argued that the production of Canadian introductory textbooks involved a general failure to create an Indigenous sociology, though there were Indigenous writers in the 1970s whose work could correct that flaw—Harold Cardinal, George Manuel, and Howard Adams, to name just three. I have made an effort in this book to correct that omission, but more work needs to be done. There are Canadian perspectives, not a Canadian perspective. Different voices need to be heard.

What Do YOU Think?

How might an introductory sociology textbook written in Canada be different from a "Canadianized" one originally written in the United States?

Different Kinds of Sociology

Sociology did not take on a uniform appearance as it grew as a discipline during the nineteenth century: instead, it diversified. European and North American social thinkers had differing views of what sociology was, what it could do, and how it should be applied. Consequently, sociology developed into several different schools that varied according to their particular applications and the perspectives (historical, political-economical, feminist, and so on) of those who were using it.

In this section, we will explore two ways of distinguishing the various kinds of sociology. The first is based on the approach used; the second is based on the intended audience for the work and how socially critical the sociologist is.

1. Sociology by Approach

The traditional way of representing different kinds of sociology in introductory textbooks is to break it down into the different approaches sociologists use to pursue their inquiries:

- structural functionalism
- conflict theory
- symbolic interactionism
- feminist theory
- postmodern theory.

These terms are typically presented in the introductory chapter of a textbook and then repeated throughout most, if not all, of the subsequent chapters. The linguist Edward Sapir said, "all grammars [i.e. explanations of language] leak." I have long felt that this particular "grammar of sociology" leaks too much (think: flooded basement) to sustain using it throughout the text. Nevertheless, the distinctions do reveal some key differences in philosophy, so they are worth explaining and illustrating here.

Structural Functionalism

The **structural-functionalist** approach has deep roots in sociology. As the name suggests, the approach contains two dimensions. *Functionalism* focuses on how social systems, in their entirety, operate and produce consequences. The work of Émile Durkheim, Robert Merton, and Talcott Parsons (discussed in Chapter 13, on health and medicine) represents the functionalist approach.

The functionalist approach was fused with *structuralism* as a way of explaining social forms and their contributions to social cohesion. It uses an *organic*, or biological, analogy for society. How? Nursing students, when they take the dreaded Anatomy and Physiology course, have to learn all the different *structures* of the human body as well as the *functions* each one performs. The structural-functionalist approach treats society in a similar way: *This is the part of society we call "organized religion." This is what it does for society* . . .

While the structural-functionalist approach was popular for much of sociology's history, it has lost favour in recent decades. It is too much of a stretch, for example, to talk about the *functions* of poverty or inequality and how they contribute favourably to social order. Poverty and inequality don't really serve the interests of society at large, just the narrow class interests of those who profit from

others' misfortunes. In addition, functionalism is not good at promoting an understanding of conflict or social change. While sociologists still draw on the classic works and essential concepts of structural functionalism, few contemporary sociologists are committed to the theoretical practice itself in their research and writing.

Durkheim and Social Facts

To get a better sense of the functionalist approach, let's look at the work of **Émile Durkheim** (1858– 1917), one of the founders of sociology. His description of the **social fact** is an important early sociological concept. Social facts are patterned ways of acting, thinking, and feeling that exist outside of any one individual but exert social control over all people. Think about how different social characteristics—aspects of your social location such as gender, age, religion, ethnicity, "race," sexual orientation, your role as sister or brother or as student or teacher—exert a compelling social force over you and lead you to act in sociologically predictable

Gary Moore/CBC

A makeshift encampment in downtown Fredericton offers temporary shelter from snow and cold to a few of the city's homeless population. A functionalist would argue that homelessness is a natural social consequence of our economic system, and that it benefits society by providing citizens with an incentive to work hard. Would you agree?

ways. These ways of acting based on social characteristics are social facts.

Every social fact has three essential characteristics:

1. It was developed prior to and separate from any individual (i.e. no one person invented or is synonymous with it).
2. It can be seen as characteristic of a particular group (young Canadian men, for instance, like to watch sports while drinking beer—a social fact that explains why so many beer commercials feature young men watching sports).
3. It involves a constraining or coercing force that pushes individuals into acting in a particular way (like when young men watching sports succumb to "beer pressure" and begin yelling, high-fiving, and displaying other behaviour associated with this social fact).

You can see how looking for social facts would be a useful way for a sociologist to get beyond focusing on individuals to examine larger social forms and how different parts of society function.

In *Suicide* (1897), Durkheim examined suicide as a social fact. He found that in late nineteenth-century France, certain groups were more likely to commit suicide than others: military officers more than enlisted men, Protestants more than Catholics, and unmarried people more than married people. He drew a correlation between suicide and the degree to which individuals were connected or committed to society, finding that those with a very strong dedication to society were more likely to commit suicide than those with a weaker commitment. Officers are responsible for the soldiers in their charge. It makes sense that a heightened sense of honour might make them suicidal when they make a mistake that results in the death of one of "their men." But Durkheim also concluded that having too weak a connection to society could produce suicide. Protestants were in the minority in France and thus had weaker bonds to both the country in which they lived and its culture.

In Canada today, men commit suicide more often than women do. This is a social fact. Why men commit suicide more often than women do is a complicated matter. It has to do in part with the fact that women are more likely to share their problems with other people than to "suck it up" and remain silent. Women are more likely to have a network of friends with whom they can communicate about serious matters, and they are more likely to go seek treatment for depression and mental illness, which lowers their likelihood of committing suicide. Women attempting suicide are also more likely to use less efficient means: pills and slashed wrists over the more deadly male choice of guns.

What Do YOU Think?

The author of this textbook considers himself fairly enlightened, with feminist sympathies. Yet a woman reader commented that it was obvious this commentary was written by a man: women, she pointed out, are less likely to commit suicide because of their childcare responsibilities, not because they're incapable or are more likely to "share their feelings." Do you agree?

Merton's Manifest and Latent Functions

Robert K. Merton (1910–2003), one of the leading American sociologists of the mid-twentieth century and a major contributor to functionalist thinking, identified three types of functions:

1. **Manifest functions** are both intended and readily recognized, or "manifest" (i.e. easily seen).
2. **Latent functions** are largely unintended and unrecognized.
3. **Latent dysfunctions** are unintended and produce socially negative consequences.

This last group is often studied using the conflict approach, making Merton's brand of functionalism something of a bridge to conflict theory (which we will examine in the next section). The three examples in Table 1.4 illustrate the differences among Merton's three functions.

Conflict Theory

Conflict theory is based on the "four Cs":
- conflict
- class
- contestation
- change.

TABLE 1.4 Examples of Robert Merton's Three Functions

Example 1	Postsecondary education
manifest function	Postsecondary education provides students with the skills and knowledge to find a profitable career in order to become productive, self-sufficient citizens.
latent function	It provides a social network that will make the search for employment and a marriage partner easier.
latent dysfunction	From a left-wing perspective, postsecondary education reinforces class distinctions, since people in the lower socioeconomic classes cannot afford to attend; from a right-wing perspective, it exposes students to (dangerous!) socialist ideas.
Example 2	**Religion**
manifest function	Religion fulfills spiritual and emotional needs, and answers important existential questions that many people have.
latent function	Religion creates a social support network and marriage market.
latent dysfunction	Religion provides justification for judging outsiders ("non-believers") negatively.
Example 3	**Doughnut shops**
manifest function	Doughnut shops provide customers with coffee, snacks, and light meals, served quickly and conveniently.
latent function	Doughnut shops serve as places to meet and socialize with others.
latent dysfunction	Doughnut shops provide late-night venues for drug dealing.

The approach is based, first, on the idea that *conflict* exists in all large societies. The stress lines are factors such as sex and gender, "race" and ethnicity, religion, age, and class—the sociological ingredients of a group or individual social location. Second, it asserts that *class* divisions exist and are a source of conflict in all large societies. Third, it contends that the functions of society, as laid out in traditional structural-functionalist theory, can be *contested*, or challenged, based on the question, *What group does this function best serve?* Finally, the approach involves the assumption that society either will or should be *changed*.

A major figure in the early history of sociology was German economist and political philosopher **Karl Marx** (1818–1883). For Marx, conflict was all about **class**: the division of society into a hierarchy of groups, with each group's position determined by its role in the production of wealth. Marx saw class conflict as the driving force behind all major social change over time. He believed that conflict between the class of capitalists (the **bourgeoisie**) and the class of workers (the **proletariat**) would initiate a socialist revolution that would produce a classless, or **egalitarian**, society. A classless society has never existed in more complex social communities, but many of Marx's insights about class conflict and capitalist production are still valid. This is true on a global scale, if you think of transnational corporations

headquartered in Western societies as the capitalist "owning class" and underpaid workers in poorer countries (say garment workers in Bangladesh producing cheap clothes for Canadian shoppers) as the ultimate "working class."

The territory of conflict theory now stretches well beyond Marxism and incorporates applications in feminist sociology, critical disability thinking, queer theory, anti-colonialism, and other approaches that fall under the umbrella of "critical sociology," which we will encounter shortly.

Symbolic Interactionism

Symbolic interactionism is an approach that looks at the meaning (or symbolism) of our daily social interactions. For example, two male students approach each other and, with a slight incline of the head, say, "'Sup, yo," lightly bringing their fists together in greeting. What are they communicating to each other about their relationship, their shared interests, and their role models? In Newfoundland in the 1970s, when I lived there as a graduate student, the greeting in passing was likely to be a tilt of the head to the left. In giving and receiving this greeting, I felt accepted into the society.

The symbolic-interactionist method was pioneered by American social psychologist **George Herbert Mead** (1863–1931), who examined the way

bonnie jacobs/iStockphoto

The relationship between a teacher and their students is a social fact. What patterned ways of acting influence this teacher's behaviour toward her students? How might the teacher, should she not conform to the behaviour expected of her, be punished, either in some formal way (i.e. by the school board) or in some informal way (i.e. by her peers or her students or their parents) depending on the nature of the transgression? What are some of the patterned ways of acting that influence students' behaviour?

the individual self is constructed as we interact with others and how the self allows us to take on social roles, reflect on ourselves, and internalize social expectations. **Herbert Blumer** (1900–1987), a pupil of Mead's, coined the term "symbolic interaction." Blumer (1969) argued that social systems are simply abstractions that do not exist independently of individual relations and interactions. In other words, social systems (friendship patterns, education, the economy, etc.) are simply by-products of our personal dealings with one another.

The symbolic-interactionist approach, with its focus on individuals rather than larger social structures, represents one part of another distinction used to differentiate various kinds of sociology: **macrosociology** versus **microsociology**. When sociologists engage in research and writing that focus primarily on the "big picture" of society and its institutions, they are engaging in macrosociology. Weber, Durkheim, Merton, and Marx were all

primarily macrosociologists. When the focus is, instead, more on the plans, motivations, and actions of the individual or a small group, then a microsociological approach is involved.

A good example of how microsociology and a symbolic-interactionist approach are used to understand people's actions comes from the work of **Erving Goffman** (1922–1982). Born in Alberta, Goffman received his BA from the University of Toronto and his MA and PhD from the University of Chicago. His work was highly original, as evidenced by the many terms he introduced to sociology. One example is **total institution**, an expression he coined in *Asylums* (1961). He defined it as any one of "a range of institutions in which whole blocks of people are bureaucratically processed, whilst being physically isolated from the normal round of activities, by being required to sleep, work, and play within the confines of the same institution" (quoted in Marshall, 1998, pp. 669–70). Examples include psychiatric hospitals, prisons, army barracks, boarding schools, concentration camps, monasteries, and convents—institutions whose residents are powerfully regulated, controlled, or manipulated by those in charge.

Goffman carried out his research for *Asylums* in 1955–6, when he engaged in fieldwork at a mental hospital in Washington, DC. He wanted to learn about the day-to-day social world of the inmates. He did this by pretending to be an assistant to the athletic director, a position that allowed him to pass his days with the patients. Goffman stressed the importance of learning the *subjectivity* of people, meaning the views and feelings they have. He denied both objectivity and neutrality in his research methodology, and sided with the patients rather than the professionals who managed them in the hospital.

Feminist Theory

Two branches of conflict theory now comprise such an extensive collection of research and literature that they demand to be considered in their own right. These two branches are feminist theory and postmodern theory.

Western European feminism arguably began with Mary Wollstonecraft's *A Vindication of the Rights of Woman* (1792). But like anything that has existed and evolved for well over two hundred years, feminism is difficult to pin down with a tidy, hard-and-fast definition. We can say that feminism involves correcting centuries of discrimination and male-dominated conceptions of gender roles in order to gain and present an accurate view of the social condition of women. Another way to put it is that feminism tackles centuries of **patriarchy**, a social organization in which men hold political, cultural, and social power. Contrary to what some male students believe, you don't have to be a woman to be a feminist. You do have to accept that recognizing a female perspective (or "standpoint") is absolutely critical to forming an accurate appraisal of the roles women play in society (or so says the bearded author of this textbook).

One of the earliest Western sociologists to carry out a careful examination of women's roles in

Vitchanan/iStockphoto

Words are simply one aspect of constructing meaning in our day-to-day interactions. In this conversation, how is meaning being generated?

All the World's a Stage: Applying Goffman to Research

I'm a Goffman fan. His books are readable, and his concepts are readily adaptable to research, as I discovered in 1972, when I spent a year studying a religious group in downtown Toronto for my honours thesis. I needed a theoretical base for my research, and so I turned to Goffman's *The Presentation of Self in Everyday Life* (1959). In this book he introduced the **dramaturgical approach**, a way of conducting research as if everyday life were taking place on the stage of a theatre. According to an often-told anecdote, Goffman was on the Hebrides Islands, off the coast of Scotland, looking for a topic for his doctoral dissertation. While sitting in a restaurant, he noticed that the waitstaff acted differently when they were on the "**front stage**"—that is, in the public eye—than when they were "**back stage**" in the kitchen, away from the dining customers. He considered this an act of **impression management**, which he described as the ways in which people conduct themselves in specific roles and social situations. His doctoral thesis and bestselling book were born that day—or so the story goes.

The religious group I was studying was managing their impressions for two different audiences. One included street kids and other youthful lost souls who might be in need of spiritual guidance. For this audience, representatives of the religious group put on a hip, anti-establishment face. However, in order to obtain food donations from supermarket chains to feed their flock, and to achieve respectability in the eyes of both corporate sponsors and the neighbouring businesses in their rather exclusive downtown area, they had to present a more conservative face.

I predicted that the group would split according to the two "stages," the two audiences to which they were presenting themselves. This happened just a year later, when the organization developed two distinct branches, one dealing with youth outreach and the other handling charitable donations. Thanks, Erving.

Brian Losito/Air Canada

Can you apply Goffman's dramaturgical approach to the work of a flight attendant? Who makes up the "front stage" audience? Where is the "back stage"? Which audience(s) are the pilots part of?

society was British writer and social theorist **Harriet Martineau** (1802–1876). She wrote over 6000 articles, many of them on the social condition of women. In 1834 she began a two-year study of the United States, which she documented in the three-volume *Society in America* (1837) and in *Retrospect of Western Travel* (1838). Her feminist thinking can be seen in her comparison of women to slaves in a chapter of the former work revealingly called "The Political Non-Existence of Women." After travelling to the Middle East, she published *Eastern Life: Present and Past* (1848), in which she briefly departed from her intended sociological spirit of impartiality to condemn the practice of polygyny (one husband with more than one wife).

Martineau's goal of remaining impartial was in keeping with the sociology of her time. In contrast, most feminist theorists today believe that the best way to understand the social condition of women involves trying to view life through the eyes of the women they're studying. It sounds obvious, but it was a revolutionary idea, and a foundational figure in the movement was a Canadian sociologist, **Dorothy Smith** (b. 1926). While doing graduate work at the University of California–Berkeley, Smith experienced firsthand the kind of systemic sexist discrimination that would become the subject of her first work. She moved to Canada in the late 1960s, when she was given a rare (for a woman) teaching opportunity at the University of British Columbia. It was the start of a distinguished academic career that also includes 20 years at the University of Toronto's Ontario Institute for Studies in Education.

Smith developed **standpoint theory** directly out of her own experience as a woman discriminated against by male colleagues in the academic community. Her standpoint theory challenged traditional sociology's preference for **objective** (depersonalized and distanced from everyday life) as opposed to **subjective** (personalized and connected to everyday life) research and analysis. Traditionalists held that the objective approach to research was more scientific and therefore truthful, while the subjective position was **ideological**, based on biases and prejudices, and therefore distorted. Smith argued that knowledge is always developed from a particular lived position, or "standpoint." Sociology, having developed from a male standpoint, had long denied the validity of the female standpoint and overlooked the everyday lives of women—an oversight that feminist researchers today are still working to correct.

What Do YOU Think?

1. How does Smith's standpoint theory fit with Mills's notion of the sociological imagination?
2. Consider the list of early sociologists and their contributions provided in Table 1.2. How might early developments in the growth of sociology have differed if the female standpoint had been given greater consideration?

Feminism's "Waves"

Some historians have attempted to trace the development of feminism through successive generations, or "waves," each characterized by a different agenda. According to this conception, first-wave feminism is associated chiefly with the campaign for civil and political rights, specifically the rights to vote and hold political office, which began in the nineteenth century. Canada's "Famous Five," a group of social leaders and activists who petitioned to have women recognized as "persons" under British and Canadian law in the early twentieth century, are examples of first-wave feminists in this country.

After securing political rights in most North American jurisdictions, the women's movement began to wane in the first half of the twentieth century. It gained new life during the civil rights movement that began in the 1960s, fuelled by the fight for equality in the home and in the workplace, including equal opportunities for employment and pay. The activists of this generation saw themselves as successors to the "first wave" of activists, who had won voting and other rights. Second-wave feminism differed, though, by tackling not just public rights—like the right to take a job in traditionally male-dominated professions—but also private rights, including reproductive rights and freedom from domestic violence (Hunter College & Simalchik, 2017).

Beginning during the 1980s, third-wave feminism is associated with the campaign for social justice for women left out of the more mainstream agenda of second-wave feminism, traditionally set by white women from middle- and upper-middle-class backgrounds. Some critics view it as a backlash against second-wave feminism. Third-wave feminism represents the interests of LGBTQ2 (lesbian, gay, bisexual, trans, questioning, Two-Spirit) women, as well as women from racial and ethnic minorities and women living in poverty. It is closely tied to the notion of intersectionality defined earlier in this chapter.

So where are we now? Many feminist activists today are using social media as a way to draw attention to issues including sexual harassment and violence, online bullying and shaming, media representations of women, and questioning whether there is an "ethical" pornography. Some see this millennial-driven activism as a fourth wave. Others say it's merely third-wave feminism carried out using the tools of technology. Others still argue that the idea of waves is an outdated concept that was problematic to begin with: after all, where do you situate black feminists of the 1960s and 1970s, who were arguing way back then that race was being left off the feminist agenda (Hunter College & Simalchik, 2017)? Maria Campbell's *Halfbreed*, first published in 1973, spoke powerfully of her experience as a Métis woman in a way that pointed to the need of an intersectional feminism (even though the term did not exist at that time). What is clear is that there are many feminisms, defined by different (sometimes competing) interpretations of the movement and its objectives.

Stephen Sinclair

Tahani (*left*), married at the age of six, and Ghada (*right*), also a child bride, stand with their husbands in Hajjah, Yemen. According to UN figures for 2017, 32 per cent of girls are married by the time they are 18, and 9 per cent by the time they are 15. Girls who marry early often abandon their education, and the incidence of maternal and infant death is high for women under 18 who give birth. How important are the factors of "race" and gender in telling the story of these girls? What might a Western, white, male sociologist, or female journalist miss? What insights might a sociologist raised with child marriage as part of their culture add that could otherwise be missing? How does this compare with states such as Kentucky and Idaho that allow for child (under 16) marriage?

Postmodern Theory

A good way to think of postmodern theory is to consider the concept of *voices*. In all societies, there are different voices that speak, and together they represent a diversity of life experiences and social locations. Postmodern theory is concerned with recognizing that there are many such voices, and that they should not be drowned out by the powerful voice of those who are dominant in society (traditionally, white heterosexual men from middle- and upper-class backgrounds).

A leading figure in postmodern theory was the French philosopher and historian **Michel Foucault** (1926–1984). In his groundbreaking article "Two Lectures" (1980), Foucault talked about the misleading nature of what he termed **totalitarian discourse**. A totalitarian discourse is any universal claim about how knowledge or understanding is achieved. Western science, for example, is at the centre of a totalitarian discourse used by those who claim that it is the only legitimate path to discovering the "truth" about the causes and cures for different diseases, while dismissing alternative forms of medicine that are popular and trusted in many non-Western cultures.

"Totalitarian" in this context should be easy enough to understand: it describes a set of beliefs or ideas that dominates ("totally") all others. The other part of this term, "discourse," is not as easily understood. A **discourse** can be defined as follows:

> A conceptual framework with its own internal logic and underlying assumptions that may be readily recognizable to the audience. A discourse involves a distinct way of speaking about some aspect of reality. [Use of the term] also suggests that the item under discussion is not a natural attribute of reality but socially constructed and defined. (Fleras & Elliott, 1999, p. 433)

A discourse is not necessarily wrong or false. The term really just refers to a particular treatment of a topic that has been created through a given set of assumptions, a vocabulary, rules, logic, and so on. However, to call something a *totalizing* (or *totalitarian*) discourse is to condemn it as overly ambitious and narrow-minded, or dangerously manipulative.

Foucault was concerned with how those in positions of power could shape and use a discourse to "control the message" and ultimately control the people.

A good example of a totalitarian discourse is the American Dream, the idea that success, in terms of wealth, fame, or social prestige, can be achieved by any determined, hardworking American citizen, regardless of their "race," ethnicity, social class, gender, or degree of ability. The dark side of that discourse, the "American nightmare," is that if you fail it is because you haven't worked hard enough or wanted it enough. This is what **William Ryan** (1976) called blaming the victim. The supposed universality of the American Dream flies in the face of sociological statistics that say that your social location is the best predictor of your personal success. There is no level playing field.

2. Sociology by Audience

Another way of categorizing sociology is based on the *audience* for whom the work is intended and how critical the sociologist is. We borrow here from Michael Burawoy (2004), who divided sociology into four types:

- professional
- critical
- policy
- public.

Professional Sociology

Professional sociology has as its audience the academic world of sociology departments, scholarly journals, professional associations, and conferences. The research carried out by professional sociologists is typically designed to generate very specific information, often with the aim of applying it to a particular problem or intellectual question. Consider some of the articles that appeared recently in the *Canadian Review of Sociology* (2018–19):

- "The Corporate Elite and the Architecture of Climate Change Denial: A Network Analysis of Carbon Capital's Reach into Civil Society"
- "The Stratification of Attendance at Cultural Activities in Canada"

- "Gender, Artifacts, and Ritual Encounters: The Case of *Tomboy Tools* Sales Parties"
- "The Experiences of and Responses to Linguicism of Quebec English-Speaking and Franco-Ontarian Postsecondary Students"
- "Wanting to Be Remembered: Intrinsically Rewarding Work and Generativity in Early Midlife"

These articles address specific sociological questions, centring around the key issues of gender, work, culture, and the state of sociology in Canada. Written in technical or specialized language, they target an academic or professional readership, but can usually be read by interested students.

Critical Sociology

The main role of **critical sociology**, according to Burawoy (2004), is to be "the conscience of professional sociology." It performs this role in two ways:

> Critical sociology reminds professional sociology . . . of its value premises and its guiding questions. It also proposes alternative foundations upon which to erect sociological research. In other words, critical sociology is critical in two senses, first in bringing professional sociology into alignment with its historical mission and second in shifting the direction of that mission. (Burawoy, 2004, p. 261)

Critical sociology, then, addresses the same audience that professional sociology does, but with a different purpose. Its aim is to make sure that professional sociologists do not lose sight of the goals of sociological inquiry, specifically to bring about meaningful social change.

Much of what we call conflict theory would fit into this category. Two giants of critical sociology, Michel Foucault and Dorothy Smith, are known for having examined the production of knowledge in relation to power—in other words, which groups in society get their views heard and accepted as true. Foucault discussed the conflict between "scientific experts" and other producers of knowledge, whose voices tended to be drowned out by the former group, while Smith discussed conflict in terms of gender relations.

Policy Sociology

Policy sociology is about generating sociological data for governments and large corporations, to be used in developing laws, rules, and long- and short-term plans. Education, health, and social welfare are three main areas that policy sociology serves, but they are by no means the only ones. For example, a government might commission a study on crime prevention to see whether tougher sentences or better rehabilitation programs are more likely to reduce the rate of criminals reoffending: this would be an example of policy sociology.

Not all works of policy sociology are initiated by government lawmakers. Think tanks are policy organizations that try to bring about social change by persuading governments to adopt or amend certain laws (the right-wing Fraser Institute and the left-leaning Broadbent Institute are two examples). When they commission studies to generate findings that support their lobbying efforts, this is another example of policy sociology.

Public Sociology

Public sociology addresses an audience that is not part of the academic world of colleges and universities or the political establishment. Herbert Gans (1989) has identified three key traits of public sociologists:

> One is their ability to discuss even sociological concepts and theories in the English of the college-educated reader. . . . Their second trait is the breadth of their sociological interests, which covers much of society even if their research is restricted to a few fields. That breadth also extends to their conception of sociology, which extends beyond research reporting to commentary and in many cases social criticism. . . . [T]heir work is intellectual as well as scientific. A third, not unrelated, trait is the ability to avoid the pitfalls of undue professionalism. (Gans, 1989, p. 7)

By "undue professionalism" Gans is referring to professional sociology's overly cautious style, its tendency to footnote almost everything, and its inclination to bury analysis in statistics.

My nominee as the consummate public sociologist is C. Wright Mills, introduced earlier in this chapter, but there have been many important works of sociology that have reached a wide public audience:

- In *Ain't I a Woman?* (1981), bell hooks argues that black women in America, facing both sexism and racism, occupy the lowest status in society.
- Judith Butler's *Gender Trouble* (1990) introduced the idea that gender is not innate but is something rehearsed and performed according to cultural expectations. It has become a landmark text of queer studies.
- George Ritzer's *The McDonaldization of Society* (1993) looks at how the principles of managing a fast-food business have come to dominate many other aspects of our social life.
- Robert Putnam's *Bowling Alone* (2000) argues that the demise of traditional clubs and social societies has led to a decline in North America's "social capital"—essentially, the feeling of fellowship among citizens.
- Barbara Ehrenreich's *Nickel and Dimed* (2001) is an undercover look at the working poor and the challenges they face in just getting by.

- Malcolm Gladwell's *Outliers* (2008) sets out to undercover the social conditions that allow some people to succeed while other, equally talented and determined people do not. It challenges the discourse of the American Dream, discussed earlier.
- Guy Standing's *The Precariat: The New Dangerous Class* (2011) looks at the causes and effects in society of the development of a class of people whose jobs have no benefits or security.
- In *Why Young Men: Rage, Race, and the Crisis of Identity* (2018), Jamil Jivani, drawing on his own upbringing in Toronto, looks as what draws black men into violence, and sees parallels with white nationalists and Islamic terrorists.

Naturally, works of sociology intended to reach the masses aren't limited to book form. Many documentaries and podcasts can also be considered works of public sociology.

Professional, Critical, Policy, and Public Sociology: A Review

Distinctions among the four types of sociology are not watertight. It is common for individual sociologists to engage in more than one area, even on a single piece of work. Criticisms can flow easily from people who see themselves as practitioners of one form only. Professional sociologists criticize critical sociologists for low professional standards and for being "troublemaking radicals." Critical sociologists accuse professional sociologists of being far too conservative, and of taking small bits of data and overanalyzing them, dazzling their reading audience with statistical science while actually saying little. Public sociologists could accuse professional sociologists of speaking only to a very small audience made up exclusively of peers; at the same time they accuse the policy sociologists of selling out to corporate and government "mouthpieces." But policy and professional sociologists can counter-accuse the public sociologists of being in it just for the fame, of being no more than "pop sociologists" or simply "popularizers"—a dirty term among many in the academy.

If you've ever watched reruns of *The Flintstones*, you'll know that the titular hero Fred and his "bosom buddy," Barney, attend regular meetings of the Loyal Order of Water Buffaloes and play together in one of Bedrock's bowling leagues. What activities and organizations today foster the sort of social capital that Robert Putnam believes is in decline in America?

What Do YOU Think?

1. Consider the four types of sociology we've just discussed. Where do you imagine your sociology instructor would fall in this scheme? Where would you place the author of this book?
2. Have you ever seen or heard a broadcast interview with a sociologist? If you haven't, why do you think this is so? Is "popular" sociology—sociology for the masses—any more or less important than the other kinds (professional, critical, policy)?

Wrap it Up

Summary

In this chapter, I tried to give you a sense of what sociology looks like. You likely won't have formed a really good opinion of what sociology is until you've reached the end of the book. You've learned a bit about what my approach to writing sociology is like, and my aim of making this a textbook not like the others. You have been introduced to some of the main players that will strut the stage in the chapters that follow: Marx, Durkheim, Weber, three of the modern discipline's founders; Goffman, Foucault, and Smith, pioneers of critical sociology; the structural-functionalist Merton and the symbolic-interactionist Mead. Others you have met only in passing, but you can expect to read a lot more about them in later chapters.

In addition to becoming familiar with some of the discipline's key figures, you have discovered two different ways of categorizing sociology: by approach (structural functionalism, conflict theory, symbolic interactionism, feminism, and postmodernism) and by audience (professional, critical, policy, and public). References to these categories turn up frequently throughout the book. Finally, you have tasted some of sociology's Canadian flavours. Expect plenty more Timbits and maple syrup in the chapters to come.

Think Back

Questions for Critical Review

1. What is the relationship between a sociological narrative and a person's social location? Why are narratives important to the study of sociology?
2. What are some of the factors that gave rise to the birth and growth of sociology in Europe and the United States? To what extent was sociology in Canada shaped by the same factors?
3. How did the Chicago school influence sociology in Canada?
4. Explain the term *vertical mosaic*. Who coined it, and what situation did it apply to?
5. What is the difference between structural functionalism and symbolic interactionism? How do these terms relate to macrosociology and microsociology?
6. Define the term *social fact* and provide an example. Who introduced the concept?
7. Pick one of the examples below to explain the difference between a manifest function, a latent function, and a latent dysfunction.
   a. children's organized sports
   b. large organized walks, runs, or bike rides for social causes
   c. religion
8. What is standpoint theory? Why is it an important element of a feminist approach to sociology?
9. What qualities make a book, a documentary, or a podcast a good work of public sociology?

Read On

Suggested Print and Online Resources

Arianne Hanemaayer and Christopher J. Schneider (2014), *The Public Sociology Debate: Ethics and Engagement* (Vancouver: UBC Press).
- The authors in this collection present a powerful discussion of public sociology as it relates to the Canadian context.

Canadian Journal of Sociology (CJS), 2009, 34, no. 3, https://journals.library.ualberta.ca/cjs/index.php/CJS/issue/view/380
- This special issue of *CJS* devoted to professional, critical, policy, and public sociology features articles by and about Michael Burawoy, as well as features on sociological practice in French Quebec and what public sociologists do.

C. Wright Mills [1916–1962], www.genordell.com/stores/maison/CWMills.htm
- This very useful website features a short profile of the eminent sociologist, as well as lists of works by and about Mills and links to online copies of some of his books and articles.

Dorothy Smith (1989), *The Everyday World as Problematic: A Feminist Sociology* (Boston: Northeastern University).
- This is probably the most often read work by the Canadian pioneer of standpoint theory.

Anna Bessendorf, *From Cradle to Cane: The Cost of Being a Female Consumer.* www1.nyc.gov/assets/dca/downloads/pdf/partners/Study-of-Gender-Pricing-in-NYC.pdf
- New York City's Department of Consumer Affairs commissioned a study of gender pricing in 800 products sold at over two dozen retailers in the Big Apple. Released in December 2015, the report documented evidence of the "pink tax" on everything from toys and children's clothing to adult apparel and personal care products.

FrontPage: Sociology through Documentary Film, http://sociologythroughdocumentary-film.pbworks.com/w/page/17194965/FrontPage
- Originally created by Jessie Daniels, a PhD student at Hunter College and CUNY, this wiki list catalogues sociology-themed documentaries. The films are organized by category ("Culture," "Family," "Education," and so on), so you can pick out something that suits your mood, or you can create an account to add to the list yourself.

Marx & Engels Internet Archive, www.marxists.org/archive/marx
- This is a comprehensive guide to the works of the two fathers of socialism, complete with an image gallery and a sophisticated search feature that allows the reader to find specific words and phrases.

Mary Jo Deegan (2009), *Jane Addams and the Men of the Chicago School, 1892–1918* (New York: Transaction).
- The author explores Addams's influence in America's leading sociology department.

Max Weber [1864–1920], www.sociosite.net/sociologists/weber_max.php
- Created by Dutch sociologist Albert Benschop, this site contains links to books and articles by and about Max Weber.

Michael Hviid Jacobsen, ed. (2009), *The Contemporary Goffman* (New York: Routledge).
- This collection of readings by various authors imagines what kind of research Goffman might be involved in if he were living in the twenty-first century.

Mona Zhang (2017), "The Crimes of Reefer Madness," *High Times* (Sept. 30), https://hightimes.com/culture/crimes-reefer-madness
- This piece discusses the history and nature of the anti-marijuana campaign.

Tanya Talaga (2017), *Seven Fallen Feathers: Racism, Death, and Hard Truths in a Northern City* (Toronto, ON: House of Anansi).
- An award-winning sociological investigation into the deaths of seven Indigenous youths in Thunder Bay from 2000 to 2011, by Anishinaabe journalist Tanya Talaga.

The Durkheim Pages, http://durkheim.uchicago.edu
- Created by University of Illinois historian and sociologists Robert Alun Jones, this site contains abundant information on the French sociologist, including a biography, summaries of some of his works, and a glossary of terms important to understanding Durkheim's work.

Doing Sociology: Social Research Methods

2

Reading this chapter will help you to ...

- Articulate the difference between fact, theory, and hypothesis.
- Understand the role of the scientific method in social science research.
- Name some strengths and limitations of insider and outsider perspectives.
- Distinguish between qualitative and quantitative social research.
- Outline the value of narratives to sociological research.
- State the significance of operational definitions in quantitative research.
- Recognize and give examples of spurious reasoning.
- Explain why care must be taken with using statistics.
- Respect the importance of treating research subjects ethically.

For Starters

Fact, Theory, Hypothesis, and Wondering Why People Speed Up When I Pass Them

It's easier to observe than it is to explain. I can observe people speeding up on the highway when I pass them, but I can't really explain why they do it. Is it because the bee-like buzz of my car's engine wakes them up from a semi-sleeping state? Or is it their competitive spirit that awakens when I—an aging hippie in a Toyota Corolla—pass them in their shiny, high-priced, high-powered vehicles?

That people speed up when I pass them is a **fact**: an observation that, as far as can be known, is true. It does not happen all the time. I have observed it often enough to call it at least a tentative fact. But if I want to use important qualifiers such as "almost all of the time," or "most of the time," or the easier to prove "often," then I have to find a way to quantify this fact—for example, by saying: "I passed 100 vehicles, and 37 were observed to speed up." I should also be more specific about the situation involved by adding "on Highway 50, northwest of Toronto"; "while driving in the slow lane, passing someone who is in the passing lane"; "commuting from work, travelling north around four o'clock." This is how I quantify and qualify my fact: by giving details about how often it occurs and under what conditions.

Now I need a **theory**. A theory is an attempt to explain a fact or observed phenomenon. My theory of why people speed up when I pass them is that I make them aware that they are travelling more slowly than they thought they were. My theory becomes a hypothesis when I set out to verify it by providing some kind of concrete test of its validity. What kind of test can I provide? Obviously, I can't pull people over on the highway and ask them why

they just sped up when I passed them. However, I could develop a questionnaire for people who use that highway. First, I might ask a question such as, "Do you frequently speed up when people pass you on a highway?" I might follow up with a multiple-choice question such as the following:

What is your best explanation for speeding up when people pass you on a highway?

a) Being passed makes me realize that I am driving slower than I thought.
b) I do not like people passing me.
c) I am very competitive.
d) Other (explain): _____. (e.g. I use the highway to re-create my favourite movie scenes from *The Fast and the Furious*.)

Then, I would proceed to test the hypothesis.

Introduction: Research Methodology Is No Joking Matter

Nothing is more contentious in sociology than **research methodology**, the system of methods a researcher uses to gather data on a particular question. There's a running joke:

(Q) How many sociologists does it take to change a light bulb?

(A) Twenty: one to change the light bulb and nineteen to challenge that person's methodology.

I didn't say it was a *funny* joke. The point is, there is no single best way to do sociological research. In fact, researchers often combine several research methods in their work.

In this chapter, we'll take a look at some of the different methods used in sociological research, pointing out the pluses and pitfalls of each one. We begin, though, with a few comments about the history of sociology research and some challenges to be aware of.

How Do You Know That? Generating Knowledge in the Social Sciences

A question I have repeatedly asked my students—and one that I encourage them to ask me—is simply, *How do you know that?* It can sound confrontational.

But in an age of "alternative facts" and the notion that a 6 could easily be a 9 if you just looked at it differently, it is an important way to distinguish sociological fact from ill-formed opinion.

Here's an example. A friend of mine recently asserted that "all Americans love guns." We Canadians can sometimes be a little smug and self-righteous when it comes to discussing our southern neighbours' attitudes to gun control and gun ownership. In this case, my friend was off base, and I knew it.

How do you know that? I challenged.

"Just look at the news," he replied. But "the news" over-communicates (to borrow a phrase from Erving Goffman) certain events, making them seem more common than they actually are.

How do *I* know my friend's declaration was false? I have my own anecdotal evidence, based on discussions I have had with a good number of Americans who do not love guns, but I also came to the conversation armed (sorry) with statistics. Drawing on a recent Pew Research Center survey (2016), I could claim that as of August 2016, only 52 per cent of Americans believed it was more important to protect the right to own guns than to control gun ownership. Moreover, certain groups prioritized gun control over gun rights more than others:

- women (54 per cent) over men (37 per cent)
- Gen Xers (52 per cent) over millennials (45 per cent)
- Hispanics (67 per cent) and blacks (65 per cent) over whites (37 per cent)
- liberals (70 per cent) over conservatives (29 per cent)

- urban residents (59 per cent) over rural residents (29 per cent)
- people living in the American West (53 per cent) and Northeast (52 per cent) over people living in the South (42 per cent) and Midwest (40 per cent).

These statistics come from just one research company, and as we shall see in this chapter, not all statistics are created equal, but thanks to these research findings, my opinion on this matter is more fact-based, and therefore is a position with more truth value.

A related question concerns the distinction between "many" and "most." Students of mine over the years have seen the dreaded stroke of the red pen crossing out the *most* in an exam paper or essay and replacing it with a *many*. Why? *Many* is easily observed, and is difficult to challenge. *Most* is a statistical statement, and usually requires some kind of numbers behind it. In classroom discussions, I have often challenged a student who says "most" with the question, *How do you know that it is "most"?* It can be a nasty question, and it may sound picky, but sociology is, after all, a social science, and it must be held to scientific standards of evidence, or it loses credibility.

The Scientific Method

As a social science, sociology employs the **scientific method**, a series of steps leading to proof. A first step is observation, which involves noticing a repeated action or situation. Cars in the fast lane will speed up when I pass them: that is an example of an observation that I discussed earlier this chapter. Here is another example, which I touched on briefly in Chapter 1.

At the college where I worked, I frequently taught the introductory sociology course to nursing students. It was a required course for them, as it should be, since we expect nurses to treat patients as social beings, not just bodies.

The first thing I would observe—and it was obvious—was the gender imbalance in the classroom. The vast majority of the students were female. This observation was expected, and would be easily proved by a simple head count. The next observation concerning gender involved the social characteristics

of the male students. When compared with female students, the male students were more often older than the typical college student. I also observed that the male students were more likely to speak with a non–North American accent, usually eastern European. (I was often able to confirm this observation in speaking with them, since they would tell me something of their personal history.)

So, I had observed a pattern of behaviour, which led me to a question: How does the background of male nursing students differ from the background of female nursing students? This question is important because it helps to define the **hypothesis**, or the prediction we make about what we have observed. In this case, my hypothesis was that male nursing students in my North American classroom are generally older and more likely to be of eastern European background than are female nursing students. Had I been engaged in a formal sociological study of the subject, I would have needed to prove the hypothesis by generating statistics on both male and female nursing students over, probably, a 10-year period at least. I should also have consulted the sociological literature to see whether anyone had already written on the subject.

Let's assume I had been able to generate enough data to substantiate my hypothesis. I would now have been prepared to answer the question *How do you know that?* should anyone have challenged my hypothesis. But if I were engaged in a formal study, I would have gone on to the next step in the scientific method: theory. A theory is not an observation but an explanation, and it is more difficult to validate than an observation is. Think about how easily we make casual observations with respect to other humans. Girls talk more than boys do. Boys are more aggressive than girls are. Women in their thirties who are named Jennifer are often involved with yoga (personal observation). Gathering data to prove our observations is hard, but explaining our observations—and testing that explanation—is even more difficult.

In the case of my sociological look at male nursing students, I do have a theory: I believe there is a strong social factor that keeps young men born and raised in North America from wanting to become nurses. I think a strong association exists in the minds of many (you'll notice I didn't say most) North Americans between male nurses and femininity. It is an association that is reflected in and perpetuated by film and television representations of male nurses. Think of Ben Stiller's character in *Meet the Parents* (2000) and *Meet the Fockers* (2004): Stiller plays a male nurse named Gaylord, who is teased by his in-laws for his "sissy" career choice. A 2014 study published in the *Journal of Advanced Nursing* provides more evidence to substantiate this theory. The study found that male nurses on American TV "were often subject to questions about their choice of career, masculinity, and sexuality, and their role [was] usually reduced to that of prop, minority spokesperson, or source of comedy" (Weaver, Ferguson, Wilbourn, & Salamonson, 2014). The researchers note that even the programs that apparently set out to challenge misconceptions about men in nursing actually "reinforced stereotypes in more implicit ways."

This research doesn't really prove my theory; it merely gives it some weight. In other cases, research findings may cause us to re-evaluate or even discard our theory. In this way, the scientific method is a cycle in which theories are proposed, tested, revised, and retested many times over, with each step generating a new understanding of the research topic and bringing us closer to truth.

Social Science Debate #1: Insider versus Outsider Perspectives

It was the French philosopher **Auguste Comte** (1798–1857) who coined the word *sociology* and established the discipline as a social science. Comte's sociology was rooted in **positivism**, a belief that the social sciences could be studied using the methods used to study the natural sciences, namely, experiment, measurement, and systematic observation—in other words, the steps that make up the scientific method. Positivism also assumes that the supposed objectivity of these methods can be applied just as well to the social sciences with no accommodation made for the biases of the social scientist.

Although the positivist mode of thinking had a long run, many sociologists today do not believe it is possible for an "outsider" to study a group with complete objectivity. Indeed, one way to contrast the different methods of sociology research is to look at how researchers treat **insider** and **outsider perspectives**. In Comte's view, the outsider was the "expert" and occupied a privileged position over the

subjects of study. Most of sociology's history reflects this privileging of the outsider perspective. Of the four audience-based types of sociology discussed in Chapter 1—professional, critical, policy-based, and public—policy sociology is the one most likely to reflect the outside expert ideal.

By contrast, critical sociology, particularly feminist sociology, rates the insider view highly while questioning the outsider's presumed objectivity. Dorothy Smith's standpoint theory, also introduced last chapter, states that social characteristics such as gender, "race," ethnicity, age, and sexual orientation strongly condition both the questions sociologists ask and the answers they receive. **Michel Foucault**, in volume 1 of *The History of Sexuality* (1978), criticized the outsider approach in his discussion of the "sexual confession." Foucault described the sexual confession as an approach to treating sexual deviance in which the "deviant" patient admits to "impure" thoughts, fantasies, and taboo sexual practices in the presence of an "expert"—typically a doctor or psychotherapist. The people being treated provide information based on personal experience. But according to Foucault, this information is not recognized as "authentic" until it has been interpreted by an "objective" outsider expert, who is placed in the privileged position of deciding which parts of the insider's account are true and which are fabricated or imagined. The subject is not allowed to have a **voice** that is heard without translation from the outsider/expert. This is how sociologically important messages get lost.

To see how an outsider perspective can be flawed, imagine yourself as a non-Indigenous sociologist studying a First Nations reserve. Taking an outsider approach, you conduct your study by looking only at statistics, covering such subjects as unemployment, housing, crime rates, and suicide. Not including the voice of the people who live on that reserve means that you will miss key elements of interpretation. First, some definitions could be problematic. Take "unemployed." Is a man providing for his family by hunting, trapping, fishing, gathering plants for food and medicine, and cutting wood for home heating and cooking "unemployed"? Technically he is, as he does not have a "job" that pays money. Second, typical statistical surveys of Indigenous communities leave unanswered the question of why so many people choose to live on reserves when there is so much more unemployment,

Quick Hits

Steps in the Scientific Method

My doctor's office is next door to a large, fancy coffee shop, where people often sit with their laptops. The same people who are there when I go into my doctor's building are usually there when I leave. Are they working? Are they looking for work? Are they just passing time with social media? How much time do they spend there? Does length of time relate to seriousness of purpose? Let's apply the scientific method to this situation.

1	Make an Observation	We notice that patrons of a coffee shop sit for long periods with their laptops.
2	Identify a Research Question	We articulate the main question we are trying to answer. It could be *What percentage of patrons use laptops at the coffee shop?* or *What is the main reason people use laptops at the coffee shop?*
3	Conduct Background Research	We need to see if anyone has already investigated this situation. If so, their findings might help us refine our research question, or we might see if our own experiment replicates their findings. If our experiment records something different, we should attempt to explain it in terms of possible social differences between our group and the group in their study.
4	Formulate a Hypothesis	Here we come up with a prediction that we wish to test. It is a tentative answer to our research question. It could be *Twenty-five per cent of patrons at our coffee shop use laptops* or *Length of time spent in the coffee shop correlates with the seriousness of their laptop activity.*
5	Select a Research Design	How will we test our hypothesis? We could sit in the coffee shop from 8 a.m. to 5 p.m. and count how many people use their laptops and for how long. We could ask some of the people with laptops what they're doing, or we could try peeking at their screens to avoid having to ask them, but this would be performing research without their consent, which is unethical (as we will see later in the chapter).
6	Gather Data	We have selected a research design to test our hypothesis, and now we can carry out our research.
7	Analyze Data	After we have completed our experiment, we summarize the results to see if they confirm the prediction we made with our hypothesis. Were we right? Were we close? Were we way off base?
8a	Revise Hypothesis or	If our results do not confirm the prediction we made, we need to go back to step 4 and revise our hypothesis, performing more research and checking the results against what we predicted.
8b	Present Results	Once we have results that confirm our hypothesis, we can write them up and share them with other sociologists who may find our research useful.

Our research may uncover a group of reluctant freelance workers who do not have the infrastructure—the office space and internet access—to work from home; they spend long hours at the coffee shop because it is the only place where they can do work. Or it may show us a group of people who stop in at the coffee shop to check social media on their way from one activity to another. Either way, our findings should help us formulate some theories about the situation and open up avenues for further research. As you read about the methods described throughout this chapter, try to imagine how each might be used to investigate this example.

crime, and overcrowding than in non-Native communities of comparable size. You need to hear the people's voices to answer this question.

Brian Maracle is a Kanyen'kehaka (Mohawk) who left his home reserve when he was five years old but returned as an adult. *Back on the Rez: Finding the Way Home* (1996) is his account of the first year of his return to the Six Nations reserve near Brantford, Ontario. This reserve is very different from the more troubled Indigenous communities—Davis Inlet and Attawapiskat, for example—commonly described in sociology textbooks. The people of the Six Nations reserve have lived there for over 220 years, since the land was granted to them for siding with the British during the American Revolution. In the introduction to *Back on the Rez*, Maracle points out that reserves can be considered homelands because they function as refuges from non-Indigenous society:

> The reserves mean many things. . . . On one level, these postage-stamp remnants of our original territories are nagging reminders of the echoing vastness of what we have lost. On another, they are the legacy and bastion of our being. They are a refuge, a prison, a madhouse, a fortress, a birthplace, a Mecca, a resting-place, ·Home-Sweet-Home, Fatherland and Motherland rolled into one. (1996, p. 3)

Maracle writes of the importance of the reserve as the home of the Mohawk Elders, who interpret past traditions and adapt them to the present. In this way, he emphasizes that the reserve is the home of Indigenous culture. However, reserves are not always homeland to everyone. They can be places where men with physical strength and social connections can oppress women and sexually abuse children. They can be

What Do YOU Think?

Think of a community that you are particularly involved in—a club or team, a religious group, your college or university residence, or some other. How easily could it be studied by an outsider? Which insider voices would an outsider need to listen to in order to get an accurate picture of it? What biases would be reflected if they asked only you?

places where young people feel despair and alienation, caught between the ancient traditions that make up their heritage and the rapidly modernizing practices of a globalizing world. While recognizing the importance of the insider's view in sociological research, remember that a range of voices have to be heard.

My position is that complete objectivity is impossible whenever one human being studies others. However, complete subjectivity can be blind. A judicious balance of insider and outsider vision is the ideal.

Social Science Debate #2: Quantitative versus Qualitative Research

Another ongoing debate in sociology concerns the relative merits of quantitative research and qualitative research. **Quantitative research** focuses on social elements that can be counted or measured, which can therefore be used to generate statistics. It often involves working with surveys, questionnaires, and polls. **Qualitative research** involves the close examination of characteristics that cannot be

Quick Hits

The Weaknesses of the Insider View

Have you ever been told you were too close to a situation to judge it fairly? Many of Maracle's insights come from his position as both an insider and an outsider. Imagine the perceptual weaknesses of an investigation of the Prime Minister's Office conducted by the prime minister or a cabinet minister. Think of how a marriage counsellor can see the flaws in a marriage that are invisible to the couple. The point is, while insider views are vital to a proper sociological understanding of a situation, a critical view often requires a certain measure of distance.

Do you find the sight of a police officer on your street comforting or alarming? Your perspective is likely to be shaped by your age, your "race," your class, sex, sexual orientation, and other social characteristics. How would you overcome this challenge as an outsider sociologist studying the relationship between the police and a particular community?

counted or measured. Unlike quantitative research, which is typically used to find the patterns governing whole structures or systems, communities, and so on, qualitative research may be used to study those smaller cases that don't fit into the larger model.

Proponents of quantitative research accuse qualitative researchers of relying on data that are "soft," "anecdotal," "too subjective," or "merely literary." In turn, champions of the qualitative approach dismiss quantitative researchers as soulless "number crunchers" operating under the delusion that it is possible for humans to study other humans with complete objectivity. The debate between quantitative and qualitative researchers may remind you of the distinction made in Chapter 1 between macrosociologists, with their big-picture approach to social issues, and microsociologists, concerned with the actions and behaviours of individuals and small groups.

So which side is better? In true twenty-first-century fashion, everyone gets a medal. Quantitative

research and qualitative research both have merits, and sociologists can draw valuable insights from each. It's wrong to think that the two methods are mutually exclusive. Good quantitative researchers know that their research always has a subjective component to it and always involves choice and some personal bias; they usually acknowledge as much in the abstracts or introductory comments of their research articles. Qualitative researchers, similarly, often benefit from using quantitative data to provide some context for the cases they are focusing on.

Many researchers today embrace **triangulation**, or a **mixed-methods approach**, in which qualitative research is used to confirm or expand on the results of quantitative research, or vice versa. For example, a researcher might poll all of the students in the sociology department to measure their level of support (on a scale from 1 to 5) for online textbooks, and then supplement those findings with open-ended interviews of a sample of the students.

GerryRousseau / Alamy Stock Photo

Imagine you wanted to study the impact of fentanyl use on a community like Vancouver's Downtown Eastside. How would you use quantitative data in your study? What insights could qualitative data (e.g. interviewing addicts, police officers, doctors, and therapists) give you?

We will spend the next few sections of this chapter taking a closer look at different methods of qualitative and quantitative research. We will see how they measure up and how they can be used together.

Qualitative Research

Qualitative research permits—often encourages—subjectivity on the part of both researcher and research subject in a way that quantitative research oriented around "hard data" does not. Among the various qualitative methods are **ethnography** and the **case study approach**, which differ mainly in their breadth of focus. The former typically takes a broader view by attempting to describe the entirety of a culture, while the latter adopts a narrower focus to study individual cases.

Ethnography

Robert P. Gephart, who teaches research methods at the Alberta School of Business, describes ethnography as relying on "direct observation and extended field research to produce a thick, naturalistic description of a people and their culture. Ethnography seeks to uncover the symbols and categories members of the given culture use to interpret their world" (1988, p. 16).

A classic example of the ethnographic approach in sociology is William Whyte's *Street-Corner Society: The Social Structure of an Italian Slum (1955)*. Beginning early in 1937, Whyte spent three-and-a-half years living in the neighbourhood of Boston that he called "Cornerville," following a standard research practice of assigning a fictitious name to the community studied in order to preserve the anonymity of the subjects. Whyte spent 18 months living with an Italian American family. His research methodology involved **semi-structured interviews**—informal, face-to-face interviews designed to cover specific topics without the rigid structure of a questionnaire but with more structure than an open interview—and **participant observation**, which entails both observing people as an outsider would and actively participating in the various activities of the studied people's lives. Participant observation enables the researcher to achieve something resembling an insider's perspective.

Researchers engaged in ethnography typically depend as well on **informants**, insiders who act as interpreters or intermediaries while helping the researcher become accepted by the community studied. Whyte's informant was a gang leader in his late twenties who went by the name "Doc." Whyte met Doc through the latter's social worker in a meeting Whyte describes in the book:

> I said that I had been interested in congested city districts in my college study but had felt very remote from them. I hoped to study the problems in such a district. I felt I could do very little as an outsider. Only if I could get to know the people and learn their problems first-hand would I be able to gain the understanding I needed. (1955, p. 291)

Doc replied,

> "Well, any nights you want to see anything, I'll take you around. I can take you to the joints—gambling joints—I can take you around to the street corners. Just remember that you're my friend. That's all they need to know. I know these places, and, if I tell them that you're my friend, nobody will bother you. You just tell me what you want to see, and we'll arrange it." (Whyte, 1955, p. 291)

Doc and Whyte would discuss Whyte's research interests and findings to the point where Doc became "in a very real sense, a collaborator in the research" (Whyte, 1955, p. 301). Whyte learned to speak Italian so that he could talk directly to the older generation from Italy. He participated in the second generation's activities of going to "gambling joints," bowling, and playing baseball and cards. He called his work "participatory action research" because he wanted his research to lead to actions that would improve the lives of the people studied.

In Canada, Whyte's study influenced Carl Dawson's work with Prairie communities, as well as the Quebec community studies of Everett Hughes (*French Canada in Transition*, 1943) and Horace Miner (*St Denis: A French-Canadian Parish*, 1939).

What Do YOU Think?

William Whyte's *Street-Corner Society* was published without a co-author, despite the fact that Doc's involvement was instrumental to the research. What does this say about the power imbalance between research subject and researcher?

Institutional Ethnography

Institutional ethnography is a relatively new method of research, based on the theories of **Dorothy Smith**. This method of research differs from traditional sociological research in that it does not reflect the view that a neutral stance is necessarily more scientific than an approach that explicitly involves "taking sides" (Campbell & Gregor, 2002, p. 48).

Institutional ethnography recognizes that any organization can be seen as having two sides, each associated with a different kind of data. One side represents **ruling interests**: the interests of the organization, particularly its administration, and/or the interests of those who hold power in society. The data associated with this side are text-based, comprising the institution's written rules and practices. When the workers in the institution follow these rules and practices, they are activating **ruling relations**: that is, they are helping to serve the needs of the organization, often at the cost of their clients and themselves.

The other side of an organization is that of the informant, someone who works in the institution outside of management. The data associated with the informant's side are **experiential**, based on the informant's experience. Institutional ethnography recognizes that there is a **disjuncture**, or separation, between the knowledge produced from the perspectives of these two sides. In pointing out this disjuncture, institutional ethnographers generate information that they hope will lead to institutional change.

Schools offer a good example of the kind of organization that institutional ethnographers study. York University professor Alison Griffith asserts that teachers rely on parents (typically mothers) to get children to do the work and acquire the skills necessary to succeed at school. Campbell and Gregor refer to this reliance on parents as "downloading educational work" (2002, p. 43). This practice serves the ruling interests of boards of education and provincial governments, who can then spend less on schools and teachers. Teachers and parents, by complying with the demands of school administrators, are activating ruling relations. At the same time, they are also biasing the system in favour of students from upper- and middle-class households, whose parents are in a better position to provide the resources (including their own time and knowledge, as well as computers and high-speed internet access and a quiet study space) to best serve this end. Lower-class students are poorly served by the system, as they are more dependent on the school and its resources.

The problem is made worse in provinces such as Ontario, where it is illegal for school boards to pass deficit budgets. Local boards, meeting the ruling interests of the provincial government, have been forced to consider closing pools and cutting music and athletic programs, putting more pressure for children's health and enrichment onto the parents. This creates a second disjuncture—between the provincial government and its boards—in addition to the one between boards and administrators and parents/children. This kind of information, generated through institutional ethnography, can be used to recommend improvements to the school system.

What Do YOU Think?

1. Which side do you think researchers typically take in institutional ethnography?
2. Who should be most responsible for ensuring that children get the exercise they need: school boards and the province, or parents?

Peter Graham/Nova Scotia Health Authority

Managers and charge nurses at the QEII Health Sciences Centre in Halifax meet to identify how many beds will be available for patients coming from scheduled surgeries and the emergency room. The hospital is a common subject for institutional ethnography. Who represents the ruling interests? Who is responsible for ensuring that those ruling interests are met? What individuals or groups are likely to give the most consideration to patient needs? Who is most likely to receive criticism from patients and their families?

An Example of Institutional Ethnography: Aileen Ross's Research on Homeless Women in Montreal

In 1977–8, Canadian sociologist **Aileen Ross** engaged in pioneering sociological research in two women's shelters in Montreal, one run during the day, the other at night. Both shelters had just opened when she began her research in the summer of 1977. The methodology she chose, and her reasons for choosing it, are instructive in understanding the limits of sociological research as she saw them:

> This study began without case histories that could be analyzed in terms of the usual neat hypotheses gleaned from previous studies. One reason for this omission was that very little sociological research has been done which throws light on Skid Row men, still less on homeless women. Another reason was that the staff of the day shelter held tenaciously to their basic philosophy that the women would not be questioned about themselves. . . . "Don't sit eyeball to eyeball with them. If they think the shelter is being researched, they won't come back. No questions, please, and <u>no</u> questionnaires" (Staff member).

> The data were collected through careful observation of and informal interviews with the women and through accounts of their behaviour by the staffs of the two shelters and several other shelters. Interviews also were obtained from the directors of the Women's Shelter Foundation and from many professionals, including psychiatric, medical, and other social workers. . . . The records kept at the night shelter and the log written up each night at the day shelter were other sources of information. (Ross, 1982, p. 107)

In the description of her methodology, Ross notes that she gathered information not just from observations and interviews but from logs kept by the staff of the shelter. These kinds of records can be valuable to social research as they provide clues to what goes on in a person's life. Consider "Lily," one of the homeless women Ross wrote about. Lily was a 30-year-old anglophone resident of Montreal. She had held a steady job until she injured her leg skiing. During a painful recovery, she became addicted to painkillers, which led her to homelessness. The following is just part of an account of her interactions with local institutions during the period of Ross's study:

Date	Institution	Problem	Result
1977			
19 June	hospital	drugs—couldn't speak	discharged
2 July	hospital	stomach pains	discharged
6 August	night shelter	crying at door in early morning frightened, scratches and bruises	—
7 August	hospital	stoned, shaky, grave condition	discharged
19 August	night shelter	strongly medicated, couldn't stand	—
23 August	hospital	drug overdose	discharged next day
26 August	hospital	could not stand, poor respiration	discharged next day
28 August	detention centre	upset as she had to go to court	did not show in court
29 August	hospital	stomach ulcers	discharged
2 September	jail	one day for shop-lifting	sent to hospital
9 September	hospital	drugs and sore legs	discharged next day
23 September	hospital	suicide attempt (set fire to room)	sent to another hospital
28 September	hospital	drug overdose	left

The Case Study Approach

British sociologist Gordon Marshall describes the case study approach as

> [a] research design that takes as its subject a single case or a few selected examples of a social entity—such as communities, social groups, employers, events, life-histories, families, work teams, roles, or relationships—and employs a variety of methods to study them. (1998, p. 56)

The case study approach is often used to investigate or compare situations that are considered either very typical or very different from the norm. The approach is a key tool of policy sociology, used to identify and describe **best practices**—strategies with a proven history of achieving desired results more effectively or consistently than similar methods used in the past by a particular organization or currently by similar organizations. The case study typically begins by introducing an organization or department that exemplifies the best practices under review, before describing the practices in terms of the organization's success. The case study is often geared to finding out whether certain best practices can be applied with comparable success elsewhere.

Case Study of a Best Practice: First Nations Policing in Kitigan Zibi Anishinabeg

Located about 130 kilometres north of Ottawa, Kitigan Zibi Anishinabeg, with a registered population of 3,466 (as of April 2019), is the largest of nine

Wollertz/Shutterstock

Why might a homeless person fear being questioned by someone in a position of authority?

communities that make up the Algonquin Nation in Quebec. The community first had its own policing services in 1981, when, like other Quebec First Nations, it began operating a community police force under the auspices of the Amerindian Police Service (the APS). The APS is usually seen as a failure by Quebec's First Nations, whose officers were typically given limited, second-class roles as "special constables." In 1985, Kitigan Zibi moved ahead of other Indigenous communities by transferring police services to its own independent force.

Following the introduction of the federal First Nation Policing Policy in April 1992, the community entered into a three-year tripartite agreement that allowed the Kitigan Zibi Police Department (KZPD) to become a fully functional force, with powers equivalent to those of any non-Indigenous force in Canada. By 2002, the KZPD had a chief of police, five full-time officers, and one part-time officer. Community satisfaction with the department's work was high: in a 2002 survey, 91 per cent of community members surveyed felt that the KZPD was the best police organization to meet the needs of the community. This compares favourably to the 55 per cent of community stakeholders who, in a First Nations Chiefs of Police Association survey, felt the self-administered police services in their communities were effective.

What Do YOU Think?

1. What can you learn from examining the record of Lily's interactions with institutions? What questions does it leave unanswered? Does it only show the negative side of her life?
2. In what ways can Ross's study be considered an institutional ethnography?

There are four keys to the success of the KZPD. Unfortunately, two of them cannot be replicated in most other First Nations. First, Kitigan Zibi has a very stable political environment. At the time of the study, the chief councillor of the band had been in the position for over 20 years. During that time there had been few changes in the makeup of the band council. Further, there were no apparent political factions within the community, making it unlike many First Nations. Second, the KZPD has a reasonably harmonious relationship with the Quebec provincial police, a rarity for a First Nations force in Quebec.

Two remaining keys to the KZPD's success offer lessons for police forces operating in other First Nations. One is the strong relationship between the KZPD and the youth of the community. In 1995, the KZPD took part in a pilot project with Indigenous youths aged between 12 and 24, who were paired with police officers to ride in cruisers, observe police duties firsthand, and visit the homes of their police mentors. Commenting on the mentoring experience, one officer said, "I took great pride in seeing the barriers fall and the sense of openness that developed in our communication" (Aboriginal Policing Directorate, 1995, p. 3).

The final key is the KZPD's dedication to training. One condition of the 1992 tripartite agreement signed with federal and provincial governments was that constables already in the force would earn the basic training equivalency diploma. This would enable the officers to assume powers equal to those of any other officer in Quebec. All of the KZPD's officers successfully completed the training. The chief of police went beyond the qualifications required in the agreement, taking managerial courses for senior officers and additional courses offered at the Canadian Police College in Ottawa. When the Quebec Police Act was amended to include more training for provincial officers, the chief of police prepared a five-year forecast of the training needs of his force.

Narratives

The **narrative** is perhaps the purest form of the insider view. Narratives are the stories people tell about themselves, their situations, and the others around them. They have long been part of sociology. An early Canadian example of narrative research is **Aileen Ross**'s *Becoming a Nurse* (1961), based on her analysis—for an introductory sociology course—of 259 term papers written by nursing students between 1948 and 1959.

In spite of their history and the value of narratives to sociological inquiry, the positivism of early sociology and the discipline's emphasis on statistical evidence kept narrative study in a minor role until the late 1980s. In 1993, D.R. Maines proclaimed the growing interest in narratives among sociologists as "narrative's moment." He saw in this trend a dual focus for sociological study, aimed at both examining the narratives of the subjects of study and at the same time "viewing sociologists as narrators" (Maines, 1993, p. 17). The use of narratives in research is important because it can give voice to people who do not usually get to speak directly in research. Voice is the expression of *a* (not *the*) viewpoint that comes from occupying a particular social location.

Consider the two narratives presented below. Both give voice to viewpoints not often heard in mainstream media. In the first, a young, male, Muslim college student talks about fasting. His voice is different from the voices of other

Kitigan Zibi Police Department

Justin Petonoquot is an Algonquin police corporal and investigator with the Kitigan Zibi Police Department. What makes the KZPD a good subject for a case study? How does the study combine qualitative and quantitative research?

Muslims—those of young women, or of local religious leaders, but it speaks a truth because it reflects the speaker's life experience. It carries value because it gives the non-Muslim reader a sense of what it is like to be a young, male Muslim living in Canada. The second narrative provides a perspective on what it is like to be a young Palestinian-Canadian woman growing up in a small suburban community in Ontario. Consider the factors shaping her **social location**, the vantage point from which she speaks: age, gender, ethnic background, nationality, the site of her upbringing, her status as a student, even the political climate at the time of writing. All contribute to her unique perspective.

Content Analysis

Content analysis involves studying a set of **cultural artifacts** or events and interpreting the themes they reflect. Cultural artifacts may include children's books, billboards, novels, newspaper articles, advertisements, artwork, articles of clothing, clinical records—even textbooks. These items

What Do YOU Think?

Consider an issue raised in one of the two narratives you've just read. What further research could you do to deepen your understanding of the topic?

all have two distinct properties not normally found in the subjects studied using other types of qualitative methodology. First, they have a "found" quality because they are not created specifically to be studied. Second, they are *non-interactive* in that there are no interviews used or behaviours observed to gather the data (Reinharz, 1992, pp. 146–8).

Feminist approaches to content analysis investigate the way gender is portrayed in the media, particularly as it reflects a culture of persistent **patriarchy** (male domination) and misogyny (hatred of women). American sociologist Elaine Hall (1988), in "One Week for Women? The Structure of Inclusion of Gender Issues in Introductory Textbooks," demonstrated how women's issues are treated as

Telling It Like It Is

A Student's POV

Fasting

"Hey Moe, come join us for lunch."
"I can't, guys. I'm fasting."
"Fasting, what's that?"

This passage may be heard every year, asked by anyone and almost everyone. It bothers me to consider that the average person doesn't know what fasting for Muslims is. Fasting is an Islamic tradition practised for centuries, where a Muslim is subjected to no food or drink from sunrise to sunset. This is done to remind Muslims where we came from, to remind us that we started with nothing. It teaches us to value what we have and to value our gracious religion. There is fasting in almost every religion, yet the people who know the basic term *fasting* don't know what type of fasting

Muslims commit to. Many people [I have spoken to] were shocked to hear that during Ramadan [fasting month] not only can you not eat, but you also cannot drink [from sunrise to sunset]. Many people thought that water was allowed in any fasting, but it isn't for the Muslim type of fasting.

When someone asks me what fasting is for Muslims, I reply with such fatigue from saying it over and over that I simply reply, "Well, we (Muslims) basically can't eat or drink anything when the sun is up." I simply gave a quick answer because I get that question asked every year, by anyone and almost everyone.

—Mohamed Abseh

Telling It Like It Is

Canadian by Birth, Palestinian by Culture

My name is Nadine and I am Canadian-born, but Palestinian by culture. My father was born in Palestine and my mother was born in Egypt to Palestinian refugees. Nowadays, being of Palestinian origin is quite difficult, even when you're living in a so-called multicultural nation. I guess it's not as hard for me as it has been for my parents because I am Canadian-born, and my parents came to Canada knowing little about the country. However, the difficult aspect in my life was that I grew up in a one-cultured town [the predominantly Italian Canadian town of Woodbridge, in southern Ontario], which made it extremely difficult for my brothers and I to fit in. I have never been able to have any close relationship with anyone. Why? I guess that children needed a common ground in order to establish a relationship, and not possessing the same culture as those around me made my assimilation even more difficult. Within homogeneous groups one can be easily singled out and that happened to me. Furthermore, as I grew up it became harder for me to engage in any real relationship with boys or girls because my culture became stronger for me and as well for them, which made us even grow farther apart. Maybe it was because I didn't speak or dress like them, or because I was darker than them, it didn't matter—basically I was just different.

Entering college, it was a bit easier for me to make acquaintances, though I realized how uneducated and ignorant people could be. It was particularly difficult for me after the events of 9/11 because, automatically, the Arab world would get blamed for it and most people, ignorant as they are, believed everything that the media's propaganda had been telling them. I was in college at that time, and explaining to people my point of view was tremendously challenging. Media brainwash had its toll on the majority of those around me. Furthermore, getting into debates with individuals about what's occurring in Palestine and my views as a Palestinian was almost impossible. Right now my oppressed and displaced people who have been legitimately resisting occupation since 1948 are the bad guys. Maybe in a couple of years it will be another group, but for me now it's hard because I'm still singled out by my friends and the media. Maybe it would be a little bit easier if individuals would become open-minded about what goes on in the world. Then, people could understand who we are and who I am. Knowledge is responsibility and, to most, responsibility is a heavy burden to take. It is pretty sad what's going on in the twenty-first century is that people like me, Canadian-born, have difficulties growing up because of who they are and where they're from!

—Nadine Dahdah

an afterthought in introductory-level texts. Judith Dilorio, in a paper presented in 1980, used content analysis to examine scholarly articles on gender role research and found that their methods *naturalized*, or normalized, social facts that diminished women and promoted male-oriented conservatism (in Reinharz, 1992, pp. 147, 361).

In *Gender Advertisements*, Erving Goffman (1976) undertook a content analysis of commercial pictures depicting gender in print media. The women in the magazine ads he examined were overwhelmingly shown as subordinate and submissive. The magazines Goffman studied represented both mass media and popular culture, having been selected on the basis of their availability and their circulation size. Taken together, these magazines (available in supermarkets, convenience stores, and drug stores) act as cultural objects, reflecting the social world. This relationship, however, is bi-directional: cultural objects such as magazines reflect the social world, and the social world, in turn, is influenced by cultural objects (Griswold, 1994, pp. 22–3).

Popular magazines give us both a snapshot of the social world and also, if we look carefully, an indication of how the social world is being constructed through mass media.

Sut Jhally (1990), argues that magazine ads are neither completely true nor completely false reflections of social reality. They are partial truths and falsehoods. Ads depicting gender do not truly or falsely represent "real" gender relations or **ritualized** gender displays. Rather, for Jhally, they are "hyper-ritualizations," exaggerations that emphasize certain aspects of gender display and de-emphasize others (1990, p. 135).

While content analysis is considered a qualitative method of research, it can often involve some quantification of the data. Elements may be systematically counted to see which ones dominate. Consider Alan J. Sofalvi's (2008) content analysis of 39 condom ads, in print and online. Affiliated with the Health Department at the State University of New York at Cortland, Sofalvi believed that his study could help high school and college educators begin a discussion about media literacy and health literacy. Underlying his study was the question of whether advertising succeeds in delivering messages about public health. To answer this question, Sofalvi looked for the benefits touted in the condom ads and tallied them up. His results are summarized in Table 2.1.

One of Sofalvi's main conclusions was that, compared with condom ads from an earlier time, the emphasis of the 39 ads he studied was decidedly more on pleasure for the two participants (a theme often presented with humour) than on disease and pregnancy prevention (topics that, frankly, aren't as funny). Only 12 ads—less than one-third of the total sample—mentioned safe sex. One reason for this, he explained, was that some American media outlets, more conservative by nature, would not air commercials addressing pregnancy prevention.

A topic that Sofalvi did not fully explore in his study was how condom ads varied in their messaging depending on the target audience—male versus female, gay versus straight, North American versus Russian or Indian, and so on. This sort of research could be carried out without too much difficulty by students with the time, inclination, and internet access to do so.

TABLE 2.1 Features or Benefits Specified in Condom Advertisements, 1997–2007

Condom feature/benefit	Number
Pleasure	26
None specified	9
Protection (unspecified)	9
Disease prevention	8
Sensitivity	6
Lubricated	5
Comfort	4
Larger size	4
Pregnancy prevention	4
Thinness	3
Strength	2
Low latex odor	1
Non-lubricated	1

Source: Sofalvi, 2008, p. 12.

Discourse Analysis

Foucault defined *discourse* as "a conceptual framework with its own internal logic and underlying assumptions that are generally recognizable." There are two types of **discourse analysis** used by sociologists. One analyzes discourse as the term is commonly understood: that is, as a conversation, a speech, or a written text. Sociologists may examine the "discourse" found in a given ethnography, in an open-ended interview, or in a narrative. They might also focus on other kinds of "text," such as court transcripts, newspaper stories, movie trailers, and advertisements.

Another type of discourse analysis considers a broader definition of "text," going beyond individual works and authors to include large "fields" of presentation of information over a period of time, such as movies in general or in the early twenty-first century, reality shows, introductory sociology textbooks, Canadian historical writing, and so on. A "field" comprises all known discourse on a particular cultural concept or idea—"masculinity," for instance.

The role of the researcher is to examine a discourse through time and to decode it, looking at it a way of constructing knowledge that benefits its creator. A discourse analysis could, for instance, focus on a government's messages around

► ►❙ ◄》 0:01 / 0:15   ⚙ ▭ ⟦⟧

In 2017, Trojan introduced a new line of condoms marketed to women, with pretty purple packaging and a wholesome ad campaign empowering female consumers to "trust themselves" and "have the confidence to be who they want to be." Wait, aren't women interested in novelty flavoured warming lubricants and a pleasure-enhancing configuration of riffles and dots? Why should ads targeting men and women be different when the principal aim of the product—prevention of disease and unwanted pregnancy—should be of equal importance to both sexual partners?

immigration—in ads, in speeches, in press briefings, in tweets—to understand how that discourse advances a political agenda by conditioning a segment of the voting public to view outsiders in a particular way.

Genealogy

In discourse analysis, **genealogy** is a method of examining the history of the second type of discourse defined above. Foucault, in his later works, used a genealogical method to trace the origins and histories of modern discourses as they collide, fragment, and adhere to other cultural practices and discourses over time. Foucault's genealogical work captures the dynamic nature of such discourses as mental illness (1961), the penal system (1975), and sexuality (1978).

Edward Said's study of Western attitudes toward Eastern culture, *Orientalism* (1979), offers another example of genealogical research. The Palestinian-born Said (1935–2003) developed the genealogy of **Orientalism**, broadly defined as a Western fascination with or romanticization of the "exotic" culture of Middle and Far Eastern societies. For Said, Orientalism could not be studied or understood without the concept of discourse:

My contention is that without examining Orientalism as a discourse one cannot possibly understand the enormously systematic discipline by which European culture was able to manage—and even produce—the Orient politically, sociologically, militarily, ideologically, scientifically, and imaginatively during the post-Enlightenment period. (1979, p. 3)

Mary Evans / Grenville Collins Postcard Collection

JIM WATSON/AFP/Getty Images

(*left*) What does this 1904 postcard from Constantinople (present-day Istanbul, Turkey) tell us about how Westerners thought of "the Orient" at this time? Compare it with a more recent reflection of Orientalist thought (*right*). In each case, how does the discourse of Orientalism reflect, in Said's words, "a Western style for dominating, restructuring, and having authority over the Orient"?

Orientalism, for Said, refers to "a corporate institution for dealing with the Orient—dealing with it by making statements about it, authorising views of it, describing it, by teaching it, settling it, ruling over it: in short, . . . a Western style for dominating, restructuring, and having authority over the Orient" (Said, 1979, p. 3). Orientalism, then, refers to the ways in which the "Orient" was, and continues to be, constructed in the western European and North American imagination. What is important to understand is that the discourse of Orientalism has was created and has been revised over time to further expansionist goals of Western powers by dominating and controlling this part of the world.

What Do YOU Think?

Now decidedly old-fashioned, *Oriental* was once the common term to describe what many people today consider *Asian*. But what does "Asian" mean to you? If you're North American, it likely refers mostly to China and Japan. If you're British, you probably associate it with India and Pakistan (countries we in Canada might refer to as "South Asian"). What countries do the terms *Southeast Asian* and *East Asian* suggest to you? What term might you use for someone from Siberia or Mongolia?

Quantitative Research

Understanding Statistics

Sociologists have mixed feelings about **statistics**, a science that, in sociology, involves the use of numbers to map social behaviour and beliefs. Social scientists relish the opportunity to show off by quoting numbers. And yet, sociologists are also critical of other people's statistics. There are more jokes about the science of statistics than about any other kind of sociological research method—and we can prove that statistically. But here is some anecdotal evidence:

- "It shames me some to hear the statistics about us in class. The shame burns holes in whatever sympathy I may have for Indians, not my mom though."—the Native protagonist of Indigenous writer Lee Maracle's novel *Sundogs* (Maracle, 1992, p. 3)
- "There are three kinds of lies: lies, damned lies, and statistics."—Benjamin Disraeli
- "There are two kinds of statistics: the kind you look up, and the kind you make up." —Rex Stout
- "An unsophisticated forecaster uses statistics as a drunk man uses lamp-posts—for support rather than illumination."—Andrew Lang
- "Smoking is one of the leading causes of statistics."—Fletcher Knebel
- "Statistician: A man who believes figures don't lie, but admits that under analysis some of them won't stand up either."—Evan Esar, *Esar's Comic Dictionary*
- "Statistics: The only science that enables different experts using the same figures to draw different conclusions."—Esar

In the sections that follow, we will look at the ways that statistics can either enhance or impair good sociological research.

Measuring the Centre: The Median, the Average, and the Mean

Let's take a moment to consider that last statement above and the idea that experts can draw different conclusions from the same statistics. How is that possible? One way is by using different measures of centre to analyze the statistics. A *measure of centre* is a way of taking all of the data you have gathered on a particular subject and finding the most representative result. Two of the most common measures of centre are the median and the average. The **median** represents the number, score, or result that separates the higher half of all results from the lower half of results in a given set of data. If you have a set of five scores, in order from lowest to highest, the median will be the one in the third position. In the series 6, 8, 10, 11, 14, 16, 18, the median is 11: it is the number

in the fourth position, separating the bottom three scores from the top three scores.

How is the median different from the **average**? You find the average by adding up all the scores and dividing the total by the number of scores you have. In the series above, the average would be 6 + 8 + 10 + 11 + 14 + 16 +18 = 83 ÷ 7 =11.9. The average is not always higher than the median. For the sequence 4, 7, 9, 11, 12, 14, 16, the median—the score in the middle—would be 11, and the average would be 10.1. Another measure of centre is the **mean**, which is usually calculated in the same way as the average. However, for weather (and other purposes), it can be determined by taking the two extremes and dividing by two. If the daily low is 0 degrees Celsius and the daily high is 10, then the daily mean is 5.

To see why this matters, let's consider an example. A small hardware store employs seven sales associates to help customers with their purchases. Two of the sales associates believe they are significantly underpaid: they both make $14.75 an hour. They pluck up the courage to talk to the store's owner, who explains that the median salary of the seven employees is $15.00—not much more than what the two employees make. End of story? Not quite.

The two employees decide to ask their coworkers what their hourly wages are, and this is what they discover:

Employee	Hourly Wage
1	$22.50
2	$21.00
3	$19.75
4	$15.00
5	$14.75
6	$14.75
7	$14.00

The median hourly wage, represented by Employee 4, really is $15.00. However, the average salary, found by adding all of the wages and diving the total by 7, is $17.39—quite a bit more than what the two employees make. The employees would make good sociologists: they did their own analysis of the data and came up with a different interpretation to the one they were given. The average is not necessarily more reliable than the median: the two scores can be very different, though, so it's good to look at both if you can.

Quick Hits

The Value of Using the Median: All Those "Indian Chiefs" Making So Much Money

Members of the conservative news media suspicious of the way First Nations bands manage their funds will occasionally draw attention to the exorbitant salaries of band chiefs. An analysis that appeared in the *Toronto Star* gave me material for a good reply to these criticisms, and a teaching moment for readers. The numbers shown in Table 2.2 come from the former federal Department of Indigenous and Northern Affairs.

What you can expect from critics of Canada's First Nations would be a focus on all of the band chiefs getting paid $240,000, or else the $180,000+ earned by the list's top ten. However, when analysts at the *Star* looked for the median salary earned by First Nations chiefs, they arrived at a figure of $64,697. Other figures could have been used to get across the same idea: for instance, 79 per cent received less than $80,000, and about 67 per cent (or roughly two-thirds) received between $20,000 and $79,999. This approximates the pay of a low-level bureaucrat or a lower middle manager in a large company.

TABLE 2.2 Median Pay for First Nations Band Leaders

Salary Range ($)	Number of First Nations Chiefs	Running Total
$0	8	8
$1–9999	34	42
$10,000–19,000	41	83
$20,000–39,999	100	183
$40,000–59,999	140	323
$60,000–79,999	190	513
$80,000–99,999	70	583
$100,000–119,999	28	611
$120,000–139,999	14	625
$140,000–159,999	8	633
$160,000–179,999	4	637
$180,000–199,999	5	642
$200,000–209,999	2	644
$210,000–219,999	0	644
$220,000–239,999	0	644
$240,000+	3	647

Source: Smith, 2015, pp. A1, A8.

Using Operational Definitions

Knowing that different measures of centre can produce different interpretations of the data is one area of quantifiable research in which a sociology student can learn to challenge the research of professionals. Another involves the use of **operational definitions**. These definitions take abstract or theoretical concepts—"poverty," "abuse," or "middle class," for example—and transform them into concrete, observable, and measurable entities. But "operationalizing" abstract concepts can be difficult to do.

The *Handbook for Sociology Teachers*, by British sociologists Roger Gomm and Patrick McNeill (1982), contains a brilliant exercise illustrating the importance of operational definitions. Students are presented with a table showing the number of thefts that have occurred at a number of schools. Included in the table are the following factors that may have a bearing on the findings:

- size of the school
- social class of the school's students
- whether the school is single-sex or co-educational.

Students are asked to determine if there may be a cause-and-effect relationship between any of these factors and the number of thefts. Having given the students a chance to reach tentative conclusions, the teacher gives them a handout showing that each school in the study defined *theft* differently. With no consistency in the operational definition, the students' efforts to compare schools were sociologically worthless (although pedagogically rewarding).

Quick Hits

So You Think You Know What a Single Parent Is?

Arriving at an operational definition for a concept that appears to be obvious can sometimes be difficult. Take a category as seemingly self-evident as "single parent" (or "lone parent"). Identify which of the following you would count as a single parent, and then address the questions below.

	Yes	No
a) a mother whose husband is dead	☐	☐
b) a 41-year-old separated mother who lives with her 22-year-old son	☐	☐
c) a father whose 4-year-old daughter sees her mother every weekend	☐	☐
d) a mother whose 10-year-old son lives with his father every summer	☐	☐
e) a father whose two daughters live with their mother every other week	☐	☐
f) a mother whose husband lives in the same house but contributes nothing financially or in services to the raising of her children from a previous marriage	☐	☐
g) a gay man who, along with his live-in partner, is raising his two sons without any assistance from the children's mother	☐	☐
h) a mother who, along with her son, is completely supported financially by her ex-husband	☐	☐
i) a mother whose husband in the armed forces and stationed overseas for most of the year	☐	☐

What Do YOU Think?

1. How would you define *single parent*?
2. Do you think that "single-parent family" is a category that would be easy to do research with? Why or why not?

Measuring Poverty: Operational Definitions in Action

To get a sense of how operational definitions are used, consider **poverty**. There is no standard definition for "poverty" or "poor." There are, however, various conventional methods for defining poverty. One is to establish a **poverty line**, an income level below which a household is defined (for statistical or governmental purposes) as being "poor."

How is a poverty line established? There is no universally accepted procedure, though a few methods are prevalent. One is to link it to the availability of basic material needs: food, clothing, and shelter. Anything below the minimum income level needed to secure these necessities is considered **absolute poverty**. But this varies across countries and provinces. Consider, for example, how housing costs vary across Canada. It costs more for a resident of Vancouver to pay rent on an apartment than it costs a citizen of Moncton living in a comparable dwelling.

Since 1997 Statistics Canada has used the **Market Basket Measure** (MBM) to establish a poverty line for different regions across the country. As Giles explains,

> The MBM estimates the cost of a specific basket of goods and services for the reference year, assuming that all items in the basket were entirely provided for out of the spending of the household [i.e. that none of the items were purchased for the householders by family or friends]. Any household with a level of income lower than the cost of the basket is considered to be living in low income. (2004, pp. 6–7)

The "basket" includes five types of expenditures for a reference family of two adults and two children:

- food
- clothing and footwear
- shelter
- transportation
- "other" (school supplies, furniture, recreation and family entertainment, personal care products, and phone and internet access).

Different levels are calculated for 19 specific communities in Canada and 30 theoretical communities based on province and population size (Statistics Canada, 2013). To give you an idea of what the Market Basket Measure looks like, Table 2.3 shows the MBM thresholds for Saskatchewan in a given year, to show how they differ.

Another way to define *poor* is to use a **relative poverty** scale, which defines poverty relative to average, median, or mean household incomes. An example is the **low income cut-off**, which is calculated based on the percentage of a family's income spent on food, clothing, and shelter. Since 1992, Statistics Canada has judged any household that spends more than 63 per cent of its total after-tax income on food, clothing, and shelter to be in low income (Statistics Canada, 2011).

What Difference Does It Make?

Poverty measures are used to determine how government assistance is distributed. You can imagine, then, that groups with different views on how much government funding should go to reducing poverty

might adopt different definitions of what it means to be poor.

Take conservative-minded analyst Christopher Sarlo. Sarlo argues that measures of relative poverty are really just measures of inequality, a condition that exists even in prosperous societies. The focus, he argues, should be not a person's standard of living compared to that of a neighbour but rather a person's "absolute level of well-being and ability to acquire basic necessities" (Sarlo, 2013, p. 3). With that in mind, Sarlo developed the Basic Needs Poverty Line (BNL), which is favoured by the Fraser Institute, a conservative think tank. Like the Market Basket Measure, the BNL is a measure of absolute poverty based on a household's ability to purchase a certain set of necessities. In this case, regional variations are not considered. This differs from MBM thresholds, which are adjusted higher for families living in larger cities and lower for those living in rural areas. Table 2.4 shows the BNL thresholds for households of one to five people compared with the MBM thresholds for the most and least expensive regions, according to Statistics Canada.

The table shows that Statistics Canada considers a family of four in Toronto to be living in poverty if its total household income after taxes is less than $36,861. The Fraser Institute considers the same family to be in poverty only if its total household income is less than $26,619. There's a difference of over $10,000 in these two measures of poverty. Why? Statistics Canada is a public organization that gathers and supplies statistics based on the federal census and other means. The Fraser Institute is a private think tank appealing to conservative policy makers with policy recommendations

TABLE 2.3 MBM Thresholds for Saskatchewan, 2015

MBM Region	Persons not in economic families	2 persons	3 persons	4 persons	5 persons
Rural areas	$18,779	$26,558	$32,526	$37,558	$41,991
Small population centres with less than 30,000 persons	$19,329	$27,335	$33,479	$38,658	$43,221
Medium population centres with a population between 30,000 and 99,999 persons	$18,216	$25,761	$31,550	$36,431	$40,731
Saskatoon	$19,055	$26,948	$33,004	$38,110	$42,608
Regina	$18,807	$26,569	$32,574	$37,613	$42,053

Source: Statistics Canada, Income Statistics Division, 2017, www12.statcan.gc.ca/census-recensement/2016/ref/dict/tab/t4_5-eng.cfm

TABLE 2.4 MBM and BNL Thresholds for Households Ranging in Size from 1 to 5 Members

Household Members	Statistics Canada's Market Basket Measure (2015)		Fraser Institute's Basic Needs Poverty Line (2014)
	High[a]	Low[b]	
1	$19,976	$16,436	$13,310
2	$28,250	$23,243	$18,824
3	$34,599	$28,467	$23,054
4	$39,951	$32,871	$26,619
5	$44,667	$36,751	$29,762

a Province of British Columbia, Vancouver census metropolitan area

b Province of Quebec, medium population centre with a population between 30,000 and 99,999

Source: Statistics Canada, Income Statistics Division, www12.statcan.gc.ca/census-recensement/2016/ref/dict/tab/t4_5-eng.cfm; Lammam & MacIntyre, 2016, p. 3, Table 1.

that promote free enterprise and limit spending on social programs. The lower the poverty line, the lower the number of people considered poor in the analysis of statistics, and the lower the need for social programs such as welfare and legal aid.

Research Surveys and a Lesson in Interpreting Poll Results

Polls, surveys, and questionnaires are frequently used in both quantitative and qualitative research. Quantitative research uses *closed-ended questionnaires*, in which respondents are asked to reply to set questions by selecting the best answer from a list of possibilities. "What college or university do you presently attend?" would be an example of a closed-ended question, and you can see how the results would be easy to summarize in numbers. Closed-ended questionnaires can be administered online, over the phone, or in person. They are generally administered to a sample, a selection of the population under investigation, such as a sample of college and university students or a sample of Canadians. The sample must be representative of the broader population so that the results of the survey can be extrapolated and applied to the whole. You could not do a study of student debt by interviewing only students from families with a total household income of over $175,000: that would not be a representative sample.

Qualitative research relies on open-ended questionnaires, in which respondents are encouraged to answer freely to each question without having to select a predetermined response from a list. Open-ended questions are most effective when they cannot be answered with a simple *yes* or *no*. "How would

you describe your first year of college or university?" is an open-ended question. You can see how this question might give you a more informative response than one that asks you to rate your first year of college or university on a scale from 1 to 5, although it can be more difficult to summarize the results of open-ended questionnaires.

The term *poll* usually refers to a quantitative survey designed to measure respondents' views on a particular topic or set of topics. The wording of poll questions is important, since polls may be manipulated for political ends rather than scientific accuracy. Consider the following example. In 2015, Conservative Member of Parliament Lawrence Toet sent a pamphlet out in his Winnipeg riding to promote the federal Conservatives' anti-terrorism legislation, Bill C-51. The mailer included the following poll question designed to be answered by the recipient and returned to the riding office:

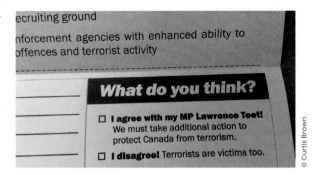

Can you see the problem with this question? In logic terms it represents the fallacy known as a false dichotomy, where two positions are presented as though they were opposites and mutually exclusive, so that if you disagree with one premise, you must naturally agree with the other. In fact, this is not a choice between two opposites. The moral is that polls can be used to guide, rather than gauge, public opinion. As a sociologically aware consumer of polls, you should always ask yourself, *who funded this poll?*

> ### What Do YOU Think?
>
> How would you turn the question in Lawrence Toet's pamphlet into an unbiased poll question?

Variables and Correlations

Here are a few concepts necessary for understanding and carrying out quantifiable research (and even certain forms of qualitative research). The first one is variable: a concept with measurable traits or characteristics that can vary or change from one person, group, culture, or time to another. One variable can cause another variable to change, or it can be affected by another. The average temperature of Nunavut's capital, Iqaluit, can be a variable, as can the average amount of clothing a resident of Iqaluit wears. Clearly, the first variable can affect the second one.

Sociologists commonly refer to two different types of variables: independent variables and dependent variables. **Independent variables** are presumed to have some effect on another variable. In the example given above, the average temperature of Iqaluit is the independent variable. **Dependent variables** are those that are assumed to be affected by an independent variable. In our example, the average amount of clothing worn by the Iqalungiut ("people of Iqaluit") would be the dependent variable. Table 2.5 presents a list of possible independent and dependent variables from examples presented in this chapter.

Another key term is **correlation**. A correlation exists when two variables are associated more frequently than could be expected by chance. Both variables might increase together, or one might increase while the other decreases. A **direct or positive correlation** exists when the independent variable and the dependent variable increase or decrease together. Table 2.6 shows some examples. An **inverse or negative correlation** exists when the two variables change in opposing directions—in other words, when the independent variable increases, the dependent decreases, and vice versa. Table 2.7 gives examples of inverse correlation.

TABLE 2.5 Independent and Dependent Variables: Three Examples

Study	Independent Variable		Dependent Variable
opening narrative	Car passes another car	⇒	The passed car speeds up.
schoolwork	Middle-class parents take an active role in children's education	⇒	Middle-class children achieve better results.
fasting	Muslim student mentions Ramadan.	⇒	Non-Muslim classmates ask what fasting is.

TABLE 2.6 Direct Correlation of Independent and Dependent Variables: Three Examples

Independent Variable		Dependent Variable
smoking	⇒	rates of lung cancer
education level	⇒	(1) income level (2) tolerance for difference (e.g. regarding "race" and ethnicity, sexual orientation, etc.)
parents' income level	⇒	likelihood of child becoming a dentist, doctor, or lawyer

TABLE 2.7 Inverse Correlation of Independent and Dependent Variables: Three Examples

Independent Variable		Dependent Variable
average temperature	⇒	average amount of clothes worn
woman's education	⇒	number of children she will have
age (of an adult)	⇒	support for legalizing cannabis

Spurious Reasoning: Correlation Is Not Causation

In the discussion of correlations above I've said nothing about **causation**, the linking of effects to causes. We may *observe* that women with postsecondary education have fewer children than those who do not, but we can't assume, based on that correlation, that being engaged in postsecondary education *causes* them to have fewer children. We have to prove it, by testing hypotheses about why this is so (for example, women who attend college and university delay childbirth while they complete their studies and begin a career).

While correlation is relatively easy to prove, causation is not. Claiming that a cause-and-effect relationship exists based on correlation alone, without sufficient evidence, is known as *spurious reasoning*. Spurious reasoning is a concept that's hard to grasp with just the definition. Sociology instructors are challenged to explain and identify it. It usually takes lots of examples. So I'll begin here with the definition and then present examples.

Spurious reasoning exists when someone sees *correlation* and falsely assumes *causation*. Remember that a correlation is easy to determine; causation is not. The journey from one to the other is long and difficult. It involves proving—or else disproving—the existence of the critical **third variable**, the outside factor that influences both correlating variables.

Here are the examples, some silly, some serious.

Example #1: Birds and Leaves

There is a correlation in Canada between birds flying south and leaves falling. We can see both phenomena occurring roughly at the same time. It would be spurious reasoning to say that the birds see the leaves falling and therefore decide to migrate. If we look for a third factor, we'll find that the angle of the sun's rays affects both dependent variables.

Example #2: Fire Trucks and Fire Damage

There is a direct correlation between the number of fire trucks that go to a fire and the amount of damage that takes place at the fire. The greater the number of fire trucks, the greater the amount of fire damage. It would be spurious reasoning to say that the large number of fire trucks *causes* the extensive damage done at the site of the fire. Seek out the third variable: the seriousness of the fire affects both the number of fire trucks that appear and the amount of damage caused.

Example #3: Older Men and Younger Wives

Older men who marry significantly younger women tend to live longer than the cohort of men their own age. Spurious reasoning would lead us to conclude that marrying young women keeps old men active and healthy. But before declaring that we've found the fountain of youth for old men, we must look for a third variable. If the older man is relatively strong and healthy for his age, then he is both more likely to attract and keep a younger bride and also more likely to live longer.

Example #4: Cohabitation and Divorce

There is a direct (but not strong) correlation between a couple's living together prior to marriage and the likelihood of divorce. People who live together first are more likely to divorce than those who go directly from living apart to living together in marriage. It would be spurious reasoning to say that a couple's greater likelihood of divorce comes from the fact that they lived together first. Seek out the third variable and you will find it in social liberalism and social conservatism (the latter possibly a cause or effect of that difficult-to-pin-down social factor "religiosity"). Socially liberal people are more likely *both* to live together *and* to leave a marriage if they feel it is bad. More socially conservative people are *both* more likely to begin living together with marriage *and* more likely to stay in a marriage, even if it is horrible.

Example #5 Divorce and Suicide

Durkheim detected a direct correlation between divorce rates and suicide rates during a 10-year period from 1870 to 1880; some of his findings are recorded in Table 2.8.

There was a positive correlation between divorce rates and suicide rates over this period. However, it would be spurious reasoning to say that greater rates of divorce produced higher suicide rates. For Durkheim, the third variable was **anomie**, a societal state of breakdown or confusion, or a more personal one based on an individual's lack of connection to society. Anomie, concluded Durkheim, was the real cause of increases in both divorce and suicide rates.

tyler olson/istockphoto

Spurious reasoning might lead us to conclude that this man will live long because he is married to this young woman. What do you think? What "third variable" might help to explain the correlation between marrying a younger bride and living longer?

TABLE 2.8 Correlation between Divorce and Suicide Rates in Four Countries, 1870–1889

Country	Divorce rate (per 1,000 marriages)	Suicide Rate (per 1 million people)
Italy	3.1	31.0
Sweden	6.4	81.0
France	7.5	150.0
Switzerland	47.0	216.0

Source: Durkheim, [1897] 1951.

Critical Thinking and Statistics

Sociologist Joel Best (2001), author of *Damned Lies and Statistics: Untangling Numbers from the Media, Politicians, and Activists*, presented the following example illustrating why we should approach statistics critically. He was on the PhD dissertation committee of a graduate student who began his dissertation with a questionable statistic. The student cited the following stat from an article published in 1995:

> Every year since 1950, the number of American children gunned down has doubled.

This certainly gains the reader's attention. But wait a minute, said Best: do the math. Say the 1950 figure was 1. Here is how it would add up from 1950 to 1995:

1950	1
1951	2
1952	4
1955	32
1957	128
1959	512
1960	1012
1961	2058
1965	32,768 (there were 9,960 homicides in total that year)
1970	1 million +
1980	1 billion (approximately more than four times the total population of the United States at the time)
1983	8.6 billion (nearly one-and-a-half times the world's population)

Source: Based on Best, Joel (2001). *Damned Lies and Statistics: Untangling Numbers from the Media, Politicians, and Activists.*

What the author of the original article—the one cited by the PhD student—had done was misquote a 1994 document stating (accurately) that the number of American children killed each year by guns had doubled since 1950; the number itself had not doubled *each year.*

Best advises us to approach statistics critically. That involves recognizing that all statistics have flaws, and that some flaws are more significant than others. Best presents the following useful series of questions for sociology students to consider when encountering a statistic in a news report, magazine, newspaper, or conversation:

> What might be the sources for this number? How could one go about producing the figure? Who produced the number, and what interests might they have? What are the different ways key terms might have been defined, and which definitions have been chosen? How might the phenomena be measured, and which measurement choices have been made? What sort of sample was gathered, and how might that sample affect the result? Is the statistic properly interpreted? Are comparisons being made, and if so, are the comparisons appropriate? Are there competing statistics? If so, what stakes do the opponents have in the issue, and how are those stakes likely to affect their use of statistics? And is it possible to figure out why the statistics seem to disagree, what the differences are in the ways the competing sides are using figures. (2001)

The Point Is ...

Misreading Statistics Can Have Grave Consequences

Failing to give proper scrutiny to a statistic is not just a student mistake: journalists, politicians, and other professionals have been guilty of misinterpreting, misusing, or placing too much trust in reported evidence, sometimes with devastating consequences.

According to the US Centers for Disease Control and Prevention (CDC, 2018), nearly 218,000 people in the United States died from overdoses related to opioid-based prescription narcotics between 1999 and 2017. The situation is just as grave here in Canada, where, according to the federal Public Health Agency, there were over 115,000 apparent opioid-related deaths in a three-year period from January 2016 to December 2018 (Special Advisory Committee, 2019).

Opioid painkillers such as oxycodone are highly effective but highly addictive: up to one in four people using prescription opioids long-term struggle with addiction (CDC, 2016). So why are opioids so widely prescribed if they carry such risks? It is possible the risks may have been misunderstood, thanks in part to a one-paragraph letter published in a 1980 issue of the *New England Journal of Medicine* (Porter & Jick,

1980, p. 123). A recent American study found that the letter, published under the headline "Addiction Rare in Patients Treated with Narcotics," was cited "heavily and uncritically . . . as evidence that addiction was rare with long-term opioid therapy . . . even though no evidence was provided by the correspondents" (Leung, Macdonald, Dhalla, & Juurlink, 2017).

The problem is that the letter's claim was based on an informal, unsystematic study of patients in hospital (whose use of medication is easier to monitor and regulate; patients outside of hospital are much more likely to misuse prescribed medications). The letter was cited as evidence that opioid addiction was rare in 439 separate articles, some of which "grossly misrepresented the conclusions of the letter" (Leung et al., 2017). Greater scrutiny of the original letter might have prompted additional research on the subject, or at least reduced the propensity for prescribing opioid-based narcotics for chronic pain.

Ethics and Research

An important consideration in sociological research today, and one that is more important now than it was historically, is the **ethics** of research. Practising good research ethics largely involves demonstrating respect for the research subjects, specifically concerning their privacy, their understanding of what the research will require of them, and their capacity to choose to be researched or not. When participants indicate their understanding and acceptance of the research conditions, they are providing what is known as **informed consent**. Colleges and universities now have research committees or entire departments responsible for vetting the research that sociologists and other faculty members engage in. In times before such oversight was common, breaches of ethics might not have been detected until after the research had been completed, if they were detected at all. As you consider the cases described below, you can consider how the research would have been different had it been proposed today.

The Ethics of Deception: Tales of Covert or Undisclosed Research

Laud Humphreys and the Tearoom Trade

Robert Allen "Laud" Humphreys (1930–1988) was an American sociologist best known for his published PhD dissertation *Tearoom Trade* (1970), which has been viewed both as a pioneering study of male homosexuality and as an egregiously unethical case of sociology gone wrong. For his doctoral thesis,

Humphreys engaged in ethnographic research of anonymous male–male sexual encounters in public toilets. ("Tearoom" was a code word for these meeting places; a quick search of *Urban Dictionary* suggests it's not in common use today.) Fairly obviously, Humphreys did not disclose to the men he encountered that he was performing sociological research; instead, he posed as a voyeur and "watch queen"—a scout keeping a lookout for approaching police.

Conducting research without advising his subjects, much less gaining their consent, was already an ethical no-no, but Humphreys went a step further. By recording their license plate numbers, he was able to find names of the men he was studying, and their addresses. Disguising himself as a public health official performing a social survey, he interviewed about 50 of the men. The research yielded interesting findings. Humphreys discovered that many of his research subjects appeared to the world to be heterosexual. Many were married, with wives who apparently knew nothing about their husbands' extramarital activity. Humphreys's thesis was that the people he studied used a conservative public persona that conformed to societal norms and values to conceal a private self that was participating in a deviant (at the time, illegal) practice. Interestingly, Humphreys was in a position similar to that of many of his research subjects: he was married for 20 years before coming out as gay.

The deceptive, or covert, nature of Humphreys's research turned out to be a divisive issue in the Department of Sociology at Washington University in St Louis, where he received his PhD in 1968. Some faculty members wanted to rescind his doctorate. It was one of the issues that ultimately caused the disbanding of the department in 1989.

"Unethical" Fieldwork in Religion: 1972–3

This case is not as well known. It concerns my own work as an undergraduate.

In Chapter 1, I described how I applied the theories of Erving Goffman to a newly formed religious group as part of my honours thesis. What I didn't mention was how I conducted my research. The group was known as the Process Church, or the Church of the Final Judgement. The *Toronto Sun* had labelled them a Satanist cult. They weren't, as it turned out, but the rumour alone was enough to make them particularly interesting to me.

My research method was *undisclosed* participant observation. This means that I did not tell them that I was doing research. I was working "undercover." I presented myself as an unemployed drummer (which I was); I did not tell them I was also an undergraduate sociology student. My research subjects were not willing participants who knew that they were being studied. I felt that my research had to be undisclosed because the Process Church had received negative publicity from the local media, and its members were nervous about outsiders, especially if they felt they might be reporters posing as faithful congregants to observe their meetings.

The Process Church was located in downtown Toronto, where they operated a soup kitchen and held different services every night. Once a week from September to February, I would participate in the evening activities, which could include their own music (no choir or church organ here; think sitars and bongos) and a sermon. The speaker did his best to "keep it real," in the words of the day. He would be hip and funny, but he also dispensed good advice. On some nights there

would be workshop sessions in which people in groups would talk to each other, sometimes at a very personal level. I grew close to a number of people there, including those who worked in the soup kitchen, where I often hung out. Once the evening's session was over, I would head to the subway, take a pad of paper out of my pocket, and write notes like crazy.

Speed Bump

When the need for informed consent gets in the way of research progress, it can be tempting to forgo or lessen ethical standards to get things done. Why is it important to retain your ethical integrity, even at the cost of potential sociological insight? Who do ethics polices benefit?

The Point Is ...

Ethnographic Research Can Turn a Sociologist into a Witness

Alice Goffman (b. 1962), Erving's daughter, is a sociologist whose book *On the Run: Fugitive Life in an American City* (2014) draws on fieldwork she carried out to study the impact of policing on the lives of young black men in Philadelphia. Positive reception came quickly from both the academic world (her thesis, the basis for the book, received the American Sociological Society's Dissertation Award for 2011) and the popular press (*The New York Times* listed it as one of the 100 most notable books of 2014). But the academic world is intensely competitive, and with the accolades came fierce scrutiny and harsh criticism of Goffman's research methodology. An unsigned, untraceable 60-page document (single-spaced!) was sent to hundreds of sociologists across the country, detailing what the document's author felt were the flaws, big and small, of the book. Two stand out because of how they relate to current ethical practices.

The first is that Goffman did not begin her work with a discussion of positionality (her social location, essentially). In other words, she did not address the limits of her understanding (i.e. that she could not know from her own life experience what poverty and racism feel like). Nor did she acknowledge the exercises of privilege that came from her being a rich, white sociologist studying a mixed-income black community (i.e. she could invade their lives, but they could not invade hers).

The second issue relates to illegal practices she observed. During her fieldwork, she heard about and may have witnessed plans to break the law. She even drove with a young man who was armed and out for revenge on an individual he suspected of killing one of his gang members. This presented her with an ethical dilemma: protect the confidentiality of her research participants or prevent the commission of a crime (or several crimes). The guidelines for sociological research at the University of Pennsylvania, where Alice Goffman studied, were clear: she was not to divulge the identity of the individuals she was writing about, and she was expected to burn her fieldnotes (which ran to thousands of pages).

What Do YOU Think?

Which do you consider a greater breach of ethics: failing to report illegal activity or failing to protect an informant's confidentiality? When would you stop being a sociologist to honour your civic duty as a citizen?

Social Research Methods: A Final Word

In this chapter we've considered a number of ways to carry out sociological research. In all the talk about quantitative and qualitative methods, independent and dependent variables, correlation and statistics, it's easy to lose sight of an important point: the subjects under investigation are people, and the moment you begin to study them, you start a relationship that will not always be equal. Students, soldiers, and inmates of prisons and asylums are often studied because they have little power to say no. If I can ask questions about your life but you can't ask questions about mine, then I have a kind of power over you that you do not have over me. People who are poor or who belong to racialized (e.g. black) or colonized (e.g. Indigenous) groups have often been studied by white, middle-class researchers for purposes that serve more to control or exploit the subjects of the research than to give them power over their lives. The Maori of New Zealand have been through that experience. Maori researcher Linda Tuhiwai Smith (1999), in *Decolonizing Methodologies: Research and Indigenous Peoples*, writes,

> From the vantage point of the colonized . . . the term "research" is inextricably linked to European imperialism and colonialism. The word itself, "research," is probably one of the dirtiest words in the indigenous world's vocabulary. When mentioned in many indigenous contexts, it stirs up silence, it conjures up bad memories, it raises a smile that is knowing and distrustful. . . . The ways in which scientific research is implicated in the worst excesses of colonialism remain a powerful remembered history for many of the world's colonized peoples. . . .

It galls us that Western researchers and intellectuals can assume to know all that it is possible to know of us, on the basis of their brief encounters with some of us. It appalls us that the West can desire, extract and claim ownership of ways of knowing, our imagery, the things we create and produce, and then simultaneously reject the people who created and developed those ideas and seek to deny them further opportunities to be creators of their own culture and own nations. (1999, p. 1)

If your interest in sociology comes from a desire to effect positive social change, the critical tone of this statement might shock you. Let it serve as a reminder. Treat research participants with respect and represent the data fairly. You will go a long way toward sociology's goal of bringing clarity to social issues.

Wrap it Up

Summary

This chapter has taken you on a flight over a large piece of land known as Sociology's Contested Ground—otherwise known as "the things over which sociologists argue the most." Among the main fault lines along which sociologists differ are theories, approaches, and perhaps most bitter of all, social research methods. If sociologists worked with Santa Claus, they would challenge him on his operational definitions of "naughty" and "nice."

Ideally, the study of sociological research can lead students to develop reliable "fact checkers" or "bullshit detectors" that will automatically kick in when it comes to assessing the many forms of social information they receive through a variety of media. Asking such questions as *How did they define . . . ?*, *What social voices or locations were being heard or excluded?*, *How do they know that?*, and *Who paid for the research?* should enable you to be critical of even professional researchers. Keep these questions in mind as you read the chapters that follow.

As you encountered the diverse and, at times, opposing research strategies presented here, it has hopefully become clear to you that the facts do not speak for themselves. Knowledge is created: social "facts" and hypotheses are tested by human researchers with human biases who occasionally (and perhaps unintentionally) allow these biases to manufacture distortions rather than the ever-elusive "facts" or "proof." In short, be critical.

Think Back

Questions for Critical Review

1. Distinguish between qualitative and quantitative research. Give examples of each.
2. What value do narratives bring to sociological research?
3. Explain the relationship between insider views and qualitative research, on the one hand, and outsider views and quantitative research, on the other.
4. How could you combine qualitative and quantitative research methods in an institutional ethnography of your school's sociology department?
5. In 2018, an Ottawa hospital let go of 130 nurses. Yet employees responding to a public online survey developed by the hospital's administration expressed positive attitudes toward the hospital. (You can see the results for yourself at www.glassdoor.ca/Reviews/The Ottawa-Hospital-Reviews-E116113.htm.) Why do you think that employees' attitudes were so positive? What might be a more accurate way of finding out what the employees think?

6. How would you carry out a content analysis of current crime shows on Netflix to investigate what is sometimes called the "dead girl trope," or the way female victims are portrayed? Would you use qualitative or quantitative research methods, or both?

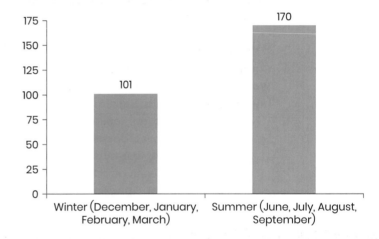

Fatal Traffic Collisions in Ontario, 2016

Source: Road Safety Research Office, 2016, Table 3.5.

N'we Jinan Artists – "HOME TO ME" // Grassy Narrows First Nation

In 2016, N'we Jinan Artists recorded a video for their song "Home to Me," about their connection to Grassy Narrows First Nation, in northern Ontario. You can view the video on YouTube: www.youtube.com/watch?v=EgaYz8YWsO8 (googling "Grassy Narrows Home to Me" is probably easier). What could you learn from a content analysis of the 500+ comments on YouTube?

7. According to a report for the province's Ministry of Transportation, there are more fatal traffic accidents in Ontario during the summer (June–September) than during the winter (December–March). Can we conclude, based on these data, that in Ontario, road conditions are safer in winter than in summer? What other variables might affect this relationship?

8. Imagine you wanted to study binge drinking on campus among students. How would you go about operationalizing your key terms?

9. You have received scores of 30/40, 22/30, and 20/30 in three sociology tests. Which would you rather have as your mark: your average percentage or your median? And shouldn't you have studied harder for the third test?

Read On

Suggested Print and Online Resources

Ginger Gorman (2019), *Troll Hunting: Inside the World of Online Hate and Its Human Fallout* (Richmond, Australia: Hardie Grant).

- After being trolled online, Gorman, an Australian journalist, decided to investigate the phenomenon, first by studying the incidence of trolling (with help from the Australia Institute), and then speaking with psychologists, victims, and trolls themselves, whom she met by embedding herself in their online world. The work offers a good example of a sociological study combining qualitative and quantitative research methods.

James Paul Gee (2014), *How to Do Discourse Analysis: A Toolkit*, 2nd edn (London: Routledge).

- A relatively accessible introduction to discourse analysis by a professor of literature.

Joel Best (2012), *Damned Lies and Statistics: Untangling Numbers from the Media, Politicians, and Activists*, updated edn (Berkeley: University of California).

- Now in an updated edition, this relatively light-hearted but helpful sociological guide to understanding the manipulation of statistics was so popular that it spawned a sequel, *More Damned Lies and Statistics: How Numbers Confuse Public Issues* (2004).

John L. Steckley (2008), *White Lies about the Inuit* (Toronto: University of Toronto).

- This genealogical work puts to rest three discourse myths about the historic Inuit: that Inuit elders are sometimes abandoned on ice floes; that there are blond, blue-eyed Inuit descended from Norse ancestors; and that the Inuit have 52 (or more) words for snow.

Marie Campbell & Frances Gregor (2002), *Mapping Social Relations: A Primer in Doing Institutional Ethnography* (Aurora, ON: Garamond).

- The insights of Dorothy Smith inform this insightful work on institutional ethnography.

Michael Blastland & Andrew Dilnot (2007), *The Tiger That Isn't: Seeing through a World of Numbers* (London: Profile Books).

- A Scottish journalist and an English economist teamed up to produce this useful guide to interpreting statistics.

"Orientalism: How the West Views the Rest of the World," www.youtube.com/watch?v=NExfbX7E42o

- This 13-minute video, posted in 2017, gives a good explanation of Orientalism and how it shapes Western ideas of "the East" today.

Tri-Council Policy Statement: Ethical Conduct for Research Involving Humans (2014), www.pre.ethics.gc.ca/pdf/eng/tcps2-2014/TCPS_2_FINAL_Web.pdf

- This policy statement defines ethical research in the social sciences, natural sciences, health sciences, and humanities in Canada. It is long, but you should know where to find it for guidelines on such topics as consent, confidentiality, and conflicts of interest.

Culture

Reading this chapter will help you to . . .

- Describe Canada's dominant culture.

- Explain what it means for culture to be contested.

- Recognize the difference between a subculture and a counterculture.

- Know how the concept of agency relates to popular culture and mass culture.

- Understand how folkways, mores, and taboos differ.

- Explain how values and language contribute to culture.

- Define *ethnocentrism* and explain its significance with regard to culture.

◄ © Ed Begley

For Starters

When Does Culture Need Protecting?

Photograph by Jacob Chimilar; pictured, Thomas Wilson (@Twcosplay)

Someone once wrote that the difference between Americans and Canadians is that Americans don't care about the difference between Americans and Canadians. It's true: in the mainstream, Canadians are very conscious of how we differ from Americans. When travelling, we bristle when someone mistakes us for American; we really bristle when we correct them and they say, "Same thing." (Although we love it when they then apologize and buy us a beer, which has happened to me in Scotland.)

We imagine ourselves having a rich cultural tradition that differs from that of our global trendsetting neighbour to the south. Yet we feel pride when one of our own achieves success on the American cultural scene, like Drake, Shawn Mendes, Samantha Bee, Alessia Cara, Ryan Gosling (or Reynolds—take your pick of the Ryans), or

Margaret Atwood. And we tend to be very conscious of how our culture is viewed in America. The day after Sandra Oh hosted *Saturday Night Live* in March 2019, some mainstream Canadian news outlets reported on how many references to Canada she made. A month later, an episode of *The Simpsons* set in Canada made headlines in many mainstream Canadian media outlets both before and immediately after it aired, reflecting first anticipation at how our culture might be portrayed and then disappointment that it was largely reduced to simple cultural stereotypes.

American content swamps our airwaves, and we are happy consumers of it. Many Canadians would rather stream *Game of Thrones* illegally because they don't have HBO than watch any original programming that airs on the CBC. Many Canadians could easily sketch the family tree of the Kardashians but hardly know the talented and successful (in a mostly Canadian way) Dale sisters, Cynthia (of Stratford and *Street Legal*) and Jennifer (Mystique in the animated X-Men movies).

Does it matter? Is it important to have and protect a distinct national culture (or national cultures)? It is important enough that our broadcast regulator, the CRTC (Canadian Radio-television and Telecommunications Commission), has rules requiring Canadian television and radio networks to air a specified amount of made-in-Canada programming during daytime hours. (Needless to say, American broadcasters do not face similar regulations.) Our Canadian content (Can Con) quotas are designed to ensure that we see ourselves and hear our music and stories reflected in Canadian broadcasting. Can Con regulations helped homegrown bands like the Guess Who get a strong start in the smaller Canadian market. The same quotas undoubtedly contributed to the success of Nickelback, the Barenaked Ladies, Avril Lavigne, and many others in the time before streaming services diminished the influence of local radio stations.

We have Canadian content regulations to thank for folksy, small-town sitcoms such as *Corner Gas*, *Schitt's Creek*, and *Letterkenny*. Perhaps, if you live in a small town as I do, you see yourself reflected in those shows. But then we have the second-hand Canadian versions of shows like *American Idol* and *Real Housewives* (recently ". . . of Toronto"), which are of questionable value as products of Canadian culture and are questionable generally.

We really lose out in the movie category. The Canadian film industry is booming with American productions shot in Toronto, which stands in for New York or Chicago, and in Vancouver, the body double for Los Angeles or Seattle. We seldom see movies that reflect our own stories of World War I and II. And think about how many times you have seen an actor play the president of the United States, and then how many times you've seen an actor play the prime minister (although Canada's prime minister as of 2019 was a drama teacher).

In short, Canadians fret a good deal about our Canadian culture—what is it, is it protected, is it different enough, is it inclusive enough, does it leave anyone out, is it unique? Our American cousins have no such insecurities. Should they? Should we? Or is our culture doing just fine, despite the presence of the American elephant in the culture room.

Northwood Entertainment

A scene from *The Grizzlies* (2018), about a group of Inuit teens who come together to form a lacrosse team in an Arctic community scarred by the legacy of colonialism. Canada is home to award-winning directors (Denys Arcand, Deepa Mehta, for instance), and Canadians have made award-winning feature-length films set in the North (*Atanarjuat: The Fast Runner*, 2001) and Quebec (*The Barbarian Invasions*, 2003). But most products of our flourishing film industry are big-budget American movies. Why aren't there more movies set in Canada, made by and about Canadians?

Introduction: What We Mean by Culture and Why It's Contested

The word *culture* has a lot of different meanings. Some people equate it with a sophistication of manners and tastes, something you either have (if you enjoy, say, the opera, ballet, and fine dining) or lack (if your idea of a good breakfast is cheap beer and leftover pizza). But that's just one kind of culture—*high culture*—which we'll get to a bit later on.

More broadly, **culture** is a system of behaviour, beliefs, knowledge, practices, values, and concrete materials including buildings, tools, and sacred items. In this sense, everyone has culture. In fact, everyone can claim more than one. But although I've described culture as a system, I'm not suggesting there is total agreement concerning any one culture and its constituent parts. Those who belong to a particular society (the collective group) may disagree about what the culture of that society does or should include.

Let's talk hockey. Just about everybody would agree that hockey is part of Canadian culture—but that's where agreement ends. Does success by Canada's national teams in international competition mean we've succeeded as a culture? Not everyone would say so. Is fighting an integral part of the Canadian game? You don't have to be Don Cherry to get into an argument on that point. Does the sport's long history in this country make it more culturally important than soccer, even though the latter has higher youth participation rates and tends to be played by boys and girls in more equal numbers, representing a far broader range of ethnic and socioeconomic backgrounds? A 2012 study commissioned jointly by Hockey Canada and equipment company Bauer found that only 10 per cent of Canadian families have children playing hockey (Ralph, 2013)—a surprising finding if hockey is, indeed, a dominant thread in our cultural fabric. Periodically, a brazen historian will offer evidence that—brace yourselves, hockey fans—the sport was not even invented here but traces its origins to some other nation (see Gidén, Houda, &, Martel, 2014, for example). All of which goes to show that hockey as part of our national culture is **contested**.

In more serious cases, aspects of a culture may be contested when they become instruments of oppression. Anne McGillivray and Brenda Comaskey (1999), in *Black Eyes All of the Time: Intimate Violence, Aboriginal Women and the Justice System*, argue that we should not assume that Aboriginal women who have suffered spousal abuse "will view 'cultural' solutions in the same way as Aboriginal men" (p. 18). Aboriginal justice typically calls for forgiving offenders and reintegrating them into the community. This is part of Indigenous cultures. However, many of the women McGillivray and Comaskey interviewed said that they would prefer that their male abusers spend time in jail to give the abused time to feel safe again. Under these circumstances, these aspects of Indigenous justice—forgiveness and keeping offenders in the community—become contested.

Culture often becomes contested over the question of **authenticity**. Culture involves traditions but is not confined by them. It is dynamic, changing over time. Authenticity carries the idea of being true to a particular time, place, or context, yet think of how broadly the word *authentic* can be applied and understood. For some, an "authentic Italian meal" may be something you can get from the pizzeria down the street; for others, it is something you would have to fly to Tuscany to experience. But even once you touch down in Pisa, your experience may be carefully stage-managed. You have bought a vacation package that places you in a district designed for tourists, where your "authentic Italian meal" is overpriced and prepared with inferior ingredients. It isn't authentic at all. Urban sociologist Dean MacCannell (1999), drawing on Goffman's dramaturgical approach (introduced in Chapter 1), explains that tourists, in seeking out authenticity, are looking for the "back stage" of a cultural setting; what they often get is really a sanitized version prepared to meet the needs of the modern visitor, "a front region that has been set up in advance for touristic visitation" (p. 101). MacCannell finds this *staged authenticity* in many settings, including the re-created period town, a city's historic district, and, yes, the restaurant promising authentic cuisine.

Authenticity becomes a problem when a colonial society studies a colonized culture and claims to know the secret of its authenticity. Edward Said, in *Orientalism*, criticized Western intellectuals for forming their impressions of the Middle East and Asia from historical accounts written by nineteenth- and twentieth-century Western scholars. Once they had formed an idea of what "the Orient" was, these intellectuals negatively compared their rather romanticized (think *Aladdin*) notions of the Eastern world's traditions to their negative perceptions of its present. In effect, they said, "You are a corruption of what you used to be." That's like someone saying to you, "I understand you better than you do, and you were better before."

It is a common mistake to view one's own culture as being dynamic and complex, while holding a narrow view of other cultures as somehow simple and fixed. This leads to unhealthy cultural stereotypes—that all Americans are *jingoistic* (extremely nationalistic), warmongering bullies with guns in their homes, or that Irishmen are always drunk and fighting but make up for it by singing sweetly. It is important to appreciate that all cultures are contested and subject to change.

What Kinds of Cultures Are There?

There are different kinds of culture, apart from culture in the general sense just outlined. These can be seen in terms of two oppositions:

1. dominant culture *versus* subculture and counterculture
2. high culture *versus* popular culture and mass culture.

As we examine each of these oppositions, you will gain a better idea of why we say that culture is contested.

Dominant Culture versus Subculture and Counterculture
Defining Canada's Dominant Culture

Look around, and it isn't hard to see the signs of the dominant culture in Canada. The **dominant culture** is the one that, through its political and economic power, is able to impose its values, language, and ways of behaving and interpreting behaviour on a

NiglayNik/Shutterstock

Popular among tourists, the town of Helen, Georgia, bills itself as a Bavarian alpine village—in the American Appalachians. The local business community, in an effort to revive the struggling town, turned it into a Bavarian-themed village in the 1960s as a way to attract tourism. Canadian cultural geographer William Norton (2006) comments, "Tourists to theme parks such as Epcot Center are aware that they are visiting simulations, but towns such as Helen implicitly suggest that the ethnic landscape has foundations in the settlement of the area" (p. 371). How does Helen represent MacCannell's concept of staged authenticity?

given society. The people most closely linked with the cultural mainstream are sometimes referred to as **dominants**. Although statistically their share of the overall population has dropped significantly in the last 20 years, it is fairly safe to say that Canada's dominants are white, English-speaking people of Christian and European stock. It is also fair to say that the dominant culture is middle-class. How do we know what the dominant culture looks like? Think of what culture is typically represented in Canadian morning shows like *Breakfast Television*, in commercials played on Canadian airwaves, and in television programs generally. Think of the expectations they express about what people own, what their concerns are, and how they live.

We can narrow our picture of Canada's dominant culture by taking a regionalist perspective. People living in the Atlantic provinces have good reason to suspect the dominant culture lies in central or western Canada, where banks and multinational companies have their head offices, and where most of the national population is situated. But western Canada has several times produced political parties (the Social Credit, Reform, Wildrose, and, most recently, Alberta parties, for instance) to protest the West's exclusion from the dominant political culture and its unfair treatment at the hands of institutions dominated by and situated in central Canada (like the big banks and the agencies of the federal government). Power and wealth tend to be concentrated in large cities, and central Canada is home to the country's two largest metropolitan areas, Toronto and Montreal.

Feminists argue that Canada's dominant culture is male. Let's look at our House of Commons. Of the 335 members of Canadian Parliament in May 2019, 244 were male and just 91 were female; in other words, women made up roughly 37 per cent of the seats. On the positive side, this is up from 2014, when it was 25 per cent. There was a nine-month period in 2013 when women led six of Canada's provinces and territories (Nunavut, British Columbia, Alberta, Ontario, Quebec, and Newfoundland and Labrador); as of May 2019, none of Canada's provincial or territorial leaders are women. What happened?

Thunderbird TV

Television both reflects and contributes to our sense of culture. Pick a sitcom you're familiar with (it's probably American, unless, like me, you're a big fan of *Kim's Convenience*, shown here). In your opinion, does it reflect the dominant culture we've just described? What are the principal attitudes, concerns, and occupations of its main characters? What sexualities and ethnic backgrounds do they represent (and represent positively, not just as the subject of jokes, which can be a form of marginalizing people)? How much are the main characters like you?

Adding age to the picture, we can say that those who are just starting or who have just ended their careers often feel peripheral to the dominant culture. Other factors to consider are sexual orientation, level of education, and overall health (since those with disabilities or chronic medical conditions often feel they are outside the dominant culture). To summarize, our portrait of Canada's dominant culture looks something like this: white, English-speaking, heterosexual, male university graduates of European background between the ages of 30 and 55, in good health, who own homes in middle-class neighbourhoods of cities in Ontario or Quebec. (I came *so* close—but I'm too old, and my town is too small for city status. How well do you fit the portrait of Canada's dominant culture?)

Minority Cultures, Subcultures, and Countercultures

Minority cultures are those that fall outside the cultural mainstream. As a multicultural society, Canada is home to a diverse abundance of cultures defined by religion (Sikh culture), language (francophone culture), ethnicity (Indo Canadian culture), and "race" (Africadian culture). Canadian law protects cultural pluralism as a core political value and social good, meaning that these cultures are not assimilated into the broader mainstream culture just described but are allowed (in fact, encouraged) to preserve the characteristics that make them stand out in the Canadian **cultural mosaic**. But although multiculturalism is enshrined in law, in reality the cultures that sit outside the dominant culture are not treated equally, as John Porter (1965) described in *The Vertical Mosaic* (see Chapter 1). There is, according to Porter, a hierarchy according to which certain minority cultures, particularly those based on ethnic background, are favoured more than others.

Some minority cultures fall within one of two subcategories: countercultures and subcultures. **Countercultures** are minority cultures that feel the power of the dominant culture and exist in opposition to it. **Subcultures** are minority cultures that differ in some way from the dominant culture but don't directly oppose it. Subcultures may be organized around occupations or hobbies and typically exhibit a fairly neutral contrast to the mainstream: there is no significant opposition

Quick Hits

Are You Excluded from the Dominant Culture?

		Yes	No
1.	Are political leaders (your prime minister, premier, local federal or provincial representative, mayor, etc.) like you in sex, religion, clothing style, language, and ethnic background?	❏	❏
2.	Do the homes portrayed in most television shows you watch look like yours?	❏	❏
3.	Do the leading characters in movies live lives like yours?	❏	❏
4.	If you work, is your boss of the same sex, ethnicity, "race," and age as you?	❏	❏
5.	Do the people who get arrested on reality-based police shows look like you and your neighbours?	❏	❏
6.	Are people like you frequently made the subject of news stories for demonstrating or protesting something?	❏	❏
7.	Are there a lot of derogatory slang terms that refer to people like you?	❏	❏
8.	Are people like you described as a "special interest" group?	❏	❏
9.	Are people like you often told they're "too sensitive" or "too pushy"?	❏	❏
10.	Are you often asked, "Where do you come from?"	❏	❏

A "no" answer to questions 1–4 equals exclusion from the dominant culture; for questions 5–10, a "yes" answer equals exclusion from the dominant culture.

to the dominant culture. Examples include anime artists, Bollywood fans, sociologists, and stamp collectors.

Countercultures are defined oppositionally. They are groups that reject elements of the dominant culture, such as clothing styles or sexual norms. Examples of counterculture range from the relatively harmless hippies of the 1960s and early 1970s to dangerous biker gangs like the Hells Angels. In the 1990s, *alternative* was the watchword for a culture of music and fashion that defined itself in contrast to the mainstream. Today we might use the word *indie*, which applied first to artists who were independent of major media companies and then to anyone or anything independent of mainstream commercial culture. You could say that indie culture is now fairly mainstream, and this is, in fact, a key aspect of counterculture: it may have to evolve to keep ahead of the mainstream or risk being absorbed by it. Think, for instance, of the "mountain man" beard that was once a defining feature of hipster culture: it has now become so widespread that it is firmly established in the dominant culture it was once intended to subvert. My own beard, which predates the hipster era, is too scruffy to belong to the trend, making it and me decidedly countercultural.

High Culture versus Popular Culture

High culture is the culture of the elite, a distinct minority. It is associated with theatre, opera, classical music, and ballet, "serious" works of literary fiction and non-fiction, "artsy" films (note: *films*, not *movies*) that may be difficult to appreciate without having taken courses on the subject, and a "cultivated palate" for certain high-priced foods and alcoholic beverages. High culture is sometimes referred to as "elite culture," which Canadian sociologist Karen Anderson describes as

> produced for and appreciated by a limited number of people with specialized interests. It tends to be evaluated in terms of "universal" criteria of artistic merit and to be seen as a sign of prestige. Appreciation of elite culture usually entails a process of learning and the acquisition of specific tastes. (1996, p. 471)

The Point Is ...

A Subculture Offers Its Members a Sense of Belonging

Furry fandom is a subculture of people who enjoy dressing up in animal costumes and meeting up with others who share their passion for "fursuits" and anthropomorphic animal role-play. If you are familiar at all with furry fandom, you may think it has to do with animal fetishes and sex. I'll remind you here that it is wrong to presume you have someone else's culture figured out based on stereotypes and a few things you've heard.

So who are furries, and why do they dress up? For answers, we turn to a report published by a team of American and Canadian social scientists at the University of Waterloo (Plante, Reysen, Roberts, & Gerbasi, 2016). Their International Anthropomorphic Research Project involved a five-year study of furries in North America.

According to the report, the majority of furries—75 per cent of those studied—are adults in their early to mid-twenties. Older furries may be labelled "greymuzzles," a term considered either a sign of respect or an insult. Furries are predominately white (83.2 per cent), and two-thirds of them are male. They tend to be well educated, either having a degree or working toward one, and 45 per cent of those studied were living with their parents (which is consistent with the non-furry population of 20- to 25-year-old postsecondary school students).

People involved in furry fandom adopt different "fursonas" and don their costumes for regular conferences and smaller meet-ups. Fursonas are usually large predator species, such as wolves, dogs, big cats, and dragons.

Why do people join this subculture and stay in it for years? The number one reason, according to their report, is that furry fandom participants enjoy being part of a group and having a sense of belonging with other like-minded individuals, with whom they frequently form close friendships. The second biggest reason is that furry fandom offers a form of escapist entertainment. But what about the sex? It is exaggerated: of the group studied, 23 per cent said that it had little or nothing to do with their becoming involved with the furries, while 37 per cent said that it was a small part of their interest. The activities members identified as being most central to furry fandom are art and craft work (e.g. designing and crafting pictures and the clothes of their fursonas).

French sociologist **Pierre Bourdieu** (1930–2002) coined the term **cultural capital** to refer to the knowledge and skills needed to acquire the sophisticated tastes that mark someone as a person of high culture. The more cultural capital you have, the "higher" your cultural class.

Popular culture, on the other hand, is the culture of the majority, particularly of those who do not have power (the working class, the less educated, women, and racialized minorities). Serious academic discussion of popular culture has grown with the rise of **cultural studies** courses and programs. Cultural studies draws on both the social sciences (primarily sociology) and the humanities (primarily literature and media studies) to cast light on the significance of, and meanings expressed in, popular culture, a topic previously neglected by most academics.

Popular Culture and Mass Culture

A crucial distinction exists between popular culture and mass culture. The two differ in terms of **agency**, the ability of "the people" to be creative or productive with materials given to them by a dominant culture. Sociologists disagree on how much agency people have. Those who believe that people take an active role in shaping the culture they consume (e.g. the clothing they buy, the music they listen to, the websites they visit and contribute to, the TV shows and movies they watch) use the term *popular culture* to describe the consumers and producers of culture outside the world of the cultural elite.

Peter Steffen/AFP/Getty Images

LARPers don elaborate costumes to engage in live-action role-play, re-enacting battles from history or fantasy. Subculture or counterculture?

Those who believe people have little or no agency in the culture they consume and produce use the term **mass culture**. They tend to believe that multinational companies (such as Walmart, Disney, Google, and Apple) and powerful governments dictate what people buy, watch, wear, value, and believe. Mass culture is *not* benign. Critical theorists Theodor Adorno (1903–1969) and Max Horkheimer (1895–1973), who belonged to what is know as the Frankfurt school, called mass culture the output of the culture industry. In *Dialectic of Enlightenment* (1944), a work they co-authored, they described how cultural products—particularly movies but also radio shows and magazines (1944 was pre-television)—are mass-produced to keep society happy and submissive. To them, mass culture stifles creative freedom and individuality while keeping people dependent on these products of capitalism.

The internet was once seen as a boon for popular culture, enabling users to have their stories, social commentaries, photos, videos, and so on, seen by an enormous audience without any intervention by large media companies. Today, however, these products of popular culture are mediated by dominant technology services such as Facebook, Google, and YouTube, which control the results that appear at the top of your search while promoting the content most likely to generate clicks by consumers.

One feature of mass culture is what French sociologist **Jean Baudrillard** (1929–2007) called **simulacra**. Simulacra are stereotypical cultural images produced and reproduced like material goods or commodities by the media and sometimes by scholars. For example, Inuit are often represented by simulacra of described practices (e.g. rubbing noses, abandoning elders) and physical objects (e.g. igloos, kayaks). These images tend to distort contemporary Inuit "reality." Consider the way the inukshuk, the Inuit stone figure, has become a Canadian cultural symbol, with models of these stone figures sold in tourist shops across the country. It has such cultural currency that it was incorporated into the logo for the 2010 Winter Olympics held in British Columbia—a province with no Inuit community.

Indigenous people are often represented by simulacra of described practices, such as shape-shifting and performing magic. These simulacra account for some of the strange questions my Native American Facebook friends receive, such as

- Can you interpret my dreams?
- Do you talk to animals?
- Can you teach me to be a shaman?
- Are you a shape-shifter?

This image, which I call the "hyper-spiritual Native American" simulacrum, does not come from talking to and being with Indigenous people; instead, it comes from popular media, particularly novels.

Baudrillard describes simulacra as being "hyperreal"—that is, likely to be considered more real than what actually exists or existed. He illustrates the principle with an analogy of a map, but we will consider a GPS system instead. Imagine you are driving down a country road on a winter night. Your GPS system tells you to turn right onto a major road that will lead you straight home, yet all your eyes see is a narrow dirt road covered in snow. If you follow that road and get stuck at a dead end, the GPS system was hyperreal to you: you believed the information it was giving you was more real than what your eyes detected. This information is thus a simulacrum. When sociologists encourage their students to be critical of what the media present, they are hoping their students will be able to detect simulacra.

British sociologist John Fiske (2010) takes the popular culture position. He does not believe that people are brainless consumers of mass culture; rather, he believes that the power bloc—the political and cultural institutions with the greatest influence on society—merely supplies people with resources that they resist, evade, or turn to their own ends. He recognizes agency and warns about the dangers of sociologists presenting people as mere dupes of mass media.

An important distinction between the two positions involves the contrast, identified by Michel de Certeau (1984), between *decipherment* and *reading*. **Decipherment** involves looking in a text for the definitive interpretation, for the purpose (conscious or unconscious) the culture industry had in mind in creating the text. For sociologists who believe that mass culture predominates, decipherment is about looking for the message that mass media impose on consumers, who are left without the opportunity to challenge it or reject it by substituting their own.

Sociologists who believe that popular rather than mass culture predominates tend to use the term *reading*. **Reading** is the process in which people treat what is provided by the culture industry as a resource, a text to be interpreted as they see fit, in ways not necessarily intended by the creators of the text. The sociological technique of reading involves analyzing the narratives of those using the text in this way.

🔴 reddit   ⓣ r/tumblr   ▾   🔍 Search r/tumblr   〰

ⓣ r/tumblr

Posts

▲
423   Posted by u/dylanna who lives, who dies, who clears my history 2 years ago
▼   **"The Cask of Amontillado" meme**
    i.imgur.com/wkZuRs... ⧉

    wehaveallgotknives:

    brinnanza:

        my favorite thing about the cask of amontillado meme (which I LOVE) is that it displays, yet again, how difficult millennials on the internet are to predict. oh, giant company, you want your advertisement to go viral? well this week the kids are obsessed with a short story written in 1846 good fucking luck

        oh my dear marketing man, you want me to explain how to track this? well, I could show you a chart that indicates the next five big memes. it is down in my basement, though it is quite cold, and surely you have another engagement to attend.

    💬 10 Comments   ↗ Share   🔖 Save   98% Upvoted

If you were born this century, you have grown up with the world's most powerful medium for creating, transmitting, and consuming cultural products. Do you consider what you engage with online to be popular culture or mass culture?

Cultural Norms

Norms are rules or standards of behaviour that are expected of members of a group, society, or culture. There isn't always consensus concerning these standards: norms may be contested along the sociological lines of ethnicity, "race," gender, and age. A quick illustration: a student of mine once told

The Point Is ...

There Aren't a Lot of Goth Grandparents ... Yet

What happens when a youth counterculture ages? Does it just disappear with the youth of the members? Or does it last as part of their lives into middle age?

Let's apply this question to goth counterculture, which is still in evidence today. You can probably summon up a rough image to fit the term: dyed black (or, less often, blue) hair, dark clothes, and white makeup that contrasts sharply with clothing and hair colour. You may associate goths with their fascination with death and with art, especially music and film that reflects this fascination. If you can't picture goth, picture emo: while the two are not synonymous, emo counterculture has much in common with goth counterculture and is sometimes seen as an offshoot or descendant of it.

Goths tend to be young, white people from middle-class families. Their opposition to dominant culture is expressed most clearly in their dress and overall appearance, but it goes beyond the visual. Goths of the 1980s rejected the yuppie world of financial self-indulgence and conservative politics. They pursued a life concerned with less world-exploitive politics and cultish small-market arts. Generally, they find beauty in things the mainstream culture finds repulsive, frightening, or ugly.

Some bloggers claim that there are three generations of goths, each not so aware of its predecessors or reincarnations. Because of this generation gap, the goth lifestyle is invented and reinvented by the youth cohort of the time. So what happens to goths when they grow up? Sociologist Paul Hodkinson (2011, 2013) studied

Philartphace/iStockphoto

Hodkinson's research suggests that most youths in a counterculture—goths excepted—withdraw from the counterculture as they age. Why do you think this is so? Can you think of why goths may differ in this regard?

Continued

people who entered the goth counterculture during the 1980s in their teens and early twenties. He followed them as they aged, using participant observation at goth events, observing goth communication online, and doing in-depth interviews with 19 men and women aged 27 to 50. He noted that from the late 1990s, "the previously very small number of older goths in the scene began to grow and, as a result of the coincidence of this with slower recruitment of youngsters, the average age of the scene rose, to the extent that some events now are thoroughly dominated by over-thirties. The goth scene therefore provides an example of a subculture dominated by 'the same body of continuing participants' (Smith, 2009, p. 428), something which contrasts with the isolated older participants in otherwise adolescent cultures focused on in my other studies...." (Hodkinson, 2013, p. 1077)

As they aged, the goths followed dominant cultural practices by getting married and becoming parents (to "baby bats" or "gothlings"). Women were more likely than men to withdraw from the goth scene as they settled into more conventional domestic arrangements. Aging goths turned to monthly goth festivals that included supervised children's activities. They subscribed to online countercultural magazines and blogs that included discussions of goth-themed baby outfits and children's clothes. When they did go out at night, they spent less time preparing their appearance, drank less, and came home sooner—and with their spouses, not with someone they had just met. Nevertheless, it's clear that not all goths grew out of the counterculture; instead, the counterculture has evolved to accommodate its aging members.

me he remembered being embarrassed, as a child, when his grandmother refused to "pick up" after her poodle. Although stoop-and-scoop laws weren't yet in effect, it had become common custom, as far as the boy was aware. Yet his grandmother was completely unselfconscious, even as the neighbours eyed her and her poodle with annoyance. Many years later, when the boy, now a young man, was engaged to be married, he was reprimanded by his grandmother for failing to write out the invitations individually, by hand. "It is bad form," she told him, "to send *printed* invitations unless you are inviting more than one hundred guests." Coming from different generations, the student and his grandmother recognized different norms of behaviour.

Norms are expressed in a culture through various means, from ceremonies that reflect cultural customs (a wedding, for example) to symbolic articles of dress (the white dress worn by the bride). In the following sections, we'll consider different ways in which norms are expressed and enforced.

Sanctions

People react to how others follow or do not follow norms. If the reaction is one that supports the behaviour, it is called a **positive sanction**. It is a reward for "doing the right thing." Positive sanctions range from small gestures like a smile, a high five, or a supportive comment, to larger material rewards like a bonus for hard work on the job. A hockey player who gets into a fight is positively sanctioned by teammates at the bench banging their sticks against the boards, or by the cheering crowd.

A **negative sanction** is a reaction designed to tell offenders they have violated a norm. It could be anything from a glare, an eye roll, or a sarcastic quip to a parking ticket or the fine you pay at the library for an overdue book. When someone around me says, "Hey, look—it's Santa Claus," I know that behind the apparent joke is a negative sanction about my well-proportioned frame and my bushy, grey beard.

Folkways, Mores, and Taboos
Folkways

William Graham Sumner (1840–1910), the first person in North America to teach a course called "sociology," distinguished three kinds of norms based on how seriously they are respected and sanctioned. He used the term **folkways** for norms governing simple day-to-day matters. These are norms that you *should* not (as opposed to *must* not) violate. They are the least respected and most weakly sanctioned. The term *etiquette* can often be applied to folkways. George Costanza, on the TV show *Seinfeld*, continually violated folkways by, for instance, double-dipping chips at a party or by fetching a chocolate pastry out of the garbage.

Mores

Mores (pronounced like the eels—*morays*) are taken much more seriously than folkways. You *must* not violate them. Some mores—against rape, killing, vandalism, and most forms of stealing, for example—are enshrined in the criminal code as laws. Violation of some mores, even if they are not laws, will meet with shock or severe disapproval. Booing the national anthem of the visiting team prior to a sporting event is likely to cause offence among supporters of the visitors and even anger or embarrassment among fans of the home side. Mores are complicated and may be contested. Mores of cleanliness, for instance, are in the cultural eye of the beholder. In Britain, dogs are allowed in pubs; in Canada, they are not. This does not mean that bars in Canada are more sanitary than those in Britain. Differences in mores of cleanliness can lead to serious problems when, for instance, an overdeveloped Western sense of what is hygienic jeopardizes the health of a hospital patient (see the discussion of Hmong refugees on page 410 of Chapter 13, on medical sociology).

Like folkways, mores change over time. A young woman sporting a tattoo would once have been seen as violating the mores of acceptable behaviour for "a lady." Today, many women have tattoos and display them without arousing the kind of shock or condemnation generally produced when mores are violated.

Taboos

A **taboo** is a norm so deeply ingrained in our social consciousness that the mere thought or mention of it is enough to arouse disgust or revulsion. Cannibalism, incest, and child pornography immediately come to mind. Taboos affect our dietary habits. Eating dogs, cats, or other animals that might be considered family pets is taboo in North American culture. There are religious taboos surrounding the consumption of

"#114: Another Terrible Combination" from NYC Basic Tips and Etiquette by Nathan W. Pyle. Copyright © 2014 by Nathan W. Pyle. Reprinted by permission of HarperCollins Publishers.

You can think of folkways as unwritten rules of etiquette established through custom and enforced through social coercion. How might someone—an irritated fellow pedestrian or, for that matter, a grumpy social cartoonist—show their disapproval of the violation depicted above?

certain foods—pork by Jews and Muslims, beef by Hindus. Some cultures recognize gender taboos, such as those surrounding women who interfere with or attempt to partake in typical male activities. Like folkways and mores, taboos differ from culture to culture.

Culture Symbols

Symbols are cultural items that hold significance for a culture or subculture. They can be either tangible (i.e. physical) material objects (as illustrated in the narrative on page 82) or intangible, nonmaterial objects, such as songs or even remembered events. Just as culture itself is contested, culture symbols are likely to be interpreted differently by people inside and outside of the culture they represent.

Symbols of nationality tend to take on tremendous cultural significance. Think of the maple leaf a Canadian tourist stitches to the backpack they wear when travelling in Europe. It's meant to stand not just for their country of origin but for a whole set of qualities that we like to think make up the Canadian cultural identity—courtesy, tolerance, knowledgeableness, peacefulness, and so on. To the European who sees and recognizes it as a symbol of Canadian cultural identity, the maple leaf might conjure up a very different set of qualities: our rejection of the Kyoto agreement on climate change, our tar sands, our seal hunt . . . Some of these are recent developments, illustrating another point: the cultural significance of symbols can change over time.

The Point Is . . .

An Important Culture Symbol May Puzzle an Outsider

In the fall of 1989, I travelled through rural Virginia on a short lecture tour, having been invited by staff and students of Southwest Virginia Community College who had attended a lecture of mine during their spring break. I spent the first night of my stay at the home of the college president. It was elegant, finely furnished, with everything in its place. While there, I noticed something that surprised me. In a glass case—the kind normally used to hold curios and objets d'art, such as glass and china figurines—I saw two six-pointed objects, each one made of three nails. They reminded me of the jacks I had played with as a child, but bigger, and menacing. Why had these mean-looking items been placed on display?

The next night I stayed with a coalminer's family. There I learned about the dynamics of a months-long coalminer's strike in the one-industry area. I was taken on a tour of the strike centre, where bunk beds were being built to accommodate the families of striking workers who had been thrown out of their homes for failing to pay the rent. The people I met there were friendly, but the long strike was crushing their spirit.

The mining company was owned by people from outside the area—foreigners, in the eyes of the locals. The company owners had circumvented the picket lines by trucking the coal out at night, but striking miners in camouflage had found ways to thwart their efforts.

The next day, at the college, I spoke to a sociology class about symbols. Near the end of the class, I asked students to name some local symbols. One student shouted out "jackrocks." When I asked what "jackrocks" were, I got a description of the six-pointed objects I had seen in the president's glass case, as well as a bag full of jackrocks handed to me by a student who went to his car to get them. I was told that one of the tactics used to keep the coal trucks from shipping out the coal was to toss these jackrocks underneath the tires. The jackrocks had become symbols of the miners' resistance. They appeared in store windows in the town nearest the mine, and I was given a pair of small, aluminum jackrock earrings. I then understood why the college president kept the two jackrocks in the glass case. He was from Florida, and therefore a "foreigner" to the area. By keeping the jackrocks in a place of honour, he was expressing solidarity with his students and their community.

What Do YOU Think?

1. What cultural significance did the jackrocks have for the local people of southwestern Virginia?
2. Why do you think the college president kept jackrocks in his glass case at home? Do you think he fully appreciated their significance?

The Hijab as a Symbol for Some Canadian Muslim Women

Few clothing symbols have a greater power to evoke emotions than the **niqab**, the veiled head covering worn by some Muslim women. To many in the West, it is a symbol of patriarchal domination by religious extremists, similar in effect to the full-length, screen-faced *burqa* that many Afghan women wear and to the *chador* that Iranian women are forced by law to wear. Even the *hijab*, which covers the head and hair but not the face, may be seen by non-Muslims as a symbol of religious oppression. In the lead-up to the 2015 federal election, Canadians debated whether the *niqab* aligned with our national cultural values. The issue came to the fore when a young woman, Zunera Ishaq, wanted to take her oath of Canadian citizenship while wearing the veil. The federal government under Conservative Prime Minister Steven Harper attempted to deny her that right on the grounds that most Canadians would find it offensive. The Supreme Court overruled the government's motion, upholding Ms Ishaq's right to keep her face covered during the public ceremony. In October 2015, shortly before the election, she took her citizenship oath while wearing the *niqab*.

It is important to understand why women of various cultures—especially in Canada—choose to wear a *hijab* or *niqab*. For this information there can be no better source than the community of Canadian Muslim women who have considered the choice themselves. Some of them have provided the narratives that appear on pages 84–85. What stands out, as we read their views, is that to some Muslim women in Canada, taking the veil is a matter of choice, not command.

The perspectives featured on pages 84–85 are part of a ground-breaking study carried out by Iranian Canadian anthropologist Homa Hoodfar (2003) in Quebec, where the right of public servants—from politicians to school teachers, bus drivers, and nurses—to wear symbols of religious faith continues to be a source of political debate. The voices Hoodfar recorded speak compellingly of their choice to wear the veil as a way of opposing restrictions placed on them (and not their brothers) as teenagers by parents concerned that their daughters would fall prey to the irreligious sex-, alcohol-, and drug-related behaviours of North American culture. Some of those interviewed saw the decision to wear the *hijab* as a step,

What Do YOU Think?

1. Could you sociologically predict which social characteristics—age, religion, sex, etc.—might make a person more likely or less likely to oppose the wearing of the *niqab* during an oath of Canadian citizenship?
2. Do you see the *niqab* or *hijab* as a symbol of personal choice, patriarchal oppression, religious honour, or something else? How, if at all, did the narratives presented on pages 84–85 affect your view?
3. Missing from this box are narratives reflecting the views of young Muslim women in Canada who have chosen not to wear the *niqab* or *hijab*. What might we learn from their perspectives?

together with Qur'anic study and banding together with Canadian Muslim women of different cultural backgrounds, down a path of opposition to some of the patriarchal mores of their specific cultures. In addition, taking the veil gave some women the opportunity to defend their faith against the ethnocentric ignorance of some of their fellow Canadians.

Values

Values are the standards used by a culture to describe abstract qualities such as goodness, beauty, and justice, and to assess the behaviour of others. Values have long been a topic of interest to sociologists. Max Weber's identification of the **Protestant (work) ethic** is one early example of a sociological study of values. Many others have followed since. But in spite of these studies, values remain difficult to understand and to represent accurately. What makes the issue especially puzzling is that the values that people claim to have are not always the ones they act upon. In other words, there is a discrepancy between the **ideal culture** that people believe in and the **actual culture** that really exists. Do we recognize, then, the value that is professed or the value that is reflected in human action? Is the person who preaches a value but fails to honour it in everyday life necessarily a hypocrite?

Telling It Like It Is

The Hijab as Worn by Young Canadian Muslim Women in Montreal

MoralSO/Thinkstock

The Narrative of a 19-Year-Old Palestinian-Canadian Woman

The veil has freed me from arguments and headaches. I always wanted to do many things that women normally do not do in my culture. I had thought living in Canada would give me that opportunity. But when I turned 14, my life changed. My parents started to limit my activities and even telephone conversations. My brothers were free to go and come as they pleased, but my sister and I were to be good Muslim girls. . . . Life became intolerable for me. The weekends were hell.

Then, as a way out, I asked to go to Qur'anic classes on Saturdays. There I met with several veiled women of my age. . . . None of them seemed to face my problems. Some told me that since they took the veil, their parents know that they are not going to do anything that goes against Muslim morality. The more I hung around with them, the more convinced I was that the veil is the answer to all Muslim girls' problems here in North America. Because parents seem to be relieved and assured that you are not going to do stupid things, and your community knows that you are acting like a Muslim woman, you are much freer. (cited in Hoodfar, 2003, pp. 20–1)

The Narrative of a 17-Year-Old Pakistani-Canadian Woman

Although we did not intermingle much with non–Indian Canadians, I very much felt at home and part of the wider society. This, however, changed as I got older and clearly my life was different than many girls in my class. I did not talk about boyfriends and did not go out. I did not participate in extracurricular activities. Gradually, I began feeling isolated. Then, my cousin and I decided together to wear the veil and made a pact to ignore people's comments; no matter how much hardship we suffered at school, we would keep our veils on ....

At first it was difficult. At school people joked and asked stupid questions, but after three months they took us more seriously and there was even a little bit of respect. We even got a little more respect when we talked about Islam in our classes, while before our teacher dismissed what we said if it didn't agree with her casual perceptions. (cited in Hoodfar, 2003, pp. 28–9)

The Narrative of Mona, an Egyptian Canadian Woman

I would never have taken up the veil if I lived in Egypt. Not that I disagree with that, but I see it as part of the male imposition of rules .... The double standard frustrates me. But since the Gulf War, seeing how my veiled friends were treated, I made a vow to wear the veil to make a point about my Muslimness and Arabness. I am delighted when people ask me about my veil and Islam, because it gives me a chance to point out their prejudices concerning Muslims. (cited in Hoodfar, 2003, p. 30)

A Response to the Narratives by a Muslim Feminist

[The following was written by a 19-year-old university student in Alberta, who describes herself as a Muslim feminist (not a contradiction in terms). After reading the above narratives in a previous edition of this textbook, she felt compelled to comment.]

Hijab and the veil are religious decisions to be made between the person choosing to wear it and God. It is highly disrespectful to belittle the value of Hijab, making it to be something as simple as a political statement or a statement to your classmates or parents. If you're wearing Hijab simply so your parents can treat you the same as your brother, you are using a religious statement to combat culturally driven inequality (which, in fact, goes against Islam).

These responses made Hijab seem entirely misogynistic, when it is in fact the exact opposite. Compare it with the following. In almost any magazine, book, advertisement, or movie you encounter, women are overly sexualized. Women are used to sell products, and are constantly treated as no more than just eye candy. Magazines injected with unrealistic beauty standards tell you "How to Lose 10 Inches Off Your Waist!" and "How to Be the Sexiest Woman in the Room!"

In movies and TV shows, girls are constantly purchasing cosmetics and discussing weight loss, talking about boys, and competing with one another to impress boys. Everything about Western media values women according to appearance, sexualizing and exploiting us in every way possible, just to please the male-kind. From a young age, women are trained to prioritize our physical appearance so that we can "fit in" and be "normal."

When young women fail to meet these unfair beauty standards naturally, we see millions of dollars spent on cosmetics and cosmetic surgery. Money aside, we also find an increase in eating disorders (i.e. anorexia and bulimia) as well as mental disorders (i.e. depression and anxiety), resulting from a lack of self-worth and self-esteem, which can ultimately lead to drug abuse or suicide.

Now back to the topic about Hijab. I chose to wear Hijab to protect myself from all of that. Hijab and the veil create a barrier between the woman choosing to wear it and the rest of the world. It forces people to actually listen to what she has to say, rather than to pass judgments solely on her physical appearance. Hijab gives me the comfort and liberty of knowing that I'm being judged according to my intellect rather than my sexual appeal. I know that I can freely stroll down the street without feeling insecure because men are staring at my body or talking about it to others. Not that they should in the first place, but Hijab and the veil ensure that they don't have the opportunity.

Canadian and American Values

As I noted at the start of this chapter, Canadians sometimes wonder about where we fit in the North American cultural landscape, and whether Canadian culture really exists as something other than American culture + more snow, colourful banknotes, and the metric system. The exercise becomes more difficult when considering cultural *values*, which are not as easy to pinpoint as cultural *symbols*. This is why Canadians, finding themselves at a loss to summon up uniquely Canadian values, will sometimes define themselves in contrast to Americans, as in "Canadians are like unarmed Americans with better health coverage." That doesn't really say much for Canadian values.

Michael Adams, of the Environics Research Group, has been conducting and publishing opinion polls since the early 1980s. During the 1990s, he measured and tracked 100 "social values" among Canadians and Americans, including such things as acceptance of violence, obedience to authority, penchant for risk, and sexual permissiveness. He published the results of his work in *Fire and Ice: The United States, Canada and the Myth of Converging Values* (2003). His thesis was that Canadians and Americans are becoming more different rather than more alike in their values. It certainly seemed so in 2003, when the American military was heading into Iraq and Canada was not, and when a modest majority of Canadians supported gay marriage and the liberalization of marijuana laws, which a majority opposed in the United States.

Adams based his findings on data from Environics polls conducted in the United States and Canada in 1992, 1996, and 2000. It's always important to look at the data critically. For instance, the polls invited respondents to "talk" about their values. But you will recall that there is often a difference between the values we profess and those we act upon. Another point: Is the time period—from 1992 to 2000—long enough to produce evidence of what he called "long-term shifts"? All of the data were gathered before the September 11 terrorist attacks, which occurred in 2001. Adams speculated that the events of 9/11 would only make the differences he had identified greater.

In the early first decade of the twenty-first century, Canada and the United States underwent some significant changes that caused Adams to revisit his thesis. During the period of his initial study, the United States had a conservative Republican administration led by George W. Bush, and Canada had a Liberal administration headed by Jean Chrétien. However, from 2006 until 2015, Canada had a prime minister, Stephen Harper, with very conservative values, on par with those of American Republicans; in contrast, Americans elected a liberal Democratic leader and first ever black president, Barack Obama. In a 2014 presentation at the Woodrow Wilson Center in Washington, DC, Adams asked whether Americans and Canadians were trading places. He then answered his own question with a resounding *no*: he found that Canadians and Americans remained far apart on certain values (see Table 3.1). However, there were some surprising findings. Consider one of the value clusters Adams identified: **patriarchy**, or the acceptance of men in positions of political, cultural, and social power. One of the statements used to measure patriarchy was the following:

> "The father of the family must be master in his own home."

Respondents were asked whether they agreed with this statement. Figure 3.1 shows the results over a 24-year period from 1992 to 2016. Note the increase in the difference after each four-year period from 1992 to 2004. During that time, even the regional ranges of the two countries did not intersect: in the 2000 poll, the *highest* rate of agreement with this statement among Canadian respondents was 21 per cent, in Alberta; that is 8 percentage points below the *lowest* rate of agreement among US respondents, 29 per cent, in New England (the highest rate of agreement that year was 71 per cent in the Deep South) (Adams, 2017). In other words, the *most* patriarchal region of Canada was less patriarchal than the *least* patriarchal region of the United States.

Between 2004 and 2012, with Obama and Harper in office in the United States and Canada, respectively, the margin between the two countries narrowed to 1992 levels. How much did these changes have to do with the prevailing political climate? Likely a lot. Here in 2019, as I'm writing this book, Canada has, once again, a Liberal prime minister, whose outlook on many social issues sets him

TABLE 3.1 Values on Which Canadians and Americans Differ the Most (2012)

Stronger in Canada	Stronger in the US
• flexible families	• national pride
• ecological concern	• fear and acceptance of violence
• cultural assimilation	• work ethic
	• spiritual quest
	• propriety
	• religiosity
	• patriarchy

Source: Adams, 2014

in stark contrast to his Conservative predecessor. The United States is currently governed by a controversial Republican demagogue who came to power thanks largely to his regressive anti-immigration, anti–free trade stance, and his divisive "us versus them" rhetoric. Adams's polling data from 2016 indicates that the patriarchy margin has widened again, as Figure 3.1 shows (Adams, 2017).

A critic of Adams's conclusions might argue that his analysis relies too much on the one question about the father's role in the household. Indeed, this is just one of 50 values that Adams's polling company has been tracking recently. To Adams, patriarchy is worth honing in on because it "is highly correlated with other values such as religiosity, parochialism, and xenophobia, and views on issues

> **What Do YOU Think?**
>
> 1. Adams has argued that American and Canadian social values are becoming less alike. How convincing do you find his argument?
> 2. If the difference is indeed growing, what do you think is the cause? What role do you think factors such as religion, politics, and the economy play in the difference?

such as abortion, guns, and the death penalty" (2017). Nevertheless, to boil US and Canadian cultural differences down to this one value may be too narrow-focused.

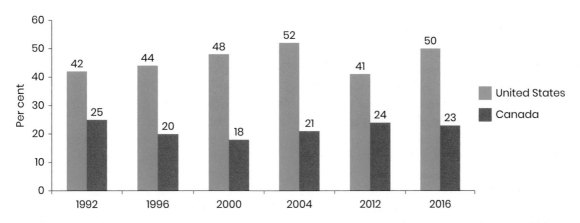

FIGURE 3.1 Percentage Agreeing with the Statement "The Father of the Family Must Be Master in His Own House," US and Canada, 1992–2016

Source: Adams, 2017.

The Point Is . . .

The Maple Leaf and the Stars and Stripes Carry Very Different Strings of Meaning

Culture symbols that are physical objects are sometimes called **cultural artifacts.** Like other culture symbols, artifacts have strings of meaning attached to them, giving them special significance to particular cultural groups. The more strings of meaning that are attached to an artifact, the more powerful it is as a symbol of the culture for whom it has relevance.

Let's consider flags as cultural artifacts. Specifically, we'll compare the strings of meaning attached to the flags of the United States and Canada. I will begin with a statement that may be controversial (and goodness knows, I try to avoid controversy at all costs): the American flag has more cultural value for Americans than the Canadian flag has for Canadians. This is because the Stars and Stripes has more cultural strings of meaning.

Let's start with the star-spangled banner. First, there is the apocryphal story of the flag's origins: that it was first sewn by a young Pennsylvania seamstress, at the request of the future first president, during the American War of Independence. That the patriotically romanticized account has been disputed by some historians in no way diminishes the power of the flag's origin story.

The story of the flag's connection to America's revolutionary history is invoked whenever the US national anthem is played, reminding us that the flag was around at the dawn of American nationhood and making it a symbol of the country's successful fight for independence. That isn't even the only song about "Old Glory." There is also the patriotic song "You're a Grand Old Flag," which is dated but occasionally still sung in American schools on Memorial Day, and newer homages such as Toby Keith's "Courtesy of the Red, White, and Blue" (2002) (neither of which is, thankfully, sung before NHL games hosted by Canadian teams).

Third, the American flag has important visual symbols on it: 13 stripes for the 13 colonies that revolted against the British Crown, and 50 stars for 50 states, updated as necessary (there were just 48 stars when I was born). These symbols give the flag a universal significance: whether you live in Alamosa, Colorado, or Kittery Point, Maine, your place in the country is represented on the flag.

Fourth, there is the pledge of allegiance to the flag, a solemn exercise performed with right hand over heart at the start of the school day and the commencement of government meetings. Americans may take the pledge for granted; how could they know that it is a practice that America shares with very few other countries.

Fifth, there is the strong association between the flag and the military. This goes back to the flag's introduction during the American Revolution, but it was solidified by the classic picture of five US marines and one navy corpsman raising the flag on the Pacific island of Iwo Jima during World War II. In both world wars, the Korean, and subsequent wars, the flag has been with the troops.

Sixth, there are serious laws against any desecration of the flag. You may not decorate your ceiling with it, make it into an article of clothing, or fly it carelessly so that it touches land, water, or the floor. And you certainly may not burn it.

The Maple Leaf is internationally recognized as a symbol of Canadian identity, but Canada's flag carries far fewer strings of meaning than the Stars and Stripes does. When I used to ask my students when the Canadian flag was first used, hardly anyone could give me the correct answer without googling it on their phone. (It was February 1965, nearly 100 years after Canada became a country.) I couldn't imagine a student knowing that the

© Charla Sylvester

Titled "Home and Native Land," this photo was taken by Charla Sylvester, a 25-year-old student from the Beausoleil First Nation. As a culture symbol, what do you think the Maple Leaf means to her?

man who designed the flag was historian Colonel George Stanley.

The flag was not the product of any revolution, although it was the subject of fierce debate in Parliament when the first suggestions that it replace the Union Jack were raised. I don't need to tell you we don't pledge allegiance to it, and I challenge you to find an iconic patriotic picture of it or contemporary song about it. And we have no flag desecration laws in Canada.

The central symbol of the flag is the leaf of a tree that isn't native to much of Canada. The red on both sides represents that the country spans from sea to sea, although there is no red line at the top to represent the Arctic Ocean. Our national anthem does not include reference to the flag. In 1867, when Canada achieved its nationhood, the soldier and poet Alexander Muir wrote a rousing tune called "The Maple Leaf Forever," which did include some references to historic battles. It was an unofficial national anthem for a time, but it never made it officially because it was strongly rooted in British heritage and celebrated the defeat of Canada's French population at the hands of the British. The "Maple Leaf" in the song's title and chorus is an emblem on the national coat of arms. It is not a reference to the flag, which was created 60 years after Muir's death.

Canada's armed forces have served under various flags. Land forces in World War I most commonly used the Union Jack, but merchant seamen used numerous never-officially-approved versions of the red ensign, a red flag with a Union Jack in the upper left-hand corner and a central shield with different emblems. Two versions of the red ensign are used today as the provincial flags of Manitoba and Ontario.

In 1996, the federal government established 15 February as National Flag of Canada

Continued

Day, although it is not a holiday and I'll bet you were unaware of the occasion before I mentioned it just now. By comparison, in the US, Flag Day has been observed nationally since 1916, and it is a holiday in some parts of the country.

Canadians may proudly wear a modest pin with the flag on it when they go to other countries, but the Maple Leaf still lacks the strong cultural meaning attached to the Stars and Stripes.

What Do YOU Think?

Feel free to disagree: Could you argue that our flag has more cultural value for Canadians than the American flag has for Americans? How could you study this?

Ethnocentrism

Ethnocentrism occurs when someone holds up a culture (usually one's own) as the standard by which all cultures are to be judged. It follows a simple formula: all cultures like the gold-standard culture are good, praiseworthy, beautiful, moral, and modern; those that are not are bad, ugly, immoral, and primitive. Ethnocentrism can manifest itself in many forms, but it often entails declaring that there is only one right way (the way of the cultural model) to run a business, handle finances, or manage social policy.

The term was coined by William Graham Sumner (1906), the author of *Folkways*, whom we encountered about ten pages ago. A staunch anti-imperialist, Sumner saw evidence of ethnocentrism in the arguments made by imperial governments to justify colonizing other, supposedly less-civilized nations. He was particularly critical of America's suppression of Philippine nationalism in the aftermath of the Spanish–American War (1898), when the United States gained control of the Philippine islands, previously a colony of Spain.

Generally, Sumner was of the opinion that "outsiders"—governments, imperial powers, or authority figures—should not meddle with or impose their values on the cultures of "insiders," such as the people of the Philippines, American citizens, or bankers and businessmen. Were he alive today we might call him a libertarian—a rare ideology for a sociologist—since he believed strongly in free-market capitalism, where businesses are free to operate without government restrictions. He was ordained as an Episcopal priest in 1869 but chose a career outside of the church, in part because he felt that ministers were expected to speak out against the rich, instructing them to do more to help the poor, who, he believed, should be doing more to help themselves.

Ethnocentrism is often the product of ignorance, something experienced by Hmong refugees who arrived in the United States from Southeast Asia during and after the Vietnam War. The Hmong were targeted in the United States in part because of their supposed practice of stealing, killing, and eating dogs. Lack of evidence or truth did not deter an ethnocentric public from spreading these stories about a "foreign" culture. The false stories followed particular themes, as Anne Fadiman explains in her book on Hmong Americans:

> [Rumored] methods of [dog] procurement vary. Some are coaxed home by Hmong children. Some were adopted from animal shelters. . . . Others are strays. The most common accusation is theft, often from backyards, sometimes leaving the head and collar as mute testimony to Rover's passing. . . . The dog is usually an expensive one, often owned by a doctor. The theft is observed, the license plate number is marked down. When the police check, the dog is already in some Hmong family's pot.

> The supposed proof varies. That fixture in the urban legend, the garbage man, reports the presence of canine remains in Hmong garbage cans. Carcasses are seen hanging

in the cellar by meter readers, salesmen, or whomever. Freezers are said to be full of frozen dogs. A bizarre touch is that the dogs are supposedly skinned alive to make them more tasty. (Fadiman, 1997, pp. 190–1)

On a larger scale, ethnocentrism has played a role in the colonizing efforts of powerful nations imposing their political, economic, and religious beliefs on the indigenous populations of lands they "discovered." The following discussion highlights how Canada's First Nations were forced by an ethnocentric government to abandon a traditional custom.

Potlatch and Peyote: Ethnocentrism and Indigenous Cultures

The Potlatch Act of 1884

The **Potlatch** is a traditional ceremony of Northwest Coast Indigenous people living in the United States and Canada. It often involves the acquisition or affirmation of hereditary names. These hereditary names carry more than just symbolic significance: they are connected with rights to fish, hunt, or forage for plants in particular territories, and with the responsibility to conserve the living entities in those areas. Potlatches thus serve to maintain the strength and social unity of the group.

An important aspect of the Potlatch is the giving away of gifts and possessions. Traditionally, a high-ranking man could prove he was worthy of his position by making gifts of the possessions he had acquired. The hierarchical nature of Northwest Coast culture made this competitive, as those holding or aspiring to high rank gave away a great deal. The level of competition rose after European contact, because of the sudden availability of European manufactured goods. The population of the Kwakwaka'wakw or speakers of Kwak'wala of Vancouver Island, for example, dropped from roughly 8000 in 1835 to around 2000 in 1885. When diseases decimated lineages entitled to important names, more distant relatives would vie for prestigious family names. In some cases, competition could become socially divisive, and there were even incidents in which property was destroyed as a show of wealth

("I am so rich, that this property means nothing to me"). Such incidents appear to have been rare, but overreported in the literature.

This aspect of the Potlatch gained the notice of government officials in Canada, who saw the ceremony as an impediment to assimilation. For one thing, the Europeans who had settled in North America viewed the drive to accumulate wealth as an important lever in their burgeoning capitalist economy. The notion of redistributing wealth among people who had not earned it through hard work was difficult to understand and potentially dangerous. In the nineteenth century, the people of the Northwest Coast were already wealthy, but the prevalence of the Potlatch and the quantity of goods given away gave Europeans the impression that Indigenous people were poor and, perhaps worse, lazy because a good number of them were benefitting from handouts (Lutz, 2012, p. 306). Christian missionaries also disliked the Potlatch, which did not fit within the model of religion they were attempting to establish among the Indigenous population.

In 1884, the Canadian government banned the Potlatch, making participation in the ceremony a misdemeanour. In 1921, 45 of the highest-ranking Kwakiutl were arrested. Twenty-two were sentenced to prison terms of two to three months. The people lost many sacred Potlatch items that were taken as a condition for the release of community members arrested but not charged. The items became the property of the minister of Indian Affairs, who distributed them to art collectors and museums.

In 1951, the Potlatch ban was repealed. But it wasn't until 1975 that the National Museum in Ottawa declared it would return the sacred items—provided they be kept in museums. The Royal Ontario Museum returned its items in 1988, and the National Museum of the American Indian in New York repatriated some of its holdings in 1993. Some items were never recovered.

Outlawing Peyote

When Spanish explorers arrived in Mexico in the sixteenth century, they encountered an Indigenous population that practised a *monotheistic* (literally "one god") religion they could relate to because of its similarity to their own Christian belief. It revolved around an omnipotent and omnipresent "Great Spirit" who had created the universe very much like the Christian God the Spanish believed in. There was an important difference, however. Central to the Indians' religious practice was a small, spineless cactus known as the peyote. The people believed the Great Spirit had provided the peyote to help them cure disease, gain spiritual enlightenment, and communicate with the Great Spirit (James, 2009).

The edible buds of the peyote contain mescaline, a hallucinogenic substance. The Spaniards did not approve, and they attempted to ban the use of peyote among the native inhabitants. This merely pushed practitioners of the peyote-based religion into hiding and, eventually, over the border in the southwestern United States, where the religion flourished. During the nineteenth century, the peyote-based religion combining traditional Indigenous practices with elements of Christianity spread to the American southwest. As a narcotic, peyote helped the many nations that had been dumped into Indian Territory (later to become Oklahoma) deal with the harsh realities of life confined to reservations (Fikes, 1996). Again, it met resistance from state authorities, who attempted to outlaw the substance beginning in the late 1800s. To gain an exemption from harsh state-level drug laws, the peyotists banded together to form the Native American Church, which was officially recognized as religion in 1918. They continued to face persecution until the passing of the American Indian Religious Freedom Act in 1978. Card-carrying members were permitted to take peyote in ceremony. A similar act was passed in Canada in 1953.

This did not end the legal difficulties of the Native American Church. In 1990, a Supreme Court decision sided with the state of Oregon in the case of the *Employment Division of Oregon v. Smith*. Two Native Americans had been fired from state jobs, and because it was a "drug firing," they were denied unemployment benefits. The response to this perceived threat to the First Amendment from both liberal and conservative groups resulted in the Religious Freedom Restoration Act, which was passed in Congress in 1993. The lack of effectiveness of the provisions of this act concerning Native American religion resulted in the passing of the Religious Freedom Act Amendment of 1994.

Today, the Native American Church has roughly 80 chapters coming from 70 nations in Mexico, the

United States, and Canada, numbering around 250,000 members (Fikes, 1996).

Eurocentrism

Eurocentrism involves taking a broadly defined "European" (i.e. western and northern European, plus North American) position to address others, and assuming that the audience shares that position. It can be seen in historical references to the "known world"—that is, the world as it was known by Europeans—and to Christopher Columbus "discovering," in 1492, continents that were already home to millions of people. It foregrounds discoveries and contributions that are Western, and backgrounds those that are not. Did you know that our standard numbering system is known (poorly) as the Hindu–Arabic system? Did you know that chocolate and vanilla, corn, squash and pumpkins, most beans, peppers, potatoes, tomatoes, and sunflowers were first grown by Indigenous people? The Eurocentric perspective of many textbooks used in the West tends to champion advances made by people of European stock while downplaying or altogether ignoring important non-European developments such as these.

Cultural Globalization

Global studies expert Manfred Steger defines *cultural globalization* as "the intensification and expansion of cultural flows across the globe" (2003, p. 69). Our concern is with the one-way flow of culture from the West, or what we might call the "Americanization" of the world. Think of the factors. First of all, English has emerged as by far the most prominent language of science, of the internet, and of other powerful media. Second, American movies and television are seen in almost every country in the world. But to label this "American" culture is perhaps giving it

Telling It Like It Is

Plastic Shaman on my Dashboard: The Appropriation of Indigenous Culture Symbols

Cultural appropriation in a new pernicious form is directly hurting First Nations cultural revitalization and the financial well-being of our Peoples. With the advent of the internet and social media, the number of people offering "shaman" teachings or First Nations drum making, or Indigenous spirituality teachings, has exploded. A simple web search will turn up a number of people in your area offering a wide variety of services for a fee (usually substantial) either loosely or directly tied to the teachings of First Nations People.

The practitioners of these ersatz services are directly damaging cultural recovery/revitalization in our communities and affecting the incomes of Indigenous artisans. Their teachings perpetuate harmful stereotypes and offer unauthentic teachings that are compilations of pan-Indian practices from many Nations. The fees they charge and the products of their workshops are not authentic and directly compete with the Indigenous artisans. Authentic Indigenous teachings are never given for a fee or offered as a one- (or several-) year study format.

These teachings can be harmful. For Indigenous peoples struggling to find their way home, the unauthentic or pan-Indian teachings can cause ethno-stress. For others it can

be very risky. Indigenous healers spend a lifetime learning the correct use of medicines. The person instructing may simply have observed smudging at a powwow yet feels qualified to teach.

It is common for these practitioners to claim Indigenous heritage. When asked to identify their Nation, clan, family, and home community, they will either not answer or be evasive. One group in Toronto claims to donate 15 per cent of their profits to First Nations communities as hedge against scrutiny. It does not specify which Nation is the beneficiary of these proceeds. None of the group's practitioners is Indigenous to Turtle Island.

If you are interested in our teachings and medicines, build a relationship with a local community. Understand that the knowledge is not yours to use for profit. Be respectful of the people and the teachings. Always refer others to actual Indigenous peoples and communities. Appropriation of this type is harmful in many ways and requires direct action by allies to stop the practice.

—Thohahente yontiats. Kanien'kehá:ka ní:'i nok wakenáthen. Tsi Kenhteke nitiwaké:non. They call me Thohahente. I am Mohawk Turtle Clan from the community of Kenhteke (from which the Bay of Quinte takes its name). I am a researcher and advocate working for language and cultural revitalization, and Kanien'kéha sovereignty.

too broad a scope. It is just a small number of transnational companies—AT&T, Verizon, Comcast, Viacom, and Disney in the United States, as well as the European companies Bertelsmann and Vivendi, and Sony in Japan—that control most of the media. Not only do these companies reap enormous dividends by exporting their respective brands of Western culture to consumers across the globe, but as Steger points out, they draw audiences abroad away from the culture of their own countries into a global "gossip market" that revolves around the "vacuous

details of the private lives of American celebrities like Britney Spears, Jennifer Lopez, Leonardo DiCaprio, and Kobe Bryant" (Steger, 2003, p. 77). We could update this list to include the Kardashians, Taylor Swift, Jay Z, and Canada's own Justin Bieber.

It's worth noting that interpretations of globalized items of Western culture are not necessarily the same abroad as they are in their countries of origin. The classic study of a cultural reading of a Western cultural item by a non-Western audience is described by American anthropologist Laura

Constantino Brumidi, Fresco, c. 1875, Senate wing, U.S. Capitol.

Columbus and the Indian Maiden (c. 1875) is one of a series of frescoes adorning the vaulted ceiling of the US Capitol Building in Washington, DC. It was painted by Italian-born American historical artist Constantino Brumidi (1805–1880). Works of art are important cultural artifacts that are used to tell the story of a culture. What story does this mural tell about Columbus and America? What culture is it intended for? And what do you mean you find it "creepy"?

Bohannan (1966) in "Shakespeare in the Bush." In the article she describes her experience of telling the story of *Hamlet* to the Tiv of West Africa, and the reading they put on it. The article concludes with the words of a Tiv elder. After admitting that he had enjoyed Bohannan's story, told "with very few mistakes," the elder said,

> Sometime . . . you must tell us some more stories of your country. We, who are elders, will instruct you in their true meaning, so that when you return to your own land your elders will see that you have not been sitting in the bush, but among those who know things and who have taught you wisdom. (Bohannan, 1966, p. 47)

Cultural Relativism

Cultural relativism is an approach to studying and understanding an aspect of another culture within its proper cultural context. Because of the *holistic* nature of culture—because a culture is a complex system in which everything is connected—no single cultural practice can be understood in isolation, outside of its social, historical, and environmental context. Just as you cannot understand a single part of a car without understanding the system of which it is a part, you cannot attempt to understand individual aspects of culture without looking at their cultural context.

Unlike what Spock used to say in the original *Star Trek series*, logic (as a pure entity) does *not* dictate. Logic is a cultural construct, and every society has its own cultural logic. Any explanation of a cultural practice or belief must in some way incorporate this logic. This is especially important in medicine. Western medicine is dominated by a kind of ethnocentric logic that states that nothing worth knowing comes from non-Western traditions. Yet in order to cure or to heal, it's important to respond to the way the patient envisions the healing process. This point comes across with striking clarity in Anne Fadiman's (1997) study of Hmong refugees in America, mentioned earlier in this chapter. The book describes the way American doctors and nurses failed to respect, among other things, the Hmong people's spiritual connections to medicine, the importance of encouraging their belief that a cure is available, and the role this belief plays in the curing process.

Cultural relativism is about not just how we *understand* cultural practices that are not our own but how we *judge* those practices. One prevailing viewpoint argues that individuals should not be judged by the practices of their culture. They have relatively little choice in what they do. After all, those living today no more invented those customs that you might find objectionable than you invented customs in Canadian culture that others may find strange. Consider the Maasai, an African people with a strong warrior tradition, who have a custom in which boys, at the onset of puberty, are circumcised. It is frightening and painful, but it is an important initiation ceremony: only once he has gone through the ceremony is a Maasai boy treated as a man and permitted to have sex with women. It is easy for Canadians to judge this custom negatively, to be critical of those who perpetuate what they consider a cruel and barbaric ritual. But is that right? The Maasai might identify as a sign of our cultural weakness the fact that most Canadian boys are never ritually transformed into men.

Judging the Past by Present-Day Standards: Cultural Relativism versus Presentism

The doctrine of cultural relativism becomes problematic when studying historical practices and views that were once widespread but are now considered abhorrent and offensive. The city of Halifax recently had to consider the appropriateness of honouring its founder, Edward Cornwallis, who, as governor of

What Do YOU Think?

Is judging practices and attitudes of the past by the moral standards of today a form of ethnocentrism? Why or why not?

Nova Scotia, endorsed the use of violence to eliminate the colony's Mi'kmaq population in what some have called an act of genocide. In 2010, a new statue of women's rights activist Nellie McClung in Winnipeg touched off similar debates. While McClung was instrumental in winning Canadian women the right to vote and hold public office, she was also a proponent of eugenics, the movement to improve the population by sterilizing people with mental and physical disabilities, as well as people of races deemed "inferior." Not even Canada's first prime minister is safe: in 2016, the board of governors at Wilfrid Laurier University shelved a plan to erect on campus a statue of John A. Macdonald—and 21 other past prime ministers—after students and instructors protested, citing in particular Macdonald's racist policies toward Indigenous people.

The Go-Between, a 1971 movie based on a novel of the same name written by British writer L.P. Hartley, begins with the line, "The past is a foreign country: they do things differently there." That captures the spirit of the doctrine of cultural relativism, which suggests we should judge figures like Cornwallis, McClung, and Sir John A. not by today's moral standards but by the standards of their own time; failing to do so is known as **presentism**. But can we really let bygones be bygones when assessing certain cultural practices that are so repugnant?

Cultural Relativism, Ethnocentrism, and Smell: Two Stories

Our senses—the way we perceive what is beautiful or ugly, pleasant or disgusting—are culturally conditioned. Think of female beauty. For many North Americans, the image that comes to mind is that of a skinny model with very white teeth. Do you think this is true in other cultures?

What about our sense of smelling "good" or "bad"? Part of how we smell is determined by the food we eat (e.g. dairy products, meat, garlic, curry), but there is more to it than that. As a member of the Peace Corps, an organization of volunteers operating in developing countries, Tom Bissell observed how his colleagues working in the central Asian country of Uzbekistan reacted to sharing space with local inhabitants who were overdressed for the weather and, understandably, hot and sweaty. He observed,

> When I was in the Peace Corps, one of my least favorite things was when my fellow volunteers complained about Central Asian body odor. . . . But Gandhi probably smelled bad. Surely Abraham Lincoln smelled. William Shakespeare was, in all likelihood, rank. . . . Most certainly Jesus and Julius Caesar and the Buddha all smelled terrible. People have been smelly for the vast majority of human history. By gooping up our pheromonal reactors with dyed laboratory gels, could it be that we in the West are to blame for our peculiar alienation? Might not the waft from another's armpit contain crucial bioerotic code? Could it be by obscuring such code we have confused otherwise very simple matters of attraction? (Bissell, 2003, p. 98)

In a very different setting, Emma LaRocque, a Métis writer, came to a similar conclusion:

> Several summers ago when I was intern-teaching on a northern reserve, one of the teachers told me how she "had to get used to" the smells of the children. She insisted it was not just stuffiness but a "peculiar odor." . . .
>
> Oddly enough, the "peculiar" smell was a redolent mixture of spruce, moosehide, and woodsmoke. All the while this teacher was complaining about the smell of the children, the children reported a "strange" odor coming from the vicinity of some of the teachers and their chemical toilets. And it never seemed to occur to the teacher that she could be giving off odors.
>
> More to the point, both the teacher and the children attached value judgements to the unfamiliar odors. As a friend of mine noted, "to a person whose culture evidently

prefers Chanel No. 5 or pine-scented aerosol cans, moosehide and woodsmoke can seem foreign." The converse is true, I might add. (1975, p. 37)

As we have seen, ethnocentrism and cultural relativism are opposing ways of looking at cultures, both our own and those of others. Ethnocentrism is laden with negative judgment, while cultural relativism is characterized by a greater appreciation for context in understanding and evaluating culture. This is not to say that everything is relative, or that there are no universal standards. Certain practices, such as killing, are not unique to one culture and may be widely rejected by many cultures. Practices such as female genital mutilation, the use of land mines and child soldiers, and the torture of political prisoners can be added to this list.

The point to take from this is that it's important to realize how easy it is to make an ethnocentric assessment of a different culture. It is important to try to understand why different cultures do what they do. And, while true appreciation of aspects of other cultures might not always be possible, it is worth the trip to take a few steps down that path.

Sociolinguistics

Sociolinguistics is the study of language as part of culture. Language exists at the centre of communication between individuals and groups. It is a source both of understanding and of misunderstanding. It is also the main vehicle for transmitting culture, and a culture cannot be understood without some sense of the language(s) it uses and the way those languages fit with other aspects of culture. Sociolinguistics thus looks at language in relation to such sociological factors as "race," ethnicity, age, gender, and region.

Dialect as a Sociological Term

A **dialect** is a variety of a language, a version that is perhaps different from others in terms of pronunciation, vocabulary, and grammar. To the sociologist, the distinction between dialect and language is interesting because it can be as much a product of social factors as of linguistic ones.

Dutch and German, for instance, are considered separate languages, although going strictly on linguistic criteria they could be called dialects of the same language. For some German speakers living near the Netherlands, Dutch is easier to understand than dialects of German spoken in Austria or Switzerland.

Dialects, unlike languages, are often evaluated according to whether they represent proper or improper, casual or formal, even funny or serious versions of a language. These judgments usually depend on the social status of the dialect's speakers. In Britain, the "Queen's English" is an upper-class dialect, more highly valued in formal communication than regional dialects like that of the city of Manchester. The latter is often used by characters on TV shows such as *Coronation Street*, where it signifies that the characters are "real people" rather than upper-class people with what are called BBC accents. A few years ago, a commercial for an SUV featured a voiceover spoken in a Newfoundland accent. The accent here was used to put the audience in a receptive mood by evoking the famed good nature and affability of the people of Newfoundland and Labrador. You might not hear that same accent extolling the marketable features of a Lexus.

The Point Is . . .

Speakers of the Same Language Don't Always Share a Culture

I was enjoying a midday meal with colleagues in the Flemish city of Leuven, Belgium. My companions were three Belgian academics, two of them professors at the local Catholic university, the third a PhD candidate. We were studying an eighteenth-century grammar of Wendat (Huron) written by a Belgian Jesuit missionary, but took a break to enjoy the weather and a beer in a courtyard surrounded closely by several old buildings. It was all very "civilized," as my second wife would have said.

Our quiet conversation was suddenly disturbed by a boisterous group of students, who passed so close to our table that they bumped us, without an apology or any sign they were aware of their rude intrusion upon our peaceful lunch. It took only an instant for one of my colleagues to identify them as Dutch. This was followed by a short lecture on the difference between the Dutch and the Flemish (the people of Flanders), who speak dialects of the same language but apparently share little else in terms of their culture. The Flemish were part of the United Kingdom of the Netherlands until the Belgian Revolution of 1830. They opposed the authoritarian rule of the Dutch King William I, and being Catholics, they were uneasy with the dominance of Protestants in the kingdom. Belgium became a country in 1839, but Flanders has maintained a connection with the Netherlands because of their shared border and language (elsewhere in Belgium, French and German dominate).

The discussion of how the Flemish differ from the Dutch reminded me a lot of conversations I had been part of comparing Canadians with Americans and New Zealanders with Australians. In each pair, one group is considered loud and brash, the other quieter and more respectful.

That night, one of my colleagues told me about how the Dutch spelling system changes about every 10 years, so that Flemish people have trouble understanding Dutch people, either writing or speaking. An article I read recently filled in more details about the linguistic differences. Entitled "Explainer: 'I Speak Dutch Not Flemish,'" its author (who I assume is Dutch) describes the symbolic importance of differences in the Dutch and Flemish dialects (like the symbolic importance for some Canadians of spelling *colour* with a *u*) (Van de Poel, 2018). She also comments on the "usually boisterous persona" of the Dutch compared with the "unassuming behavior" of the Flemish. And, yes, she spelled *behaviour* with an American *-or*.

Linguistic Determinism and Relativity

The relationship between language and culture is sometimes discussed in terms of the **Sapir–Whorf hypothesis**, which posits the existence of **linguistic determinism (or causation)**. The principle of linguistic determinism suggests that the way we view and understand the world is shaped by the language we speak. Like theories of biological or social determinism, the Sapir–Whorf hypothesis can be cast either as strongly or weakly deterministic—that is, language can be seen to exert either a strong or a weak influence on a person's worldview. I tend to favour a weak determinism: I believe that linguistic differences are a valid form of cultural relativism, that exact translation from one language into another is impossible, and that knowing the language of a people is important to grasping the ideas of a people.

Noun Classes and Gender

Consider linguistic determinism in the context of the following statement: the different noun classes that exist in a language can reinforce the beliefs its speakers have within their culture. English speakers in Canada have some awareness of difference in noun classes through the presence of gender exhibited by the Romance languages to which they are exposed (e.g. French, Italian, Portuguese, Spanish, and other languages based on Latin, the language of the Romans). Students struggling through French classes may wonder why every French noun has to be masculine or feminine. Why are the words for *tree* (*arbre*) and tree species masculine, while the parts of trees—roots, leaves, branches, bark, blossoms—are feminine?

While it does not have noun classes labelled as "masculine" or "feminine," English does have a certain degree of grammatically mandated gender, with our use of *he, him, his,* and *she, her, hers.* Take the following two sentences: *One of my sisters is called Ann. She is younger than I am, and her hair used to be the same colour as mine.* In the second sentence, the words "she" and "her" are grammatically necessary but do not add any new information. Am I assuming that you have forgotten the gender of my sister? We already know from the nouns "sister" and "Ann" that the person spoken about is female. The

Indo-European languages—the family of languages that includes almost all the languages of Europe plus Farsi (Iranian) and the languages of Pakistan and northern India—all impose gender grammatically in some way.

Algonquian languages, which together make up the largest Indigenous language family in Canada and the United States, have no grammatically mandated gender, in either the French or the English sense. They have no pronouns meaning "he" or "she." They are not alone in that respect. Almost every Indigenous language spoken in Canada does not recognize gender grammatically. Does this mean that Algonquian speakers were traditionally more flexible about gender roles than their European contemporaries, or that there was a greater degree of equality between the sexes? The latter was certainly true at the time of contact, but whether that can be related to the absence of grammatical gender in their language is difficult to determine.

There have been campaigns to bring gender-neutral pronouns to English. In 2014, the Vancouver School Board agreed that students should have the right to be referred to by the pronoun of their choice, including the gender-neutral options *xe, xem,* and *xyr* (Brean, 2014). The decision was made to accommodate transgender, gender-fluid, and gender–non-conforming students for whom neither *he/him* nor *she/her* was appropriate. When assessing the validity of the Sapir–Whorf hypothesis, consider how you might feel as a transgender person repeatedly referred to as "him" or "her": How would you feel about yourself knowing that neither option adequately described you?

A Final Thought

Sometimes the terms that a language *doesn't* have tells you something significant about the culture. I have worked with the Wendat (Huron) language for 40 years. I have noticed that it doesn't have terms for the following concepts:

- guilt or innocence
- best or worst
- command or obey.

What do you think might be the cultural implications of these "holes" in the Wendat language?

Wrap It Up

Summary

Not only do cultures differ, but cultures are viewed and lived differently by people who occupy different social locations, based on gender, sexuality, "race," ethnicity, age, and so on. Similarly, although humans, as intensely social creatures, cannot live without culture, they can also feel oppressed by their culture, if their social location is not one of power and influence.

Remember, as well, that cultures are contested, that not everyone is in agreement concerning the rightness or goodness of every aspect of their mainstream culture. This is why there are minority versions that exist in contrast or opposition to the dominant culture. Subcultures tend to organize around preoccupations—we might call them hobbies or pastimes—not found within the dominant culture. Countercultures oppose the defining elements of the dominant culture, but there's something inherently attractive in a counterculture—people like to cast themselves as rebels—and so a counterculture sometimes must reinvent itself repeatedly to keep from becoming mainstream. Even high culture, which occupies a privileged position, is a minority culture, concerning itself with sophisticated pursuits that may be beyond the reaches of the masses. Which brings us to popular culture or mass culture: the label you use depends on whether or not you believe people create culture independent of the powerful and manipulative influence of large commercial interests.

Think Back

Questions for Critical Review

1. What does Canadian culture mean to you? What parts of your definition might be contested by other Canadians?
2. Beer producers, banks, and coffee shop chains are just some of the companies that tap into the theme of Canadian culture in their advertising. How does this benefit them? What impact does their advertising on people who belong to the kind of culture they describe? What is the impact on people excluded from their vision of Canadian culture?
3. Using your own examples (as opposed to those mentioned in the chapter), explain the difference between a subculture and a counterculture.
4. What are some norms associated with being online? How are these norms reinforced through positive and negative sanctions?
5. Use examples to explain the difference between a folkway, a more, and a taboo.
6. Imagine you wanted to study how Canadian values differ from province to province and territory. What questions could you ask in a survey? How else could you investigate value differences?
7. In 2015, students at Princeton University in New Jersey lobbied to have Woodrow Wilson's name and image stripped from the university. A Nobel Peace Prize winner, Wilson had been president of the university before being elected president of the United States in 1912. While in office, he passed progressive legislative reforms that included voting rights for women. He was also a racist, having endorsed segregation and the Ku Klux Klan. What do you consider an appropriate response to a situation like this?
8. Canadians and Americans speak the same language but observe many spelling differences: *colour* versus *color*, *centre* versus *center*, *plough* versus *plow*. Why do you think these spelling differences have not been reconciled?

Read On

Suggested Print and Online Resources

Anishinaabemowin, http://imp.lss.wisc.edu/~jrvalent/ais301/index.html

- This is an excellent introduction to the grammar and other key aspects of the Ojibwe language. Students can consider linguistic determinism as they enjoy an introduction to an Indigenous language.

Cannabis Culture, www.cannabisculture.com

- This Vancouver-based online retailer and information site reflects the viewpoints of the marijuana counterculture, particularly in Canada. Students can consider the aspects that define it as a counterculture at a time when recreational marijuana use has become legal. Is it still a counterculture?

Jennifer Carlson (2015), *Citizen-Protectors: The Everyday Politics of Guns in the Age of Decline* (New York: Oxford University Press).

- The author of this ethnographic study bought a gun and took courses to become trained as an instructor for the National Rifle Association. Her interviews with 60 gun owners in Michigan helped her discover that many young Americans, especially young men, carry guns out of a sense of responsibility to help maintain civil order.

John Fiske (2010), *Understanding Popular Culture*, 2nd edn (London: Routledge).

- A classic sociological study of popular culture, recently updated.

Michael Bibby & Lauren M.E. Goodlad, eds (2010), *Goth: Undead Subculture* (Durham, NC: Duke University Press).

- This edited collection of scholarly essays covering all aspects of goth subculture—from music and film to fashion and aesthetics—includes a study of individualism within the subculture by British sociologist Paul Hodkinson, an authority on youth subcultures.

Sajida Sultana Alvi, Homa Hoodfar, & Sheila McDonough, eds (2003), *The Muslim Veil North America: Issues and Debates* (Toronto: Canadian Scholars' Press).

- This insightful look into the cultural image of the niqab focuses especially on the North American (particularly Montreal) experience of the 1990s.

TED: Culture, www.ted.com/topics/culture

- The non-profit organization dedicated to "ideas worth spreading" has a good collection of curated TED talks on cultural themes ranging from "misconceptions of Islam and Muslim life" to "pop culture obsessions."

4

Socialization

Reading this chapter will help you to . . .

- Define *socialization* and describe the role is plays in human lives.

- Explain how the concepts of agency, biological determinism, and social determinism relate to our understanding of socialization.

- Explain, with examples, what it means to be an agent of socialization.

- Outline the basic ideas of Freud, Mead, and Cooley as they apply to sociology.

- State the difference between broad and narrow socialization.

- Explain the relationship between primary socialization, secondary socialization, and resocialization.

For Starters

Playing for Fun vs Playing to Win: Sports as an Agent of Socialization

"Straight from Canada, the land of loonies, politeness, and socialized medicine, comes the latest concept to baffle Americans—a youth sport that doesn't keep score." (John Keilman, Chicago Tribune)

Organized sports have long been a way of socializing Canadian children. As well as promoting fitness through exercise, organized sports provide an environment for children to learn key values from their peers and from adults. These values include teamwork, co-operation, work ethic, practice, and even friendship. They also include competitiveness.

It is well known that when it comes to competitiveness, parents and coaches do not always model healthy behaviours. They may holler abuse at players, officials, and each other. I have seen riled-up parents confront one another in the stands; I have seen a mom vehemently shout, "Kill her!" at a girls' house league hockey game. When fistfights break out in the stands, these anecdotal cases become news stories, as one did in February 2019, when the Ontario Provincial

Police were called in to break up a 30-parent donnybrook in Simcoe. When an isolated case of parental rage becomes a pattern of devastating abuse, someone may write a book about it, as former NHL player Patrick O'Sullivan (2015) did.

The perceived overemphasis on competition has caused some people to question the value of organized sports as a socializing agent for children. As a result, some youth athletic associations in Canada have made the move to no-score sports. In 2013, the Ontario Soccer Association announced that it would stop keeping score in matches involving under-12 teams in its recreational, or "grassroots," leagues. A number of associations across the country followed suit, adopting the "festival" format and the philosophy of "No scores, no standings, no trophies" (OSA, 2015). The aim of no-score programs is to lower the stress associated with the pressure to win (see the discussion of hurried child syndrome later this chapter) and to focus instead on fostering skill and love of the game among child athletes.

The immediate response was predictable. Newspaper editorials supported by online comments warned that no-score sports would blunt the "natural" human trait of competitiveness and encourage young people to believe in a world with no winners and losers, setting them up for failure when they encounter "real world" hardships and adversity. They'll just keep score anyway, some critics argued. This is true. Kids, living in a culture that stresses "better" and "best" will "naturally" compete and measure themselves against their peers: this is an important part of their socialization into Canadian culture. They will do this with or without adults bellowing encouragement from the sidelines or the stands. Kids will know who the best and the worst teams are and whether their team is winning or losing; they will still have to learn how to take failure well, how to lose with pride, and how to win with grace. And while end-of-season participation awards can seem meaningless to a 15-year-old tired of hearing that everyone's a winner, they matter a great deal when you're five and earning your first trophy. My son once received an award in hockey not for first place or MVP but for being the most improved player on his team. That gave him a sense of pride and showed that real achievement can be celebrated without keeping score.

What Do YOU Think?

1. What values did you learn from participating in youth competitive activities—chess club, gymnastics, tennis, baseball, video games, robotics? Who reinforced those values: Your peers? Your parents? Your coaches? Someone else?
2. John Keilman, author of the quotation at the start of this box, writes, "I'm hard pressed to identify anything good that comes from sorting [kids] into winners and losers at so young an age." Can you? Do you think the no-score policy makes athletic programs more beneficial or less beneficial to young people? How would you design a sociological study to research the issue?

Introduction: Socialization Is a Learning Process

Socialization is an area of sociological study that brings the discipline close to psychology. The intersection of sociology and psychology is clear from the fact that a good number of the leading socialization theorists are psychologists.

Socialization is something we all experience. It is a learning process, one that involves figuring out or being taught how to be a social person in a given society. It brings changes in an individual's sense of self. This applies both in the earliest socialization we undergo in childhood, generally known as **primary socialization**, and in socialization that occurs later in life, which is sometimes known as **secondary socialization**.

If socialization is a learning process, it stands to reason that there are teachers, too—many of them, in fact. You have probably had many teachers before now, some of them better than others. So it is with agents of socialization, the people and institutions who contribute to our socialization. We will meet these agents shortly, but first we will look at some of the ideas underpinning theories of socialization.

Determinism: Nature versus Nurture

Central to any discussion of socialization are two contentious topics:

- *determinism versus free will* and
- *biological determinism versus social determinism.*

When we speak of determinism, we are talking about the degree to which an individual's behaviour, attitudes, and other "personal" characteristics are *determined*, or caused, by something specific. That something specific could be your genetic makeup or the people in the environment in which you were raised. Has anyone ever told you that you're just like your mother or father? If so, they were implying that your behaviour was passed down by one of your parents, either through inheritance or through upbringing, and that you had little or no role in shaping your own character. In other words, they were endorsing a deterministic view of personality formation.

Most sociologists and social psychologists accept that determinism plays a role in socialization, but there are "hard" and "soft" versions of determinism. Champions of hard determinism claim that we are, in essence, programmed to think and act in a particular way, either by our biology or by the society we live in. Proponents of soft determinism believe biology and society play a part, but they also believe there is some room in everyone's life for free will, or the exercise of agency. Agency involves personal choice above and beyond the call of nature or nurture. We'll set agency aside for the moment while we take a closer look at these two kinds of determinism, based on biology and society.

Biological Determinism

Biological determinism ("nature" in the old "nature versus nurture" debate) states that the greater part of what we are is determined by our roughly 26,000 genes. Biological determinism has become a popular subject of discussion and debate in the mainstream media, owing in large part to the rise of human genetic research generally and, in particular, the Human Genome Project, which involves a painstaking count of the number of genes we have and investigation into what each of those genes codes for (if anything), either singly or in combination.

Certain abilities seem to fall into the "nature" category. We all know of people who are "naturally good" at sports, music, art, and so on. However, we have to be very careful in making even tentative statements about biological determinism and the influence of nature. A cautionary tales comes from a notorious research study into XYY males that began in 1962. The standard pattern of chromosomes in men is XY; the corresponding pattern for women is XX. During the 1960s, the atypical XYY chromosome pattern was found in some men studied in hospitals for dangerous, violent, or criminal patients with emotional/intellectual problems, first in England and then in the United States and Australia (see Jacobs et al., 1965; Price & Whatmore, 1967; Telfer, 1968). The XYY pattern was hastily declared the "criminal gene."

The problem was that researchers at first focused only on people institutionalized in prisons or special security hospitals after being convicted of crimes. When the study was extended to the general population, researchers discovered that roughly the same percentage of men outside the institutionalized population (about 1 in 1000) were XYY (Brown, 1968). There remain some well-documented associations of XYY males with above-average height, a tendency to have acne, and somewhat more impulsive and antisocial behaviour and slightly lower intelligence, but there is no evidence to conclude that XYY males are more likely than XY males to engage in criminal activity.

Softer forms of biological determinism focus on predispositions that people have (for shyness, for aggressiveness, and so on). These findings tend to have a stronger foundation and are easier to support than the more sensational claims of hard determinism—the ones beginning "*We have found the gene for _____*"—that sometimes make the news. What we are is based on too complex a mixture of social and biological factors for any one gene to be an absolute determinant of behaviour or personality.

Sigmund Freud: Balancing the Biological and the Sociocultural

I mentioned that socialization is a meeting point for sociology and psychology. Let's take a moment, then, to consider **Sigmund Freud** (1856–1939), father of **psychoanalysis**, whose ideas about the processes that shape human nature influenced generations of theorists who have attempted to explain the role of socialization in personality development.

Central to Freud's psychodynamic theory was his belief that the human mind has three parts: the id, the superego, and the ego. Think of it as a team with three players, but three players who don't get along and are often in conflict. Human personality is shaped by that conflict and how it is resolved in childhood and adolescence.

The **id** is the driving force of personality, an expression of two motives that demand gratification in all humans. The two motives (which you can think of as **i**nstinctive **d**rives) are *eros* and *thanatos*. **Eros** (related to the word *erotic*) is the drive that tends to be stressed by Freud's fans and critics. It is a "life drive" that is dedicated to pleasure seeking—particularly, but not exclusively, sexual pleasure. **Thanatos**, the less celebrated of the two drives, is the "death wish," an instinct for aggression and violence.

To get along in society, humans must learn to control the instinctive drives for pleasure and aggression, and this is where the **superego** comes in. It is the part of the mind that polices the id. Think of it as your conscience. It takes in the normative messages of right and wrong that your parents, family, friends, teachers, and other socializing agents give you, and *internalizes* them. In other words, it adopts them as a personal code of moral behaviour. Picture a caped crusader with a big "S" on its chest, saying "Don't hit your sister or want to have sex with your mother—those are wrong!"

In Freud's thinking, the id and superego often come to blows. Failure to manage the conflict can take years of psychotherapy to resolve. If one of the drives is too strong, a person may grow to become either too unrestrained or too controlled. The **ego**, meanwhile, is the main agent of personality, driven by the id and its demands but restrained by the superego. As the ego matures, it learns and develops strategies to satisfy the id's demands in socially acceptable ways. This maturation occurs through a sequence of stages that begin in infancy and end in adolescence. Freud called them *psychosexual stages* because each one is associated with sexual pleasure from a different part of the body.

Freud, we can say, saw biological and social factors as contributing equally to the development of human personality. But personality, for Freud, was pretty well set by the end of the last psychosexual stage, when the superego is fully formed, and sexual maturity is achieved. Psychoanalysts who followed in Freud's footsteps agreed that early experiences were critical to personality formation, but they believed that the ego continued to grow over the lifespan. **Erik Erikson** (1902–1994), for instance, recognized the influence that society has on ego development well into old age. He believed that each stage of life, from infancy to maturity, is defined by a central crisis (trust versus mistrust, intimacy versus isolation, etc.) that has a significant bearing on individual personality development. A pivotal stage is adolescence, from about age 12 to age 20, which is defined by a conflict between identify and identity confusion. It is during this stage that humans chart the course for their adult lives by choosing a career, selecting a mate, and adopting a worldview. I don't need to tell you that these are pretty weighty decisions, but put them off at your peril, warned Erikson: doing so will produce an *identity crisis*, a state of doubt and uncertainty resulting from the failure to resolve the conflict between identity and identity confusion.

Social (or Cultural) Determinism, a.k.a. Behaviourism

Behaviourism is a school of thought in psychology that takes a strong cultural-determinist position. It emphasizes the power of learning ("nurture" in the "nature versus nurture" debate) in the development of behaviour. For the behaviourist, the social environment is the prime mover in the development of personality; biology and agency count for little. One cautionary statement about this school of thought is that much of the research on which it is based involved non-human animals: Pavlov's dogs, Thorndike's cats, B.F. Skinner's rats and pigeons. Critics say that the theory disallows the existence of choice, of agency, which even a dog, pigeon, or rat can be seen as possessing (try training a dachshund, for example, if you doubt the existence of agency in dogs).

One of the earliest principles of behaviourism is the **law of effect**, introduced by **Edward Thorndike**

(1874–1949) in his book *Animal Intelligence* ([1911] 1999). The law of effect has two parts. The first says that if you do something and it is rewarded, the likelihood that you will do it again increases. The rewarded behaviour is said to be "reinforced." On the other hand, according to the second part, if you do something and it is punished or ignored, the likelihood of your doing it again decreases. It boils down to the idea of the carrot (reward) and the stick (punishment). Accordingly, if the screaming child in the grocery store lineup is given a lollipop to be quiet, the reward reinforces the screaming: expect it to happen again. If a student is ridiculed when giving an answer in class, that student will likely never raise their hand in that class again.

There are debates about what constitutes a reward for an individual, and about what behaviour is or is not being rewarded. For example, if you punish a child who is acting out at school by making them sit in the corner and the objectionable behaviour persists, could it be that they see the "punishment" as a reward? Are they getting attention? Is that their goal? If you pick up a crying baby, does that teach them that they can get anything they want by crying? Or does it reward communication, which, once they learn to speak, becomes words and not tears? Attempting to change someone's behaviour using this kind of approach is called **behaviour modification**. When you scold a dachshund for peeing on the floor and praise her for peeing on the lawn (*not* the steps leading *to* the lawn), you are attempting to practise behaviour modification. What the dachshund does is another matter; if she's like my dog Trudy, she may be highly resistant to behaviour modification, like a dachshund Jedi master—the Force is strong in her breed.

Hard social determinism claims that just about any behaviour can be taught and learned. A powerful expression of this view comes from **John B. Watson** (1878–1958), the founder of behaviourist psychology:

> Give me a dozen healthy infants, well-formed, and my own specified world to bring them up in and I'll guarantee to take any one at random and train him to become any type of specialist I might select—doctor, lawyer, artist, merchant-chief and yes, even beggar-man and thief, regardless of his talents, penchants, tendencies, abilities, vocations, and race of his ancestors. There is no such thing as an

inheritance of capacity, talent, temperament, mental constitution and behavioral characteristics. (1925, p. 82)

Sounds like it comes from a scary science fiction movie: *Attack of the Rat Psychologists*. Indeed, some of Watson's research methods were controversial. His most famous experiment, the "Little Albert" study (Watson & Rayner, 1920), involved conditioning fear of a white rat in an 11-month-old infant ("Little Albert" was the infant, not the rat). It is hardly surprising that someone who felt that manipulating humans was so easy would write popular books and articles on parenting, and eventually enter a career in advertising.

What Do YOU Think?

How much of your own behaviour do you think is influenced by your social environment—by friends, family, your charismatic sociology professor—and how much were you simply born with?

Jeff Harper/Starmetro File Photo

Let's make a connection to the last chapter. A parking ticket is a negative sanction issued to someone who has violated a norm. What role do negative and positive sanctions play in behaviour modification? Who is doing the socialization in this case, and what is the lesson being taught?

The Point Is . . .

Socialization Encourages Good and Bad Habits

I am not a gambler, but I am no stranger to casinos. When I visit Oklahoma to teach the Wyandotte language, the hotel I stay at is attached to a casino. It has a decent restaurant where I go for breakfast. When I arrive and sit down, usually around 7:00 a.m., I see people playing the slot machines. I wonder why, and have to restrain myself from asking. But I know that the answer has a lot to do with Edward Thorndike's law of effect.

The first slot machine, called the Liberty Bell, was invented by San Francisco native Charles Fey. Depositing a coin and pulling a lever would set three reels spinning, each one decorated with the same set of colourful symbols. The aim for players from the beginning was to get three matching symbols to line up when the reels stopped spinning. Over the years, different kinds of fruit, especially cherries, became common symbols on the machines. This is why in Britain, where the machines are often found in pubs, they are called "fruit machines."

Obviously, the odds have always been against the players—hence the term "one-armed bandits"—but for most of the twentieth century these were what I would call "natural odds" having to do with the mechanics of the machines. During the last few decades, the machines have been computer-programmed, their levers replaced by buttons or touch screens. This technology has allowed manufacturers of the machines to manipulate the results. The newer machines, known informally as "cherry dribblers," are behaviourist-driven socializing agents. They offer a good number of rewards, small payouts, and bonus rounds in which the possible prizes are higher. They also serve up a relatively high number of two-of-a-kind "near wins," so people think that they are this close to winning. They are not. There is no payout for almost winning. There is only winning and losing.

What Do YOU Think?

When is a human like a rat? Or, how does the law of effect apply to someone sitting at a casino slot machine? In what other situations are humans trained to behave a certain way by the promise of an occasional small reward?

The Oversocialized View of Human Behaviour

Critics of the social determinist perspective argue that it is important not to view humans as merely passive recipients of socialization. Canadian sociologist **Dennis H. Wrong** (1961), for example, warned against taking an **oversocialized** view of people. Wrong argued that people do not completely conform to the lessons of their socialization, automatically doing what socializing agents dictate. Rather, they can elect to resist their socialization. Put another way, they have a greater degree of agency—the power to influence the outcomes of one's life—than a behaviourist like Thorndike would allow.

Wrong's critique of the social determinist position came during the 1950s, a period associated with growing commercialism and conformity to norms in North America. His arguments resonate in the **branding** days of the twenty-first century, as advertisers try to socialize children at younger and younger ages into thinking that they can acquire social acceptance through branded products. It is also worth considering this point in terms of the debate, discussed in the last chapter, between proponents of mass culture (who see individuals as passive recipients of cultural messages) and champions of popular culture (who view individuals as having agency in producing and interpreting culture).

Finally, in the debate between determinism and agency, consider the story of Luis Aguiar, who teaches sociology at the Okanagan campus of the University of British Columbia. Born in the Azores, off the coast of Portugal, Aguiar grew up in Montreal and experienced the "working-class socialization" of his parents, who encouraged him to adopt a trade rather than pursue a postsecondary education. They could not understand the idea of finding a "career," and they considered boys who preferred mental to physical work "sexually suspect" and "unmanly" (Aguiar, 2001, pp. 187–8). Aguiar's father even supplied his son with examples of men who "became insane as a result of too much reading and studying" (2001, p. 180).

Ultimately Aguiar did go to university, demonstrating agency by overcoming his parents' attempts to socialize him into entering a trade. However, he was not unaffected by their efforts, which left him with feelings of guilt, since he could not, because of the length of his schooling, help provide for the family until relatively late in life:

> Today I still feel terribly guilty because of my selfish educational pursuits that deprived my parents from owning a home or car or having some higher level of comfort in their retirement years. My parents never complained about my lack of financial contribution to the family, but my sense is that they are extremely disappointed at not achieving the immigrant dream of owning their own home. To my mind, only immigrant students of working-class background feel this heavy load of class guilt. (Aguiar, 2001, p. 191)

The Point Is . . .

Cold Mothers Don't Cause Autism

The tendency to adopt an oversocialized view of certain behaviours has caused experts to ascribe biological conditions to ineffective socialization, usually with the parents to blame. Male homosexuality was once commonly attributed to poor socialization involving a smothering, over-attentive mother and a weak or absent father. Joseph Nicolosi is a clinical psychologist who still holds this outdated view. In a 2002 handbook for parents, he warns that

> if a father wants his son to grow up straight, he has to break the mother–son bond that is proper to infancy but not in the boy's best interest afterward. In this way, the father has to be a model, demonstrating that it is possible for his son to maintain a loving relationship with this woman, his mom, while still maintaining his own independence. (Nicolosi & Nicolosi, 2002, p. 27)

Thankfully, not many clinical psychologists today subscribe to this oversocialized view.

Ineffective parenting and faulty socialization were once also blamed for the behaviours associated with autism. **Autism spectrum disorder** encompasses several conditions and may be associated with social communication difficulties, repetitive or fixated behaviours, and sensory problems. No cause has been discovered, though autism appears to have a strong biological or genetic component. The influence of the effects of socialization is strongly contested. There was a time, though, when it was widely believed that so-called **refrigerator mothers**, described as "cold" women who withheld affection from their sons, were responsible: they had supposedly socialized their children into not expecting warmth from a parent. This oversocialized view developed in the 1940s, when autism was first described, and then expounded single-mindedly with great influence by child psychologist Bruno Bettleheim (1903–1990). Bettleheim's oversocialized explanation of autism has been rejected today, but only after two generations of women were blamed for their children's autism through ineffective socialization.

Agents of Socialization

Luis Aguiar's parents were among his most influential **agents of socialization**, meaning the people who had a significant impact on his socialization. Many individuals, groups, and institutions can act as agents of socialization—and the list varies from person to person—but the following are considered to be highly influential agents of socialization for most people:

- family
- peer group
- neighbourhood/community
- school
- mass media
- the legal system
- culture generally.

The impact of each of these agents is severely contested, both in the sociological literature and in the day-to-day conversations of people in society. In the following sections, we'll take a closer look at some of the debates surrounding their influence.

Significant Other, Generalized Other, and Sense of Self

The American psychologist **George Herbert Mead**, whom we introduced as a symbolic interactionist in Chapter 1, saw all agents of socialization falling into one of two categories he named "significant other" and "generalized other." He believed that children develop their sense of self by internalizing values and behaviours modelled by these "others" in their lives.

Significant others are those key individuals—primarily parents, to a lesser degree older siblings and close friends—whom young children imitate and model themselves after. Picture a mother or father doing yardwork with a young child imitating the practice (for instance, clearing leaves with a toy rake). The parent, in this case, is a significant other to the child. Please note: your boyfriend/girlfriend, your spouse, or your partner is *not* your significant other in the sociological sense. When people ask me to bring my significant other to a party, I inform them that my parents are dead. (I hope that somewhere Mead is chuckling.)

Mead's concept of the **generalized other** is a bit harder to grasp. The generalized other is not one person; it's more like a composite of all the people who make up a group, such as a team, a local community, or society writ large. As children age, they become aware of the attitudes and expectations of various generalized others, and as they do so, they adjust their own behaviour to conform to the social expectations of these different groups.

Mead also identified a developmental *sequence* for socialization, just as Freud and Erikson did. Mead's sequence begins with the **preparatory stage**, which involves more or less pure imitation on the part of the child. The next step is the **play stage**, where the child engages in **role-taking**: this is where children become aware of the viewpoints of significant others—parents, grandparents, siblings, and so on—and imagine what those others are thinking as they act. The third stage is the **game stage**, in which a child is able to consider several roles and viewpoints simultaneously. A seven-year-old playing soccer, for instance, will understand that the goalie has a different role from other players on the team, and that

Quick Hits

Political Leaders as Agents of Socialization

The presidency of Donald Trump (a.k.a. the Dark Age of American leadership) has coincided with a marked increase in public displays of racism by white nationalists. Is this a case of correlation or causation? Trump's racism is readily apparent, from his poor treatment of Puerto Rico to his vilification of Mexicans as criminals and rapists, fueling his pledge to build a wall between the United States and Mexico (and not just to block Americans from obtaining cheaper health care there). The question is this: If we consider Trump a role model for many Americans, do you think his public comments have influenced white people (especially men) to hold more racist views? Or has he made people more likely to express publicly views they held before he was elected?

By permission of M.Media & Design Ltd

A British campaign warned parents of the harm their cellphone use might be doing to their children. What lessons might the child in this ad be internalizing from his significant other? How might that affect his behaviour as he ages?

players on an opposing team will have different objectives than those of the players on their own team. Where younger children tend to make up rules, children at this stage can understand and follow the rules for organized sports, card games, and so on.

Significant and generalized others continue to exert strong socialization influences later on in the life of an individual, with important consequences for the individual's self-concept. Mentors and other role models can be important significant others to an adolescent or adult. The media, meanwhile, is a leading source of generalized others that can have a powerful impact on the individual's sense of self. Advertisers cultivate generalized others to great effect. When an Old Navy commercial presents a group of young, attractive, and Old Navy–dressed people dancing and having a good time, the advertising agency is trying to

tell you that this is what your cool, young community likes, and you should, too. At the same time, advertisers also use celebrity spokespeople—a star athlete, the latest pop sensation—they hope will be viewed as significant others by consumers in their target market. This can backfire, of course: when celebrity spokespeople transgress the moral norms of a society, they lose their marketability as role models. In May 2018, Vancouver's transit authority, TransLink, suspended announcements broadcast over its SkyTrain system when the reader of those announcements, actor Morgan Freeman, was accused of sexual harassment. Two months later, TransLink announced Seth Rogen as the new voice of a series of etiquette tips for its Sky-Train riders. Why do you think a public transit system needs a celebrity to remind passengers to keep their feet off the seats?

Another symbolic interactionist, **Charles Horton Cooley** (1864–1929), put forth the idea of the **looking-glass self**. This is a self-image based on how people think they are viewed by others. In Cooley's poetic words, "each to each a looking glass / Reflects the other that doth pass" (quoted in Marshall, 1998, p. 374). The looking-glass self has three components:

1. how you imagine you appear to others
2. how you imagine those others judge your appearance
3. how you feel as a result (proud, ashamed, self-confident, embarrassed).

The relationship between body image and self-esteem, especially in young women, illustrates this well. Harvard educational psychologist and respected feminist **Carol Gilligan** (1990) noted how the self-esteem of girls declines during their teenage years. Studies show that this happens more with girls and young women than with boys. The harsher standards of body type that we apply to women have rightfully been associated with this difference in self-esteem.

What Do YOU Think?

You and your peers belong to the most photographed generation in history. Do you think this gives you a more fragile or a more robust self-image than that of past generations?

Family

The family is an individual's first agent of socialization, and often the most powerful one. Significantly, just as families differ across cultures, so do the means and goals of families in socializing the child. Consider the narrative on page 112, which is based on research done on the Rajput of Khalapur in northern India, carried out by **John T. Hitchcock** (1917–2001) and **Ann Leigh Minturn** (1928–1999) in the early 1960s. Their work was part of a classic study of cross-cultural socialization, Beatrice Whiting's *Six Cultures: Studies of Child Rearing* (1963).

Class and the Passing on of Parental Values to Children

In a classic study of socialization, American sociologist Melvin Kohn (1959) investigated the relationship between social class and the way parents socialize their children. The study was done in Washington, DC, with children aged 10 and 11. Kohn drew his research subjects from 11 census tracts: four were predominately working-class, four were mostly middle-class, and the remaining three were made up of working-class and middle-class households in roughly equal numbers. His sample contained 200 families in which the father had a white-collar job, and 200 families in which the father had a "manual occupation" (Kohn, 1959).

Parents were presented with a set of 17 value-based characteristics and asked to indicate which characteristics they most valued in their fifth-graders. While some characteristics were valued by both middle-class and working-class parents, certain qualities were valued more highly by one class or the other (see Table 4.1).

An important conclusion of the study was that middle-class parents valued self-control or inner control, while working-class parents put a higher valuation on external control. As Kohn himself put it in a reassessment of the work, "Middle-class parents . . . are more likely to emphasize children's *self-direction*, and working-class parents to emphasize their *conformity to external authority*" (1977, p. 34). What does this mean? Essentially, Kohn believed that working-class families were raising their children to value qualities that would make them successful members of that class—notably, obedience to authority and conformity—while middle-class families were socializing

COSMOPOLITAN UK

Plus-size model Tess Holliday's appearance on the UK edition of *Cosmopolitan* was seen as a positive step for a magazine better known for its tips on how to achieve a standard of beauty represented by much skinnier models. Praise for the magazine was not universal, though. English commentator Piers Morgan called the cover "dangerous and misguided," viewing Holliday as a negative role model in light of Britain's "ever-worsening obesity crisis." As an agent of socialization, is Tess Holliday a positive or a negative role model? What about Piers Morgan?

their children into white-collar occupations by emphasizing self-reliance, independence, and curiosity. Kohn noted that it was the wives of men with the more highly educated jobs, such as the professionals and highly educated businessmen, who put the highest value on these characteristics.

Kohn revisited this research in his influential work *Class and Conformity: A Study in Values*, first published in 1969 and then in 1977 with an added commentary. He later carried out comparative

The Rajputs: Child Rearing and Personality in a North Indian Village

Although Rajput infants will be picked up and attended to when they are hungry or fussing, for the most part they are left in their cots, wrapped up in blankets. . . . Except for anxieties about a baby's health, it is not the centre of attention. A baby receives attention mainly when it cries. At that time, someone will try to distract it, but when it becomes quiet, the interaction will stop. Adult interaction with babies is generally aimed at producing a cessation of response, rather than stimulation of it. Infants and children of all ages are not shown off to others. . . . Children are also not praised by their parents, who fear that this will "spoil" them and make them disobedient.

Rajput children . . . are never left alone, yet neither are they the centre of interest. The child learns that moodiness will not be tolerated. Few demands are put on Rajput children; they are not pressured or even encouraged to become self-reliant. Weaning, which generally occurs without trouble, takes place at two to three years; but if the mother does not become pregnant, a child may be nursed into its sixth year. There is no pressure for toilet training. . . . Babies are not pressured, or even encouraged to walk. They learn to walk when they are ready, and mothers say they see no reason to rush this. . . .

Village women do little to guide children's behaviour by explaining or reasoning with them. There is also little direct instruction to small children. Small children learn . . . the customs and values of the group through observation and imitation. In the first five years of life, the child moves very gradually from observer to participant in village and family life. . . .

[C]hildren are not encouraged in any way to participate in adult activities. The chores a child is given are mainly directed to helping the mother. . . . There is little feeling that children should be given chores on principle in order to train them in responsibility. . . . Rajput children take little initiative in solving problems by themselves. Instead, they are taught whom they can depend on for help in the web of social relations of kin group, caste, and village. . . . Although chores increase somewhat as the child gets older, it is not a Rajput custom to require children to work if adults can do it. Children are not praised for their work, and a child's inept attempt to do an adult job is belittled. Thus children are reluctant to undertake what they cannot do well.

—J.T. Hitchcock & A.L. Minturn

What Do YOU Think?

1. How would this be interpreted by a behaviourist?
2. What values are being taught with this form of socialization?
3. How does this compare with your upbringing?

studies in Poland, Ukraine, and China to see if he could replicate his findings there.

Family Socialization through the Lens of Culture and Personality

I mentioned that the impacts of certain agents of socialization are contested. One of the more debated mechanisms of socialization is the focus of the **culture and personality** school of thought, which emerged during the first half of the twentieth century, drawing on sociology, anthropology, and psychology. Proponents of this school attempted to identify and describe idealized personalities or "personality types" for different societies, and attach to each one a particular form of family socialization.

TABLE 4.1 Areas of Significant Difference in Working-Class and Middle-Class Rankings of Values

As Judged by Mothers					
Valued in Boys ("That he . . .")		Valued in Girls ("That she . . .")		Valued Overall ("That he or she . . .")	
Middle Class	Working Class	Middle Class	Working Class	Middle Class	Working Class
• is happy • is curious about things	• obeys his parents well	• is considerate of others	• is neat & clean	• is happy • is considerate of others • has self-control • is curious about things	• is honest • obeys his/her parents well
As Judged by Fathers					
Valued in Boys ("That he . . .")		Valued in Girls ("That she . . .")		Valued Overall ("That he or she . . .")	
Middle Class	Working Class	Middle Class	Working Class	Middle Class	Working Class
• is happy • is considerate of others • is dependable	• obeys his parents well	• is considerate of others • is dependable • has self-control • is ambitious	• is honest • obeys her parents well • is able to defend herself • is popular with other children • is a good student • is liked by adults	• is happy • is considerate of others • is dependable • has self-control	• obeys his/her parents well • is a good student • is able to defend him/herself

Source: Kohn, 1977, Tables 2.1 & 2.2.

What Do YOU Think?

1. Do you think that Kohn had similar findings in Poland, Ukraine, and China? Why or why not?
2. Kohn first published his findings in a 1959 article, which he followed up with longer commentaries in 1969 and 1977. How would you expect his findings to be different if he were conducting the same study toady, among twenty-first-century North American families?

During World War II and in the early years of the Cold War standoff between the West and the Soviet Union, the scope of these studies broadened to examine **national character**, the personality type of entire nations. These studies typically drew conclusions about how the primary socialization of child-raising was linked with a country's national character.

An example is *The People of Great Russia* (1949), in which Geoffrey Gorer and John Rickman proposed the **swaddling hypothesis**. They identified moodiness as a supposedly typical Russian character trait, citing extremes of controlled and out-of-control behaviour (for example, intense bouts of alcoholism), and attributed it to the *swaddling*—as

in bundling up—of infants commonly practised among Russian families. Theories like this that attempt to generalize about such large populations are extremely difficult to prove.

Studies attempting to link child socialization practices to national character could very well be sitting on the dusty shelf of old theories that no longer affect us if it weren't for a persistent preoccupation with trying to understand overarching personality traits of certain populations. Since the September 11 attacks on the United States and the rise of groups like Daesh (the self-styled Islamic State) and al-Shabaab, there has been a great deal of focus in the media and among Western political and military leaders on the "Arab mind." Raphael Patai's book of this very title, first published in 1973 and revamped in 1983, was reprinted in 2002, the year after the September 11 attacks. It gained media attention in 2004, after American journalist Seymour Hersh (2004) singled it out as "the bible of neocons on Arab behaviour" in an article for *The New Yorker*. According to Hersh, the book enjoyed considerable influence in upper military circles in the United States. *The Arab Mind* replicates the negative excesses of the national character study publications, both by oversimplifying the psychological makeup of very sociologically diverse peoples and by tying that broad portrait to overgeneralized child-raising practices. Think of the significant class differences between oil-wealthy Saudi princes on the one hand, and Arab shop-owners and camel-herders on the other, as one manifestation of how Arabs experience life in a broad variety of ways.

Families in different cultures socialize their children differently, but no culture exhibits complete uniformity in its socialization practices. Think of how a parenting practice such as spanking can generate considerable debate and variety of viewpoints when a newsworthy incident raises it in the Canadian media. Remember the point made in Chapter 3: it is a common mistake to view one's own culture as complex and dynamic while viewing others as fixed and easy to characterize. All cultures have elements that are contested, and a population of over 200 million people cannot be reduced to a single set of personality traits or mindset.

Peer Group

An important agent of socialization is the **peer group**, a social group sharing key characteristics such as age, social position, and interests. The term is usually used to talk about children and adolescents.

The term **peer pressure** refers to the social force exerted on individuals by their peers to conform in behaviour, appearance, or externally demonstrated values (e.g. not appearing excited about something that isn't deemed acceptable or "cool"). Peer pressure is socialization in action.

A classic sociological study that argues for the influence of the adolescent peer group is Paul E. Willis's (1977) *Learning to Labour: How Working Class Kids Get Working Class Jobs*. Willis studied the informal culture of a group of 12 teenage boys attending a working-class, all-male school in the industrial town of Hammerstown, England. Willis wanted to know why working-class boys settled for labouring jobs rather than directing their energies to getting the kinds of jobs obtained by middle-class kids in their cohort. He believed the boys were not passive recipients, through socialization, of the informal working-class culture. Rather, he speculated that, as an act of minority-culture resistance to the dominant culture, they were active participants both in the creation of this culture, with its belief and values systems and rules of behaviour, and in socializing newcomers into the culture. Among the evidence Willis found to support his theory were vocalized disdain for and humour directed against more conformist middle-class peers, ridicule of the "effeminate" nature of the mind-centred work done in school and in offices, and denunciation of middle-class values in general. The minority-culture resistance also involved manipulating the classroom (by controlling attendance and the level of work done, for example) and educational figures of authority in ways that the youths would repeat in the "shop floor" environments of factories and warehouses and with the middle-management figures they encountered there. Their classroom behaviour prepared them for their future.

Community and Neighbourhood
Risk Behaviour

Community and neighbourhood can be important agents in child and adolescent socialization. It is one of the reasons parents debate whether they should live in the city or in a town or suburb outside the big city where they work. It's also why urban planners are concerned about creating mixed-class

What Do YOU Think?

1. Do you think the power held by the Hammerstown peer group was related more to the fact the students attended a single-gender school or to the fact they were from working-class families?
2. Do you think these individuals had as much agency as Willis claimed that they had? If not, then what sort of determinism were they subject to?

Telling It Like It Is

An Author's POV

Experiencing Peer Pressure

Growing up, everyone is exposed to peer pressure. How we respond to the powerful influence exerted by our peer group helps to mould us into the adults we become.

When I was 10, I had a small group of classmates I hung out with. I felt they were "cooler" than I was, so I was susceptible to peer pressure from them. I was up for pretty much any of their hijinks, even when I knew they weren't the wisest things to do. We never did anything seriously wrong. We begged candy from a local candy manufacturer and stole chocolate bars from the neighbourhood drug store. We played "chicken" with trains on the railroad tracks. We threw snowballs at passing cars. Peer pressure made me do things I knew were wrong and would never have done otherwise.

But it's important to recognize that, while leading us to do some pretty silly things, peer pressure plays a vital role in forging personality. Peer pressure hits us hardest when we're insecure adolescents striving for acceptance among people outside our immediate family. By encouraging a degree of conformity, peer pressure helps children develop friendships and find acceptance among others their own age, fostering both self-confidence and independence. I belonged to a class of smart kids culled from various schools in the district, and it was easy to feel separate, different. My classmates and I formed a close circle from which we all gained a sense of belonging. It also gave us a safe place to test norms and values. I don't (often) throw snowballs at passing cars anymore. And perhaps, by remembering these stories, I will be less likely to judge younger people who do similar things.

IHeart Street Art

How does the peer group you interact with in person differ from the peer group you interact with online? And what kind of socializing influence does your online community exert on you? Is the peer pressure you might experience online different from the peer pressure described in the feature above? If so, how?

urban neighbourhoods rather than ghettoizing the economically disadvantaged in government-assisted housing projects.

Studies during the late twentieth century showed that young people living outside large cities were at lower risk of becoming involved in crime, drug and alcohol abuse, and other risk behaviour. **Risk behaviours** include driving at dangerous speeds, engaging in unsafe sexual activities, drinking to excess, experimenting with different drugs, and so on. Much of this research was carried out in the United States, although American developmental psychologist Jeffrey Arnett and Danish-born sociologist Lene Balle-Jensen (1993) performed a cross-cultural study of adolescents in the United States and in Denmark. Their findings showed a correlation between risk behaviour and city size (Arnett & Balle-Jensen, 1993). As the authors explained,

> City size was related to adolescents' reports of sex without contraception, sex with someone known only casually, marijuana use, heavy marijuana use, shoplifting, vandalism, and cigarette dependency. For most types of risk behavior, adolescents in the larger city were more likely to report the risk behavior than adolescents in the smaller city. (Arnett & Balle-Jensen, 1993, p. 1849)

More recent research suggests that rates of drug and alcohol use in rural areas of North America have caught up to and in some cases surpassed the rates in cities. A 2015 review of the literature for the Canadian Centre on Substance Abuse reports that "Among American youth, those living in a rural setting are more likely to report use of alcohol, compared to those living in urban areas," and that "the former group is also more likely to report heavy drinking on one occasion and risk behaviours, such as drinking and driving, or driving under the influence of illicit drugs" (McInnis, Young, & Working Group, 2015, p. 4). Drawing on studies of Canadian students from across the country, the researchers found that students in rural schools in Canada were more likely than students in urban schools to report alcohol use, heavy drinking, and driving while under the influence of alcohol or cannabis (McInnis, Young, & Working Group, 2015, p. 17). There were no significant differences in rural and urban rates of using illicit or prescription drugs.

Broad and Narrow Socialization

Let's return to Arnett and Balle-Jensen's (1993) study to see how they accounted for the fact that adolescents in certain communities were especially prone to engaging in risky behaviour. The authors recognized that there is a biological component to such behaviour—a genetic predisposition to certain kinds of behaviour that is present naturally in certain individuals—but they also stressed the large role that socialization plays in encouraging or discouraging risk behaviours. In presenting their argument, they made an important distinction between **narrow socialization** and **broad socialization**, describing them as follows:

> In cultures characterized by *broad socialization*, individualism and independence are promoted, and there is relatively less restrictiveness on the various dimensions of socialization. This allows for a broad range of expression of individual differences on the developmental tendencies (such as sensation seeking) that contribute to risk behavior, and leads to higher rates of risk behavior. Cultures characterized by *narrow socialization*, in contrast, consider obedience and conformity to the standards and expectations of the community to be paramount (enforced through the parents and the school as well as through members of the community), and punish physically and/or socially any deviation from the norm. The result is greater obedience and conformity, a narrower range of expression of individual differences, and low rates of antisocial adolescent risk behavior (although risk-taking tendencies may be directed by such cultures into avenues that serve a culturally approved purpose, such as warfare). (Arnett & Balle-Jensen, 1993, p. 1843)

In Kamsack, Saskatchewan, population 1825, two men wait for drug store to open so they can pick up their methadone. What resources for opioid addicts may be scarce in a small, rural community?

In other words, young people in cultures characterized by broad socialization have greater freedom to act independently and make choices—about what they will study at school, how they will spend their time when they're not at school, where they will work, whom they will socialize with, and so on. By contrast, in cultures based on narrow socialization, young people face greater pressure—from families, from the authorities, and from society in general—to act a certain way and to conform to widely held expectations regarding behaviour. Adolescents in these societies, according to Arnett, are less likely to participate in risky activities.

To test his hypothesis, Arnett and Balle-Jensen undertook a cross-cultural study of adolescent socialization in Denmark. While that country has a tendency toward broad socialization, the researchers noted ways in which Denmark has narrower socialization than the United States. For instance, they cite the fact that the legal driving age in Denmark is 18, reflecting, according to Arnett, narrow socialization

elements in the legal system and in the cultural belief system. It reflects, too, a different cultural consensus concerning the balance between ensuring the individual autonomy of the teenager who wants to drive a car and the good of the community, through fewer traffic fatalities and fewer cars on the road. This narrower socialization means, according to Arnett, that in Denmark fewer adolescents engage in the risk behaviour of unsafe driving than in North America.

Mass Media

Questions about the role communication for the masses plays in socializing young people go back at least as far as the ancient Greek philosopher Plato, who felt that art (in his day, plays) aroused primal instincts, stimulating violence and lust. Plato's student Aristotle believed that violence depicted in art actually produced among those viewing it an experience of *catharsis*, a relief from hostile or violent emotions, leading to feelings of peace. Theatre, of course, is not

A Mckeone Carolyn/Getty Image

Growing up, you might have felt as though your parents were on your back all the time. Overall, would you say your upbringing was characterized by narrow socialization or broad socialization?

really mass media, and so it wasn't until the middle of the twentieth century, after television arrived on the scene, that researchers began to wonder about and investigate the socializing effects of media.

A Canadian-born clinical psychologist, Albert Bandura, made a major contribution to the research with a series of experiments he conducted in the 1960s. Cast your mind back for a moment to Edward Thorndike, the "rat psychologist" we met earlier this chapter. The central tenet of his theory of behaviourism was that behaviour is learned through rewards and penalties. If someone compliments me on my new leather pants, I may wear them again tomorrow; if someone points and laughs, I probably will not. (I actually have a pretty thick skin, and I would never, ever own leather pants, but you get the idea.)

Bandura wanted to see if behaviour could be learned without rewards and penalties. To that end, he set up an experiment in which children were placed individually in a room with an adult, an inflatable clown (a "Bobo doll"), and an assortment of toys, including stickers, tops, mallets, and bats. Children in one group—the "control group"—were invited to play with the toys while the adult sat in an opposite corner. Children in the other group—the "experimental group"—watched as the adult abused the Bobo doll physically and verbally. In both scenarios, the adult left the room for a period, leaving each child alone in the room with the doll.

Can you guess what happened? Children in the control group paid little attention to the doll, but children who had witnessed the doll being struck or shouted at repeated these behaviours when left alone. In variations of the experiment, the adult was either praised or scolded by the experimenter for their treatment of the doll, and this had an effect on how the children behaved. The key, though, was that the children themselves were not receiving any direct rewards or penalties. This becomes an important part of Bandura's social cognitive learning theory: first, people (children and adults) learn by observing the behaviour of other people (that's the social part); second, we are able to assess the pros and cons—the rewards and penalties—of demonstrated actions and be fairly judicious about how and when we perform those learned behaviours.

Bandura's research wasn't specifically designed to test the effects of watching violent images on television, but you can probably understand why people made that link. His research helped touch off a debate that has yet to be settled: Do mass media—through action movies that make heroes out of vicious criminals, video games that promote war and crime, and TV shows that glorify death and murder—socialize young people, especially adolescent males, into committing violence, or at least into being desensitized to violence and the pain of others? Or do they provide a safe outlet for pent-up hostile emotions? Competing viewpoints in the contentious debate are offered in the following passages by Rowell Huesmann and Jib Fowles. First up, arguing for a link between media violence and criminal activity, is Rowell Huesmann, a professor of communication studies and psychology:

> True, media violence is not likely to turn an otherwise fine child into a violent criminal. But, just as every cigarette one smokes increases a little bit the likelihood of a lung tumor someday, every violent show one watches increases just a little bit the likelihood of behaving more aggressively in some situation. (Bushman & Huesmann, 2001, p. 248)

Arguing for the other side is communications professor and sociologist Jib Fowles (1999), in *The Case for Television Violence*:

> Television is not a schoolhouse for criminal behaviour. . . . Viewers turn to this light entertainment for relief, not for instruction. Video action exists, and is resorted to, to get material out of minds rather than to put things into them. . . . Television violence is good for people. (1999, pp. 53, 118)

Having whetted your appetite for the debate, we'll take a closer look at how Huesmann and Fowles arrived at their views.

Huesmann's Longitudinal Studies

Huesmann's pioneering work on the effects of television violence on children involved the use of **longitudinal studies**, which examined data

gathered on research subjects over an extended period. His first was a 22-year study of 856 youths in New York State. At the beginning of his study the participants were all in Grade 3, about 8 years of age. Huesmann followed up by interviewing them again when they were 19, and then again at 30 (Huesmann & Eron, 1986). Among male subjects, the relationship between viewing television violence and engaging in aggressive behaviour roughly 10 years later was both positive and highly significant—in other words, there was a link, and it was a strong one. These findings were consistent for males of different social classes, IQ scores, and levels of aggressiveness at the start age. When the male subjects were checked again at age 30, the relationship between violent television viewing and aggressive behaviour—both self-reported and as documented in criminal records—was just as strong.

Huesmann and his colleagues (2003) also studied 557 Chicago-area children from Grade 1 to Grade 4, beginning in 1977. Fifteen years later, they interviewed as many of them (and their spouses and friends) as they could, and also looked at public records and archival material. The researchers were able to gather reasonably complete data for 329—roughly 60 per cent—of the original research participants (153 men and 176 women, all then in their early twenties). The results of this study were similar to those of the earlier study, with the only difference being that the link between TV violence and aggressive behaviour was evident among women as well as among men. The researchers concluded their study as follows:

> Overall, these results suggest that both males and females from all social strata and all levels of initial aggressiveness are placed at increased risk for the development of adult aggressive and violent behavior when they view a high and steady diet of violent TV shows in early childhood. (Huesmann et al., 2003, p. 218)

Huesmann proposed two theories to explain the data. One, **observational learning theory**, states that children acquire what he termed "aggressive scripts" for solving social problems through watching violence on television. The other, **desensitization theory**, states that increased exposure to television violence desensitizes or numbs the natural negative reaction to violence.

Telling It Like It Is

treechangedolls.com.au

Tree Change Dolls/Sonia Singh

before   after

Australian artist Sonia Singh takes girls' toys (such as the Bratz dolls, *left*) and repaints them to make them more realistic, makeup free, and more childlike (*right*). What do you think the impact of playing with the doll on the left versus the doll on the right would be on a child's understanding of "growing up"? Are toys like Bratz dolls harmless fun or roads to self-objectification?

Fowles's Defence of Television Violence

Jib Fowles has argued that sociologists and others who condemn violence on television are really using TV violence as a pretext to tackle other issues: class, "race," gender, and generation. He calls television violence a "whipping boy, a stand-in for other clashes":

The attack on television violence is, at least in part, an attack by the upper classes and their partisans on popular culture. In this interpretation, . . . the push to reform television is simply the latest manifestation of the struggle between the high and the low, the dominant and the dominated. (Fowles, 2001)

A Sociologist's POV

Branding Consciousness, Selling Pretty

In an era in which feminism has made many legislative gains toward gender equity, and more women are entering into professional and non-traditional fields for their gender, the world of children's media seems unable or un-willing to keep up. Most toys are still marketed along strongly demarcated gender lines of what constitutes femininity and masculinity. Through pervasive marketing campaigns of many different toy brands, girls are compelled to obsess, and enjoy obsessing, about clothes, makeup, shopping, boys, and babies. They are also given the message that to be physically attractive you must also be sexy.

Through product lines and advertising, the gender roles young girls are frequently and re-peatedly labelled with include Diva, Princess, Angel, and Pop-Star. These roles are not usually seen by parents as part of gender socialization. Girls who are labelled as such are often seen by parents as sweet, cute, and girly; however, these roles embody and encourage traits such as vanity, self-centredness, and an "all about me" attitude, while encouraging, normalizing, and rewarding girls' preoccupation with their bodies over their minds.

Marketing toward young girls is not just stuck in the past; in many ways, it is worse than in the past. The Bratz doll emerged as a hyper-sexualized version of Barbie, Mattel upped the ante with "Lingerie Barbie," and there is an array of T-shirts that objectify and impose an adult sexuality on toddlers and young girls through slogans like "Future Trophy Wife," "Hot Tot," "Made You Look," and "Born to Shop." Costume stores feature many provocative costumes for pre-teen girls, one of which is "Major Flirt"—a provocative "military" uniform complete with high, black, leather-look boots with a platform heel, kilt-style miniskirt, and studded black leather belt and choker.

Everywhere they turn—family, toys, ad-vertising, media, and school—girls learn that beauty, narrowly defined and sexualized, is of utmost importance. This definition of beauty is also dependent on the consumption of beauty aids and products. "Salon" and "spa" birthday parties aimed at little girls as young as three years old are gaining popularity, providing a venue for girls to indulge in a range of services from manicures and pedicures to full makeup and hair extensions. One website for such ser-vices (replete with descriptors such as "diva" and "little princess") suggests that such ex-periences "build confidence," a statement re-flecting the sad reality of girls who are taught that their self-worth is dependent on valida-tion they receive from others in response to their physical and sexual attractiveness.

—Angela Aujla

Fowles draws upon the work of **Pierre Bourdieu** (1930–2002), a French thinker best known for his work on the connection between class and culture. Fowles applies two of Bourdieu's key concepts in particular: habitus and reproduction. **Habitus** (somewhat differ-ent in meaning from the English word "habits") is a wide-ranging set of socially acquired characteristics, including, for example, definitions of "manners" and "good taste," leisure pursuits, ways of walking, even whether or not you spit in public. Each social class has its own habitus, its set of shared characteristics. **Reproduction**, in Bourdieu's definition, is the means by which classes, particularly the upper or dominant class, preserve status differences among classes. As Fowles phrases it, "the reproduction of habitus is the key work of a social class" (2001, p. 3).

Fowles's main point is that sociologists who condemn television violence are merely fighting proxy wars aimed at reproducing the habitus of the dominant class by condemning the habitus of the dominated class. It is ironic that he uses Bourdieu's writing to do this, as Bourdieu (1996) was a severe critic of television.

What Do YOU Think?

1. Do you think that Fowles's arguments are valid? What other criticisms of mass media might be challenged using this kind of approach?
2. In a number of cities, police forces put more officers on duty on nights when the latest instalment of *The Fast and the Furious* franchise is opening. Is this a statement about the socialization potential of these movies?

Education
The Teacher's Role in Socialization

Education can be a powerful socializing agent. Schools often are the first source of information that children receive about social groups other than their own. Teachers, curriculums, textbooks, and the social experience of being in the classroom and in the playground all play a part. We will focus here on the role teachers play in the socializing function of education.

What we call the "social location" of the teacher—the teacher's gender, age, ethnicity, and so on—can have a powerful effect on the educational socialization of the student. The fact that the early years of schooling are dominated by women teachers will have different effects on female and male students. The fact that science and math courses in high school are usually taught by men and English courses by women will also have different effects on girls and boys. Being of the same ethnic background

Chesnot/Getty Images

Online video games like the hugely successful *Fortnite: Battle Royale*, in which players fight one another to the death, are attracting younger and younger participants. Which is more likely: that this young man is becoming desensitized to violence, or that he is ridding himself of aggression?

or "race" as the teacher can have a positive effect on a child's socialization experience, as Kristin Klopfenstein (2005) points out in her article "Beyond Test Scores: The Impact of Black Teacher Role Models on Rigorous Math Taking." In the introduction to her article she notes that

> Poor [in terms of income] black students, amongst whom teachers are often the only college-educated people they know, are in particular need of role models who (a) are interested in their educational progress; (b) understand the school system as an institution [i.e. as being located in the middle class and more in "white culture" than in "black culture"]; and (c) actively encourage academic excellence and the pursuit of challenging curriculum. Culturally similar teachers may take more interest in mentoring black students and have more credibility with those students. Given the importance of a rigorous mathematics curriculum and that math is frequently a gate-keeper subject for black students [i.e. success in math determines whether or not they will advance to postsecondary education], same-race math teachers play a potentially vital role in preparing black students for their academic and working futures. (Klopfenstein, 2005, p. 416)

Klopfenstein looked for a correlation between having a black math teacher in grade 9 and the kinds of math courses a black student would take the following year. She found that black students who had had a black math teacher in grade 9 were more likely to enrol in a more challenging math class in grade 10. These students, she found, also had a greater chance of postsecondary entry and success than students who had not had a black math teacher.

The socialization effect of having black teachers does not end there. Klopfenstein quotes Pearl Rock Kane and Alfonso J. Orsini's assertion that "Teachers of color are important role models to white students, as they shape white students' images of what people of color can and do achieve" (2003, p. 10). Though you probably didn't notice, the prevailing demographics of the teachers you had growing up—their age, sex, ethnic background, and so on—played a role in your socialization.

Gendered Achievement in Reading, Writing, and Arithmetic

There is a common belief among both parents and educators that boys have a greater aptitude for the so-called STEM subjects—science, technology, engineering, and math—while girls have a higher ability in language and literature. Concerns that young female students are not succeeding at math and that boys are falling behind in reading have generated a large body of research into the accuracy of these assumptions and the causes.

The Organisation for Economic Co-operation and Development (OECD) tracks student achievement in its 35 member countries with its Program for International Student Assessment, more commonly known as PISA. The program tests 15-year-old students every three years in math, science, and reading, to see how different countries compare in turning their academic policies and funding into success. According to the results of the 2015 PISA survey, Canadian girls outperformed Canadian boys by an average of 26 points on the reading literacy scale (p. 383); however, boys outperformed girls by 1 point on the science literary scale (p. 383) and by 9 points on the literacy scale for mathematics (OECD, 2016, pp. 328, 383, 395). This appears to confirm the belief that boys do better in math and (by a narrow margin) science, while girls do better in reading.

PISA also generates some interesting findings on the career expectations of participating students. The 2015 survey found that 33.9 per cent of Canadian students expected to be working in a science-related field by the time they were 30. That's well above the OECD average score of 24.5 per cent, and well ahead of student scores for such countries as Germany (15.3 per cent), Israel (27.8 per cent), Japan (18.0 per cent), Sweden (20.2 per cent). In fact, the only OECD countries with a higher percentage of students expecting to find work in the science professions were Chile (37.9 per cent), the United States (38.0 per cent), and Mexico (40.7 per cent). The Canadian results are also notable for the difference in male and female students' expectations. Across the OECD, male and female students expected to find work in the sciences in roughly equal percentages (25.0 per cent for boys, 24.0 per cent for girls). Among Canadian 15-year-olds, girls (36.5 per cent) were more likely than boys (31.2 per cent) to expect to work in science-related professions (OECD, 2016, p. 364). As Figure 4.1 shows, much of the difference has to do with girls expecting to enter health professions, as doctors, dentists, veterinarians, nurses, and so on.

To what extent does socialization influence these results? Sociologists and educators today recognize that socialization plays a big part in shaping student academic success and expectations. Beyond the actual instruction they provide, parents and teachers give cues to children about what is expected of them in these subjects. Some of these cues are fairly explicit, as when a parent tells a girl struggling in the supposedly male STEM subjects not to worry: "You aren't expected to do well in math," or "You won't need to know it." Other cues can be subtle, as when a teacher gives a male student a graphic novel to read instead of the traditional, picture-less novel his female classmates are reading.

A recent study published in the online journal *Psychological Bulletin* offers some interesting thoughts on the role of socialization in female students' math and science marks. The authors of the study, Daniel Voyer and Susan Voyer (2014), performed a meta-analysis on grades awarded by teachers in 30 countries between 1914 and 2011. The researchers focused on year-end grades awarded by teachers, and found that girls (particularly in middle school) performed consistently better than boys not just in language and literature but also—by a smaller margin—in math and science (Voyer & Voyer, 2014, p. 1194). They acknowledge that these findings contradict analyses based on the results of standardized "performance tests" like the PISA assessment, but suggest that school marks provide a broader measure of long-term overall success than point-in-time tests. Among the explanations proposed by the authors for the stronger-than-expected math and science results of female students, the one that caught my attention has to do with parental socialization. The authors suggest that because parents typically attribute grades in math and science to natural ability in boys and to effort in girls, they "encourage more effort in females than in males, at least in math courses. This differential amount of encouragement

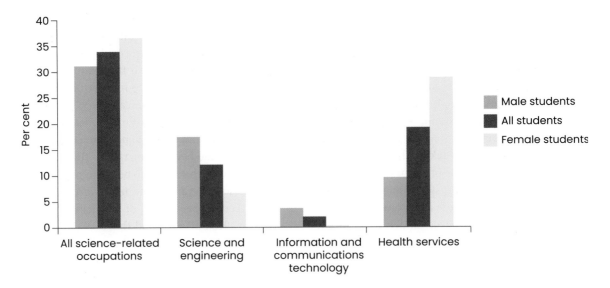

FIGURE 4.1 Percentage of 15-Year-Old Canadian Students Who Expect to Work in Science-Related Occupations at Age 30

Source: OECD, 2016, Table 1.3.10b, Table 1.3.11a–c.

The Point Is . . .

Parents May Be to Blame for the "Disappearance of Childhood"

David Elkind studies culture as an agent of socialization. One of his interests is the negative effects on children whose lives have been over-programmed by their parents, with little free time built in for spontaneous play. On this topic, Elkind's tone is dire: "[The] traditional culture of childhood is fast disappearing," he warns. "In the past two decades alone, according to several studies, children have lost 12 hours of free time a week, and eight of those lost hours were once spent in unstructured play and outdoor pastimes" (Elkind, 2003).

Spontaneous play, Elkind argues, has been replaced by a programmed schedule of organized sports and extracurricular learning. Technology is partly to blame: digital communication enables us to do more, faster, giving us a false feeling that we can accomplish much more than we used to. We extend this push for accomplishment to our children, putting pressure on them to take part in more after-school activities, play more organized sports, do more homework, and learn languages and other academic subjects at an earlier age. All of this is part of what Elkind calls the **hurried child syndrome**, which causes kids to feel adult-like levels of stress and guilt. It also contributes to the sometimes crippling apprehension that postsecondary students feel about deadlines and their career—"I'm 21 and I don't know what I want to be." It doesn't help that television and the movies often present people in their twenties as being financially successful.

Elkind was echoing concerns expressed a generation earlier by media commentator and cultural critic Neil Postman (1931–2003), who made an important contribution to the discussion of primary socialization with his book *The Disappearance of Childhood* (1982). Early in the book, Postman speaks of the disappearance of children's games. By "children's games" he means the kind of game that "requires no instructors or umpires or spectators, . . .uses whatever space and equipment are at hand, . . . [and] is played for no other reason than pleasure" (Postman, 1982, p. 4). Examples he cites include jacks, blind man's bluff, hide-and-seek, and rhyming games played with a bouncing ball, to which I would add skipping games (which my sisters did all the time), marbles, capture-the-flag, and tag. He contrasts these kinds of games with organized sports such as Little League Baseball and peewee football, which are played by children following adult practices: maximizing adult-level competence through professional-style coaches and trainers. This leads him to the following series of questions, and a tentative conclusion:

> Why should adults encourage this possibility [i.e. adult-level competence]? Why would anyone wish to deny children the freedom, informality, and joy of spontaneous play? Why submit children to the rigors of professional-style training, concentration, tensions, media-hype? . . . What we have here is the emergence of the idea that play is not to be done for the sake of doing it but for some external purpose, such as renown, money, physical conditioning, upward mobility, national pride. For adults, play is serious business. As childhood disappears, so does the child's view of play. (Postman, 1982, p. 131)

What Do YOU Think?

1. The children Postman was writing about in 1982 have grown up to become the "helicopter parents" sometimes criticized for overscheduling their children's lives today. Do you think this trend in the way parents are socializing their children is changing? If so, why do you think that is?
2. Elkind also warned that advances in technology were affecting socialization by dissuading children from enjoying "traditional games" and thereby stifling opportunities to exercise imagination, originality, and autonomy. Do you agree or disagree with his assessment?

could account in part for the slight female advantage in math" (Voyer & Voyer, 2014, p. 1193).

On the other hand, another study suggests that well-meaning parents can actually make their children's struggles worse. Researchers Ruchi Bhanot and Jasna Jovanovic (2005) found that when parents offer their children unsolicited help with homework, they may be undermining their children's confidence. As the researchers explain, "parents tend to provide such unsolicited—or intrusive—support when they perceive that their child is not doing well in school" (Bhanot & Jovanovic, 2005, p. 598). Since many parents expect male students to struggle with English and female students to struggle with math, they will provide their uninvited assistance accordingly, reinforcing the stereotypes.

How might parents and educators change their approach to socialization in order to diminish the gender differences in literacy and math and science skills? Many education experts recognize that boys and girls have different learning styles, and this view has led to experiments with single-sex classrooms and schools. However, the benefits of single-sex learning environments are difficult to assess. A 2012 report by a council of educators concluded that "the existing research on single-sex schooling is inconclusive and too tenuous to support a widespread move to single-sex classrooms or schools" (Ungerleider, Thompson, & Lavin, 2012). If classroom

socialization is not the problem, what is? The commentary suggests that "Parents may play a role in the different performance levels achieved by boys and girls in math and reading," adding that "girls may be doing better in reading and boys may be doing better in math because of parents' own beliefs about boys' and girls' natural abilities. . . . Children absorb their parents' beliefs about their own abilities and then those beliefs become powerful determinants of their school success" (Ungerleider, Thompson, & Lavin, 2012).

Secondary Socialization and Resocialization

At the start of the chapter, I touched on the difference between *primary socialization*, which occurs early in childhood, and *secondary socialization*, which occurs usually in adolescence and early adulthood. Secondary socialization also differs from primary socialization in that

a) it typically involves a group that is smaller than society in general, such as a new school or a new neighbourhood; and
b) it usually takes place outside of the family (unless it involves a "new" blended family with step-parents and step-siblings).

Secondary socialization involves learning life lessons from a different source—from classmates at school or teammates on the ice instead of from parents at home. What you learn during secondary socialization may contradict some of what you've learned in primary socialization. Any time you switch from one experience of socialization to another—whether as a child or an adult—you undergo **resocialization**. This is a process that typically involves both learning and unlearning. In its extreme form, the individual unlearns all of the behaviours, attitudes, and values that were appropriate to the previous social environment while learning those that make it possible to fit into the new situation.

Karen Armstrong describes her process of unlearning values in *Through the Narrow Gate*, which chronicles the period when, as a teenager, she joined a strict order of nuns in Britain. In the following passage she recollects what the Mother Superior said to

What Do YOU Think?

1. Why do you think so many more Canadian girls than boys expect to enter the health professions? What socializing agents could be shaping female students' expectations about their future roles as doctors, veterinarians, dentists, and nurses?
2. Blaming the parents seems to be a recurring theme in our chapter on socialization. Do you think the criticism is fair when it comes to gender differences in classroom performance? What other socializing influences are at play? Which one do you think has the greatest bearing on academic performance?

her and others who had just joined the order as *postulants*, candidates vying for admission to the order:

> Novices and postulants are kept in a particularly strict seclusion. They may not speak at all to seculars [i.e. to those who are neither nuns nor priests]. If a secular speaks to you, you must never reply. It is only by severing yourself absolutely from the world that you can begin to shed some of its values. Again no novice or postulant may ever speak to the professed nuns unless she is working with them and those few necessary words are essential for the job. The professed are in contact with the world, and even that indirect contact might seriously damage your spiritual progress. . . .
>
> You have to be absolutely ruthless in your rejection of the world, you know, Sisters. So many of its attitudes, even in really good people, are permeated with selfish values that have nothing at all to do with the self-emptying love of God. You yourselves are riddled with these ideas; you can't help it—it's not your fault. (Armstrong, 2005, pp. 92–3)

Resocialization can be voluntary or involuntary. *Voluntary resocialization* occurs when someone starts school or moves to a new school, when someone begins a job with a new company, when someone retires from work (willingly), or when someone undergoes a religious conversion (which can also, in extreme circumstances, be involuntary, as with cults). Associated with this kind of resocialization is the **rite of passage**, which is a ritual marking a life change from one status to another, typically following some form of training. A wedding is a rite of passage; so is a funeral. Other examples include the Christian practices of baptism and **confirmation**, and the Jewish **bar mitzvah** (for boys) or **bat mitzvah** (for girls), when adolescents become "adults in the faith" after a period of instruction.

Involuntary resocialization occurred in First Nation residential schools, like the one in Shubenacadie discussed in the narrative on page 130, where the language, religion, and customs of Indigenous children were brutally beaten out of them. Other examples of involuntary resocialization include

being drafted into military service, being put in prison, being committed to a psychiatric hospital, and being subjected to mandatory retirement. Goffman (1961) called institutions where involuntary resocialization takes place **total institutions**, as they regulate all aspects of an individual's life. A significant part of the unlearning process associated with involuntary resocialization is what has been termed a **degradation ceremony**, a kind of rite of passage where a person is stripped of his or her individuality. Hazing, whether of Grade 9 students, first-year college or university students, or rookies on amateur and professional sports teams, is a degradation ceremony in which being made to perform acts of minor (sometimes major) humiliation informs the initiates that they are in a new social world where they are mere beginners.

Sometimes voluntary and involuntary resocialization can occur together. Consider, for instance, programs for treating alcoholism or obesity, which begin with the sufferer's decision to change his or her lifestyle but then involve a strict and rigorous regime that is imposed for the duration of treatment.

Hazing as Resocialization

Hazing is a way of using ritualized initiation ceremonies to resocialize new members of some group or organization, such as a high school, a university fraternity or sorority, a sports team, or a military unit. It is like a test in which the initiate must demonstrate, by successfully undergoing a demeaning or uncomfortable experience, that they are "tough enough" to be a member.

Hazing rituals have long been practised in amateur, professional, and collegiate athletics. They typically involve some form of degradation ceremony imposed on the team's rookies by the veterans, who as first-year members had to go through the same trial themselves. For instance, male players might have to shave their heads, or wear women's clothing, or dress like a chicken in a public place. Sometimes, the rituals can cause serious harm to the individual being hazed, particularly when the activity involves nudity and sexualized activities. In 2005, sports hazing made national headlines when a member of the McGill University football team quit after he and other rookies were forced to participate in a hazing ritual: nude and gagged, they were made to

The Point Is...

The Vision Quest: A Modern Indigenous Rite of Passage

A traditional rite of passage for Indigenous people is the **vision quest**, which once marked the passage from childhood to adulthood. After receiving months of informal instruction from Elders, the individual would embark on a journey away from the home community to an isolated location. Then, they would fast for days, and possibly go without sleep, in the process of seeking a vision. A vision could be a song that comes to mind, or the appearance in dreams of an animal or other spirit who instructs the dreamer and initiates a connection with him or her that will continue until death.

More recently, adults have used the vision quest as a way of resocializing themselves with traditional ideals following a period of difficulty. The following is a generalized example of the Ojibwa vision quest as it has been practised recently in northeastern Ontario (Steckley & Rice, 1997, pp. 226–7). It begins in a sweat lodge, a dome-shaped structure built around overlapping willow poles, covered with skins or tarpaulins and used as a kind of sauna. The participants throw sacred tobacco on a fire to thank the Creator. They are told the story of how the sweat lodge came to the people from a little boy who was taught about healing from the seven grandfather spirits. Water is put onto the seven stones that represent those spirits. The Elder sings ceremonial songs.

After the sweat, the participants are led to their own small lodges, where they fast and meditate. The Elder visits them to ask about their spiritual experiences. The participants fast for three nights and four days. What they learn changes with each night:

> The first is described as the night of doubt, where participants pray but are uncertain about what will happen. Hunger is mitigated by a feeling of excitement. The second night is one of fear, sometimes known as the dark night of the soul. Participants realize that their bodies are beginning to weaken, and they may question their resolve. The third night is the night of the spirit. It is often said that if something meaningful is going to happen, it will occur between the beginning of the spirit night and when the fast is finished. (Steckley & Rice, 1997, pp. 226–7)

After the final sweat there is a feast with gift-giving to the Elder and to those who have assisted the individuals in their resocialization.

bend over while being prodded up the backside with a broom. This was nothing less than sexual abuse. At around the same time, a 16-year-old rookie on the Windsor Spitfires of the Ontario Hockey League became the subject of media attention after refusing to go through a hazing ritual called the "sweat box." This entailed crowding, naked, with other rookies into the washroom at the back of the team bus, with the heat turned up high enough to make the participants perspire.

Traditionally hazing has been much more a male than a female activity. Establishing one's toughness has long been viewed as a manly thing to do. But this may be changing. In September 2009, the Carleton University's women's soccer team was suspended by the university for holding a rookie initiation party that ended up with a player becoming so drunk that she had to be rushed to hospital by ambulance. Interestingly, while the suspension made the national news, the ensuing decision to reduce the suspension to just two games did not.

The last three decades have seen the emergence of a solid body of sociological literature on hazing, including why it exists, the various forms it can take, its harmful consequences, and even, rarely, its benefits as an instrument of socialization (see, for example, Kirby & Wintrup, 2002; Waldron & Kowalski, 2009). Sociologists have several questions to address.

First is whether hazing has always existed at the same level. Is it more out of control today, or has the privacy lid been opened up so that it is simply reported more often? Michelle Finkel (2002) argues that victims of hazing, like victims of domestic violence, are difficult to identify and may not come forward "out of embarrassment or the desire to protect their perpetrator(s)" (p. 231). Is it possible that greater social awareness is emboldening victims to report cases of hazing in greater numbers than in the past?

Second, if hazing rituals are becoming more dangerous and more widespread, why is that so? Does hazing perform a necessary socializing function? And if we consider hazing a form of resocialization, which by definition involves unlearning

certain social values and taking on a set of beliefs and behaviours associated with a new social community, what norms of behaviour does hazing encourage in initiates?

A final question comes from a finding by Waldron and Kowalski (2009), that among athletes who reported engaging in risky, hazing behaviours, "both the values of sports as well as the desire to be accepted by teammates encouraged hazing." What are the "values of sports" that hazing supposedly promotes? How do they overlap with the values of organized sport we identified in the box at the start of the chapter? If those values are worth promoting, can we find a healthier way to promote them in clubs, teams, and organizations for adolescents and emerging adults?

Aflo Co. Ltd. / Alamy Stock Photo

As part of its new anti-hazing and anti-bullying policy, Major League Baseball no longer permits teams to force players to dress up as Hooters Girls, Dallas Cowboys cheerleaders, or players from the All-American Girls Professional Baseball League. Being forced to dress in women's clothing is degrading for young men socialized in a patriarchal society that emphasizes masculine behaviours, especially in hyper-masculine endeavours such as male professional sports. Who benefits from hazing rituals in professional sports? Who may be harmed by a highly publicized degradation ceremony such as this? (A hint: Think not just of players but of fans, journalists, and others involved in the game.)

Resocializing the Mi'kmaq

The Shubenacadie Indian Residential School operated for 45 years, beginning in the early 1920s, under the auspices of two Roman Catholic orders in the small Nova Scotian community of Shubenacadie. Mi'kmaq students at the school suffered terrible abuse at the hands of the staff, whose mission was to resocialize students by beating their traditional culture out of them—literally, if necessary. The abuse is illustrated graphically in the words of anthropologist and former student at the school Isabelle Knockwood, who provides the following account of a young Mi'kmaq girl caught speaking in her native language:

The nun came up from behind her and swung her around and began beating her up. . . . Then the Sister pinched her cheeks and her lips were drawn taut across her teeth and her eyes were wide with terror. . . . Then the nun picked the little girl clean off the floor by the ears or hair and the girl stood on her tiptoes with her feet dangling in the air. . . . The nun was yelling, "You bad, bad girl." Then she let go with one hand and continued slapping her in the mouth until her nose bled. (Knockwood, 1992, p. 97)

Resocialization at the Shubenacadie Indian Residential School. Notice that the boys have more freedom in what they can wear than the girls do. Why do you think that was so?

Wrap It Up

Summary

Whether you're a lab rat or a dachshund, a young teen buying her first bra, a rookie at training camp, or a first-year student at frosh week, everyone's undergone processes of socialization and resocialization. (To see what human life without socialization would be like, check out the 1970 film *The Wild Child*, based on the true story of a young boy who grew up entirely on his own in the wilds of France.) How we become the people we are depends significantly on the agents of socialization we've grown up around—parents and family, educators, peer groups, culture, and the media. Sometimes these agents work together, but sometimes they send conflicting messages (you might have very different ideas about how to dress from your parents and your friends). How influential are these messages? Well, to a cultural determinist, who you are depends almost entirely on the messages you receive from your social environment. Others, though, like Dennis Wrong, believe we have the power to choose which messages we hear—that we have agency, in other words.

Postsecondary educators (myself included) are heavily engaged in resocialization, in preparing students for careers, and for making them think critically about how they have been and are being socialized. In fact, this chapter (like the ones that precede and follow it) has been written in an effort to resocialize you. Did you notice? Do you think it worked?

Think Back

Questions for Critical Review

1. Explain, in your own words, what socialization is. When does it begin in humans? When does it end?
2. Under what circumstances can socialization be harmful? Give some examples.
3. Identify at least five different agents of socialization and outline their roles.
4. What is the difference between biological determinism and social determinism? Which one allows for a greater degree of agency?
5. Career, clothing, hobbies: do you believe each of these is more socially or more biologically determined?
6. How do Mead's concepts of significant and generalized others relate to primary and secondary socialization?
7. What are some things you learned from your family that you unlearned from forces of secondary socialization, including friends, classmates, educators, and the media?
8. As an agent of socialization, what has been the impact of media—including television, video games, movies, and the internet—on your life?
9. Do organized sports represent a positive or a negative form of socialization? Consider the chapter's opening narrative and the views of Elkind and Postman discussed later in the chapter. Draw on your own experience as well.
10. If you were a parent of a boy and a girl, what could you do to ensure they had the best opportunity to succeed equally in STEM and non-STEM subjects?
11. Does the continued prevalence of hazing in spite of new laws to combat it stem from the fact that there are no socially sanctioned and encouraged rites of passage from adolescence to adulthood in modern North American society?

Read On

Suggested Print and Online Resources

Isabelle Knockwood (1992), *Out of the Depths: The Experiences of Mi'kmaw Children at the Indian Residential Schools at Shubenacadie* **(Lockeport, NS: Roseway).**

- Knockwood's work is an insightful ethnography on the residential school experience by one who survived the experience herself.

Karen Armstrong (1981), *Through the Narrow Gate: A Memoir of Spiritual Discovery* **(New York: St Martin's Griffin).**

- Karen Armstrong's recounting of her time inside a Catholic convent provides a window into religious training and spiritual life.

Laurie Kramer (2009), "Siblings as Agents of Socialization: New Directions for Child and Adolescent Development," *New Directions for Child and Adolescent Development* **126 (Winter).**

- A look at how brothers and sisters act as socializing agents in ways similar and different to those of parents, and as differing in different cultures and classes.

National Longitudinal Survey of Children and Youth (NLSCY), http://www23.statcan. gc.ca:81/imdb/p2SV.pl?Function=getSurvey&SDDS=4450&lang=en&db=imdb&adm=8&dis=2

- Launched in 1994 by Statistics Canada and Human Resources and Development Canada, the NLSCY is a 15-year study of Canadian children designed to follow their development and well-being from birth to early adulthood.

Patrick O'Sullivan with Gare Joyce (2015), *Breaking Away: A Harrowing Story of Resilience, Courage, and Triumph* **(Toronto: HarperCollins).**

- A former NHL player discusses growing up with an abusive hockey dad and how it affected his adolescence—a model of how not to socialize children.

Ruth Benedict (1946), *The Chrysanthemum and the Sword* **(Boston: Houghton Mifflin); David Riesman (1950),** *The Lonely Crowd: A Study of the Changing American Character* **(New Haven, CT: Yale University Press).**

- These two books are classic examples of national character studies.

Shirley Steinberg & Joe L. Kincheloe, eds (2011), *KinderCulture: The Corporate Construction of Childhood,* **3rd edn (Boulder, CO: Westview Press).**

- An important look at how corporate marketing is socializing small children and teenagers.

Sigmund Freud (1953), *On Sexuality: Three Essays on the Theory of Sexuality and Other Works* **(New York: Penguin).**

- This collection features three of Freud's key articles on sexuality, ranging in scope from sexual abnormality to puberty.

Social Psychology Network, http://huesmann. socialpsychology.org

- Maintained by Wesleyan University professor Scott Plous, the Social Psychology Network is dedicated to psychological research and teaching. This page presents an overview of the work of Rowell Huesmann, with free access to some of his articles.

"Play, Love and Work", www.youtube.com/ watch?v=IOWbh8qqTGU

- David Elkind, who pioneered the concept of hurried child syndrome, talks about the importance of play in this YouTube video.

Social Roles, Interaction, and Organization

5

Reading this chapter will help you to ...

- Understand what sociologists mean by the term *status*, and how ascribed and achieved statuses differ.

- Describe what it means to hold several statuses at once, and the complications that arise from this.

- Explain the relationship between status and role.

- Define *role conflict*, *role exit*, and *role strain*, and explain the effect these can have on an individual.

- Be familiar with the characteristics of male and female organizational structures.

- Discuss the impact of bureaucracy and formal rationalization on the lives of Canadians.

For Starters

Learning to Be a Stepfather

Charles Dickens's novel *David Copperfield* features the archetype of the evil stepfather in the cruel, domineering Edward Murdstone, whose sadistic treatment of young David includes beating him for falling behind in his schoolwork and then sending him away from home to work in a factory. That character was the model I hoped to avoid when I acquired the status of stepfather in the early 1990s, when I gained, through marriage, stepsons who were seven and eight. During my first years as a stepfather, I felt that of all the statuses I had, it was the one that caused me the most grief. I couldn't sort out what my responsibilities were. They weren't clearly defined. I wasn't "their dad," and yet I felt I was expected to take on the responsibilities that go along with being a father of sons.

In some ways, I felt as though I was making up my job as stepfather as I went along. What do you do when a seven-year-old boy grasps your hand and walks with you in public? What do you do when a 10-year-old won't go out the front door because there's a bee outside? I wished there were a manual—Stepfathering for Dummies—that I could consult.

At first, I was anxious to win them over by acting like the uncle I already knew how to be—the one who spoils nephews and nieces with presents and crazy antics, and then leaves Mom and Dad to deal with their rambunctious children inspired to reckless hijinks by my very physical humour. But I didn't want to be like the stepfather I had once met whose stepson could get away with anything. I had stayed with this acquaintance's family for a few days, and the boy soon learned that I wasn't soft like his stepfather. When he wouldn't wash his face, as part of the routine I was asked to supervise, I took a cloth and gave him a good, hard scrub. Next time, he did it himself. In that case, though, I wasn't emotionally attached to him or his mother, so I really had nothing to lose.

In this new relationship, I had to be more like a father: strict but fair. Not an easy path to take for a "live and let live" kind of guy. It was good that I loved sports, as they did. I went to all their hockey,

A. Steckley

baseball, and lacrosse games. I coached Rob in baseball, and drove Justin all over the countryside when he made the local rep baseball team.

I found that people are sometimes suspicious of stepfathers. When the school called or I went for parent–teacher interviews, I felt that my status was being judged. Sometimes after I'd explained the nature of my relationship to the boys, I perceived a certain knowing look in the eyes of teachers, principals, and office staff: a look that said, "Well that explains it."

Now that both boys are in their thirties, I have become comfortable with my stepfather status. I refer to them as "my sons." When Rob had a near-fatal car accident and he asked me to drive him home when he was confined to a hospital bed, I was moved to tears. Justin's co-workers call me "Justin's dad." I'm happy with that. Although I know I made lots of mistakes, I feel I know what it means to have the status of "stepfather."

And perhaps I can write Stepfathering for Dummies.

What Do YOU Think?

1. Why is the status of stepfather a complicated one? What does this status entail?
2. Imagine the narrative the author's stepsons might write in response to this. Do you think they would have found the status of stepson just as complicated?

Introduction: Why Sociologists Obsess over Status

Unlike some of the sociological concepts we've encountered so far, *status* is a term that probably has meaning for you already. You might think of it as something along the lines of high social standing, credibility, or a favourable reputation. In this sense, status is something you either have or don't have, something you can gain or lose. You might also think of status in terms of the update you post to your favourite social media site to give followers some insight into your condition, state of mind, or romantic relationships. In this sense, status is something singular that can change as often as you post to Facebook.

To a sociologist, status is something different. For one thing, status isn't something you either have or you don't: everyone has a status. In fact, everyone has *several* statuses that they hold at the same time. Moreover, while some statuses can change and be replaced, others do not change, or they change very infrequently. I gained a status when I became a stepdad; that was over 25 years ago, and I still have

that status. In March 2019 I gained the status of grandfather.

Our statuses are vitally important to how we see ourselves and how others see us. When we interact with people, much of what goes on both in thoughts and in behaviour relates to the statuses we hold and the way we perform the *roles* attached to those statuses. The interaction may be relatively simple when the expectations are well understood by both parties. But if a status is more complex because the set of expectations attached to it is not well established, the exchange may be more difficult, as with stepparents and stepchildren. Sometimes, too, the expectations associated with one status interfere with those of another.

The sociological concept of status is important to understanding how people interact in pairs and in small groups. Later in the chapter, we will broaden our focus to look at the social dynamics existing in large groups and organizations. We will see that small- and large-group dynamics differ in a very important way: while the statuses we hold help us establish ourselves as individuals in small groups, the principles at play in large social organizations seem designed to strip our individuality away entirely.

Social Status

Status and role: it sounds like nothing more than a quick breakfast order, but this pair of concepts is critically important to helping us establish social identity. A **status** is a recognized social position that a person occupies. It contributes to a person's social identity by imposing responsibilities and expectations that help define that person's relationships to others. You don't have just one status; you have many over your lifetime, and in fact, you can have several statuses at once—daughter, mother, wife, CEO, volunteer board member, soccer coach, and on and on. The collection of statuses you have is your **status set**. For instance, you could have the statuses of son, brother, uncle, teacher, drummer (for your band), neighbour, taxpayer, white person—all at the same time. These would make up your status set. We gain and lose statuses as we age, so we possess, dozens of statuses over our lifetimes, some of them only briefly, others for as long as we live.

Bill Mooney/RCMP

Born in Inuvik, Northwest Territories, Darcie Bernhardt grew up in Tuktoyaktuk and was the first Inuit person from that city to participate in the RCMP's pre-cadet training program for Indigenous people. She later studied at the Yukon School of Visual Arts and the Nova Scotia College of Art and Design in Halifax, taking on the more "traditional" status of Inuit artist. Why might the achieved status of artist put less pressure on an Inuit person than the achieved status of police officer?

Ascribed and Achieved Status

One way of classifying our many statuses is to distinguish between statuses that are *achieved* and those that are *ascribed*. A status is considered **achieved** if you have entered into it at some stage of your life, but you weren't born into it. If you are a college or university student, then that is an achieved status. Presumably you are also a high-school graduate, which is also an achieved status. A professional position (assuming it's not a job in the family business), a role in a hobby or recreational activity, a brief stint as a contestant on *Jeopardy*: all are achieved statuses. They assume some kind of personal ability, accomplishment, or voluntary act, although very few statuses are completely achieved (for instance, an accomplished drummer has *some* natural ability).

An **ascribed** status is one that you were born into ("daughter" or "son," "black" or "Latino," etc.) or one you have entered into involuntarily ("teenager," "elderly person," "cancer survivor," "unemployed person"). Circumstances trump choice in ascribed statuses.

Some statuses can be both achieved and ascribed. The degree to which a status is achieved or ascribed often depends on how much **social mobility** exists. Consider a professional title, like doctor or prime minister: normally, a title of this kind is achieved. However, in a society with little social mobility, where a small ruling elite dominates, the statuses of president, judge, or rich business owner can be more ascribed than achieved. Some Hindu societies of South Asia have traditionally been organized socially according to a system of ranked social classes, or *castes*, that people are born into and that are associated with different occupations. For example, Brahmans are people born into the highest caste, associated with priesthood; Vaisyas occupy the third caste, comprising merchants, farmers, and craftspeople. People traditionally have not been permitted to move beyond their caste, meaning that a status such as general in the military, which would be an achieved status in most societies, is an ascribed status where the system of hereditary castes prevails, and social mobility does not.

Your race—white, black, Asian, Latino, and so on—is, for the most part, an ascribed status. However, people from a racialized group who want to avoid discrimination and whose appearance does

What Do YOU Think?

You may wonder why it matters if a status is ascribed or achieved. Consider, then, the status "poor person." First, do you think this is an ascribed or an achieved status? Now imagine you're a politician responsible for drafting social welfare policies. How would your policy proposals differ depending on whether you considered being a poor person to be primarily an ascribed status or primarily an achieved status?

not clearly put them into that group can sometimes successfully claim (or "achieve") a racial status that society judges to be more favourable. This process is known as **passing**. It is not unusual for Indigenous people in Canada to "pass" for white, or at least to try, particularly in big cities.

Sexual Orientation and Status: A Problem Area

Sexual orientation is primarily an ascribed status. Heterosexuality is natural for some, and homosexuality is natural for others. Others still feel naturally *asexual* (having no feelings of sexual attraction), bisexual, *demisexual* (sexually attracted only to someone with whom one has a strong emotional bond),

sapiosexual (sexually attracted to people with high intelligence), and so on.

There are those who believe that homosexuality is simply a "lifestyle choice," one that can be overcome with heavy doses of therapy (see Dr Joseph Nicolosi, Chapter 4), drugs, religion, or conservative politics. Remember, homosexuality was against the law in Canada until 1969. The scholarly literature strongly argues that sexual orientation is a physical/psychological predisposition that may or may not be acted upon at some point. According to this definition, regardless of whether you live in a gay or lesbian relationship, you are homosexual if your sexual fantasies are overwhelmingly about people who are of the same sex as yourself.

Of course, sexual orientation is much more complicated than this. One problem with naming it as either an achieved or an ascribed status has to do with the way one's own sexuality is recognized by others. Someone who is gay but who marries into a heterosexual relationship because of social pressure would not be socially recognized as homosexual (this is another example of passing, defined in the section above). In terms of statuses, that would mean the status of sexual orientation is, at least partially, achieved because it involves a decision to behave in a way that conforms with social norms and expectations about how a gay or a straight person should act. Status, then, lies in what you do, not in what you feel; in this case, choice can trump circumstances.

Telling It Like It Is   A Student's POV

Being Casually Queer in a Heteronormative World

There's a weird sort of liminality to being "out" as bisexual. A lot of LGBTQ2 people know that coming out is never just one moment, you're constantly coming out to everyone you meet. But when you're bi, I feel like you don't even get those moments in a satisfying way, either. You just kind of exist, not sure if you're saying too much or too little about yourself.

I've had people know me for months, and be surprised when it comes out that I'm bisexual. "Well, the subject just never came up," I can say,

and shrug it off. But it still feels like I've been hiding something from them. This part of myself which I never try to conceal—no big deal, right? just let it come up naturally—has suddenly become this really personal thing that you only get to unlock with a high enough friendship level. But if I bring it up too soon, who knows how they might react? With lots of people, you can tell what they would say if you told them you were gay. But telling them you're bi? It's way harder to gauge. Lots of times, even they don't know. They know what

Continued

they think about gay people, but they still don't know what to make of bisexuality. It's confusing. It's a lot of things at once. "Wait, so how do you choose, then?" they might ask. "Do you think you'll end up gay or straight?"

I'll listen to my gay and lesbian friends talk among themselves, and wonder if I'm allowed in that conversation. I'll listen to my straight friends talk about their relationships, and wonder if I'm allowed in that conversation. I'll hear a female friend gush about how gorgeous she thinks a female celebrity is, and I'll wonder if she's like me, or if this is just the way that straight girls appreciate aesthetic beauty (usually it is). I'll try to find a way to casually

tell people—colleagues, friends, people I trust— "hey, by the way, this is who I am! But also, it's no big deal!" But if it's no big deal, then I shouldn't have to say anything, right? But if I don't, then why do I feel like I'm hiding something?

If anyone ever asked me if I'm bi—anyone at all—I'd say yes. I have no problem telling people, whoever they are. So I guess that means I'm "out." But I don't really feel "out," because no one ever really asks. They make their assumptions one way or another, and I just don't deny them. But it's hard to put into words what it feels like to be so separate from who people think I am. Sometimes it's enough to make me wonder who I am at all.

What Do YOU Think?

1. Why is bisexual a complicated status for the student writer of this narrative?
2. Sexual orientation is an ascribed status, but as the writer explains, it is largely invisible. What are some other ascribed statuses that are invisible? How might they complicate the lives of people who hold them in ways that visible statuses (such as "race") do not?

Master Status

Everett C. Hughes (1897–1983) introduced the concept of master status in "Dilemmas and Contractions of Status" (1945), published when he worked at the University of Chicago. He applied the term in the context of race in the United States:

> Membership in the Negro race, as defined in American mores and/or law, may be called a master status–determining trait. It tends to overpower, in most crucial situations, any other characteristics [i.e. statuses] which might run counter to it. (Hughes, 1945, p. 357)

The term **master status** signifies the status that dominates all of an individual's other statuses in most social contexts, and plays the greatest role in the formation of the individual's social identity. You can learn a lot about people by asking them what they consider their master status to be. Canadians, upon being introduced to someone, will often ask,

"What do you do?" This implies that a person's occupation is their master status. It isn't always the case, though: ethnicity and gender can be master statuses, even when someone doesn't want them to be. During his presidential campaign, Barack Obama's master status was his race. For some conservative Americans, it still is.

What Do YOU Think?

1. Hughes called "black" a master status because in most interactions it was more significant than statuses based on sex, age, or class. Do you think that "white" only exists as a master status for white nationalists? Do you think that your "race" affects your answer to this question?
2. Has there ever been a time in your life when your "race" or ethnicity was your master status? How did you know?

Quick Hits

Labelling Theory

Sociologist **Howard Becker** (b. 1928) developed **labelling theory** in the 1960s to explain the negative effects a label can have when applied to a group outside of the majority. Part of this theory states that when negative labels are attached to a status, a powerful master status can be created and internalized both by the individual and by others. The process is well portrayed in the following excerpt from a study of drug culture:

> [I]f people who are important to Billy call him a "druggie" this name becomes a powerful label that takes precedence over any other status positions Billy may occupy. Even if Billy is

also an above average biology major, an excellent musician, and a dependable and caring person, such factors become secondary because his primary status has been recast as a "druggie." Furthermore, once a powerful label is attached, it becomes much easier for the individual to uphold the image dictated by members of society, and simply to act out the role expected by significant others. (Hanson et al., 2009, p. 76)

A label like "druggie" thus becomes a master status that can follow a person for their entire life, despite efforts to change it.

Status Hierarchy

Statuses can be ranked from high to low based on prestige and power; this ranking is referred to as **status hierarchy**. For each of the basic social categories—gender, race, ethnicity, age, class, sexual orientation, and physical ability—one status tends to be valued above the others. In Canadian society we tend to rank male over female, white over black or brown, British heritage over eastern European and Asian, upper-class over middle- and working-class, heterosexual over LGBTQ2, and able-bodied over disabled.

Applying the status hierarchy to age is complicated. Power is concentrated in the hands of those who are middle-aged, yet because we live in a society that promotes the cult of youth—the desire to look, act, and feel young—youth also has some prestige. The middle-aged often abuse their bodies, injecting poison (e.g. Botox) into their faces, undergoing facelifts, and fighting to hold onto their youthful appearance through fitness regimes and the masking effects of makeup. We could also call this a form of passing, as those who engage in such rejuvenating practices are trying to achieve higher status by "passing" for younger than they really are.

Status Inconsistency

Some people seem to hold all the statuses favoured by society. Federal and provincial governments, for instance, tend to be clubhouses for people who are male, white, of British heritage, rich, heterosexual, and able-bodied: that is a winning status set, consisting of mostly ascribed statuses, that gives anyone who holds it a significant life advantage. Likewise, there are a lot of black or Indigenous women living at or below the poverty line; the deck is stacked against those born into that status set.

Status consistency is the condition a person experiences when all of their statuses fall in the same range in the social hierarchy. However, there are cases in which a person holds social statuses that are ranked differently and do not align; this condition is known as **status inconsistency**. A middle-aged white man born to wealth but working as a receptionist at a dentist's office is a case of status inconsistency. An Indigenous woman who is a lawyer and high-ranking federal cabinet minister (as Jody Wilson-Raybould was) is another example.

When a person's statuses do not add up—when an individual holds one highly valued status and other less-valued ones, or vice versa—the situation

The Point Is . . .

Statuses Change through Time

Norman Kwong (1929–2016) was born in Canada six years after the Chinese Exclusion Act was passed. Though it did not stop Chinese immigration to Canada, the act required all Chinese people—even those born in the country—to register with the government. In this way, it gave Chinese Canadians a legal status different from that of other Canadians, a diminished one. The act was in place until 1947, when Normie Kwong was 18 years old. His master status as a child would have been Chinese Canadian. Among his other statuses were son, brother, and student.

The year the act was repealed, Kwong became a star junior football player. The next year, he began his professional football career, playing first for the Canadian Football League's Calgary Stampeders (1948–50) and then, after a trade to the team's fiercest rival, for the Edmonton Eskimos (1951–60). During this time, professional football player was his master status in a status set that also included Chinese Canadian, husband, and father.

When he retired from football, Kwong became involved in sports management, both for the Calgary Stampeders and for the National Hockey League's Calgary Flames, a team he helped bring to the city and part-owned. This was but one of several business interests he was involved in during this time. It is hard to know what his master status was then, although Chinese Canadian would still have been prominent.

From 2005 to 2010 Kwong served as lieutenant-governor of Alberta. His appointment was not surprising, given his high profile as an athlete and sports executive and his connections with the then-ruling provincial Conservative Party. This political position would be his master status at the time.

When we look at Norman Kwong's life, we can see that he has held many different statuses, some ascribed and some achieved, as well as at least three different master statuses (Chinese Canadian, professional football player, provincial lieutenant-governor).

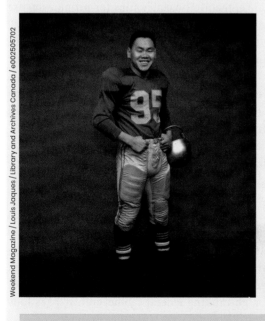

Weekend Magazine / Louis Jaques / Library and Archives Canada / e002505702

CP PHOTO/Jeff McIntosh

What Do YOU Think?

1. Norman Kwong had at least three master statuses. In each case, how did it become his master status? Did he choose it?
2. Why you think that I chose Norman Kwong for an example and not a white football player?

that results can cause social tension. The same tension can occur when the value of statuses shifts over time. Hughes noticed this pattern at work in Quebec during the 1930s. He found that when people of "lower" status moved into occupations typically held by people with more favoured statuses, they became targets of certain strategies their colleagues used to reduce the apparent inconsistency. One strategy was to modify the stereotype surrounding the lowly regarded status. As Hughes explained,

> the idea that French-Canadians were good only for unskilled industrial work was followed by the notion that they were especially good at certain kinds of skilled work but were not fit to repair machines or to supervise the work of others. In this series of modifications the structure of qualities expected for the most-favoured positions remains intact. But the forces which make for mobility continue to create marginal people on new frontiers. (Hughes, 1945, p. 356–7)

In other words, these upwardly mobile people would become alienated both from others sharing their low ascribed status and from people defined by the more highly regarded, achieved status. When he called these individuals "marginal people," Hughes was drawing on the work of **Robert E. Park**, who described the figure he called "marginal man." The male bias implied in the term is the main reason it's no longer used; however, it is historically important and preserved in the commonly used term **marginalization**, which refers to the process by which groups are assigned into categories that set them at or beyond the margins of the dominant society.

Status Inconsistency and White Male Violence

Let's consider a more contemporary example of how changing status values can lead to tension. This case, which can help us understand the rise of white nationalism and the alt-right movement, concerns the white working-class Christian male in

Courtesy of the Northern Affairs Institute of Technology

There is a high demand in Canada for workers in skilled trades, such as electrical work, plumbing, construction, heavy equipment technician, and so on. What would cause young people to shy away from careers in these well-paying industries? What role could status inconsistency play in career decisions?

the United States. Forty years ago, this was a highly valued status set, likely to translate into prosperous employment, a place at the head of the household, and a secure position within the middle class. Higher education was not a prerequisite for success: in 1979, there were close to 20 million Americans employed in manufacturing, most of them men without college degrees (Thompson, 2016).

Since that time, a number of things have happened to diminish the value of this status set. First, the number of manufacturing jobs in America has declined steadily and currently sits around 12 million. As Derek Thompson (2016) explains, work has shifted toward lower-paying jobs in the service sector, where women without degrees have fared better than men without degrees. The growing participation of women in the workforce has contributed to the decline in the employment rate of men without degrees. According to a report by the Hamilton Project, the full-time employment rate among men aged 30 to 45 without a degree fell from 76 per cent in 1990 to 68 per cent in 2013, while the portion of this group that did not work at all rose from 11 per cent to 18 per cent (Kearney, Hershbein, & Jácome, 2015, p. 2). Median earnings for these men fell from $31,900 in 1990 to $25,500 in 2013, representing a 20 per cent decrease (Kerney, et al., 2015, p. 3). This has left workers of all races and ethnicities feeling vulnerable, but according to a poll conducted for *The Washington Post*, Kaiser Family Foundation, and Harvard University, white Americans are far less likely than Americans of other races "to think their children will be better off than they themselves are now" (Fletcher & Cohen, 2011). As Thompson (2016) puts it, "Many of these first beneficiaries of the franchise now feel disenfranchised. The original middle class feels cut out of the American Dream."

The devaluation of the status set representing the white, working-class, Christian male in the United States has had a profound effect on American society. This group became the target audience for Donald Trump's "Make America Great Again" speeches during the 2016 election campaign. As Robert Jones (2017) explains, "Trump's promise to restore a mythical past golden age—where factory jobs paid the bills and white Protestant churches were the dominant cultural hubs—powerfully tapped evangelical anxieties about an uncertain future." The insecurity of white Americans has fuelled the rise of movements opposing immigration, feminism, globalism—in short, any "-ism" that might threaten the privileged status of white, Christian men. White men without a university degree also make up the group most likely to own guns, according to a Pew Research Center study, and while there are many reasons for owning a firearm, some have drawn a link between gun ownership and the declining status of the American male. In an interview, Canadian-born conservative political commentator David Frum made the following observation:

> [T]he typical man finds himself less needed than he was 20 or 30 years ago. . . . [He] is less likely to be married, less likely to be supporting a family. In many ways he's become superfluous to society. But there's one thing he can do. For just a few hundred bucks, he can pick up godlike power to dispense death . . . to dozens or hundreds of people. And he may or may not do that, but you know that you can. And how can you be a loser if you can kill so many people? (2017)

Frum's comments pertained specifically to the shooting deaths of 59 people in Las Vegas in October 2017, but they could just as easily apply to the October 2018 attack on the Tree of Life Synagogue in Pittsburgh, the January 2017 shooting at the Islamic Cultural Centre in Quebec City, or the March 2019 shooting at two mosques in Christchurch, New Zealand, carried out by an attacker who described himself as an ordinary white man, born to a working-class but low-income family, and the product of a "regular childhood."

What Do YOU Think?

Entitlement is the expectation that holding a particular set of statuses will guarantee a certain kind of success. Can this definition explain the rise of white nationalism? What about violence against women? Can it explain the Incel (involuntary celibate) rebellion proclaimed by the perpetrator of the 2018 Toronto van attack that killed 10 people and injured 16?

For a very brief time in 2016, this flyer could be found on telephone and hydro poles in Toronto. Canada has white nationalists and alt-right groups. Why do you think the visibility of these groups is less than it is in the United States?

Social Roles

A **role** is a set of behaviours and attitudes associated with a particular status. Roles attached to a status may differ across cultures. For example, people holding the status of elder in traditional cultures of China and Africa and Indigenous communities of North America are expected to have acquired a certain level of wisdom. The same expectations seldom exist in mainstream Canadian culture, where the status of elder has few positive role expectations attached to it; the status is more "old person" than it is elder. One reason that Western social scientists were slow to question the myth of Inuit elder abandonment—the idea that it was once common for Inuit communities to abandon their elders during food shortages and other tough times—is that Western culture lacked its own positively defined role of elder, making the myth much more credible in their eyes.

A given status may be associated with more than one role. **Robert Merton** (1968) developed the idea of the **role set**, which comprises all of the roles that are attached to a particular status. As professors, we have the role of teacher to our students, but we are also colleagues to our peers, employees to our schools, sometimes demanding children to our support staff, and of course, trouble-making underlings to our administrators. Students have a peer role with classmates in addition to their student role with instructors. To the college or university, they are paying customers.

Role Strain

Role strain develops when there is a conflict between roles within the role set of a particular status. For example, if a student complains to his instructor about a teacher in another class, the instructor is placed in a conflict between her role as educator, in which she has the student's best interests at heart, and her role as colleague, in which she must be loyal to the professor teaching the other class. Similarly, a student who catches a classmate cheating on an exam is at once a member of the academic community with a responsibility to report the offence and a member of the student body who wouldn't rat out a peer. Role strain can even affect a single role. Consider the parent who feels more at ease with one of his children than with the other but tries to balance his attentions between them. It can be a very difficult game to play.

Role Conflict

Another useful concept for understanding social tensions is role conflict. **Role conflict** occurs when a person is forced to reconcile incompatible expectations generated from two or more statuses they hold. If you are both a mother and a student, then you know all about role conflict. Imagine: it's the night before the big exam and you need to study—part of the set of behaviour expectations attached to being a college or university student; however, your daughter needs help with her homework, your son is ill, and your husband is out with friends watching the big game—he's been looking forward to it for weeks. You're on your own with the demands of conflicting statuses of mother and student. These clashing sets of expectations illustrate role conflict. Role conflict occurs when people turn down promotions because they do not want to move into a position where they might have to reprimand peers and friends who suddenly occupy a lower position within the organization.

Role Exit

Role exit is the process of disengaging from a role that has been central to one's identity, and attempting to establish a new role. **Helen Rose Fuchs Ebaugh** (an ex-nun turned sociologist) has studied role exit processes extensively. Her findings are summarized in *Becoming*

Quick Hits

Status and Role: What's the Difference?

A number of sociology students over the years have had problems distinguishing between status and role. This stems largely from the fact that both have somewhat different meanings outside the sociology classroom. Status in a non-sociological sense often refers to importance or prestige (CEO being high-status and cleaning staff being low-status). Role is commonly linked to the characters that actors play in a movie or TV show; in essence, a TV role is closer to what sociologists would call status.

So here are essential differences between the two sociological concepts. A status is a position that is recognized in society. It can be a job, such as teacher, minister, banker, lawyer, accountant, or nurse. Status can also be a recognized position in a family: mother, uncle, grandmother, brother, daughter, and spouse. It can also include neighbour, citizen, student, driver, and pedestrian.

A role is a set of socially shared expectations about the behaviours and attitudes that belong to a given status. Take the roles associated with being a student. You may have received a document from your college or university outlining the expectations for students attending your school. These expectations include such things as attending classes regularly, completing homework and other assignments, not plagiarizing or cheating on tests and exams, being diligent and responsible. These expectations reflect the role your school associates with the status of student. You and your friends or roommates may have other expectations that define the role you associate with being a student: studying late into the night or morning, being tired all the time, drinking late into the night or morning, having the freedom to live by your own set of house rules. Your parents, meanwhile, will have their own expectations about the role associated with your student status: that you will be costing far more money than you earn, that you will go long stretches without calling or texting, until you need something, and that you will be bringing home laundry for them to do. In each case, the status is the same, but the expectations that make up the role differ depending on the person judging it.

Pictorial Press Ltd / Alamy Stock Photo

In the movie *Black Panther*, King of the Wakanda is a role; in sociological terms, it's a status.

an EX: The Process of Role Exit (1988). According to Ebaugh—who wrote about not just ex-nuns but also ex-priests, ex-convicts, and recovering alcoholics—role exit involves shifting your master status. If you were forced to retire and had always defined yourself by what you did ("I am a nurse"), you might feel uncomfortable when asked, "What do you do?" If you are a stay-at-home mother and your children grow up and move away, you have lost a very important purpose in your day-to-day life that is not easily replaced (and grandmother might be far away in the future). If you are a father and your parental role is reduced because your ex-wife gains primary custody of the children, then becoming a part-time dad may feel like a role exit.

The role exit of married people who become single through separation, divorce, or death of a spouse is difficult, as it entails shifting from "we" to "I." Previous relationships with friends and family change, and in the case of divorce, people often take sides. Some people you've been close to might start avoiding you, treating your divorce like something contagious and you as a carrier of the "failed relationship" virus. On the other hand, others might begin to pay you more attention, and in ways you

© Cindy Moser, used with permission

Imagine trying to study for an exam during a shift at your part-time job. What role conflict do you think this student experiences?

Matt Rourke/AP

A tearful Allen Iverson announces his retirement from the National Basketball Association in October 2013, over two-and-a-half years after his last appearance in an NBA game. Do you think he struggled with role exit? What changes does retirement entail for a professional athlete?

The Point Is . . .

Half-Elf Paladin Is a Status Set . . . in Dungeons & Dragons

Before video games, there was E. Gary Gygax's Dungeons & Dragons (or D&D), the first world-wide **role-playing game**. During the 1970s and 1980s it sold millions of copies as a pen-and-paper, sit-at-the-table game before it joined the computer world.

D&D was set in any one of a number of fantasy worlds populated by such creatures as elves, trolls, gnomes, dreaded orcs, and wyverns, all borrowed from Tolkien's *Lord of the Rings* and the fantasy works of Michael Moorcock, H.P. Lovecraft, and Roald Dahl. Players entered these worlds as sorcerers, knights, and holy warriors, their fate in encounters with various monsters or sealed passages determined by the roll of any one of a number of different dice. As for the dungeons, they weren't jails but settings invented by the person acting as the "dungeon master" (the DM). You could call the DM a sort of referee, but for author Mark Barrowcliffe, "To call the DM a referee is a bit misleading. His role is nearer to that of a god. He creates a world, sets challenges for players' characters, and rewards or punishes them according to the wisdom of their actions" (2008, p. 32).

Barrowcliffe's *The Elfish Gene: Dungeons, Dragons and Growing Up Strange—A Memoir* (2008) is a good introduction to D&D as a sociological phenomenon. Barrowcliffe grew up in working-class England, and began playing D&D in 1976 at the age of 12. Explaining his fascination with the game, Barrowcliffe notes that he and his friends didn't aspire to their parents' simple and (from their perspective) dull lives, characterized by predictability and stability. Instead, they sought the kind of magic that was missing from their "real" world. They were, in Barrowcliffe's estimation, intelligent (particularly in the mathematical calculations necessary to be a successful player), but not necessarily school-smart. They certainly were not jocks or tough guys, and they weren't concerned with fashion or appearance.

What does D&D have to do with status and role? For a generation of adolescents—almost exclusively boys—their D&D characters formed a status that was recognized by other players, and that was as significant as traditional statuses such as son, brother, friend, and student. The roles played in Dungeons & Dragons were more engaging than those occupied in real life, though some real-life "truths" were learned through playing.

Players adopted their statuses from among a number of different character classes. Initially, these were simple: fighter (warrior), cleric (priest), and magic-user (wizard). As the game evolved, however, the number of character classes grew to include alchemists, assassins, berserkers, druids, ninjas, paladins, and female characters such as witches and the bizarrely sexual houris—"a cross between sorcerers and prostitutes" (Barrowcliffe, 2008, p. 227). By rolling dice and recording the results, players would determine the strength, magical ability, charisma, and intelligence of their characters, and they would speak and act as they imagined their characters would. According to Barrowcliffe,

> People . . . identified very strongly with their characters. . . . This is where it differs from a computer game. You can't reboot if your character is killed. In D&D if the character dies, he's dead, which . . . is a serious threat to his future. Losing a character that you've had for . . . years can be a major emotional experience. At fourteen years old it can be the first real grief you've known in your life. It's like having an imaginary friend but one you get to actually look at, that other people will discuss as if they're real and may even attempt to kill. (2008, p. 35)

The game socialized young males, giving them self-knowledge, opportunities to exercise creativity, and experience in the competitive world of adults. Just as important, it allowed them to invent for themselves an alternative status set, one that gave them the control to choose a number of statuses that are typically ascribed, like sex, age, and social position.

Wikipedia

D&D was played with dice and a map sketched on a sheet of graph paper, typically around the dining room table. How do you think that would affect the status formation of those who played? How might it differ from the experience of participants in today's online gaming community, who may never meet one another face to face?

What Do YOU Think?

What lessons does participating in role-playing games produce? Does it matter that they are learned while playing out fictional rather than real statuses?

haven't been used to. As a "single," you are expected to be "out there" meeting other eligible singles. Role exit is something we all experience throughout our lives.

Studying Social Interaction in Small Groups

As we have seen, status and role are important concepts in understanding individual identity-formation. The statuses we hold are crucial to how we see ourselves. But they also lay the groundwork for interaction with others. A man walks into a bar (seriously). His statuses as male and customer establish certain expectations around the interaction he will have with the woman waiting his table, who holds the statuses of female and server. Before either of them says a word to the other, we can predict how each one might act based on the statuses that each one holds in that situation. Statuses related to age and whether or not the customer is a "regular" will also have an effect: my own advancing age and my status as a long-term patron of my local pub affect the way I play the role of customer.

In small-group settings, statuses can be a valuable way to establish the **pecking order**, or who is in charge. It's not uncommon for criminal gangs to have a hierarchy of statuses, ranging from president to associate, soldier, and wannabe. Each of these statuses carries its own set of roles, or expected behaviours. A gang member's status—be it official or unofficial—sets out his (usually his) responsibilities and the reporting structure: whom does he take orders from, and who answers to him?

Quick Hits

Pecking Order

In the 1920s, Norwegian zoologist and comparative psychologist Thorleif Schjelderup-Ebbe introduced a term that, when translated into English, became *pecking order*. It originally applied to chickens (hens in particular), with reference to who can get away with pecking whom. If no one pecks you (and you are chicken), then you are at the top of the flock's social hierarchy, or pecking order. With the eight parrots I live with, it is different: there is a tail-pulling order. Gus, a cockatiel and the smallest of our birds, has had his tail pulled by all seven of the others, demonstrating that he occupies the lowest position on our parrots' social hierarchy.

Humans coexisting in small groups neither peck nor pull tails—not literally. What kinds of behaviour do humans use to establish a pecking order?

Small-Group Studies and the Definition of the Situation

The study of small-group interaction came early to sociology with the pioneering work of German sociologist **Georg Simmel** (1858–1918), who was among the first to narrow his focus to the daily, one-on-one social interactions of individuals. He was a microsociologist and a forerunner of the symbolic interactionists whom we met in Chapter 1. Others working in this tradition around the turn of the twentieth century include **Charles Cooley** (1864–1929), whose concept of the looking-glass self we discussed last chapter, and **Frederic Thrasher** (1892–1962), whose classic study of gangs in Chicago (Thrasher, 1927) represents a study of group interaction rooted in fieldwork. He saw the gangs that he studied as small clusters of intense interaction socially separated from the larger world:

> An immigrant colony . . . is itself an isolated social world. . . . [T]he gang boy moves only in his own universe and other regions are clothed in . . . mystery. . . . [H]e knows little of the outside world. (1927)

Thrasher's ethnographic research on gangs and small-group interaction was carried on brilliantly in William Whyte's *Street-Corner Society* (1955), which we considered in Chapter 2. The social interactions of North American gang worlds continues to be an area of study for sociologists, including Sudhir Venkatesh, whose *Gang Leader for a Day* (2008) is a "rogue sociologist's" look at New York street gangs, and Humber College criminologist Mark Totten, author of *Nasty, Brutish and Short: The Lives of Gang Members in Canada* (2012) and *Gang Life: 10 of the Toughest Tell Their Stories* (2014).

Another key contribution to the study of small-group interaction—and another study of European immigrants entering North America during the first two decades of the twentieth century—came from the symbolic interactionist William I. Thomas, whose monumental work with Polish sociologist Florian Znaniecki, *The Polish Peasant in Europe and America* ([1918–20] 1996), illustrated the important part narratives play in defining situations. Thomas showed that the way people interpret their own lives was a sociological element well worth studying. As he expressed it, the "situations we define as real become real in their consequences" (Thomas, 1966, p. 301). This idea, which came to be known as the **Thomas theorem**, influenced other developments in symbolic interactionism, including a concept known as the **definition of the situation**. The term refers to the notion that two or more people might define a given situation differently and in contradictory ways, based on their own subjective experiences. For this reason, understanding how an individual defines a situation is crucial to understanding the individual's actions and responses to it.

A classic case of how different ways of defining a situation can lead to misunderstanding and mistrust surrounds the practice that Europeans referred to as "Indian giving." In traditional Indigenous culture, people would give gifts as statements that they wanted to strengthen the bonds between them. In the Wendat (Huron) language of the trading people, the verb meaning "to trade" translates literally as "to give to each other." Accepting a gift was an important gesture: it was the first step in acknowledging and accepting the wish to strengthen bonds. Returning the favour was the second, equally important step: it confirmed the desire to establish friendly terms. From the European perspective, when a gift-giver expressed a desire for a return gift, it was looked upon as demanding and selfish.

Interaction Process Analysis

During the 1950s, a Harvard research team headed by social psychologist **Robert F. Bales** (1916–2004) brought the study of small-group interaction to the laboratory. Bales and his colleagues developed a system of coding for social interaction in small groups, called **interaction process analysis** (IPA). It dealt initially with ways of determining whether groups and their members were task-oriented or relationship-oriented. The researchers later developed the methodology to identify patterns of behaviour such as dominant/submissive, friendly/unfriendly, and accepting of authority/non-accepting of authority.

Most sociologists today are not involved in studying small-group interaction, for several reasons. First, the work was very much the product of a structural-functionalist perspective, which has become a minority perspective in twenty-first-century sociology. Second, small-group studies at the time when they were popular seemed to lack a proper consideration of gender, "race," ethnicity, and other sociological factors that are now considered essential to any rigorous inquiry. Imagine how the dynamics of a group of women change when a man is part of the group. Imagine how the opportunities and strategies for leadership differ in a small group of women and a small group of men. And what if we were to bring "race" into the discussion? Third, many contemporary sociologists view the study of small groups—especially in a lab setting—as artificial.

Studying Social Interaction in Large Groups: An Introduction to Social Organization

So far in this chapter we've looked at status and role and how these serve to structure one-on-one and small-group interactions. Whenever we look at individuals and small groups, we're taking a microsociological approach. For the remainder of the chapter we'll be moving from micro to macro as we look at social organization from a bird's eye view.

When we think of the term *social organization*, we might think of the way a society and its institutions—the family, organized religion, the legal system, the government, and so on—are organized. What we seldom consider is that the basis for social organization, whether imagined or real, rests on a particular set of principles.

In the sociological literature, *social organization* is rarely defined, and when it is, it's often *conflated* (i.e. blended together) with the terms *social structure* or *social institution*, as though they were all synonymous. They are not. While social institutions *are* social structures and *are* socially organized, social structures and social organization are *not* social institutions. So, what is social organization?

We can think of **social organization** as the social and cultural *principles* around which people and things are structured, ordered, and categorized. In this way, we are able to speak about the social organization of cultures, of social institutions, or of corporations. For example, a community may be socially organized around the principle of **egalitarianism**, a social organization based on the equality of members; or, the community could be organized on the principle of hierarchy, a social organization based on clear, well-defined ranks or levels. (The Hindu caste system discussed earlier this chapter reflects this hierarchical model of social organization.)

Organizational Structure

Under the old European system of feudalism, which was a particular kind of social organization, a citizen owed allegiance to, in order, God, the king, the feudal lord, and finally, the country. Over time, this social organization was replaced, as European societies moved from being states organized around religion (**theocracies**) to **secular**, non-religious states, and from kingdoms or monarchies to democracies. With this new social organization known as democracy, the nation-state or country became the main focus of allegiance and loyalty. Consider this: when we go to war, we fight for our country more than we fight for our religion or our leader. And yet, in spite of the emotional feelings—pride, loyalty, sentimentality—that are aroused when we sing the national anthem or win an Olympic gold medal, Canada is an imagined and somewhat artificial geopolitical space. It is a large territory with a diverse population that is unified through symbols such as the anthem, the flag, and our Constitution. Canada is not a "natural" social form. It is, like any country, a socially organized invention based on certain collectively shared principles. Its organizing principles are upheld by shared cultural beliefs and maintained through a network of social relations. If you find this a challenging idea to wrap your head around, it might help you to think of it this way: for the vast majority of human history, there were no countries at all. The idea of countries was largely an invention of the twentieth century.

At the heart of organizing principles are the ways in which a culture produces knowledge about the world based on a particular **cosmology**. A cosmology is an account of the origin and ruling principles of the universe, especially the role of humans in relationship to non-humans (living and non-living). Cosmologies and corresponding myths are often seen as a high form of truth.

Indigenous cosmologies are rooted in the belief that all matter, both inanimate and animate, is interdependent: everything is connected. They emphasize the interdependence of humans and nature. Judeo-Christian and Islamic cosmology emphasizes human dominion over nature as decreed by God. This cosmology, together with the emergence of modern science beginning in the Enlightenment, has helped establish "control over nature" as an important organizing principle of our Western culture. Consider the fact that both sides of the climate change debate in some senses believe that humans control the environment. Those who deny that climate change is a problem believe that humans can easily minimize the effects of carbon emissions and manufacturing waste, whereas those who are concerned about global warming think that we are not controlling these effects well enough and must change our behaviour to minimize the impact.

The Study of Organizations

To recap: organizational principles are based on our knowledge or understanding of the world, which is informed by our cosmology. These principles determine not just how our culture and society are organized but how other social bodies are organized, whether we're talking about social institutions such as the family and education, or bureaucracies and corporations, or community-based organizations. What is important in the study of organizations is to distinguish both the level of organization and the level of analysis.

Interest in the sociological study of organizations picked up after Max Weber conducted his detailed work on bureaucracy, and again when the study of organizations filtered into the business sector and commerce degree programs that began to be offered at colleges and universities during the 1980s. The study of organizations shifted from the examination of social institutions to the examination of business corporations as a way to uncover more effective and efficient management practices. The result was an explosion of studies in the fields of **organizational theory** and **organizational behaviour** (see Mills & Simmons, 1995).

During the last twenty-five years, the study of organizational behaviour has expanded by integrating approaches from other disciplines. Anthropology, for

Maria Janick/Alamy Stock Photo

What principles make up the social organization of your college or university? Democracy versus hierarchy (e.g. in administration–faculty and faculty–student interaction)? Freedom versus strict control of discussion and debate? Commercialism? Elitism versus access? How would you detect the presence and influence of these factors?

instance, has contributed to the study of organizations through its understanding of corporations as communities in which an **organizational culture**, with "organizational rituals" and "symbolic acts," is an aspect of organizational dynamics. An *organizational ritual*, as defined by Islam and Zyphur, is "a form of social action in which a group's values and identity are publicly demonstrated or enacted in a stylized manner, within the context of a specific occasion or event " (2009, p. 116). TV shows such as *The Office* and *Parks and Recreation* and the comic strip *Dilbert* make fun of such organizational rituals as the office Christmas party, employee-of-the-month awards, "town hall" meetings, the company picnic, and the charity golf tournament—events intended to project a specific identity the organization wants to convey. A sociologist may also study the informal organization of a company to determine how decisions are made or how information actually flows—processes that may not quite follow the mandated, formal structure of the organization itself.

With the spread of globalization, there has been increased study of cross-cultural organizations, which are of particular interest to businesses and those who study organizational behaviour. In the 1980s, organizational structures based on models derived from the productive corporate culture of Japan were implemented in North America. They failed, however, in part because they did not account for the organizational principles of Japanese culture, which are more *collectivist* than the *individualist* organizational principles favoured in Canada and the United States. Organizational structures based on a *collective* model, in which employees work in teams, did not have the same success when applied to the competitive individualism found in North American business culture and society generally.

Much of the increase in organizational studies has been fuelled by Western capital, invested by companies in an effort to find ways to increase profits by managing employee behaviour and practices more efficiently. This has led to questions about the ethics of controlling worker behaviour, not to mention the inherent ethnocentric and capitalist assumptions in organizational theory given the context of global culture. These critiques have fostered the growth of **critical management studies**, which challenge traditional theories of management. Mills and Simmons (1995), for example, have challenged the assumptions of mainstream accounts of organization. They point out that there is little in the literature of organizational theory and behaviour that deals with "race," ethnicity, class, or gender, despite the high participation rates of women and visible minorities in the labour force. They also note that there is too little attention given to the impact organizations have on the social and psychic life of individuals and groups affected by organizations. Despite the demonstrated link between organizational life and lack of self-esteem, a sense of powerlessness, segregated work life, stress, physical injury, pay inequality, sexual harassment, and racism, standard organizational theory and behaviour studies continue to ignore it (Mills & Simmons, 1995).

Organizational Structure and Gender

In October 2017, a single tweet encouraged women to share their stories of workplace sexual harassment under the hashtag #MeToo. As the movement went viral, it exposed the prevalence of gendered sexual violence in patriarchal organizations ranging from corporate boardrooms and movie studios to political offices and churches. The issue brought calls to advance women to positions of power within organizations as one way to limit the ability of men in positions of authority to prey on female employees. And yet, as of 2018, there were fewer women in powerful executive positions within Canada's largest

Photo by FOX Image Collection via Getty Images

Television's favourite NYPD detectives get into the holiday spirit in a classic episode of *Brooklyn Nine-Nine*. Dressing up for Halloween is a plotline staple of office-based sitcoms. Can you think of other rituals, events, or symbolic acts that reflect the organizational culture where you have worked or where you go to school? What message do these organizational rituals communicate to or about the organization?

companies than there had been five years earlier. An analysis of companies on the TSX 60 index revealed that not one of Canada's 60 largest publicly traded companies had a woman as chief executive officer, and just three had a woman listed as its chief financial officer. Those figures were down from one and eight, respectively, in a similar study conducted in 2012 (Ligaya & Deschamps, 2018).

Why is this the case? It isn't that women are ineffective leaders. A summary of relevant research by the American Psychological Association (APA) found that women and men are equally effective as leaders (APA, 2006), yet their leadership styles tend to differ. Male leaders are more likely to adopt what the APA describes as a "command-and-control" approach, which emphasizes strong, central leadership that extends from the top of a hierarchy down through the ranks. Female leaders, in contrast, tend to adopt a transformational style of management, a more collaborative approach that revolves around coaching, mentorship, and shared decision-making (APA, 2006). Coincidentally, or not, the research showed that male leaders were more effective than female leaders in male-dominated organizations, while women were more effective when leading female-dominated organizations. We can surmise from this that there is a female organizational structure that differs from traditional male organizational structures. The former is more democratic and involves a greater distribution of power and responsibility, while the latter is more autocratic and hierarchical.

The military may provide the best example of a male organizational structure. Where might we see female social organization at play? In her study of feminist organizations, Carol Mueller (1995) identified three models that typify the kind of organizational structure that has developed in contrast to traditional, male forms:

1. **formal social movement organizations**, which are professional, bureaucratic, and inclusive, and which make few demands of their members (examples include organizations dedicated to basic women's rights)
2. **small groups or collectives**, which are organized informally, and which require large commitments of time, loyalty, and material resources from its members (examples

include publishing companies dedicated to promoting women authors)
3. **service-provider organizations**, which combine elements of both formal and small-group organizations (examples include organizations dedicated to specific women's rights, such as providing counselling services and protection to victims of domestic abuse).

Mueller found that these organizational forms varied in the degree to which they practised typical feminist organizational principles, such as inclusivity and democratic participation. She also found these forms combined in a variety of structural configurations ranging from coalitions to complex social movement communities.

> ### What Do YOU Think?
>
> 1. Why do you think inclusivity and shared decision making would be qualities favoured by feminist organizations? Why do you think these qualities would be absent from traditional organizations dominated by men?
> 2. Do you think that Indigenous forms of organization will provide similar challenges?

Bureaucracy

The Origins of Bureaucracy

As Israeli American sociologist Amitai Etzioni pointed out, "organizations [and bureaucracies] are not a modern invention" (1964, p. 1)—and that was over fifty years ago. In fact, we can trace the origins of the bureaucracy back nearly 5000 years, to a time when organized states and writing systems were just coming into existence.

As empires emerged and grew, administrative bureaucracies expanded at a pace to match imperial expansion. In Han Dynasty China (fifth century BCE), the bureaucratic system developed out of Confucius's concern with creating social stability, which required a system of administrators to ensure good

Jane Hynes

The Terra Nova Chapters is one of five book clubs active in the small town of Glovertown, New-foundland and Labrador. According to sociologist Elizabeth Long (2003), women use reading clubs to openly discuss their own experiences in the context of the books they're reading, and in this way consider the place of women in society. What makes the book club a typically female organization? And why aren't there more book clubs for men?

governance. Administrators were appointed based on the merit of examinations (i.e. written tests). What became known as the imperial examination system continued in China until the early twentieth century.

The term *bureaucracy* originated in eighteenth-century France and comes from the word *bureau*, meaning "writing desk"—in other words, the place where officials work. The cumbersome processes of bureaucracies are sometimes referred to as "red tape," which dates back to nineteenth-century Britain, when government officials used red ribbon to tie up official documents until they were needed. Red tape, then, refers to the slow procedures associated with acquiring and dispensing bureaucratic information. Most of us have encountered bureau-cratic red tape in our federal, provincial, or mu-nicipal agencies—when applying to replace a lost

passport or driver's licence, for instance—but this is not confined to government agencies. Many private companies, including banks, the cable company, your internet provider, maybe even your college or university admissions office, are known for their red tape. Trying to reset or recover a lost password can involve plenty of red tape. As we will see, despite their inefficiencies and the difficulties in changing bureaucratic organization to meet individual and societal needs, bureaucracies are necessary for the successful functioning of complex societies.

Bureaucracy and Formal Rationalization

Max Weber's extensive work on bureaucracy is still frequently cited today. It was part of his larger study of the process of rationalization—specifically, his examination of **formal rationalization** (or **rationality**). *Rationalization* is a term frequently used in business reports, where it serves as a euphemism for firing workers and cutting jobs in an effort to reduce costs and become more efficient. This is an example of formal rationalization, which, according to Weber, has four basic elements:

- efficiency
- quantification
- predictability
- control.

We will look at the implications of these terms shortly, in the section on McDonaldization.

Formal rationalization, with its emphasis on forms, differs from other models of rationalization, like **substantive rationalization**, which involves the substance of values and ethical norms. Organizations governed by substantive rationalization are constantly asking themselves, *are we reflecting our values?* By contrast, organizations governed by formal rationalization tend to ask, *have we instituted the most efficient or predictable forms in our organization?* Take, for example, Indigenous organizations. Democracy, spirituality, and respect for Elders are all important values among Indigenous people. Forms that reflect those values are open meetings, where anyone can speak and be listened to, and prayers spoken by Elders. How do you think Indigenous organizations at opposite ends of the substantive rationalization–formal rationalization spectrum would act?

Weber was critical of both formal rationalization and bureaucracy, arguing that the former led to the "irrationality of rationality" and that the latter was dehumanizing by nature. Workers within the rational, bureaucratic organization of various companies and political bodies came to be viewed as "cogs in the wheel," reminded frequently that they could always be replaced. You may feel similar effects even when you're not part of the bureaucracy but are confronted by the impersonal nature of its public face. When you're told, "Your call is important to us," you know that it isn't (see Laura Penny's *Your Call is Important to Us: The Truth about Bullshit, 2005*). These examples speak to the dehumanizing feelings we experience daily through our interactions with bureaucratic organizations.

The "irrationality of rationality" involves the "disenchantment of the world," an important concept

in Weber's writing. Weber believed that with the increase in formal rationalization, the West was becoming increasingly **disenchanted**—lacking in magic, fantasy, and mystery—which could only lead to further alienation on the part of individuals. Enchantment is a quality that cannot be efficient, quantified, predicted, or controlled. Disney's "Magic Kingdom," for instance, is anything but magical: it is a rationalized system of pre-packaged enchantment commodities—there are to be no surprises. Weber worried and warned about the oncoming danger of the "iron cage of rationality," meaning a world in which every aspect of life is controlled by the formal rationalization of bureaucracy, a world dehumanized and over-controlled.

The Evolution of Formal Rationalization

The Industrial Revolution, which occurred in the late eighteenth and early nineteenth centuries, was the starting point for the development of formal rationalization. **Francis Galton** (1822–1911), considered the father of modern statistical analysis, was a pioneer in developing methods to measure the capabilities and productivity of individuals. He had a natural love of numbers and made formal rationalization a part of his everyday life. An example: he spent many hours getting the quantities (temperature, volume, etc.) just right for the "perfect" pot of tea (he was English, after all).

Along these same lines, **Frederick W. Taylor** (1856–1915) developed the practice he referred to as **scientific management**. Based on "time-and-motion" studies, scientific management (later known as **Taylorism**) was designed to discover the *one best way* of doing any given job. Taylor and his team of "efficiency experts" studied the time, methods, and tools required for a proficient worker to do a particular job. His objective was to eliminate wasteful or "inefficient" (i.e. slow, non-productive) motions or movements. Frank Gilbreth, a follower of Taylor's, undertook an intensive study of a bricklayer's job and reputedly reduced the number of motions involved in laying a brick from 18 to just 5. Assembly line work also used Taylor's methods to the maximum efficiency, though Henry Ford is credited with making the assembly line an industry standard.

One of the weaknesses of Taylorism/scientific management is that it didn't allow the individual worker to develop a broad set of skills, because he or she was asked to perform a single set of actions over and over again. Workers often became alienated from their work, with little sense that they had anything to do with the overall manufactured product.

Taylorism, slightly modified, was still practised in North America during the 1980s and 1990s. At that time, the success of Japanese auto manufacturing prompted North American businesses to implement "non-Tayloristic" Japanese business practices in their training sessions. Among these practices was the team approach, which incorporated worker input and fostered the idea that workers could be involved in several stages of the manufacturing process, generating a greater sense of product ownership. (If you thought this might be an instance of substantive rationalization, you'd be right.) This approach was first adopted by car manufacturer Saturn, which, until the downturn in the automotive sector in 2008, was very successful, in large part because it managed to reduce the sense of alienation among its workers.

The McDonaldization of the World

George Ritzer, in *The McDonaldization of Society* (2004), draws on Weber's concept of formal rationalization in his conception of **McDonaldization**. McDonaldization is similar to "Disneyfication," "Walmartitis," and "Microsoftening"—in Ritzer's words, "the process by which the [rationalizing] principles of the fast-food restaurant are coming to dominate more and more sectors of American society as well as the rest of the world" (2004, p. 1).

Ritzer applies the four fundamental elements of Weber's formal rationalization—**efficiency, quantification, predictability,** and **control**—to his

Do you think you would be happier performing one task in the assembly of twenty vehicles or several tasks in the assembly of five? The first approach reflects formal rationalization principles such as maintaining quotas. The second reflects the substantive rationalization principle of worker ownership of the work and the product. Why do you think some instructors feel as though their college or university endorses the first of these two approaches to education?

examination of contemporary fast-food restaurants. To see how McDonaldization is affecting other areas of everyday life, let's apply his theory to the world of postsecondary education.

Efficiency relates to the streamlined movement in time and effort of people and things. This efficiency is achieved mainly by breaking up larger organizational tasks into smaller, repeated tasks performed by individuals who are separated from each other by a division of labour. Smaller tasks are often performed later on by machines rather than by people. It should be noted that efficiency has different meanings in the different layers of a social organization. What is efficient for a college administrator might not be efficient for a college professor (for example, the former finds efficiency in the networking of printers, rather than allowing the prof to use his own little printer and not wait in line when print requests are heavy—personal experience here). And being efficient in this way is not the same as being *effective*, although it's possible for a process to be both efficient and effective. Think of the potential differences between being an efficient teacher—one who teaches quickly and articulates a great number of concepts—and an effective teacher—one who successfully communicates to students all or almost all that is taught. A teacher can be one or the other, both, or none of the above. At college and university, the multiple-choice test is a classic example of bureaucratic efficiency: questions are often provided by the textbook's publisher, and they can be marked quickly or, if they're delivered online, graded automatically. But are they the most effective means of promoting and testing learning? Would you be surprised that the author of this textbook never uses multiple-choice questions?

Second, formal rationalization in bureaucracy involves the *quantification* of as many elements as possible. The efficiency, or "success," of the process is measured by the completion of a large number of quantifiable tasks. For instance, the success of call centres is primarily measured by how many calls are handled rather than how many clients are actually satisfied. When educational administrators pressure instructors to quantify the type and exact percentage of tests on a course syllabus, this is a type of formal rationalization—the logic being that if courses are equally quantified, then students are equally served. With bureaucratic education, administrators and instructors can quantify the number and length of interactions between students and professors through computer platforms that monitor such things as the number of e-mails and the number and length of "chats." In the classroom, instructors can monitor students by having them use electronic clickers to respond to questions, which is an attempt to counteract the impersonal nature of large, "efficient" lectures with increased and quantifiable electronic interaction.

Next, *predictability* means that administrators, workers, and clients all know what to expect from employees, underlings, colleagues, and companies; this is the "uniformity of rules." A Big Mac in Moscow is the same as a Big Mac in Calgary. You can wake up in a Holiday Inn anywhere in the world and not know where you are until you look out the window. Hollywood, too, is all about predictability—if you've seen one Will Ferrell movie, you've seen them all—and if you liked the last one, you'll be sure to see the next one. With the advent of rationalized, bureaucratic education, teachers are replaceable in the delivery of predictable, pre-packaged courses, and creative, innovative input is minimal. Students who have already taken a course can tell others almost exactly what to expect and what will be taught. Prepackaged online courses cut down on the time spent planning lessons, thus making class prep more "efficient," leading to what might be called the "silicon cage" of rationalization. However, in a recent lecture, culture critic Henry Giroux (former director of the McMaster Centre for Research in the Public Interest and a distinguished visiting professor at Ryerson) noted that it is the value of the indeterminate in education—in effect, the value of the unpredictable—and the free-flowing "don't know where this is going" instructor–class discussion that makes for an inspiring classroom experience. This creative process, however, is lost through formal rationalization and the imposition of predictability.

Finally, *control*, for Ritzer, is always hierarchical. He characterizes the hierarchical division of labour in the following passage:

> Bureaucracies emphasize control over people through the replacement of human judgment with the dictates of rules, regulations, and structures. Employees are controlled by the division of labor, which allocates to each office a limited number of well-defined tasks. Incumbents must do the tasks, and no others, in the manner prescribed by the organization. They may not, in most cases,

devise idiosyncratic ways of doing those tasks. Furthermore, by making few, if any, judgments, people begin to resemble human robots or computers. (2004, p. 27)

This control is exercised over both workers and clients. People who work at McDonald's are taught exactly what they have to do, while customers have their selection controlled by the menu board. Even the uncomfortable seating is part of the process, helping to control how long customers stay in the restaurant. We can see the formally rationalized, bureaucratic package at its most extreme in the following overview of material from a 1958 copy of the McDonald's operations manual, cited in John F. Love's *McDonald's: Behind the Arches* (1986):

It told operations *exactly* how to draw milk shakes, grill hamburgers, and fry potatoes. It specified *precise* cooking times for all products and temperature settings for all equipment. It fixed *standard* portions on every food item, down to the *quarter ounce* of onions placed on each hamburger patty and the *thirty-two slices per pound* of cheese. It specified that french fries be cut at *nine thirty-seconds of an inch* thick. And it defined quality *controls* that were unique to food service, including the disposal of meat and potato products that were held more than *ten minutes* in a serving bin. (quoted in Ritzer, 2004, p. 38)

As with people who have only ever eaten French fries from McDonald's, never real "chips" cut and prepared on site, students experiencing today's increasingly bureaucratized education might become less able to judge the quality of what they are receiving.

Telling It Like It Is

Little Boxes: Mass Produced Suburban Communities

After the end of World War II, which marked the start of North America's "baby boom," there was a fairly severe housing shortage in both Canada and the United States. One response was the development of mass-produced suburban communities. The first and standard-setting effort in this regard was the series of "Levittowns" built in the eastern US. Between 1947 and 1951, Levitt and Sons built 17,447 houses on Long Island, New York, creating an instant community of about 75,000 people. This model would soon be reproduced in Pennsylvania and then New Jersey. The company began by building warehouses for their supplies, their own workshops for wood and plumbing manufacture, and gravel and cement plants. Ritzer describes the rationalization of the house-building process in the following excerpt:

The actual construction of each house followed a series of rigidly defined and rationalized steps. For example, in constructing the wall framework, the workers did no measuring or cutting; each piece had been cut to fit. The siding for a wall consisted of 73 large sheets of Colorbestos, replacing the former requirement of 570 small shingles. All houses were painted under high pressure, using the same two-tone scheme—green on ivory.... The result, of course, was a large number of nearly identical houses produced quickly at low cost. (Ritzer, 2004, p. 36)

The owners of the construction company knew that their employees did not enjoy many of the intrinsic rewards experienced by skilled independent tradespeople, but they felt that the extrinsic rewards of money would make up for that:

The same man does the same thing every day, despite the psychologists. It is boring; it is bad; but the reward of the green stuff seems to alleviate the boredom of the work. (A. Levitt, 1952, quoted in Ritzer, 2004, pp. 35–6)

This kind of rationalized uniformity can come at the cost of oppression of minoritized people. In

Formal Rationalization in the Digital Age

In their wildest dreams, Francis Galton and Frederick Taylor could not have imagined a world where a hungry customer could, from their home, place an order for food, without having to speak to anyone, and have it delivered within 30 minutes by an independent contractor on wheels or on foot. The internet allows for an enormous degree of formal rationalization. And in spite of Weber's warnings about the "iron cage of rationality," we welcome it into our lives. We shop online in growing numbers, reducing the need to make time-consuming trips to the mall. We can leverage the reach of the internet to crowdsource start-up companies or raise funds for the needy, as concerned global citizens did for the families of the victims of the Humboldt Broncos bus crash. We are nearing a time when we may never again need to set foot in a grocery store, because our provider of groceries and other household products, tracking our daily consumption, will replenish our stocks automatically, via drone. I plan to be the last holdout against this trend, because I like going to stores, handling the wares, speaking with the sales staff. Although, there is a small family-run business in the town where I live, whose owner, nearing retirement age, will eventually pass the business on to his son, a poor manager and lazy worker who does not seem particularly interested in extending his father's legacy. The business's better employees have no incentive to overachieve because, not being part of the family, they can never rise to the top of the small corporate hierarchy. Could a measure of formal rationalization save it as our purchasing moves increasing online?

An Author's POV

the case of Levittown, the covenants (agreements signed by homeowners with the developer) included racial segregation. Blacks were not allowed. The story of how one family "conspired" to bring a black family into Levittown, and how it was resisted, sometimes violently, by neighbours and social organizations illustrates this (see Kushner, 2009). This leads to the question: Does extreme rationalization of organization lead automatically to social oppression?

In Canada, the neighbourhood of Don Mills, constructed during the early 1950s, became known as Toronto's "first planned community." I grew up there beginning in 1956. It had the city's first shopping centre, the first Country Style doughnut shop, and the first Shopper's Drug Mart. As a teenager, I was a "plaza boy"—a term for someone who spent his leisure hours hanging around the mall. Famous Canadians from this community include comedian Rick Green (of *The Red Green Show*), "Martha" of the 1980s band Martha and the Muffins, and singer and writer Dan Hill. It also produced an outstanding Canadian sociologist: Neil Guppy of the University of British Columbia. And yours truly, of course.

Did I feel alienated by the rationalism of my planned community? I definitely grew up to be a rebel, pushing back against anything I thought confined me. I grew my hair long (which it still is, although on top it is long gone), and the bands that I was in were blues bands whose lyrics reflected the trials of life in the south side of Chicago more than the suburbs of Toronto. I generally disliked conformity in its many forms, and that is still true. I may have been a product of the times (the 1960s) as much as I was a product of the environment (the suburbs), but that the planned community in which I was raised was a significant contributor to my socialization is undeniable.

What Do YOU Think?

Think of a suburb you're familiar with. What aspects of it do you think reflect formal rationalization or "McDonaldization"? Do you think these qualities are beneficial or not?

xijian/istockphoto

Smartphone: check. Fitbit: check. Were he alive today, what would Weber say about rationalizing technologies that keep us connected, on time, and on pace at all times?

Social Order through Social Organization

Social organization and social stability are fundamental aspects of the human condition. We couldn't really dispense of all social organization without falling into chaos. However, the foundational principles and forms of organization themselves can have a profound effect on society and the lives of individuals, and so they deserve to be critically examined and questioned.

As we have seen, social organization impacts everything from the environment (through our relationship with nature) to the places where we work, study, and live, where the dehumanizing effects of formal rationalization sometimes prevail. Large, bureaucratized organizations, instead of serving the needs and interests of people, often dictate our values and interactions (think of your most recent shopping experience at a mall or big box store). And the perils of bureaucracy and formal rationalization that Weber warned of long ago have only gotten worse, if we use Ritzer's work on McDonaldization as an indicator. The inefficiency of efficiency seems to dominate organizations from the military and businesses to hospitals and postsecondary institutions. Red tape, long lineups, quantity over quality, apathy, and even violent reactions (going "postal," road rage, fighting with the registrar's office or school board) have become the norm both within and outside of organizations and bureaucracies. In short, we need the **social order** that organizational structures promote, but there is evidence that bureaucracy has lost sight of the "greater good" of a greater number and a broader world. Through a perversion of means and ends, in which the means become ends in and of themselves, organizational bureaucracies become increasingly self-serving, behaving as though they were self-sustaining communities with no meaningful positive social connections to the other citizens of the planet.

Wrap it Up

Summary

While there is a lot to learn in this chapter, a lot of terminology to remember, I would stress one basic thing. There is more choice involved in both social interaction and social organization than what might seem to be "out there." Often that choice is between oppressive forms that have been practised over years and less oppressive, and more empowering, ways that have been little tried, or that have come from groups outside the mainstream. The oppressive forms are not as "natural" as they may seem, especially if you have grown up never knowing a time before we had Netflix to tell us what to watch.

It is important to see that much of the frustration that we feel on a daily basis flows from the fact that we lead complicated lives. This complication arises from the increasing array of statuses we have and the many roles (including virtual roles we maintain online) that we perform at the same time. Think of the way our master statuses change as we go through life. Shifts are not easy. At the same time, we all deal with large organizations—banks, service providers, the local motor vehicle office—that often frustrate us with their lack of flexibility and human contact. Studying organizational behaviour, as we have done in this chapter, should, hopefully, enable you to see these personal frustrations through the lens of the sociological imagination. Don't take it personally—it's not just your call that isn't important to them, but everybody's.

Think Back

Questions for Critical Review

1. Describe your own status set. How does your status set change over the course of a day, as you move, say, from home to school to the coffee shop to work to Facebook, and so on? Which of your statuses are ascribed and which ones are achieved? What would you consider your master status to be?

2. Is gender an achieved or ascribed status? What about sexuality? (Consider returning to this question after you've read Chapter 9, on gender and sexuality, to see if your perspective has changed at all.)

3. In Chapter 1 we considered Goffman's dramaturgical approach, the idea that people behave differently depending on whether they're on the "front stage" or the "back stage." How can this idea help us understand the various social roles associated with a particular status? Consider the role set associated with the status of high school teacher. Which of these roles are performed on the front stage? Which ones are performed behind the scenes?

4. Identify and describe the social roles associated with an online status you're familiar with—gamer, blogger, Snapchat poster, movie reviewer, etc. How do certain roles—competitor, critic, friend, etc.—differ depending on whether the status they belong to is online or offline?

5. It's time for your annual performance review, where you will be sitting down with your boss to discuss your accomplishments over the past year and your goals for the future. How might you and your manager have different definitions of this situation?

6. At some point in your school career, you probably took part in a school concert. Consider the school concert as an organizational ritual. What goals is it designed to achieve?

7. Take a social organization that you are part of—a family, business, religious organization, or school. How do formal and substantive rationalization influence these organizations?

8. Music, television, and movie streaming services use your media consumption habits to formulate playlists and recommendations for you. Does this example of formal rationalization improve your life or diminish its enchantment?

Read On

Suggested Print and Online Resources

Amitai Etzioni (1975), *A Comparative Analysis of Complex Organizations*, rev. edn (New York: Free Press).

- In this landmark text, sociologist Amitai Etzioni examines a wide range of social organizations, from prisons, hospitals, and schools to communes, churches, and businesses.

***Book Club* (2015) (Winnipeg, MB: National Screen Institute), www.nsi-canada.ca/2015/05/book-club; Elizabeth Long (2003), *Book Clubs: Women and the Uses of Reading in Everyday Life* (Chicago: University of Chicago Press).**

- The short, 15-minute video by Canadian filmmaker Kate Yorga imagines what book clubs would be like if they operated more like Fight Club—or, in sociological terms, what happens when the principles of male organizational structure are applied to a typically female organization. Watch it in conjunction with Elizabeth Long's qualitative study of 77 all-female reading groups in Texas.

George Ritzer (2014), *The McDonaldization of Society*, 8th edn (Thousand Oaks, CA: Sage); John F. Love (1995), *McDonald's: Behind the Arches*, rev. edn (Toronto: Bantam).

- Ritzer's work is a classic and readable study of how the means and methods of McDonald's are reproduced in many areas of our lives. Read it in conjunction with John F. Love's history of the fast-food burger empire.

Laura Penny (2016), *Your Call Is Important to Us: The Truth about Bullshit*, reprint edn (New York: Broadway Books).

- Penny's work is a refreshing look at how corporate behaviour says one thing but really means another.

Howie's Home Page, www.howardsbecker.com

- Now in his nineties, Howard Becker, the sociologist who brought us labelling theory, has his own website, which features news and views, along with photos and—this may be of greatest interest to you—an invitation to contact him if you are writing a paper about him or need to prepare for an exam. This may be the best sociological help desk ever.

Mark Barrowcliffe (2009), *The Elfish Gene: Dungeons, Dragons and Growing Up Strange* (New York: Soho).

- This memoir of how a British man spent his youth playing Dungeons & Dragons provides some insights into socialization, virtual status, and interactive role-playing games before the age of the internet.

"Maysoon Zayid: I Got 99 Problems . . . Palsy Is Just One," www.youtube.com/watch?v=buRLc2eWGPQ

- In this 15-minute TED Talk, Maysoon Zayid, an Arab American comedian with cerebral palsy, promises that "if there was an oppression Olympics, I'd win the gold medal." Watch the talk and see if you can trace her evolving statuses. Which would you say is now her master status?

***Paperland: The Bureaucrat Observed*, www.nfb.ca/film/paperland**

- Students may enjoy this one-hour 1979 National Film Board documentary by Donald Brittain, which criticizes "the absurdities of bureaucratic behaviour . . . with humour and irreverence." The film targets the originators of bureaucratic practices, not those tasked with implementing them.

Robert Kanigel (2005), *The One Best Way: Frederick Winslow Taylor and the Enigma of Efficiency*, paperback edn (Cambridge, MA: MIT Press).

- This readable introduction to Taylor's life and ideas gives a good account of the effects of Taylorism.

Deviance and Crime

6

Reading this chapter will help you to ...

- Avoid some of the leading misunderstandings of the term *deviant*.
- Distinguish between *overt* and *covert* characteristics of deviance.
- Discuss the reasons that deviance is sometimes associated with ethnicity, culture, "race," gender, sexual orientation, disability, and class.
- Explain how deviance is socially constructed and contested.
- Define some of the leading theories of criminal deviance, including *strain theory*, *subcultural theory*, *labelling theory*, and *social control theory*.
- Discuss recent trends in Canada's crime rate.

For Starters

Greta Thunberg and Uncomfortable Deviance

Greta Thunberg is a deviant. She knowingly participated in demonstrably deviant behaviour. This is not to say that either she or her behaviour is good or bad. It is just to say that she did something different, engaging in unexpected activities that fall outside the boundaries of what is considered normal behaviour.

And it made people very uncomfortable.

Here is her story. On Friday 20 August 2018, Greta Thunberg, then 15 years old, skipped school to sit outside the parliament building in the Swedish capital of Stockholm. There she handed out leaflets that read, "I am doing this because you adults are shitting on my future." Beside her where she sat was a large, hand-painted sign that read *Skolstrejk för Klimatet*, which translates as "School-Strike for Climate." She continued her strike for 20 days. In September, she started striking just on Fridays.

What made this deviant? First, it was different from what other schoolchildren were doing. Greta Thunberg was not acting on behalf of any group or organization, or because her parents wanted her to. Her actions were her own, and they deviated from what is considered normal behaviour for a person of her age and position in society.

Second, her behaviour was subversive. In Chapter 3, I described the dominant culture as middle-aged and male. Not only does Greta fall outside that culture, but in criticizing adults who were failing to act—and, by extension, adults in positions of power—she was acting in opposition to the mainstream culture. Her actions inspired thousands of teenage students in Europe and Australia to go on a similar strikes, and in May 2019, there was a nationwide Friday strike in Canada.

Michael Campanella/The Guardian/Eyevine/Redux

Following Greta Thunberg's initial protests came predictable attempts to discredit her. Deviance is hard to ignore, and because it makes people uncomfortable, a common strategy is to push it further toward the margins. And so, there were accusations that Greta was not acting independently but was part of a larger, carefully orchestrated campaign or conspiracy. There were hints that she was receiving attention mainly because she is on the autism spectrum. But then, when attempts to diminish her failed, something interesting happened. She was invited in November to give a TED Talk in Stockholm, and a month later to address the United Nations at a climate change conference. In January, she travelled by train to Davos to speak at the World Economic Forum, and in February she was asked to address the European Union's Economic and Social Committee. Large political and economic organizations made up of the very kinds of powerful adults that Greta was criticizing were now trying to align themselves with her. This is another strategy for dealing with deviance: absorb it into the mainstream where it is less likely to be noticed.

What Do YOU Think?

The case of Greta Thunberg may remind you of the students of Marjory Stoneman Douglas High School in Parkland, Florida, after the shooting deaths of students there in 2018. How are the cases similar? Would you consider the actions of the Parkland students deviant?

Introduction:
What Is Deviance?

Many people, when they hear the word *deviance*, think of behaviour that is immoral, illegal, perverse, or just "wrong." But **deviance** is better thought of as a neutral term. It simply means "straying from what is normal." It does not mean that the deviant—the one engaging in deviance—is necessarily bad, criminal, perverted, "sick," or inferior in any way. The word is based on the Latin root -*via*-, meaning "path." To deviate is simply to go off the common path.

When looking at deviant behaviour it helps to distinguish between **overt characteristics** of deviance—the actions or qualities taken as explicitly violating the cultural norm—and **covert characteristics**, the unstated qualities that might make a particular group a target for sanctions. Covert characteristics can include age, ethnic background, "race," sexual orientation, sex, and degree of physical and mental ability. In an example presented on pages 174–5, the *overt* characteristics of the young people associated with "zoot suit" culture include their clothing, hairstyle, and taste in music—fashions that violated the cultural norm. The *covert* characteristics are age (they were mostly teens) and race (they were mostly Latino or African American).

Deviance, then, comes down to how we define "the norm." It is also about *who* defines the norm, and the power of those who share the norm to define it and treat others as inferior or dangerous. And we must recognize that just as the norm changes—over time and across cultures—so does deviance.

When we invoke "the norm," we are usually referring to what we defined in Chapter 3 as the **dominant culture**. As you read through the different sections of this chapter, keep in mind that the dominant culture in Canada is white, English-speaking, of European heritage, Christian, male, middle-class, middle-aged, urban, heterosexual, able-bodied, and without visible signs of mental disability. Remember that behaviour that deviates from that of the dominant culture may be labelled deviant, but that doesn't make it wrong.

Another term to revisit here is **subculture**. This is a group existing within a larger culture and possessing beliefs or interests at variance with those of the dominant culture. Subculture is the focal point of one of two early theories of deviance that we will examine later in detail.

Kim Valliere/Radio-Canada

In 2016, the Toronto Raptors commissioned graffiti murals in six Canadian neighbourhoods, including the Glebe in Ottawa. Does graffiti lose some of its deviant quality when it is commissioned and features sponsor logos?

Conflict Deviance

Deviance Is Contested across Cultures

What gets labelled deviant differs from culture to culture. Consider tattoos, for example. In mainstream Western culture, tattoos have been associated negatively with certain marginalized groups considered deviant. These groups include prisoners, sailors, prostitutes, and performers in circus sideshows (sometimes called "freak shows"). But around the world, tattooing is a longstanding and highly respected practice among many cultural groups, including the Aborigines of Australia, the Austronesian peoples of the Pacific Islands, and Canada's Inuit. Among some of these cultures the practice died out during generations of colonial oppression. Ashleigh Gaul (2014) describes how, in the North, tattooing the face of young women went from being "a widespread rite of passage and a source of Inuit pride to a mark of shamanism in a Christianized community." The practice has recently undergone a revival in Northern communities, sparked by young

Quick Hits

Getting Deviance Straight

- **Deviant** just means *different from the norm, the usual.*
- **Deviant** *does not mean bad, wrong, perverted, sick, or inferior* in any way.
- **Deviant** is a category that *changes with time, place, and culture.*
- Definitions of **deviance** often *reflect power.*

Indigenous people and cross-cultural contact with interested young people of dominant Western cultures. They view tattooing both as a link to the past and a way to display how "modern" they are.

Tattooing highlights three important aspects of deviance. First, deviance differs across cultures: what one culture defines as deviant may be considered a venerable practice in another. Second, deviance changes over time. In the North, tattooing was a respectable practice for generations before becoming a cultural taboo. In mainstream Western culture, tattoos have now become so common that they may no longer be seen as deviant. We may in fact have hit "peak tattoo": when your mom suggests getting matching mother–daughter tats, the practice loses some of the value it once held as an act of rebellion. Third, deviance is contested: whether something is

CBC

Marjorie Tahbone, an Inupiaq woman from Alaska, chose to have three vertical lines inked onto her chin to signify her coming of age, reviving an ancestral tradition that, she says, "a lot of the elders don't really know or understand because it's been asleep for so long" (Hanlon, 2015). Why do you think she decided to get this this traditional tattoo when previous generations did not? Is this tattoo more or less deviant than the tattoo you might see on a Hells Angels gang member? A mom at spin class? A Holocaust survivor?

or is not considered deviant can become a source of conflict among people within a community. This can have unfortunate social consequences when a dominant culture condemns as deviant the practices of a minority culture and, by extension, the minority culture itself.

Deviance Is Contested within Cultures

Definitions of deviance differ not only *across but within* cultures. It is true that the culture defines deviance—that deviance is essentially a social or cultural construct—but it is important to remember that there is seldom total or even near total agreement within a culture as to what is deviant. Deviance, like other elements in a culture, can be **contested**: not everyone agrees.

When deviance is contested, we have a situation known as **conflict deviance**. Conflict deviance is a disagreement among groups over whether or not something is deviant. It may be a sign that a practice long condemned as deviant is gaining wider acceptance in mainstream culture. Consider marijuana use, for example. In Canada, marijuana was made a prohibited substance in the 1920s. Those who flouted the law were cast as deviant: they faced public condemnation and arrests by police. During the late twentieth century, efforts to have marijuana possession and use decriminalized made cannabis a focal point of conflict deviance. In 2001, the government made it legal to possess small amounts of marijuana for medicinal purposes. In 2012, a Canadian Community Health Survey suggested that 3.4 million people aged 15 and older had used marijuana at least once in the previous year, a finding that went a long way toward changing public perceptions and normalizing the practice. Debates over whether possession of small amounts of marijuana for recreational use should be legalized entered the mainstream in 2015, when the Liberal Party of Canada successfully campaigned on a promise to legalize recreational cannabis use. It is now legal to buy and sell marijuana, and as of writing, brick-and-mortar cannabis retailers are open across Canada. This won't convince all Canadians that smoking up is a safe, responsible, and respectable activity, meaning that it is still a subject of conflict deviance.

The Point Is...

Being Deviant Is Not about What Is Right or Left

Deviance is not always a random violation of norms. It can be carefully signified by symbols and gestures set out in "the rules," which may be written or unwritten.

I discovered this in the 1980s, when I was sharpening my writing skills and supplementing my income by penning articles about my sociological insights for local newspapers and magazines. I had an idea to write a piece on men who wear earrings.

The prevailing style of dress for young men in the 1980s was very conservative. The trend was known as "preppy," and it was characterized by polo shirts in pastel shades of pink or green tucked into khaki trousers, with an argyle sweater draped over the shoulders like a cape (don't ask me why). Preppies were clean-cut: there were no hipster beards, and even stubble was an odd choice (until it was popularized in the show *Miami Vice*). Anyone with a tattoo was assumed to be a sailor on shore leave or a "skinhead," a member of the anti-preppy set inspired by British punk rock bands like The Clash. For a man, to wear a single stud earring was an act deeply imbued with deviance.

My choice of newspaper topic was deeply personal: I was 40 years old and living on my own, between marriages, and I was thinking of getting an ear piercing myself. But first I had to be sure of the rules. For years, it was commonly believed that a left ear pierced meant drug dealer, while a right ear pierced meant gay. Both were deviant: drug dealing was, of course, illegal, but gay men were cruelly persecuted during the 1980s, partly because of the perceived association between homosexuality and AIDS. In the 1980s, it took more courage to admit you were gay than to admit you were a drug dealer.

The hypothesis I adopted for my article was that the vast majority of the men I observed with pierced ears would have their piercings on the left side—that the many who were not actually drug dealers would choose to signify their deviant nonconformity by aligning themselves with street criminals rather than with gay men. Sure enough, over the months that I observed men with pierced ears, I saw that rule followed religiously. I took note of over 100 men wearing earrings, and all of them had the earring on the left ear. A few had earrings in the right ear as well, but the showier of the earrings (they never matched) was always on the left side.

Having these quantitative data in hand, I confidently had my left ear pierced, following convention so that my act of deviance would be interpreted the way I intended. Today, I wonder if my small gesture of subverting social norms was really so rebellious, given how self-conscious I was about the decision. What do you think: can you follow the rules and still be deviant?

Social Constructionism versus Essentialism

One of the reasons deviance is contested has to do with the differing viewpoints of social constructionism and essentialism. **Social constructionism** is the idea that certain elements of social life—including deviance, but also gender, "race," and other social characteristics—are not natural but artificial, created by society or culture. **Essentialism**, on the other hand, reflects the view that there is something natural, true, universal, and therefore objectively determined about these characteristics.

When we look at certain social phenomena, we can see that each of these two viewpoints applies to some degree. Alcoholism, for instance, is a physical condition, so it has something of an essence or essential nature. However, whom we label an alcoholic and how we as a society perceive an alcoholic (i.e. as someone who is morally weak or as someone with

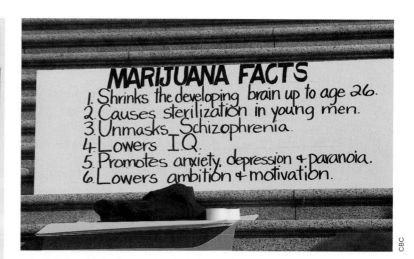

Fast-forward to October 2018, when a coalition of groups concerned about the health risks of marijuana voice their concerns in Vancouver on the very day recreational cannabis use became legal. What overt and covert aspects of deviance are raised in the poster?

Reefer Madness (1936) came out as a propaganda film at a time when exaggerated accounts of the drug's dangerous effects were causing panic among North American parents and lawmakers. It continued to be shown as an educational film in the 1940s and 1950s, in spite of its misinformation and low-budget production values. During the early 1970s it made a comeback among college students (personal experience) and became a cult classic thanks to its dated message, its lurid depiction of drug use, and its campy acting. It returned again in on 20 April 2004, or 4/20: a date circled on the calendars of many pot users.

a mental illness) is a social construct, one that will vary from society to society.

The interplay between social constructionism and essentialism receives excellent treatment from Erving Goffman in his study of stigma and deviance (1963). A **stigma** is a human attribute that is seen to discredit an individual's social identity. It might be used to label the stigmatized individual or group as deviant. Goffman identified three types of *stigmata* (the plural of *stigma*):

- **bodily stigmata**
- **moral stigmata**
- **tribal stigmata**.

He defined them in the following way:

First there are abominations of the body—the various physical deformities. Next there are blemishes of individual character perceived as weak will, domineering or unnatural passions, treacherous and rigid beliefs, and dishonesty, these being inferred from a known record of, for example, mental disorder, imprisonment, addiction, alcoholism, homosexuality, unemployment, suicidal attempts, and radical political behavior. Finally there are the tribal stigma of race, nation, and religion, these being stigma that can be transmitted through lineages and equally contaminate all members of a family. (Goffman, 1963, p. 4)

Quick Hits

How Canadians and Americans Differ on Issues of Conflict Deviance

In July 2016, American research company Gallup and Canadian research company Abacus surveyed North Americans to gauge their views on certain topics that, sociologically speaking, we might call matters of conflict deviance. Here are the percentages of Americans and Canadians who considered the listed behavio(u)rs morally right:

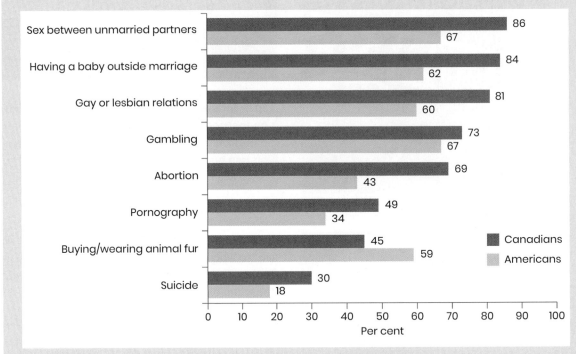

Source: Based on Bruce Anderson & David Coletto (2016, July 9), Canadians' Moral Compass Set Differently From That of Our Neighbours to the South; Abacus Data: https://abacusdata.ca/canadians-moral-compass-set-differently-from-that-of-our-neighbours-to-the-south/

According to this definition, bodily stigmata exist physically, putting them within the essentialist framework. And yet, how we define "blemished" is socially constructed: think of descriptions such as "too fat" or "too thin." People in a variety of societies "deform" their bodies to look beautiful according to social standards—for instance, by engaging in extreme dieting and exercising, by piercing their bodies, or, in certain cultures, by putting boards on their children's heads to give them a sloping forehead, all to achieve socially constructed standards of beauty and avoid certain bodily stigmata associated with deviance. Meanwhile, people who hear voices and see what is not physically present may be considered religious visionaries in some cultures,

but they may be thought to require psychiatric treatment in others, where the tendency to experience visions is constructed as a moral stigma. Racializing groups based on their ethnicity or religion is another social process, one that give rise to tribal stigmata: national identity is a social construct open to change over time, and a religion given privilege and respect in one society is very likely to be cast as deviant in another.

In this textbook, I take a view of deviance that is more social-constructionist than essentialist. Following Howard Becker's classic work *Outsiders* (1963), I do not see deviance as being inherently "bad," conformity to a norm being inherently "good." Instead, I generally follow the rule that, in Becker's words,

You can see that deviance is contested along national lines, but within Canada, deviance is also contested along age lines:

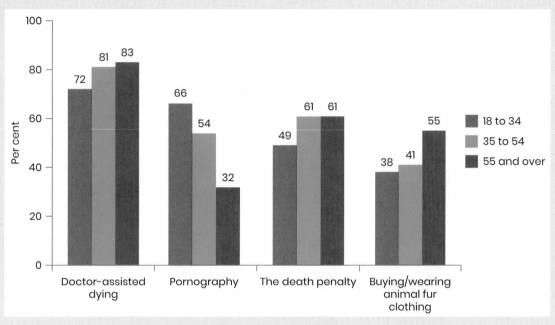

Source: Based on Bruce Anderson & David Coletto (2016, July 9), Canadians' Moral Compass Set Differently From That of Our Neighbours to the South; Abacus Data: https://abacusdata.ca/canadians-moral-compass-set-differently-from-that-of-our-neighbours-to-the-south/

What Do YOU Think?

How do you account for the difference in scores between Canadians and Americans? How much of the difference do you think has to do with the greater presence of evangelical Christianity in the United States?

social groups create deviance by making the rules, whose infraction constitutes deviance, and by applying those rules to particular people and labelling them as outsiders. . . . Deviance is *not a quality* of the act the person commits, but rather a consequence of the application by others of rules and sanctions to an "offender." (Becker, 1963, pp. 8–10)

The Other

An important concept in the sociological study of deviance is "the Other," or "Otherness." **The Other** is an image constructed by the dominant culture to

characterize subcultures; it may also be used by a colonizing nation to describe the colonized. When the United States took over Haiti (between 1915 and 1934), Hollywood and the Catholic Church helped to make deviant the native religion of the Haitians by casting it as "Other." Voodoo, which combines elements of Catholic ritual with traditional African magical and religious rites, became an example of how Haitians deviated from "civilized" norms. Along with sympathy and aid for Haiti following the January 2010 earthquake came criticism of Haitians, mostly in the conservative media, for their "fatalistic" or "superstitious" views and adherence to voodoo, which, some critics argued, made the people incapable of helping themselves. The

KatarzynaBialasiewicz/iStockphoto

Feminist critics of pornography say it degrades women and encourages sexual violence. A counter-argument states that by validating women's sexuality, some sexually explicit materials (characterized as "ethical pornography") can be empowering. Assess pornography as an issue of conflict deviance. Can there ever be "ethical" porn?

"Other" label, once applied, can be extremely difficult to erase.

The Other can be depicted as mysterious, mystical, or mildly dangerous, but somehow it is ultimately cast as inferior. **Edward Said**, in his discussion of **Orientalism**, characterized the West's treatment of the Middle East as the creation of an Other. The dominant culture in Canada typically defines "Indigenous" as Other. English Canada has portrayed French Canada the same way. In "slacker movies," written and directed by men and aimed at underachieving, socially inept, young white men, "woman" is constructed as an Other.

Deviant behaviour, once it has been associated with Otherness, is often subject to negative sanctions or punishment. But should deviant behaviour be punished? Certain acts of deviance, those that fall under our criminal justice system, are considered illegal and have sanctions attached, ranging from

a judge's warning to fines and jail time for more serious offences. But remember that deviance is not synonymous with criminality: it simply means anything outside the norm. Young people trying to establish their independence and individuality will often breach societal norms when it comes to fashion and style of dress. This can make them targets of the negative sanction of *bullying*—aggressive behaviour that includes shaming, ridiculing, physical attacks, and generally having unwanted attention drawn to their Otherness. Should this kind of deviance be punished?

Children with allergies may be targeted for deviance: they differ from the norm and make up a minority of the population of children. Although school boards are increasingly making efforts to accommodate their difference (e.g. by prohibiting classmates from bringing peanut-contaminated products and certain other foods in their lunches), these measures draw attention to

The Point Is . . .

A Comic Strip Contributed to the Social Construction of a Deviant Group

An instructive case of deviance labelling and sanctioning surrounds the "Zoot Suit Riots" that occurred in June 1943 in Los Angeles, California. The targets were racialized groups—young African American and Latino men—who were convenient targets for wartime tension.

In the early 1940s, Los Angeles was undergoing rapid change. The city's population was growing, and its demographics were changing. Large numbers of Mexicans and African Americans were coming to the city. Teenagers made up a large share of the population, as older men and women had gone off to join the war effort. With a surplus of well-paying jobs left available by older brothers and sisters drafted into the military, the young people who remained made money that they were able to spend on music and clothes. These teens—black and Latino males in particular—adopted a unique style of dress, a distinctive haircut (the "duck tail," or "duck's ass"), and a musical style that were countercultural. The music was jazz, rooted in the African American experience and only slowly gaining general acceptance in the United States. The dancing (the jitterbug) was more sexual than dancing of the 1930s. The clothing was the zoot suit: a jacket with broad shoulders and narrow waist, ballooned pants with "reet pleats," "pegged cuffs," and striking designs. Participants in zoot-suit culture swaggered with a distinctive bold strut and posing stance, and communicated with new slang words unknown to parents and other adults.

How did the zoot suit get labelled as deviant? The main media vehicle was the comic strip *Li'l Abner*, by Al Capp. In a time before television, comic strips were a major part of popular media. *Li'l Abner,* with maybe 50 million readers a day, was one of the most popular strips of the time. Its influence is difficult to overstate.

Al Capp identified the zoot suit as a target for his negative sanctioning humour. From 11 April to 23 May 1943, the strip presented the story of "Zoot-Suit Yokum," an invention of US clothing manufacturers bent on taking over the country politically and economically. In Capp's strip, these industrialists had conspired to create a national folk hero, who would popularize their zoot suits by performing feats of bravery clad in this signature costume. The triumph of conservative clothiers was proclaimed in the third frame of the 19 May strip,

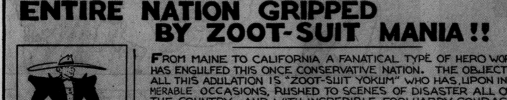

ENTIRE NATION GRIPPED BY ZOOT-SUIT MANIA!!

FROM MAINE TO CALIFORNIA A FANATICAL TYPE OF HERO WORSHIP HAS ENGULFED THIS ONCE CONSERVATIVE NATION. THE OBJECT OF ALL THIS ADULATION IS "ZOOT-SUIT YOKUM" WHO HAS, UPON INNUMERABLE OCCASIONS, RUSHED TO SCENES OF DISASTER ALL OVER THE COUNTRY—AND, WITH INCREDIBLE, FOOLHARDY COURAGE, PERFORMED AMAZING FEATS OF STRENGTH AND HEROISM. NATURALLY, "ZOOT-SUIT YOKUM" HAS BECOME THE IDOL OF ALL RED-BLOODED YOUNG AMERICANS—AND THIS IDOL-WORSHIP HAS LED MILLIONS OF MEN TO IMITATE HIS PECULIAR COSTUME, KNOWN AS THE "ZOOT SUIT." CLOTHING STORES REPORT THAT THERE HAS BEEN A MAD RUSH TO BUY "ZOOT SUITS"—WHILE THE REGULAR MEN'S CLOTHING MARKET HAS HIT ITS WORST SLUMP IN ONE HUNDRED YEARS.

ZOOT-SUIT YOKUM

Continued

Los Angeles police detain a group of young men in their zoot suits, under suspicion of being part of the riots of 1943. Do they look like troublemakers to you?

which displayed the mock headline: "GOVERNOR ISSUES ORDER BANNING ZOOT-SUIT WEARERS!!" (Mazón, 1984, p. 35).

Beyond the pages of dailies carrying the *Li'l Abner* comic strip, hostility emerged between mainstream society and the zoot-suit counterculture. One LA newspaper ran a piece on how to "de-zoot" a zoot-suiter: "Grab a zooter. Take off his pants and frock coat and tear them up or burn them. Trim the 'Argentine ducktail' that goes with the screwy costume" (Mazón, 1984, p. 76). Whether it was intended with humour or not, instructions for the negative sanctioning of zoot-suiters were carried out by people opposed to the counterculture.

The conflict reached a climax in early June 1943, when thousands of young white men—soldiers, marines, and sailors on weekend leave from nearby military installations—launched a campaign to rid Los Angeles of zoot-suiters by capturing them, buzzing their hair down in a military style, and destroying their clothing.

Historian Mauricio Mazón describes the extent of the riots and police intervention:

> They were not about zoot-suiters rioting, and they were not, in any conventional sense of the word, "riots." No one was killed. No one sustained massive injuries. Property damage was slight. No major or minor judicial decisions stemmed from the riots. There was no pattern to arrests. Convictions were few and highly discretionary. (Mazón, 1984, p. 1)

The conflict lasted just under a week, and was brought to an end with two acts. First, the military reined in their troops. More significantly, on 9 June, Los Angeles City Council issued the following ban:

> NOW, THEREFORE, BE IT RESOLVED, that the City Council by Resolution find that wearing of Zoot Suits constitutes a public nuisance and does hereby

instruct the City Attorney to prepare an ordinance declaring same a nuisance and prohibit the wearing of Zoot Suits with reet pleats within the city limits of Los Angeles. (Mazón, 1984, p. 75)

This, the culmination of a series of increasingly explicit and punitive sanctions, shows how humour with a social edge and a large audience can be used against a particular group.

What Do YOU Think?

1. Why do you think the zoot-suiters were targeted? What were the overt and covert aspects of their deviance?
2. Can you think of parallels between zoot-suiters of the 1940s and any group today?

the otherness of children with allergies and can actually increase the potential for the negative sanction of bullying. An article in the *Annals of Allergy, Asthma & Immunology* (Lieberman et al., 2010) reported the results of an American study in which 353 questionnaires were completed by parents of food-allergic children and by food-allergic teenagers and adults. Twenty-four per cent of the survey participants reported having been "bullied, teased, or harassed" because of their

Debra Wiseberg/iStockphoto

Canada's Mennonites are known for their belief in adult baptism, their commitment to non-violence, and the modest everyday fashion worn by the group's conservative members, all of which keep them outside of the cultural mainstream. Which type of stigma is demonstrated here? Would you consider it socially constructed or essentialist?

allergy. Of the reported incidents, 82 per cent had occurred at school, and 80 per cent had been perpetrated by classmates. Disturbingly, 21 per cent of the respondents reported having been bullied by teachers or other school staff. Also surprising is that the greater part (57 per cent) of the reported incidents were physical: victims were touched with the allergen, had it thrown or waved at them, or had their food deliberately contaminated with the substance.

Deviance and the Moral Panic

When Otherness is sensationalized in the media, it can become the source of a **moral panic**. A moral panic is a campaign designed to arouse concern over an issue or a group. The issue at the heart of a moral panic is typically something very small that has been exaggerated so that it seems like a significant threat to social order; in some cases, the issue has been fabricated entirely. To use a phrase I learned in my first sociology class, the moral panic is about a problem that is more apparent than real. It is also volatile: it rises and falls quickly in the public eye and consciousness.

A moral panic is spearheaded by a **moral entrepreneur**—someone who has something to gain from public fear around the issue. The term was coined by Becker (1963) to describe a person who tries to convince others of the need to take action around a social problem that they have defined. The moral entrepreneur could be a journalist sensationalizing an issue as clickbait, or an activist trying to draw supporters to a cause, or a politician hoping to advance a policy agenda. The moral entrepreneur often has a recommended course of action that is disproportionate to the actual threat, the proverbial hammer to kill a fly. Al Capp could be considered a moral entrepreneur for his part in stoking moral panic around zoot-suiters.

A recent Canadian example of a moral panic, discussed in Chapter 3, concerns Zunera Ishaq, a Muslim woman who fought to wear her *niqab* while taking the oath of Canadian citizenship in 2015. In its efforts to uphold the ban on covering the face during citizenship ceremonies, the federal Conservative government created a moral panic, calling it "offensive" that anyone should want to "hide their identity at a time when they are committing to join the Canadian family" (Quan, 2015). In fact, Ishaq removed her *niqab* before an official, in private, prior to the ceremony to confirm her identity. In this case, the moral panic was socially constructed for political gain, although it would appear to have failed. An older Canadian example of a moral panic is described on page 177.

"Race" and Deviance: To Be Non-White Is Deviant

To racialize deviance is to link minority ethnic groups—particularly visible minorities—with certain forms of deviance, and to treat these groups differently because of that connection. We see this in movies and television shows that portray all Italians as being involved in organized crime, and news reports that link young black men with gangs and gun violence. We see it when a person of Arab background is suspected of being a terrorist. Muslims who wear the *niqab* are seen as deviant for concealing their faces. Part of **racializing deviance** is making ethnic background a covert characteristic of deviance, as though all people of a particular ethnic group are involved in the same supposedly deviant behaviour.

Despite the public promotion in Canada of **multiculturalism**—the set of policies designed to encourage respect for cultural differences—the pressure to **assimilate** (i.e. become culturally the same as the dominant culture) is persistent. Immigrants who have experienced the embarrassment of having Canadians stumble over their names—sometimes deliberately for supposed comic effect

The Point Is . . .

Drugs and Immigrants Are Common Features of Moral Panics

In the 1920s, Canada experienced a moral panic around racialized deviance and illegal drugs. The "race" was Chinese Canadians, and one of the people who gave fuel to the panic was Emily Murphy. Journalist, activist, and self-taught legal expert, born of a prominent and wealthy Ontario family, Murphy was a gender heroine of first-wave feminism. In 1916, she became the first woman magistrate in the British Empire. She would later play a role in the historic "Persons Case" (1928), which ended when the British Privy Council overturned a Supreme Court ruling that women were not "persons" eligible to hold public office.

In 1922, Murphy published *Black Candle*, a collection of her articles, many of which had originally appeared in *Maclean's* magazine. Murphy's four books of personal sketches, written under the pen name "Janey Canuck," were well known when she published *Black Candle* to expose the insidious details of the Canadian drug trade. The collection cast Chinese Canadians as the main villains in the trafficking of illegal drugs—particularly opium, heroin, and cocaine—although blacks were also singled out for censure. The main theme was that Chinese men—those bachelors who, because of the restrictive head tax on Chinese immigrants, could neither be reunited with their wives nor find companionship among women "of their own race"—were corrupting white women through drug dealing, "ruining them" and making them accomplices in their dealing. The following excerpt from a chapter titled "Girls as Pedlars" is typical:

> Much has been said, of late, concerning the entrapping of girls by Chinamen in order to secure their services as pedlars of narcotics. The importance of the subject is one which warrants our closest scrutiny: also, it is one we dare not evade, however painful its consideration. (Murphy, [1922] 1973, p. 233)

Murphy believed that the "yellow races" would use the drug trade to take over the Anglo-Saxon world, and she warned North American readers to be wary of these "visitors":

> Still, it behooves the people in Canada and the United States, to consider the desirability of these visitors . . . and to say whether or not we shall be "*at home*" to them for the future. A visitor may be polite, patient, persevering, . . . but if he carries poisoned lollypops in his pocket and feeds them to our children, it might seem wise to put him out.
>
> It is hardly credible that the average Chinese pedlar has any definite idea in his mind of bringing about the downfall of the white race, his swaying motive being probably that of greed, but in the hands of his superiors, he may become a powerful instrument to this very end. . . .
>
> Naturally, the aliens are silent on the subject, but an addict who died this year in British Columbia . . . used to relate how the Chinese pedlars taunted him with their superiority at being able to sell the dope without using it, and by telling him how the yellow race would rule the world. They were too wise, they urged, to attempt to win in battle but would win by wits; would strike at the white race through "dope" and when the time was ripe would command the world. (Murphy, [1922] 1973, pp. 187–9)

As a moral entrepreneur, Emily Murphy was a success. *Black Candle* had a huge impact on the perception of the drug trade and on drug legislation in Canada. Chapter XXIII, "Marahuana—A New Menace," was the first work in Canada to discuss cannabis use. It contained a lot of damning half-truths and anecdotes but nevertheless led to the enactment of laws governing the sale and use of marijuana in Canada.

(as when Don Cherry knowingly mispronounces French and Russian names)—may feel pressure to anglicize their names to make themselves more "Canadian."

Racial profiling is one way in which deviance is racialized. Ontario's Human Rights Commission defines racial profiling as

> any action undertaken for reasons of safety, security or public protection that relies on stereotypes about race, colour, ethnicity, ancestry, religion, or place of origin rather than on reasonable suspicion, to single out an individual for greater scrutiny or different treatment. (OHRC, 2003, p. 6)

The report notes that racial profiling can arise from a combination of these factors, and that age and gender may can also "influence the experience of profiling."

Racial profiling assumes that visible characteristics of an individual can be used to predict engagement in illegal activity. This is not the same as criminal profiling, which "relies on actual behaviour or on information about suspected activity by someone who meets the description of a specific individual." Racial profiling uses a person's otherness as grounds to single the individual out for different treatment, often involving some sort of sanction.

Racial profiling can occur in a variety of contexts involving various agents and individuals. Examples include incidents involving

- law enforcement personnel, such as police and border control agents;
- security personnel, such as private security guards;
- employers—for example, in conducting security clearances of staff;
- landlords—for example, when a property owner assumes that certain applicants or tenants will be involved in criminal activity;
- service providers—for instance, an Uber driver who refuses to stop at night for certain people; and
- the criminal justice system, such as courts.

Racial profiling is commonly associated with *carding*, a police intelligence-gathering procedure in which officers stop, question, and document people when no offence is being committed. Individuals may be carded during police street checks or "community engagement" initiatives, carried out in neighbourhoods with high rates of crime. The practice has come under criticism from human rights groups, who argue that it disproportionately targets black youths, Indigenous people, and other racialized groups. And it can provoke a response that becomes an excuse for arrest.

Gender and Deviance: To Be Female Is Deviant

Feminist sociologists teach us that in a patriarchal society (one dominated by men), what is "male" is treated as normal, while what is "female" is treated as Other and seen as inherently deviant. Male values and behaviours are **normalized** (i.e. made to seem normal, right, and good), through customs, laws, and culture production. Two related concepts are important here: misogyny and patriarchal construct. **Misogyny** means literally "hating women." In a patriarchal or male-dominated society, images of women are often constructed in ways that contain and reflect misogyny. **Patriarchal construct** refers to social conditions considered or structured in a way that favours men and boys over women and girls. Think, for example, of highly prized and well-paying jobs—corporate lawyer, investment banker, emergency room doctor—that have been constructed so that the job-holder is forced to place family in a distant second place to employment. This gives advantages to men, who in Canadian society are expected to fulfill fewer domestic and childrearing duties than are women are.

Menstruating women in North America are cast as deviant. How so? You have probably never had to take your own toilet paper into a public washroom, or pay by the sheet for what is provided. Yet feminine hygiene products are not universally available in public washrooms; when they are, they are often sold from a vending machine. Women are essentially penalized for a naturally occurring bodily function.

This "women only" subway car in Tehran, Iran, exists with the officially declared purpose of protecting riders from sexual harassment. Is separating women—treating them as "Other"—the best way to crack down on groping and other sexual attacks?

Casting women as deviant is not new. Take the witch-hunts waged in Europe and, later on, in colonial America from about the fourteenth to the seventeenth centuries. Women identified as witches were tried and, if found guilty, executed. Here we have a good example of moral panic surrounding deviance that was entirely fictitious. While some of those tried may have committed criminal acts, their alleged powers and connections with Satan were not real. Why were they believed to be involved in dark magic? The vast majority of those accused were women (the figure usually cited is 85 per cent). The word *witch* itself is closely associated with women, conjuring up negative images of pointed black hats, warty faces with pointed noses, and flying broomsticks: bad clothes, bad looks, and bad use of a female-associated cleaning implement. In a patriarchal society, this image of deviance is very much associated with femaleness, its opposite—normalcy—with maleness.

In the eighteenth and nineteenth centuries, European doctors and psychotherapists used a diagnosis of "female hysteria" to account for natural emotional states that, in women, were considered unacceptable or deviant (see Scull, 2009). Excessive emotionality, restlessness, and sexual desire were among the symptoms of the supposed neurological disorders. Much like accusations of witchcraft (only with less severe punishment), the diagnosis of hysteria was used to account for and sanction behaviour that was considered deviant because it occurred in women.

"Fallen Women": Sexual Deviance as Gendered

The double standard that has long applied to male and female sexual activity is evidence that deviance can be gendered. The Magdalene asylums serve as a case in point.

Magdalene asylums existed in Ireland, Australia, and North America from the eighteenth to the late twentieth centuries. Their stated purpose was to house "fallen women": prostitutes and unmarried women who were sexually active, but also women deemed by the Church to be at risk of being led astray. This includes very attractive and "feeble-minded" women who might be easily talked into unmarried sex. Moral purity was the Church-imposed standard for women, one that was to be preserved at all costs. Anything short of that standard constituted deviance. As a result, many women were incarcerated against their will, and with no formal trial. They were stripped of their rights and their children. It seems hardly worth noting that men were not held to the same standard.

In Ireland, it is believed that up to 30,000 unmarried women were incarcerated because they either were or could become sexually active (J.M. Smith, 2007). They were held in institutions commonly known as **Magdalene laundries**, because the inmates were required to perform the hard physical labour of washing clothes (this was well before there were washing machines). The women laundered the uniforms of other prisoners, priests, and nuns, which enabled the institutions to be financially self-supporting. When not working, the women were forced to spend long periods of time praying, or at least remaining silent. They could not leave. The doors to the outside were locked, and there were iron gates, guarded by nuns.

Mari Steed was one of thousands of children born in Ireland and brought without her permission to the United States, where she was put up for adoption. She now works for an organization seeking restitution for survivors of the Magdalene laundries. In an interview, she described the relationship between the nuns and the inmates this way:

> [The nuns] may have started with the best of intentions, but by the very nature of Irish society and repression of women's sexuality, they began to see these women as less than human, and treat them that way. That's where we're seeing a lot of the abuse, and really torture, at the end of the day. (Matthews, 2014)

Referring to J.M. Smith's description of Ireland's "architecture of containment" for dealing with social deviants, she adds,

> You had these industrial schools, the Magdalene laundries, the mother and baby

What Do YOU Think?

Why were the women taken to the Magdalene laundries perceived to be deviant?

homes, all with different remits, but the basic model was to contain and segregate anything that was deemed morally inferior by society, whether that's children, unwed mothers, the women in the Magdalenes, etc. (Matthews, 2014)

The last of Ireland's Magdalene laundries did not close until 1996.

Being *Incorrigible*: Gendered Deviance in Ontario

Canada has its own history of gendered deviance. From 1913 to 1964, thousands of women in Ontario were put into reformatories under the *Female Refuge Act*. Among the "offences" for which young women would be placed in these institutions was being sexually active outside of marriage. This kind of behaviour and the women guilty of it were branded "incorrigible."

In 1939, Velma Demerson, 18 years old and white, became sexually involved with a Chinese man. They intended to get married. When she became pregnant, her parents reported to the authorities that she was "incorrigible." Velma was arrested and sent to a "home" for young girls, then to the Andrew Mercer Reformatory for Women, Canada's first prison for women (16 and over), in operation from 1872 to 1969. She was confined to a cell that was seven feet long and four feet wide, one bare light bulb, a cot, a cold-water tap, and a basin. A covered enamel pail was provided for use as a toilet (Demerson, 2004, p. 5).

Class and Deviance: To Be Poor Is Deviant

Poverty can be considered a covert characteristic of deviance. Marginally illicit activities like overindulgence in alcohol are more likely to be considered deviant in poor people than in middle-class or "rich" people. Jeffrey Reiman, in *The Rich Get Richer and the Poor Get Prison*, argues that the criminal justice system has a distinct class bias. This bias appears in the way we define what constitutes a crime, and in our processes of arrest, trial, and sentencing. Each step shows bias against the poor. As Reiman explains,

> [T]he criminal justice system keeps before the public . . . the distorted image that crime is primarily the work of the poor. The value of this to those in positions of power is that it deflects the discontented and potential hostility of Middle America [the American middle class] away from the classes above them and toward the classes below them. . . . [I]t not only explains our dismal failure to make a significant dent in crime but also explains why the criminal justice system functions in a way that is biased against the poor at every stage from arrest to conviction. Indeed, even at the earlier stage, when crimes are defined in law, the system primarily concentrates on the predatory acts of the poor and tends to exclude or deemphasize the equally or more dangerous predatory acts of those who are well off. (Reiman, 1998, p. 4)

This is how behaviours associated with poverty and criminality become synonymous with deviance, while criminal activity associated with wealth and celebrity is often labelled "good business." Martha Stewart, media star and founder of a business empire aimed at aspiring home decorators and entertainers, was convicted of contempt of court for lying under oath during a probe into alleged insider trading, and yet she received a standing ovation from a mostly supportive public and press following a hearing at which she was sentenced to five months in prison.

From School to Prison: The Deviance of Students in Low-Income Neighborhoods

Class bias is at the centre of what is known in the literature as the *schools-to-prison hypothesis*: the idea that in schools located in poorer, often racialized neighbourhoods, there is a biased application

of practices such as "zero tolerance," which creates a misleading perception of higher crime rates. Greater rates of suspension and expulsion, higher numbers of random locker and student searches, and tough anti-violence measures like the installation of metal detectors, the hiring of security guards, and even periodic police raids characterize the schools in these poorer neighbourhoods, but these measures are greatly out of proportion to the amount of violence and crime actually occurring at the schools.

While most of the literature relates to the American situation, the schools-to-prison hypothesis applies in urban Canada as well. In a 2009 *Toronto Star* article, journalists Sandro Contenta and Jim Rankin reported that Ontario's Safe Schools Act, in force from 2001 to 2008, produced startlingly high numbers of suspensions and expulsions. The *Star*'s analysis, which examined school suspension rates for 2007–8 alongside sentences and postal code data for inmates in Ontario provincial jails, showed that the highest rates of suspension tended to be in those areas that also had the highest rates of incarceration. This is a positive correlation, which suggests that punishing youths from the city's poorest neighbourhoods with zero-tolerance measures reinforces the higher incarceration rate in those areas.

"But wait," I can hear you say, "Isn't it possible that low-income neighbourhoods naturally produce crime, and that greater rates of true crime, not increased levels of scrutiny or harsher application of zero-tolerance policies, are responsible for higher incarceration rates corresponding to these neighbourhoods?"

Indeed, lower-class people are overrepresented in the statistics on criminal convictions and admission to prison. That means that per population they are more often convicted and admitted to prison than are middle- and upper-class people, and this contributes to the idea that lower-class people are criminally deviant. However, a closer look at the statistics helps us see why they do not give us an accurate picture of the lower classes.

Crime in Low-Income Communities

"Lower class" is a designation that is often established by looking solely at recorded income, but it covers a broad and far from homogeneous set of individuals.

The Point Is...

White-Collar Crime Is a Serious Business

In a speech to the American Sociological Society in 1939, criminologist **Edwin Sutherland** (1883–1950) introduced the term **white-collar crime**. He defined it as "crime committed by a person of respectability and high social status in the course of his occupation" (1949, p. 9). His article "White Collar Criminality" was published the next year in the *American Sociological Review* (Sutherland, 1940). He later published a book on the subject (Sutherland, 1949).

Sutherland's work was a landmark in the sociological study of criminology. Previous work had focused on the crimes of the poor, creating a biased and very limited survey. But Sutherland's definition is not flawless. Associating certain kinds of criminal behaviour with a particular class reflects a class bias and a misleading view of the situation. After all, you don't have to be a person of "high social status" to commit identity theft, which tends to be classified as a white-collar crime. Sutherland's original definition implied that only people of the higher classes are capable of planning and carrying out crimes that are essentially non-violent. In this way it fails to recognize that industrial accidents caused by unsafe working conditions created by a negligent business owner are in a real sense crimes of violence.

More recent works have refined the definition of white-collar crime to remove the class bias associated with Sutherland's original definition. Clinard and Quinney (1973) went further, splitting white-collar crime into categories they named **occupational crimes and corporate crimes**. They defined the former as "offenses committed by individuals for themselves in the course of their occupations [and] offenses by employers against their employees" (1973, p. 188). Embezzlement and sexual harassment are examples. The latter include "offenses committed by corporate officials for their corporation and the offenses of the corporation itself" (1973, p. 188), including bribery, false advertising, and industrial accidents. The difference is one of beneficiaries and victims: occupational crimes benefit the individual at the expense of other individuals who work for the company; corporate crimes benefit the corporation and its executives at the expense of other employees, other companies, and the general public. This latter definition, by placing less emphasis on the individual, hones in on the negative aspects of corporate culture and the way that individuals and corporations work together to commit illegal acts against consumers and the common public.

Some are part of the working class, who labour for long hours with little financial reward. Others are on welfare. These two subgroups of the lower class are probably not significantly more involved in criminal activity than are middle-class or upper-class people. In fact, it's a separate subgroup, representing a small minority of the lower class that is responsible for a high percentage of the crimes. These people are lumped together with the first two groups statistically because of their low reported income, giving a misleading forensic picture of the working poor.

Another reason for the overrepresentation of the lower class in crime statistics has to do with **social resources**. In this context, *social resources* refers to knowledge of the law and legal system, the ability to afford a good lawyer, influential social connections, and capacity to present oneself in a way that is deemed "respectable." Lower-class individuals generally have access to fewer social resources than middle- and upper-class people do, and this makes them more likely to be convicted of charges people from the wealthier classes might be able to avoid. Tepperman and Rosenberg explain the importance of social resources:

> Social resources help people avoid labelling and punishment by the police and courts. For example, in assault or property-damage cases, the police and courts try

to interpret behaviour and assess blame before taking any action. They are less likely to label people with more resources as "criminal" or "delinquent" and more likely to label them "alcoholic" or "mentally ill" for having committed a criminal act. (Tepperman & Rosenberg, 1998, p. 118)

The authors make use of Goffman's concept of **impression management**, which they define as "the control of personal information flow to manipulate how other people see and treat you" (Tepperman & Rosenberg, 1998, p. 118). The upper classes are better at managing impressions than are people who belong to the lower class. Therefore, they conclude,

Official rule-enforcers (including police and judges, but also social workers, psychiatrists and the whole correctional and treatment establishment) define as serious the

deviant acts in which poor people engage. On the other hand, they tend to "define away" the deviant acts of rich people as signs of illness, not crime. They are more likely to consider those actions morally blameless. (Tepperman & Rosenberg, 1998, pp. 118–19)

Sexual Orientation and Deviance: To Be Gay is Deviant

Homosexuality has long been socially constructed as deviant to varying degrees around the globe. Cultures differ in terms of how and what kind of social sanctions are applied. Homosexuality was not legalized in Canada until 1967, and prior to a US Supreme Court ruling in June 2003—less than

AP Photo/Mindaugas Kulbis

Male homosexuality tends to be sanctioned more heavily than female homosexuality, and there are some countries (e.g. Jamaica, Uzbekistan) where only male homosexuality is illegal. Why do you think male homosexuality is viewed as more deviant than female homosexuality?

20 years ago—sexual activity between consenting adult homosexuals was still against the law in 13 American states. Same-sex marriage was recognized nationwide in Canada in 2005 and 10 years later in the United States.

Around the world, homosexuality remains illegal in over 60 countries, with penalties ranging from flogging and imprisonment to death (see Figure 9.6). The countries with the most severe penalties for homosexuality are Islamic countries of Africa and the Middle East where Sharia law is practised. In March 2019, the small Asian kingdom of Brunei joined the list of countries to make homosexuality punishable by death.

In countries where homosexuality is protected by law, it continues to be punished through powerful sanctions. In Canada, young men continue to sanction behaviour perceived as effeminate or weak statements like, "Don't be so gay." This practice, reflecting what is sometimes called the **ideology of "fag,"** is a way of pressuring individuals to behave according to gender role expectations.

Disability and Deviance: To Be Disabled Is Deviant

Society, as we have seen, punishes deviance with negative sanctions, and offers positive sanctions to those who adjust their behaviour to conform to standards set by the mainstream. A negative sanction can be fairly mild, like a rude hand gesture from a driver, but we also have an institutionalized criminal justice system that exists to identify and punish those whose behaviour is judged as deviant according to law. Legal penalties for deviant behaviour typically involve restriction of freedoms and measures to diminish the independence and self-respect of the person convicted.

A reasonable sociological question to ask is whether society punishes disabled people for their disability. For example, do the ways in which we design and build houses (with steps to the front porch and narrow interior stairways), public buildings (with revolving doors), sidewalks (without sloping edges to meet the road), public transport (cramped buses too small in which to manoeuvre a wheelchair), and shelving in grocery stores essentially punish—by limiting freedom, independence, and self-respect—those who cannot walk?

Lennard Davis and the Politics of the Disabled Body

Lennard J. Davis is a leading figure in the sociological study of disability. In his article "Constructing Normalcy," he writes,

> To understand the disabled body, one must return to the concept of the norm, the normal body. So much of writing about disability has focused on the disabled person as the object of study, just as the study of race has focused on the person of color. But as with recent scholarship on race, which has turned its attention to whiteness, I would like to focus not so much on the construction of disability as on the construction of normalcy. I do this because the "problem" of the disabled is not the person with disabilities; the problem is the way that normalcy is constructed to create the "problem" of the disabled person. (Davis, 2006, p. 3)

The politics of disability involves promoting respect for difference, as opposed to just respecting the "normal" and treating anything else as a problem to be solved. For example, proud and politically active members of the Deaf community have represented cochlear implants (surgically implanted electronic devices that assist the deaf in sensing sound) as an attempt to "normalize" people with hearing disabilities while disrespecting Deaf culture, with its long history of using sign language. Deafness, they argue, is merely a difference in ability and not a disadvantage to be corrected.

We all have different sets of mental and physical abilities; the world does not divide easily into those who are disabled and those who are not. Davis's point is that the social problem of disability is actually created by those people (typically able-bodied people) who view and treat those with a different set of abilities as "Other" rather than accepting their difference.

Pamela Moore/iStockphoto

In what ways does society punish disability? Does the failure to better accommodate people with disabilities arise simply from carelessness, or can it be taken as a negative sanction of disability?

Henry Goddard and the Eugenics Movement

When it comes to "punishing" disability by failing to accommodate differences in physical ability, the sanction is often an act of omission. It is not that disabled people have been singled out; it's that they haven't been taken into account at all. But there are many cases in which people with disabilities have been targeted because of their difference. Consider the eugenics movement.

The **eugenics** ("good genes") movement was based on the mistaken beliefs (1) that intelligence can be measured easily, and (2) that it is inherited, transferred directly from one generation to the next. A popular philosophy during the first half of the twentieth century, it led to efforts to have the so-called "feeble-minded" sexually sterilized so that they could not reproduce.

A pioneer of the eugenics movement was American psychologist Henry H. Goddard, who promoted the idea that "feeble-mindedness" (then an accepted clinical term in psychology) was hereditary. In an article published in a 1911 issue of *American Breeders Magazine*, Goddard attempted to demonstrate the inheritance of feeble-mindedness among inmates in an institution for people suffering a range of poorly diagnosed mental health conditions. He was widely considered to be the "father" of intelligence testing, having earned the reputation at Ellis Island, where he screened thousands of prospective immigrants to the United States. His assessments of institutionalized inmates were based on intelligence tests (flawed, even more than now, by cultural biases) and, I suspect, on "eyeballing" the inmates. The very fact of being in an institution or having been previously diagnosed could be enough for Goddard to conclude

Telling It Like It Is   A Student POV

Mental Health and Deviance

As a child, I was labelled quiet, shy, and introverted. I was celebrated for these characteristics because family, teachers, and other adults saw me as sweet and polite. It took until adulthood for me to realize that I am actually talkative, outgoing, and extroverted. Undiagnosed mental health issues prevented me from expressing my personality, and my environment encouraged my introverted coping mechanisms. In 2018, at the age of 24, I was diagnosed with Generalized Anxiety Disorder (GAD), Obsessive Compulsive Disorder (OCD), and symptoms of periodic depression.

As a Millennial from a small town in southern Ontario, I was taught in elementary and secondary school about bullying and its effects but rarely about mental health as a whole. In rural communities, mental health is considered "new age" hippie urban thinking. It's abnormal to talk to a counsellor or therapist unless you have severe mental illnesses. Even in tragedy, you are expected to rely on your family and community for emotional support even though they are rarely certified to help you. In middle school, mental health education was taught through the effects of bullying. I was taught that suicide was a side effect of cyberbullying and could be prevented by blocking online harassment. But I was rarely bullied, and I contemplated suicide.

When I was diagnosed, my mother was shocked that I would have my mental health evaluated and expressed her fears for me: "What if a future employer finds out? You have a file now! You won't be hired if they know you have mental issues!" My mother, like others from the baby boomer generation, has an anxiety around the documentation of mental health. Once it's on paper, it's harder to hide. While I have confidence in the security of my medical files, I am also not ashamed of my diagnoses. For me, they are no different than a medical file documenting a flu I had years ago.

GAD, OCD, and depression have hindered 24 years of my life. I wish my culture had given me the tools and confidence to talk about my issues. I am a better and stronger person for my experiences, and for me I wouldn't change that. However, I worry about the generations following me who are increasingly absorbed in virtual reality and are losing touch with their bodies and minds. I worry that if our culture and our education system do not start normalizing mental health, then we will be facing a new adolescent epidemic.

What Do YOU Think?

1. How do the writer and her mother differ in their views of mental health and deviance?
2. How do you view mental illness: as something that is safe to discuss openly or as something that should be kept private? How do you think your attitudes are shaped by your age, your gender, and your ethnic background?

that an individual was a "moron" (a term he coined for clinical use, not for taunting classmates or heckling referees). He was strongly opposed to the notion that the social environment had any impact on a person's mental health, making him a biological determinist as we defined the term in Chapter 4.

Despite its now obvious flaws, Goddard's work on eugenics was very influential in the early twentieth century. We can see its influence in Alberta's Sexual Sterilization Act, which was in effect from 1928 until 1972. The act reflected the belief that controlled breeding could be used to improve the population by increasing the occurrence of favourable heritable characteristics and limiting the reproduction of unfavourable ones. Essentially, the Alberta act was designed to make it impossible for people deemed "mentally inferior" to reproduce. It also punished racial and ethnic deviants. Many of those targeted were Indigenous (see Karen Stote's *An Act of Genocide: Colonialism and the Sterilization of Aboriginal Women*, 2015) and eastern European, illustrating how racial and cultural difference is often cast as deviance and punished. But the act principally targeted people living with mental disabilities. The signal case in this regard is that of Leilani Muir.

In 1955, Leilani Muir was confined at what was then called the Red Deer Training School of Mental Defectives (later the Michener Institute). At the age of 14 she had taken an IQ test (one reflecting a number of biases concerning class, culture, and ways of evaluating intelligence) and had scored 64, earning her the official designation of "moron." ("Normal" intelligence is confirmed by any score around 100.) In 1989, Muir would take another test and score a "normal range" 87. By then it was too late. Following the earlier test she was informed that she would be taken into surgery to have her appendix removed; instead, at the age of 14, she had her fallopian tubes destroyed. This was the negative sanction for Leilani Muir's mental difference. In 1996, the Alberta government admitted she had been wrongfully sterilized and agreed to a court-appointed settlement of $740,280.

Criminal Deviance

Over the course of this chapter we have seen examples of how people in power have sanctioned deviant behaviour by making it illegal. Zoot-suiters, niqab-wearing Muslims, "fallen women," homosexuals, and the "feeble-minded" have all been persecuted under the law for deviant behaviour that places them outside of the mainstream.

Of course, while deviance and crime are not synonymous, deviance does encompass criminal behaviour. A growing area of sociology is **criminology**. You would get no marks on a test for defining criminology simply as the study of crime. In fact, criminology involves the sociological (and psychological) study of crime in terms of such elements as causation, prevention, management or control, and the statistical patterns of crime. When I taught students in the Police Foundation program, I would open my first class by stating that I had much (perhaps most) of the sociological profile of a serial

killer: I am male, white, middle-class, and highly [in]telligent, and I am deviant in a number of ways [I] have a big beard, do not own a cellphone, do o[wn] eight parrots, and make fun of skinny white men in suits who drive black BMWs; they are often the villains in my short stories). The point is, criminology is about studying patterns in criminal behaviour to learn more about how crime can be predicted, prevented (or at least managed), and sanctioned.

Theories of Criminal Deviance
Strain Theory: Robert Merton

Early sociological theorist **Robert Merton** (1938) developed **strain theory** to explain why, in his opinion, some individuals "chose" to be criminally deviant. The "strain" Merton identified was a disconnect between society's culturally defined goals and the unequal distribution of the means necessary to achieve those goals. Merton was describing a situation in which social reality—the real-life circumstances of many individuals—inhibits the attainment of "the **American dream**." The American dream is essentially success, however you choose to define it (e.g. fame, wealth, or social prestige), mythologized as an opportunity that any American citizen, regardless of background or circumstances, can seize provided they put in the hard work to get it.

Merton was aware that success was most available to those with upper- and middle-class resources (wealth, expensive postsecondary education, and social connections). When those without these resources find themselves prevented from achieving society's culturally achieved goals, they experience a sense of social disconnection or exclusion that Durkheim called **anomie** (see Chapter 1). Merton's term for the realization that one lacks legitimate means to achieve success was *strain*, and people respond to it, he argued, in one of five ways:

1. They conform, striving against the odds to attain idealized goals through socially acceptable practices, such as upgrading their education and working hard for small promotions.
2. They lower their sights, showing the hard work that society expects but secretly setting less ambitious goals that are more within their means.

3. They give up on society's goals, and may wind up dropping out of school, engaging in very low-paid work, or living on the streets.

4. They reject and rebel against the established system of social goals, advancing new goals while attempting to subvert the prevailing social order.

5. They innovate, pursuing material success using improvised techniques that deviate from socially accepted, legitimate means.

It is the last of these groups that concerns us here. The rebels score high in intelligence and ambition, but without the means to attain success the "right" way, they turn to unconventional means, specifically crime.

Subcultural Theory: Albert Cohen

Albert Cohen developed **subcultural theory** to challenge and refine certain aspects of Merton's work. He was also building on foundations laid by Frederic Thrasher in his studies of gangs and by **E. Franklin Frazier** (1894–1962), who had carried out pioneering studies of African Americans in Chicago.

Cohen's study of teenage gangs (1955) presents a model of what he called the **delinquent subculture**, made up of young, lower-class males suffering from **status frustration**. Failing to succeed in middle-class institutions, especially school, they become socialized into an oppositional subculture that inverts the values of the school. For example, the youths he studied engaged in delinquent stealing that was primarily **non-utilitarian**—in other words, the objects weren't stolen because they were needed for survival but because the act of stealing was respected within the delinquent subculture.

Cohen stressed that becoming a member of the delinquent subculture is like becoming a member of any culture. It does not depend on the psychology of the individual; nor is the subculture invented or created by the individual. When members of the delinquent subculture grow up and leave the gang (to join adult gangs or mainstream society), the subculture persists. Cohen asserted that

> delinquency is neither an inborn disposition nor something the child has contrived by himself; that children *learn* to become delinquents by becoming members

> of groups in which delinquent conduct is already established and "the thing to do"; and that a child need not be "different" from other children, that he need not have any twists or defects of personality or intelligence in order to become a delinquent. (Cohen, 1955, pp. 11–12)

We can use Cohen's model to review other ideas presented earlier in the textbook. First, the **norms** of the delinquent subculture—the rules or expectations of behaviour—would be different, at least in part, from those of the dominant culture. The difference, according to Cohen, comes from the inverting of norms. In Cohen's words, "The delinquent's conduct is right, by the standards of his subculture, precisely *because* it is wrong by the norms of the larger culture" (1955, p. 28). Likewise, there is an inverting of the **sanctions**: the **negative sanctions** of non-gang members—the ways in which society shows its disapproval of the delinquent behaviour—are viewed as **positive sanctions** by members of the delinquent gang.

Labelling Theory: Howard Becker

One weakness of subcultural theory is that it stresses subcultural values as developed in opposition to mainstream society. The theory is only partially useful, and generally inadequate, to address social situations in which subcultural values, beliefs, and practices considered deviant by mainstream society in fact flow from the history and traditional culture of the people involved. Consider, the way Canada's Indigenous people are often cast as deviant. You could not argue that most of their cultural differences have been consciously shaped to oppose the culture of mainstream Canadian society. Certain aspects of their situation might be better explained by **Howard Becker's labelling theory**.

Becker theorized that labels applied to individuals and groups outside the mainstream become internalized both by those cast as deviant and by the majority group. Take the image of the "Indian drunk." Cree playwright Tomson Highway described it as "our national image":

> That is the first and only way most white people see Indians. . . . In fact, the average white Canadian has seen that visual more

frequently than they've seen a beaver. To my mind, you might as well put an Indian drunk on the Canadian nickel. (as quoted in York, 1990, p. 191)

Yet when an image like this gets applied to an individual and becomes a **master status**, dominating all other statuses, it may eventually become internalized.

A few facts should be presented here. One is that Indigenous people, in greater percentages than any other group in Canada other than Muslims, abstain entirely from alcohol: they do not drink. According to the 2012 Aboriginal Peoples Survey, 26 per cent of First Nations people aged 15 and over had not consumed alcohol in the previous 12 months, versus just 21 per cent of the total Canadian population (Rotenberg, 2016, p. 9). Second, Indigenous people who drink are more likely to be *binge drinkers* (i.e. people who have five or more drinks at a time). Third, there is no conclusive evidence that Indigenous people have lower tolerance of alcohol than other racialized groups. What effect do you think the image of the "Indian drunk" has on the first two statistics presented in this paragraph?

Another criticism of strain theory and subcultural theory is that while both have been used productively to address deviance in what can be termed "male culture." The research in this area falls short when applied to "female culture."

Social Control Theory: Travis Hirschi

Merton, Becker, and especially Cohen devoted much of their research to the question of why young people become delinquent. It is a complicated issue that involves such factors as **agency** (personal choice), family, religion, racism, and the extent to which social inequality denies young people the full range of choices, such as with regard to work.

For **Travis W. Hirschi** (1935–2017), a key factor was social bonding. He set out his argument in *Causes of Delinquency* (1969), in which he outlined his version of social control theory. A delinquent, or juvenile delinquent, is someone who is not yet an adult and becomes involved with acts considered deviant or antisocial—primarily, of course, breaking the law.

Hirschi was critical of strain theory for failing to account for why so many young delinquents grow up to become law-abiding adults, even when their position within the economic structure—the apparent source of their frustration—remains "relatively fixed" (Hirschi, 1969, p. 6). He also rejected—with italics—strain theory's tendency to link crime with the frustrations of people from the poorer socio-economic class: "Delinquency is not confined to the lower classes," he wrote (Hirschi, 1969, p. 7).

According to Hirschi, "Control theories assume that delinquent acts result when an individual's bond to society is weak or broken" (1969, p. 16). That "bond" encompasses attachment, commitment, involvement, and belief. The theory went that if a child is bonded with such social institutions as family, religion, athletic teams, and school, then that child is unlikely to engage in delinquent activities. The child has accepted the positive social values of the institution and therefore will not commit antisocial acts.

If you have been studying for an upcoming sociology test or quiz, you might recognize that this is a functionalist theory. If you have just finished reading or re-reading Chapter 1 of this textbook, you might find that Hirschi's theory fits comfortably with Émile Durkheim's idea of anomie, a lack of connection between citizens and their social institutions that Durkheim felt was a significant cause of both divorce and suicide. Even a casual reading of this textbook will tell you that I am primarily a conflict theorist, so I am critical of any theory that fails to look at how such factors as institutional racism and the exploitation of the poor by wealthy corporations contribute to delinquency.

This being said, I am a strong believer that kids should be involved with sports, for both physical and social reasons. I coached a baseball team that my youngest son was on and saw the positive effects of that bond to both his team and the sport. I was very happy to see both my boys become involved in organized baseball, hockey, and lacrosse. It was also a good opportunity for me, as a stepfather, to increase my stepsons' bonding to me and to our family.

Crime in Canada Today: Going Up or Going Down?

A 2017 report by the Canadian polling firm EKOS reveals that many Canadians believe the crime rate is rising, and that the increase is being driven by violent crime. The report was based on a survey conducted in

Photo by Martin Bazyl

Hosted by the University of Toronto in partnership with Toronto Community Housing, this Midnight Madness basketball league offers youths from high-risk communities the chance to learn drills and skills in a structured environment that also offers educational opportunities and life-skills workshops. In an ethnographic study of urban gang culture, self-described "rogue sociologist" Sudhir Venkatesh describes how community groups in Chicago used midnight basketball to keep at-risk kids on the hardcourt and off the streets. How does sport foster a positive bond with community?

2015. On the question of whether crime had increased over the previous five years, 45 per cent of those surveyed said that it had, while 20 per cent thought that it had stayed the same. Only 31 per cent guessed—correctly—that crime had decreased over the previous five years (EKOS, 2017). When asked how many crimes out of 100 they believed to be violent, close to a quarter of the respondents put the figure anywhere between 60 and 80. The correct answer—that fewer than 20 reported crimes are violent—was given by just 18 per cent of those surveyed (see Figure 6.1).

Before we look at why Canadians tend to over-estimate the rate of crime generally and of violent crime in particular, let's take a look at actual trends in the crime rate. Before we start, though, you should know that Statistics Canada relies on two rates of police-reported crime. The traditional crime rate is usually expressed as the number of crimes committed per 100,000 Canadians. The second rate is the crime severity index (CSI), which weighs serious crimes (like homicide) more heavily than less serious crimes (like jaywalking). The weight of the crime is based on the average prison sentence given for a conviction.

Figure 6.2 shows the police-reported crime rate in Canada from 1998 to 2017. Figure 6.3 tracks the crime severity index in Canada over the same period. Take a moment to look at these two graphs. Would you say that crime in Canada is on the rise or on the decline?

If you answered "sort of," you would be right. The two graphs are consistent in showing an overall drop in the rate of crime since 1997—that's the good news. In fact, in the 10 years from 2007 to 2017, the crime rate dropped by 23 per cent, and the crime severity index fell by 24 per cent. However, both graphs show an increase in crime since 2015—that's the bad news. Why the sudden increase? Part of the jump in serious crime has to do with a 13 per cent

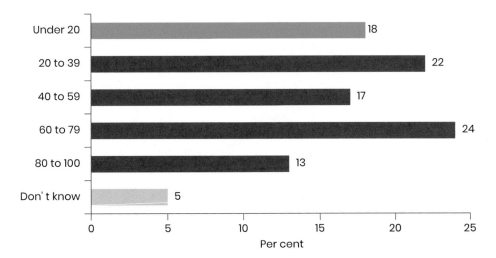

FIGURE 6.1 "Out of 100 crimes committed by adults and reported to police, roughly what number do you think involve violence or the threat of violence?"

Source: EKOS, 2017, p. 15.

increase in reported cases of sexual assault between 2016 and 2017 (see Figure 6.4). Sexual assault accounted for 6 per cent of all violent crimes in 2017 (Allen, 2018). We know that cases of sexual assault often go unreported, but 2017 saw the start of the #MeToo campaign to embolden victims of sexual assault to speak about and report these crimes. At the same time, police departments across the country committed to investigating sexual assault allegations more thoroughly than they had in the past.

Taken together, these two factors likely contributed to the increase in reported cases of sexual assault.

In spite of the uptick in crime since 2015, there has been a significant overall drop in reported crime since the early 1990s. In 1991, the overall police-reported crime rate in Canada was 10,040 (per 100,000 population); in 2017, it was 5334, representing a decrease of close to 47 per cent. The decrease was mirrored by a similar drop in the crime rate over the same period in the United States, meaning that

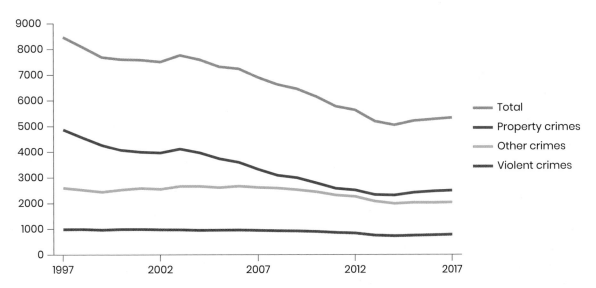

FIGURE 6.2 Rate of Police-Reported Crime in Canada, per 100,000 Population, 1998–2017

Source: Allen, 2018.

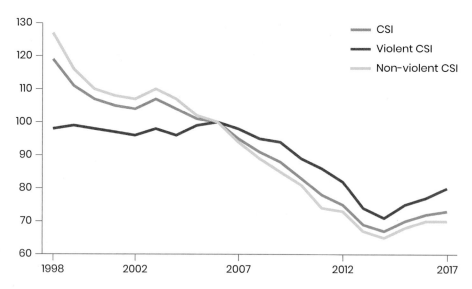

FIGURE 6.3 Police-Reported Crime Severity Index in Canada, 1998–2017

Source: Allen, 2018.

this is not a uniquely Canadian phenomenon. So, how can we account for what one journalist and political commentator in the United States described as "one of the most stunning statistical and sociological mysteries of our time" (Hayes, 2017, p. 172)? No one explanation has emerged in the literature, although many factors have been considered (see Ford, 2016; Gramlich, 2017; Hayes, 2017; Zimring, 2007). Here are a few of them; some more credible than others.

All the Young Criminals Are Growing Up

Demographics is likely one of the larger factors in the declining crime rate. The huge bulge in the population created by the baby boom is moving into the senior section. Young men commit a disproportionately high number of crimes, and the percentage of adult men who are young has dropped drastically on

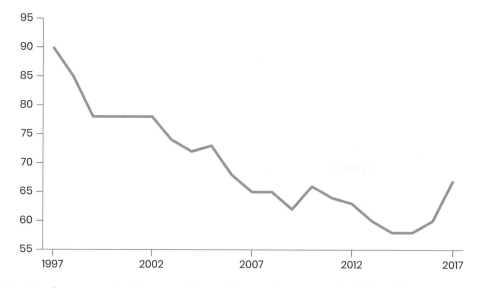

FIGURE 6.4 Police-Reported Cases of Sexual Assault in Canada, 1997–2017

Source: Allen, 2018.

both sides of the Canada–US border. Some support for this idea comes from the fact that other countries that experienced a baby boom in the wake of the Second World War have also had a lowering of the crime rate.

The Criminals Are All in Jail

This proposed explanation applies particularly to the American situation, where mass incarceration is a factor. With such high numbers of people in prison, the criminal element outside of prison should be much smaller. Hayes (2017) questions the validity of this explanation, though, given that American states that have recently tried to reduce their incarceration rates have not seen accompanying increases in crime.

The "Crack Years" Are Over

The mid-1980s are known in criminological circles as the "crack years." Crack cocaine entered big cities across North America at that time, and battles over territory and marketing led to increased crime rates. Once these battles were fairly settled, so the theory goes, the crime rate dropped.

The Number of Crimes Is Seriously Underreported

In 2015, according to a US study, only 47 per cent of violent crime was reported to police. When it comes to more serious violent crime—the sort that causes injury—55 per cent was reported to police, but in the very large category of property crime, the reporting level was just 35 per cent (Truman & Morgan, 2016, p. 5).

There are several reasons why people do not report crimes, including shame or embarrassment, lack of faith in the justice system, and the feeling that a crime is too small to be of interest to the police. But these factors are nothing new, and according to Truman and Morgan (2016, p. 5), there has been no statistically significant change in the percentage of violent crimes and property crimes reported to police since 1993. For the underreporting of crime to be considered a factor in the lowering of the crime rate, there would have to be another factor that caused reporting levels to fall—say, a demonstrated

growth in the number of violent gangs responsible for crimes that victims are usually reluctant to report for fear of reprisal. But this does not appear to be the case.

The Police Have New Laws and New Methods to Fight Crime

What about policing practices and the institution of new laws? While police in some jurisdictions are using new and more sophisticated methods to track, predict, and prevent crime, the idea that these new methods are a leading cause in the declining crime rate is generally discounted by researchers. For one thing, the decline in crime is something we're seeing even in parts of the world where these new methods are not in use. In addition, the timing is wrong: many of these methods were introduced after the crime rate had already begun to fall.

Why Are Canadians More Afraid of Crime?

We can debate the reasons why Canada's crime rate is declining, but we cannot dispute the decline itself: the evidence shows that reported crime has declined steadily over the past 25 years. And yet, as I noted at the start of the last section, a large number of Canadians believe crime has been increasing, violent crime in particular. As sociologists, we have to ask: What's going on?

One explanation is the rise of 24/7 news reporting. Media outlets are in fierce competition for viewers, readers, and clicks, and a story about a local stabbing or shooting tends to attract more eyeballs than an article about foreign policy initiatives or international trade. America's first cable news

What Do YOU Think?

1. Of these individual factors, which do you think has had the greatest effect in the lowering of the crime rate?
2. Are there factors beyond those considered here that you believe have had an impact?

network, CNN, launched in 1980 but didn't become everyday viewing for Americans until 1991, when it came to prominence with its coverage of the first Gulf War. By that time, Canada's own all-news network, CBC Newsworld, was just two years old. Fox News launched in 1996. It is not unreasonable to see a connection between the rise of the cable news networks in the 1990s and the increasing fear of crime. The growth of the internet and social media platforms like Twitter and Facebook means there are more ways than ever for stories of crime to circulate and reach people.

The rise of international terrorism since the September 11 (2001) attacks has helped to make people more fearful of crime. As media scholar Nikki Usher explains, terrorism succeeds in an environment where cable news networks and websites give events happening around the world an immediacy to viewers and readers at home:

> [N]ews organizations help people form their understanding about the world. So with increased coverage of terrorism, more people are thinking about terrorism as part of their daily world experience. This is compounded in another way, though, because now you have an entire conversation of people taking place online through Twitter, through comments on news stories. And so there's almost a compounding effect as people remind each other why there's a reason to be scared. (Usher, 2016)

Our fascination with crime has made us voracious consumers of crime entertainment. Whether is the legion of procedural crime dramas on Netflix or the growing number of true-crime documentaries like *Making a Murderer* or CBC's *Somebody Knows Something* podcast, the menu of shows about killings and psychopaths seems to grow and grow. With their focus on the most gruesome of crimes, these shows not only exaggerate but distort the picture of crime in North America. Property crime far outweighs violent crime in both reported and unreported cases (Truman & Morgan, 2016, p. 7), and yet shows about serial killers outnumber shows about burglary and theft.

As media consumers, we should be able to distinguish between fictional crimes and real ones, and between distant events and those happening close to home. However, communications scholar George Gerbner (1919–2005) and others have argued that all of these media messages combine to make us believe the world is a frightening place. Gerbner coined the term *mean world syndrome* to describe this phenomenon: the more we hear about, for instance, terrorist attacks in Belgium or France or New Zealand, the more we come to see the world as a dangerous place.

It is no coincidence that the EKOS poll on Canadians' perceptions of crime was conducted in the run-up to the 2015 federal election. There are politicians at all levels of government who will raise the spectre of criminal activity to support a law-and-order platform that comes with a promise to crack down on a crime epidemic that doesn't truly exist. Insurance agents, home-security companies, and gun shops are just some of the other groups that benefit when public fears around crime increase.

Wrap it Up

Summary

Deviance can be examined from one of two positions: essentialism and social constructionism. This chapter has taken a social-constructionist perspective, reflecting the belief that deviance is not natural but is socially constructed, artificial, and something that can vary from culture to culture and can change over time. What's more, the social construction of what is considered deviant is often contested or challenged within a culture. There is a power element found in deviance, with those who hold power in society getting to define what is deviant and what is "normal." The dominant culture's definition of deviance (in

North America, a predominantly white, male, English-speaking, middle-aged, middle-class, and ableist definition) can override the definitions of deviance that come from people less powerful in the same society. People may be classified and treated as deviant not because of their behaviour but because of their ready identification as belonging to a group outside of what makes up the dominant culture. Once branded as deviant, these groups may find themselves the targets of social sanctions designed to punish members of minority cultures and people with "alternative" lifestyles.

Some deviant acts that do not meet standards of behaviour established by the dominant culture are relatively benign. Attending multiple comic book conventions dressed as your favourite superhero (when you are not paid to do so) isn't hurting anyone. However, some deviant acts, from begging and loitering to assault and homicide, have been socially constructed as criminal and are prohibited by law. Looking at criminal deviance in Canada presents us with a contradiction: the crime rate is dropping, and yet people fear crime more than ever. Neither trend has a simple explanation.

Think Back

Questions for Critical Review

1. Describe, with examples, what is meant by the term *deviant*. Is deviance always bad for society?
2. Assess tattoos as a subject of conflict deviance. How do public perceptions of tattoos change over time and place, and depending on the situation?
3. From the moment they learned to draw, humans have been producing sexually erotic or explicit materials on cave walls, pottery, sketchpads, newsprint, film, and video. It will be no surprise to you that the internet has made all of this material much more widely accessible than ever before, though there is disagreement about the extent and the effects of North Americans' consumption of pornography. Is pornography strictly deviant, or are attitudes changing?
4. In sociology, what is meant by "the Other"? How is the concept of the Other related to deviance?
5. Outline how deviance can be associated with disability.
6. Find a recent example of a moral panic. What agenda does it serve? How is it spread? Who are the moral entrepreneurs behind it, and what do they stand to gain?
7. Those who study linguistics distinguish between **marked** and **unmarked terms**. The unmarked term is the usual one, while the marked term has a label added to distinguish it from the common term. "Field hockey," "light beer," "white chocolate," and "decaffeinated coffee" are all marked terms. What does the marked term *white-collar crime* suggest about the way crime is viewed in the mainstream?
8. Michel Foucault said that "the guilty person is only one of the targets of punishment. For punishment is directed above all at others, at all the potentially guilty." What do you think he meant by that?
9. The theories of criminal deviance discussed in this chapter were designed to explain primarily male gangs and behaviour around the mid-twentieth century. How well do these theories explain delinquent youth gangs—male and female—today?

Read On

Recommended Print and Online Resources

Andrew Scull (2009), *Hysteria: The Disturbing History* **(Oxford, UK: Oxford University Press).**

- A sometimes funny, always readable, and very instructive sociological history of the eighteenth- and nineteenth-century diagnosis of a "woman's emotional/mental disturbance."

Claudia Malacrida (2015), *A Special Hell: Institutional Life in Alberta's Eugenic Years* **(Toronto, ON: University of Toronto Press).**

- A powerfully written book about the Michener Institute, where people were imprisoned for being deemed "mental defectives."

critcrim.org: Critical Criminology Information and Resources, www.critcrim.org/index.php

- Affiliated with the American Society of Criminology, this site provides a forum for organizations and individuals who are working to critically analyze, and change, the American justice system.

James William Coleman (2002), *The Criminal Elite: Understanding White-Collar Crime*, **5th edn (New York: Worth).**

- Coleman's work offers an in-depth analysis of how white-collar crime affects society, and an evaluation of the legal remedies.

Jeffrey Reiman (2007), *The Rich Get Richer and the Poor Get Prison: Ideology, Class, and Criminal Justice*, **8th edn (Boston, MA: Allyn & Bacon).**

- Reiman's timeless work gives an excellent look at how class and deviance go hand in hand.

John Steckley (2011), *Learning from the Past: Five Cases of Aboriginal Justice* **(Whitby, ON: De Sitter).**

- This short work outlines the deviance of being Indigenous in Canada through five notorious cases.

Kim Rossmo (1995), "Place, Space and Police Investigations: Hunting Serial Violent Criminals," in D. Weisburd & J.E. Eck, eds, *Crime and Place* **(New York: Criminal and Justice Theory).**

- Canadian criminologist Kim Rossmo developed methods of geographic profiling to map, predict, and prevent violent crime and pinpoint the home base of the offender.

Leilani Muir (2014), A Whisper Past: Childless after Eugenic Sterilization in Alberta (Calgary, AB: Friesen).

- Leilani Muir describes in her own words the events that led to her incarceration in the Red Deer Training School for Mental Defectives and sterilization under Alberta's Sexual Sterilization Act.

Sandro Contenta & Jim Rankin (2009), "Suspended Sentences: Forging a School-to-Prison Pipeline?" *Toronto Star* **(June 6).**

- A readable news feature on class and criminal deviance.

SocioWeb: Criminality and Deviance, www.socioweb.com/directory/sociology-topics/criminology-and-social-deviance

- The SocioWeb is a guide to sociology resources on the internet. This page gives links to websites covering topics in criminology and deviance.

Sudhir Venkatesh (2008), *Gang Leader for a Day: A Rogue Sociologist Takes to the Streets* **(New York: Penguin).**

- A study of poverty, gangs, and drugs in Chicago, based on ethnographic research.

Velma Delmerson (2004), *Incorrigible* **(Waterloo, ON: Wilfrid Laurier University Press).**

- The autobiography of a white woman who was incarcerated for having a sexual relationship with a Chinese man.

Social Inequality

Reading this chapter will help you to . . .

- Describe Marx's class structure and how it differs from Weber's.

- Differentiate between "class" and "stratum."

- Comment on how wealth is distributed in Canada.

- Define *ideology* and give examples of a dominant ideology and a counter-ideology.

- Explain the difference between a minimum wage and a living wage.

- Discuss who uses food banks in Canada and what that information tells us about poverty.

For Starters

A Picture of Poverty in Canada's Backyard

Situated on the west coast of James Bay in Ontario's north, Attawapiskat First Nation gained international attention in October 2011 when its leaders declared a state of emergency, citing inadequate housing and poor sanitation. It was not the first time the Cree community had resorted to this measure. In May 2008, hundreds of residents had been evacuated from their tents, trailers, and shelters because of serious flood conditions. And yet, in the fall of 2011, the media seized on stories of poverty and overcrowded, substandard housing as though they were new developments, while politicians claimed to have had no idea how bad the situation was.

How bad was it? You can read statistics about lack of housing, but to me, this account tells the story much more vividly:

In a one-room, tented shack where Lisa Kiokee-Linklater is watching television with her two toddlers, two mattresses lie on the floor. Each is a bed for three. Mould is creeping across one mattress even though Ms Kiokee-Linklater just bought it last summer. It cost her $1000.

There is no running water, no bathroom, and cold comes through the uninsulated floor. There is little room for her four children to play. The broiling cast-iron wood stove that takes up one corner of the room represents a burn hazard and eliminates the notion of the rambunctious play that is the norm for most young kids.

Moving into the tent was Ms Kiokee-Linklater's choice. It seemed a step up from her previous home next door, where she shared a single bathroom with 20 other people until it became too much for her and her growing family.

THE CANADIAN PRESS/Adrian Wyld

"It's kind of better, yeah," she said.... "But during the winter, it's hard. I cut back on the baths because it is so cold." (Scofield, 2011)

A situation like that doesn't just develop overnight. Nor is it quickly resolved. A year later, Attawapiskat Chief Theresa Spence began a hunger strike to draw attention to the desperate circumstances of her own community and others across the country. The reaction in Ottawa and in the media focused on the alleged mishandling of funds in her community, a "red herring" that distracted the public from the real issue: the desperate state of Indigenous housing in Canada. Then, in April 2016, Attawapiskat again declared a state of emergency, this time because of an eight-month-long epidemic of suicide attempts. In one month alone, 28 people in the community of 2000 tried to kill themselves (Rutherford, 2016). The crisis was acute among young people suffering from bullying, sexual abuse, drug and alcohol addiction, and the dismal prospects they face in a town where jobs, housing, and even drinkable water are in short supply. Once again, politicians expressed shock at how grave the situation had become, as if it had happened overnight.

Attawapiskat had not always been a town in crisis. In 2003, anthropologist Bryan Cummins characterized Attawapiskat as a model of self-sustainability. His extensive fieldwork revealed how successfully the Attawapiskat Cree used their land for food, clothing, and building supplies. That was less than 20 years ago. So what caused the community's fortunes to turn around?

In 2008, months after the town experienced disastrous flooding, a wealthy neighbour took up residence less than 100 kilometres away. This was the international mining giant De Beers, which opened up a diamond mine in the James Bay Lowlands. The operation was not good for local wetlands and wildlife, and it had a mixed effect on Attawapiskat's residents. Some locals recount that the mining development attracted a sudden influx of outsiders, who brought, acquired, and spent big money during their short stay in Cree country, creating short-term jobs for the locals and giving a tantalizing taste of what could be. But short-term wealth brings trouble, too—corruption, alcohol, drugs. In spring 2019, the mine closed for good, leaving a large open pit and questions about the community's future.

When it comes to poverty, neither causes nor solutions are easy to identify. Examining the situation from afar, politicians, newspaper columnists, and other citizens of the South, many of them well meaning, have mused that the community should simply resettle somewhere where there are jobs, schools, hospitals, and better economic prospects. This commentary ignores centuries of problems caused by "repeatedly hustling [Indigenous people] into new and unfamiliar environments," notes Tristin Hopper (2016), adding that non-Indigenous Canadians, descended from immigrants, have a uniquely favourable view of leaving home in search of greener pastures. Poverty is seldom simply a matter of setting; indeed, wherever it exists—in a northern Indigenous community, a drought-stricken farming region, a once prosperous Atlantic fishing village, a rundown urban neighbourhood—it is a complex problem. There is rarely one cause, never one solution.

Introduction: Is Social Inequality Inevitable?

For there will never cease to be poor in the land. Therefore I command you: "You shall open wide your hand to your brother, to the needy and to the poor, in your land." (*English Standard Version Bible*, Deuteronomy 15:11)

The disposition to admire, and almost to worship, the rich and the powerful, and to despise, or at least, to neglect persons of poor and mean condition ... is ... the great and most universal cause of the corruption of our moral sentiments. (Adam Smith, *The Theory of our Moral Sentiments*, [1759] 1976)

The study of social inequality has long been a part of the sociological tradition. You could argue that modern sociology evolved from the writings of eighteenth-century economists such as **Adam Smith** (1723–1790) and **Thomas Malthus** (1766–1834). Smith, quoted above, was an early proponent of laissez-faire economics, the idea that governments should not try to manage or interfere in the so-called free market. To those who believe in laissez-fair economics, "interference" is anything that regulates or slows down how businesses operate. (It does not include the financial incentives, tax benefits, and bailout packages that governments sometimes offer to big businesses; that kind of interference is apparently okay.) To critics of laissez-faire economics, there is no such thing as a "free" market when it is dominated by multinational corporations with near-monopolistic power.

Smith was optimistic that a market free of government interference would raise standards of living for everyone, though he might have agreed with the idea that there will always be at least some "poor in the land." Malthus wasn't nearly as optimistic about the prospects for the poor. He predicted that dramatic population growth would inevitably lead to a scarcity of food and other resources. He warned that famine, disease, and war would "naturally" limit population growth unless other measures, including birth control and celibacy, were adopted.

Is poverty really inevitable? Is offering a handout to "the needy and the poor" really the best we can do? I like to think that most sociologists would say no to both questions. The political philosopher **Karl Marx** (1818–1838), whose writings we will consider in a moment, certainly didn't see inequality as inevitable—and he was prepared to do something about it. Perhaps that is why he is often seen as one of the founders of sociology. But it would be wrong to suggest that all sociologists share his view. Indeed, few areas are more contentious in the sociological, economic, and political study of societies than the study of social inequality, the long-term existence of significant differences in access to material goods and opportunities among social groups.

Inevitable or not, social inequality is a function of many factors, only some of which we will cover in this chapter. Ethnicity, "race," and gender are discussed in their own chapters, but they all have an impact on the economic well-being of an individual or family. This chapter will focus mainly on two related concepts, class and stratification, beginning with an introduction to the writings of Karl Marx. There is a special language involved in interpreting Marx, and I apologize in advance for the volume of bold terms you will find bearing down on you as you read the following sections.

Marx and Weber: Historical Approaches to the Study of Social Class

The main term used to talk about social inequality is *class*, but its definition has been the subject of much debate since Marx popularized the term. Near the beginning of *The Communist Manifesto* (1888), Marx and his co-author, **Friedrich Engels** (1820–1895), give us some clues about their understanding of class:

> The history of all hitherto existing society is the history of class struggles. Freeman and slave, patrician and plebian, lord and serf, guild-master and journeyman, in a word, oppressor and oppressed, stood in constant opposition to one another, carried on an uninterrupted, now hidden, now open fight, a fight that each time ended, either in a revolutionary reconstitution of society at large, or in the common ruin of the contending classes. . . .
>
> The modern bourgeois society that has sprouted from the ruins of feudal society has not done away with class antagonisms. It has but established new classes, new conditions of oppression, new forms of struggle in place of the old ones.
>
> Our epoch, the epoch of the bourgeoisie, possesses, however, this distinct feature: it has simplified class antagonisms. Society as a whole is more and more splitting up into two great hostile camps, into two great classes directly facing each other— bourgeoisie and proletariat.

"Opposition," "fight," "antagonism," "hostile camps"—if you gleaned anything from these paragraphs, you will understand that Marx saw society as divided into two groups embroiled in a bitter rivalry. That sets the tone for much of what he says about the distribution of wealth in society.

Class, as Marx described it, is **relational**: it reflects the relationship of people to what he called the **means of production**—the resources needed to produce goods (and hence, wealth). In the pre-industrial Europe that Marx studied, the chief means of production was fertile land: wealth was produced by growing food crops and raising livestock. Once Europe began to become industrialized during the nineteenth century, when Marx and Engels lived, the means of production became **capital**, the money needed to build factories, purchase raw materials, and pay labourers to turn those raw materials into manufactured products. In spite of the fact he devoted an entire book (*Das Kapital*) to the topic, the precise meaning of Marx's term *capital* has been contested. For our purposes, we can understand it as the funds and properties necessary for large-scale manufacturing and trading.

For Marx, there were only two possible relationships to the means of production: either you owned them or you worked for those who did. In pre-industrial Europe, the owners were called **aristocrats** and the workers, **peasants**. Marx called the owners of capital in industrial-era Europe **capitalists**; he referred to the members of this class collectively as the **bourgeoisie**. The class of **workers**, which succeeded the peasant class of the pre-industrial era, made up the **proletariat**.

Two centuries after his birth in 1818, an imposing statue of Marx is unveiled in his home town of Trier, Germany. Marx looms large in the political discourse and popular imagination of the twenty-first century. Is it the vision of a classless society? The promise to topple the capitalist order? The big hair? What about Marx and his teachings resonates so much with academics, activists, and economic theorists today?

The Point Is...

Today's Working Class Is Precarious

There is a useful new term that has begun popping up in the sociological literature: *precariat*. Coined by British economist Guy Standing, it combines the word *precarious* (as in precarious employment) with Marx's term *proletariat*. According to Standing (2011), the precariat was born in the 1970s, in the early days of the globalization movement, when large corporations and conservative governments started demanding greater "labour flexibility" from a previously secure and stable working class. The goal was competitiveness. Labour flexibility was achieved through a number of corporate and political strategies, including "downsizing" (the great euphemism for laying off workers), "outsourcing" (sending work to lower-paid labourers abroad), and in the United States, "right to work" legislation (another euphemism, meaning the right to work without having to join a union).

As a business strategy, labour flexibility turned steady work into precarious employment and gave rise to the precariat, a vulnerable, unstable version of the Marxian working class. As Standing explains, Marx's proletariat usually signfies

> a society consisting mostly of workers in long-term, stable, fixed-hour jobs with established routes of advancement, subject to unionisation and collective agreements, with job titles their fathers and mothers would have understood, facing local employers whose names and features they were familiar with. (Standing, 2011, p. 6)

How does this differ from the precariat? For Standing, the precariat

consists of people who have minimal trust relationships with capital or the state.... [I]t has none of the social contract relationships of the proletariat, whereby labour securities were provided in exchange for subordination and contingent loyalty, the unwritten deal underpinning welfare states. Without a bargain of trust or security in exchange for subordination, the precariat is distinctive in class terms. (Standing, 2011, p. 8)

Recall for a moment Marx's prediction about the proletariat: he imagined that workers would eventually tire of being taken advantage of and would attempt to overthrow the capitalist system through revolution. In most capitalist countries, this didn't happen—partly, we could argue, because workers accepted their "bargain," as Standing puts it: the proletariat would submit to the capitalist class, giving their labour in exchange for stable, guaranteed employment and wages.

Today's precariat enjoys no such social contract or relationship of trust with either the state or the capitalist class. As a result, Standing argues, members of this new working class "are prone to listen to ugly voices, and to use their votes and money to give those voices a political platform of increasing influence" (Standing, 2011, p. 1). In other words, the success of populist leaders like Donald Trump can be attributed directly to the spread of precarious employment, in Standing's view. I would add that the gig economy, characterized by disruptive innovation (see Airbnb, Uber, and Lyft as examples) began as a more pragmatic, typically millennial response to precarious employment.

Marx identified various sub-classes—the **petty** (or **petite**) **bourgeoisie**, made up of small-time owners with little capital, and the **lumpenproletariat**, the small-time criminals, beggars, and unemployed—but these terms do not have the significance of his two primary classes, the "two great hostile camps" referred to in the final sentence of the passage quoted above.

Marx's Historical Context

If you wonder at Marx's black-and-white view of society, remember the conditions he saw, and the context in which he lived. Britain, where Marx lived from 1850 until his death in 1883, was operating according to those laissez-faire market practices advocated by Smith and others, in which business was supposed to take care of itself without any interference from government. The Factory Act of 1833, which targeted primarily the booming textile mills of Britain, was considered radical at the time. The mill-owning bourgeoisie claimed that the act interfered with the "natural course" of business by "severely" limiting the hours that people were allowed to work. They complained that the act would ruin them financially, even drive them out of business. What limits did the Factory Act put on business? First, the act stipulated that the working day was to start no earlier than 5:30 a.m. and end no later than 8:30 p.m. It also included these provisions:

- "[N]o person under eighteen years of age shall [work] between half-past eight in the evening and half-past five in the morning, in any cotton, woollen, worsted, hemp, flax, tow, linen or silk mill. . . ."
- "[N]o person under the age of eighteen shall be employed in any such mill . . . more than twelve hours in . . . one day, nor more than sixty-nine hours in . . . one week. . . ."
- "It shall not be lawful . . . to employ in any factory . . . , except in mills for the manufacture of silk, any child who shall not have completed his or her ninth year."
- "It shall not be lawful for any person to employ . . . in any factory . . . for longer than forty-eight hours in one week, nor for longer than nine hours in one day, any child who shall not have completed his or her eleventh year. . . ."
- "Every child restricted to the performance of forty-eight hours of labour in any one week shall attend some school." (*Statutes of the Realm*, 3 & 4 William IV, c. 103)

These limits on the length of the working day and working week for people under 18 were the aspects of the Factory Act that mill owners thought would ruin them. We hear the same kind of concerns from business representatives today whenever someone proposes improving worker rights by raising the minimum wage or granting sick days to unsalaried employees.

Class as a Social Identity

Another characteristic of class in Marx's view is that it has a **corporate** (or **organic**) **identity** as a real social group. In other words, there is a shared sense of purpose among members of each class. A related term, **class consciousness**, means having an awareness of what is in the best interests of one's class. Marx believed that the owner class always possesses class consciousness, always knows what is in its best interests, and attempts to shape society in ways that promote those interests. Witness the **Highland Clearances** of the late eighteenth and early nineteenth centuries. Land-owning aristocrats in Scotland, aware of the rising value of wool to the rapidly industrializing textile industry, began evicting tenant farmers from their estates to make room for sheep. The clearances caused extreme hardship among the evicted "crofters," whose families had been on the land for generations. Many were forced to emigrate, notably to North America. The aristocrats knew that they would benefit in the long run from evicting the crofters.

The worker class does not always have such an awareness. On the contrary, it often has **false consciousness**, a belief that something is in its best interests when it is not. Marx believed that the proletariat's false consciousness kept them from waging open revolt against a system that was not working in their favour. Factors that could contribute to false consciousness include religion, which may be used to argue that poverty and wealth are parts of some divine plan; politics, which are often used to persuade low-income voters that pro-business policies will benefit everyone; and patriotism, which underlies protectionist policies that limit free trade between countries.

Weber's Critique of Marx

Another early sociologist to look at inequality was **Max Weber**, whom we met in Chapter 1. Weber didn't quite agree with Marx's theory of class relations, and though the two men were not contemporaries (it is

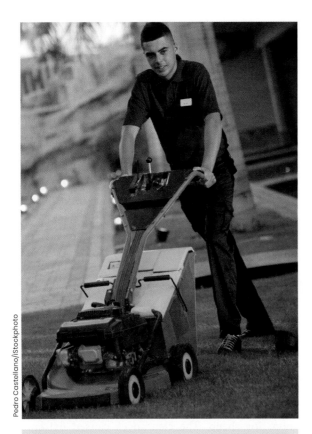

Pedro Castellano/iStockphoto

This young man owns two gas-powered lawnmowers and, with the help of his buddy Jake (whom he pays $18 an hour), operates his own small landscaping business. Assess his class position from both a Marxist and a Weberian perspective.

find so often among Super Bowl quarterbacks. Prestige is the degree of respect with which individuals, their socially valued possessions, and their master statuses are viewed by the majority of people in a society. Prestige can be turned into various forms of *social power*, which is usually defined as the ability of individuals or groups to achieve their goals despite the opposition of others.

One example of a person embodying (literally!) wealth, prestige, and power is Arnold Schwarzenegger. As a young man, his good looks and muscular body were his wealth, earning him prestige as a bodybuilder (then his master status) and winner of the Mr Universe competition. The respect accorded him for his physical appearance enabled Arnie to change careers and become an actor, which brought him further prestige. This he turned into real social and political power, first by marrying a Kennedy relative (more prestige) and then by being elected governor of California in 2004. He followed a course laid out by an earlier governor of California, Ronald Reagan, who had parlayed his own prestige as an actor into presidency of the United States. From a Weberian perspective, what is important is that Schwarzenegger's membership in the dominant social class was not about controlling the means of production in a Marxist sense.

sometimes said that Weber engaged in theoretical discussions with Marx's ghost), their views on the subject are frequently compared. (Hint: the topic makes a good exam question.)

Like Marx, Weber viewed society as divided into different economic classes, but he believed that Marx's materialist approach was too simplistic, that there was more to social inequality than just who owned the means of production. In particular, Weber stressed three elements—*wealth*, *prestige*, and *power*—as contributing to social inequality. For Weber, wealth, or material resources, includes not just factories and other property used to make money but also properties that are highly respected by members of the society in question: in Western society, the flashy car, the expensive house, the trophy spouse, the winning good looks you seem to

Using Class to Study Social Inequality Today

There are some problems with applying a traditional Marxist interpretation of class to contemporary societies in countries such as Canada. For one thing, there are many people who, as employees of big businesses (bank presidents, corporate CEOs, business lawyers, hospital administrators, professional hockey players), would belong to Marx's class of "workers," even though their incomes put them in the top 1 per cent, on a par with the wealthiest of capitalists. Likewise, there are farmers, store owners, and other small business operators who have incomes that are more like those of workers. And unlike Marx, who was concerned with the binary opposition of the bourgeoisie and proletariat, we can argue for the existence of a very large middle group with a powerful sense of itself as a class.

The Point Is...

The Gig Economy Is Nothing New

The "gig economy" is a trendy term for those who get by performing assorted casual, part-time jobs, typically with hours flexible enough that a person can fit two or more kinds of work in around other commitments, such as going to school. To a musician, a gig is a one-night performance, and if you have ever known a working musician, you will know that it takes a lot of gigs to pay the rent and keep food on the table.

When we talk about the gig economy, we tend to think of ride-hailing services like Uber and other internet-mediated peer-to-peer services that connect people with underused assets (a spare bedroom, a cube van, a background in computer science) with people willing to pay for them. These arrangements are sometimes seen as disrupting the traditional economy, giving savvy millennials a way to undermine traditional capitalist structures. But stringing together part-time jobs is nothing new, and it isn't restricted to the generation that grew up with the internet on their iPhones. The gig economy is good for retired people like me. I retired from full-time work in 2015 but was hired to work part-time as the tribal linguist for the Wyandotte Nation of Oklahoma. I have a contract with Oxford University Press to update the

IAN KUCERAK / POSTMEDIA

While it's not quite the violent overthrow of capitalist machinery that Marx was hoping for, the growth of ride-hailing services like Uber does present a challenge to the traditional business models—or does it? Is it just another way for large multinational companies to exploit workers with low pay and no benefits? Or do you see a hint of Marxist revolution in the gig economy?

Continued

textbook you're reading. Like a good number of baby boomers, I supplement my pension with the money earned from these gigs. This brings undeniable benefits: I set my own hours, and I work from home (sometimes, like now, with a parrot resting on my head), meaning I don't have to commute to work or attend staff meetings.

But the gig economy also means job insecurity, no medical benefits, and low income. Like many academics, I experienced that early in my career, before I had a regular teaching job. I did an 11-month contract for the Ontario Ministry of Natural Resources, developing wildlife programs for students in grades 4 to 6. Before that I taught English part-time at a small private school, while writing articles for newspapers and magazines and teaching a few courses at Humber College, where I was eventually hired full-time. I could not afford to have my teeth done, never went on vacation, and constantly worried whether I would ever have a "real career."

Within the Canadian context, we can draw on the work of Curtis, Grabb, and Guppy (1999) to amend Marx's class paradigm by arguing that there are essentially three different classes in this country:

1. A **dominant capitalist class** "composed mainly of those who own or control large-scale production." This would include the presidents and CEOs of large businesses (including universities), who may not own their companies but who are paid handsomely for running them.
2. A **middle class** representing "a mixed ... middle category of small-scale business people, educated professional-technical or administrative personnel, and various salaried employees or wage-earners possessing some certifiable credentials, training, or skills." This group includes small-business entrepreneurs, teachers and nurses, academic researchers, and those who have been able to translate a postsecondary degree into a modest but respectable job in an office or skilled trade.
3. A **working class** or **proletariat**, "made up of people who lack resources or capacities apart from their own labour power": people in construction or manufacturing, retail employees, and others in the service industry. (Curtis, Grabb, & Guppy, 1999, p. ix)

We will consider the middle class in greater detail later in this chapter.

Class Divisions and Popular Sport

There is a strong connection between class and sport at both the professional and recreational levels. The traditional association of sports like golf and tennis with the wealthy classes has been reinforced through the prohibitive cost of—and prestige surrounding—country club membership. Weber might recognize belonging to an exclusive Vancouver golf club as a form of wealth. Compare that with membership in a bowling league, where players enjoy a sport generally seen as having greater working-class appeal. Marketers and advertisers involved in professional sports often exploit these associations to attract a particular fan base to their sport, in spite of the fact that most professional athletes earn lucrative salaries that put them in the top 1 per cent.

Sports that offer people from poorer socioeconomic backgrounds the chance to reap large financial rewards as professional athletes are called **mobility sports**. Any sport can be considered a mobility sport if it is cheap to play (with low costs for equipment and participation), if it offers people of all classes the chance to "be discovered," and if it provides middle-to upper-class incomes for the select few who "make it." Boxing is a sport with a tradition of providing young men raised in poor and sometimes violent circumstances an alternative to "the mean streets." Professional boxers rarely come from the middle class. The highest-paid athlete in 2018 was boxer Floyd Mayweather Jr, who grew up with poverty and abuse in New Jersey. He never completed high school but was wearing boxing gloves as soon as he

pumkinpie/Alamy Stock Photo

A youth in Cochin, India, wears the soccer jersey of Lionel Messi, ranked second on Forbes's list of wealthiest athletes in 2018 with an income of USD$111 million (Forbes, 2018). How would you situate Messi within Marx's class framework? And what would it take for this youth to follow in his hero's footsteps? Is "the beautiful game" also the world's greatest mobility sport?

could walk (Snowden, 2013). Boxing today has lost some of its popularity and prestige to mixed martial arts and its professional embodiment, UFC (the Ultimate Fighting Championship), which has developed a loyal and increasingly mainstream fan base rooted in lower- and middle-class North America. During the last 40 years, basketball in North America and soccer globally have been mobility sports for racialized young people.

When a Mobility Sport Becomes an Elitist Sport

Canadian hockey lore is filled with stories of poor young men from farming communities in the West or mining towns in the East rising from poverty and humble beginnings to achieve celebrity playing in the NHL. Gordie Howe, who was born in 1928, was one of nine children raised on a failing farm in Depression-era Floral, Saskatchewan; he became a

superstar, arguably (among older fans) the greatest player ever. Born in 1935, Johnny Bucyk grew up in a rough neighbourhood of north Edmonton, the son of Ukrainian immigrants. In a memoir he recalls learning to play hockey with "road apples," without sticks, pads, or skates:

> I can remember playing street hockey when I was a kid, maybe seven or eight years old. In those days you couldn't afford to buy hockey sticks, nobody in our group could. I was from a poor family and I really didn't know what it was to own a hockey stick, so I didn't care. I played a lot of street hockey and we used brooms for sticks. We couldn't afford pucks either, so we'd follow the milk wagon which was pulled by a couple of horses, waiting until the horses did their job, dropping a good hunk of manure. Usually it would be a cold day, anytime between

Quick Hits

Minor Hockey, Major Cash

The cost of outfitting a child for hockey depends on what level the child is at, where you shop, and how much you're willing to pay. Below are two extremes based on the new equipment a 10-year-old might typically wear to play forward or defence (goalie equipment is even more expensive).

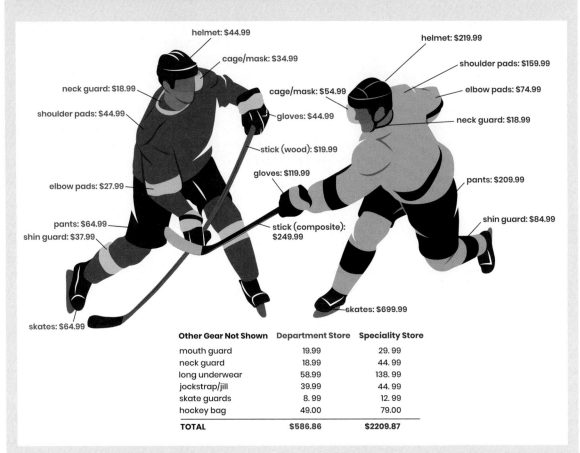

Left player (Department Store): helmet: $44.99; cage/mask: $34.99; neck guard: $18.99; shoulder pads: $44.99; gloves: $44.99; stick (wood): $19.99; elbow pads: $27.99; pants: $64.99; shin guard: $37.99; skates: $64.99

Right player (Speciality Store): helmet: $219.99; shoulder pads: $159.99; elbow pads: $74.99; cage/mask: $54.99; neck guard: $18.99; gloves: $119.99; pants: $209.99; stick (composite): $249.99; shin guard: $84.99; skates: $699.99

Other Gear Not Shown	Department Store	Speciality Store
mouth guard	19.99	29.99
neck guard	18.99	44.99
long underwear	58.99	138.99
jockstrap/jill	39.99	44.99
skate guards	8.99	12.99
hockey bag	49.00	79.00
TOTAL	**$586.86**	**$2209.87**

Other Basic Costs

- average registration for boys' or girls' house league: $700
- average registration for boys' or girls' competitive league: $3000–$4000
- ice time for extra practices
- power-skating lessons
- summer hockey schools
- gas, food, and accommodations for "away" games and out-of-town tournaments
- skate sharpening.

Source: Ormsby, 2007; Rutherford, 2009.

What Do YOU Think?

Do you think that hockey in Canada can still be seen as a mobility sport, or has it become solely an elitist sport? What arguments can be made for each position? How could you test your hypothesis?

the start of October through the end of April, and we'd let it freeze up solid. We'd use it as a hockey puck. . . . I didn't get my first pair of skates until I was about 10 years old. It was a pair of my older brother Bill's, which he outgrew. (Quoted in Lowe, Fischler, & Fischler, 1988, pp. 43–4)

Bucyk played in the National Hockey League from 1956 to 1978, most of that time with the Boston Bruins, and was inducted into the Hockey Hall of Fame in 1981.

Players like Howe and Bucyk earned decent livings playing hockey, though they came nowhere near the earnings of professional athletes in North America today. They grew up at a time when the cost of playing organized sport was relatively low. Over the last 30 years, the costs associated with raising a potential professional hockey player have risen astronomically. Beyond the price tag for the latest equipment and league fees, a player who shows skill enough to play for a touring competitive team will incur travel costs and higher registration fees.

The rise in costs is a feature of the **professionalization** of elite minor hockey, which now depends heavily on professional coaches and trainers. The trend is evident not just in other sports but in activities such as music, drama, and dance. In some cases, it reflects the diminishing role of schools in delivering extracurricular activities. School boards facing tight budgets may be forced to cut dedicated gym and music teachers, leaving athletic and arts programs starving for staff and funding. It also reflects changing middle- and upper-class expectations concerning extracurricular activities, as parents indulge in the dream that, with sufficient funds, their

THE CANADIAN PRESS/Darryl Dyck

Fans packed Vancouver's Rogers Arena to watch teams compete for USD$25 million in prize money during a week-long _Dota 2_ tournament in August 2018. The past decade has seen the rise of professional videogaming, which attracts huge audiences live and online. Fans can wager on their favourite pro teams, like the Vancouver Titans, owned by the NHL's Vancouver Canucks. Universities are offering scholarships to students who join their varsity eSport teams, and there's a push to add eSports to the Olympics. Is online videogaming a mobility sport? Is it a sport at all?

children may one day become highly paid professionals. Many lower-class families cannot afford the same experience for their children, giving middle- and upper-class families a distinct advantage and making various sports—hockey in this case—much less of a mobility sport.

Social Stratification: Another View of Social Inequality

The class structure that Marx introduced remains a useful way to talk about social inequality, but it is imprecise. For example, many North Americans identify as middle class, which makes sense: no matter how comfortable you are, there will always be others with more and less than what you have, and what you have never seems like enough; that puts you in the middle, right? Politicians exploit this when they pledge (if elected) to help the middle class: most voters see themselves as likely beneficiaries of those promises.

The trouble comes when we try to define what it means to be middle class. Definitions vary so much that it can be hard to know who belongs. Does it have to do with what you own or what you earn? Is it more nuanced than that? A CBC article from 2015 quotes Scott Brison, then a federal member of Parliament and finance critic for the Liberal Party, as saying the middle class includes "the broadest swath of Canadians whose working income gives them the capacity to provide decent housing, quality of life, and a good education for their families, while saving for retirement" (Blatchford, 2015). If that sounds vague to you, then you are thinking like a sociologist and not a politician. After all, shouldn't we be able to *quantify*, or measure, what it means to be middle class?

This brings us to social stratification. When we talk about social stratification, we are borrowing a geological term to describe society as though it were divided into a series of layers. In geology, a stratum is a single level or layer of rock made up of tiny particles deposited together; if you look at a cross-section of sedimentary rock, you will be able to see the different strata and note the differences.

In sociology, a *stratum* is a group to which people belong depending on their level of income,

education, or another social variable. It is usually each of several equal groups into which a population has been divided for comparison. **Strata** are used as units of analysis in stratified sampling, a research method in which equal samples are drawn from each stratum of the population instead of drawing one larger sample at random from the whole population. Stratified sampling produces a more representative sample to analyze.

Using Quintiles to Identify the Middle Class

Studies using stratified sampling to divide the population into even segments for analysis use quintiles, quartiles, or deciles. A **quintile** is a segment, or stratum, representing each of five equal groups into which the population is divided; each quintile represents 20 per cent of the population. (Quartiles use four strata, deciles ten.)

Let's say that we wanted to divide the population into quintiles according to household (family) income. Using Statistics Canada's definition, a household is a person or group of people who occupy the same dwelling as their primary place of residence. Grattan (2003) offers a good explanation of how we would arrive at our quintiles:

> Imagine that all families are placed in a line, a family's place being determined by its income level. The poorest family is placed at the front of the line, followed by the next poorest, and so on, until the last family, with the highest income, is placed at the end. Next, the line is split into five equal groups. The first group, or quintile, is composed of the first 20 per cent of the line. Obviously, this group will consist of the poorest people. The next group consists of the next 20 per cent. A similar process occurs in selecting the third, fourth, and fifth groups. The fifth group, of course, comprises those families with the highest incomes. (Grattan, 2003, pp. 64–5)

Figure 7.1 shows what you would find if you conducted that very procedure using Canadian families and their household incomes in a particular year. You can see that this gives us one basis for

Quintile	Household Income Range
Highest 20%	$125,010 and above
Upper-middle 20%	$88,075 to $125,009
Middle 20%	**$61,929 to $88,074**
Lower-middle 20%	$38,755 to $61,928
Lowest 20%	$0 to $38,754

FIGURE 7.1 Stratification of Canadian House-holdsᵃ by income, 2013ᵇ

a. Estimates for 2013 were compiled by *MoneySense* magazine based on Statistics Canada 2011 data.

b. A household is any family of two or more people.

Source: Data from Hodges & Brown, 2015.

defining *middle class*. We could define it narrowly as any family in the middle quintile—meaning the middle 20 per cent of Canadians—or more broadly as any family in the middle three quintiles, representing 60 per cent of Canadian families. Politicians prefer the latter of these two definitions, which gives them the largest group of "middle-class voters" to pitch their promises to. But consider this: Is it realistic to treat the middle three quintiles as a single group when their household incomes range from a meagre $38,750 all the way to $125,000?

Assessing the Distribution of Household Wealth in Canada

Quintiles are useful for comparative purposes, both across time periods and across regions. Figure 7.2 repeats the exercise just described using total household wealth held by Canadian families over a four-year period. A family's total wealth, or net worth, is what it has left once the value of its liabilities (i.e. debt) has been deducted from the value of its assets (mostly real estate and savings). Using Grattan's method, imagine that we have placed all Canadian families in a line, beginning with families having the lowest total wealth and ending with the families having the highest total wealth. Then we divide the families into five equal groups and calculate the average household wealth for each group. Now imagine that we perform that exercise every year from 2014 to 2018: this is what Figure 7.2 represents.

Figure 7.2 shows us a couple of things very clearly. First, the average family in the highest quintile has nearly as much wealth as the families in the other four quintiles combined. Second, while overall household wealth in Canada rose between 2014 and 2018, the share of wealth held by families in each quintile remained more or less constant. Table 7.1 adds detail to this picture by showing how

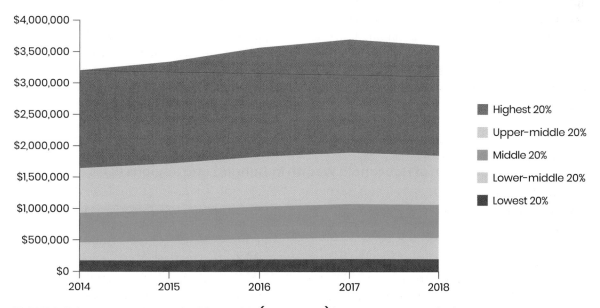

FIGURE 7.2 Average Household Wealth (Net Worth) in Canada, by Quintile, 2014–2018

Source: Statistics Canada Table 36-10-0586-01, Distributions of household economic accounts, income, consumption, and saving, by characteristic.

TABLE 7.1 Distribution of Household Wealth in Canada (%), by Quintile, 2010, 2014, and 2018

	2010	2012	2014	2016	2018
Highest 20%	50.4	49.3	48.7	48.7	48.7
Upper-middle 20%	22.0	22.0	22.0	22.2	21.7
Middle 20%	13.6	14.6	14.7	14.5	14.7
Lower-middle 20%	8.5	8.6	9.1	9.3	9.5
Lowest 20%	5.4	5.5	5.4	5.4	5.5

Source: Statistics Canada, Table 36-10-0586-01, Distributions of household economic accounts, income, consumption, and saving, by characteristic.

the distribution of total household wealth by quintile changed between 2010 and 2018. You can see that between 2010 and 2018, the share of wealth held by families in the top two quintiles dropped by 2 percentage points, while the share of wealth held by families in the middle and lower-middle quintiles rose by 1 percentage point each. The share of wealth held by families in the lowest quintile remained nearly constant over the 8-year period.

Keep in mind that if household wealth were distributed equally across Canada, then each of the five quintiles would have 20 per cent of the total. Because wealth is not distributed equally, the highest quintile will always have the largest share, well above 20 per cent; the lowest quintile will always have the smallest share of wealth, well below 20 per cent. The narrower the gap between the highest and lowest quintiles, the greater the equality. So, another way to assess income inequality is to find the ratio of wealth controlled by families in the highest and lowest quintiles. In 2018, Canada's top quintile held 48.7 per cent of all household wealth, while the bottom quintile held 5.5 per cent. The ratio is 48.7 to 5.5, or 8.85 to 1—an improvement over 2010, when the ratio was 10.27 to 1.

Comparing the Distribution of Wealth across Regions

Table 7.1 gives us a picture of how household wealth is distributed across quintiles in Canada, but how does this national picture compare with the situation in different regions? For that view, we turn to Table 7.2, which shows the distribution of total household wealth in a single year (2018), again by quintile, for all of Canada and five different regions. Take a quick look at the table and see if you can predict, based on the data, which regions will have the greatest and least wealth equality. You can confirm your prediction by referring to Figure 7.3, which shows the high-to-low quintile ratios for Canada and the five regions profiled in Table 7.2, in order from most to least equality.

When looking at Figure 7.3, remember that the lower the score, the greater the degree of wealth equality. Here, only Quebec and Atlantic Canada have wealth equality scores below (i.e. better than) the national rate. As shown in Table 7.2, these are also the two regions with the greatest share of wealth held by families in the middle quintile. Meanwhile, in Ontario, British Columbia, and the Prairies

TABLE 7.2 Distribution of Household Wealth in Canada and Regions (%), by Quintile, 2018

	Lowest	Lower-Middle	Middle	Upper-Middle	Highest
CANADA	5.5	9.5	14.7	21.7	48.7
British Columbia	5.6	9.0	11.2	20.4	53.8
Prairie Region	4.8	6.8	11.0	21.5	55.9
Ontario	5.3	8.6	14.0	21.8	50.2
Quebec	6.5	13.4	22.6	22.4	35.1
Atlantic Region	6.1	13.7	16.3	22.7	41.2

Source: Statistics Canada, Table 36-10-0586-01, Distributions of household economic accounts, wealth, Canada, regions, and provinces.

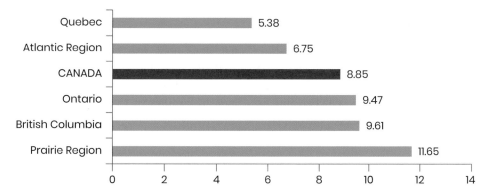

FIGURE 7.3 Income Inequality, Canada and Regions, Using High to Low Ratios of Household Wealth Quintiles

Source: Statistics Canada Table 36-10-0586-01, Distributions of household economic accounts, wealth, Canada, regions, and provinces.

Quick Hits

The Mean and the Median

In Chapter 2 we looked at how the **mean** and the **median** could give very different impressions of the same set of figures. You will remember (I hope) that the *mean* (or *average*) is what you get when you add up a set of figures and divide the total by the number of figures in your set ($2 + 2 + 4 + 10 + 12 = 30 \div 5 = $ **6**). The *median* is the figure in the middle of the ordered set (2, 2, **4**, 10, 12). If you've been waiting four-and-a-half chapters to demonstrate your mastery of the concept, here's your big chance. Have a look at the figure below, which compares the mean and median wealth for households in Canada and the five regions Statistics Canada uses for its analysis.

In Canada and each region, the median household wealth is less than 50 per cent of the mean household wealth. Why in each case are the mean and median values so different? What does that difference tell us? Which measure would you use if you belonged to a lobby group advocating for an increase to the minimum wage? Which measure would you use if you were a politician opposed to such a recommendation?

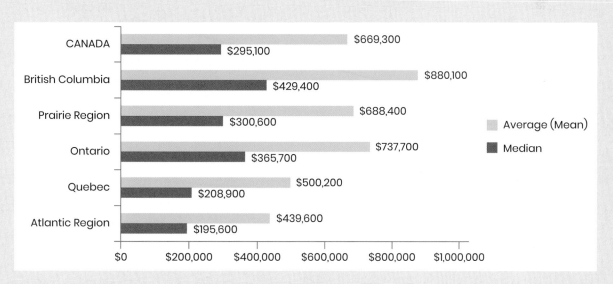

Mean and Median Household Wealth, Canada and Regions, 2016

Source: Statistics Canada Table 11-10-0016-01, Survey of Financial Security (SFS), assets and debts held by economic family type, by age group, Canada, provinces, and regions.

(Alberta specifically), where many wealthy multinational companies are headquartered, the wealth gap between the top and bottom quintiles is above the national score. Based on Table 7.2 and Figure 7.3, we can argue that when it comes to total household wealth among Canadian families, Quebec and Atlantic Canada have the lowest degree of inequality in Canada.

A Few Final Thoughts on Social Stratification

Let's return to our question about Canada's middle class with one last figure. Figure 7.4 shows the change in average household wealth from 2010 to 2018 for Canada's highest, middle, and lowest 20 per cent of families (I've omitted the upper-middle and lower-middle quintiles from this graph). In percentage terms, the middle quintile experienced greater growth than either the highest or the lowest quintile: over the 8-year period, wealth per household in the middle quintile rose by 54 per cent, compared with 38 per cent and 45 per cent, respectively, in the highest and lowest quintiles. This suggests the gap is narrowing slightly between the top and the middle, and to a lesser between the top and the bottom.

If that does not seem to match what you see in Figure 7.4, it's because the line graph charts the growth of each of the three quintiles in actual dollars. Families in the highest quintile saw their wealth per household rise by 38 percentage points but $480,516 in actual dollars. That is over two-and-a-half times the increase in net worth, in actual dollars, of families in the middle quintile ($185,450), and nearly eight times the dollar growth per household in the lowest quintile ($62,012). This serves as a reality check on the health of Canada's middle class relative to country's highest income earners. It also makes us wonder if that 54 per cent increase for the middle quintile is significant.

Throughout this section we have been basing our analysis on household wealth, or net worth, because it is a variable that is easy to trace over time (thanks to the friendly agents at our federal statistics bureau). When considering economic disparities between the rich and the poor, there are many other quantitative factors we could consider. Household income is one; debt as a percentage of income is another. And as I noted in Chapter 2, when we considered **poverty**, it is important to take regional differences into account: that toonie in your pocket will go further in Moncton than it does in Calgary. This is why some measures of middle class rely on *purchasing power*, which is the value of your wealth based on the cost of living in your city, town, village, or hamlet.

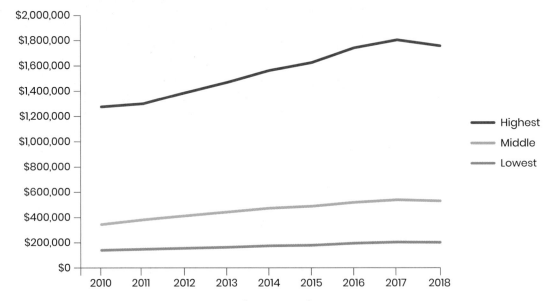

FIGURE 7.4 Average Household Wealth (Net Worth) in Canada, Lowest, Middle, and Highest Quintiles, 2010–2018

Source: Statistics Canada Table 36-10-0586-01, Distributions of household economic accounts, wealth, Canada, regions, and provinces.

The Point Is...

How You Experience Poverty Depends on Your Social Location

I completed my master's degree in the mid-1970s at Memorial University in Newfoundland. During that time, I was statistically poor. My annual income consisted of a $2500 fellowship combined with a $2500 salary for my work as a research assistant. During my first year, I supported my wife and my dog on just that much money, paying monthly rent of $150 for a unit in a large apartment complex.

Although we were poor by pure statistical measures, there were unmeasurable factors that made life easier. We didn't pay for our furniture: we built our own, using planks I "liberated" from various undisclosed building locations. A neighbour who worked on the ferry that travelled between Newfoundland and the mainland regularly supplied us with free toilet paper. On Saturday and Sunday mornings I would walk the dog to places where teenagers drank beer so that I could collect empty bottles, worth five cents each. That can add up when you have a shopping cart full of empties. I learned which nearby fields had wild blueberries, raspberries, and partridgeberries (a Newfoundland favourite, related to cranberries). I had friends who hunted moose.

There were still things we had to pay for, but they were things you could get cheaply if you knew who to talk to or where to go. I bought fresh cod—then a staple of the Newfoundland diet—for forty cents a pound from a guy who sold fish from the back of his pickup truck in the parking lot of a shopping plaza. In our second year we obtained, third-hand, a weather-beaten Ford pickup that needed a new starter motor. As I was under the truck removing the old one, I saw a pair of boots approach the vehicle. When I pulled myself out from under the truck, the person standing in the boots told me he could get me a new starter motor cheap, if I didn't care how it was obtained. I didn't. It cost me a bottle of screech.

It was not a glamorous life, but we were buoyed by the optimistic belief that living in poverty was but a short-term condition. I was a graduate student with prospects. I was expecting to become a college professor and move up into the middle class. The books on my homemade shelves reminded me of possibilities: the hope I would one day have a store-bought bookcase featuring books that I had written (I do). It took a little more than 10 years and a lot of short-term contract work in a variety of jobs for me to realize that dream, but the dream always kept me from feeling poor.

In short, there are many ways to define Canada's middle class, based not just on wealth or income but also employment status, occupation, and education. Some even argue that when discussing Canada's middle class, *qualitative* variables must also be taken into account—that belonging to the middle class is about cultural values or state of mind. Perhaps a better question to ask is why politicians, the media, economists, and, yes, sociologists devote so much time to contemplating the middle when it's the families in the lowest stratum we should really be worried about.

Ideology: Explaining Social Inequality

Dominant Ideology

When political economists write and speak about social inequality, their arguments and ideas are typically shaped by their ideology. An **ideology** is a set of beliefs about society and the people in it, usually forming the basis of a particular economic or political theory. A **dominant ideology** is the set of beliefs put forward by, and generally supportive of, society's dominant culture and/or classes. In Marxist terms, it reflects the class consciousness of the ruling capitalist class and is used to defend or justify the status quo.

An example of a dominant ideology in North America is **trickle-down theory**. The term refers to a view that if the wealthy are given the freedom to generate more wealth, others in society will benefit: new jobs will be created, more money will be spent on consumer goods, and a good part of the generated wealth will eventually find its way into the hands of members of the middle and lower classes. American author and historian William Blum described it as "the principle that the poor, who must subsist on table scraps dropped by the rich, can best be served by giving the rich bigger meals" (2003, p. 20). As a dominant ideology, trickle-down economic theory is used to justify policies that favour wealthy business owners. These policies include government subsidies for certain industries and low corporate taxes and other incentives for businesses that promise to "invest" in Canada by setting up offices and manufacturing plants here.

Neoliberal Ideology

Neoliberalism, or **neoliberal ideology**, is a dominant ideology that views the individual as a more or less independent player on the sociological scene. Drawing on classical economic liberalism of the eighteenth and nineteenth centuries (*neo-* means "new"), it reflects a belief in a great deal of **social mobility**—the ability of individuals to move (generally upward) from one class, or stratum, to another—and downplays concerns over social inequality. According to neoliberal ideology, when people are successful, it is because they have justly earned that success, not because they have benefited from the social privileges of "race," ethnicity, class, or gender. The **American dream**—the belief that anyone can "make it" if they are willing to work really hard for it—reflects neoliberal ideology. Failure to achieve the American dream (resulting in the "American nightmare" of poverty) is likewise placed solely on the individual. **William Ryan** referred to this as **blaming the victim**, assigning individuals responsibility for events or circumstances that have broader social causes, such as the quality of a person's upbringing and education or a lack of the resources and social connections that help a person secure a well-paying job. Other examples of blaming the victim include the following arguments:

- People become alcoholics because they lack willpower; biological factors (genetic predisposition) and sociological factors (racial or ethnic stereotypes, systematic oppression) need not be considered.
- People receiving employment insurance are on welfare because they don't have a strong work ethic, not because they come from poor families with the odds of success stacked against them.
- People convicted of crime offend and reoffend because they have a "criminal mind," not because they were raised in socioeconomically disadvantaged circumstances, or because they belong to a group disproportionately targeted by the criminal justice system.

Note that classical liberalism and neoliberalism derive their names from the core belief in the right of citizens to conduct their affairs free ("liberated") from government interference. Adam Smith, discussed briefly at the start of this chapter, was a classical liberal in this sense. Over the course of the twentieth century, the term *social liberalism* came to describe the movement to loosen laws around such practices as homosexuality and abortion. This makes things complicated because political parties that champion neoliberal economic policies tend to oppose social liberal policies. In Canada, political parties most closely associated with a neoliberal ideology on financial matters tend to describe themselves as conservative (or Conservative). Political parties taking a liberal stance on social policy issues like same-sex marriage, cannabis legalization, and safe-injection sites for drug addicts may describe themselves as liberal (or Liberal), even though they tend not to be the strongest proponents of unregulated financial markets.

Counter-Ideology

Not everyone embraces the dominant ideology. Consider the critique of trickle-down theory presented by Linda McQuaig and Neil Brooks in *Billionaire's Ball: Gluttony and Hubris in an Age of Epic Inequality* (2012). She is a journalist; he is a college instructor in tax law and policy. They see "Reaganomics," a nickname for the economic policies adopted to help bring the United States out of a recession in the 1980s under president Ronald Reagan, as ushering in a period of uneven growth in income and wealth:

> Between 1980 and 2008, the incomes of the bottom 90 percent of the population grew by a meager 1 percent, or an average of just $303. Meanwhile, over those same years, the incomes of the top .01 percent of Americans grew by 403 percent, or an average of a massive $21.9 million. The richest 300,000 Americans now enjoy almost as much income as the bottom 150 million. (McQuaig & Brooks, 2012, p. 5)

The authors point out that this contrasts greatly with the pre-Reagan period, when, from 1950 to 1980, the bottom 90 per cent experienced "income growth of 75 percent, or an average of $13,222" (McQuaig & Brooks, 2012, p. 6).

A **counter-ideology**, then, is one that offers a critique of the dominant ideology, challenging its justice and its universal applicability to society. People promoting a counter-ideology are typically looking to create significant social change. Classical Marxism, which predicted the overthrow of the capitalist classes by the proletariat, is an obvious example of a counter-ideology. The Occupy movement, though it did not have a well-defined set of objectives, is another example. Its basic premise, that 99 per cent of the world's wealth is concentrated in the hands of 1 per cent of the world's population and must be subject to greater taxes in order to be distributed more equitably, challenged the dominant ideology of trickle-down theory.

The 2011–12 Montreal student protests represented a counter-ideology. The largest student group, CLASSE, demanded that universities cut research programs (which, they argued, benefited private interests) and advertising with an aim to making college and university tuition-free (Bruemmer & Dougherty, 2012). And for some time a counter-ideology has been developing among contemporary Indigenous people in Canada, who are drawing on traditional values and who are critical of the capitalist/materialist society that has oppressed them. In 2012, the movement coalesced around Chief of the Attawapiskat First Nation Theresa Spence under the banner Idle No More, drawing attention to the federal government's elimination of environmental protections in order to fast-track pipeline construction and industrial development. This fight was taken up in 2018 by the Secwepemc (pronounced suh-wep-muh), a Salish people, in their resistance to the expansion of the Trans Mountain pipeline in the interior of British Columbia.

Hegemony

Antonio Gramsci (1891–1937) was a critic of the dominant ideology. The Italian-born political theorist and activist was a co-founder and leader of the Italian Communist party and an opponent of fascist dictator Benito Mussolini. Jailed in November 1926, he remained a political prisoner for nearly 10 years. During that time he developed the concept of hegemony.

Gramsci used **hegemony** to mean non-coercive methods of maintaining power. He believed that the

Prototype for New Understanding #23 (2005), by Dane-zaa (people-real) artist Brian Jungen, who lives in Vancouver. What do you think the message of this artwork is? What ideology could it be critiquing?

ruling classes relied on something more than their military and police forces to keep society running smoothly while quietly oppressing the masses. In her study of Gramsci, Kate Crehan defines *hegemony* as all the ways by which "the power relations underpinning various forms of inequality are produced and reproduced" (2002, p. 104).

Hegemony can take many forms. It is expressed in the reproduction and celebration of the idea that the path to prosperity is available to everyone equally, and that inequality exists not because of problems in "the system" but because some people are willing to work harder than others. Hegemony can also be seen in the rampant materialism of people waiting in long lines for the latest iPhone or other tech gadget considered a must for those who want to keep up with changing trends.

Recalling the case of Attawapiskat described at the start of this chapter, we can consider the response of the federal government under then Prime Minister Stephen Harper as an instance of hegemony. In November 2011, Harper defended his government's handling of the crisis, arguing that they had spent $90 million on Attawapiskat since taking office and suggesting the funds had been mishandled by the community. In 2013, he sent an auditor to examine the community's finances, later ordering the First Nation to pay back $1.8 million it had been unable to account for. He thereby shifted blame *onto* the people and the handling of their money by the chief and council, and *off of* the inadequate measures taken by the federal and provincial governments and the exploitative practices of the powerful mining company. That exercise of hegemony worked, as the government managed to avoid any serious backlash for failing to avert a crisis that had been building for years.

Even an introductory sociology textbook could become an instrument of hegemony. Say its author portrayed Canadian society as though there were no destructive social splits based on "race," ethnicity, gender, ability, and class—in other words, as though there were none of the social divisions that create and sustain social inequality. In this sense, the textbook would be playing a part in maintaining the power of the ruling classes by suggesting that there were no problems of social inequality that needed to be addressed.

Poverty and Excess: The Real Effects of Social Inequality

So far in this chapter we have looked at how social inequality is talked about by theorists, how it is measured by economists, and how it is sometimes explained or justified by policy makers. In this final section we will look at some of the ways social inequality affects society. Since studying social inequality is often about looking at the extremes, we will start with the people using Canada's food banks and end with the country's top 1 per cent of earners and where they stand in relation to the average Canadian.

Food Banks

Changing Rates of Food Bank Use

One indicator of the social inequality that exists in Canada comes from statistics concerning the use of food banks. A **food bank**, as defined by Food Banks Canada, is a "central warehouse or clearing house, registered as a non-profit organization for the purpose of collecting, storing and distributing food, free of charge, directly or through front line agencies which may also provide meals to the hungry" (Food Banks Canada, 2004). Food Banks Canada is a national charitable organization that supports provincial agencies and community groups dedicated to fighting hunger. Each year the organization issues *HungerCount*, a report on national food bank use. The statistics presented in the report are generated from a survey distributed annually in February to food banks across the country, so *HungerCount* provides a good snapshot of food bank use that can be tracked from year to year, serving as an indicator of how Canada's neediest citizens are faring. Note that *HungerCount* covers just one aspect of efforts to relieve hunger in Canada: it does not include the efforts of other free food providers such as soup kitchens, shelters, and breakfast programs for schoolchildren.

In March 2016, food banks in Canada helped 863,492 people. That figure is 28 per cent higher than the total in March 2008, when 675,735 received help from food banks (Food Banks Canada, 2017). When considering that dramatic increase, it is important to

TABLE 7.3 Food Bank Use in Canada, 2008 and 2016, by Province

Region	Total Assisted March 2008	Total Assisted March 2016	Difference 2008–2016 (%)
British Columbia	78,101	103,464	32.5
Alberta	33,580	79,292	136.1
Saskatchewan	17,751	31,395	76.9
Manitoba	40,464	61,914	53.0
Ontario	314,258	335,944	6.9
Quebec	127,536	171,800	34.7
New Brunswick	15,638	19,769	26.4
Nova Scotia	16,915	23,840	40.9
Prince Edward Island	2892	3370	16.5
Newfoundland & Labrador	27,260	26,366	−3.3
Canada	**675,735**	**863,492**	**27.8**

Source: Food Banks Canada, 2017, p. 6.

keep in mind that graphs of statistics seldom rise or fall in a straight line; they will typically do both over a significant period of time. We need to look at what happened over that eight-year interval to produce an overall 28 per cent increase in food bank use.

In 2009, a short recession began in North America, causing an increase in food bank use across the country. In 2010, Alberta and Ontario had more people visit food banks than ever before: 59,311 Albertans and 402,056 Ontarians received help from food banks that year. By 2014, however, those figures had fallen to 49,766 and 374,698, respectively.

The peak year for food bank use in Canada was 2012, when 872,379 individuals visited food banks in March (Food Banks Canada, 2017). But from 2013 to 2015, four provinces—Ontario, New Brunswick, Nova Scotia, and Newfoundland and Labrador—saw declines in the number of March food bank visitors, and the number of March food bank visitors in Canada overall declined to 852,137.

From March 2015 to March 2016, food bank use increased everywhere except in Ontario and Manitoba. Factors that likely contributed to the increase include a sudden drop in oil prices in mid-2014, which caused a downturn in the economies of Alberta and Saskatchewan. Another factor contributing to the year-over-year increase in food bank use was the intake of refugees from Syria, many of whom depended on food banks during their resettlement. Food Banks Canada (2017) attributes a 17 per cent increase in food bank use in Surrey, BC, to this factor. Not reflected in the March 2016 statistics is the increased use of food banks by Albertans displaced by wildfires in Fort McMurray, beginning in May 2016.

All of this is to say that the number of food bank visitors in Canada varies from year to year and from province to province. It is a mistake to think that food bank users represent a single homogeneous group, when an unexpected job loss or an unprecedented environmental disaster can turn someone living in a stable financial position into a food bank user in the blink of an eye. Consider that in March 2014, 10 per cent of all food bank visitors were using a food bank for the first time. Many Canadians simply do not have the financial reserves to withstand a sudden change in circumstances.

Who Uses Food Banks?

So who do you think the typical food bank user is? Some of the details might surprise you. First, just 5 per cent of food bank users are homeless, a category that includes those living temporarily with family or friends. Roughly 66.5 per cent of food bank users pay market rent, while 22 per cent live in subsidized housing. The remaining 7 per cent own their own homes (Food Banks Canada, 2015, p. 17).

In March 2018, 45 per cent of all food bank visits were made by people living in single-person households. (Note that in its 2019 report, Food Banks Canada counts visits rather than visitors, complicating year-over-year comparisons). Another 19 per cent of visits were made by single parents with children. And yet, only 6 per cent of visits were made by people reporting no income (Figure 7.5). Taken together, these findings point to the difficulty of living on a single source of income, whether that income comes in the form of a salary or government assistance.

In terms of age, 35 per cent of people served by food banks in March 2018 were children under the age of 18. People aged 45 to 64 made up the next largest group of food bank visitors (23 per cent), while over 6 per cent of those served by food banks were aged 65 and over (Figure 7.6).

Minimum Wage and Living Wage

In any jurisdiction, the minimum wage is the lowest hourly rate a person can be paid for their work. Setting the minimum wage is a provincial responsibility, and the rate varies widely across the country, from a low of $11.06 in Saskatchewan to a high of $15.00 in neighbouring Alberta (as of October 2019; see Table 7.4). Some provinces, such as British Columbia, have plans to increase the minimum wage incrementally over the coming years, but a change of government can bring about a swift change to such plans. Witness Ontario, where in 2018, the newly elected Conservative government made cancelling a planned minimum wage increase one of its first orders of business.

Minimum wage increases are often a source of fierce debate among labour and anti-poverty activists, on one hand, and business supporters on the other. Pro-business politicians argue that raising the minimum wage hurts workers by forcing

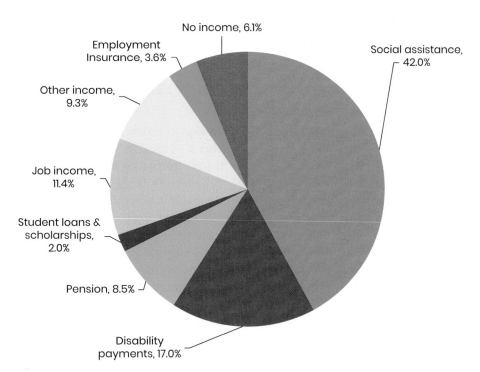

FIGURE 7.5 Household Primary Income Source among Food Bank Visitors, March 2018

Source: Food Banks Canada, 2019.

small-business owners to lay off employees in order to offset the increase in labour costs. Keeping the minimum wage low allows businesses to flourish, preserving or even creating those precious (albeit low-paying) jobs. (If this sounds to you like something a champion of neoliberalism and free-market capitalism would argue, you are spot on and have clearly been paying attention.)

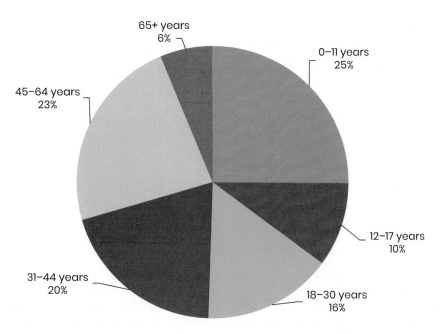

FIGURE 7.6 Age of Those Served by Food Banks, March 2018

Source: Food Banks Canada, 2019.

The Point Is...

Are Students on Campus Hungry? You Bet They Are!

I remember the first time my research team learned that students on college campuses were going hungry. It was 2008, and we were conducting an evaluation of a financial aid program. Going out to talk to students across Wisconsin, we had one simple question [a very, very open-ended question]: "How's college going?" Most spoke of challenges paying for school, fitting in, or doing the academic work. But a few surprised us, speaking instead of difficulty finding food, even being distracted from class by persistent hunger. (Goldrick-Rab, in Dubick, Mathews, & Cady, 2016, p. 1)

This comes from the preface to *Hunger on Campus: The Challenge of Food Insecurity for College Students*, published in 2016 by James Dubick, Brandon Mathews, and Clare Cady. The author of the preface, public sociology activist Sara Goldrick-Rab, teaches sociology at Temple University in Philadelphia. I will admit that when I first heard there was a food bank (or food pantry) at the college where I taught, I, too, was surprised. Food was never a problem for me as an undergraduate. My first year, when I lived in residence, I had a good meal plan, and my last three years I lived at home and was very well fed.

For this ground-breaking study, the researchers interviewed 3765 students using food banks and food pantries in 12 American states, at 34 colleges and universities. The researchers' revelations broke several stereotypes of the typical food bank user. For instance, of the students surveyed, roughly 75 per cent received some form of financial

University of Alberta

aid, and 43 per cent had some kind of meal plan. Still, they needed to rely on food banks. Another 56 per cent of the students using food banks had a paying job.

The authors define *food insecurity* as "the lack of reliable access to sufficient quantities of affordable, nutritious food" (Dubick, Mathews, & Cady, 2016, p. 6). It is usually associated with other indicators of poverty. For instance, roughly two-thirds of the students surveyed were also coping with housing insecurity: they faced frequent change of residence, couch surfing, and even periods of homelessness.

What Do YOU Think?

1. If your sociology instructor asked the class, "Who has used the food bank on campus?" and you had, would you put up your hand? Why or why not?
2. Do you know if there's a food bank on your campus? (Hint: there probably is.) Do you know where to find it?
3. What do you think would be the best way of dealing with food insecurity among college students?

TABLE 7.4 Minimum Hourly Wage in Canada, by Province and Territory (October 2019)

Saskatchewan	$11.06
Newfoundland & Labrador	$11.40
New Brunswick	$11.50
Nova Scotia*	$11.55
Manitoba	$11.65
Prince Edward Island	$12.25
Quebec	$12.50
Yukon	$12.71
Nunavut	$13.00
Northwest Territories	$13.46
British Columbia	$13.85
Ontario	$14.00
Alberta	$15.00

*Nova Scotia has a separate wage of $11.05 per hour for inexperienced employees.

Source: Data from Retail Council of Canada

In an interesting, and detailed, analysis of an earlier minimum wage increase in Ontario, *Huffington Post* journalist Daniel Tencer (2019) concluded that raising the minimum wage did not stall job growth in the province, either overall or in the two sectors of the economy where minimum-wage jobs are concentrated: food services and retail. He also found that wage growth among workers aged 15 to 24 (who tend to be overrepresented in minimum-wage jobs) grew above the provincial average, suggesting a clear link to the increase. On the downside, there was an overall trend of jobs shifting away from those younger workers to workers aged 25 to 54. Tencer concedes this may have been a result of the minimum wage hike, although there may have been other factors at play: for instance, minimum-wage jobs are often the easiest ones to replace with automation.

Social activists and sociologists who study poverty often argue about the need for what they call a **living wage**. It is a vague term, but it generally represents a target above the existing minimum wage, which is considered too low for the "working poor" to live on. People paid minimum wage often have to use food banks, especially if they can find only part-time work and if they are supporting or helping to support a family. You could safely say that anyone using a food bank is not paid a living wage.

As a sociologist in training, how would you calculate a living wage? The Vancouver-based Living Wage for Families Campaign uses the **Market Basket Measure (MBM)**, which we examined in Chapter 2. As you will recall, the MBM is based on the cost of a standard set of goods required to support an individual or family, and it is adjusted to account for regional variations in the cost of housing, food, and other necessities. A visit to the organization's website (www.livingwageforfamilies.ca) provides living wages for 21 municipalities in southern British Columbia and Vancouver Island. Vancouver and Victoria have among the highest hourly living wages ($20.91/hr and $20.50/hr, respectively), because of the high cost of accommodation in BC's two largest metropolitan centres. However, coming in third is in the small island community of Clayoquot Sound ($20.11), where the scarcity of affordable childcare makes the cost of living greater.

As of October 2019, the minimum wage in BC is $13.85. It is set to rise to $14.60 in June 2020, and $15.20 by June 2021. If you are a migrant worker employed by one of BC's many farms, your pay is based on what you can harvest by hand, ranging from 16.3¢ per pound for Brussels sprouts to 39.6¢ per pound for blueberries (plus they taste better). According to the Living Wage for Families Campaign, the lowest living wage in the province is $16.51 in Prince George and the province's North Central Region.

The "Mincome": A Manitoba Town's Modernist Experiment

During the 1970s, the Manitoba town of Dauphin was home to a progressive social experiment around a simple idea: What if every family in the town received a guaranteed, unconditional annual income? Would citizens become lazy, knowing their income was guaranteed no matter how hard they worked? Would they stop working altogether?

The pilot project was introduced in 1974 under the province's NDP government and the Liberal government of Canada. Under the plan, families were guaranteed a minimum income based on family size. The guaranteed minimum income (or "mincome," as it came to be known) would be reduced by 50 cents for each dollar the household earned.

Creative Touch Imaging Ltd./NurPhoto via Getty Images

At a news conference announcing her government's intention to roll back plans to raise the province's minimum wage to $15, Ontario's minister of Labour, Laurie Scott, vowed to "reduce the regulatory burden for anyone willing to create jobs in Ontario" (Bouw, 2018). What kind of ideology does this statement reflect?

During the four years the project lasted, it was studied by anthropologists, sociologists, and economists. It was stopped in 1979 by Conservative governments that came to power at the provincial and federal levels. As Dutch historian Rutger Bregman explains in his book *Utopia for Realists* (2016), hardly any of the results were analyzed by staff overseeing the project. Boxes of paper files and questionnaires were left to rot in the archives.

Twenty-five years later, University of Manitoba researcher Evelyn Forget unearthed the documents shortly before they were to be destroyed. She found that during the time of the study, the town recorded fewer work-related injuries, fewer mental-health visits, and an 8.5 per cent drop in hospital visits overall (Forget, 2011). There were only minor reductions in the number of hours worked by Dauphin residents, except among young adults, where the decrease was greater. However, the decrease in hours worked meant that young adults were more likely to complete their high school educations, and young families were likely to devote more time to the care of young children.

The argument in favour of providing a guaranteed minimum income is that it benefits people living in poverty, providing them with the stability and time to find employment (or more lucrative employment) or to upgrade their skills through education. At the same time, the cost of administering a guaranteed income is less that the cost of administering the many other government social assistance programs it would replace. The chief arguments against the policy are that it would diminish the incentive to work while being far too costly to implement.

In 2017, the Liberal government of Ontario announced its own plans to pilot a guaranteed basic income in three jurisdictions over a three-year period. The participants chosen for the study were all living on a low income, defined as less than $34,000 per year for single people or $48,000 per year for couples, with or without children. The participants would be given up to $16,989 less 50 per cent of earned income for single people, and up to $24,027 per year less 50 per cent of earned income for couples. Two years into the study, the newly elected Conservative government announced plans to end the pilot project,

arguing that the cost was too great, with benefits going to too few.

Canada's "1 Per Cent"

In the fall of 2011, protesters in cities around the world joined the Occupy movement to draw attention to the fact that 1 per cent of the world's population controlled 99 per cent of the world's wealth. Does the ratio apply in Canada?

On 3 January 2012, Canadians beginning their work year learned that by noon that day, each of the top 100 chief executive officers (CEOs) in Canada had already earned as much as the average Canadian would make in an entire year ("Canada's Top CEOs," 2012). The report, prepared by the non-profit Canadian Centre for Policy Alternatives, was based on figures from 2010, when the average Canadian was earning $44,300 per year, while the average annual salary for the top 100 CEOs was $8.4 million. These CEOs include the heads of well-known companies including Canadian Tire, Rona, Air Canada, Loblaws, Rogers, Shaw, Telus, and Cineplex (no wonder the popcorn is so expensive) as well as a significant number of oil and mining companies and the "big six" banks.

Reports like this are meant to shock us by sensationalizing a situation we all know exists. Issued in the early days of the calendar year—a notoriously slow time for news—they play well in the media. As students of sociology, we have to look at the

Quick Hits

Who Are the Top 1 Per Cent of Earners in Canada?

In a 2015 study for the Institute for Research on Public Policy, economists Thomas Lemieux and W. Craig Riddell developed a profile of the top 1 per cent of earners in Canada. Here's a snapshot of what they found.

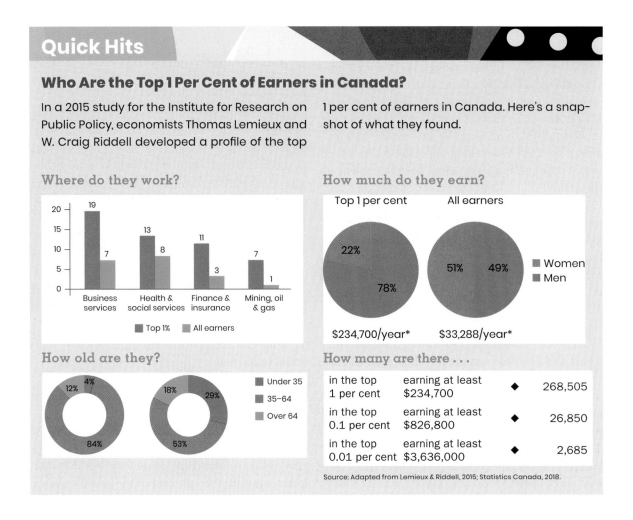

Where do they work?

Top 1% / All earners
- Business services: 19 / 7
- Health & social services: 13 / 8
- Finance & insurance: 11 / 3
- Mining, oil & gas: 7 / 1

How old are they?
- Under 35
- 35–64
- Over 64

4% / 12% / 84%
18% / 29% / 53%

How much do they earn?

Top 1 per cent: 22% Women, 78% Men — $234,700/year*
All earners: 51% / 49% — $33,288/year*

How many are there . . .

in the top 1 per cent	earning at least $234,700	◆	268,505
in the top 0.1 per cent	earning at least $826,800	◆	26,850
in the top 0.01 per cent	earning at least $3,636,000	◆	2,685

Source: Adapted from Lemieux & Riddell, 2015; Statistics Canada, 2018.

statistics critically. Here, then, is some context. The figure cited as the average salary of the top 100 Canadian CEOs in 2010—$8.4 million—represents an increase of 27 per cent over the previous year, while the average Canadian salary went up by 1.1 from 2009 to 2010 (Flavelle, 2012). Another way of looking at the situation: the highest salary of a Canadian CEO in 2010 was 189 times that of the average wage earner in 2010. Compare this with the situation in 1998, when the best-paid CEO made 105 times what the average Canadian earned, and in 1995, when the wealthiest CEO's salary was 85 times that of the average Canadian (Flavelle, 2012). This suggests

that social inequality in Canada is growing, not diminishing.

More recent figures released in 2018 by Statistics Canada confirm this trend (Canadian Megatrends, 2018). They found that from 1982 to 2014, the share of income earned by the bottom half of all earners fell by 28 per cent, while the share earned by the top half increased by 5 per cent. While that increase sounds modest, the biggest gains over the period were made by the top 1 per cent of earners, whose share of income rose by 53 per cent. The top 0.1 per cent saw their earnings rise by 90 per cent, and the earnings of the top 0.01 per cent rose by 133 per cent.

Wrap it Up

Summary

We began the chapter with a hefty question: Is social inequality inevitable? Karl Marx didn't think so. What was inevitable, he thought, was that society's poor workers would rise up against their wealthy masters in a revolution aimed at levelling the playing field. Things haven't played out quite as Marx imagined. There have been popular movements to challenge a system organized around class divisions—the Occupy movement and Idle No More, to name just two—but the ideology that prevails in the West perpetuates the idea that if a small percentage of the population is allowed to generate enormous wealth, everyone else will benefit.

Social inequality seems less unjust when there are good avenues for mobility, which might give someone from a lower class a decent chance to climb the socioeconomic ladder. Education is one: you may feel very poor now, but just think of the riches that await you once you complete your honours sociology degree. Alternatively, you might be spending the time you aren't in soc class playing *Fortnite*, hoping to join the eSports circuit to make your fortune in one of the fastest-growing mobility sports. (It's a faint hope, I'm afraid.) Most people looking for a road out of poverty rely on social assistance: policies involving minimum wage, living wage, and guaranteed basic income are very real to them. Even with that social assistance, they may have to rely on food banks and other charitable organizations. Food bank user statistics give us a good idea of who is poor in Canada; they also suggest that social inequality isn't going away any time soon.

Think Back

Questions for Critical Review

1. Is social inequality in Canada inevitable? Explain your answer.
2. Explain why the class structure that Marx described does not fully apply to contemporary Canadian society.
3. Explain what is meant by the term *precariat*, and describe its relationship to (a) populism and (b) the gig economy.
4. Identify what quintiles are and explain how they are used. What is the relationship between quintiles and class?
5. What goes into defining Canada's middle class? Is it something you can quantify, based on wealth or income alone? And does the middle class have class consciousness in the way that Marx defined the term?
6. Where would you find the greatest degree of economic equality in Canada? What factors might give one region greater equality than others?
7. Identify what neoliberal ideology is. Who supports it, and on what grounds? Who opposes it, and on what grounds?
8. Imagine that you have been asked to study trends in the use of food banks in Canada and put forward recommendations to help reduce Canadians' reliance on them. Which of the following policies would you recommend, and why?
   a. implement a "living wage" to replace the minimum wage
   b. increase the age of retirement
   c. increase family allowance cheques
   d. introduce a guaranteed basic income
   e. crack down on employment insurance fraud to ensure there is more money in the system for deserving families
   f. increase the availability of low-cost housing
   g. implement free or minimal-cost daycare

h. subject employment insurance recipients to drug testing and provide counselling services as necessary

i. create incentives for businesses to hire and train unemployed people

j. make postsecondary education free

k. raise the tax rate on the top 1 per cent of earners.

l. write your own: _____

_____

_____

_____.

Read On

Recommended Print and Online Resources

Bryan D. Cummins, *Only God Can Own the Land*, Canadian Ethnography Series Vol. 1. (Toronto, ON: Pearson, 2003).

• This book looks at how the life of the Attawapiskat Cree changed once diamond exploration and mining began in Ontario's north.

Ed Grabb and Neil Guppy, eds, *Social Inequality in Canada*, 5th edn (Toronto, ON: Pearson, 2008).

• An insightful collection of articles, edited (and with some articles written) by two leading Canadian sociologists studying social inequality in Canada.

Food Banks Canada, www.foodbankscanada.ca

• On its website Food Banks Canada documents the hunger problems of the poor in Canada and proposes policy solutions. Its annual report, *HungerCount*, gives details of the organization's activities and findings on a yearly basis.

Kristina Rutherford, "Is the Cost Keeping Kids Out of Minor Hockey? Absolutely, Players and Parents Say" (2009), www.cbc.ca/sports/ hockey/ourgame/story/2009/01/16/hockey-costs-too-much.html

• This feature article on the CBC's website gives an informative, journalistic look at the high price of hockey in Canada, which may be to blame for falling minor hockey registration numbers.

Living Wage for Families Campaign, www.livingwageforfamilies.ca

• Visit this website for more information on how the BC-based organization calculates its living wage for different metropolitan centres and why a living wage is important.

Micah M. White, *The End of Protest: A New Playbook for Revolution* (Toronto: Knopf, 2016).

• A former editor with Vancouver-based Adbusters and a co-founder of the Occupy Wall Street movement, Micah White calls for a new approach to social activism given that the disruptive tactics behind some of the largest protests in history have failed to fundamentally change society.

Michele Simon, "Walmart's Hunger Games: How America's Largest Employer and Richest Family Worsen the Hunger Crisis" (2014), www. eatdrinkpolitics.com/wp-content/uploads/ Walmarts_Hunger_Games_Report.pdf

• In the early part of this decade, Walmart drew some bad press over its treatment of employees. This seven-page report argues that Walmart "builds their wealth off of workers' inability to afford food" by underpaying their employees and then redeeming the food stamps their low-paid workers rely on. The report is subtitled "A Call for Walmart's Owners to Change," and you can research the company online to see if, in the years since 2014, they have changed, and if their practices differ in Canada.

Patrizia Albanese, *Child Poverty in Canada* (Don Mills, ON: Oxford University Press, 2009).

• An important work by a Canadian sociologist on theories of, and possible solutions to, child poverty in Canada.

Zygmunt Bauman, *Collateral Damage: Social Inequalities in a Global Age* (Malden, MA: Polity Press, 2011).

• A readable look by a prolific sociology author about how contemporary society is producing an underclass of disposable people.

"Race" and Ethnicity

8

Reading this chapter will help you to . . .

- Define "race" and *ethnicity*, and explain why they are social, rather than biological, constructs.

- Understand how Indigenous people, blacks, and Asians have been racialized in Canada.

- Apply different approaches to studying and understanding ethnicity.

- Cite the contributions of some pioneering black sociologists in North America.

- Distinguish between different forms of racism, including systemic racism, friendly racism, and colourism.

- Demonstrate how Canadian immigration laws reflect institutional racism.

For Starters

On White Privilege and Being Invisible

Like a lot of white North Americans, I am, for all intents and purposes, invisible.

I blend into the crowd at a concert or a ballgame. I pass through the security gate without anyone double- or triple-checking my bag; no one gives me a second glance.

Pedestrians don't cross the street to avoid me; passengers don't change cars when I get on the subway. No one becomes visibly agitated when I board their flight.

I can walk past a police officer without fear of being stopped and asked to empty my pockets or show my ID.

Strangers don't tell me they wish they had my hair, my fascinating complexion, or my innate talent for dancing or math (although I'm surprisingly good at both).

I've never had to interrupt an awkward conversation with someone who has mistaken me for another white person who looks just like me.

Being white and invisible is like having a superpower that keeps me safe. We could call this superpower white privilege. It's something easily taken for granted.

I haven't always been invisible. In the 1960s, I became visible for a time because of my long hair. With this new status (that of the counter-cultural hippie) I took a few baby steps down the long path of unmasked prejudice. Police, folks from small towns, and denizens of the big city's "greaser" neighbourhoods all made me highly aware of my visibility, causing me to feel vulnerable to the emotions of others. Once, waiting for a bus in northern Ontario, dark from a summer's work in forestry, straight hair hanging well below my shoulders, one of the people working at the bus depot thought I was Indigenous. I got a glimpse—very brief—of what it was like to be the object of racial disdain.

White people do not automatically lose status as a function of being white, even when they are visible. In fact, visible white people sometimes enjoy a rise in status. When I went to Taiwan, my visibility brought prestige. Children

watched me with respect. They would practice English with "the expert." In the mid-sized city of Hualien, long before the advent of cellphones, a group of taxi drivers helped me use the payphone, even when I told them I wouldn't be needing a ride. Would a Taiwanese visitor to a mid-sized, racially homogeneous American city have been treated that well? For the first time in my life I went an entire day without seeing another white person. Far from being able to disappear anonymously into crowds, I parted the throngs like Moses through the Red Sea (the beard might have helped). I felt as though I was always on stage, but with a friendly audience.

When I returned to North America, I became invisible once again. I was home, and I felt safe. Many North Americans who do not enjoy white privilege as I do may never know what that feels like.

What Do YOU Think?

Think of a situation when your race or another social characteristic—your sex, your age, your accent—made you feel visible. What was it like to stand out? Did your visibility cause you to gain or to lose status?

Introduction to "Race": Why the Scare Quotes?

The term "race" was first applied to humans during European colonial expansion in the sixteenth and seventeenth centuries. Use of the term has long reflected beliefs about biological superiority and inferiority in the context of colonial power. It does not always follow the formulas *lighter skin = good* and *darker skin = bad*. Russian racism was directed at white Siberian communities speaking languages related to Finnish and Hungarian. Japanese governments and citizens have long exhibited racism toward the indigenous Ainu. The Chinese government has long established racist practices against Tibetans and the Muslim Uighurs. However, white supremacy—involving discrimination against anyone not of western European ethnic background—has been the prevailing pattern since people began discussing humans in terms of different "races."

Why have I put quotation marks around "race"? It is to remind you that races do not exist as distinct biological entities among humans. When early scientists tried to divide humans into three "races"—Caucasian, Mongoloid, and Negroid—there were always groups left over, such as the Ainu of Japan or the Aborigines of Australia. Differences *within* supposed races often outnumbered those *between* races. "Negroid" people included both the tallest and shortest people in the world, and people of greatly varying skin colour and build. Human biologists and physical anthropologists

Ann Ronan Picture Library/HIP/The Image Works

A nineteenth-century artist's representation of five "human races": (*clockwise from top left*) American, Malayan, Mongolian, Ethiopian, and Caucasian. What role do you think politics and religion might have played in scientific efforts to prove the existence of different races during the eighteenth and nineteenth centuries?

have for over 60 years established that there is but one human species, one race, albeit one that displays variation among its members—rather like *Ursus americanus*, the black bear, which can be black, cinnamon brown, and even white (the "spirit bears" of British Columbia).

"Race," Racialization, and Visible Minorities

While the idea that the world's human population can be separated, biologically, into different "races" has been disproven in science, race in real life is a very real concept. Humans have made it so. When we form judgments about others based solely on the colour of their skin—when we think we know something about a person we've never met simply because of the way they look—we are perpetuating the idea that people who share physical characteristics can be viewed in a certain way. In this context, race is a social construction rather than a biological construction, the product of a practice called **racialization**. Racialization is a social process in which human groups are viewed and judged as essentially different in terms of their intellect, morality, values, and innate worth because of perceived differences in physical appearance or cultural heritage. Racialization is directly connected to racism, which we'll consider later in the chapter.

Race is not just an informal social construct. Canada's federal government collects information on race every five years in the population census. While the questionnaire avoids the term *race* in favour of the less politically charged *population group*, Statistics Canada states explicitly that the question is asked "to derive counts for the visible minority population," defining **visible minority** as "persons, other than Aboriginal peoples, who are non-Caucasian in race or non-white in colour" (Statistics Canada, 2017c). Here are the options available to non-Indigenous respondents in the 2016 census questionnaire:

- White
- South Asian
- Chinese
- Black
- Filipino
- Latin American
- Arab
- Southeast Asian
- West Asian
- Korean
- Japanese

There is a write-in option if none of these applies, and respondents are permitted to select more than one option. Why does the government collect information on "race"? The stated purpose is to create programs that promote equality in access to employment opportunities, health care, education, and other services. You will see that it also allows sociologists to write about population trends, and textbook publishers to create colourful graphs.

"But wait," I hear some of you saying. "In the United States, white voters helped elect a black president. Black recording artists are among the most successful in North America. Audiences of all stripes made a movie about a black superhero, featuring a predominantly black cast and production crew, a historic box office hit, and *Crazy Rich Asians* is certified fresh on Rotten Tomatoes. Does race still matter?" It does, and we are still a long way from becoming a post-racial society. In this chapter we will examine some of the many areas of society where "race"—with or without the scare quotes—continues to exert a powerful influence.

What Do YOU Think?

Visible minority is a uniquely Canadian term that gained legitimacy when it was written into the 1986 Employment Equity Act. Critics argue that it's imprecise, lumping together non-white populations whose experiences are very different. Do you think we need a word for non-Caucasian, non-Indigenous Canadians?

The Point Is...

Hispanic Is Not a Race, According to the US Census Bureau

In the hands of governments, the social categories of "race" become deeply political.

Like the Canadian government, the government of the United States collects information on "race" in its census (conducted every 10 years, not 5). In its 2010 census questionnaire, there were just five options to choose from: white, black, American Indian, Asian, and Native Hawaiian/Pacific Islander. There was no option for Hispanic or Latino. So, in the 2010 census, 94 per cent of Americans chose one of the five official categories, while 6 per cent of respondents—including 37 per cent of Latino respondents—ticked the box labelled "some other race" (Gonzalez-Barrera & Lopez, 2015).

In the proposed questionnaire for 2020, the broad category "Asian" has been replaced by more specific options—Chinese, Filipino, Vietnamese, and so on—and Pacific Islanders can choose to identify specifically as Samoan or Chamorro. However, Hispanic and Latino continue to be absent from the list of possible races. Why is this so?

The Census Bureau explains that people who identify as Hispanic or Latino may be of any race. They may be black, or they may be white; they may be American Indian. Supporters of the questionnaire in its present form argue that these racial categories are the most important ones, since people of Hispanic and Latin American ancestry may have very different experiences depending on whether they are light- or dark-skinned (i.e. white or black). Yet for many US citizens of Mexican or Latin American descent, none of these options fits comfortably.

Why does it matter? First, it is true that Hispanics typically have a mixed genetic heritage of white, black, and Native American. But it is also true that they are sociologically racialized: they are treated differently, usually negatively, because of being Hispanic, whether they are identified by physical characteristics (such as the darkness of their skin) or by cultural ones, such as language, accent, food, clothing, or

Consider these two Americans. For each one, would you describe their race as white, black, or Native American?

Continued

music. But consider also what it is like to identify as Hispanic and to have to choose from a set of races that do not accurately capture your lived experience. This is a situation encountered every year by American high school students applying for college, since most American college applications include a question about race.

Apart from Hispanic and Latino Americans, who else might have trouble identifying an appropriate race category on the US census? What races are missing from the Canadian census question on population groups?

The Racialization of Visible Minorities in Canada: A Brief History

When they say that history is written by the winners, that history is what Michel Foucault called the master narrative. A **master narrative** is the story a nation tells about itself to celebrate its past and present. It evolves over time, reproduced and refined in schoolbooks, museums, government propaganda, and popular culture. To a greater or lesser degree, depending on the honesty of the nation involved, the master narrative will often gloss over or omit altogether certain unpleasant events that complicate the national self-identity. Stories about the exploitation of Indigenous people or the repression of ethnic or religious minorities may be excluded, becoming what Foucault (1994) called "buried knowledge."

Canada's master narrative is the story of a harmonious multicultural society made prosperous by its open-arms acceptance of immigration and diversity. While there is much evidence to support this narrative, it does not include some buried knowledge about the treatment of various racialized groups. Canadians have recently been coming to terms with certain elements of buried knowledge, particularly around this historical mistreatment of Indigenous people, but there is still a lot to be unearthed. In the following sections, we will have a chance to dig up some of episodes that make up Canada's buried knowledge.

Indigenous People in Canada

When I was in school, the "official" version of early Canadian history presented in our textbooks described how First Nations people co-operated with Europeans to make the fur trade successful by obtaining the furs, teaching Europeans how to use canoes and snowshoes, and providing the Europeans with new foods, such as pemmican (buffalo jerky) and corn. Of course, this account overlooked the exploitation and social destruction that occurred when Europeans introduced alcohol into the fur trade, setting off a pattern of ruinous colonial intrusion into the lives and culture of Indigenous people. Canada has begun to address the buried knowledge surrounding the government's relationship with Indigenous people, issuing formal apologies to survivors of residential schools and the Sixties Scoop (see Chapter 10), but the recent Inquiry into Missing and Murdered Indigenous Women and Girls shows that we have a long way to go to address the racialization of Indigenous people in Canada.

The racialization of the Indigenous population of the Americas began in the sixteenth century in Europe, with a discussion of whether or not Indigenous people were human and had souls. To western Europeans, Indigenous people were so different in terms of their ways of life, their languages, and their approaches to religion (all considered unsophisticated by Europeans). They also differed in their physical appearance. Racialization became a way to explain the whole set of differences. It was used to justify colonial occupation of lands inhabited by this inferior "race" of darker-skinned people.

Indigenous people have been living in what is now Canada for at least 14,000 years. The first Europeans (the Norse or Viking explorers) did not arrive on Canada's eastern shores until roughly 1000 years ago, and they left shortly thereafter. We can say that roughly 93 per cent of Canadian history is Indigenous alone. Yet as Métis writer Emma LaRocque explains, sociologically, Indigenous people have been studied most often not as founders but as problems:

> Several years ago in a sociology class on social problems, I recall wondering if anyone else was poor, because the professor repeatedly referred to Native people as statistical examples of poverty. . . . Not for one moment would I make light of the ugly effects of poverty. But if classroom groups must talk about Indians and poverty, then they must also point out the ways in which Native people are operating on this cancer. To be sure, the operations are always struggles and sometimes failures, but each new operation is faced with more experience, more skill, more confidence and more success. (1993, p. 212)

It does not help that the voices of Indigenous people have barely been heard in the sociological study of their people (Steckley, 2003). Indigenous people have only recently been able to take advantage of graduate-level work in Canadian universities, and Indigenous studies remains one of several research areas sociology that continue to privilege outsiders. Thus, it will be a while yet before the Indigenous voices we are beginning to hear will speak loudly in Canadian sociology.

Indigenous Status

Indigenous people are defined by a complex system of legal statuses that separates them from non-Indigenous people, and from each other. The main designations, as defined in Canadian legislation, are

- **registered Indian**
- Bill C-31 Indian

- band member
- reserve resident
- treaty Indian (a category with its own subdivisions, as each treaty is different)
- Métis
- Eskimo.

The legal differences come from the Indian Act, which was administered by the federal Department of Indian Affairs (now called Crown–Indigenous Relations and Northern Affairs Canada). Passed in 1876, the Indian Act enshrined a sexist definition of "Indian" as (1) any man of "Indian blood" reputed to belong to a particular band, (2) any child of such a man, or (3) any woman married to such a man. A man kept his status no matter whom he married, but a woman, if she married someone not legally an Indian, lost her status, and her children would share that fate. A non-Indian woman could gain Indian status by marrying an Indian man. This discriminatory law was in force until 1985, when Bill C-31 was passed, enabling people who had lost their Indian status through marriage or through the marriage of their mother to apply to be reinstated. (Incidentally, if "Indian" and "Eskimo" strike you as old-fashioned, they are. The terms are found in legislation written before the 1970s and should be used only in that context; the Quick Hits box on page 236 offers some guidelines on how to refer to Indigenous people.)

Inuit (from a word in their language meaning "people"; the singular is "Inuk") differ from "Indians," having been in Canada for a shorter time—somewhere between 5,000 and 10,000 years. It was not until 1939, when the federal government wanted to assert territorial claims in the Arctic, that Canada officially took responsibility for the Inuit. Each Inuk was given a metal disc with a number that was to be used as a token of their status. Today, about 60 per cent of Inuit have disc numbers. The lives of many Inuit changed on 1 April 1999, when the territory of Nunavut ("Our Land") came into being. Inuit make up nearly 85 per cent of the territory's 35,580 residents. They own 18 per cent of the land, have subsurface rights to oil, gas, and other minerals for about 2 per cent of Nunavut, and will receive royalties from the extraction of those minerals from the rest of

Quick Hits

Which Terms to Use and Avoid When Discussing Indigenous People

When sociologists talk about Indigenous people living in Canada, they are referring to the earliest inhabitants of this land and their descendants. The Canadian government recognizes three distinct groups of Indigenous people: First Nations, Métis, and Inuit.

While it is appropriate to speak of Indigenous people *in* Canada, you should try to avoid the expressions "Indigenous Canadians," since not all Indigenous people embrace Canadian citizenship, and "Canada's Indigenous people," which reinforces centuries of paternalistic treatment by Canadian governments. "People" is used when referring to a group of individuals or the entire Indigenous community; "peoples" is used only when referring to distinct groups (as in, *the Gitksan, Nisga'a, and other Indigenous peoples*). "Aboriginal," when used as an adjective, is an acceptable synonym for "Indigenous," but it has become less common since Canada officially adopted the UN's Declaration on the Rights of Indigenous Peoples in May 2016. Do not use "Aboriginal" as a noun (as in "Aboriginals living in Canada").

Although it is embedded in the Indian Act, the word "Indian" has gradually given way to "First Nations," just as "Eskimo" has been replaced by "Inuit" (plural) or "Inuk" (singular). Wherever possible, use the self-defined name of the community you are discussing instead of more general terms (e.g. *a Mi'kmaq woman*, instead of *a First Nations woman* or *an Indigenous woman*). Keep in mind that most of the names that identify specific Indigenous peoples in history books are not the people's names for themselves (e.g. "Huron" rather than "Wendat").

An excellent resource for further information is *Elements of Indigenous Style*, by Greg Younging (Brush Education, 2018).

---

the territory. They do not require a licence to hunt or fish to meet their basic needs. Nunavut is one of four regions that make up Inuit Nunangat, the Inuit homeland in Canada; the other three regions are Nunangit, Nunavik, and Nunatsiavut.

The term **Métis** is used in two ways. It is commonly used, often with a lowercase *m*, to refer to anyone of mixed Indigenous and non-Indigenous heritage. With an uppercase *M* it usually refers to the descendants of French fur traders and Cree women. Starting in the late eighteenth century, the Métis developed a culture that brought together European and First Nations elements. Over time, they achieved a sense of solidarity from their shared legal struggles with the Hudson's Bay Company (HBC) over the HBC's trade monopoly. The HBC owned most of the prairies and about half of present-day Canada, thanks to a 1670 charter granted by the English King Charles II, who knew little about the land. In 1867, the HBC negotiated the sale of most of its lands to the federal government, which, with no regard for Métis land rights, set up a colony in Manitoba. In 1869, a college-educated 25-year-old, Louis Riel, led the Métis in a military takeover, setting up an independent government to negotiate with Ottawa. The Manitoba Act of 1870 established the province and recognized the rights of the Métis. The Métis were given *scrips*, certificates declaring that the bearer could receive payment in land, cash, or goods. But government officials and land speculators swindled the Métis out of their land, buying up the scrips for next to nothing. Most Métis moved west. In 1885, with western expansion again threatening their rights to the land, the Métis, led again by Louis Riel (who had been leading a peaceful life in Montana before he was asked to lead his people), made a stand in Saskatchewan. Canadian forces attacked and defeated them. Riel was hanged for treason.

The Métis settled in a patchwork of rural prairie communities and nearly disappeared altogether. But during the 1930s, Alberta Métis pushed for the creation of communal settlements similar to First Nations reserves. In 1938, eleven Métis "colonies" were formed (eight remain). These colonies carry some political rights, making them like rural municipalities. However, they do not have rights to the royalties for oil and gas extracted from their land. Beyond the colonies, the Métis are represented by the Métis National Council and provincial organizations in Ontario and the western provinces.

Indigenous People in Canada: What the Census Tells Us

Indigenous people make up just under 5 per cent of the population of people living in Canada, but their population is growing at a rate over four times that of the non-Indigenous population (Figures 8.1 & 8.2). In the 10 years between the 2006 and 2016 censuses, the population of Indigenous people rose by 42.5 per cent, including a 51 per cent increase for Métis. The most likely reason for this increase is a heightened tendency to self-identify as Indigenous, but increased life expectancy and high fertility rates also play a role. The Indigenous population is young—the average age (32) is 9 years younger than the average age of non-Indigenous Canadians—which means that their population growth will likely continue to outpace increases in the non-Indigenous population.

Blacks in Canada
Black Communities in Atlantic Canada

Black communities have existed in Nova Scotia since the British Proclamation of 1779 offered freedom to slaves who left their American masters to fight on the British side in the American Revolution. More came north in the first half of the nineteenth century. They were offered significantly less land and fewer opportunities than white immigrants were, and they endured incredible hardship and prejudice. Despite having been in Canada for more than 200 years, Nova Scotian blacks are treated as an anomaly when they travel west in Canada; "But where are you really from?" is a question they are often asked.

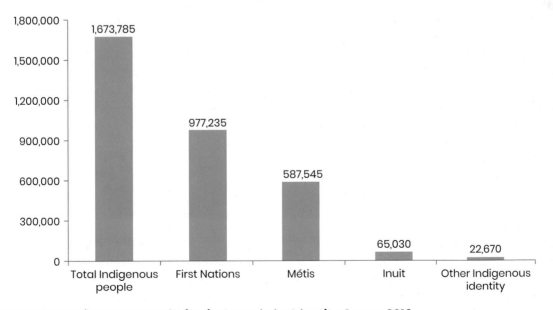

FIGURE 8.1 Indigenous Population in Canada by Identity Group, 2016

Source: Statistics Canada (2015), p. 6, Chart 2; Statistics Canada (2018).

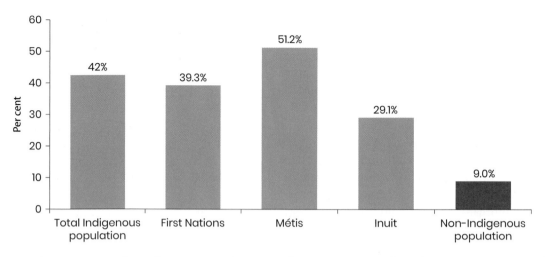

FIGURE 8.2 **Increase in Indigenous and Non-Indigenous Populations in Canada by Identity Group, 2006–2016**

Source: Statistics Canada (2017a).

No wonder the Métis population is on the rise: from the runway to the summer music festival, "going native" has become cool. For those seeking what Tuck and Yang (2012) describe as a "move to innocence," Métis ancestry is ripe for appropriation because it is perceived to be harder to disprove than First Nations official status. What's wrong with donning a ceremonial headdress in kinship with Canada's earliest inhabitants? No, seriously: What is wrong with it?

The Point Is . . .

Colton Boushie and Helen Betty Osborne: The Racialization of Indigenous People in the Criminal Justice System

Imagine you are an Indigenous woman, a Cree mother whose 22-year-old son was killed by a white man. You are in the courtroom and you look around. The judge is white, the lawyers are white, in all probability the bailiff and other court officials are white, the witnesses called by the defence lawyer are white, and very significantly so are all of the members of the jury who will decide guilt or innocence of the white killer. How would you rate the chances that your son's killer will be found guilty?

In August 2016, Colten Boushie, from the Cree community of the Red Pheasant First Nation in Saskatchewan, was killed by gunshots fired by Gerald Stanley, a white 56-year-old farmer. Boushie and four of his friends were out in an SUV when it got a flat tire. They had been drinking. They drove up Stanley's driveway to where a number of vehicles were parked (Stanley worked part-time as a mechanic). The SUV collided with one of the vehicles, and one of Boushie's friends started an ATV that was parked nearby. Stanley became aware of the commotion and took action. Armed with a loaded semiautomatic pistol and accompanied by his 28-year-old son, he approached the youths and fired two warning shots. Boushie was sitting in the driver's seat of the SUV, asleep, when Stanley arrived at the vehicle. As Stanley reached in to turn off the ignition, his gun went off, firing two shots and killing Boushie. Stanley later claimed that it was hang fire, which occurs when a gun delays in firing.

Stanley was arrested and tried for second-degree murder. In February 2018, he was acquitted by a jury of his peers.

Jury selection involves assessing lists of potential candidates. In a practice known as *peremptory challenge*, a lawyer can have a jury candidate excluded. The reasons for the challenge do not have to be stated clearly. In the trial of Gerald Stanley, the defence lawyer exercised peremptory challenge for all of the Indigenous candidates; as a result, Stanley was tried before an all-white jury.

This has happened before, notably in the case of Helen Betty Osborne. She was a Cree woman from Norway House, Manitoba, who was kidnapped and killed in 1971 by a group of young white men looking for sex (see Steckley, 2013). Her case remained unsolved until the late 1980s, when two of the four men implicated in her murder were charged. Notably, a lawyer for one of the accused men, defending his use of peremptory challenge, stated, "There was no deliberate campaign to keep the Natives off [the jury]. . . . But we didn't want these men to be convicted for all of the ills of society" (Priest, 1989, p. 143). In the end, one of the accused men was acquitted, while the other was convicted and released after serving 10 years of a life sentence. The Osborne case later became the subject of the Aboriginal Justice Inquiry, which recommended replacing peremptory challenge in such cases. It did not happen.

What Do YOU Think?

1. Do you think that peremptory challenge is an instrument of institutional racism in Canada?
2. How do you think the case of Colten Boushie should have been handled?

The Point Is . . .

North American Team Sports Are Racialized

If you are a fan of North American football, you have watched this scene countless times: a white guy (the centre), flanked by four white guys (offensive guards and tackles), snaps the ball to another white guy (the quarterback), whom all five white guys try to protect. This white guy looks up, sees that there are several, mostly black guys coming after him, and so hands the ball off to a black guy (the running back, sometimes jokingly called the running *black*), who gets tackled by the onrushing players. If the running back is stopped before advancing 10 yards, another white guy might come in to try to kick a field goal.

Racialized positions—positions associated with different racialized groups—are common in North American professional sports. The two most racialized positions in American football

are place kicker and running back. The former is exclusively white. A well-researched sports blog indicates that since 1966—the beginning of the National Football League's modern era—there have been just five black place kickers in a league where 60 per cent of the players are black (Matthews, 2011).

In contrast, running backs are nearly all black. A few explanations have been proposed. First, a number of players who broke the colour bar in American football were running backs: Jim Brown, Gale Sayers, and the now infamous O.J. Simpson paved the way for Walter Payton, Marcus Allen, Emmitt Smith, and LaDainian Tomlinson. A list of the 25 greatest running backs could easily not feature a single white player. Precedent and role modelling helped establish a stereotype around the running

AP Photo/Charles Krupa

Tom Brady (*left*) and Brandon Bolden play the positions of quarterback and running back for the New England Patriots. Can you guess which of them plays which position?

back position (as they did, perhaps, with white place kickers).

Prejudice has also played a role. Some black running backs took up the position only after they were told they would never make it to the NFL as a quarterback, a position of authority once reserved for white players. (Others, such as Chuck Ealey and Warren Moon, left the United States to play quarterback in the Canadian Football League, which was more receptive to black quarterbacks.) Worth noting: there are strict rules in place to protect quarterbacks and kickers; there are no special rules to protect running backs. Also worth noting: the average NFL playing career is 3.3 seasons. Kickers (4.87 seasons) and quarterbacks (4.44 seasons) have the longest average careers, while running backs (2.57) have the shortest (Statistica.com).

A similar situation exists in Major League Baseball. Most of the game involves "two white guys playing catch." At the start of the 2016 season, for example, there were just 14 African American pitchers, representing 3.1 per cent of all MLB pitchers (Nightengale, 2016). Canadian Russell Martin, whose father is black, is currently the league's only black catcher. Pitcher and catcher are, like the quarterback in football, positions of authority and have long been white. Outfielders tend to be black

(see Figure 8.3), as the first "Negro" players to break the colour bar and be stars were outfielders: Jackie Robinson, Willie Mays, and Hank Aaron. Latino players dominate the middle infield positions—shortstop and second base—as the first Latino player to star in professional baseball was Luis Aparicio, a shortshop.

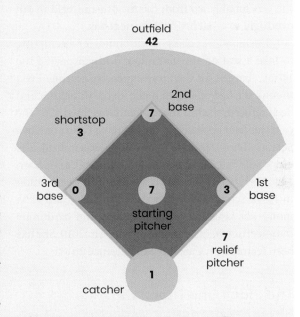

FIGURE 8.3 African American Players on MLB Rosters by Position, 2016

Source: Adapted from: Bob Nightengale (2016, April 5), "As MLB celebrates Jackie Robinson, dearth of black pitchers concerns many," USA Today.

What Do YOU Think?

Is this a discussion of sport or society? What are the broader sociological implications of the findings discussed in this box?

Tensions have long existed between black and white communities in Nova Scotia, and so it is little surprise that the province was home to a Canadian civil rights hero who has only recently gained the national recognition she deserves for her role in opposing racial discrimination. Viola Desmond (1914–1965) grew up in Halifax, in a well-respected, middle-class black family. Inspired by her father, a successful independent businessman, she aspired to open a beauty parlour in her hometown. However, she was unable to train as a beautician in Halifax,

since very few of the city's schools accepted black students, and so she pursued her education first in Montreal and then in the United States. When she returned to Halifax she established a hair salon, a beauty school, and her own line of beauty products.

On a fall evening in 1946, as she was travelling on business to Sydney, her car broke down in the town of New Glasgow. Since she would have to wait several hours for repairs, she thought she would take in a movie at New Glasgow's Roseland Theatre. She bought a ticket and proceeded to a seat on the main floor. After taking her seat, she was advised that her ticket entitled her to sit in the balcony, not on the main floor, where seating was more expensive. She offered to pay the difference but was informed that she would not be permitted to sit on the main floor; she soon became aware that blacks were expected to sit in the balcony, and that the main floor was reserved for whites. When she refused to surrender her seat, she was forcibly led from the theatre and held in jail overnight to await her trial the next day.

Desmond was charged with fraud for attempting to take a seat on the main floor without paying the 1¢ tax charged for the more expensive seating. Even though she had offered to make up the difference and been refused, she lost the case and was fined $26. The case was later appealed to the Supreme Court of Nova Scotia, where Desmond's conviction was upheld. She eventually left Nova Scotia for Montreal and, later, New York, where she died at the age of 50. Segregation in Nova Scotia was legally ended in 1954, and Desmond was issued an official apology and pardon by the government of her home province in 2010. She has been featured on Canada's $10 bill since 2018.

The Black One Thousand: Black Settlement in Alberta

In the late nineteenth century, many black Americans living in the eastern United States migrated west to find a place where they would be free from prejudice and discrimination. In Oklahoma, they established all-black communities, but many of these towns' black residents, feeling crowded out and unwelcome, travelled north in search of a new frontier to settle. Western Canada was a promising destination. Harrison Sneed, a minister from an all-black town called Clearview, went first to scout the land. The federal government granted him land far north in Alberta, where white settlers did not want to live and farm. And so, in 1909 Sneed returned to Alberta with a group of 194 men, women, and children. They carried more than just their hopes for the future: they brought 200 rail cars filled with their baggage, livestock, and other possessions. A group of 200 black settlers followed shortly after, and in the years that followed, black settlements spread across the countryside.

The white citizens of Edmonton responded predictably in 1911. They issued a petition to the federal government, signed by roughly one-quarter of the city's 24,000 residents. It began,

We, the undersigned residents of the city of Edmonton, respectfully urge upon your attention and upon that of the Government of which you are the head, the serious menace to the future welfare of a large portion of Western Canada, by reason of the alarming influx of negro settlers. . . . Last year several hundred negroes arrived in Edmonton and settled in surrounding territory. Already this season nearly three hundred have arrived; and the statement is made . . . [that] the advent of such negroes as are now here was most unfortunate for the country, and that further arrivals in large numbers would be disastrous. We cannot admit as any factors the argument that these people may be good farmers or good citizens. It is a matter of common knowledge that it has been proved in the United States that negroes and whites cannot live in proximity without the occurrence of revolting lawlessness and the development of bitter race hatred. . . . (from the *Edmonton Capital*, 25 April 1911, as quoted in Cobb, 2017, p. 19)

Canadian Prime Minister Wilfrid Laurier (the guy on our $5 bill) accepted the petition that year, declaring a prohibition of "any immigrants belonging to the Negro race, which race is deemed unsuitable to the climate and requirements of Canada" (Cobb, 2017, p. 19). By 1914, the immigration that had resulted in the settlement of "The Black One Thousand," as they were known, had ceased.

The Black Population in Canada Today

The black population of Canada has declined several times. In 1792, nearly 1200 black Loyalists left for the new African colony of Sierra Leone. Many more left Canada for the United States following the Civil War. Between 1871 and 1911, there was a slow decline in Canada's black population, from 21,500 to 16,900, and a further drop (following a brief resurgence) from 22,200 to 18,000, between 1941 and 1951. It was not until the 1970s that the black population began to increase consistently, rising from 34,400 in 1971 to 239,500 by the end of the decade (Milan & Tran, 2004, p. 3).

According to the 2016 census, close to 1.2 million people who identified as black were living

Glenbow Archives NA 704-5

Once a thriving black farming community, Amber Valley was large enough to have its own baseball team; today, it is a ghost town. How is this story of black settlement in Alberta at odds with the prevailing narrative of how western Canada was settled?

in Canada, representing the third-largest visible minority population in the country (Figure 8.4). Roughly 37 per cent of black Canadians were living in Toronto, where they made up 7.5 per cent of the city's population (Statistics Canada, 2019). Montreal, where blacks are the largest visible-minority group, had the second-largest black community in Canada, thanks to recent immigration from former French colonies such as Haiti, Rwanda, Chad, and Cameroon. In fact, the black population in Quebec grew by 142 per cent from 1996 to 2016, and by 70 per cent from 2006 to 2016 (Table 8.1).

TABLE 8.1 Canada's Black Population by Region: Total, Percentage, and 10-Year Growth Rate (2006–2016)

Region	British Columbia	Prairie Provinces	Ontario	Quebec	Atlantic Provinces	Territories
Total black population	43,505	174,655	627,710	319,230	32,080	1,350
Share of total population	1.0%	2.8%	4.7%	4.0%	1.4%	1.2%
Growth rate 2006–16	+53.6%	+157.5%	+32.5%	+69.7%	+27.2%	+125.0%

Source: Statistics Canada, 2019.

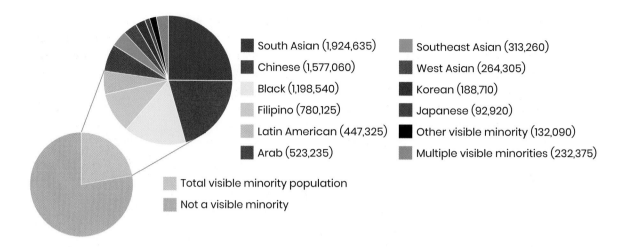

South Asian (1,924,635)   Southeast Asian (313,260)

Chinese (1,577,060)   West Asian (264,305)

Black (1,198,540)   Korean (188,710)

Filipino (780,125)   Japanese (92,920)

Latin American (447,325)   Other visible minority (132,090)

Arab (523,235)   Multiple visible minorities (232,375)

Total visible minority population

Not a visible minority

FIGURE 8.4 **Visible Minority Populations in Canada, 2016**

Source: Statistics Canada, 2017c.

Asian Canadians

As of the 2016 census, two-thirds of visible-minority Canadians were of Asian ancestry, with South Asians and Chinese Canadians making up the two largest visible-minority populations in the country (see Figure 8.4). Asian Canadians do not always face the same barriers to success that other racialized minorities do, and so they are in some ways the heroes of the master narrative of Canada that I described earlier. But this ignores many pieces of buried knowledge.

Chinese immigrants began to settle on Canada's west coast in the mid-nineteenth century, arriving first from American cities such as San Francisco and then directly from China. They were driven from China by poverty and political upheaval, and drawn to British Columbia by opportunities to work. Thousands of Chinese labourers (estimates range from 7,000 to 15,000) helped complete the Canadian Pacific Railway, risking their lives for very little reward. Not only did their contributions go unrecognized, but in 1885—the same year the last spike of the CPR was driven at Craigellachie, BC—Chinese immigrants were targeted by Canada's first "head tax."

Head Taxes and an Act to Prevent the Employment of Female Labour

From the time they arrived in British Columbia, Chinese immigrants were viewed by the predominantly white European settler population with suspicion

verging on disgust. To stall the influx of undesirable immigrants, the federal government, in 1885, imposed a $50 head tax on any Chinese migrant entering the country. There were similar policies in place in the United States, New Zealand, and Australia, but, in Canada, no other immigrant group was targeted with an entry fee. In 1900, when it was clear the policy was not stalling immigration enough to appease anxious British Columbians, the government doubled the head tax to $100 and then, under continued pressure from politicians and residents of the province, increased the tax to $500 in 1903. To put this in perspective, it has been estimated that the average Chinese labourer made around $300 a year (Chan, 2019).

The new tax had a dramatic effect on Chinese immigration, as it was meant to do. For the overwhelmingly male population of Chinese immigrants who had already settled in Canada, it meant the chances of marrying a Chinese woman were greatly reduced (the ratio of Chinese men to Chinese women in Canada in 1911 was roughly 28 to 1). While this limited population growth among Chinese Canadians, the gender imbalance became a new cause for panic among white Canadians, who worried that white women would be subjected to unwanted advances by desperate Chinese men. It was this kind of worry that led the government of Saskatchewan, in 1912, to create the Act to Prevent the Employment of Female Labour in Certain Capacities. It declared,

No person shall employ in any capacity any white woman or girl or permit any white woman or girl to reside or lodge in or to work in or, save as a *bona fide* customer in a public apartment thereof only, to frequent any restaurant, laundry or other place of business or amusement owned, kept or managed by any Japanese, Chinaman or other Oriental person. (quoted in Backhouse, 1999, p. 136)

Two months after the legislation was enacted, restaurant owner Quong Wing was convicted and fined for employing two white women. His appeals to the supreme courts of Saskatchewan and Canada failed. Twelve years later, in 1924, a Regina restaurateur, Yee Clun, challenged the law. He had strong support from members of the city's Chinese and non-Chinese communities. But local newspapers were spreading poorly researched stories of Chinese men bringing opium into Saskatchewan and turning white women into "drug fiends." Clun won the case in court but found his efforts foiled by the Saskatchewan Legislature, which passed another statute authorizing any municipal council to revoke the court ruling. The act was not repealed until 1969.

In 1923, amid renewed immigration from China, the Canadian government enacted its firmest anti-immigration measure to date. The Chinese Immigration Act, sometimes called the Chinese Exclusion Act, banned nearly all Chinese migrants from entering Canada. At the time, roughly 82,000 Chinese immigrants had come Canada since 1885, paying around 23 million dollars in taxes to do so. It would take 24 years for the act to be repealed (it violated the Charter of the United Nations, which Canada signed in 1945) and 20 years after that for Chinese immigration to Canada resume.

Japanese Canadian Soldiers in World War I

During the Second World War, roughly 22,000 Japanese Canadians were placed in internment camps and dispossessed of their property. It is a shameful but fortunately well-known episode in Canadian history. Less well known is the story of Japanese Canadian soldiers who volunteered to serve in the Canadian Expeditionary Force in World War I. At first, they were turned away, just as many Indigenous volunteers were. But by 1916, year three of the war, at least 222 had been admitted. It is interesting that although the majority of them lived in British Columbia, only 28 enlisted in that province, while 169 enlisted in Alberta, where they believed their chances of being accepted in the army were better. Japanese Canadian soldiers tended to be grouped together in sections of the battalions to which they belonged. Some fought and died at Vimy Ridge, in a battle that has become an important part of Canada's national narrative.

Japanese people had been in Canada since the 1870s. Many came from Japanese fishing villages and, once in Canada, settled in fishing communities along the west coast. Their service in the First World War earned them no favours from the federal government. In 1919, the year after the war ended, the Federal Department of Marine and Fisheries responded to growing concern that Japanese Canadian gill net salmon fishers were "taking over" at the expense of white Canadian fishers. In the words of Port Alberni MP Major R.J. Burde, reported in the Victoria *Colonist* in May 1920, "they have become so arrogant in their feeling of security that many white settlers are reaching the limit of tolerance" (quoted in Adachi, 1976, p. 105). In response, the government drastically reduced the number of licences that Japanese Canadian fishers could obtain. The new law had a swift impact: in just three years, white fishers gained 493 licences (an increase of 33.5 per cent), while Japanese fishers lost 974 licences (a drop of 48.9 per cent).

In 1920, the same year a Japanese Canadian War Memorial was dedicated in Vancouver's Stanley Park, the Japanese Canadian veterans association lobbied for the right to vote in provincial elections; this was not granted until 1931. Eleven years later, when Canada declared war on Japan, the perpetual light shining on the Japanese Canadian War Memorial was extinguished. A branch of the Canadian Legion that was home to many Japanese Canadian veterans was shut down and many of its members interned. Among them was the branch's head, Masumi Mitsui, who had been awarded the Military Medal for his leadership in the First World War. In 1985, at the age of 98, Mitsui was part of a ceremony commemorating the relighting of the Japanese-Canadian War Memorial (Dick, 2010).

Not Wanted on the Voyage: The *Komagata Maru*

Most of the first South Asians to come to Canada were Sikhs, who had been given special status by the British as soldiers and police serving imperial purposes throughout the world. In 1904, they began to arrive in small numbers, many of them settling in Port Moody, east of Vancouver. By 1906, their numbers had increased considerably, with as many as 5000 Sikhs entering the country between 1905 and 1908 (Johnston, 1989, p. 5; Burnet & Palmer, 1988, p. 31). They were young men, most of them single, though a good number had wives back in India. They arrived in British Columbia at a time when there was a shortage of labourers willing to work in the sawmills, on the roads, and in the bush cutting wood and clearing land. Some were greeted with a measure of respect, because they were British army veterans, and they soon earned a reputation for their hard work. An October 1906 report in the Vancouver *Daily Province* quoted one employer as saying, "I would have White labourers of course if I can get them. . . . But I would rather give employment to these old soldiers who have helped fight for the British Empire than entire aliens."

BC's natural resources–based economy has long fluctuated between periods of success and recession. Slow times produce unemployment, and newcomers are accused of taking jobs from whites. It wasn't long before the initial acceptance of the hard-working Sikh immigrants was undermined by a growing unease over their rise in numbers. The local press fuelled the simmering discord with stories about the unfamiliar cultural practices of these "Hindus" (as South Asians collectively were called, regardless of their religion). "Hindus Cover Dead Bodies with Butter" announced a headline in the *Daily Province in October 1906* (quoted in Johnston, 1989, p. 3).

Amid a growing moral panic, Vancouver police began taking Sikh immigrants directly from the immigration shed to the BC interior to keep them out of the city. In spite of the deplorable accommodations in which they were placed, the Sikhs showed tremendous resilience, as Johnston records:

Two thousand had arrived during the latter half of 1906. By the end of December, with the exception of some 300 who had taken steamers for Seattle and San Francisco, all but fifty or sixty had found employment in British Columbia, most of them in saw mills. The authorities would gladly have deported any convicted of vagrancy, but there were few such cases; those who were out of work were looked after by their companions, and . . . none became a public charge. (1989, p. 3)

Facing pressure from both white British Columbians disconcerted by the influx of Sikh immigrants and British government officials in India who wanted to curtail emigration, the Canadian government responded with clever discrimination. They passed a law requiring that all Asian immigrants entering Canada possess at least $200—a large sum for people who typically earned about 10 to 20 cents a day. They also prohibited the landing of any immigrant arriving directly from any point outside of India—significant because most Sikhs were making the journey from Punjab province by way of Hong Kong—while pressuring steamship companies not to provide India-to-Canada service or to sell tickets to Canada from Indian ports. These measures brought Sikh immigration to a halt. Unable to bring their wives and families over, denied the right to vote or hold public office, and facing open discrimination, Canada's Sikh population became discouraged.

Opposition to Sikh immigration continued to grow. In December 1913, the *Daily Province* claimed that the "Hindu problem" had assumed "a most serious and menacing aspect" (Johnston, 1989, p. 22), even though only 39 Sikhs had entered the area that year. The following spring, the Japanese steamship *Komagata Maru* left Yokohama, Japan, headed for Canada. Rented by a 55-year-old Sikh, Bhai Gurdit Singh, the ship contained 376 passengers: 340 Sikhs, 24 Muslims, and 12 Hindus. News of the ship's approach was announced in the dailies with headlines such as "BOAT LOADS OF HINDUS ON WAY TO VANCOUVER" and "HINDU INVASION OF CANADA." When the ship reached Vancouver in May 1914, the local South Asian community was ready with lawyers, funds, and food to assist the passengers. Local immigration officials, politicians, and vigilante groups were also ready. For about two months, the ship's passengers were forced to endure legal battles and severe shortages of food and water. In July 1914, the *Komagata Maru* was forced to leave. Only 24 passengers were permitted to enter Canada.

Little changed afterward. After 1918, a few of the men were able to bring over to Canada their long absent wives and children, but most could not afford such an expense. By 1941, there were no more than 1500 South Asians in Canada. Most were men, many aged between 50 and 65. Only when India was granted its independence from British imperial control in 1947 were South Asians given the vote and full citizenship status.

When Immigrants Are Refugees

We have seen that East Asian immigrants arriving in large numbers are greeted with suspicion by Canadians. What if they are refugees?

A case to consider is that of Vietnamese Canadians. In 1954, the French regime in Vietnam was overthrown by a resistance force in the north, backed by China and led by Ho Chi Minh. The country was partitioned into two states, the northern one communist, the southern one not. Enter the United States. Eager to contain the spread of communism, the Americans aligned themselves with the government in the south, and devoted massive amounts of soldiers, weapons, and money to the fight they could not win. In 1973, they withdrew from the war, which ended two years later with the reunification of the country under communist rule.

Following the war, Vietnamese people from the south, fearing retaliation and oppression, began to leave their country, many in small boats barely capable of making the dangerous journey across the Pacific. With these "boat people" heading for Canadian shores, the federal government in 1976 passed new legislation that defined refugees

Sikh passengers aboard the *Komagata Maru*. Despite the fact that Sikhs have been in Canada since 1904, their visibility still prompts the question, *Where are you from?*

as a separate class of immigrant. Refugees would not have to meet the admission criteria imposed on other immigrants.

In 1979–80, Canada received some 60,000 refugees from Vietnam and neighbouring Cambodia and Laos. The federal government promised to aid the refugees by matching funds raised by individual citizens, churches, and other private organizations. During that summer, while working at Sainte-Marie among the Hurons, I took part in two fundraisers: a musical (I played drums) and a historical interpretation (I played a Jesuit missionary). It was a positive contribution I could make after strongly opposing the American presence in Vietnam.

The striking thing about this episode is the empathy with which Canadians viewed the Vietnamese boat people. I wonder if Canadians today continue to regard Vietnamese people more positively than they do immigrants from other East Asian countries. Likely not, given how long ago this occurred. (I have a special interest in the question because I have a Vietnamese Canadian granddaughter.) I also wonder if Canadians feel the same degree of acceptance toward refugees generally versus other immigrants. How would you research such a question?

Ethnicity

Ethnicity and Race: What's the Difference?

Earlier in the chapter I commented on historical attempts to identify different human "races." These quasi-scientific efforts were based mostly on analyzing biological features, including skin, hair, and eye color, facial profile, height, and even (in some cases) brain size. While we have established, scientifically, that there is but one human race, the legacy of those efforts is that we continue to lump people into different categories of race based primarily on visible characteristics.

Race is something you are born into. It has nothing to do with your nationality, the language(s) you speak, or your cultural practices: it is based on how you look to others, and throughout your life you will be judged by it, favourably or unfavourably. You did not choose your race and

cannot opt into another race. I could not, for instance, stand in front of a room of students and claim to be Filipino, since it would be apparent to everyone that I am not.

Ethnicity is different. It refers to membership in a cultural group that has roots in a particular place in the world and is associated with distinctive cultural practices and behaviours. Ethnicity differs from race in several ways. First, most people identify with just one race but may have many ethnicities. Imagine you were born in Italy and moved to Canada with your family as a child. Your father is Italian; your mother is Canadian and Jewish. You may consider yourself mostly Canadian, since you grew up in Canada, but your sympathies may lie with Italy during soccer's World Cup, and though you are not religious, you may, because of your mother's heritage, feel a deeper connection to the suffering of Jews when your class is studying the Second World War.

Unlike race, ethnicity is something you can opt into, as many people do when they cite a distant forebear from Ireland as a pretext to celebrate St Patrick's Day. This leads to another key difference between race and ethnicity: physical appearance seldom yields any clues to our ethnic affiliations. This is why I *could* stand before a class and claim a whole range of ethnicities—Manx, Walloon, Abruzzi, Cajun—that no one could contest.

Your ethnicity is not the same as your nationality, though it may be (if, for instance, your family has lived in Canada for so many generations that you feel no connection to the culture of your distant ancestors who came to this country from somewhere else). And ethnicity is no clue to your race.

To understand the difference between nationality, ethnicity, and race, imagine you were born in Canada to parents who immigrated to Quebec from Haiti. Your nationality is Canadian. That may also be your primary ethnic affiliation, though you may feel equal or greater connection to various other ethnicities, including Haitian (the nationality of your parents), Caribbean (reflecting the broader culture of the Caribbean islands), Québécois (emphasizing a strong cultural connection to the province), or francophone (signifying an affinity with the broader French-speaking community). Your race is likely to be black, reflecting the predominant population group of Haiti.

Approaches to the Study of Ethnicity

Everyone belongs to at least one ethnic group. Membership in an ethnic group can be a source of pride, but differences among ethnic groups living together can also be a source of conflict.

There are many ways to study ethnicity, but I will concentrate on five approaches that are particularly useful in understanding ethnic conflict. The first three—*social constructivism, instrumentalism,* and *essentialism*—are commonly used in political sociology. Canadian sociologist Wsevolod W. Isajiw, who specializes in ethnic studies, discusses the third of these, essentialism, in relation to the *epiphenomenal approach*, which is helpful to consider here as well. Finally, I will introduce a fifth approach, *postcolonialism*, because it is essential to understanding ethnicity in the context of the case study I am about to present.

One of the most savage, destructive ethnic conflicts of recent times involves two rival tribes, the Hutu and the Tutsi, in the central African country Rwanda. Rwanda was a colony of Germany and then of Belgium from 1890 until 1962, when it gained independence. The period that following was punctuated by uprisings by the disenfranchised Hutu majority against the ruling Tutsi elite, causing the deaths of hundreds of thousands of civilians in both groups. The violence peaked in the spring and summer of 1994, when Hutu military forces massacred between 500,000 and 1,000,000 of the Tutsi minority, sending more than a million destitute Hutu civilians, fearing reprisals from the surviving Tutsi population, fleeing to refugee camps in neighbouring Zaire (now the Democratic Republic of the Congo) and Tanzania.

What causes neighbouring ethnic groups to become so hostile toward one another? It is easy to put it all down to tribal violence, but the situation is more complicated. We can better understand it by looking through the lens of our five theories of ethnicity.

Telling It Like It Is   An Author's POVs

My Silent Ukrainian Identity

I was an adult when I informally learned of the *Holodomor*. During the 1930s, [the Soviets, under Communist Party leader Joseph] Stalin systematically starved and killed millions of Ukrainians. That horrid history lesson was absent from the social studies classes I attended as a youth. My Ukrainian grandfather never spoke of the genocide, and I think I know why. In 1933, my grandfather was the tenth of ten children born to Ukrainian immigrants. Had my great-grandparents decided to stay in the motherland instead of departing for Canada in 1907, the Ukrainian branch of my family tree might have never existed.

Our surname caused my grandfather grief. Throughout his later life, I heard my grandfather recount the attempts some made to discredit his ethnicity. His acquaintances would say that "Kondro" isn't a Ukrainian name. It doesn't end in "ski," they'd say. You don't have a proper Ukrainian name, they'd say. You're not Ukrainian, they'd say. Nonetheless, my grandfather always identified with his Ukrainian ethnicity; he appreciated the food and the ethnic sense of humour.

My Ukrainian family members have performed extensive genealogical work. We can now accurately trace our own ancestry back to the mid-eighteenth century. However, there was an emotional and ethnic existential cost for our ancestral knowledge. Our Ukrainian family has ties to Poland; an uncle to my grandfather has Polish birth records. My grandfather was deeply troubled when he learned that he *could* be Polish. I remember him saying, "I don't want to be Polish."

Continued

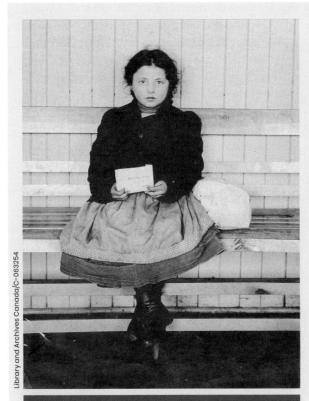

Library and Archives Canada/C-063254

A young "Galician" immigrant in Saint John, NB, in May 1905. Canada's Ukrainian population is among the highest in the world outside of Ukraine and Russia, yet during World War I, many Ukrainian Canadians were put in internment camps, since much of present-day Ukraine was then territory of the Austro-Hungarian Empire, with whom Canada was at war. Was this a case of ethnic prejudice or a practical necessity in wartime?

What was more troubling was that my grandfather's uncle was placed in an internment camp in Banff, Alberta, during World War I; he was deemed an enemy alien and forced to perform manual labour. Various documents show he escaped in exile, first to Saskatchewan and then to the United States. The uncle left for Russia in 1920. After 1937, he wasn't heard from again.

I wasn't sure of how I should feel when I learned of the interned relative and the genocide. I never saw myself as a Ukrainian like my grandfather and his immediate family saw themselves. Though my white identity is not threatened with starvation or unjust internment, I silently identify with the Ukrainian portion of my ethnic genes. I was always the closest to my Ukrainian grandfather.

The horrid history lesson of the *Holodomor* gave my silent Ukrainian identity a new emotional identity. It was a bad time for Ukrainians, but my family was simply lucky. When some stayed, others took a chance on Canada. Their gamble is paying dividends to their descendants. The sadness I feel for my distant relatives is silent. My white privilege consciously mutes it.

Now that my grandfather is dead, I expend more thinking than I ever have before on his life and his immigrant parents' lives. I took for granted that my grandfather was uniquely Ukrainian and though he spoke sparingly of the attempts to discredit his ethnicity, I never recognized the full implications of his family's immigration to Canada.

—Jonah Kondro

Essentialism

Essentialism (sometimes called **primordialism**) is the view that every ethnic group is defined by a "laundry list" of traits carried down from the past to the present with little or no change. So, for instance, we could look at the traits that differentiated the Tutsi and Hutu. The Tutsi were, on average, taller and thinner than the Hutu, with longer and thinner faces. One study (Chrétien,

1997) found that the Tutsi averaged 1.75 metres in height, while the Hutu measured 1.66 metres. The tribes also differed in terms of occupation: before colonialism, the Tutsi were mostly pastoralists who owned and herded cattle; the Hutu were agriculturalists, growing crops.

Essentialism presents a static view of ethnic culture, in which culture does not change without the influence of outside forces. Applied to our case study, it ignores the fact that the differences were not absolute: some Hutu herded cattle, some Tutsi grew crops, and intermarriage between the two groups was not uncommon. Adopting the essentialist view uncritically leads to believing that the ethnic conflicts in Rwanda have a deep history that existed long before colonialism, and that these conflicts reignited only after the "stabilizing influence" of the colonial power left. In this way, it absolves colonial powers of any blame.

Postcolonialism

Colonialism is the economic and political exploitation of a weaker country or people by a stronger one. Typically—historically—it involves a European state dominating an African, Asian, or American people, though it is not limited to this. The Chinese exercise colonial control over Tibetans and Uighurs (European language–speaking Muslims), and we don't need to look far to see how, in Canada, European settlers and successive federal and provincial governments wielded colonial control over Indigenous Peoples.

Postcolonialism is a framework that analyzes the destructive impact colonialism has on both the colonizer and the colonized. It was first developed by writers such as **Franz Fanon** (1925–1961) and **Albert Memmi** (b. 1920) to examine French colonies in North Africa and their fight for independence from France. Fanon, born in the French West Indian colony of Martinique, was radicalized by his work as a doctor and psychiatrist in Algeria during the fight for independence there. His influential works *Black Skin, White Masks* (1952) and *The Wretched of the Earth* (1961) address the psychological effects of colonization and have inspired considerable sociological study. Memmi was a Jew born in predominately Muslim Tunisia, which gained its independence in 1956. In *The Colonizer and the Colonized* (1957), he demonstrated how the two groups negatively conditioned each other, and how no party could be "neutral" in the relationship between the two.

Postcolonial theory, as it applies to ethnicity, identifies colonialism as a factor in the conflict between ethnic groups. In the African context, it is usefully applied to study situations involving **indirect rule**, a governance policy in which a European nation uses the members of a tribe or ethnic group as its intermediaries in ruling African territory.

In Rwanda prior to the colonial period, a person's sense of identity was derived mainly from lineage and clan. Lineage heads were important figures, and a single clan could include members of both Hutu and Tutsi ethnic groups. Under colonialism, lineage heads lost power to chiefs appointed by colonial administrators. Drawing on the conclusions of European social scientists, these administrators saw the Tutsi as a superior conquering race, based on the physical differences noted earlier and the fact the Tutsi appeared to have come to Rwanda after the Hutu. As a result, when appointing chiefs, the colonial administrators overwhelmingly favoured Tutsi. The blurred lines of distinction between Tutsi and Hutu became solid, reinforced by the fact that Rwandan citizens now had to carry identification cards showing their ethnic group. This produced an ethnic-based class system with Tutsi at the top and Hutu at the bottom.

Ethnicity as Epiphenomenal

"Epiphenomenal" describes a secondary effect that arises from, but does not causally influence, a separate phenomenon. **Marx** first applied it in a sociological context. He believed that economic structure was the main causal factor in society, and everything else was epiphenomenal.

Epiphenomenal theory suggests that any ethnic conflict is just a by-product of the struggle between economic classes. Thus, the strife in Rwanda stems from a situation in which the country's wealthy elite (the Tutsi) were exploiting its poor (the Hutu and the poorer Tutsi). Ethnicity made it impossible for Hutu and poorer Tutsi with shared class interests to overcome their oppression by the Tutsi elite. This was because poorer Tutsi identified with the wealthy Tutsi more than they identified with the Hutu who were, like them, being exploited. There is a measure of truth in the epiphenomenal explanation, yet it fails to fully account for why the poor identified with the rich.

Instrumentalism

Traditionally presented as opposite to essentialism and compatible with the epiphenomenal approach is instrumentalism, which focuses on emerging ethnicity rather than on long-established ethnic characteristics. It acknowledges that elites can mobilize others who identify with them ethnically. In the words of political scientist Catharine Newbury, ethnic groups are created or transformed when they "gain self-awareness (become 'self-conscious communities') largely as the result of the activities of leaders who mobilize ethnic followings in order to compete more effectively" (1993, p. 15).

Elite members who mobilize ethnicity for personal gain are called **ethnic entrepreneurs**. The classic example of ethnic entrepreneurship is Adolf Hitler's construction and manipulation of the German "Aryan race." In our case study, an instrumentalist approach better explains how frustrated

Hutu leaders could invoke the injustice of Tutsi oppression to draw poorer Hutu into their political parties and their acts of revolution; it also explains why poorer Tutsi identified closely with the Tutsi elite.

Social Constructivism

Social constructivism is the view that ethnicity is artificial, constructed by individuals to serve some agenda. Like instrumentalism, it explains how ethnicity is constructed by the elite. However, it suffers as a theory of ethnicity by overstating the influence of the elite. It generally fails to attribute the non-elite members any agency, any power to act without being manipulated. A social constructivist theory of ethnicity would look to the motivations of the broader group.

The social constructivist approach makes sense in the case of Rwanda, which was, for most of the twentieth century, a very crowded land, where

AP Photo/Ben Curtis

Twenty-five years after the 1994 Rwandan genocide, children play in the streets of Mbyo, one of six "reconciliation villages," where convicted perpetrators who have been released from prison after publicly apologizing for their crimes live side by side with genocide survivors who have professed forgiveness. How do villages such as Mbyo undermine social agents for divisive ethnicity? What stumbling blocks might they encounter?

many people, particularly Hutu, experienced malnutrition because their farms were insufficient for their needs. People suffered through famines and cattle diseases even as the country's population rose, causing farm size to shrink as a result. Social constructivism thus helps explain why the rural Hutu became so thoroughly engaged in driving off and killing local Tutsi.

Summary

What happened in Rwanda? We can say that prior to colonialism, the experience of being a member of an ethnic group was not a major part of the day-to-day lives of most Rwandans: it did affect the people's sense of identity the way that lineage, clan, and chiefdom did. Under the Belgians, a dual colonialism developed in which Europeans and elite Tutsi collaborated to forge a rigid ethnic divide between Hutu and Tutsi. And when Belgian rule ended in 1962, the common oppression experienced by Hutu of all classes sparked a social revolution in which the majority Hutu overthrew their oppressors, only to set up an ethnic dictatorship of their own. Ethnic violence was a predicable outcome, and an easily fanned racial hatred, combined with a powerful need for land, led in 1994 to the massacre of the Tutsi and neutral Hutu.

Landmarks in the Sociological Study of "Race"

Standpoint theory, which we encountered way back in Chapter 1, argues that the perspective sociological researchers bring to their work is strongly influenced by their social location, their perspective as it is shaped by gender, age, ethnicity, sexual orientation, and other social characteristics. This does not mean that sociologists should study only "their own people." But pioneers in the sociological study of specific groups—women, for instance, or black people—are often those who belong to the group themselves. They bring unique and valuable insights to the study. In this section, we will look at some of the pioneers in the sociological study of race in North America.

W.E.B. Du Bois: First Black Sociologist

W.E.B. Du Bois (1868–1963) was the first African American sociologist. He researched and wrote about the major problems concerning Africans, both those living in the United States and those living elsewhere. He was a "pan-Africanist," meaning he looked at the connection between the oppression or success of Africans and that of their descendants around the world.

Du Bois's sociology had an applied perspective to it. He was one of the founders of the National Association for the Advancement of Colored People (NAACP). He used his position as editor-in-chief of their magazine, *Crisis*, to advocate for causes such as opening up training schools for black military officers and initiating legal action against white people who lynched African Americans. He was a prolific writer, producing several landmark studies, including *The Suppression of the African Slave Trade in America* (1896), *The Philadelphia Negro* (1896), *The Souls of Black Folks* (1903), *Black Reconstruction* (1935), and *Dusk of Dawn* (1940). The following excerpt captures his oratorical power and sense of justice:

> It is the duty of black men to judge the South discriminatingly. The present generation of Southerners are not responsible for the past, and they should not be blindly hated or blamed for it. . . . The South is not "solid"; it is a land in the ferment of social change, wherein forces of all kinds are fighting for supremacy; and to praise the ill the South is today perpetuating is just as wrong as to condemn the good. Discriminating and broad-minded criticism is what the South needs—needs it for the sake of her own white sons and daughters, and for the insurance of robust, healthy mental and moral development. (Du Bois, 1903)

Daniel G. Hill: First Black Canadian Sociologist

Although he was not born in Canada, Daniel G. Hill (1923–2003) is considered the first black Canadian sociologist.

Born in Missouri, Hill moved to Canada in his late twenties to study sociology at the University of Toronto, receiving his MA in 1951 and his PhD in 1960. His primary writings include *Negroes in Toronto: A Sociological Study of a Minority Group* (1960) and *The Freedom Seekers: Blacks in Early Canada* (1981). However, Hill is best known for his applied sociology work. He was a researcher for the Social Planning Council of Metropolitan Toronto (1955–8), executive secretary of the North York Social Planning Council (1958–60), and assistant director of the Alcoholism and Drug Addiction Research Foundation (1960). In 1962, Hill became the first full-time director of the Ontario Human Rights Commission, and 10 years later, he became Ontario Human Rights Commissioner. He formed his own human rights consulting firm in 1973, working at various times for the Metropolitan Police Service, the Canadian Labour Congress, and the government of British Columbia. From 1984 to 1989, he served as Ontario's ombudsman, fielding complaints from citizens concerning their treatment by provincial government agencies. In 1999, he was made a Member of the Order of Canada.

Crenshaw, Collins, and Intersectionality Theory: Tracking "Race" and Gender

Intersectionality is an increasingly important concept in current sociological research. It refers to the way different social factors—race and ethnicity, gender, sexuality orientation, class, age, and disability—combine to shape the experience of a minoritized group. It recognizes that, for instance, the discrimination and prejudice experienced by a young black woman is different from that experienced by a young white woman or a young black man.

Intersectionality theory was first developed by **Kimberlé Crenshaw**, and then elaborated shortly thereafter by critical sociologist **Patricia Hill Collins** in *Black Feminist Thought: Knowledge, Consciousness and the Politics of Empowerment* (1990). Intersectionality theory argues against the notion, promoted by early white liberal feminists, that the experience of being "female" is basically the same for all women. It states that gender is experienced differently, with unique forms of oppression when

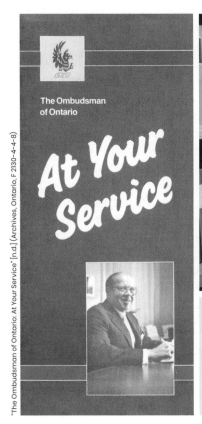

"The Ombudsman of Ontario: At Your Service" [n.d.] (Archives, Ontario, F 2130-4-4-8)

Al Dunlop/Toronto Star via Getty Images

[left] In his work as director of the Ontario Human Rights Commission and, later, as ombudsman of Ontario, Daniel Hill reached out to Ontarians of all ethnic and cultural backgrounds. The pamphlet shown here testifies to the importance he placed on the accessibility of his position to all provincial citizens. **[top]** Daniel G. Hill, ombudsman of Ontario, circa 1985.

combined with negatively valued social locations, such as certain minoritized ethnicities (e.g. African American, Hispanic, Indigenous, and South Asian). Gender-based stereotypes, when combined with racial prejudice, create an **interlocking matrix of domination** significantly more powerful and oppressive than gender alone.

In Canada, the interlocking matrix of domination has been experienced painfully by many Indigenous women. This led to the five-year National Inquiry into Missing and Murdered Indigenous Women and Girls, which heard testimony from 2386 people, including 1484 family members of victims. The release of the inquiry's final report, in June 2019, coincided with the publication of a book (Jolly, 2019) about Tina Fontaine, an Anishinaabe teen from the Sagkeeng First Nation in Manitoba, whose lifeless body was found in Winnipeg eight days after she was reported missing in August 2014. Her body had been wrapped in plastic and dumped into the Red River, weighted down with rocks. The publicity surrounding her case, in which the man charged with her murder was found not guilty, triggered the call for the national inquiry. Her case led social service agencies and volunteer groups to establish new programs to help at-risk Indigenous girls and women. The stories are told. It is time now for action to take place.

What Do YOU Think?

Indigenous groups have organized to provide safe places, night transport, and counselling for vulnerable girls and women, many of whom have escaped violent situations at home at home only to find themselves homeless and without the means to secure stable housing in cities such as Vancouver, Toronto, and Winnipeg. What should federal, provincial, territorial, and municipal governments do to remedy the situation? How can other organizations help?

William Julius Wilson and the Culture of Poverty

How you explain racial inequality may depend on where you fall along the political spectrum. At one end of the spectrum are far-right conservatives who attribute high rates of poverty, incarceration, and substandard housing among black people to two factors: the individuals and their culture. According to this view, which has been criticized as "laissez-faire racism," black people are individually responsible for the situations they find themselves in, but through hard work they can find their way out of poverty. Government assistance fails because it keeps them from taking ownership of a situation they control. At the left end of the spectrum are liberals who ascribe poverty among blacks and other racial minorities to systemic, or institutional, racism that is built into the social structure. Liberals accuse conservatives of blaming the victim; conservatives accuse liberals of making excuses for people who have made bad choices. The best explanation is far more nuanced and lies somewhere between these oversimplified, polarized views.

An interesting explanation was proposed by American anthropologist Oscar Lewis (1914–1970), who studied poverty among villagers in Mexico, Puerto Rico, and northern India. In each of these cases, he observed what he called a "culture of poverty." Essentially, he saw among the poor he studied an entrenched set of attitudes that were handed from one generation to the next, keeping the people from aspiring to better circumstances. These attitudes include widespread feelings of powerlessness, inferiority, and "personal unworthiness" (Lewis, 1998).

Enter black sociologist William Julius Wilson (b. 1935), with his important and controversial work *More than Just Race: Being Black and Poor in the Inner City* (2009). Wilson argues that both structural and cultural forces are involved in the urban poverty of black people. Structural forces include what he calls *social acts*—"stereotyping; stigmatization; discrimination in hiring, job promotions, housing, and admission to educational institutions," and so on—and *social processes*, which are "laws, policies, and institutional practices that exclude people on the basis of race or ethnicity" (Wilson, 2009, p. 5).

These structural forces that Wilson identifies as contributing to black poverty are uncontroversial. Where his argument takes a more contentious turn is in his discussion of the cultural forces that keep blacks from finding middle-class jobs and inclusion in the broader society. Wilson's cultural forces fall into two categories: national views and beliefs on race, and cultural traits. National views come from the stereotypes perpetuated uncritically through news and entertainment media. These views are reinforced when white people experience black people in settings that confirm those stereotypes. White people may only "see" the homeless black person pushing a shopping cart's worth of belongings into a downtown alleyway; they may not notice the black investment banker, lawyer, or schoolteacher.

Cultural traits, according to Wilson, may also "contribute to the perpetuation of poverty." He describes these as

> shared outlooks, modes of behavior, traditions, belief systems, worldviews, values, skills, preferences, styles of self-preservation, etiquette and linguistic patterns that emerge from patterns of intragroup interaction in settings created by discrimination and segregation and that reflect collective experiences within those settings. (2009, pp. 14–15)

Wilson argues that certain beliefs and behaviours that are prevalent among black people can keep them from climbing out of poverty. As an example he describes "street smarts," a set of behaviours adapted to get by in tough neighbourhoods:

> It is wise to avoid eye contact with strangers and keep to yourself. This mind-set may also lead someone to approach new situations with a certain level of skepticism or mistrust. Although such an approach is logical and smart in an unsafe neighborhood, the same behavior can be interpreted as antisocial in another setting. Moreover, this street-smart behavior may, in some cases, prevent individuals from performing well on job interviews, creating a perception that they are not desirable job candidates. (Wilson, 2009, pp. 17–18)

A clip from the TV show *Cops* shows a suspect being taken down in Fontana, California. The immensely popular reality show, which has been running since 1989, has generated controversy over its portrayal of poor and racialized minorities. How might Wilson view the role of shows like *Cops* in perpetuating black poverty?

Another set of behaviours could be called the "code of shady dealing," to borrow a term coined by Wilson's student Sudhir Venkatesh in *Off the Books: The Underground Economy of the Urban Poor* (2006). The back-alley market for drugs, stolen goods, and other legal and illegal items exists as "a response to circumstances in inner-city ghetto neighborhoods, where joblessness is high and opportunities for advancement are severely limited" (Wilson, 2009, p. 19). The underground economy is not random or unregulated: it is governed by its own code of rules, and operating in this space requires a very particular set of skills. These are not the same skills required for legal modes of commerce, and they are not things you would want to put on a resumé.

> ### What Do YOU Think?
>
> By citing cultural factors that contribute to black poverty, are Lewis and Wilson blaming the victims?

Current Issues in the Study of Race and Ethnicity

Racism

Racism can be understood as the product of four linked elements. The first is *racialization*, the construction of certain groups of people as different and biologically superior or inferior. This fosters ideas of relative worth and quality, which leads to **prejudice**, the "pre-judgment" of others on the basis of their group membership. The third element is **discrimination**, which involves individuals treated differently—rewarded or punished—based on their group membership. Finally, there is *power*, manifested when institutionalized advantages are regularly handed to one or more groups over others. American psychologist and educator Beverly Daniel Tatum touches on the importance of power in this equation:

> People of color are not racist because they do not systematically benefit from racism. And equally important, there is no systematic cultural and institutional support or sanction for the racial bigotry of people of color. In my view, reserving the term *racist* only for behaviors committed by Whites in the context of a White-dominated society is a way of acknowledging the ever-present power differential afforded Whites by the culture and institutions that make up the system of advantage and continue to reinforce notions of White superiority. (2003, p. 10)

In other words, without power, non-white people can be prejudiced but not racist. They can perform discriminatory acts, but they cannot be racist without institutional, structural, ideological, and historical support.

This is certainly true of systemic racism, which by definition involves power. Recently, though, sociologists have been studying how racism exists even among people of the same ethnic or racial group. **Colourism**, sometimes called shadeism, refers to the unique experience of a racialized person based on how light or dark their skin is. For instance, in a study of people living in Vancouver and Toronto, sociologist Gerry Veenstra found that darker-skinned black people were more likely than lighter-skinned black people to report poor mental and physical health, "indicating that colourism, processes of discrimination which privilege lighter-skinned people of colour over their darker-skinned counterparts, exists and has implications for well-being in Canada" (2011, p. 1152). Colourism is also evident in the preference for lighter skin shown by people outside but also within a particular racialized group, such as blacks, Latinos, and South Asians.

There are different kinds of racism. **Racial bigotry** is the open, conscious expression of racist views by an individual. When racist practices, rules, and laws become institutionalized, then we have **systemic** (or **institutional**) **racism**. The Chinese Exclusion Act (1923–47), which prohibited the immigration of Chinese people from China and other countries, is an example of systemic racism. Canada's residential school system, aimed at suppressing Indigenous culture, is another example.

Sometimes, racism can be subtle, hidden behind a smile or words that seem friendly to the person performing the gesture. This is called **friendly** (or **polite** or **smiling**) **racism**. Henry Martey Codjoe provides an example:

> The realtor who showed our house to prospective buyers quietly hinted that if I wanted my house to sell quickly, I would have to remove all traces of anything that indicated that Blacks had lived in the house: no family pictures, no African art or crafts, everything Black or African must go, and we must be out of the house before he showed the house to prospective buyers. He would call and let us know. No matter what we were doing, we must leave. One time we were late in getting out and we ended up hiding in our minivan in the garage. When he showed the garage, we ducked. It was a shameful and degrading experience. The house sold, but my wife and I never did meet the family that bought it. (2001, p. 286)

A common form of friendly racism is the *microaggression*, a casual remark or gesture that reflects racial prejudice and causes offence. Most microaggressions aren't intended as insults; they may even be misguided compliments or attempts at conversation. Even so, they are offensive. Though the comments may be spoken without any intent to cause insult or self-consciousness, they are hurtful because they reflect the speaker's awareness of racial difference and preconceptions based solely on the visible racial characteristics of the person

addressed. A good example of a microaggression is contained in the title of a book by Ojibwa writer Drew Hayden Taylor, who called his 1996 collection of essays, *Funny, You Don't Look Like One: Tales of a Blue-Eyed Ojibway*. Here are some remarks that are considered microaggression:

- Where are you really from?
- What are you?
- I never think of you as black.
- You're really pretty for a . . .
- But you sound white.

What Do YOU Think?

1. Should we be concerned about microaggressions when so much overt, intentional racism still exists?
2. Are people today too sensitive about "race"?

Carding and Racial Profiling

Despite their long history in this country, particularly in Atlantic Canada and Southern Ontario, black people are often regarded as relative newcomers. Canadians are sometimes smug about our role in helping slaves escape the American South during the eighteenth and nineteen centuries, but slavery was also practised in pre-Confederation Canada, and many freed American slaves were treated with hostility and contempt upon their arrival here.

Black people today continue to be racialized by mainstream Canadian society. Blacks are greatly overrepresented in our prisons: from 2005 to 2015,

Quick Hits

Racism

Racism is the product of four linked elements:
- racialization
- prejudice
- discrimination
- power.

Different kinds of racism include
- racial bigotry
- systemic (institutional) racism
- friendly (polite/smiling) racism
- colourism.

"Fair skin has been in favour for, what, the past hundreds of years. But, now the pendulum has swung back. Black is in fashion!" Starring Daniel Kaluuya (shown here), Jordan Peele's 2017 horror comedy *Get Out* satirizes white liberal envy of black people and culture. Is Peele's target systemic racism or friendly racism?

the black inmate population grew by 69 per cent (versus 10 per cent for the inmate population overall), and the rate of incarceration for black people is three times their rate of representation in society, according to Canada's correctional investigator, Howard Sapers (2015). There is evidence—difficult to obtain because Canada does not keep race-specific crime data—that while blacks may be overrepresented in some forms of violent crime, they are also victims of bias in policing and the administration of criminal justice (Owusu-Bempah & Wortley, 2014). Like Indigenous people, blacks are often targets of racial profiling, a form of prejudice in which people are suspected of criminal activity based solely on racial

Telling It Like It Is   A Black Canadian's POV

The Skin I'm In: Being Interrogated by Police— All Because I'm Black

When I was 22, I decided to move to Toronto. . . . In Toronto, I thought I could escape bigotry and profiling, and just blend into the crowd. By then, I had been stopped, questioned, and followed by the police so many times I began to expect it. In Toronto, I saw diversity in the streets, in shops, on public transit. The idea that I might be singled out because of my race seemed ludicrous. My illusions were shattered immediately. . . .

I was carded for the first time in 2007. I was walking my bike on the sidewalk on Bathurst Street just south of Queen. I was only steps from

Continued

my apartment when a police officer exited his car and approached me. "It's illegal to ride your bike on the sidewalk," he informed me. "I know, officer, that's why I'm walking it," I replied edgily. Then, the cop asked me for ID. After sitting in front of the computer inside his car for a few minutes, the officer returned nonchalantly and said, "Okay, you're all set." I wanted to tell him off, but thought better of it and went home. I still don't know what he saw when he ran my name.

Over the next seven years, I was carded at least a dozen times. One summer evening in 2008, two friends and I were stopped while walking at night in a laneway just north of my apartment, only a few hundred metres from where I was carded the first time. Two officers approached in their cruiser, briefly turning on their siren to get our attention. Once they got out of the car, they asked us what we were doing. "We're just walking, bro," I said. The cops immediately asked all of us to produce identification. While one officer took our drivers' licences back to his car, the other got on his radio. I heard him say the word "supervisor," and my stomach turned. Within 60 seconds, a second cruiser, marked S2, arrived in the laneway, and the senior officer at the wheel got out to join his colleagues.

The officer who had radioed for backup returned and asked us to empty our pockets. As the supervisor watched, the radio officer approached us one at a time, took our change and wallets and inspected them. He was extremely calm, as if he was thoroughly accustomed to this routine. "I'm going to search each of you now to make sure you didn't miss anything," he explained. I knew it was my legal right to refuse, but I couldn't muster the courage to object. The search officer approached me first. "Before I search you, I want you to tell me if I'm going to find anything you shouldn't have," he said gravely. "I don't have anything," I replied, my legs trembling so violently I thought they'd give out from under me. The officer patted down my pockets, my pant legs, my jacket, my underarms. He then repeated the search with my two friends, asking each of them before touching them if he would find anything. One of my friends spoke up: "I have a weed pipe in my back pocket, but there's nothing in it." The officer took the pipe and walked with the supervisor to the car with the officer who had taken our ID. As the policemen huddled for what felt like an hour, my friend apologized. "It's not your fault," I replied. I cursed myself for choosing that route rather than staying on Queen Street, where hundreds of people would have been walking. Here, we had no witnesses.

When the officers finally came back, they returned the pipe to my friend. "Are any of you currently wanted on an outstanding warrant?" asked the search officer. We all said no. "Okay, guys, have a good night," he said. I was still too scared to move, and apparently my friends were too; we just stood there and looked at the cops for a second. "You can go," the officer assured us. I made sure not to look back for fear they'd interpret some outstanding guilt on my part. I was certain that the police had just documented my name along with the names of my friends, one of whom was carrying a pipe for smoking an illegal substance. This information would be permanently on my record.

After years of being stopped by police, I've started to internalize their scrutiny. I've doubted myself, wondered if I've actually done something to provoke them. Once you're accused enough times, you begin to assume your own guilt, to stand in for your oppressor. It's exhausting to have to justify your freedoms in a supposedly free society. I don't talk about race for attention or personal gain. I would much rather write about sports or theatre or music than carding and incarceration. But I talk about race to survive. If I diminish the role my skin colour plays in my life, and in the lives of all racialized people, I can't change anything.

—Desmond Cole

What Do YOU Think?

What effect has carding had on the writer of this narrative? What effect do think these interactions have on police?

characteristics and other aspects of their physical appearance, such as clothing. Racial profiling is often at play in the practice of carding, in which police stop, question, and document people when no offence has been committed, ostensibly as a way of gathering intelligence in crime-prone neighbourhoods. In the fall of 2018, the Nova Scotia Human Rights Commission hired Scot Wortley, a professor of criminology at the University of Toronto, to investigate the rate and manner in which black people in Halifax were subjected to random street checks. His finding that blacks were six times more likely than white people to be stopped led to calls for an end to carding in the city (Wortley, 2019).

Race-Based Hate Crime in Canada

A hate crime is an act of aggression or intimidation motivated by prejudice against an identifiable group defined by its race, religion, or sexual orientation,

designed to harm or terrify not just the victim but the group to which the victim belongs. Hate crimes include advocating genocide, inciting or promoting hatred, or causing damage to property associated with an identifiable group (for instance, a place of religious worship).

In 2017, there were 2073 reported hate crimes in Canada (Armstrong, 2019). While the total made up just 0.1 per cent of all police-reported crime, it represented a year-over-year increase of 47 per cent, with the largest increases occurring in Ontario and Quebec. The majority of those hate crimes—43 per cent—were motivated by hatred of race or ethnicity. Figure 8.5 shows the distribution of hate crimes by racial or ethnic group. The greater part of the criminal activity motivated by hatred of race (56 per cent) was non-violent, most of it falling under the heading "mischief," which can include, for example, graffiti painted in a public place. While the number of reported hate crime incidents is low, it is worth noting that as many as two-thirds of all hate crimes go unreported (Dauvergne & Brennan, 2011).

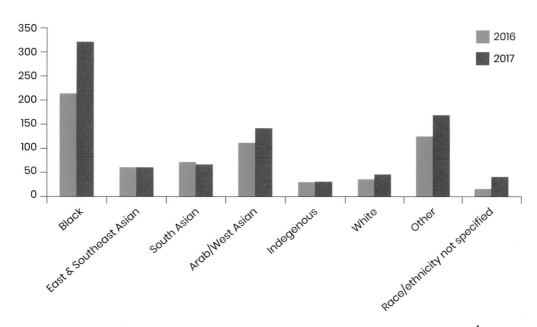

FIGURE 8.5 **Increase in Reported Hate Crimes Motivated by Hatred of Race/Ethnicity, by Group (2016–2017)**

Note: "Other/unspecified" includes motivations based on race or ethnicity not otherwise stated (e.g. Latin American, South American) as well as hate crimes that target more than one race or ethnic group (such as immigrants generally).

Source: Armstrong, 2019, Chart 6.

Wrap it Up

Summary

There are no human "races." From a sociological standpoint, "race" (or, rather, *racialization*) is a social process that reflects the ways in which people of different ethnic background are treated, and have been treated over time, by institutions such as our provincial and federal justice systems, our legislative bodies, our schools, and the media. It's also about how we view one another.

Racism is also a process, one that not only appears in personal biases and discrimination but is institutionalized in society as a whole. It's not just about the "rotten apples": the whole orchard smells. Racism certainly exists at the individual level, but it requires the support of social institutions to perpetuate itself. Fortunately, social support can be withdrawn from the features of institutions that maintain the level of racism. The apple trees can be pruned, and new trees planted and encouraged to grow.

Think Back

Questions for Critical Review

1. Explain what it means to say that "race" is a social construct rather than a biological one.
2. What is "white privilege"? What benefits does it bring to someone who is white? Are there any disadvantages to having white privilege? Any at all?
3. "Passing," in sociological terms, is the practice of downplaying or disowning an ascribed status by claiming another. Can you ever pass for a race other than the one you were born into? Can you pass for an ethnicity? Under what circumstances might you do so?
4. Are we in Canada getting closer to achieving a "post-racial society," in which race is not used as a way to categorize people and treat them differently? Is a post-racial society even possible? How much do you think your answer depends on your own race?
5. According to the 2016 Census, 1 in 5 Canadians is a member of a visible minority. What makes someone a "visible minority"? The term is used in federal legislation, but why do you think we need to distinguish between visible minorities and other ethnic minorities?
6. Provide some examples of cases in which Canadian governments enacted new laws in response to moral panics around immigration. Who, in each case, were the moral entrepreneurs? What did they stand to gain?
7. How is institutional, or systemic, racism different from other forms of discrimination?

Read On

Recommended Print and Online Resources

"Adjusting to Canada: From ABCs to -40 Degrees," www.cbc.ca/archives/entry/ adjusting-to-canada-from-abcs-to-40- degrees
- This 10-minute CBC interview from 1981 examines the experience of a Vietnamese refugee recently arrived in Canada.

Joanna Jolly (2019), *Red River Girl: The Life and Death of Tina Fontaine* (New York, NY: Viking).
- Contains all that has been discovered to date about the circumstances concerning the violence that triggered the National Inquiry into Missing and Murdered Indigenous Women and Girls.

Kay J. Anderson (1991), *Vancouver's Chinatown: Racial Discourse in Canada, 1875–1980* (Montreal and Kingston: McGill-Queen's University Press).
- A classic study of how "Chinese" and "Chinatown" have been expressed in the Vancouver area over a little more than a century.

Reclaiming Power and Place: The Report of the National Inquiry into Missing and Murdered Indigenous Women and Girls, www.mmi-wg-ffada.ca/final-report/
- The product of the five-year inquiry into the causes and effects of the disappearance and killing of Indigenous women and girls in Canada.

"Secret Alberta: The Former Life of Amber Valley," www.youtube.com/watch?v=OxXJubB2cPQ
- This 15-minute video offers a look into the history of one of the larger black farming settlements in Alberta, now deserted.

"Shades of Black: Colorism, Skin Color Discrimination," www.youtube.com/watch?time_continue=313&v=E3IzTyjhHLc
- In this 7-minute documentary by Reginald James, people of different racial backgrounds discuss their experiences of colourism.

Sleeping Tigers: The Asahi Baseball Story, **Jari Osborne, National Film Board of Canada.**
- This 2003 documentary tells the story of the Vancouver Asahi, a Japanese-Canadian baseball team formed in 1914 that often won championships and was well-known in the area. The team was forced to disband when team members were put in interment camps with other Japanese Canadians. In 2019, a Heritage Moment was produced that included narration by the last living team player.

"The Skin I'm In: I've Been Interrogated by Police More than 50 Times—All Because I'm Black," http://torontolife.com/city/life/skin-im-ive-interrogated-police-50-times-im-black/
- This is the full text of Desmond Cole's article excerpted in the narrative box on page 260, which appeared in an April 2015 issue of *Toronto Life* magazine.

Tim Stelloh, (2019, Jan.) "How *Cops* Became the Most Polariznig Reality TV Show in America: What One of TV's Longest-Running Reality Shows Says about Race and Our Relationship with the Police," https://longreads.com/2018/01/22/how-cops-became-the-most-polarizing-reality-tv-show-in-america/
- An examination of how reality TV has shaped North American understandings of race.

Wanda Robson and Ronald Caplain (2010), *Sister to Courage: Stories from the World of Viola Desmond, Canada's Rosa Parks* (Wreck Cove, NS: Breton Books).
- Viola Desmond's sister, author, and educator Wanda Robson has done much to keep her sister's story alive since Viola's death at the young age of 50. This is Wanda's account of Viola's story.

Gender, Sex, and Sexuality

9

Reading this chapter will help you to ...

- Explain the difference between sex and gender.
- Describe what makes sex and gender social constructs.
- Cite some examples of the way in which society continues to be "gendered."
- Name some of the factors that explain why men or women may be overrepresented in a particular kind of work or course of study.
- Explain what toxic masculinity is.
- Define *sexuality* and comment on how it relates to sex and gender.
- Talk about the stereotyping involved in the intersection of female gender and minoritized ethnicity/race.

For Starters

What It Takes to Be a "Real Man"

The author as he sees himself.

The author as he is.

In 1982, American writer Bruce Feirstein published a short, tongue-in-cheek guide to male behaviour. It was called *Real Men Don't Eat Quiche*, and its memorable title quickly entered public discourse, even among those who hadn't read the book. It was a standard quip in conversations about what men do (or don't do), particularly when those conversations centred on activities viewed in mainstream North America as traditionally feminine—activities like baking, gardening, or figure skating. *No, I would not like to go ballroom dancing, and I don't eat quiche, either.*

But the title of Feirstein's satire on gender stereotypes was more than a punchline. In a decade when North American society was deeply suspicious of effeminate men and openly hostile toward homosexuals, "real men don't eat quiche" became a motto that defined the quest to identify guiding principles for the would-be "macho man," an idealized cisgender heterosexual man embodying (supposedly) desirable male characteristics—good looks, sex appeal, toughness, self-assertiveness. I had my own rules, many of them formed a decade or so before Feirstein's book was published. Although I felt "secure in my masculinity," as we used to say, I would never . . .

- use an umbrella (in part because I lived in Newfoundland for a while, where "real men" were not afraid of getting wet)
- use a hair dryer (it seemed effeminate to blow my really long hair around like an actor in a shampoo commercial)
- dress in yellow, orange, or pink (male classmates of mine were given a hard time if they wore those colours)
- use a snowblower instead of a shovel, or a leaf-blower instead of a rake (rakes are easy to operate: skinny end up, wide end down)
- spend longer than five minutes getting dressed or 15 minutes shopping in any one clothing store
- shake hands in a "wimpy way"

- wear cologne or body spray (women should smell good; men should try not to smell bad)
- own more than three pairs of shoes (if I had to buy new shoes, I got rid of an old pair first)
- use the word "lovely"
- have a manicure or a pedicure.

Go on, say it: "OK, Boomer." I still use a shovel instead of a snowblower, by the way, and I try to meet a minimum standard of grip strength when shaking hands—evidence of how things we learn when we're young can become fixed in our sense of self and difficult to unlearn later.

As we will see in this chapter, masculinity is a social construct: like femininity, it is a set of attitudes—belonging to a particular time and place—about how men (or women) are supposed to behave. Where do these ideas come from? There is nothing innately masculine about the traits I listed above. They were all learned—indirectly or, in some cases, directly—from role models I had growing up as a white, straight male in North America: from male family members, male characters I admired on TV (mostly cowboys), rockers I idolized, teachers I mostly hated, and friends in my peer group who, like me, had been socialized to believe there was such a thing as a "real man" as opposed to someone we might have called a wimp, a sissy, or a "homo."

Feirstein's book is now close to 40 years old, but the myth of the "real man" persists. It is the bedrock of toxic expressions of masculinity reflecting ideas about male superiority and how real men are supposed to defend their status, control women, and settle conflicts. We will explore these ideas in the chapter as well.

What Do YOU Think?

How do you think the way you view masculinity and femininity differs from the attitudes of your parents and grandparents? Has what it means to be a man or a woman changed since your parents were your age? What socializing influences (e.g. family, friends, media, etc.) have conditioned your view of gender roles?

Introduction: Sex and Gender Are Socially Constructed

Gender is a highly contested area within sociology. Sociologists theorizing about gender and gender roles differ sharply, particularly on the degree to which gender is determined by either culture or biology. Popular culture still sometimes represents gender as an absolute duality (male–female), but there is widespread consensus among sociologists today that gender is not binary but represents a sliding scale of roles and identities. Not surprisingly, the greatest part of the critical work on gender has been carried out by women, in particular black women and women of colour, reflecting the (now) obvious fact that before the women's movement of the 1960s and 1970s, male sociologists had done an inadequate job on the subject.

Sex and Gender: What's the Difference?

Gender is different from *sex*. **Sex** refers to the biological traits that societies use to categorize people, often (particularly in the West) as either male or female. **Gender** refers to the cultural meaning that societies attach to sex categories. It consists of the behaviours that society considers "normal" for a person of a particular sex.

British sociologist **Ann Oakley** (b. 1944) was among the first to formally distinguish sex from gender in a sociological way, characterizing sex as a biological construction and gender as a social one (Oakley, 1972). Candace West and Don Zimmerman (1987), in their influential article "Doing Gender," made an important contribution to the discussion when they distinguished between a person's *sex* and their *sex category*. Sex, they agreed, was based on biology, specifically "a determination made through

The Contested Meaning of "Macho"

"Macho," from a Spanish word for a male animal, was a popular term in the late 1970s and 1980s for men showing aggressive pride in their masculinity. It became entrenched in mainstream North American discourse in 1978, when the Village People recorded their hit "Macho Man." Like their follow-up singles "YMCA" and "In the Navy," the song was a not-so-subtle tribute to gay male culture, but its double meanings were missed by listeners who thought it was simply a catchy disco homage to the heterosexual manliness believed to typify cowboys, police officers, leather-clad bikers, and construction workers—personas the

band adopted. The moniker "Macho Man" was adopted by the actor/wrestler Randy Savage, a star of the wrestling circuit in the late 1970s and 1980s. Wearing flamboyantly "gay" costumes, his character, set up as an antagonist to more "heroic" characters, would routinely bully his manager, Miss Elizabeth (actually his wife) to jeers from the audience. Savage's campy performance of the "Macho Man" type was designed to entertain and rile up the audience, but many feminists of the time criticized the term as embodying patriarchal norms of masculine behaviour, including aggression and violence toward women.

the application of socially agreed upon biological criteria" (West & Zimmerman, 1987, p. 127). However, they argued that a person could adopt a sex category that does not correspond to their assigned sex by taking on the manners and behaviours that society associates with that sex category. After all, in social settings and everyday interactions, we regularly place the people around us into sex categories—typically girl, boy, woman, man. We can't help ourselves—as West and Zimmerman explain, it's so automatic for us to do this that we may feel frustrated when we encounter someone we cannot easily characterize as male or female (1987, p. 134).

Of course, when we place others into sex categories, we are not performing DNA tests or asking to see their genitals. Instead, we look for cues that, according to custom, signify membership in socially recognized sex categories. These cues include a whole range of displayed behaviours—the way a person dresses, walks, speaks, behaves, and interacts with others. The mental checklist we keep is much longer than that, and we continue to refer to it the more we get to know a person: what kind of work do they do, what are their interests and hobbies, do they use an umbrella in the rain, and if they get wet do they blow-dry their hair, and so on.

Some of this may remind you of the symbolic interactionists we met in Chapter 1, and particularly

Erving Goffman, who considered people as though they were performing on a stage. In fact, West and Zimmerman drew on Goffman's work in describing gender as an exercise in impression management, "the activity of managing situated conduct in light of normative conceptions of attitudes and activities appropriate for one's sex category" (1987, p. 127). In other words, gender is how we behave to show that we identify as male, female, or something else. This is important because while our assigned sex and our sex category often align, they don't always. A person assigned the sex of "male" at birth may identify with and choose to adopt the female sex category; by performing the behaviours society expects a female person to engage in—by "doing gender," in West and Zimmerman's words—they gain acceptance into the female sex category.

Sex Category and the Gender Role

This brings us to the concept of **gender role**, which is a set of attitudes and expectations concerning behaviour that relates to the sex we are assigned at birth. Think of a gender role like a movie role: it is the part that corresponds to the sex category we identify with, and how we play it reflects what we understand about what it means to act within a particular category. Like any movie role—say, the part of Spider-Man in

Touchstone/Kobal/Shutterstock

Played by actress and comedian Julia Sweeney, Pat was a recurring character on *Saturday Night Live* in the early 1990s. Sketches revolved around Pat's ambiguous gender and the frustration of other characters as they tried, in vain, to discover whether Pat was a man or a woman. So popular was the running sketch that it spawned a feature-length film. Why do you think the same gag would not be well received today, less than 30 years later?

the Marvel movie universe—different "actors" may interpret the part differently, but if they stray too far from a conventional portrayal of the character, their authenticity may be questioned.

Sociologists today recognize that sex as well as gender is a social construct, a framework humans have devised to make sense of the world. In mainstream Western society, it is taken as a given that the biological sex of a child born with a penis and an XY chromosome pair is male, and that the biological sex of a child born with a vagina and an XX chromosome pair is female. If only it were so simple. In fact, not everyone fits these strict biological criteria. Consider a person born with a penis and ovaries, who menstruates, or a person with XY chromosomes and a vagina. We use the term **intersex** for anyone born with both "male" and "female" sexual characteristics. Intersex people may identify with either the male or the female sex category, or they may see

themselves belonging to a unique sex category. They may use terms like *nonconforming* and *non-binary* to signify their resistance to pressure to conform to either of the categories that Western society views as acceptable options.

On top of the biological variability, there is a strong neurological component to sex identity, meaning that someone who possesses "male" sexual characteristics may not feel male in the way society expects a male person to feel. We sometimes describe people who do not identify with their assigned sex as **transgender**, a term that reflects Western society's binary view of sex and gender (i.e. if you're not one, then you must be the other). We may use the term *gender-nonconforming* for people who identify as neither male nor female, or else as male one day and as female on another day; this term also perpetuates the use of the gender binary as a reference point, as though people who identify as neither exclusively male nor exclusively female are in violation of a universal biological standard rather than a social construct. Other cultures recognize genders beyond male and female. For example, the fa'afanine of Samoa represent a widely accepted third gender category, consisting of people who identify as neither male nor female but who display both male and female traits and behaviours. They would not view themselves as transgender because there is an established gender category for them.

In this chapter, we will be looking at sex, gender, and human sexuality. Most of this chapter concerns the way society views gender categories and how we—with considerable variation—interpret and live out our roles as "men," "women," and categories in between. The case studies that kick off the chapter show that gender is a powerful concept that can defy biology, socialization, and pressure to conform.

What Do YOU Think?

In 2019, Brooke Lynn Hytes (shown in the photo at the start of the chapter) became the first Canadian to perform on *RuPaul's Drag Race*. When not in drag, Ms Hytes (a.k.a. Brock Hayhoe) identifies as male, though many drag queens and kings are transgender. How does dressing in drag exemplify the performance aspect of "doing gender"?

Quick Hits

"Two-Spirit People" and "Manly-Hearted Women": Alternative Gender Roles among North American Aboriginal People

Indigenous people in North America have traditionally had a more complex view of gender variability than the binary view adopted by settler-colonial cultures. **Two-Spirit people** is their umbrella term to describe those who identify with one of the many gender roles beyond male and female recognized by Indigenous groups across North America. The Navaho, for example, recognize four genders, using the terms *nadleehi* for male-bodied Two-Spirit people and *dilbaa* for female-bodied Two-Spirit people. Another example is the *Ninauposkitzipxpe*, or "manly-hearted women," found among the Piegan and described in the following passage by anthropologist Alice Kehoe:

> About a third of elderly (sixty years or older) North Piegan women in 1939, and a few younger women, were considered manly-hearted. . . . Such women owned property, were good managers and usually effective workers, were forthright and assertive in public, in their homes, and as sexual partners, and were active in religious rituals. They were called "manly-hearted" because boldness, aggressiveness, and a drive to amass property and social power are held to be ideal traits for men. . . . [T]he manly-hearted woman is admired as well as feared by both men and women. (1995, p. 115)

Photo by John H. Fouch, 1877. Courtesy of Dr. James Brust.

This stereoview photograph, taken in 1877, shows "Squaw Jim" (*left*), a Two-Spirit person of the Crow Nation. Why do you think English lacks terms for genders beyond male and female?

Case Studies in Sex and Gender

David Reimer: Assigning Gender

In May 2004, 38-year-old David Reimer of Winnipeg committed suicide. His decision to take his life was likely influenced by his separation from his wife, the loss of his job, and the suicide death of his twin brother two years earlier. But there is a deeper cause to examine. David was the victim of a childhood medical accident that was compounded by an unsuccessful social experiment in assigning gender.

As infants, David and his brother were both circumcised electronically using an experimental method. During David's circumcision, too much electricity was applied, and his penis was damaged beyond repair. Desperate for a solution, David's parents consulted numerous specialists. Popular at the time was behaviourism, the psychological school of thought that emphasizes the power of socialization (nurture) over biology (nature). It was held in high regard by some feminist psychologists (both male and female) as it supported the notion that gender and gender roles were not "natural" but taught. In its extreme version, behaviourism advanced the theory that each of us starts out as a **tabula rasa**, or blank slate, on which our social environment "writes" our gender. A proponent of this school, psychologist Dr John Money, was one of the specialists contacted by David's parents. He persuaded them to have David castrated and given female hormones; their child, renamed "Brenda," would be raised as a girl.

In articles that made the case famous, Money claimed that David was adapting successfully to his new gender, socially taught and hormonally enhanced. But his view of the situation was based more on wishes than on facts. In *As Nature Made Him*, an account of David Reimer's life, author and journalist John Colapinto (2000) shows that David's childhood was highly conflicted. He felt male, not female. He didn't like wearing dresses, and he preferred roughhousing with boys to the company and play of girls his age. He was experiencing what doctors and sociologists today call *gender dysphoria*, where there is a disconnect between one's lived gender identity and the sex one was assigned (in this case surgically) at birth.

David wasn't told he had been born male until he was 13, when his parents, under pressure from Dr Money, approached him about allowing surgeons to create a vagina. David rebelled and several times attempted suicide. He abandoned his assigned female identity and sought out surgery to have his male sex restored. He later married and had stepchildren, but the effects of both the accident and the social experiment never left him.

What does the case of David Reimer tell us? David was born with traits that we categorize as male. He was forced to undergo surgery and hormone treatment to change his biological sex to female. He was raised to assume a female gender role. In spite of these efforts to change his biological sex characteristics and impose a female gender role, he continued to see himself as belonging to the male sex category. This suggests, as research confirms (Kruijver et al., 2000), that gender has a neurological component in addition to the biological features of genitals and hormones: the brain helps to shape our gender. It also clearly demonstrates the dangers of allowing social theory to impose itself into unthinking social practice.

What Do YOU Think?

In what ways, if at all, have you experienced social pressure to conform to a particular gender role? Have you ever resisted gender socialization?

Storm: Choosing Neutral

In May 2011, a Toronto couple made headlines around the world when they announced that they would not be disclosing to family or friends the biological sex of their newborn. Having raised two children who were sometimes teased for failing to conform to gender stereotypes, the couple wanted their third child, Storm, to grow up without the pressure to conform to the expectations of a particular gender role.

Two-and-a-half years later, a *Toronto Star* story reported that Storm, who was still being raised gender-neutral, would sometimes say, "I am a girl," and sometimes, "I am a boy" (Poisson, 2013). In 2016, the family disclosed that Storm, then five years old, had chosen to be referred to as "she" (Botelho-Urbanski, 2016).

Bernard Weil/Toronto Star via Getty Images

Storm (centre) with her family in 2016. Do you think that more parents will opt for a gender-neutral approach to raising their children?

What Do YOU Think?

1. How does Storm's story support the idea that we can choose which sex category we wish to belong to? Do you think Storm's gender freedom at birth led her to a gender identification she might not have made had her parents raised her differently?

2. Given that contemporary North American society sets clear boundaries between the sexes, is it easy for parents to raise their children relatively free of gender scripts? Is there a point, do you think, when sex and society take over?

Caster Semenya: Measuring Gender

Caster Semenya is a two-time Olympic medalist, having won the gold medal in the women's 800 metre race at the 2012 Summer Olympics in London

and four years later at the Summer Games in Rio. But in 2009–10, she missed an entire year of competition while the International Association of Athletics Federations (IAAF), track and field's official governing body, investigated claims that Semenya's body produced testosterone in levels far greater than those found in most women. Results of the highly invasive "gender verification test" were leaked to the media, which sensationalized her condition and turned a situation that had been kept private into a source of controversy and criticism. "World athletics is in crisis over the gender of Caster Semenya after tests revealed the South African world champion has male sex organs and no womb or ovaries," read one article in London's *Daily Telegraph* (Hurst, 2009).

Semenya was cleared to compete in her lived identity—that is, as a woman—but in April 2011, the IAAF took up the case gain. "She is a woman, but maybe not 100 per cent," said IAAF general secretary Pierre Weiss, shortly before the federation announced new gender verification guidelines based on a maximum level of testosterone an athlete may possess in order to compete as a woman. The limit, which was in place for the 2012 Summer Olympics, forced some intersex athletes to take treatments to reduce their testosterone levels to allowable standards. The rule was put on hold in 2015, but in November 2018, new rules came into effect for athletes with hyperandrogenism, the medical condition in which women have elevated levels of hormones responsible for the growth and maintenance of male traits and reproductive organs. The IAAF had identified seven events in which elevated testosterone might impact performance, but the new guidelines applied only to middle-distance races of 400 to 1500 metres—events that are typically dominated by black athletes from the global South. In a May 2019 ruling, the Court of Arbitration for Sport called the latest guidelines discriminatory but argued that "such discrimination is a necessary, reasonable, and proportionate means of achieving the legitimate objective of ensuring fair competition in female athletics" (York & Waldie, 2019).

What Do YOU Think?

1. Many world-class athletes have physical characteristics that give them a competitive advantage, including long legs and greater-than-normal lung capacity. Why do you think the IAAF views hormone levels differently?
2. Is using hormone levels an appropriate way to "measure sex" in a competitive athlete? How should we determine whether an intersex athlete is permitted to compete in their lived identity?

Raising the Profile of Transgender People

In 2015, Caitlyn Jenner brought the experience of transgender people into public consciousness. An American track and field hero, gold medallist at the 1976 Montreal Summer Olympics, and member of the extended Kardashian clan, Jenner was a well-known public figure in April 2015, when she announced in a television interview that, though biologically male, she identified as female. She was featured on the cover of *Vanity Fair* two months later, and her transition was documented in an eight-episode miniseries. She underwent sex-reassignment surgery, completing the biological transition from female to male in January 2017.

Jenner may have become the world's best-known transgender woman, but she is not the first public figure to raise awareness around the rights of transgender people. Jenna Talackova, a Vancouver-born transgender woman and model, fought for and won the right to compete in the 2012 Miss Universe Canada pageant after initially being disqualified because she was born male. Thomas Beatie, a transgender man legally married to a woman, made headlines in 2007, when he became pregnant through artificial insemination—his female reproductive organs had not then been removed. Six years later, his male identity was challenged by an Arizona judge presiding over his divorce proceedings, who ruled that because Beatie was able to carry and bear children, he could not, in the eyes of the court, be considered a man. This rendered his marriage invalid in a state that did not then recognize same-sex marriage. The ruling was overturned by the Arizona Appeals Court in 2014. And in 2013, the Netflix series *Orange Is the New Black* introduced a trans character, Sophia Burset, played by actor and transwoman Laverne Cox.

While stories such as these have helped shine a light on a community that has long been misunderstood, the cases of Jenner and Talackova in particular have glamorized an experience that has caused discrimination, social exclusion, and depression among others who lack the same degree of public support. A 2015 study by researchers at the University of Western Ontario reports that as many as 43 per cent of transgender people in North America and Europe have attempted suicide (Bauer, Scheim, Pyne, Tavers, & Hammond, 2015). The team found that the risk of suicide drops with increased social and parental support, reductions in transphobia, and greater access to transition treatments and surgeries, which are not available in all provinces and which can be costly in provinces where only some surgeries are covered by health insurance.

Trans people make up a minority of the LGBTQ2 population. They may experience discrimination within the medical system, where they face reluctance by doctors to make the necessary referral

Steve Russell/Toronto Star via Getty Images

In January 2018, Jessica Platt, a forward with the Toronto Furies of the Canadian Women's Hockey League, came out as transgender, becoming the CWHL's first openly trans player. Three months later, Harrison Browne, an openly trans man, retired from the rival National Women's Hockey League in order to begin hormone replacement therapy as part of his transition.

for surgery and reluctance by surgeons to operate (Ubelacker, 2015). In May 2016, Canada's only surgery clinic exclusively for trans people, located in Montreal, was targeted in an arson attack carried out by a man armed with a machete. The attack caused extensive damage and forced the clinic to close temporarily, putting off several scheduled surgeries. As Brightwell (2016) reports, the incident was underreported in the mainstream media and did not receive extensive coverage on social media, even among the LGBTQ2 community. Later the same month, the federal government introduced legislation to extend the rights of transgender Canadians by adding gender identity and gender expression to existing laws against discrimination and hate speech. The legislation would make it easier to prosecute attacks such as the one on the Centre Métropolitain de Chirurgerie as hate crimes.

Quick Hits

Sex and Gender: A Recap

- **Sex** is a socially constructed set of categories (or identities) based on biological factors (genitals, chromosomes, hormones) as well as neurological ones.

- **Biological sex**, as it has been constructed socially in Western society, is binary, consisting of male and female sex categories assigned at birth. However, it is far more

Continued

useful to view sex as fluid and comprising categories beyond male and female, given that sex changes over time (particularly at puberty) and that not everyone fits within the male or female sex categories. **Intersex people** possess sex characteristics that correspond to both male and female categories.

- Not everyone identifies with their assigned sex. A **transsexual** is someone with the physical characteristics of one sex category and a persistent desire to belong to another. Transsexuals feel they have been born into the wrong body and may pursue sex reassignment therapy or surgery to change their biological sex.

- **Gender** is a socially constructed set of expectations about the roles and behaviours associated with different sex categories. It is not inherently binary, and many cultures recognize genders beyond male and female. **Gender role** describes the actions people perform, naturally or self-consciously, to demonstrate affinity with a particular sex category.

- Not everyone identifies with the gender role corresponding to their biological sex. A **transgender** person is someone whose lived identity does not conform with the gender role associated with their assigned sex. Transsexual people fall under the umbrella category of transgender, but the reverse is not necessarily true.

- A male-body person who feels a greater connection to the gender role associated with being a woman is a **transgender woman** (or a **transwoman**); a female-body person who identifies as a man is a **transgender man**, or **transman**.

- A **cisgender** person is someone who feels affinity with the socially constructed sex category they were assigned at birth, typically (in Western society) either male or female.

Feminism and Gender Theory: Four Categories

Much of the critical work on gender theory has been carried out by feminist sociologists. As we saw in Chapter 1, some scholars have traced the evolution of feminism through a series of "waves," each distinguished by a different set of objectives. That is one way of viewing a dynamic movement and theoretical framework that has exerted tremendous influence on the growth of sociology. In this section we take a different approach, looking at four strains of feminist theory and how they approach the study of gender. I borrow here from the excellent work of **Beatrice Kachuck** (2003), who divides the diverse range of feminist theories into the four categories I will now describe.

Liberal Feminism

Liberal feminism, as Kachuck explains, is about securing equal rights for women in all phases of public life, including access to education, jobs, and pay. It is associated with the fight for **pay equity**, the guarantee that women in female-dominated industries (nursing, childcare, library science, for instance) receive salaries similar to those of people working in comparable (in terms of educational qualifications required, hours worked, and social value) professions typically dominated by men. Think of it this way: if we value our children so much, why do we pay so little to those in primary and early childhood education (ECE)? Feminist liberalism is credited with securing benefits for women on maternity leave, including the rights to claim employment insurance and to return to the same or an equivalent job in the same company after a fixed period of time (up to a year in Canada).

Critics of liberal feminism argue that it universalizes the position of white, middle-class, heterosexual, cisgender Western women, who have benefitted in ways that other women have not. Liberal feminism has been far less successful in promoting the interests of women who differ in class, race, ethnicity, sexual orientation, and nationality.

Essentialist Feminism

Liberal feminism argues that gender is an artificial social construct that has been used to assign men and women different roles, rights, and opportunities based on perceived differences in intellect. It argues that men and women possess the same intellectual capabilities and should therefore be treated equally. **Essentialist feminism** differs by arguing that women and men are essentially different in the way they think. Men, for example, see the world in terms of competition and opposition to others, and they have created a social order based on "paradigms of dominance and subordination" (Kachuck, 2003); women, in contrast, view the world in terms of unities. Women's "maternal thinking" (Ruddick, 1989) naturally gives women social norms and a sense of morality that (most) men do not possess. This morality is negatively valued in a *patriarchal* society (i.e. one dominated by and favouring male roles, views, and ideas).

Kachuck identifies three main criticisms of essentialist feminism:

- it universalizes women, assuming erroneously that all women experience gender alike;
- it confuses natural instincts with strategies that women have devised for coping with the demands of a patriarchal society; and
- it encourages us to see women "as social housekeepers in worlds that men build" (Kachuck, 2003, p. 66).

Thus, while essentialist feminism speaks constructively about valuing women's differences from men, it falls into the trap of generalizing from the Western model.

Socialist Feminism

Kachuck explains that **socialist feminists** "revise their Marxism so as to account for gender, something that Marx ignored. They want sexuality and gender relations included in analyses of society" (2003, p. 67). According to this school of thought, there is insight to be gained from looking at the intersections of oppression between class and gender. The struggles faced by, and resources available to, lower-class women can be different from those of middle- and upper-class women, and feminist socialism is useful in identifying these. Still, there is the danger that "race," ethnicity, ableism, and sexual orientation get overlooked in the focus on class. Black women in North America face some of the same difficulties of prejudice and stereotyping regardless of whether they come from the upper or lower classes.

Postmodernist Feminism

Postmodernist feminism takes a strong social-constructionist position, making it almost diametrically opposed to essentialist feminism. **Social constructionism** is the idea that there is no natural basis for identities based on gender, ethnicity, "race," and so on. Some postmodernists dispute the existence of biological sex categories. From this perspective, it is impossible to form scientific, universally relevant accounts of what it means to be male or female. For this reason, postmodernist feminists see women as subjects rather than objects of sociological study, allowing the perspective of the women studied to guide their research. Standpoint theory is an important product of postmodernist feminism.

Another methodology that fits within the broad-ranging perspective of postmodernist feminism is **queer theory**, notably articulated in the book *Gender Trouble* (1990) by **Judith Butler**. Queer theory rejects the idea that male and female genders are natural binary opposites. It also disputes the idea that gender identity is connected to some biological "essence," arguing instead that gender identity is related to the dramatic effect of a gender performance. Gender is seen not as one of two categories—male and female—but as a continuum with male and female at the extremes; individuals act, or perform, more one way or another along the continuum at different times and in different situations.

Kachuck's main criticism of feminist postmodernism is that it leads to no conclusions. It merely problematizes other people's conclusions and generates no solid criteria for judging better or worse positions, but satisfies itself with "constructing a 'feminine' space where intellectuals aggressively play out tentative ideas" (Kachuck, 2003, p. 81).

Applying the Gender Lens to Life

An aging white man steps to the lectern and explains gender to an auditorium full of late teens and early twentysomethings. Yes, I see the irony in that. After all, I grew up at a time when a boy who preferred reading to football was likely to be branded a sissy, and a girl who climbed trees and wouldn't wear dresses was considered a tomboy. Both would be treated as deviant for defying *gender norms*, society's expectations about what it means to be male or female.

In contrast, young people growing up in Canada today have, by and large, a remarkably sophisticated and nuanced understanding of sex and gender. And while you might not fully appreciate the fact, there has probably never been a time when people have been as free to express a range of sexual identities and gender roles as they are today. That is not to say that gender discrimination no longer exists; it does, carried out mostly, alas, by older white men. But people today, and younger people especially, are defying social expectations around gender in unprecedented ways, and are slowly succeeding in changing social attitudes around what "boys" and "girls" are allowed to do.

I mentioned that this change is slow. Try as you might to shatter the gender lens, society continues to organize itself in ways that are gendered. There are separate clothing stores, or departments within stores, for men and for women. There are different places for men and women to get their hair cut. As we have seen in earlier chapters, the same product—be it a razor or a condom—will be marketed and packaged differently for men and for women. And pink is always an option in products for girls, from bicycles and hockey helmets to slippers and bedsheets. But society can be gendered in unexpected and surprising ways. Recently, I was out for breakfast with my wife, Angie, at one of our favourite places. I ordered French toast, and for not the first time, my plate was placed in front of Angie, and not in front of me. Breakfasts are gendered, and women, apparently, are more likely than men to order French toast. Two of the waitstaff, under rigorous sociological inquiry, confirmed my suspicions: certain breakfasts are simply more "male" than others. Bacon, according to this anecdotal intelligence, is more male than female, and sausage is even more male than bacon. If French toast is being served to a table occupied by a man and a woman, it is most likely to be the woman's order, unless the other dish on the serving tray is eggs Benedict or eggs Florentine. "Fancy" eggs are female.

Telling It Like It Is   A Student POV

Walking Home Alone as a Female Student

I was studying in the library with some classmates, when my friend James suggested we grab a bite to eat afterwards. I said sure, but since my phone had died, I asked if I could borrow his to text my roommate that I'd be home later than expected.

"Do your housemates really need to know where you are at all times?" he asked.

My friend Amy and I exchanged glances. "Uh, yeah, that way they know to worry when I'm not home on time," I explained. "And they know where I was last, and who I was with."

James looked surprised. "But it's like a 10-minute walk, and it's not even dark out." At that point, Amy jumped in to explain all the precautions we take when walking on campus: that we try to stick to well-lit routes and avoid walking alone. That we'll cross the street to avoid someone we don't know. That we use the campus buddy system if we have to. And if we are alone, we carry our phone in one hand and our keys in the other. No headphones, no distractions, eyes out for any sign of trouble.

"What do you do if you're coming home late at night?" I asked him.

He took a few seconds to respond. "I just . . . walk home."

—Zoe S., McMaster University

In this part of the chapter, we will look at the difference gender makes, beginning with how society views and values women and men in the workplace.

The Feminization of Work

The **feminization** of an occupational sphere occurs when a particular job, profession, or industry comes to be dominated by or predominantly associated with women. Since the start of World War I, when women began to work outside the home in greater numbers, many occupations have become feminized, including bank teller and secretary (now financial services adviser and administrative assistant, respectively), but job feminization was occurring well before that, as the first of the two examples below describes. Typically, the feminization of an industry works to the disadvantage of those involved in it, who earn lower salaries with less job protection and fewer benefits than those enjoyed by workers outside the feminized occupational sphere.

Women's Work During the Eighteenth-Century "Gin Craze" in London

Beginning around 1720 there was a sudden rise in the sale and consumption of gin in London, England, that lasted until the middle of the century. The liquor was sold not just in bars but in the streets, from wheelbarrows and baskets, in alleyway stalls, in shady one-room gin shops, and from boats floating on the Thames River.

Anyone selling gin without a licence was operating illegally. This was the case for the majority of the thousands of women involved in the gin trade, who couldn't afford the expensive licence. They operated at great risk, and were primary targets of the Gin Acts, which were passed chiefly to restrict the selling of gin to bars owned predominantly by middle-class men. Women were more likely than men to be arrested, and were more likely to be put in prison if convicted.

Why take the chance? At the time, thousands of young women were immigrating to London from Scotland, Ireland, and rural England, looking for jobs and for husbands. The quality and availability of both were greatly lacking. So why sell gin? Historian Jessica Warner gives three reasons:

[I]t required little or no capital; it did not require membership in a professional organization; and it was one of the few occupations from which women were not effectively or explicitly excluded. It was, in other words, a means of economic survival. (2003, p. 51)

The Gin Acts often pitted women against women. Enforcement depended heavily on the accusations of paid informants, half of whom were women. Warner describes the harsh economics involved:

Consider the options of a young woman newly arrived in London in 1737 or 1738. She could work for a year as a maid and earn £5 in addition to receiving room and board, or she could inform against one gin-seller, and upon securing a conviction collect a reward of £5. There were two ways to make money, one hard, the other easy, and many people naturally chose the latter. Most did so only once, collecting their reward and then attempting to hide as best they could. (2002, p. 137)

> ### What Do YOU Think?
>
> Did the feminization of the gin trade in eighteenth-century London benefit women or harm them? What alternatives might have been available to female immigrants to London who chose not to get involved in selling gin illegally?

Women's Clerical Work in Canada, 1891–1971

The early twentieth century saw a spectacular increase in the number of clerical workers in the Canadian labour force. It also saw the feminization of the position, along with the degradation of the role, as measured in terms of wages, skill level, and opportunity for promotion. How all three trends—growth, feminization, and degradation—mesh together is a story that gives insight on both the past and the present.

Clerical work was traditionally a man's job. The male bookkeeper's varied duties required a lot of what we now call multitasking. As companies grew in size, there was much more clerical work that needed to be done, and businesses moved toward a more "rationalized" and "efficient" approach to task management, according to the principles of **scientific management** (or **Taylorism**, discussed in Chapter 5). The result was a kind of assembly-line office work, in which several clerical workers were engaged in the rapid performance of repeated simple tasks, with little variety and few opportunities to move up in the company. The growing belief (based on assumptions about women's limited capabilities) that this was ideal work for women, who were supposed to be wives and mothers first and labourers second, was reinforced by discrimination that offered them few alternatives. The thinking of the time is illustrated in the following passage from a book called *Office Management: Principles and Practice*, published in 1925 by William Henry Leffingwell, a proponent of applying scientific management to the office:

> A woman is to be preferred for the secretarial position for she is not averse to doing minor tasks, work involving the handling of petty details, which would irk and irritate ambitious young men, who usually feel that the work they are doing is of no importance if it can be performed by some person with a lower salary. Most such men are also anxious to get ahead and to be promoted from position to position, and consequently if there is much work of a detail character to be done, and they are expected to perform it, they will not remain satisfied and will probably seek a position elsewhere. (1925, p. 116)

This job transformation got a big push during World War I (1914–18), when women entered the workforce to replace men who had gone overseas to serve. During this time, the number of clerical workers in Canada jumped by 113,148—around half of them women. At the Bank of Nova Scotia's regional offices in Ontario, the percentage of clerks who were women jumped from 8.5 per cent in 1911 to 40.7 per cent in 1916. Although, overall, the number of women clerical workers in Canada fell slightly when the men returned from the war, the figure remained high and steadily grew, as Table 9.1 shows.

What Do YOU Think?

1. Where in Canada can you see evidence of the feminization of work today? What effect do you think the feminization of these workplaces has on the employees working there?
2. Is there any evidence of a reverse trend that we might call the "masculinization" of work, in which a particular type of employment dominated by men acquires greater prestige and, of course, greater pay?

TABLE 9.1 The Feminization of Clerical Workers in Canada, 1891–1971

Year	Total Clerical Workers	Women Clerical Workers	
		Number	Percentage
1891	133,017	4710	14.3
1901	57,231	12,660	22.1
1911	103,543	33,723	32.6
1921	216,691	90,577	41.8
1931	260,674	117,637	45.1
1941	303,655	152,216	50.1
1951	563,093	319,183	56.7
1961	818,912	503,660	61.5
1971	1,310,910	903,395	68.9

Source: Lowe, 1980.

Gendered Work Today and the Pay Gap

Certain jobs, as well as the college and university programs preparing people to work in those jobs, continue to be **gendered**. That means, first, that one sex will be overrepresented among the people engaged in certain kinds of work or a particular program of study. Second, as Paul Sargent puts it, "the work itself is typically imbued with gendered meanings and defined in gendered terms" (2005). What this means is that, for example, the gendered profession of nursing is described with words like "caring" and "nurturing" that are typically associated with women; nursing, and other kinds of "care work" (such as childcare, teaching, elder care, and social work), is thus characterized as a natural offshoot of the mother role. In contrast, the job of police officer (still sometimes called "policeman") is described in terms of "toughness" and the "brotherhood" of officers.

Twenty years ago, in 2000, men outnumbered women by a ratio of at least 2 to 1 in the following occupations categorized by Statistics Canada:

- the primary industries of forestry, fishing, mining, and oil and gas
- manufacturing
- construction
- agriculture (Uppal & LaRochelle-Côté, 2014).

These industries are all part of the goods-producing sector, where men made up over 75 per cent of the total labour force. The gender split was much more equal in the services-producing sector, where women made up 53 per cent of the workforce and outnumbered men by at least 15 per cent in the following categories:

- finance and insurance
- educational services
- accommodation and food services
- health care and social assistance (Uppal & LaRochelle-Côté, 2014).

In the last of these categories, the dominance was more than 4 to 1.

Data from Statistics Canada's 2018 Labour Force Survey (LFS) show that little has changed since then. Men now make up 78 per cent of the labour force in the goods-producing sector, while women occupy 78 per cent of jobs in the services-producing sector (Figure 9.1a). Figure 9.1b provides a breakdown of the 8 industries cited above and shows that women are still underrepresented in manufacturing, construction, agriculture, and primary industries, while dominating professions in educational services, health care, and social assistance. In fact, since 1991, the top three jobs for young Canadian women with a university degree have consistently been (1) elementary school or kindergarten teacher, (2) registered nurse, and (3) secondary school teacher. According to the 2016 census, 19 per cent of 25- to 34-year-old women with university degrees were employed in one of these three jobs (Statistics Canada, 2016).

Figure 9.2 shows the 10 jobs most commonly held by women and men in Canada. Figure 9.3 shows the top 10 jobs for people aged 25 to 34 who have recently graduated with a certificate, diploma, or degree from a college or university. While there are some occupations that appear in the top 10 for both women and men, the list of jobs held by men shows a greater share of roles associated with computer technology, trades, and engineering (mechanical engineer and civil engineer fall just outside of the top 10 for 25- to 34-year-old men). In contrast, the list of jobs held by women is dominated by occupations that involve care work, including nursing, education and childcare, social assistance, and food services. In 2015, 41 per cent of working Canadian women were involved in these industries, compared with just 13 per cent of working Canadian men. As Statistics Canada analyst Melissa Moyser (2017) observes, women's employment "often parallels their traditional gender roles of homemaking and caregiving" (p. 22).

Another common feature of many of the most common jobs for women is what American sociologist Arlie Hochschild called *emotional labour*. Emotional labour describes the effort required to manage our emotions and the emotions of others "in accordance with organizationally defined rules and guidelines" (Hochschild, 1983, p. 147). Imagine you're working at a coffee shop, and the patron you have just served begins berating you for using whole milk instead of two percent in the foam of his cinnamon dolce latte. Rather than confronting him with the fact he didn't specify two percent milk in his order, you apologize with servility because "the customer is always right." It has cost you a fair bit

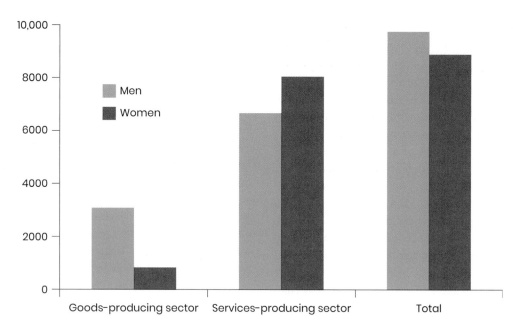

FIGURE 9.1a Labour Force Participation in Canada (× 1000), 2018

Source: Statistics Canada, 2018a.

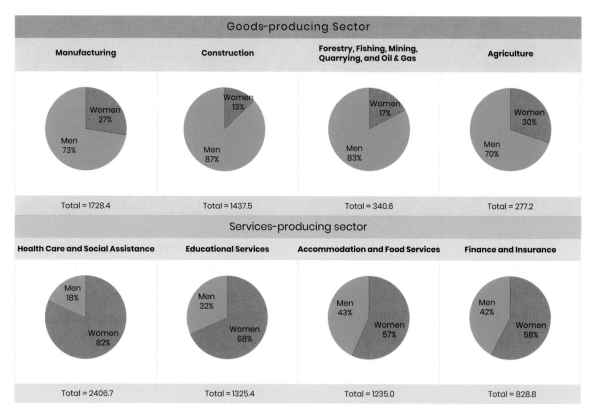

FIGURE 9.1b Labour Force Participation in Canada by sex (× 1000), select industries, 2018

Source: Statistics Canada, 2018b.

A. Women

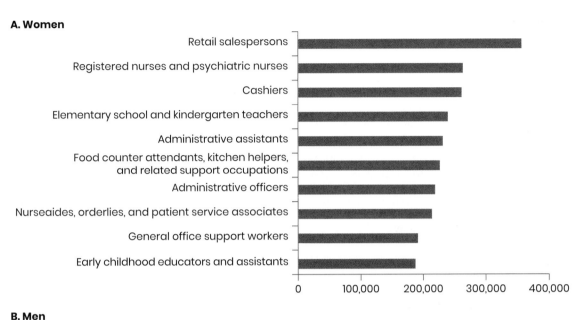

B. Men

FIGURE 9.2 Top 10 Occupations for Women and Men in Canada (2016 Census)

Source: Statistics Canada, 2016.

of emotional labour to allow the customer to leave satisfied that he has taught you a lesson.

Emotional labour involves manipulating the emotions of others through our own display of emotion. A flight attendant puts on an air of calm to put nervous airline passengers at ease; a store clerk fawns as they try to make a customer fall in love with one of the store's dresses. Hochschild made two key observations about emotional labour. First, it is used to bring about feelings of satisfaction and well-being in others, which is a role traditionally associated with women more than with men. Second, it requires us to make a

false display of emotion while concealing what we are actually feeling, and in this way emotional labour can lead to alienation and burnout over time.

It is worth noting that care work and emotional labour are hallmarks of the largest occupation not on this list: the unpaid work of raising and caring for children, which falls disproportionately on the shoulders of mothers.

So are men's jobs better? Figures 9.2 and 9.3 show that apart from retail positions, the most common jobs for men fall outside of the service industry, where emotional labour is a prerequisite, and none would

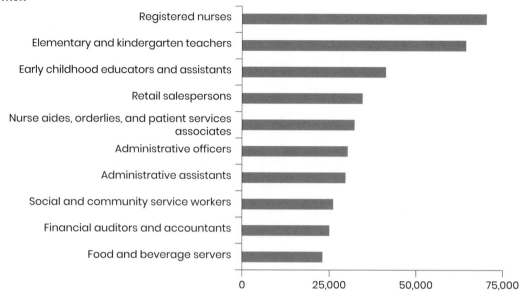

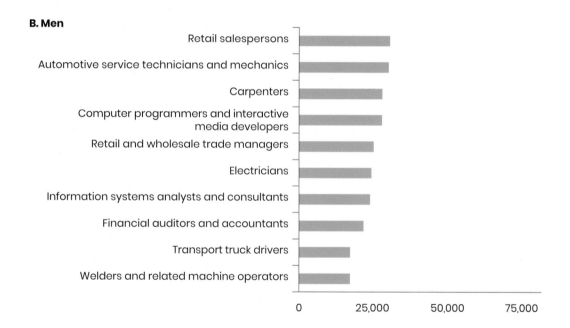

FIGURE 9.3 Top 10 Occupations for Canadian Women and Men Aged 25–34 Holding a Post-secondary Certificate, Degree, or Diploma (2016 Census)

Source: Statistics Canada, 2016.

be considered care work. In fact, the list is dominated by jobs that require minimal interaction with others, such as trucking, construction, carpentry, and electrical work. Jobs in these fields can be alienating in their own right, not to mention dangerous.

Sociology students need to look at what might cause these gender specializations to occur. A place to start would be postsecondary education, where men and women typically take different routes. We'll consider education shortly.

In 2019, Barbie celebrated her sixtieth anniversary with an inspiring campaign teaching girls that they can be anything—as long as they have long hair and less than 20 per cent body fat. (The message was surely not lost on many boys, parents, and nostalgic adults also.) Does the campaign promote a healthy or unhealthy message about gender and work?

The Point Is...

Women's Work in Canada Is Devalued

The gap between what men and women earn in Canada has narrowed since the 1980s, though as Figure 9.4 shows, women still earn just 87 cents for every dollar a man earns. Why?

In large part it is because of the different kinds of work that men and women do. Women are overrepresented in low-paying professions in health care, education, and social services. This kind of work is devalued compared with high-paying and male-dominated professions in fields like engineering, architecture, and natural resources (Moyser, 2017, p. 28).

It isn't because "men's work" requires more education or expertise. The National

Continued

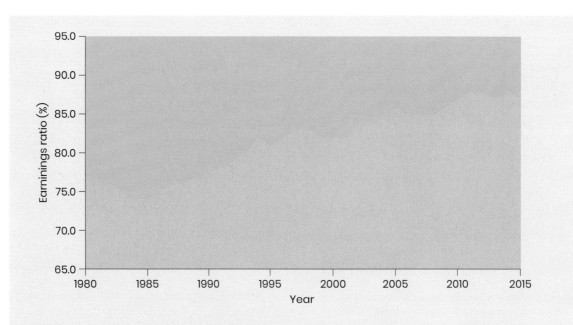

FIGURE 9.4 **Total Women's Earnings as a Percentage of Men's Earnings, 1980–2015**

Source: Moyser, 2017, Chart 17.

Occupational Classification is a tool used by the federal government to organize jobs by the amount of skill and training they require. For example, paraprofessional work in legal, social, and education services falls within the same classification as work in industrial, electrical, and construction trades: both require college education or apprenticeship training. The average rate of pay for the former is $22.57; for the latter, it is $29.76 (Moyser, 2017, Table 10). Can you guess which of those two kinds of work is dominated by women, and which one is dominated by men?

It is also the case that men and women are paid differently for doing the exact same work. Even in the "female" occupations such as nursing and teaching, men out-earn women. Moyser, in her excellent report for Statistics Canada, summarizes the possible explanations for the wage gap:

One interpretation is that women experience wage discrimination on the basis of their gender. In this case, a woman is paid less than her male colleague for doing the exact same job. An alternative . . . interpretation is that, within occupational groups, women choose the less demanding and/or more flexible positions in order to accommodate their caregiving responsibilities. Women may also be less adept at negotiating their pay or less interested in competing, as these attributes are deemed "masculine" in the context of gender socialization. (2017, p. 30)

What Do YOU Think?

Michael and Michelle graduated from university together and were hired by the same advertising company. Five years later, Michael is earning 15 per cent more than Michelle. How could you account for the wage gap in this context?

Being a Gender Minority in a Gendered Occupation

When people find themselves in gendered jobs where they belong to the minority sex, it can affect their gender performance. Sargent (2005) discusses the phenomenon among men in early childhood education. Sargent incorporates Raewyn Connell's (1995) four performances of masculinity—essentially, four ways of acting out male gender roles:

1. hegemonic masculinity
2. subordinate masculinity
3. marginalized masculinity
4. complicit masculinity.

Sargent explains them this way:

> Hegemonic masculine practices are those that serve to normalize and naturalize men's dominance and women's subordination. Subordinate masculinities are those behaviours and presentations of self that could threaten the legitimacy of hegemonic masculinity. Gay men, effeminate men, and men who eschew competition or traditional definitions of success are examples frequently cited. . . . These men are vulnerable to being abused and ridiculed by others. Marginalized masculinities represent the adaptation of masculinities to such issues as race and class. For example, a Black man may enjoy certain privileges that stem from success as a small business owner, yet still find himself unable to hail a cab. . . . Finally, complicit masculinities are those that do not embody hegemonic processes *per se*, but benefit from the ways in

jo unruh/iStockphoto

Does this ECE's hands-off celebration of a toddler's achievement look natural to you? Why do you think we're so suspicious of men who want to be daycare workers? What societal influences have conditioned our suspicion?

which hegemonic masculinities construct the gender order and local gender regimes. (2005)

Sargent argues that men working in early childhood education are caught in a conflict between performing a *subordinate masculinity* (for example, by being "nurturing") and engaging in more stereotypical masculinity performances. Men in early childhood education often have to suppress tendencies toward subordinate masculinity to avoid being associated by others with the popularly reproduced image of the homosexual–pedophile, which mistakenly conflates two very different sexualities. This is why male ECEs are not allowed the caring physical contact that female teachers are encouraged to have, and are reduced to less threatening performances of complicit masculinity, which include "high fives" and handshakes rather than hugs. This is a compromise that can be demoralizing for the male early childhood educator.

Another gender image that restricts the performance of male gender roles in the ECE environment is the "man as disciplinarian." Because it is assumed that men more naturally perform discipline, they may be assigned greater responsibility for monitoring the behaviour of "problem kids." Classrooms occupied by male teachers then become seen as sites of discipline. No matter what the male ECE's natural classroom approach may be, he may be forced to conform to a masculinity performance that reinforces male authoritarian stereotypes.

Gender and Education: What Keeps Women from Taking Math and Engineering?

Earlier we looked at how different kinds of work are gendered: how the "care work" fields of nursing and early childhood education are dominated by women, while skilled trades such as carpentry, electrical engineering, and computer programming are dominated by men. It is reasonable to expect we will find similar patterns in the postsecondary courses that women and men in Canada are taking. Let's see if that is borne out by the evidence.

In 2016, Canadian colleges and universities awarded 230,274 undergraduate degrees. Women took home close to 60 per cent of those degrees—135,000 in total (Statistics Canada, 2018b). Women received more degrees than men did in nearly every one of Statistics Canada's 13 program categories, from education and performing arts to business and public administration. The two exceptions were engineering and architecture, and math and computer science. Those programs represent the "E" and the "M" in STEM, the set of science- and technology-related courses that receives considerable attention because they offer good career prospects and because their enrolment has typically been dominated by men.

Figure 9.5 shows the distribution of undergraduate degrees awarded in STEM fields and other program types. You can see that when it comes to STEM programs, women received a greater share (58 per cent) of degrees in physical and life sciences but a much lower share of degrees in math and computer science (26 per cent) and engineering (21 per cent). This helps to account for why computer programmer, interactive media designer, and systems analyst are in the top 10 jobs for men but not for women in Figure 9.3. However, this is only part of the story.

In a study of Canadian STEM graduates, Statistics Canada's Darcy Hango (PhD in sociology) found that while the unemployment rates for young men and women graduating with non-STEM degrees were about the same (5.5 per cent and 5.7 per cent, respectively), the unemployment rate for male STEM graduates was over two points lower than the unemployment rate for women with STEM degrees (4.7 per cent versus 7.0 per cent) (Hango, 2013, p. 3). That's not all. Hango then looked at the rate of "employment mismatch." Sometimes called the "underemployment rate," the **mismatch** rate represents the percentage of university graduates in jobs requiring a high school diploma or less—jobs, in other words, for which that expensive university education really isn't required. Overall, women STEM graduates had a much higher employment mismatch rate than their male counterparts (18.3 per cent vs 11.8 per cent). Women with degrees in mathematics and computer engineering had a mismatch rate of 22.4 per cent, compared with just 10.1 per cent for men. The only STEM field in which women had the lower mismatch rate was technology (20.5 per cent vs 23.5 per cent for men); that happens to be the STEM field associated with the lowest average pay. Incidentally, the mismatch rate among those with non-STEM degrees

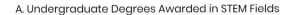

A. Undergraduate Degrees Awarded in STEM Fields

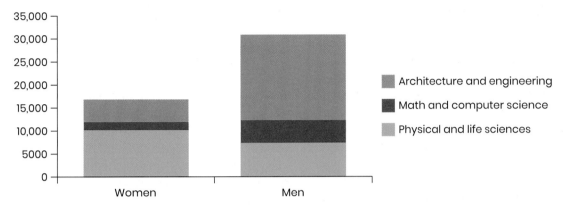

■ Architecture and engineering
■ Math and computer science
■ Physical and life sciences

B. Undergraduate Degrees Awarded in Social Science and Humanities

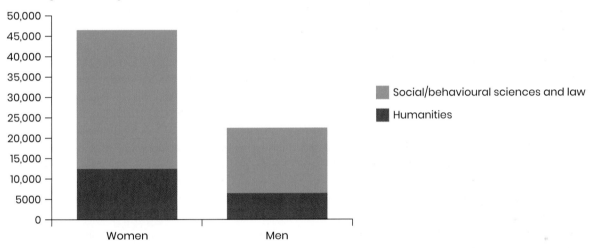

■ Social/behavioural sciences and law
■ Humanities

C. Undergraduate Degrees Awarded in Health and Related Fields

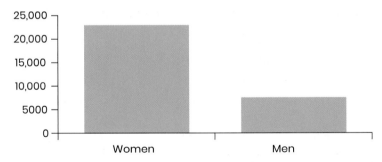

FIGURE 9.5 Undergraduate Degrees Awarded in Canada by Program Type and Sex, 2016

Source: Statistics Canada, 2018c.

was lower for women than for men (18.5 per cent vs 22.2 per cent).

Do these findings help us understand why women are underrepresented in STEM programs at Canadian colleges and universities? It may be part of the story, but it isn't the whole story. In an American study aimed at finding out why women drop out of computer science programs at a disproportionately high rate, sociologist Joanne Cohoon (2006) found that attrition rates were lower in departments where the proportion of female students was higher. The presence of more female students offers more opportunities for same-sex peer support and help to combat the notion that women do not belong in computer science (Cohoon, 2006). That finding may extend as well to engineering programs, and it suggests that we cannot simply conclude that young women are not interested in these programs, but that there may be significant barriers that, once removed, will open up these program and their many career paths to more women.

Before we leave the topic of gendered education, have a look at Part C of Figure 9.5. Health and related fields is somehow not part of STEM, despite the fact that quite a lot of science is required by those preparing for careers in nursing, human and veterinary medicine, dentistry, and pharmacy. (Perhaps the "H" would mess up the acronym.) If we are asking what keeps young women in Canada from taking math and engineering, should we also be asking why men are underrepresented in undergraduate pre-health programs? Is it a problem that needs to be addressed with the same urgency?

Race and Gender: Intersecting Oppression

Opposing Gender/Race Stereotypes

As we saw in Chapter 8, race and gender often intersect to amplify oppression. In these situations, racial prejudice reinforces gender bias, and vice versa. Prejudice often draws on stereotypes of the "other," and when gender and race intersect, the double-barrelled oppression sometimes produces a pair of opposing gender/race stereotypes.

An example of this tendency to stereotype visible minority women into extremes is described by Renee Tajima (1989) in her discussion of the **Lotus Blossom Baby** and the **Dragon Lady**, which are contrasting conceptions of gender that have sometimes been applied to East Asian women by Westerners. In Tania Das Gupta's words, the former stereotype "encompasses the images of the China doll, the geisha girl and shy Polynesian beauty. The latter includes prostitutes and 'devious madams'" (1996, p. 27).

© Christina Dun

Toronto's Ryerson University came under flak when it was reported that its engineering students were dragged through slush in their underwear as part of a hazing ritual. How do social expectations of women conflict with this controversial rite of passage? If you are a woman, would it make you think twice about applying to one of the country's engineering schools?

Black women have also faced being characterized by one of a pair of opposing race/gender stereotypes. Das Gupta describes the double image as follows:

> On the one hand there was the slow, desexed, "cow-like" mammy, evolved into the "Aunt Jemima figure"—familiar to many from older boxes of pancake mix—a servile and contented image which brings together gender and race ideologies. On the other hand, there was the sexual objectification of Black women's bodies, or body parts to be more exact. (1996, p. 27)

The sexually objectified black woman is a familiar figure in music videos. White performers have occasionally been criticized for both objectifying and dehumanizing their black female back-up dancers in their videos and on stage.

Indigenous women have long been subject to the opposing gender/race stereotypes of the "Indian princess" and the "squaw." In the United States, the **Indian princess** is a heroine at the heart of the American master narrative of how their country was built. She is the beautiful Disneyfied Pocahontas saving handsome John Smith from death, in the process abandoning her people to serve the interests of the incoming colonial power. She is Sacajawea, the Shoshone woman who aided the Lewis and Clark expedition from 1804 to 1806, helping to open up the West to "civilization" and the eventual reservation entrapment of her people.

The Indian princess is not part of the master narrative of Canada. Still, she is found here and there in Canadian history. Emily Pauline Johnson, popular Mohawk writer at the turn of the twentieth century, was billed as "The Mohawk Princess" to audiences in North America and Britain, for whom she performed her poetry. Catharine Sutton, a heroic Ojibwa woman of the nineteenth century, is known in Owen Sound, Ontario, as "the Indian Princess" (Steckley, 1999).

While the stereotype of the Indian princess has been used as a metaphor for the mythologized open-armed acceptance of European settlers by North American Indigenous people, the squaw is a figure that has been used by white writers to characterize First Nations people as savages, providing

Photo by Ezra Shaw/Getty Images

Canadian sociologist Naila Keleta-Mae calls "Formation," the debut track of Beyoncé's 2016 visual album *Lemonade*, "a complex meditation on female blackness, . . . one that is ambitious, spiritual, decisive, sexual, capitalist, loving, and communal" (2016). Yet critics say that as the most powerful woman in the American music industry, Beyoncé occupies a position of privilege that puts her out of touch with what life is like for most black women in North America. Does her social standing enhance or diminish her status as a hero of black American feminism?

ample justification for white colonial dominance (Smits, 1982). It is an offensive, derogatory stereotype of the Indigenous woman as lazy, drunk, and a target for physical and sexual abuse by men. The squaw is a central figure in the white settler narrative that characterizes Indigenous culture as primitive and barbaric, with lazy Indigenous men overworking and abusing their wives, sisters, mothers, and daughters.

Violence against Indigenous Women

Women and girls experience violence differently than do men and boys. This is primarily the case with sexual violence and murder that begins with sexual violence. Among no population is this more true than with Indigenous women. This is true even for two forms of institutionalized sexual violence involving the reproduction rights of these women: sexual sterilization and abortions without consent (informed or otherwise). I could bombard you with statistics here, but reliable statistics—that is, "official" statistics that do not underrepresent the problem—are hard to come by. I will use one reasonably representative figure that comes from Karen Stote's *An Act of Genocide: Colonialism and the Sterilization of Aboriginal Women* (2015). From 1971 to 1974, 580 Indigenous women were sexually sterilized in Medical Services Hospitals (run by the federal Department of Indian Affairs, as it was then called) in mostly northern parts of Alberta, Saskatchewan, Manitoba, and Ontario, as well as what are now the three territories of Yukon, Northwest Territories, and Nunavut (Stote, 2015, p. 79).

There have been well-selling books about murdered Indigenous women by white men. One is Lisa Priest's *Conspiracy of Silence*, about the sexually initiated killing of Helen Betty Osborne in northern Manitoba in 1971 (1989; see also Steckley, 2013, ch. 2). There is W.D. Goulding's *Just Another Indian: A Serial Killer and Canada's Indifference* (2001), about the serial killer John Martin Crawford, who killed at least four Indigenous women. Third, there is S. Cameron's *On the Farm: Robert William Pickton and the Tragic Story of Vancouver's Missing Women* (2010), about the man who has become the most notorious known serial killer of Indigenous.

Of course, there have been federal commissions, of which the most recent is the high-profile Inquiry into Missing and Murdered Indigenous Women and Girls, which published its final report in 2019. Its recommendations are too fresh to have been

implemented, and too late to spare so many Indigenous families so much agony over their stolen sisters.

Gender and Immigration

There have been several instances in Canadian history when only the men or the women of a particular ethnic group were permitted or encouraged to immigrate. We have seen, in Chapter 8, that Chinese and South Asian women were effectively blocked from entering Canada for significant parts of the twentieth century. Later in the century, women from the Philippines were encouraged to immigrate to fill labour shortages in certain feminized occupations. However, their immigration was subject to strict conditions, and they faced hardships upon their arrival.

Filipino immigration to Canada is distinctive in that allowed women to become the "pioneers." They made the journey before their husbands and other male family members, sending most of their money, together with care packages of bargain-hunted goods, back home to their families and sponsored relatives and provided them with a place to stay. There have been two periods of Filipino immigration to Canada. The first brought nurses, mostly women, while the second brought nannies, who suffer more from the **intersectionality** of gender and "race" than did the earlier generation of Filipino immigrants.

In 1981, the Canadian government instituted its Foreign Domestic Movement Program (FDMP) to address the growing need for in-house childcare that was created as more women began working outside the home. In 1992, the FDMP was replaced by the more restrictive Live-In Caregiver Program, which required selected immigrants to commit to 24 months of domestic work within a three-year period, during which time they were also required to "live in" with the family. Nannies came mainly from the Philippines, Jamaica, and Britain. Filipino nannies dominated the figures, the percentage of domestics coming from the Philippines rising between 1982 and 1990 from 10.6 per cent to 50.5 per cent. This trend occurred not just in Canada but in Hong Kong, Singapore, Saudi Arabia, Britain, and the United States. The political and economic unrest that surrounded the fall of the corrupt Marcos government made the Philippines a place many wanted to leave.

The women of the second period of Filipino immigration were older than their compatriots who had migrated earlier: those aged 30–34 predominated,

What Do You Think?

1. Why are Indigenous women and girls targeted in this way?
2. What is necessary for the situation to change? Do you think that the situation will change significantly?

with those aged 25–29 and 35–39 forming smaller but roughly equal groups, and those aged 20–24 and 50–54 sharing about the same low percentage. It was more difficult for this generation of Filipino immigrants. They were better educated than immigrating British and Jamaican nannies: among those receiving authorization for temporary employment as nannies between 1982 and 1990, 8 per cent held bachelor's degrees, 7 per cent had at least some university education, 17 per cent had some trade and technology training, and 12 per cent had other non-university training. Working as nannies made these women grossly underemployed, as sociologist Anita Beltran Chen (1998) argues. Yet only domestic work could bring them to Canada.

As women, as **visible minorities**, and as temporary and poorly paid employees subject to few industrial controls, the women were vulnerable to exploitation and physical, emotional, and sexual abuse. Those who had been trained in a specific field such as nursing also had to fight losing their skills through disuse. Between 15 and 20 per cent were married and had to endure separation from their husbands and, often, children. Those who were single returned a large portion (estimates vary around 75 per cent) of their income to their family back home, holding onto little money to look after themselves. They are restricted by the stereotypes of "race" and gender that treat Asian women as caregivers, overlooking skills that might make them productive in other areas of Western society.

Gender Abroad: Two Examples

Boyat and Deviant Gender Performance in the Arab World

In Arab countries such as Qatar and the United Arab Emirates, there is an emerging pattern of deviant behaviour that cuts across gender and ethnic lines. It involves young women who adopt a masculine style of dress, including baggy jeans or military pants, aviator shades, heavy watches and other jewellery, combat boots or running shoes, and so on; many of the women keep their hair cut short. A woman dressed this way wouldn't look out of place in North America, but in many parts of the Arab world women in public customarily wear a *burqa* or *abaya*, a full-length, loose-fitting robe that covers the whole body from the shoulders down, or at least a veil, or niqab.

The women are known as *boyat* (singular *boyah*), an Arabic word akin to "tomboy" and sometimes translated as "transsexual." But the behaviour is not sexual. It is more a deviant way of acting out and exploring gender. The conventionally masculine style of dress is liberating: *boyat* are able to talk and act more aggressively and independently than they could if they were dressed as women. But their gender performance goes beyond the "costume": the women involved consider their behaviour a way of life, and they find an important kind of solidarity with other women engaged in the same behaviour (see "Cross about Cross-Dressing," 2010; "Defying Gender Expectations," 2009; Naidoo, 2011).

What are the factors influencing the *boyat* phenomenon? Globalization has played a role, by exposing women and girls in Middle Eastern countries to images of women acting more independently than women in the Arab world are traditionally permitted to do. Social media allow *boyat* to communicate with one another anonymously, and get together online without being seen. There are also links between the *boyat* phenomenon and higher education. A college or university education prolongs the period of unmarried youth for young women. Likeminded *boyat* gathering together in women's colleges and campuses like those of the UAE's Higher Colleges of Technology are less likely to arouse suspicion with their behaviour. In such settings, their increasing number makes them the majority, putting them in a position to poke fun at and even bully their more conservative female peers.

In most settings, *boyat* remain a minority, and deviant behaviour is met with negative sanctions. Some opponents of the *boyat* phenomenon have attempted to medicalize the "problem" by proposing rehabilitation therapy and medicine. In some jurisdictions, cross-dressing has been made illegal.

Purple-Collar Workers in the Philippines

Since the start of the twenty-first century, the Philippines has seen a rapid growth in global call centres. Between 2000 and 2010, the number of Filipinos employed as call-centre operators skyrocketed from roughly 2000 to 400,000. A by-product of that growth is the emergence of an occupational niche for transgender women.

The finding comes from a study by Emmanuel David (2015), who interviewed 39 transwomen and two transmen between 2009 and 2012. Twenty-eight of these "purple-collar workers," ranging in age from 19 to 35, held university degrees, while the rest had done at least some college. David refers to the call-centre work as **purple-collar** labour, distinguishing it from the blue-collar work associated with skilled and unskilled trades, pink-collar work associated with female-defined or -oriented jobs, and white-collar office work. As David explains it, purple-collar work involves

> structural and interactional conditions experienced by transgender women workers in the labor market. Structurally, the concept refers to transgender workers' spatial location in particular work sites. The purple-collar workforce can be both densely clustered in a particular industry and systematically dispersed, vertically and/or horizontally, within particular workplaces. Interactionally, the purple-collar concept theorizes how transgender women employees' micro-interactional work is characterized by specific systems of rewards, responsibilities, and penalties. (2015)

The term *systematically dispersed* refers to the fact that the transwomen workers are not working together in one group but are spread out over all of the worksites in "patterned inclusions" (David, 2015). This is how transwomen produce what David calls **queer value** for the industry. Work at the call centre is repetitive and boring, especially for educated young people. The operators frequently have to deal with nasty remarks from potential customers in the West. The transwomen keep it light: they make co-workers happier by being entertaining or upbeat while they all work, acting as a "social lubricant" to keep the call centre operating productively. In this way, transwomen are performing "value-producing emotional labor" and providing "queer value" to their employer.

The entertainer's role is associated with what are called *bakla* in Tagalog (the national language of the Philippines). *Bakla* cannot be directly translated into "gay" or "transsexual" in English—there are too many different cultural strings of meaning. Jobs typically associated with *bakla* are hairstylist, beautician, designer, club entertainer, wedding planner, and sex worker. The transwomen in the call centres "play the role" of *bakla*. They regularly lighten the mood, fulfilling expectations of the role that are both implicit and explicit. For example, apart from being expected to lighten the mood on a day-to-day basis, the trans call-centre workers participate in ball gown and makeup contests that occur several times yearly, in "team-building" social events designed to help "foster productivity, ease workplace tensions, and boost employee morale" (David, 2015).

The trans call-centre workers occupy a class apart from the typical *bakla*. They are educated and fluent in English, and they have a job that pays fairly well for the Philippines, although it is less than 15 per cent of what call-centre workers are paid in the United States. While they are willing to follow the *bakla* stereotype to a certain degree, they recognize that there are only a few chances for upward mobility, and they have to meet a certain level of professionalism if they want to be truly successful at the job. This can create an atmosphere of competition that limits group solidarity, the kind of **class consciousness** that Marx talked about.

What Do YOU Think?

How does the "queer value" of the purple-collar workers both help and hurt their professional aspirations (i.e. their chances of being promoted to management positions)?

Masculinity and Race: Three Examples of Toxic Masculinity

Not all masculinities are the same, even within one society. Some of them can be considered "toxic," meaning not healthy either for the males involved or for the society of which they are a part. Race is a persistent factor in the production and reproduction of toxic masculinities like the ones described below.

Jamil Jivani provides three good illustrations of how ideas about masculinity are intertwined with race in *Why Young Men: Rage, Race and the Crisis of Identity* (2018). Jivani's father came from Kenya to Toronto, where Jivani was born. As a black youth, Jivani experienced deep prejudice from early on, moving always within the gaze of a suspicious mainstream society that watched him carefully once he became an adolescent:

As I grew up, I was also frequently stopped or followed by cops and security guards on my way to and from school. It's hard to feel you belong when your mere presence on the street, at the mall, and at the bus stop draws the suspicion of people who are supposed to keep our community safe. (Jivani, 2018, p. 3)

Jivani's father, who had been abandoned by his biological parents and whose adoptive parents died when he was 14, did not play a positive role in demonstrating masculinity to his son. The masculine role models that Jivani fashioned himself after were what he calls Hollywood gangster rappers. He sees correlation and argues for causation between the degree to which the people he hung out with watched and listened to gangster rap and the way they spoke, what they talked about, and how they acted:

> We adopted aspects of gang culture, including bandannas and rapper-inspired nicknames. We even gave gang names to our friend groups. . . . Some of us began smoking [marijuana] and talking about getting it from drug dealers. We would hang out and loiter, with nothing to do but share gangster fairy tales. It became normal to speak about women in disrespectful language and to pursue sexual relationships with our female classmates as sport. For kids who didn't have much money, we became oddly obsessed with expensive clothes, particularly the kind you'd see on rappers and basketball players. (Jivani, 2018, pp. 27–8)

Jivani himself cultivated a tough-guy "gangsta" image and reputation:

> In my backpack, I carried a police-style baton and a hunting knife so I could protect myself in fights and also intimidate people older and bigger than I was. I also kept an old Louisville Slugger wooden baseball bat in my locker. If I suspect a fight might break out at school, I would hide the baseball bat in the baggiest pair of jeans I owned and walk around with a limp. All these things

made me feel cool. My friends and the older guys we knew seemed impressed by this behaviour, so I kept it up. (Jivani, 2018, p. 34)

At the point where he was planning to get himself a gun, he started down a different path. He graduated from high school, and took a college program that would get him into university. At that time, he became a student of mine. The person I saw at that time was not a gangster rapper type (I had a number of those so I knew what they looked like), but an intelligent, soft-spoken young man who wanted to learn from me about his tribal heritage as a Kikuyu from Kenya.

Jivani went on to university, first in Toronto, then into a law program at Yale, where campus security guards directed a careful gaze on a student who did not look like the typical Ivy League student. He became an advocate for groups that supported young black men, both in Canada and the United States.

When a Moroccan terror cell in Belgium connected to ISIS attacked Paris in 2015, Jivani decided he needed to learn about the circumstances of these young black men. He travelled to Europe and soon found patterns in a community in Brussels, Belgium's capital city, that were similar to those he had experienced growing up black in North America. The race, religion, and immigrant status of these young men restricted their opportunities, and their capacity to identify themselves as Belgian. The opposition culture they were vulnerable to was that of Muslim terrorism. It was a way of "being a man" that garnered them a kind of respect, a kind of redemption for criminal activities and lack of financial success, a way of opposing the Western system that oppressed their people.

Insightfully, Jivani then turned his analytical eye to another racialized-based group of young men, this time white nationalists, the alt-right supporters of Donald Trump, who, like the young black men of his own time and place, and like the Moroccan Belgians he studied in Europe, are alienated from mainstream culture and express their alienation through a racialized, "toxic" masculinity. The common insult used by this group is "cuckservative," or "cuck" for short. A blend of "cuckold," an archaic term for a man whose wife has cheated on him, and "conservative," it is used with disdain to describe someone who, out of a need for acceptance, approval, and affection, has debased his masculinity by adopting liberal, especially feminist, values. To the alt-right, these men have sold out not just their masculinity but their culture and race:

> The alt-right attempts to emasculate young white men who don't identify with them and refers to them as weak beta males. The young men who gravitate to the alt-right feel disconnected from their country much as ISIS recruits do, but what's distinct is a feeling of decline. In their worldview, the West used to be theirs but is no longer because "cucks" have allowed Europe and North America to be over-taken by various minority groups. (Jivani, 2018, p. 188)

Jivani's main answer to these toxic masculinities, especially with males who have not experienced positive role modeling from their fathers, is with youth groups for young men that are run by older men who help them cope with careers, racism, and identity, in large part due to role-modelling a positive masculinity.

The Point Is . . .

Yes, Toxic Femininity Is Also a Thing

After learning about toxic masculinity, many of the men in your class, and some of the women, are asking whether toxic femininity exists as well. Typically, only the men will ask this aloud.

There are a growing number of non-academic blog posts and magazine articles on the subject, many of them written more in humour than in serious analysis (but they are funny). Perhaps we should begin by dispelling some false impressions of what toxic feminin-ity is. Keri Mangis provides a helpful list in her 2017 contribution to The Good Man Project. Toxic femininity does *not* describe the behaviour of a woman who:

- expresses her anger or outrage at legitimate offenses
- attends rallies, protests, or marches to fight for equality
- wears clothing not traditionally associated with femininity
- expresses a contrary or dissenting opinion
- refuses a man's advances
- rejects prescribed gender roles
- expresses feminist views
- isn't sexually attracted to, or only to, men.

Lync Dalton (2017) offers a description of what she believes toxic femininity to involve. She presents the following list of social beliefs or myths about femininity that she considers toxic:

- An acceptable woman presents as moral-ly pure but accommodating, refined, and nurturing. She doesn't exert direct power over others.
- An acceptable woman's power comes from her ability to charm and influence the people—particularly the men—around her to bring their own powers to bear toward her purposes.
- A woman's worth is principally determined by men's sexual desire for her.
- Women must appear to appreciate and support one another, but they're actually constantly and secretly in competition over beauty, male attention, and other things that define their worth.
- An acceptable woman's mission is to com-petently and quietly fulfill the emotional, nu-tritional, domestic, and sometimes sexual needs of the people around her. The most worthy women are the most selfless women.

The combined effect of all these myths is toxic femininity, which

> teaches us to center our looks in most matters, and hold our bodies to impossibly high beauty standards. It teaches us that if we wish to control a situation, we must do so covertly, by manipulating the people involved. It also teaches us that men are conduits to self-worth and power as much as they're individual human beings with their own sets of needs, all while overlooking our own intrinsic power and worth.
>
> And . . . men absorb these messages too, and it shapes what they see in—and expect from—the women in their lives, in obvious to subtle ways. (Dalton, 2017)

How would a sociologist study toxic femininity? Questionnaires would not be effective. I would recommend beginning with a content analysis of popular movies and television shows. Reality shows with a "survivor" theme are ripe for this kind of study. I would gather a focus group of people (particularly college and university students) to view one or more of those programs and then ask them for written and/or spoken interpretations of the behaviour of the women involved.

Sexuality

Up until this point we have considered gender and sex without addressing sexuality. While the three concepts are related, keeping them separate helps us avoid some common mistakes. For example, people sometimes assume that a person's sexuality can be accurately deduced from their gender performance—that a woman who adopts some masculine gender behaviours must be sexually attracted to women, or that a man who dresses as a woman must be attracted to other men. Neither of these assumptions is correct. It is also not correct to assume that a person assigned the male sex at birth who identifies as female is sexually attracted to men. A transgender person may be sexually attracted to people of the same or the opposite sex, or both, or neither. And of course, it would be just as wrong to assume that someone attracted to people of the same sex must secretly wish to change sexes.

All of this is to say that we can never assume a person's sexual preferences based on their gender expression or sex identity, or vice versa. For this reason, we can consider sexuality apart from sex and gender.

Sexuality refers to feelings of sexual desire and attraction and how these are expressed; like sex and gender, sexuality is fluid and often changes over time. Nevertheless, views of sexuality in North America have traditionally been shaped by two problematic ideas. The first is that we are all defined, sexually, by whether we are attracted to people of the same sex or to people of the "opposite" sex, based on a binary (male–female) understanding of sexes. According to this framework,

- a **heterosexual**, or "straight," person is sexually attracted to people of the "opposite" sex (women to men, men to women);
- a **homosexual** is sexually attracted to people of the same sex (**gay** and **queer** are, today, accepted synonyms);
- a **lesbian** is a woman who is sexually attracted to other women; and
- a **bisexual** is sexually attracted (equally or unequally) to people of "both" sexes.

The second problematic idea, premised on the first, is that of the categories defined above, the first one is "correct" or "normal," and the others are deviations from that standard. Belief in the primacy of sexual attraction to people of the opposite sex is called **heteronormativity**.

Let's take a closer look at these two outdated ideas. The first, that people are attracted to others of either the opposite or the same sex, prevailed well into the late twentieth century. This binary view of sexuality was so well entrenched that a once common notion held that bisexuality—genuine attraction to both men and women—did not exist, but that people claiming to be bisexual were really gays and lesbians who were in denial because of social pressure (see Rosario, Scrimshaw, Hunter, & Braun, 2006, for a discussion of this myth). Of course, people can be attracted to both men and women; we can also be attracted to trans men and women, adding a nuance not adequately covered by the

Telling It Like It Is

Gender Roles and Being Lesbian

People in my life in the past have tended to believe that because I am a lesbian, I automatically have more male-specific interests, and that I do not enjoy typical girl-oriented activities. Shortly after I told my brother, he invited me to a football game, stating, "You like football now don't you?" Although he was joking at the time, this is a typical comment often made to me. Although I may enjoy fixing things around the house, my partner is a sports fanatic, and while I like to sew and knit, she enjoys cooking and romantic comedies. The gender stereotyping, which is exactly what this comes down to, even goes so far as to include the style of clothes I wear. I remember one time that I went into work wearing a baseball cap, although I usually do not wear a hat to work, as I find it unprofessional. This particular day I was coming from school and in a rush. Immediately after entering work, I began to hear comments and mutters from my co-workers. It seemed that in their eyes because I was wearing a hat, I was portraying a male characteristic. They assumed that being a lesbian is the closest thing to being a male.

There is a significant difference between sexual orientation and gender identity. All of the gay people that I know, including myself, are very happy with their sex. They just happen to be attracted to the same sex as well. I am proud to be a woman. I enjoy it and would not want to change it.

For one reason or another people with little understanding of the gay population seem to need definite clarification of "who's the man and who's the woman," a question that I have been asked on too many occasions to count. In many gay relationships there are no specific roles, and each individual's identity is not masculine or feminine, but it slides on a continuum. It is ridiculous to assume that there is a male and female figure in the relationship. If I wanted a male–female partnership, I wouldn't be gay.

Many people believe that gay people, male or female, are involved in a sexual scene full of promiscuity, voyeurism, and *ménages à trois*. This is evidenced by the number of people that have made suggestive comments to me about non-committed casual sexual encounters. Although these beliefs are positive in one aspect as they break down the very untrue opinion that women cannot have the high sex drive that men are more known for, it also reflects a larger belief that being in a gay relationship is all about the sex. This leads people to believe that gay people do not commit and take part in stable, settled relationships. I remember talking with my father once about the relationship I was in and he responded, "It's alright if that's what you want, but it's unfortunate because those relationships don't last; they just don't settle." Ironically, I must say that gay relationships in fact have very little to do with sex. As a heterosexual relationship has many dimensions, so does the homosexual one, encompassing all one's needs such as emotional support, companionship, the sharing of values and spirituality, and of course, physical attraction does play its role as well. I once saw an advertisement that mocked this expectation of

binary terms *homosexual* and *heterosexual*. Today it is widely understood (perhaps even more so among your own generation than that of your instructor) that gay, straight, and bi are but three shades of the sexuality spectrum, and a growing list of terms are gaining currency to describe other hues of sexual preference. These include *asexual* (no sexual attraction), *demisexual* (sexual attraction only once an emotional bond is formed), *pansexual* (attraction to those of all sexes and genders), and *sapiosexual* (attraction to people of high intelligence).

The second problematic idea, heteronormativity, prevails, unfortunately. It is plain in the 72 countries of the world where homosexuality continues such extravagant sex lives. The poster was in a bookstore located in a gay community. The caption read, "What do lesbians do in bed?" and the picture had two women in bed wearing flannel pyjamas, one watching television and the other reading a book. I saw this as an accurate portrayal and a clever way to challenge this opinion.

Hero Images Inc. / Alamy Stock Photo

Do you think this couple spends a lot of time worrying which of them is "being the man" at any given moment?

What Do YOU Think?

What examples of heteronormativity has the author of this narrative encountered?

to be criminalized (see Figure 9.6). Criminalizing "deviant" sexuality is just one way of sanctioning it. In 2013, Russia, where homosexuality is not in itself illegal, passed a federal law prohibiting anyone from producing or distributing "propaganda of non-traditional sexual relations" among minors in a move that essentially made it illegal to equate gay and straight relationships (Elder, 2013). If you are fortunate to live in a country where such draconian measures are not in place, you can still find lots of evidence of heteronormativity, particularly in advertising, where heterosexual couples with children are emblematic of wholesome family values that companies would like their products—cars,

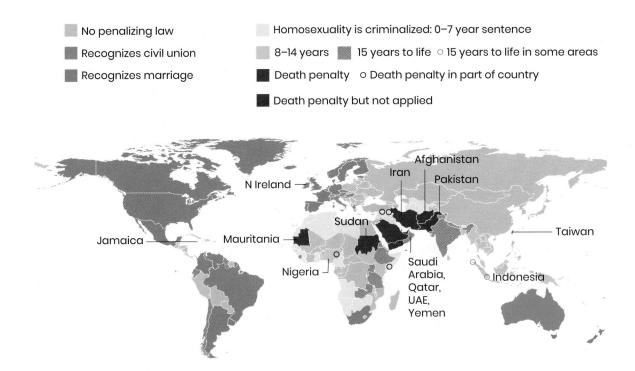

FIGURE 9.6 The Legal Status of Homosexuality around the World

breakfast cereal, furniture: you name it—to be associated with.

In this chapter and throughout the book I have used the initials LGBTQ2 (lesbian, gay, bisexual, transgender, queer/questioning, Two-Spirit) as an all-encompassing term to refer to refer to people who do not identify as heterosexual and cisgender. An "A" is sometimes added to denote asexual, and an "I" is sometimes added for intersex. Note that some Indigenous activists reject the "2" (or "2S")

addition to the initials because they consider Two-Spirit people to fall outside mainstream Western ideas of transgender. LGBTQ2 encompasses gender identities as well as sexualities, and so it is not a perfect analogue of heterosexual, which refers specifically to sexuality. It is a term that comprises disparate categories that have been grouped sociologically because they represent a shared experience of discrimination and the fight for equality and recognition.

Wrap It Up

Summary

We have seen that gender and sex are different. You are born with a sex: typically male or female, although intersex people may be born with both male and female sexual organs. Your gender is socially constructed to a significant extent. It may not fit neatly into the binary categories "male" and "female" but may sit somewhere between these two points. The social construction

of gender applies not just in obvious areas such as clothing and colours, but in occupations as well. You need be neither a woman nor a feminist to recognize that the feminization of an occupation—making it unrewarding in terms of pay, power, and social status—helps to create inequality between men and women. This inequality, reflected in pay ratio and in the greater likelihood of women working part-time, is changing very little. As sociologists, we need to investigate why this is so, and look for ways to address the inequity. We also must ask ourselves whether the separate paths that men and women take in postsecondary education lead to social inequality or just difference, an issue we considered in Chapter 4, on socialization.

Think Back

Questions for Critical Review

1. Explain, in your own words, the difference between biological sex, sexual identity, and gender.
2. What do the cases of David Reimer and Caster Semenya tell you about the relationship between biological sex and a person's lived sexual identity?
3. What does it mean to say that sex and gender are socially constructed to a significant extent?
4. The "pink tax" is a phenomenon where a product used by both sexes has a version that is marketed and sold to women or girls at a higher price. The classic example is the woman's razor, which may be identical to a man's razor except in colour and cost. Explain why razors are gendered.
5. Summarize the gender differences in Canadian postsecondary education and how they relate to the most common jobs for women and men.

What do these differences suggest about the different career paths that young women and men pursue?
6. Do you think there are still common stereotypes in North America surrounding those who transgress gendered work roles (e.g. the male nurse, the woman construction worker)? If so, do you think they can be changed? What would it take?
7. Describe how gender and ethnicity intersect to create stereotypes about women of different ethnic backgrounds.
8. How do you think gender-based immigration (i.e. with immigrants of one sex entering the country in much greater numbers than the other) affects the settling experiences of different groups, such as Filipinos?
9. Describe how the myth of the "real man" relates to toxic masculinity.

Read On

Recommended Print and Online Resources

"Converging Gender Roles," www150.statcan. gc.ca/n1/pub/75-001-x/10706/9268-eng.htm
- Katherine Marshall's article, from Statistics Canada's *Perspectives on Labour and Income*, offers a stats-based view of the extent to which gender roles may be converging in Canada.

"Cross about Cross-Dressing: Is It a Wicked Western Habit that Should be Stopped?" www. economist.com/node/154403091; "Shedding Light on the 'Boyat' Phenomenon: Conference Separates Fact from Fiction on the Issue," http://gulfnews.com/news/gulf/uae/general/

shedding-light-on-the-boyat-phenomenon-1.796816
- The *Economist* article provides an account of the "debate about fashion in Qatar," and looks at both sides of the issue of cross-dressing and *boyat* in the Middle East. The second article, from GulfNews.com, reviews a conference on the topic that was held at the Sharjah Women's College in the United Arab Emirates.

Jamil Jivani, *Why Young Men: Rage, Race, and the Crisis of Identity* (Toronto: HarperCollins, 2018); Daemon Fairless, *Mad Blood Stirring: The Inner Lives of Violent Men* (Toronto:

Random House, 2018); Rachel Giese, *Boys: What It Means to Become a Man* (Toronto: HarperCollins, 2018).

- Read together, these books give excellent insight into male violence and toxic masculinity. Jivani begins with a look at what draws young black men to violence and sees parallels with white nationalists and Islamic terrorists. Fairless interviews convicted criminals and fighters to see if the violent impulses that drive them exist near the surface in all men. Giese looks at why, at a time when gender expectations for girls are broadening, social expectations about masculinity remain as narrow as ever. Is it possible, she wonders, if young men are angry because society doesn't give them the latitude to cry in public or show other, "feminine" emotions. Consider this question in the context of Soraya Chemaly's TED Talk, in which she argues that girls and women are discouraged from showing anger, which is the moral property of boys and men.

John Colapinto (2000), *As Nature Made Him* (New York: Harper).

- Colapinto provides the definitive account of David Reimer's life and tragic death.

Judith Butler (1990), *Gender Trouble: Feminism and the Subversion of Identity* (New York: Routledge).

- Butler's pioneering work launched the study of queer theory.

Laura Bell, "Working Out Is a Minefield When You're Non-Binary," *Vice* (2018, Sept. 13), www. vice.com/en_ca/article/yw4gpx/working-out-is-a-minefield-when-youre-non-binary

- In this article for *Vice*, Laura Bell explains why working out at the gym is a challenge for non-binary people.

Melissa Moyser (2017), *Women in Canada: A Gender-Based Statistical Report*, Statistics Canada, cat. no. 89-503-X (Ottawa, ON: Minister of Industry).

- In her report for Statistics Canada, Melissa Moyser offers many insights into what defines women's work in Canada today.

Soraya Chemaly, *Rage Becomes Her: The Power of Women's Anger* (Atria Books, 2018); Chemaly, "The Power of Women's Anger," TED Talk (2018, Nov.), www.ted.com/talks/soraya_chemaly_the_power_of_women_s_anger?language=en

- In her book and in her TED Talk, Soraya Chemaly looks at how anger is gendered in such a way that anger "confirms masculinity and confounds femininity."

The Gender Book, www.thegenderbook.com

- Four Texans set out to create an illustrated guide to gender that would be accessible to children but of equal interest to adults. The website includes resources and some of the colourful hand-drawn illustrations found in the book itself (published in 2014), which is available for order through the website.

"The 'Genderless Baby' Who Caused a Storm of Controversy," www.thestar.com/news/article/1105515--the-genderless-baby-who-caused-a-storm-of-controversy-in-2011; "Remember Storm? We Check in on the Baby Being Raised Gender Neutral," www.thestar.com/life/parent/2013/11/15/remember_storm_we_check_in_on_the_baby_being_raised_genderneutral.html; "Baby Storm Five Years Later: Preschooler on Top of the World," www.thestar.com/news/gta/2016/07/11/baby-storm-five-years-later-preschooler-on-top-of-the-world.html

- These *Toronto Star* articles look at the life of Baby Storm from the eve of the infant's first birthday to the start of preschool.

Family

10

Reading this chapter will help you to . . .

- Describe the diversity of the Canadian family.

- Cite some of the ways in which the family in Quebec has differed from family in the rest of Canada.

- Discuss nine major changes that have affected the makeup of families in Canada over the past 50 years.

- Describe the different forms that conjugal roles can take, and how these roles are changing in Canada.

- Describe the varying impacts of endogamy on different racial and ethnic groups in Canada.

- Outline and comment on the argument that Indigenous families were "under attack" during the twentieth century in Canada.

For Starters

Can I Blame It All on My Family?

You probably know someone who blames their family for all of their problems—the inability to find meaningful relationships, financial success, a fulfilling career, and so on. Blaming the family is a common theme among stand-up comics and sitcom writers, who have mined the "dysfunctional family" as a source of humorous material. And venting has become a therapy prescribed by psychoanalysts who draw on Freud's notion that we all harbour a volatile mix of love and anger toward our parents that we need to bring into consciousness. Rooted in mainstream psychology of the late twentieth century, this idea gave a veneer of legitimacy to a certain breed of pop psychologists who turned blaming the family into a daytime and late-night television phenomenon known as the tabloid talk show. This variety of confessional television flourished under hosts such as Jerry Springer and Maury Povich, who encouraged guests to confront their family members in episodes that often ended in onstage fistfights and chair-throwing. While these shows may have mocked conventional family dynamics in a setting contrived to create drama, the raw emotion at the heart of many episodes was real.

Family-blaming is not restricted to trash TV and online psychology forums. Consider the anger of the following lines written by acclaimed British poet Philip Larkin (1922–1985) in the poem "This Be the Verse":

> They fuck you up, your mum and dad.
> > They may not mean to, but they do.
> They fill you with the faults they had
> > And add some extra, just for you.
>
> But they were fucked up in their turn
> > By fools in old-style hats and coats,

Who half the time were soppy-stern
    And half at one another's throats.

Man hands on misery to man.
    It deepens like a coastal shelf.
Get out as early as you can,
    And don't have any kids yourself.
(1971)

Of course, "getting out" is one thing; escaping your upbringing is quite another. We can see Larkin's poem as a very cynical take on socialization, the process of learning the values and standards of behaviour required to become members of the society to which we belong. As we saw in Chapter 4, socialization comes first through interactions with one's closest family members, and it leaves an impression that can last a lifetime.

Incidentally, this is a short poem I wrote in response to Larkin:

Larkin never married,
    But he did know how to rhyme.
He maintained non-committal relations
    With three women at one time.

He fed his family misery
    To readers down the years;

I'm glad he didn't have any kids
    To inherit all his fears. (2015)

Because as much as we may at times want to blame our families, we have to recognize the value that families bring in shaping responsible citizens of a society that functions harmoniously and advances over time.

Ultimately, you cannot run away from your family. You're better off understanding how your family made you who you are and how the family as an institution gives shape to society. By the end of this chapter, you should have some ideas.

What Do YOU Think?

1. What negative aspects of family was Larkin describing? In what ways is his poem a cynical interpretation of the process of primary socialization?
2. Are you optimistic or pessimistic about your future family life as a life partner or parent? Why, sociologically, do you think that is?
3. Do you have married uncles and aunts who have chosen not to have children? If so, why do you think that they didn't?

Introduction: Family Is Diverse

The opening line of Russian novelist Leo Tolstoy's tragic romantic novel *Anna Karenina* reads, "Happy families are all alike; every unhappy family is unhappy in its own way." I disagree. Happy families, functional families, and good families exist in many forms, and are alike only in their success at serving basic purposes, such as providing emotional support for family members, taking care of elders, and raising the next generation. In most other respects, happy families are diverse. But Tolstoy and even Larkin were right in one regard: there are many ways to screw up family.

It would be misleading to say that one family form is demonstrably better than any other for its members. And yet conservative media are filled with judgmental remarks about contemporary family forms. Even traditional sociology is not free from this bias. If you were presented with the terms **nuclear family** (which includes a parent or parents and children) and **extended family** (which might include, in addition, grandparents, aunts, uncles, and cousins), you might be led to believe that the former is "normal" and the other some kind of deviation from the regular model. This is not the case. For some cultures, historical and current, using the word *family* to mean parents and children alone would be as odd as using the term *body* to refer just to the heart.

The Wendat (Huron) language of the seventeenth century had no terms for "nuclear" or "extended" family. The common way for the Wendat to refer to

Would you call this a typical Canadian family? How many families do you know that look like this? Does yours?

family was through the noun root -*hwatsir*-, meaning "matrilineage," or the verb root -*yentio*-, meaning "to belong to a matrilineal clan." Matrilineage is the line of descendants that follows the mother's line. A woman,

her mother, and her sisters and brothers would belong to the same matrilineage. The longhouses that the people lived in would usually be dominated by one matrilineage, with married sisters and their husbands and children forming the nucleus of the people living in one house. Thus, the most common term for "family" in Wendat referred to what we would probably describe as an "extended family."

More useful than *nuclear family* and *extended family* are terms proposed by Frances Goldscheider and Regina Bures (2003) in their study of intergenerational living arrangements in the United States. They favour the terms *simple household* and *complex household*. A **simple household** consists of unrelated (by blood) adults with or without children. Conversely, a **complex household** includes "two or more adults who are related but not married to each other and hence could reasonably be expected to live separately" (2003). A simple household tends to consist of a single adult or married adults living with or without children. Probably the most common form of complex household in Canada today is one in which adult children live at home with a parent or parents. For a few years, my household was complex: my wife and I lived on the main floor, with our youngest son and his wife living in the furnished basement. (This did not even count the nine parrots who live in the aviary that used to

Quick Hits

What Is a Census Family?

For the purpose of collecting census data, Statistics Canada defines a family as

- a same-sex or opposite-sex couple, married or common-law, living together in the same dwelling, with or without the child or children, if any, of either or both spouses;
- a lone parent (single, separated, married, or divorced) living together in the same dwelling with at least one child.

The first of these is considered a *couple family*. A situation in which a child or children live with

their grandparents but not their parents is also considered a census family.

A couple family in which at least one child is the biological or adopted child of one parent only is a *stepfamily*. In a *simple stepfamily*, all of the children are the biological or adopted children of one parent only. In a *complex stepfamily*,

- there is at least one child of both parents and at least one child of only one parent;
- there is a least one child of each parent; or
- there is at least one child of both parents and at least one child of each parent.

Compare this photo with the one on page 304. Is this family any less typical of the families you know? What factors in our culture might lead us to view one family as more conventional than another?

be our living room.) They moved out, and now we're simple (cue the rimshot).

When sociologists talk of a family's diversity, they may mean one of two things. Some mean "diversity" in the sense that there are different family structures: dual-earner, single-earner/two-parent, lone-parent. I use "diversity" here and throughout this text in a broader sense that includes not just differences in structure but also cultural differences in the roles performed by each member. The discussion of the family in Quebec later in this chapter highlights this broader sense of diversity.

Nine Changes in the Canadian Family

The makeup and behaviour of Canadian families has changed dramatically over the past 40 years. I can, and in the sections that follow will, present several statistics to back up this claim, but I find that one piece of evidence is especially revealing: Statistics Canada, our national data intelligence bureau, no longer keeps track of marriages and divorces.

Let me put this in perspective. For 90 years, from 1921 until 2011, Statistics Canada published annual marriage rates for the country; beginning in 1972, the agency began publishing annual statistics on divorces as well. These data enabled sociologists and other social scientists, economists, and policy makers to track not just how many Canadians were marrying but at what age, how often, and for how long. Combined with rates of cohabitation—common-law unions that have not been solemnized in a city court or place of worship—marriage rates tell us about how Canadians are coming together in social groups for mutual comfort, care, and support. Examined against the backdrop of economic recessions and other tumultuous events, divorce rates give us a clue to the stressors that cause marriages to break down.

So why, then, did Statistics Canada in 2011 decide to stop collecting data on marriage and divorce? One explanation is that it was a cost-savings measure necessitated by budget cuts made by the Conservative government of Stephen Harper, who fought some very public battles with the federal agency and its chief statistician, Munir Sheikh. That may have played a role, but I don't think it was the main factor. What happened, I think, is that marriage and divorce became difficult to define. With the traditional church wedding on the decline, an increasing number of couples have entered into conjugal unions that resemble marriage but may or may not be recognized as such in the province where they live. In Ontario, for instance, a couple needs to be living together continuously for three years to receive some of the rights and benefits of married couples; in other provinces, the period is shorter. Not all provinces recognize "common-law marriage," though they might recognize "marriage-like relationships." In British Columbia, people living in marriage-like relationships are considered "unmarried spouses." Then consider that two people may live together for the purpose or raising a child but may not (or no longer) be intimately involved and may have romantic partners outside of that parenting union; are they "married"? What about roommates who have been sharing a dwelling because they cannot afford to live singly: they may be occasional sexual partners but would not consider themselves married, even in a common-law sense. And then while ending a marriage involves a sequence of legal steps, a marriage-like union can be dissolved without any formal procedure other than walking out the door.

The point is that while many people still aspire to a formal church wedding, Canadians are increasingly coming together in unions that resemble traditional marriage in some ways—shared costs and mutual financial support; co-parenting of a child; a sexual relationship; intimate friendship—but not in others. People in these arrangements may not consider themselves married and may even bristle at the word *couple*. And this reflects one of the ways in which the family in Canada is changing. The following are some other trends worth noting.

1. The marriage rate is decreasing while the cohabitation rate is rising.

Let's dig into the 90 years' worth of marriage rates we do have to see what trends they reveal. We can then look at the changing percentages of married people since 2008, the last year for which Statistics Canada calculated a marriage rate.

The **crude marriage rate** is the number of marriages that occur in a given year per 1000 people in a population. *Crude* refers to the fact that no statistical wizardry has been used to "refine" the rate (to use an oil analogy); it's not a social comment on marriage itself. Since the population rises over time, the crude marriage rate gives a better indication of trends than the overall number of marriages taken alone. (If the number of marriages were the same for 2002 and 2012, the actual rate of marriage would be decreasing, since the population overall is rising; a sociologist would conclude that fewer people were getting married.)

The crude marriage rate has fluctuated over the years. In 1920, it was relatively low at 6.1 per 1,000 people. Many young men (married and single) had died during World War I and the Spanish flu epidemic that followed it. When I think of that statistic, I think of two of my great-aunts who were young then—Aunt Nell the nurse, Aunt Margaret the teacher. They were gifted, intelligent women adored by the children and grandchildren of their married brothers. Neither of them ever married.

The marriage rate rose to a peak of 11.2 marriages per 1000 people in 1946, representing a post–World War II marriage boom that would precede (and contribute to) the postwar baby boom (Statistics Canada, 2011, Chart 6). After dropping a little in the years that followed, the marriage rate remained fairly high over the next three decades, peaking at 9.0 in 1972 and hovering around 8.0 for the rest of the decade (Statistics Canada, 2011b, Chart 6).

In the 1980s, Canada experienced an economic recession that contributed to a steady drop in the marriage rate, all the way to 5.5 in 1995 and 4.7 in 2001. In 2003, British Columbia and Ontario became the first provinces to legalize same-sex marriage, and they saw increased rates of marriage that year. But by 2008, Canada's crude marriage rate was at 4.4 per 1000 population, having fallen below 4.5 for the first time in history. The highest provincial rate was 6.8 in PEI, the lowest was Quebec, with 2.9. Quebec, in fact, was the only province under the national rate, accompanied only by the three territories.

Fewer *marriages* does not mean fewer *couples*. The number of **common-law** (or **cohabiting**) unions has been rising since the 1980s. There never was a "crude common-law marriage rate," comparable to the crude marriage rate, since society doesn't ritually mark the beginning of common-law relationships the way it records marriages. However, Statistics Canada does produce estimates of the population by marital status, indicating how many Canadians at any one time are single, married, living common-law, and so on. As Table 10.1 shows, the proportion of Canadian adults in common-law unions grew by over 3 percentage points between 1998 and 2018, while the percentage of married Canadians fell by nearly 5 points. Figure 10.1 provides a snapshot of Canadians aged 15 and over by marital status. Note that the categories used in Table 10.1 and Figure 10.1 are considered mutually exclusive of one another: here, only one status can apply per person. So "single" is reserved for people who have never married, and a person who was once married but is no longer in a committed relationship must be separated, divorced, or widowed. I have been divorced twice, but in the eyes of Statistics Canada I am married, reflecting not my past but my present status.

TABLE 10.1 Marital Status of Canadians Aged 15 and Over (%), 1998–2018

	1998	2008	2018
Single	27.8	29.0	29.1
Married	49.5	46.1	44.7
Living common-law	8.6	10.8	11.8
Separated	2.8	2.7	2.7
Divorced	5.3	5.9	6.1
Widowed	6.1	5.6	5.6

Note: The categories in this table and in Figure 10.1 are considered mutually exclusive of one another. So, while a person who is widowed or separated from their spouse may be single, "single" means never married

Source: Statistics Canada (2019).

The increasing share of common-law relationships raises a number of questions. First, is cohabitation replacing marriage? So far, the answer is a tentative no: despite the increase in the percentage of common-law couples since 1998, and the accompanying decline in traditional marriage, married couples still make up the predominant family structure in Canada by a wide margin, as Table 10.1 shows. Does the shifting balance signify that people today lack commitment? (Insert joke about the attention span of millennials here.) Or does it reflect the fact that an expensive church wedding is not a priority for

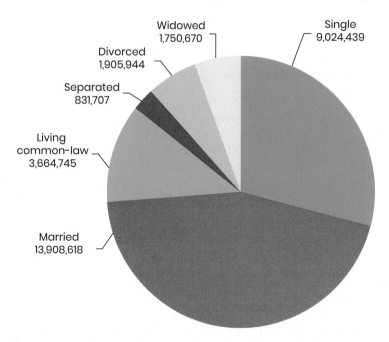

FIGURE 10.1 Marital Status of Canadians Aged 15 and Over, 2018

Source: Statistics Canada (2019).

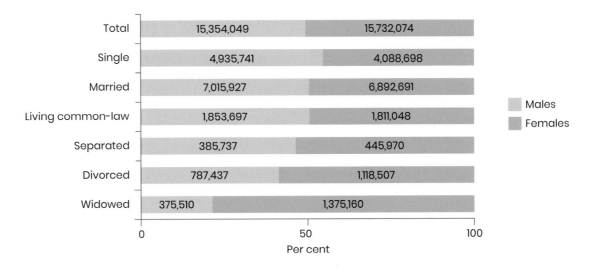

FIGURE 10.2 Marital Status of Canadians by Sex, 2018

Source: Statistics Canada (2019).

younger people who are increasingly secular and leaving university with unprecedented levels of student debt? And does cohabitation benefit men more than women? It depends on how you look at it, and possibly on your sex. As Figure 10.2 shows, the numbers of men and women who are living in common-law relationships are pretty close: among Canadians aged 15 and over, 12.0 per cent of men and 11.5 per cent of women are living common-law. The marriage numbers are also close: in 2018, 45.7 per cent of men and 43.8 per cent of women were married. More men than women are single (never married), but more women than men are separated, divorced, or widowed. Finally, how does cohabitation, compared with marriage, affect children? These are questions sociologists today are asking.

Quick Hits

How Quebec Skews the Marriage Data

In a number of areas where change in the Canadian family is occurring, families in Quebec are leading the way. This is not to say that they are "further ahead" in some kind of modernist progressive model, but that they offer the clearest evidence of certain general trends.

Consider that rates of cohabitation rate in the United States have traditionally been much lower than the rate in Canada. For instance, in 2001 the American cohabitation rate of 8.2 per cent was barely half the Canadian rate of 16.0 for the same year.

There are a number of explanations we could propose to account for this difference, including a greater attachment to religion and traditional family values in America. However,

the Quebec factor looms large in the analysis. In 2018, 11.8 per cent of all Canadians aged 15 and over were living in common-law relationships; in Quebec, the figure was nearly 10 percentage points higher, at 21.5 per cent. Figure 10.3 shows the ratio of cohabiting to married adults by province. In most provinces, cohabiting adults make up somewhere between 15 per cent and 19 per cent of the sample; in Quebec, the figure is 38.7 per cent! Quebec, in fact, is the only province with a cohabitation rate higher than the national average, which means that it is pulling the national average above the rates of all other provinces. This is why when we consider trends in the Canadian family, we have to look at Quebec to see how it aligns with the rest of the country.

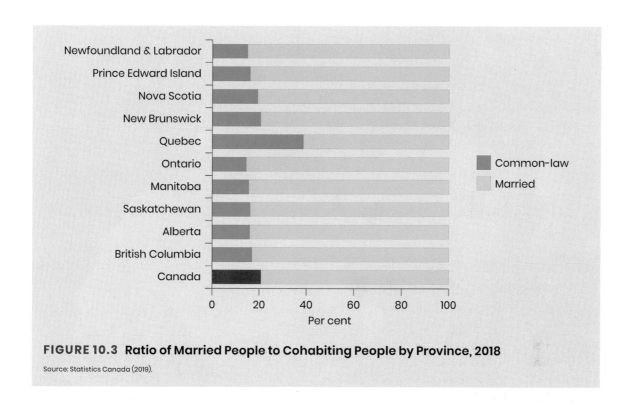

FIGURE 10.3 Ratio of Married People to Cohabiting People by Province, 2018

Source: Statistics Canada (2019).

2. The age of first marriage is rising.

The average age of first marriage in Canada has risen steadily since the early 1970s, but as Figure 10.4 shows, it wasn't until the 1990s that the figures really began to climb.

Again, because Statistics Canada stopped tracking marriage rates in 2011, we have no first-marriage

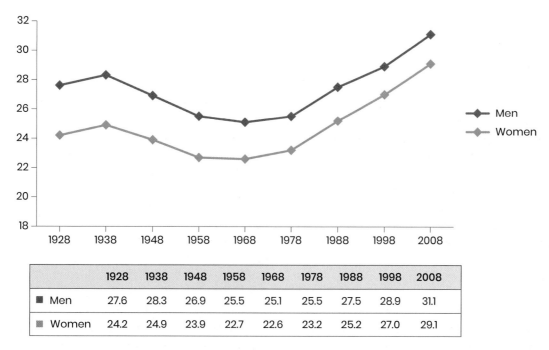

	1928	1938	1948	1958	1968	1978	1988	1998	2008
■ Men	27.6	28.3	26.9	25.5	25.1	25.5	27.5	28.9	31.1
■ Women	24.2	24.9	23.9	22.7	22.6	23.2	25.2	27.0	29.1

FIGURE 10.4 Average Age at First Marriage by Sex, Canada, 1928–2008

Source: Human Resources and Skills Development Canada (2014).

Victor de Jesus / UNP for Channel 4 TV

Shows like *Say Yes to the Dress* and *My Big Fat Gypsy Wedding* celebrate the commercial and secular aspects of the modern wedding ceremony. But even stripped of its religious significance, the wedding remains for many people an important rite of passage that distinguishes marriage from living together in an important way. To you, how important is the institution of marriage? In what ways does it differ from living together? How much do you think your answer is influenced by factors such as your age, your sex, and your sexual orientation?

rates for the years since 2008. However, we do know that the percentage of Canadians under 30 who have never married or lived common-law rose from 77.3 per cent in 2008 to 78.9 per cent in 2018 (Statistics Canada 2019). It's not a large climb, but it is a steady climb. Provincial percentages range from a low of 74.1 per cent in Alberta to a high of 82.2 per cent in Ontario (in this case, Quebec is not an outlier.) Questions arise. Will young people continue to defer marriage, or has this trend peaked? What is the cause for the high percentage of people under 30 who have never married or lived in a common-law relationship? How does this trend relate to the decline in the marriage rate noted in the last section?

What Do YOU Think?

Having recently paid a small fortune for our son's wedding, I am left wondering—sociologically, not parentally—why it is that "middle-class" weddings have become increasingly expensive over the last decade or so. Is it the influence of the shows noted in the caption to the photo above? Is it related to the decline in the religious aspect of weddings? Does it have to do with the need to put on a big show in order to make it worthwhile for family members attending from far away? What do you think?

The Point Is...

Child Marriage Is More Common Than You Probably Think It Is

As you read the title above, you may have imagined that I was going to focus on Muslim couples in South Asia or the Middle East. If you did, you were wrong. Instead, let's turn our attention to the United States, where the majority of child marriages take place between Christians.

Almost every provincial, territorial, and state jurisdiction in North America follows the principle that once you reach the age of 18, you can legally marry without parental consent; if you are 16 or 17, you need the consent of one of your parents. But almost half of the states in the United States have no minimum age for marriage, provided a judge approves the union. Remember, of course, that most judges are older men.

While accurate statistics are hard to obtain, a report published in *The New York Times* (Reiss, 2015) sheds some light on the situation in one state, New Jersey, between 1995 and 2012. During that period, the state licensed marriages involving 3481 people under the age of 18. Of that total, 163 of the people were aged 13, 14, or 15. Very rarely, these marriages may have involved two people under 18 marrying each other. However, 91 per cent of the under-18-year-olds were married to adults (18 and over), and 90 per cent of these minors were girls. According to the report, these cases involved "age differences that could have triggered statutory-rape charges, not a marriage license" (Reiss, 2015). We can speculate that a good number of these marriages were arranged by parents, and that the underage parties were forced to marry against their will. Complicating the matter is the fact that no one under 18 can legally apply for divorce.

A more recent report that appeared in the British newspaper *The Independent* (Baynes, 2017) claimed that in the United States between 2000 and 2015, a total of 207,468 marriages took place in which at least one of the partners (girls in 87 per cent of the cases) was a minor. Tennessee led the shock parade with three 10-year-old girls marrying partners who were, 24, 25, and 31. In a strange exception to the trend, an 11-year-old boy married a 27-year-old woman in the same state.

It is worth noting that the statistics that appeared in both reports came from Unchained at Last, a New Jersey–based group campaigning to abolish child marriage. At the same time, the reported figures may actually understate the real number of child marriages in the United States, since statistics on the subject are not always well managed, and some states provided no statistics at all on the subjct.

What Do YOU Think?

1. What sociological factors might contribute to child marriage in the United States? Income? Religion? What about teen pregnancy and "family honour"?
2. If you were in a position to draft policy on child marriage, what laws would you propose?

3. There are more divorces overall, but the rate is falling.

Analyzing divorce statistics can be complicated. If you ask a group of people whether they think the divorce rate is rising or falling, they would probably say that it's going up. This is not the case. The rate has jumped on several occasions over brief periods of time, but we can account for these, in part, by looking at changes to the legislation surrounding divorce.

In 1961, there were 6563 divorces in Canada, producing a divorce rate of 36.0 per 100,000 population. In 1968, the grounds for divorce were expanded in most of Canada: no longer was adultery the sole grounds for divorce. From 1968 to 1969, the divorce rate shot up from 54.8 per 100,000 to 124.5. Remember that the average age of first marriage was at an all-time low in the 1960s. This is significant as there is an inverse correlation between age at marriage and the likelihood of divorce (i.e. the younger the couple, the greater the chance the marriage will end in divorce).

By 1982, the number of divorces had peaked at a rate of roughly 280 per 100,000 population. Then, in 1985, the Divorce Act was changed again to permit divorce on the grounds of "marital breakdown." By 1987, the numbers had peaked again, this time producing a rate of 363.75 divorces per 100,000. (My divorce was in 1988, not contributing to the record.) By 2002, the numbers were back down to mid-1970s levels: a total of 70,155 divorces for a rate of 223.7.

As with other marriage data, Statistics Canada stopped collecting regular information on divorces in 2011. However, Mary Bess Kelly, for a 2012 Statistics Canada *Juristat* article, collected data on the number of divorce cases initiated in a sample of six provinces and territories (Ontario, Nova Scotia, BC, Nunavut, Yukon, and Northwest Territories). She reported that the number of cases fell by 8 per cent between 2006 and 2011, decreasing each year (Kelly, 2012). That's good news for marriage, right?

Not necessarily. It is possible that some married couples are staying together longer, particularly if we look at falling divorce rates in the context of what else we have learned in this chapter—specifically, that people are marrying later and marrying less. It suggests that people today are being more selective in their marriage choices, perhaps leading to greater levels of commitment. However, it could also be that divorce rates have fallen because a greater proportion of couples are living common-law, meaning that fewer couples require formal divorces when their relationships end. Finally, consider this: we know that the average age of first marriage in 2008 was roughly 30. Those people would have been 9 years old in 1987, when divorce was at an all-time high in Canada. What effect do you think it might have on your commitment to marriage if you grew up in a household that experienced marital discord and breakup? Is it possible you might be more likely to stay in a less-than-perfect marriage to avoid putting your own children through the kind of situation you went through growing up?

4. More women are having children in their thirties.

In 2010, the average age of a woman giving birth in Canada surpassed 30, a figure not seen since the 1930s (Statistics Canada, 2016, Chart 1). This signifies that

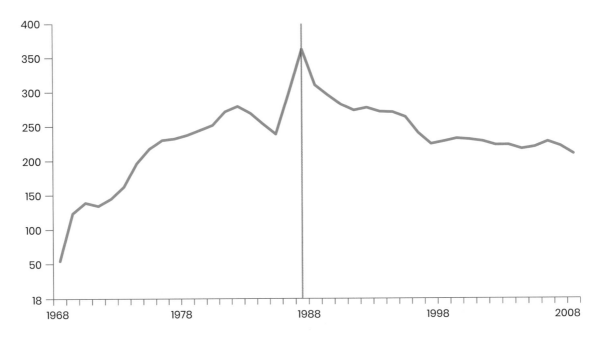

FIGURE 10.5 Crude Divorce Rate in Canada, 1968–2008

Source: Statistics Canada CANSIM Table 053-0002.

the number of women in their thirties giving birth is increasing. Not only that: the number of women in their thirties giving birth *for the first time* is also increasing. In 1987, 4 per cent of women who gave birth for the first time were aged 35 and older; by 2011, the percentage had tripled to 12 per cent. Over the same period, the percentage of first-time mothers who were over 30 increased from 15 per cent to 28 per cent.

Another way of looking at this is by considering what proportion of all births were to women aged 30 and older (Figure 10.6). As the table below shows, just under one-fifth of all births in 1975 were to women over 30; by 2015, well over half (56.4 per cent) of all births were to women over 30.

Percentage of All Births by Women over 30					Change
Year	1975	1985	1995	2005	2015	
Percentage	19.2	27.8	42.5	48.9	56.4	+37.2%

Source: Statistics Canada CANSIM Table 102-4503, Table 13-10-0416-01.

At the other end of the scale, births to mothers in their teens, we see a sharply contrasting profile. From 1995 to 2015, the proportion of births to young women under 20 decreased to just 2.5 per cent. While not the sole reason for the decrease, improved access to abortions since 1988, when the Supreme Court struck down Canada's anti-abortion laws, has certainly played a role in the decrease in teen childbearing.

Percentage of All Births by Teens					Change
Year	1995	2000	2005	2010	2015	
Percentage	6.3	5.3	4.1	3.9	2.5	−3.8%

Source: Statistics Canada CANSIM Table 102-4503, Table 13-10-0416-01.

There are significant regional differences in teen pregnancy today. In 2017, Quebec, British Columbia, and Ontario had the lowest percentages of births to mothers in their teens, at 1.4 per cent, 1.5 per cent, and 1.6 per cent, respectively (Statistics Canada, CANSIM Table 13-10-0416-01). The provinces with the highest percentages of births to young women under 20 were Saskatchewan and Manitoba (4.7 per cent). Nunavut was an extreme outlier with a rate of 17.7 per cent. The provincial/territorial differences roughly correlate with differences among urban and rural populations. Canadian regions with the highest percentages of rural residents have the greatest

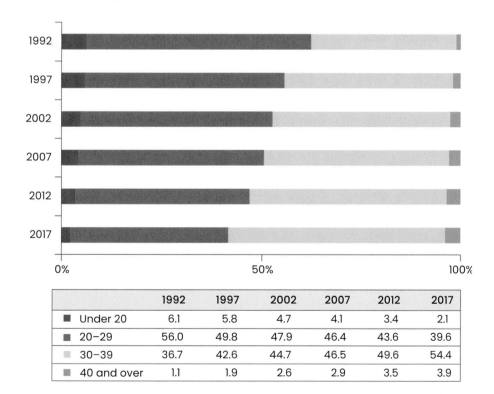

	1992	1997	2002	2007	2012	2017
■ Under 20	6.1	5.8	4.7	4.1	3.4	2.1
■ 20–29	56.0	49.8	47.9	46.4	43.6	39.6
■ 30–39	36.7	42.6	44.7	46.5	49.6	54.4
■ 40 and over	1.1	1.9	2.6	2.9	3.5	3.9

FIGURE 10.6 Percentage of Live Births in Canada by Age of Mother, 1992–2017 (Select Years)

Source: Statistics Canada, Table 13-10-0416-01, Live births by age of mother.

Average Age of Mother at Birth of First Child								
Year	1945	1955	1965	1975	1985	1995	2005	2015
Age	25.2	24.1	23.5	24.3	25.5	26.3	28.0	29.2

Source: Statistics Canada, 2016b, Chart 1; Provencher, Milan, Hallman, & D'Aoust, 2018, Table 4.

number of teenage mothers. Is this coincidence, or do you think that living in a rural community is a causal factor in teen pregnancy? What other factors might be involved?

An interesting set of statistics related to this is the average age of mother at the birth of her first child, which has a different profile:

Plotting the average age of the first-time mother in Canada shows a steady drop from the mid-1940s to the mid-1960s, followed by a gradual climb that hasn't yet stopped (Figure 10.7). It's no coincidence that the shape of this graph is nearly identical to the line in Figure 10.4, depicting the average age at first marriage. Following a decade of economic depression, the Second World War (1939–45) caused young people to delay marriage and childbearing until soldiers returned home in the mid-1940s. The age of first marriage and first birth fell from that time until the 1960s, when the women began to pursue higher education and participate in the workforce in greater numbers. At the same time, the sexual revolution changed social attitudes that had frowned upon sex before marriage and the use of contraception. The war had caused families to delay

marriage and childbearing out of necessity; the sixties brought new freedoms that enabled couples to delay marriage and childbearing by choice.

In 2014, the age-specific fertility rate for women in their early forties (10.9 births per 1,000 women) surpassed the rate for women in their late teens (10.2). You may see those two figures as being so close that they are nearly identical, but don't discount the significance of this landmark. After all, just 15 years earlier, the fertility rate for women in their early forties was barely one-quarter that the rate of women in their late teens. Historically, the age-specific fertility rate for young women aged 15 to 19 was high throughout the late 1940s all the way to the 1960s. In 1959—the peak of the baby boom—it was 59.7 births per 1000 women, nearly 6 times the 2014 rate for this age group! In general, the period throughout the 1980s to the present has seen the lowest fertility rates for young women in the data observed since 1926. Meanwhile, since 2014, the fertility rate for women aged 40–44 continues to climb and sits (as of 2016) at 11.5 births per 1000 women. While that represents the highest rate for this age group since 1970, it is still around one-fifth of the rate at its peak in 1926

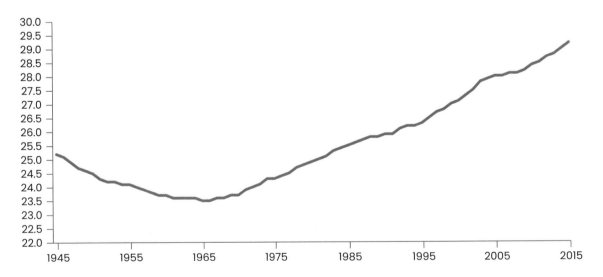

FIGURE 10.7 Average Age of Mother at First Birth, 1945–2015

Source: Statistics Canada, 2016B, Chart 1; Provencher, Milan, Hallman, & D'aoust, 2018, Table 4.

(50.6) (Milan, 2013; Provencher, Milan, Hallman & D'Aoust, 2018).

An important factor to consider when looking at delays in childbearing is **fecundity**, the physical ability to conceive. This ability changes during a woman's fourth decade. Estimates are that 91 per cent of women at the age of 30 are physically able to become pregnant. This drops to 77 per cent for women aged 35 and just 53 per cent of women at 40 (Rajulton, Balakrisnhan, & Ravanera, 1990). It could be that the fact that more women are waiting longer to have their first child is having a lowering effect on the *total fertility rate, the subject of the next section.*

5. The number of children per family has dropped below the "replacement rate."

The **total fertility rate** is an estimate of the average number of children that a cohort of women between the ages of 15 and 49 will have in their lifetime if current factors remain constant during their reproductive years. It's a projection, in other words, based on current fertility rates, even though we know that these actual rates will change.

Figure 10.8 shows the trending total fertility rate from 1921 to 2016. In 2002 the total fertility rate in Canada bottomed out at 1.51; after a short recovery, it fell again beginning in 2009, and currently (as of 2016) sits at 1.54, just a hair above that low-water

mark reached in 2002. How does this compare with the rate for other countries? Rates for the 100 most populous countries in the world in 2014 ranged from 2.22 to 6.89, with 9 of the top 10 fertility rates being in Africa. Those countries with fertility rates below Canada's include eastern European countries, such as the Czech Republic (1.43); some Mediterranean countries, including Italy (1.42), Greece (1.41), and Portugal (1.52); and several East Asian countries—Singapore (0.80), Hong Kong (1.17), Japan (1.40), South Korea (1.25), and Taiwan (1.11). In each of these countries, the population is expected to fall. Why do you think their fertility rates are so low? Is it just economics (national and family), or is some pessimistic sense of the future involved as well?

Consider the following. Of women born between 1927 and 1931, 31.0 per cent had five or more children. Compare that with women born between 1952 and 1956, of whom just 1.3 per cent had five or more children. Among the latter group, 38.3 per cent had just two children, and 33.7 per cent had one child or no children, meaning that a total of 72.0 per cent of women born in 1952–6 had two children or fewer, compared with 42.7 per cent of women born from 1927 to 1931.

Figure 10.8 also shows the **replacement rate**, the number of children that the average woman must bear if the overall population is to continue at the same level. The replacement rate is 2.1, meaning that 2.1 children must be born for every woman in

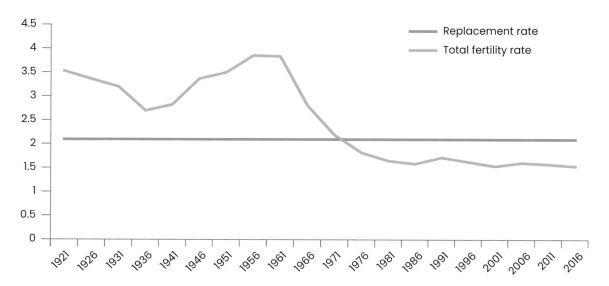

FIGURE 10.8 Canada's Total Fertility Rate since 1921

Source: Statistics Canada, Canadian Vital Statistics, Birth Database, Survey 3231, and Demography Division, Population Estimates Program.

a population aged 15 to 49 in order for the population to hold constant. As Figure 10.8 shows, it's been almost 50 years since Canada had a total fertility rate above the replacement rate.

So what does a country do when its national fertility rate is below the replacement rate? Canada makes up for its low fertility rate with high levels of immigration. Take note, however, that immigrants from countries with higher fertility rates soon begin to reproduce at a rate consistent with the fertility rate here in this country.

Are there ways to boost the fertility rate? Would government incentives—a "baby bonus"—help to offset the cost of having and raising children? Would a system of universal, publicly funded daycare change things significantly? Both of those mechanisms are used in Quebec, whose fertility rate has been falling and now sits just a little above the national average at 1.59 (as of 2016). (The highest provincial rate is Saskatchewan's, at 1.93—still below replacement; the lowest rate belongs to BC: 1.40.) Recent studies in the United States suggest that women are willing to have more children when their husbands are willing to take a greater share of responsibility for childcare and general housework. How significant a factor do you think that could be?

6. There nearly as many couples without children as with.

Related to the decline in the total fertility rate is this statistic: the proportion of couples living *with* children has been surpassed by the proportion of couples living *without* children. In 2001, couples with children made up 43.6 per cent of all census families, while couples without children accounted for 40.3 per cent. In 2006, the proportion of childless couples topped the share of couples with children for the first time (42.7 per cent versus 41.4 per cent), and by 2011, the gap had spread considerably (44.5 per cent versus 39.2 per cent).

We have to be careful not to jump to hasty conclusions. This is just a 10-year trend, which is pretty short, by demographers' standards. The 2016 census shows a modest reversal, with the ratio of couples with children to couples without at 51.1 to 48.9. Still, it's worth asking: Are these figures explained by the fact that women are waiting longer to have their first child? Or do they have more to do with the fact that Canada's overall population is aging, which means there are more older couples whose grown-up children have left home? If you're thinking the latter, consider the following.

The Point Is...

The "Typical" Family Has Changed a Lot in Sixty Years

Between 1948 and 1953, sociologists John Seeley, Alexander Sim, and Elizabeth Loosley studied a white, upper-middle-class neighbourhood in North Toronto, which they nicknamed "Crestwood Heights." The following is a brief introduction to their chapter on the family:

> The family of Crestwood Heights . . . consists of father, mother, and two (rarely more) children. The children are healthy, physically well developed, attractively dressed, and poised as to outward behavior. The mother, assured in manner, is as like an illustration from *Vogue* or *Harper's Bazaar* as financial means and physical appearance will allow. The father, well tailored, more or less successful in radiating an impression of prosperity and power, rounds out the family group.
>
> This small family unit is both lone and love-based. It is, more often than not, formed by the marriage of two persons from unrelated and often unacquainted families . . . who are assumed to have chosen each other because they are "in love." Other reasons for the choice (perpetuation of property within one family, the linking of business or professional interest, an unadorned urge to upward social mobility and so on), even

if influential, could not reputably be admitted as grounds for marriage.

This family unit is not embedded in any extended kinship system. The newly formed family is frequently isolated geographically and often socially from the parental families. It is expected that the bride and groom will maintain a separate dwelling removed by varying degrees of distance from that of each set of parents. ... The isolation of each family acts to decrease the ability of the family to transmit traditional patterns of behavior, which might otherwise be absorbed from close contact with, for instance, grandparents. The absence

of kinship bonds also tends to concentrate the emotional life of the family upon a few individuals.... (Seeley, Sim, & Loosely, 1956, pp. 159–60. © University of Toronto Press, 1955. Reprinted by permission of the publisher.)

What Do YOU Think?

Identify a middle-class neighbourhood in the city or town where you live and go to school. Give it a fictitious name, and then write a brief description of the "typical" family that lives there today. How much (or how little!) does your family sketch differ from this description of the Crestwood Heights family?

7. Children are leaving home at a later age.

The term **cluttered nest** is sometimes used to describe the phenomenon in which adult children continue to live at home with their parents (the opposite, **empty nest**, describes a household in which children have moved out to live on their own). In 1981, 33.6 per cent of women aged 20 to 24 and 51.4 per cent of men of the same age were living with a parent or parents; by 1996, those figures had risen to 50.4 per cent and 64.3 per cent, respectively (Beaujot, 2000, p. 98). The rates have levelled off somewhat since then: as of the 2016 census, 57.6 per cent of women aged 20 to 24 and 65.7 per cent of men aged 20 to 24 were living at home (Figure 10.9). Note that if you are a student away at university but you return to the home of your parents or grandparents for the summer, you are still considered to be living at home, despite the independence you probably feel from September to April.

Causation is easy to establish. First, it takes more time and education nowadays to establish a career. Some adults living with parents are "boomerang kids," who have returned home after going away to college or university, prior to setting up on their own. Second, there is the higher cost of living, including rising housing prices, and a number of

costs that earlier generations didn't have to face. (As a child, I never had to pay for wifi.) Among Canadian cities, you will find the highest proportion of young adults (aged 20–34) living with parents in Toronto, with its scarcity of affordable rental housing and notoriously high cost of living (Statistics Canada, 2017b); in fact, Ontario is home to the top 7 cities on this list. And then, with couples marrying later and later in life, it takes that much longer to set up a dual-earner household, the only model that is financially viable for some people who want to move out of their parents' home.

8. There are more lone-parent families.

The number of lone-parent families in Canada has been increasing since 1966 (which followed a 35-year period of decrease from 13.6 per cent during the Depression year of 1931). In 1966, 8.2 per cent of all families were lone-parent families; since then, the figure has risen steadily, to 12.7 per cent in 1986, 14.5 per cent in 1996, and 15.9 in 2006 (Statistics Canada, 2012, p. 5). Since then the number has dropped to 14.2 as of 2016 (Statistics Canada, Table 11-10-0017-01).

People often speculate about the negative effects on children of living in lone-parent households,

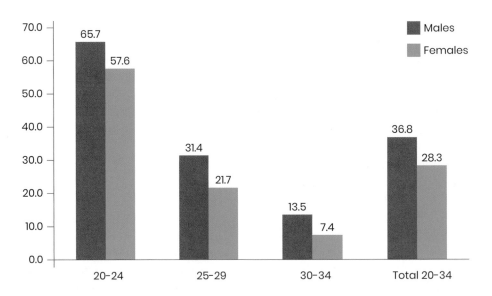

FIGURE 10.9 Percentage of Young Adults Living with Parents or Grandparents

Source: Statistics Canada, 2016 Census of Population, Statistics Canada Catalogue no. 98-400-X2016028.

Arne9001 / Dreamstime.com

Does it surprise you that young men (20–34) are more likely than young women to be living at home with their parents? Why do you think this is the case?

particularly with regard to school dropout rates and criminal activity. The critics need to be cautious here, though, as most lone-parent households began as two-parent households. It is hard to determine whether unfavourable conditions existing in the pre-divorce or pre-separation family—an abusive parent perhaps, or parental fighting—could have been the real cause of a child's crime or truancy. You can't just blame the lone-parent situation.

Another trend that must be considered, though it is difficult to document, is the planned lone-parent household, which has not resulted from the breakup of a marriage or common-law relationship. Adoption as well as advances in fertility technology give individuals today various avenues to become a parent without having to be in a traditional heterosexual union.

9. There are more people living alone.

In 1996, Beaujot (2000, p. 117) reported, 12 per cent of the entire Canadian population aged 15 and over were living alone; the rate was highest for those over 85 (48 per cent), and lowest for those younger than 55 (10 per cent). By 2016, the overall percentage of Canadians living alone had climbed to 13.9 per cent (Statistics Canada (2017a).). The percentage of adult women living alone is greater than the percentage of adult men living alone (14.5 per cent versus 13.1 per cent); the fact that women tend to outlive men contributes significantly to this difference, as Figure 10.10 shows.

A Statistics Canada publication offers an interesting comparison. In an examination of the changing percentages for one-person and five-or-more-person households, the authors note,

In 2006, there were three times as many one-person households as households with five or more people. Of the 12.4 million private households, 27 per cent were one-person households, while 9 per cent were large households of five or more people.

In 1941, 6 per cent of houses were comprised of one person, while 38 per cent were comprised of five or more people. (Statistics Canada, 2009)

We can update the picture with data from the 2016 census.

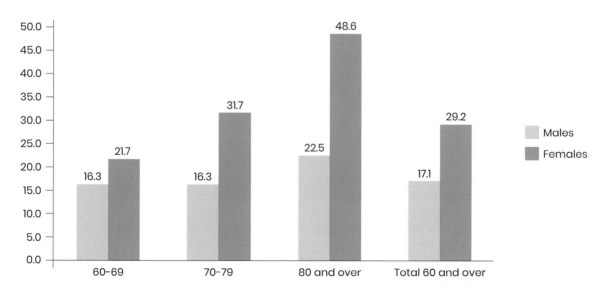

FIGURE 10.10 Percentage of Canadian Males and Females Living Alone over Age 60

Source: Statistics Canada (2017a).

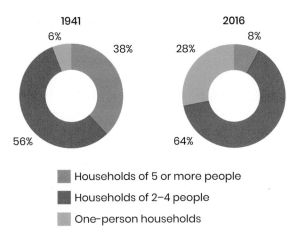

FIGURE 10.11 **Households in Canada: 1941 and 2016**

Family in Quebec

By just about every statistical measure, the family in Quebec is sociologically distinct from the family in other parts of Canada. For example, consider that Quebec has been the province with

- *the highest cohabitation rate*: 38.7 per cent of all couples, almost twice the

national average (20.9 per cent) and the second-highest provincial rate (behind only New Brunswick, at 10.6 per cent) (see Figure 10.3)

- *the lowest marriage rate*: 2.9 per 100,000, significantly lower than the next lowest rate (Ontario and Manitoba, tied at 4.9, based on 2008 data)
- *the highest divorce rate*: 69.2 per 100 marriages, far ahead of Ontario's rate of 46.7 (again, based on the latest data we have, from 2008)
- *the highest number of divorces* among couples married less than 30 years, with 61.0 per 100 marriages (Ontario's rate of 43.1 was the next highest).

Quick Hits

Delayed Life Transitions

In his article "Delayed Life Transitions: Trends and Implications," University of Western Ontario demographer **Rod Beaujot** linked together some of the trends discussed in this section as part of a phenomenon he calls delayed life transitions.

We go through a number of major life transitions in our lifetime—getting a full-time job, moving out to live on our own, getting married, having children, retiring, and so on. During the prosperous socioeconomic times of the 1950s, 1960s, and early 1970s, people went through what we could call "sped-up life transitions," making these major life changes at a relatively young age. The situation has changed considerably, as Beaujot observes, and people today are making these transitions later and later in life.

Which brings us to some questions. First, to what extent is our current speed of life transition "delayed," and to what extent is it simply "normal"? It may seem normal to you to live at home with your parents until your late twenties, when you've settled into a career and have paid off some of your student debt, but to be living at home would have seemed abnormal for a typical North American 30-year-old of your parents' generation. What are the implications for today's college and university students of having parents who went through life transitions at a much more advanced speed, perhaps at a rate that was "less normal" than now? And which version of "normal" is better, anyway?

TABLE 10.2 Support for Changing the Definition of Marriage to Include Same-Sex Unions, by Region, 2003

	Agree somewhat (%)	Agree strongly (%)	Total (%)
Quebec	*36*	*25*	*61*
British Columbia	26	25	51
Atlantic Provinces	19	26	45
Ontario	19	23	42
Prairies	16	17	33

Source: TNS Canadian Facts (2003). The study was conducted by TNS Canadian Facts (formerly NFO CF group), one of Canada's leading full-service marketing, opinion and social research organizations.

In 2011, Quebec was the province with the greatest number of total births by single (never married) women. By percentage (58.5 per cent), the province trailed only Nunavut (New Brunswick was the next closest province at 47.5 per cent). At the start of the century, Quebec also had the greatest percentage of births to women who were divorced (2.1 per cent in 2002), but has since dropped to sixth place (1.2 per cent in 2011). Why might this one ranking have changed?

Another feature unique to Quebec is the province-wide support for same-sex marriage well ahead of its legalization (see Table 10.2). In a poll conducted among 10,015 Canadian adults in August 2003, residents of Quebec showed the greatest support for changing the legal definition of marriage. In March 2004, it became the third province (following Ontario and BC) to legally recognize same-sex marriage.

In social statistician Reginald Bibby's 1995 Project Canada survey, Quebec had the highest rate of approval for premarital and extramarital sex (1995, p. 76), with 88 per cent supporting the former (compared with 82 per cent, the next highest, in BC) and 24 per cent supporting the latter (compared with 14 per cent, the next highest, in the Prairies).

Quebec residents have also shown a difference when it comes to parenting, as indicated by a *Globe and Mail*/CTV poll of 648 Canadian parents conducted by Ipsos-Reid and published in *The Globe and Mail* on 10 April 2004. The poll noted the following results:

Percentage of parents who said they spanked their children for disciplinary reasons:

Alberta	60%
British Columbia	52%
Saskatchewan/Manitoba	46%
Ontario	45%
Atlantic Provinces	42%
Quebec	22%

Percentage of parents who agreed that using flashcards at an early age makes kids smarter:

British Columbia	71%
Saskatchewan/Manitoba	67%
Alberta	63%
Ontario	60%
Atlantic Provinces	57%
Quebec	25%

In case you're wondering, section 43 of Canada's Criminal Code still permits teachers, parents, and "persons standing in the place of a parent" to use reasonable force to discipline a pupil or child under their care, provided "the force does not exceed what is reasonable under the circumstances" (Revised Statutes of Canada, c. C-34, s. 43).

What should we make of this? First, it is noteworthy that a number of the statistical indicators discussed show a major change from the situation in Quebec prior to the **Quiet Revolution** of the 1960s. Take divorce. Prior to 1968, if you were living in Quebec and you wanted a divorce, you had to seek it through federal Parliament. A growing separation from the Catholic Church since the 1960s has been cited as a possible explanation for the rising divorce rate. Yet in the 2011 National Household Survey—the last national survey that gathered information on Canadians' religious affiliation—Quebec had the second-lowest rate of residents declaring they had "no religious affiliation" (a rate of 12.1 per cent, ahead of only Newfoundland and Labrador and well below the national average of 23.9 per cent). Of course, being affiliated with the Church and being influenced by it can be two different matters. The Catholic Church considers abortion a sin, but in 2005—the last year for Statistics Canada provided this information—Quebec, the most Catholic province, led all provinces with an abortion rate of 7.6 per 1000 women, or 372.5 per 1000 live births (trailing only Northwest Territories in the latter statistic).

Can we say that family life is falling apart in Quebec? After all, since 1981, Quebec has had the highest growth in the number of citizens living alone, and in 2016 led all other provinces with 17.7 per cent of the population living alone. Three Quebec cities—Trois-Rivières, Sherbrook, and Quebec City—had the highest rates of living alone in Canada. Could this be attributed to the fact there are more older people in Quebec living on their own? It's a good guess, but it's wrong: Among people 85 and over, Quebec has a relatively low rate of living alone, thanks to a higher-than-average rate of older people living together in retirement homes (Tang, Galbraith, & Truong, 2019, p. 13). Statistics Canada proposes that "many of the sociocultural and economic developments that occurred in Quebec . . . [during] the Quiet Revolution included an evolution toward a more individualistic orientation that may have led to more persons living alone by choice" (Tang, Galbraith, & Truong, 2019, p. 13).

A more likely interpretation for Quebec's dissimilarity from the rest of Canada is that the province went through more rapid modernization and outright change during the last 40 years than any other province. The falling away of old structures does not mean the falling apart of the institutions. Québécois are perhaps best seen as reinventing family as they are reinventing other institutions—political, religious, and educational.

Telling It Like It Is   A Student's POV

Telling Your Family You're Gay

Growing up in the small town of Whitby, Ontario, I never felt the negative effects of discrimination. I am an English-speaking, Caucasian female and had never been a part of a minority group, in any sense of the word. At the age of 21, this changed, and I became aware of how easily people are judged. I am a lesbian, and from the moment I became open about my sexual preferences, I felt firsthand what it feels like to be viewed based solely on one aspect of your life, and not as an entire person. When meeting someone new in my life it was as though I was wearing a sign on my forehead reading, "I am gay," and it was perceived as "I am gay . . . that is everything you need to know about me." Once I divulge this information, almost instantly people form opinions on who I am as a person and who I should be. They develop expectations that quite often are illogical and unrealistic. By writing a paper such as this one, I am being given the opportunity to address a few of these numerous stereotypes and prejudiced beliefs. Hopefully, I can educate some to stop these beliefs from spreading.

From my experience, the original thought that people tend to have when finding out that I am gay is that it is simply a phase I am going through, a time of experimentation and rebellious behaviour. My brother's reaction was as such. He believed that it was just a phase and that it would pass. He continued to express this for an entire year after I had told him. He realizes otherwise now. . . . When telling my mother . . . , I was shocked to hear her initial reaction to what I had told her. After a moment or two of silence, she . . . said, "But I thought you wanted to get married and have kids one day." The thought of these dreams possibly fading away is what seemed to unsettle her the most. I found two things wrong and rather presumptuous about this statement. To begin with, the idea that a woman must want/need a husband and children to live a fulfilling life is old-fashioned and a step backward from the times we live in today. I figure, why can't a woman who is independent and who has a satisfying career be considered to lead a successful, happy life, despite the fact that she has no family to raise? Furthermore, my mother was correct in assuming that I did want a family, but it was not the family that she had in mind. Marriage and children are a large part of my future plans, and, with adoption, and artificial insemination, this is a very feasible option for lesbian couples. Simply because a woman falls in love with another woman, it does not mean that she didn't grow up with the same desire for nurturing children and caring for a home and family that a lot of heterosexual girls do.

Conjugal Roles

Conjugal (or **marital**) **roles** are the distinctive roles of the husband and wife that result from the division of labour within the family. The first important sociological study done on this subject was a 1957 work called *Family and Social Networks*, by Canadian/British social scientist **Elizabeth Bott** (1924–2016). Bott characterized conjugal roles as being either **segregated**—in which tasks, interests, and activities are clearly different—or **joint**, in which many tasks, interests, and activities are shared. These ideas came to be known as the **Bott hypothesis**. Her study was set against a backdrop in which men were primarily responsible for the financial support of the family, while women were primarily responsible for the housework and childcare. This was 1957, remember—how much do you think that situation has changed?

Earning and Caring: Changes in Conjugal Roles

In 2000, Rod Beaujot published *Earning and Caring in Canadian Families*. He wanted to study how conjugal roles were changing from a situation in which they were more or less *complementary* to one in which they were *companionate*. **Complementary roles** (like Bott's model of *segregated roles*) cast men primarily as earners or breadwinners, doing paid work, with women involved primarily in the unpaid work of childcare and housework. In **companionate** relationships (like Bott's *joint* relationship) the roles overlap.

Beaujot recognized that the shift from complementary/segregated conjugal roles to companionate/joint roles is far from complete. But he also stated that complete overlap was not necessarily possible, nor even desirable. Gender roles are different to a significant extent because men and women are different biologically. There is, however, a point at which we may be able to say that a basic fairness or justice has been reached. We are far from that point. As Beaujot documents, married women do more total work per day than married men do, even though married women are more likely to do part-time paid work. Married women, especially the mothers of small children, do much more *unpaid* work than married men do. And while women have caught up to men in their participation in the workforce, men have not gone as far in taking on new roles at home. This has created an imbalance in conjugal roles, where women take on what some sociologists have called a "**double burden**" or "**second shift**" (Hochschild & Machung, 1989). Canadian sociologists Pat Armstrong and Hugh Armstrong ([1978]/2010) used the term **double ghetto** to describe the marginalization working women experience in the workplace and in the home. The difficulty of correcting this imbalance in households with small children has led some women to conclude, pessimistically, that "childlessness is the easiest route to equality" (Beaujot, 2002).

In 1995, sociologist **M. Reza Nakhaie** published "Housework in Canada: The National Picture," a summary of his study demonstrating that gender was a greater factor than either relative income or amount of available time in determining how much housework an individual did. The author's most striking discovery concerned the relationship between gender, hours of paid work, and share of the housework. Nakhaie found an inverse relationship between the hours of paid work a man does and the size of his share of the housework: the more paid hours he has, the smaller his share of the housework. However, the same is not true for women. A direct relationship seems to exist over a particular number of hours of work: an increase over 30 in a woman's hours of paid work per week correlated to an *increase* in her contribution to housework.

A more recent study, by Houle, Turcotte, and Wendt (2017), appears to confirm these findings. The researchers found that mothers do more household work than fathers regardless of how much time they spend on paid work: on a typical workday, 86 per cent of Canadian mothers who worked 8 or more paid hours would spend additional time on household work, compared with 65 per cent of fathers who had worked 8 or more paid hours and 87 per cent of fathers who had participated in no paid work (Figure 10.12b). The same study found that between 1986 and 2015, the percentage of fathers who participated in household work had increased by 25 points, from 51 per cent to 76 per cent, but the percentage of mothers who performed household work did not change over the same period and was much higher (93 per cent; Figure 10.12a).

What does your reaction to this image tell you about our perception of the gender roles handed down by society?

The key to correcting the gender imbalance is to recognize that gender roles are not carved in stone. Rather, they are products of what Arlie Hochschild terms a **gender strategy**, which is "a plan of action through which a person tries to solve problems at hand, given the cultural notions of gender at play" (Hochschild & Machung, 1989, p. 15). These "problems at hand" include the fact that small children have to be taken care of. From the studies that Beaujot cites, it is clear that the typical strategy for infant care is for the mother to take time off, then to work part-time as the infant matures toward school age, eventually to try to go back to full-time work.

The responsibility for care of children is the main reason that married women are much more likely to work part-time than are married/unmarried men or unmarried women. It is also the cause of what Beaujot calls the **occupational segregation** of men and women. Women choose occupations in fields such as education and health care, which have the greatest flexibility in terms of childcare-related **work interruptions** (which include staying home to care for a sick child or taking a longer-term leave to care for a newborn). Beaujot presents something of a chicken-and-egg scenario: women seek out jobs in employment areas that offer greater flexibility, but part of the reason these jobs offer greater flexibility is that they are dominated by women. Do you think that as women enter traditionally male-dominated occupations in larger numbers, a similar flexibility will develop?

The Ethnic Factor in Conjugal Roles

One weakness of Beaujot's work is that he ignores the role of ethnocultural factors in the gendered division of household labour. A classic study of conjugal roles among North American immigrant groups is Sathi Dasgupta's "Conjugal Roles and Social Network in Indian Immigrant Families: Bott Revisited" (1992). Although the article was written over 25 years ago about South Asian immigrants in the United States, its findings have relevance to the situation in Canada today.

Dasgupta studied 25 couples and found that *segregated* conjugal roles dominated. The men were invariably the primary breadwinners and made virtually all major decisions affecting the household,

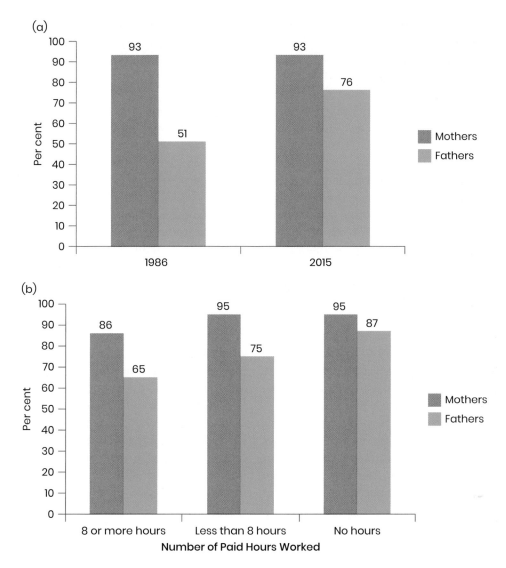

FIGURE 10.12 Percentage of Canadian Fathers and Mothers Performing Household Work

Source: Houle, Turcotte, & Wendt, 2017, Table 2.

while the women, with few exceptions, were full-time homemakers and primary caretakers of the children. Interestingly, however, there were aspects of joint conjugal roles among the immigrant families that would not be nearly as well accepted back in India. These include joint discussion of the children's education and of the couple's social life (with joint leisure activities the norm).

Change will come, as immigrants to North America adopt a more "Western" approach to dividing conjugal roles, but the ethnic factor still must be considered in any study of gender roles in the Canadian family.

Marrying "In" and Marrying "Out"

Endogamy is an anthropological term that means "marrying within." It refers to marrying someone of the same ethnic, religious, or cultural group as oneself. The opposite of endogamy, marrying *outside* of one's group, is **exogamy**.

Support for exogamy, once quite low in Canada, has increased, according to findings published by Bibby (see Table 10.3). However, I believe that this set of statistics gives a picture that is more positive than it is real. It seems more an expression of ideal

Italian Families and Conjugal Roles: Four Generations

When I think of the topic of gender in an Italian family, I laugh. The struggles between what it means to be male and what it means to be female arise so very often in my family, at every dinner and almost every conversation. The discussions are always split between the three generations because my grandmother lives with my parents and she never misses an opportunity to include her views. The eldest generation undeniably believes that the female's role in life is to be a complement to her husband; everything she does is based on his needs and his demands. All domestic duties and child-rearing except for punishment are her responsibility. Working outside the home is secondary to household work. The husband makes all decisions, although she can make suggestions. It is the male's responsibility to take care of the family financially.

My parents (second generation) feel similarly, the main difference being that the father should be very involved with the children, not solely in areas concerning punishment. Where my grandmother would discourage my father from helping around the house, my mother would welcome the help though not demand nor expect it. In this generation, family decisions are made together; however, household duties are still very divided, even with my mother working full-time outside the home. For the female, postsecondary education and career are second to marriage and family. The main female role in life is keeping a clean house, cooking good homemade food, and keeping everyone happy and healthy. The main male role is to keep the food on the table by providing the family with its main source of income.

The third generation around the dinner table changed things a little. This generation in my family consists of my husband and I, the middle brother and his wife, and the "baby brother." Most of us are in agreement that gender roles in the new Italian family have changed. No longer is the female solely responsible for all household duties. Husbands cook, clean, and change diapers, something my father had never done even with having three children! The females have postsecondary education and careers and are not a complement to their husbands, but an equal.

I also grew up with a huge double standard that affected me immensely in all areas of my life. It goes something like this: "This is what boys can do and this is what girls cannot do" (my father's infamous words). Boys can play all day and not help their mothers (girls can't), boys can fight and play rough (girls can't), boys have to do well in school (girls don't have to), boys can go out whenever they want (girls can't), boys have to play sports (girls don't have to), boys can stay out late (girls have to come home early).

"This is what girls must do and this is what boys do not have to do." Girls must cook and clean (boys do not), girls must learn the traditions (boys do not), girls must be good always (boys do not), girls must stay home to take care of the family (boys do not), girls must not be left alone with their boyfriends (boys can live with their girlfriends). I fought with my younger brothers fairly consistently growing up. The words, "that is not fair" were spoken often. I disliked one of my brothers for years. It was not until he got a family of his own that we began to grow closer together. We even talked about the jealousy we felt for one another over different family issues and how the double standards we grew up with had a great deal to do with it.

My family's views on gender have had a great impact on my life. It has carved me into the woman I am today. Much to my parents' chagrin, I cannot cook. I hate housecleaning, run away from tradition whenever I can. I am constantly in school working on a career, and even though I am married, I frequently go out with my friends and stay out late! Being married has been difficult at times also. I always have an intense instinct to run from the gender roles that surround me, and yet I realize that in many circumstances they are needed to preserve peace in a family. I now have many concerns for my daughter. I know she will not be faced with an obvious double standard, as I do not have any sons and I am fully aware that being completely opposite of the Martha Stewart–like woman is not anything to be proud of. Something in the middle would be nice. Since little girls are greatly influenced by their mothers, I know I must be really careful to set a positive female role in our family. I truly hope the difference for my daughter will be the ability for her to choose the woman she wants to be instead of madly running away from what I demand her to become.

—Alina Mucci

What Do YOU Think?

1. What kind of narrative do you think the writer's brothers would write about conjugal roles, based on their upbringing?
2. Do you foresee any gender role conflict concerning the writer and her daughter?

Blend Images / Alamy Stock Photo

Do you think Dasgupta's findings on the separation of conjugal roles among Indian families are applicable in Canada today? To what extent is the "ethnic factor" still at play?

culture than an indication of probable practice. After all, according to data from the 2011 National Household Survey, only 4.6 per cent of all married and common-law couples in Canada were mixed unions (Statistics Canada, 2014, p. 4). Table 10.4 shows which visible minority groups in Canada are most likely to form mixed unions.

For all of the visible minority groups shown in Table 10.4, only people of Japanese ancestry are more likely to form a mixed union; the majority of people in all other groups—including the two largest visible minority groups in Canada, South Asians and Chinese—marry or cohabit within their own group.

Bear in mind that this survey includes people born outside of Canada, who might have been married when they immigrated. Couples made up of people born in the same country overwhelmingly form non-mixed unions, and this is particularly the case for people born in the same country outside of Canada: 94 per cent of those couples were non-mixed. By comparison, 75 per cent of couples where both people were born in Canada were non-mixed (Statistics Canada, 2014, p. 5).

Remember, too, that at different times in its history, Canada has weighted the immigration of certain groups in favour of one sex (consider the pattern of early immigration among Filipino women, discussed in Chapter 9). What influence could factors like these have on the data?

TABLE 10.3 Canadians' Approval of Intergroup Marriage (%), 1975–2015

	1975	1980	1985	1990	1995	2000	2005	2015
Whites and Indigenous people	75	80	83	84	84	91	93	95
Whites and Asians	66	75	78	82	83	90	93	95
Whites and East Indians	58	66	72	77	80	87	91	92
Whites and blacks	57	64	72	79	81	88	92	94
Any other kinds of racial or cultural mixed unions	—	—	—	—	—	—	—	93
Protestants and Catholics	86	88	89	90	92	93	95	—
Protestants and Jews	80	84	84	86	90	91	93	—
Roman Catholics and Jews	78	81	82	85	89	91	92	—
Christians and people of other world faiths	—	—	—	—	—	90	90	89

Source: Reginald W. Bibby, Project Canada Survey Series.

TABLE 10.4 Mixed Couples by Visible Minority Group, 2011

Visible Minority Group	Number of Couples	Mixed Unions (%)		Non-mixed Unions (%)
South Asian	407,510	13.0		87.0
Chinese	351,640	19.4		80.6
Black	167,950	40.2		59.8
Filipino	155,700	29.8		70.2
Latin American	112,265	48.2		51.8
Arab	94,315	25.4		74.6
Southeast Asian	74,560	21.9		78.1
West Asian	51,300	19.5		80.5
Korean	41,370	22.5		77.5
Japanese	32,820	78.8		21.3
Multiple visible minorities	40,415	65.9		35.1
Other visible minority	27,215	52.4		47.6
All visible minorities	**1,557,060**	**27.0**		**73.0**

Note: A mixed couple is any common-law or marital relationship comprising one spouse or partner who is a member of a visible minority group and one who is not, as well as couples comprising two members of different visible minority groups.

Source: Statistics Canada, 2014.

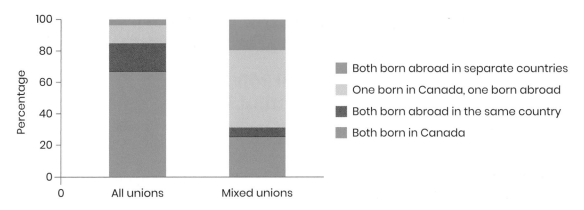

FIGURE 10.13 Composition of Canadian Unions and Canadian Mixed Unions, 2011

Source: Statistics Canada, 2014, p. 4.

What Do YOU Think?

1. Consider Table 10.4. Do you think that Canadians' attitudes toward exogamy are different from what they were 10 years ago?
2. Have you ever been involved in a relationship with someone from a different ethnic or cultural group? If so, what kinds of challenges did you face? If not, could you imagine yourself in such a relationship?

Based on findings from the 2006 census, Milan, Maheux, and Chui (2010) report that people in mixed unions "were younger, did better socio-economically, and were more likely to live in large CMAs [census metropolitan areas]" than non-mixed couples. How could you account for these facts?

Telling It Like It Is

The Religious Factor in Conjugal Roles: Polygamy and the Case of Bountiful, BC

In the aptly named commune village of Bountiful, British Columbia, there is a long history of **polygamy** (many marriages) or **polygyny** (many wives) practised by the leaders of the Fundamentalist Church of Latter Day Saints, an offshoot of the Mormon Church. The commune has attracted attention and criticism, stemming mainly from reports of forced and underage marriage and the abuse of women and children. Beginning in the 1990s, the community was the focus of policy investigations and attempts to enforce Canada's anti-polygamy laws on the commune.

The following quotations are taken from the testimony of a woman in her forties, given in a BC Supreme Court case examining the constitutionality of Canada's laws against plural marriages. The mother of nine children married one of the leaders when she was 16; her husband was already married to her older sister. She herself has nearly 30 siblings; her father had five wives. The woman is well educated, with six years of postsecondary training in nursing, elder care, and midwifery.

I did not know him well; I knew he was in good standing in the church. . . .

He (my father) told me, "You do not have to marry him if you don't want to." I felt good about him, and I married him. My sister wife and I have lived at times in the same home, we've lived in different homes. I feel that we are both very committed in having a good relationship with each other. . . .

I feel my husband really supported me through my years of education and he really has been a life-long friend to me, as well as watched my children when I went to school. . . .

CP/AP Photo/Joe Sales

Students play an afternoon game of basketball at Bountiful Elementary-Secondary School. What relationship between these women does the photo appear to convey?

I believe that there's so many people in mainstream society that make so many assumptions about us that we are treated with bias and prejudice, and that affects my everyday life. If I wanted to go anywhere and get any sort of counselling in mainstream society, I feel like I would not be accepted....

My beliefs are that living plural marriage isn't for everyone. . . . ("Plural Wife Describes Life in Bountiful Commune," 2011)

In November 2011, the chief justice of the Supreme Court in BC ruled that the ban against polygamy was constitutional, even though it violated the religious freedom of this group. Protecting the rights of the women and the children, he ruled, was of greater importance than protecting the religious freedom of the commune's residents. This paved the way for the trial of two former religious leaders of the Bountiful community on charges of practising polygamy; both men were found guilty in July 2017 and later sentenced to house arrest and community service. These were the third and fourth polygamy convictions in Canada's history; the previous two occurred in 1899 and 1906.

What Do YOU Think?

If you had been a government lawyer, what kinds of questions would you have asked the witness quoted in the narrative above? What concerns would you have voiced about plural marriage?

Family and Ethnicity

As we saw in Chapter 8, on "race" and ethnicity, there is a history in Canada of federal government policies designed to deprive racialized minorities of family. The prohibitively expensive head tax levied on immigrants from China and South Asia in the late nineteenth and early twentieth centuries made it impossible in many cases for married couples or their families to reunite in Canada. Canadian sociologists **Nancy Mandell** and **Ann Duffy**, in *Canadian Families: Diversity, Conflict and Change* (1995), noted a similar connection between government immigration policy and the denial of family for black women, calling it

> a policy of the government not to encourage the possibility of developing families among women of colour who came as domestic workers. Thus, their status as "single" and as "temporary" is deliberately organized by immigration policies. (Mandell & Duffy, 1995, p. 157).

The policy they refer to was initiated in 1910–11, during one of the country's greatest periods of immigration. About 100 black women from the Caribbean islands of Guadeloupe came to Canada to work as domestic servants, but when authorities discovered that many of the women were not as "unattached" as they had claimed to be—many had children they had been forced to leave behind—the women were sent back.

Between 1955 and 1967, a number of women from the Caribbean—primarily Jamaica—were allowed to come to Canada to work as domestics. They had to be young, of "good character," and single (in other words, not married or cohabitating). They were given the status of landed immigrants, but they could not seek other work until they had served at least a year of domestic duty. Roughly 300 Caribbean women came to Canada each year between 1955 and 1960, the number rising to about 1,000 a year during the 1960s (Bolaria & Li, 1985, p. 178). Many of them agreed to work as domestics, even though they were trained as teachers or secretaries. Many, in order to be "single," left family behind, all because it was the only way they could enter the country.

Naturally, those immigrants who had left husbands and children in the Caribbean wanted to sponsor their families to join them in Canada, but their efforts were blocked by immigration officials.

In 1976, seven Jamaican women applied to sponsor their children to come to Canada. They were ordered to be deported for having failed to report their children on their applications to come to Canada (Leah & Morgan, 1979). After an intense legal struggle, the seven women won their appeals and were allowed to stay in Canada.

Attacks on the Indigenous Family

Immigrant families are not the only ones affected by restrictive Canadian legislation. The Indigenous family has long been a target of federal policy. The following passage describes how, during the early twentieth century, an "Indian Agent" (the official title of the position) used the Blackfoot community's need for food rations as a tool to ensure the people remained monogamous:

> In my last report, I expressed thankfulness that there had been no plural marriages during the preceding year. That report was barely out of my hand when I learned that three members of the band were dissatisfied with one wife each and had taken another. I immediately directed that the rations of these families be withheld until such time as they saw fit to obey the rules in this respect. One family missed one ration, and then decided that it was better to abide by the rules. The other two families held out for several rations, and then they succumbed and put away wife No. 2. (Dosman, 1972, pp. 52–3)

This incident, in which food rations were withheld to control marriage choices, is not atypical of the kind of treatment Native families suffered at the hands of government agents.

It's important to note that actions like this were often products of well-meaning agencies and their representatives. With the benefit of modern perspective, we can see just how misguided and racist these policies were. The following section looks closely at three policies aimed at controlling Indigenous families. In some cases, as we will see, the same strategies have targeted other groups that governments have felt they needed to manage, including certain cultural and ethnic groups as well as people with physical or mental disabilities.

Residential Schools

Among the institutionalized instruments of control devised to manage the lives of Canada's Indigenous populations, the system of residential schools tops the list for the devastating effects it has had on Indigenous families. Officially started in 1910 but existing in "industrial" and "boarding" schools established before then in the nineteenth century, the **residential school** program was created with the almost explicit objective of keeping Indigenous children away from the supposedly harmful influences of their parents and their home communities. Families were ripped apart as parents reluctantly signed over legal guardianship of their children to school principals, then watched their children leave for the state- and church-run boarding schools, where they would live for most, if not all, of the year. Parents were discouraged from visiting. Those who did were closely monitored. Brothers and sisters were kept apart, sometimes not seeing each other for months on end. Many families were never reunited.

Historian J.R. Miller tells the story of a Cree woman who went to a residential school that was 19 kilometres from her reserve. For hours on end, she would stand at the corner of a fence that surrounded the school property:

> She would put her hand through the fence, because that meant she was closer to her home and family by the length of her arm and watch for her parents. She would say to herself, "the next black horse that comes along" will be drawing her parents' wagon on a visit. Disappointment only led to repetitions of the childlike incantation, a wish and a prayer that never seemed to come true. (Miller, 1996, p. 338–9)

Physical, emotional, and sexual abuse by residential school employees demoralized the students. And as those who have been abused so often become abusers, many Indigenous children grew up to bring the abuse they learned at school to their home communities.

Sexual Sterilization

In its definition of **genocide**, the United Nations includes attempts to destroy a people by imposing measures designed to prevent births within the group. This describes certain policies aimed at Canada's Indigenous population during much of the twentieth century. For instance, in 1928, the government of Alberta passed the Sexual Sterilization Act, with the intent of sterilizing "mental defectives" so that their "bad genes" would not be passed on. The act reflects the early twentieth-century belief in **eugenics**, the flawed notion that a single gene responsible for intelligence was absent in "stupid people," who would be capable of having only "stupid children"—in other words, children inheriting their parents' genetically defective intellect. We know now that there is a complex relationship between genetics and the various aptitudes that make up the biological potential known as intelligence. It is more accurate to say that we have **intelligences** of various kinds and levels (e.g., I have a talent for writing, but I am inept in drawing). This complexity makes the degree to which intelligence is inherited uncertain. We just don't know.

Eugenics has rightly been called **scientific racism**, as it was used to justify prejudices based on the supposed genetic inferiority or "feeble-mindedness" of certain immigrant groups to North America—particularly those from eastern Europe—as well as of black people and Indigenous people. Since it was used to support prejudice against the poor, it is also an instrument of **scientific classism**. The traditional yardstick for measuring intelligence is the intelligence quotient (IQ) test. This test has been rightfully criticized for its bias against people representing certain language and culture groups. The test also perpetuates the myth that we have a **general intelligence** to which a single number can be assigned.

During the history of Alberta's Sexual Sterilization Act, which lasted from 1928 to 1972, 2,832 people were sterilized, most of them women. Sterilizations of Métis and First Nations people account for a disproportionately high number of the total, an estimated 25 per cent (roughly 10 times their percentage of the total population). Eastern European immigrants (Ukrainians, Russians, etc.)—people whose English language skills and cultural capital were low—were also represented in high numbers in the sterilized group.

British Columbia passed an act similar to Alberta's Sexual Sterilization Act in 1933, the same year that the notorious Law for the Prevention of Genetically Diseased Offspring was passed in Nazi Germany. Recently, there have been accusations that, following both racial and religious prejudice, hundreds of non-Christian Indigenous people were sterilized by a United Church missionary doctor in a church-run hospital in the BC coastal community of Bella Bella, and that a good number of young Indigenous women made pregnant by residential school staff, clergy, and visiting officials were coerced into having abortions (see Truth Commission, 2001: pp. 12–13).

The Sixties Scoop

The United Nations' definition of genocide also includes attempts to destroy a people by forcibly transferring children of the group to another group. This characterizes what has been referred to as the **Sixties Scoop**, a program, beginning in the 1960s, of separating large numbers of Indigenous children from their families and home communities. Children could be removed by government-affiliated agencies for a variety of reasons: some were children of parents judged to be alcoholics, some were newborns needing hospital care taken to the nearest city (and in many cases never returned), some were living in homes considered crowded or substandard. In 1964, the number of children of all backgrounds removed from their families was 4228; roughly 34 per cent of those (1446) were Indigenous children.

Between 1971 and 1981 in Manitoba, where Indigenous families were hardest hit, over 3400 Indigenous children were removed from their homes. Many were taken from the province, and more than 1000 of them were sent to the United States, where American child welfare agencies could get as much as $4000 for each child placed. The province later launched an investigation into the practice, led by Justice Edwin Kimelman. In his summary of the investigation, *No Quiet Place* (1985), he stated,

> Cultural genocide has been taking place in a systematic routine manner. One gets

an image of children stacked in foster homes as used cars are stacked on corner lots, just waiting for the right "buyer" to stroll by. (cited in Fournier & Crey, 1997, p. 88)

But statistics and judges' reports do not give a real sense of the suffering caused. The following statement comes from a research report on the emotional return of children to their families, communities, and people:

I was sixteen years old when my daughter was taken from me. My partner at the time was drinking and at eighteen he went to prison. I had no way of looking after her and felt very alone. The social worker told me that my daughter would be better off with a "nice, normal family." I thought that I would at least be able to visit her sometimes, but she was placed in Pennsylvania and we did not meet her again until she was 20 years old. I took a bus to Windsor and that is where we met. I was alone and scared. She looked just like me when I was twenty, but with a very different attitude. She had suffered sexual abuse in her adopted home and she blamed it on me. She had a little girl of her own, but she would not let me meet her. I wish there was someone who could help us get past this pain. (Budgell, 1999, p. 6)

George Littlechild

Little Indian Foster Boy #4 is part of a multimedia art installation by George Littlechild, who was four when he was removed from his family and placed in the first of a series of foster homes. He is the child to the right of the group in this photo, trick-or-treating in Edmonton in the 1960s. In March 2018, a federal judge approved an $875 million settlement to be paid to victims of the Sixties Scoop, for their loss of identity, language, and culture, and for the abuse many suffered in foster care.

Wrap it Up

Summary

When we talk about the family in Canada, we are talking about a model of social organization that is diverse and complex, and that has long been so. This diversity expresses itself in family size and structure, in age of marriage and of having children, in qualifications for family membership, in who is and is not considered eligible for marriage into the family, in the expectations and practices of gender roles, and in the relationship between children (of all ages) and their parents. And this diversity works—the "good" family takes many forms. This is why we find such diversity in the Canadian family of the past, the present, and no doubt, the future: the family adapts, evolving to fit changing social circumstances.

Think Back

Questions for Critical Review

1. Describe the diversity of the Canadian family, both historically and today.
2. What do you think has contributed to the perception that the nuclear family is the "normal" model? Do you think this perception is changing? If so, why?
3. Describe how family in Quebec is different from family in the rest of Canada. Give some examples and some possible explanations. What is the significance of Quebec's difference when it comes to family?
4. We looked at nine different trends in Canadian families. Of those, which two or three do you think are most likely to continue, and why? Are there any trends you think might level off or reverse?
5. Identify the different forms that conjugal roles can take. How are these roles changing? Are they changing quickly enough?
6. Setting aside the church ceremony or the trip to city hall, what characteristics do you think must be present for a relationship to be considered a marriage?
7. Do you think Canada's low birth rate is a cause for concern? Why or why not? Should Canadians be encouraged to have more children? How would you do that?
8. Sociologists like to throw around fancy words like *exogamy* and *endogamy*, but does it really matter whether or not people are marrying outside of their ethnic or religious group? What does this information tell us about Canadian society?
9. Outline the measures used to place Canadian Indigenous families "under attack" during the twentieth century.

Read On

Recommended Print and Online Resources

Elizabeth Bott (1957), *Family and Social Networks: Roles, Norms, and External Relationships in Ordinary Urban Families* **(London, UK: Tavistock).**
- This classic work introduced and developed much of the terminology and ideas used by social scientists studying the sociology of the family today.

Karen Stote (2015), *Sterilization of Indigenous Women: An Act of Genocide* **(Black Point, NS: Fernwood).**
- This book delves into the hidden history of the forced sexual sterilization of Indigenous women in Canada.

Marguerita Cheng (2019, Feb. 26), "Grey Divorce: Its Reasons & Its Implications," *Forbes*

Magazine, www.forbes.com/sites/marguer-itacheng/2019/02/26/grey-divorce-its-rea-sons-its-implications/#3530d1234acd
- Baby boomers like to shake things up, and as this generation ages, we're seeing an increase in divorce in couples 50 and over. This article looks at some of the causes of "grey divorce" and its social impact, including the affect it has on adult children.

Rod Beaujot (2000), *Earning and Caring in Canadian Families* (Peterborough, ON: Broadview Press).
- One of this country's preeminent social demographers, Rod Beaujot, draws sociological conclusions about the Canadian family based on an analysis of statistical data.

"Stolen Children," www.youtube.com/watch?v=vdR9HcmiXLA
- This CBC story features interviews with survivors of Canada's residential school system.

The Vanier Institute of the Family, www.vifamily.ca
- This Ottawa-based organization researches and publishes on issues affecting the Canadian family. You can read their recent publications on such topics as family vacations, the changing role of fathers, and young people who become responsible for the care of older family members.

Wayne Hower (2006), *Does a Disabled Child = a Disabled Family?* (Authorhouse).
- This is a self-published work that combines the author's personal experience raising a disabled child with an academic and professional approach.

Nancy Mandell and Ann Duffy (2011), *Canadian Families: Diversity, Conflict, and Change*, 3rd edn (Toronto: Thompson Nelson).
- This edited collection features articles that outline a number of ways in which family operates in Canada.

Religion

11

Reading this chapter will help you to . . .

- Identify the principal elements of religion.
- Understand how new religious movements differ from established religious traditions.
- Outline Émile Durkheim's sociological approach to religion.
- Talk about how the sociological profile of religion is changing in Canada.
- Analyze the relationship between organized religion and family.
- Discuss the relationship between organized religion and gender roles.
- Detail the impact of Christian religious colonialism upon the Indigenous people of Canada.
- Explain what *laïcité* means and who is most likely to support it.

For Starters
The Christmas Rant

Starting around mid-November, the annual Christmas rant begins. Last year, a Christian Facebook friend of mine from the southern United States (she asks people not only to like but to type "Amen" for some of her posts) fired the first shot. It began something like this:

> So we are not allowed to say "Merry Christmas" to people anymore—just "Happy Holidays" or "Season's Greetings." We can't even have Christmas parties anymore, just "holiday" parties.

From there the rant goes on, concerning how the United States is a Christian country and how she, as a Christian, should be able to say "Merry Christmas" if she wants to.

I both agree and disagree with what she has to say. I was raised as a Christian in what I was brought up to believe was a Christian country. People such as this friend have said "Merry Christmas" all their lives, not usually meaning it in any religious way, just invoking the happiness that Christmas has long meant to them. I have never said "Happy Holidays" to anyone, and certainly not "Season's Greetings" (when I hear that, I often feel like replying, "Hello, Winter!").

Then the sociologist in me comes to life. Sure, Canada is a Christian country. But it is also a Muslim, Jewish, Jainist, Sikh, Hindu, Buddhist, and Baha'i country. Though roughly 68 per cent of Canadians are in some way affiliated with a Christian religion (see Table 11.2), not everyone in Canada has grown up with the cultural tradition of celebrating Christmas. If someone greets me with "Merry Christmas," I say it right back to them; in fact, if I know that the person is Christian, I might be the first to offer the greeting. Otherwise,

I don't say it. But I make an effort to recognize the holidays celebrated by acquaintances of other faiths as well. Rather than saying "Season's Greetings" to someone I know is Jewish, I will normally greet them with "Happy Hanukkah" (though I confess that the start of the holiday sometimes catches me by surprise, because its date, based on the Hebrew calendar, may fall in November). During Diwali, the Hindu Festival of Lights (held either in October or in November, based on the Hindu calendar), I might greet someone I know is Hindu, Sikh, Jain, or Buddhist with a reference to the special day. In December or January, Sikhs may also celebrate the birthdate of Guru Gobind Singh, a seventeenth-century spiritual leader (whom I knew about, though I had to double-check his birthdate). Muslims celebrate two Eids: Eid al-Adha and Eid al-Fitr. I have no idea what a proper greeting might be, but this won't be an issue for some time, as these dates, based on the Islamic lunar calendar, shift by approximately 11 days every year and won't take place in December again until 2034. I try not to eat in front of a Muslim during Ramadan, when Muslims are supposed to refrain from eating from sun-up to sundown. In other words, I compromise within my knowledge, rather than assuming that everyone shares my religious and cultural experience.

Back to my Facebook friend. If you are to have a sociological imagination, you cannot blame the individual in cases such as this. Instead, you have to look at what the various media and social institutions—the education system, the family, political leadership, and, in this case, organized religion—teach.

The "war on Christmas" has been loudly declared a problem for years by certain media outlets and churches. You might think that Americans like my friend are much more prone than Canadians are to feel threatened by people whose religious traditions differ from their own. However, as you will learn over the course of this chapter, Canada does not have a long history of religious tolerance and respect. Huguenots (French Protestants) were banned from entering Catholic New France for decades in colonial Canada of the seventeenth and eighteenth centuries. Quebec citizens of the twenty-first century face a ban on "overt and conspicuous" religious symbols in public-sector workplaces. The federal government prohibited First Nations from practising the Potlatch and the Sun Dance for over 60 years.

Why is religious tolerance so hard to come by? Because true tolerance of difference requires us to rethink long-held beliefs and behaviours, and that kind of change can be painful.

What Do YOU Think?

1. What is your response to the "Christmas rant"? Do you expect to hear the rant for years to come?
2. How do you think that the provincial governments and workplaces should deal with questions of religious holidays other than Christian ones?

Introduction: What Is Religion?

This is a nasty question, and, in my view one that should never be asked in a multiple-choice test. Religion is something people tend to think they understand until they are asked to define it; then the questions begin. How does a religion start? What kind of purpose does it have to serve?

What distinguishes a religion from a cult? Or for that matter, from that really dedicated workout group that meets in my local park at the same time every week and is always trying to get me to join? (I tell them my workout is walking my border collie every morning at six o'clock.)

A consensus on what religion is would be hard to achieve. Psychologists, philosophers, theologians, and sociologists are likely to come up with different answers that reflect the qualities of religion that are most relevant to their respective disciplines. As a sociologist, I look upon religion primarily as a social institution. So I see religion as having ritualized social practices that members can engage in alone or, more often, in groups, in a way that fosters a sense of shared experience and of belonging. With belonging, or inclusion, comes exclusion, and so religion is a powerful engine of ingroup/outgroup dynamics, where people attached to a religious association (their ingroup) may regard those outside the group (the outgroup) as threatening or inferior.

At a state fair in Lincoln, Nebraska, a man promises to reveal the likelihood of your salvation with a free two-question test. If only it were so easy. Can you guess what two questions might determine whether or not you are destined to go to Heaven? Can you imagine a booth like this being found at a fall fair in Canada?

Religions are often hierarchical and can be divided along the usual social fault lines of race, ethnicity, class, and especially gender, reflected in persistent beliefs about appropriate roles for men and women. I see religion as promoting a code of moral values that identifies right and wrong actions to help guide the social behaviour of religious members. Religious beliefs typically involve a reality that is beyond the purely physical, one in which there are spiritual or supernatural beings. These beings are part of the social world of religious members, and the relationship between human and spiritual beings may mirror the social dynamics of people on earth. If you live in a hierarchical society, then your relationship to spiritual beings will likely be hierarchical as well.

To sum up, defined sociologically, religion is a social institution with ritualistic practices, value-driven behaviour, and often socially divisive elements of "race," ethnicity, class, and gender, featuring other-than-human beings who are believed to intervene in the natural world of humans and who are venerated (or worshipped) in ways deemed socially appropriate by the group.

What Is a Cult?

In case you're still stuck on the question above, let's consider what distinguishes a religion from a cult. One way to look at it is that a cult is a religion that is deviant in its beliefs and/or practices. Remember that deviant is not a moral judgment of good or bad. Applied to cults, *deviant* means differing from, or offering an alternative to, older, established religions such as Islam, Judaism, and Christianity. Many cults are spinoffs of these established traditions, from which they may selectively borrow certain elements that they combine with secular practices into new religious forms.

Cults tend to be newly arrived on the religious scene: though cults of different kinds have existed for centuries, they came to prominence during the 1960s and 1970s, when, thanks to a few notorious (but not especially typical) cases, they became associated with the larger counterculture movement of that era. It's safe to say that the murder–suicide of 914 followers of the Peoples Temple in Jonestown, Guyana, in 1978 gave cults the world over a bad reputation. Canadian sociologist Lorne Dawson, who has done extensive research on the topic, prefers the term *new religious movement* (or NRM), which does not carry the sinister overtones hanging over the word *cult*. He identifies four types of new religious movement (Dawson, 1998, p. 14):

1. NRMs associated with Asian philosophy, meditation, and magic (e.g. the International Society for Krishna Consciousness, or ISKCON, whose beliefs are based on Hindu scripture)
2. NRMs drawing on pop psychology's "human potential movement" (the Church of Scientology fits here)
3. NRMs associated with occult revival (e.g. Wicca)
4. NRMs seeking spiritual salvation through contact with extraterrestrial beings (e.g. Heaven's Gate)

Cults may develop around a single charismatic leader or a small group of people, but don't mistake cult in this sense from the related term "cult of personality," which is an excessive admiration for someone. Donald Trump is the focal point of a cult of personality, but his supporters are not a cult in the sense described above (although there is a definite deviant Christian element among his most devout followers). A cult can develop over time to become a full-fledged religion with a general acceptability in society. Or it can die off with the passing away of the leader or leaders.

Telling It Like It Is

A Sociologist's POV

My Experience with the Baha'i Faith: The Social Support of a Religious Community

The year 1987 was a bad one for me. My second marriage was breaking up; within the year, I would be divorced. I was lonely and disheartened, believing this was my last chance at a serious relationship. Then, you might say, I got religion.

A cousin of mine and his wife were Baha'i. He had been born into a Christian household, and she was raised Jewish, but as adults they sought out a religious community that respected both faiths. Baha'i began as an offshoot of Islam, although it is generally considered a religion unto itself today. It was started by an Iranian prophet of the nineteenth century, who spoke of the truth of the prophets of all religions, and of the equality of religions. The Baha'i have been persecuted in Iran and other Muslim countries, where the faith is viewed as a renunciation of Islam. Dozens of Baha'i were executed during the last two decades of the twentieth century, including Mona Mahmudnizhad, a 16-year-old who was sentenced to death and hanged in 1983 for misleading children and youth and for being a Zionist. Canadians who grew up watching the early days of MuchMusic in the mid-1980s learned of her

case in the song and video "Mona with the Children," written and recorded by a Canadian musician, Doug Cameron (you can find it on YouTube).

My cousin and his wife intervened because they knew the state I was in. They also knew that I loved playing sports, and so they told me about Friday-night volleyball at a school not far from where I lived. Most the participants were Baha'i. It soon became the highlight of my week: volleyball followed by Pizza Hut (no alcohol; they don't drink). It later extended to Saturday-afternoon baseball . . . and Pizza Hut.

I developed some strong friendships with the people, both North American and Iranian. I was welcomed into people's homes and invited to ceremonies, which I readily attended and enjoyed. I felt a very strong sense of belonging. At no point was I pressured to make any kind of commitment to joining, although they made sure that I learned about the faith. I was referred to as a "friend of the faith," which I definitely was and still am. They helped me rebuild my confidence, and I owe a huge debt of thanks to this religious community for that.

The Sociocultural Elements of Religion

One of the earliest sociological insights into religion came from the Greek philosopher Aristotle:

> All people say that the gods also had a king because they themselves had kings either formerly or now; for men create the gods after their own image, not only with regard to form, but also with regard to their manner of life. (*Politics*, i.2.7)

Aristotle was suggesting that a society with a powerful king would likely have in its religion a commanding divine authority figure. A less hierarchical society would be more likely to have a spiritual society of gods that is somewhat egalitarian, in their relationships both with one another and with human beings. The point Aristotle was making is that people are likely to use the same language they use to describe human relationships to describe their relationship with their god or gods. In this way, the gods we worship are a mirror, reflecting our own social structure. Aristotle, it's worth noting, spent over 20 years in Athens, the birthplace of democracy, where the Greeks worshipped a host of gods who, according to their mythology, would frequently interact with humans and be influenced by them.

We can test Aristotle's insight by applying it to the religious and social practices of the seventeenth-century French Jesuit priests and the Wendat (Huron) people among whom they lived and did missionary work. The Jesuits were Roman Catholics who had come to North American from France, a country ruled by a powerful king. Central to their Catholicism was an omnipotent God. The language they used when speaking of either political or spiritual figures was one of great authority, with frequent reference to "masters" and to commanding and obeying.

By contrast, the Wendat nation had formed as an alliance of four member nations, or tribes. Each of the separate nations had a tribal leader who could recommend actions but not give orders. The Wendat word used to refer to the leader can be translated

What Do YOU Think?

How do you think a social Darwinist would have characterized the gods and level of civilization of the seventeenth-century Wendat?

as "we cause him to be a principle to imitate"—in essence, "him whom we see as our role model." There were no words in Wendat that meant "order" or "command." As for religion, the Wendat recognized a series of spiritual figures, including Yaatayentsik, the first woman on earth, who had fallen from the sky, and her twin grandsons, Ioskeha and Tawiskaron, who had transformed the earth. These and other spirits did not *command* people; rather, they *inspired* them through visions, or else they plagued them with curses.

This does not suggest that the Wendat, or other societies without strong political hierarchy, had no sense of a creator or god above all other gods. It simply means that the relationship between people and spirits was more in line with the relatively egalitarian relationships between humans.

By the late nineteenth century, this idea of the link between social and spiritual relationships became set in a **social Darwinist**, or evolutionary, model. According to this model, the most "primitive" people had pesky spirits; "barbarians" had playful or nasty but ultimately impotent gods. Only "civilized" people had religion that reflected the prevailing social order in Europe, in which power was invested in a supreme ruler. This way of thinking justified policies aimed at converting heathens in the colonies to Christianity. The methods used were often anything but civilized, as survivors of Canada's residential school system can attest.

Religion and Class in Canada

Religion and class intersect. If you are an Anglican in Canada, your income is likely to be higher than if you are a Catholic or a Baptist, and certainly higher than if you are a Pentecostal. Why so? One explanation is the **Protestant (work) ethic**. This theory, touched on in Chapter 1, was developed by **Max Weber** to explain the rise of modern capitalism. Weber was familiar with the Protestant belief in a predestined "elect" who would be saved during the second coming of Christ. A person demonstrated membership in this elect group by achieving material success through hard work. According to Weber, this religious/cultural influence spurred people to accumulate wealth, making this set of values, associated with Protestantism, a key factor in the rise of capitalism. Were he alive today, Weber might argue that the Protestant work ethic survives in the general prosperity of some religious groups over others.

But this is only part of the story. The Anglican Church (the Church of England) is a socially conservative church with a long historical connection to power in Canada. One of the issues that led to the 1837–8 rebellions in what are now Ontario and Quebec was the set of privileges that the Anglican Church enjoyed in British North America (e.g. having land specially reserved for their use or sale, called "clergy reserves"). The official wording was "for the support and maintenance of a Protestant clergy," but it was understood that "Protestant" in this context meant "Anglican only."

Class and "race" aligned with religion. The Methodist Church attracted small-scale farmers and Indigenous people. The Baptist Church long welcomed members of Canada's black community, particularly in the Maritimes, as well as white people with lower-than-average income. The Pentecostal Church is likewise racialized, and has a connection to poor people living in rural areas. The Catholic Church has been home to minoritized groups that have experienced discrimination. The earliest Catholics were French, who, living within a British colony, historically did not have the power that the English did. During the nineteenth century, many poor Catholic Irish immigrants came to Canada, only to find "No Irish Need Apply" on signs for jobs in Toronto. Subsequent periods of immigration brought Italians, Croatians, Poles, Hungarians, and other working-class groups whose presence affected the class standing of Catholics in Canada.

According to **Karl Marx**, religion generally functions as an instrument of **hegemony**. He famously called it the "opium of the people," with reference to religion's power to soothe the suffering of the working masses (Marx, [1844]/1976). Religion, he argued, serves the interests of the ruling class by dissuading oppressed members of the working class from organizing around their own class-based self-interests to challenge the inequality of society. Religion thus helps instil a **false consciousness**, Marx's term for the workers' belief that the class-based hierarchy—in which they occupied the lowest position—was justified and to their advantage. Religion, in Marx's critical view, made members of the lower class believe that God had planned society to be the way it was, and that by toiling away under oppressive conditions, they were really acting in the best interests of their class and would find their rewards ultimately in the "next life." A classic example of how religion supported the class system comes from the hymn "All Things Bright and Beautiful":

> The rich man in his castle,
> The poor man at his gate.
> God made them high or lowly
> And ordered their estate. . . .

That last line means that God determined the appropriate positions within the class system for the poor and the rich. The message: don't revolt against a God-determined social order, no matter how oppressive!

Yet religion can bear a "radical possibility," an ability to bring about positive social change. This is exemplified in Canada by the **social gospel** movement and the progressive politics of J.S. Woodsworth, Stanley Knowles, and Tommy Douglas. They were trained as ministers and became involved in the development of "radical" policies, such as socialized medicine and pensions that dramatically improved the lives of working-class people. That same Christian spirit of helping those in need is not just a fact of the past. It can be seen today in the strong, swift response of Canadian religious communities to the plight of Syrian refugees coming to Canada. Refugee sponsorship is strong in many Christian denominations, and was especially important in 2015, when the federal government under Stephen Harper was lagging behind church initiatives and public opinion on the matter.

Durkheim and the Elementary Forms of Religious Life

Although he was not particularly religious, Émile Durkheim (1858–1917) had a profound effect on how sociologists view religion. His father and grandfather were both rabbis, yet he himself felt no religious calling. His great work on religion is *Les formes élémentaires de la vie religieuse: Le système totémique en Australie*, published in 1912. In 1915 it was published in English as *The Elementary Forms of the Religious Life*.

Durkheim took sociology into areas where at first glance it did not seem to belong, including suicide (surely the realm of psychology) and religion (certainly the realm of theology). Both suicide and religion were seen as being firmly rooted in the individual, not in the group or society, and there was strong resistance to his ideas among people studying psychology and religion at the time.

Durkheim's aim was to identify the basic elements of religion. He believed he could do this by studying the religion of the most basic society then being discussed by social scientists: the Aborigines of Australia. Through this study he hoped to develop a sociological model applicable to all religions.

Durkheim's Definition

Here is how Durkheim defined *religion*:

> A religion is a unified system of beliefs and practices relative to sacred things, that is to say, things set apart and forbidden—beliefs and practices which unite into one single moral community called a Church, all those who adhere to them. ([1912]/1995, p. 44)

As Karen Fields puts it, Durkheim's view was that "religion is social, social, social" (1995, p. xxxiv). In using the term **moral community**, Durkheim was recognizing that religious groups are "made up of individuals who have mutually recognized and recognizable identities that set them, cognitively and normatively, on shared human terrain" (Fields, 1995, p. xxxiv). It is clear from this how dramatically Durkheim deviated from his contemporaries, who considered religion something experienced by the individual rather than the larger community.

Three Key Elements of Religion

There are three key elements in Durkheim's analysis of religion. The first is the equation *god = society*. Durkheim formulated this idea in the context of the totems of the Australian Aborigines.

Totem is a word that came into English in the late eighteenth century from the language of the Anishinaabe or Ojibwa people. It comes from the word *ndotem*, meaning "my clan" in Ojibwa. When Anishinaabe people introduce themselves in formal situations, they often follow the statement of their name by saying something such as *waawaashkesh ndotem*, meaning "deer is my clan." In this way, they are telling something about their identity and who they are.

Anishinaabe Elder Edward Benton-Banai, a leading figure in the tradition-based Three Fires Midewiwin Lodge and the author of *The Mishomis Book: The Voice of the Ojibway*, identified seven original clans of the Anishinaabe (1988, pp. 75–7). Traditionally, he explains, each clan was associated with a specific function and certain ideal characteristics of clan members. These characteristics connect with the clan's totem animal (see Table 11.1). The carved totem poles found on the Pacific coast of North America have images that represent different clans connected to the villages where the poles were erected.

Having some sense of what *totem* means, we can look at Durkheim's famous explanation of the *god = society* equation:

> [The totem] . . . symbolizes two different . . . things. [I]t is the outward and visible form of . . . the totemic principle or god; and . . . it is also the symbol of a particular society that is called the clan. It is . . . the sign by which each clan is distinguished from the others, the visible mark of its distinctiveness, and a mark that is borne by everything that in any way belongs to the clan: men, animals, and things. *Thus if the totem is the symbol of both the god and the society, is this not because the god and the society are one and the same? How could the emblem of the group have taken the form of that quasi-divinity if the group and the divinity*

TABLE 11.1 Clans and Totems of the Anishinaabe

Clan/Totem	Associated Characteristics
Crane Clan Loon Clan	leadership, chieftainship
Fish Clan	mediation, settling disputes; philosophy
Bear Clan	protecting the community; medicinal plants
Marten Clan	warfare and war strategy
Deer Clan	poetry
Bird Clan	spiritual leadership

Source: Benton-Banai (1988)

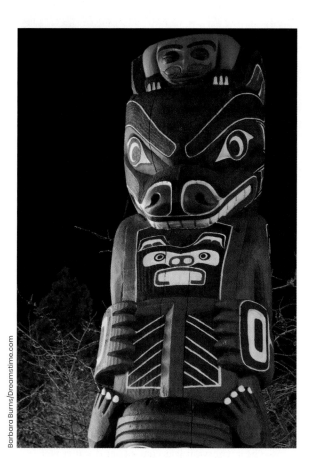

Barbara Burns/Dreamstime.com

The images in this totem pole are culturally stylized versions of the totem animals of clans of the artist's First Nation. What impression do you think these totem poles made on the Christian missionaries arriving in villages on the Pacific coast? What impression do they make on you?

were two distinct realities? Thus the god of the clan, the totemic principle, can be none other than the clan itself, but the clan transfigured and imagined in the physical form of the plant or animal that serves as totem. (Durkheim, [1912]/1995, p. 208)

A totem, then, is a symbolic representation both of a god and of the society that reveres it. Another way of looking at it is that societies fashion deities represented as having characteristics like the people themselves. These characteristics are then projected back onto both the culture and the individuals. The god and the people are one and the same.

Collective Consciousness and the Sacred and Profane

Durkheim focused primarily on the group experiences and rituals of people belonging to a particular religion. These sacred experiences foster what Durkheim called a **collective consciousness**. In Muslim countries, the cry of the Muzzin (the religious caller) over the loudspeaker calling the faithful to early morning prayer, followed by the collective deep bowing of people who are similarly dressed, is a compelling example of collective religious experience.

Durkheim distinguished between experiences, acts, and objects that are *sacred* and those that are *profane*. **Sacred** objects and acts are set apart from more ordinary (**profane**) ones as being positively regarded, holy, and therefore deserving of reverence or respect. Sacred objects include prayer beads, crosses, flags, and items in the medicine bundle of an Aboriginal shaman; sacred acts include prayer, some Aboriginal dances, and keeping kosher. But Durkheim used the term *sacred* also for that which is forbidden or taboo. The Arabic term used in Islam, *haram*, applies here. Canadian writer **Haroon Siddiqui**, in *Being Muslim*, lists the following prohibited objects and practices:

Haram Foods: Pork and its by-products, carnivorous animals (those that tear their food apart with claws, such as lions), almost all reptiles and insects, animals that died before being properly slaughtered, blood, and all alcoholic or intoxicating drinks.

Hikron/Dreamstime

Muslims pray at a mosque in Turkey. How do you think this kind of communal prayer generates a sense of collective consciousness?

Haram Lifestyle: Gambling, including lotteries; all drugs that cause intoxication, alter sensory perception (hallucinogens) or affect one's ability to reason and make sound judgments; and paying and accepting interest. (Siddiqui, 2006, p. 80)

Durkheim argued that objects were not sacred by nature but acquired their sacred status socially.

Durkheim's Study of Religion and Suicide

In his 1897 study of suicide, Durkheim stated that Protestants committed suicide more often than Catholics did. He explained the difference by arguing that Protestants were less connected to society than Catholics were. The implication was that being Catholic made a person less likely to die from suicide.

For years I made this point without questioning it in my lectures, but not now. The reason I stopped merely citing it unquestioned is that Durkheim's **social fact** concerning Catholic and Protestant suicides has been challenged. Van Poppel and Day (1996, p. 500) assert that the **operational definition** for suicide was different for the two groups: Catholics, they argue, were much less likely to count "sudden deaths" and "deaths from ill-defined or unspecified causes" as suicides than Protestants were (Van Poppel & Day, 1996, p. 500). The reason, they propose, is that in the Catholic Church suicide is considered a mortal sin, meaning that (until relatively recently) a person dying by suicide could not be buried with religious rites in a Catholic graveyard. The suggestion was that either doctors were reluctant to pronounce an unexplained Catholic death a suicide or they covered up some suicides; either way, Catholic suicides were systematically underreported. This viewpoint is not without critics (see e.g. van Tubergen, te Grotenhuis, & Ultee, 2005), but if true, it would throw into question Durkheim's assertion about the protective effects of being Catholic in France in his day.

f9photos/iStockphoto

Jeremy Richards/iStock Photo

The Kandariya Mahadeva temple, a Hindu holy site at Khajuraho, in Madhya Pradesh, India. Close inspection reveals its erotic reliefs. Sacred or profane?

Canadian Society and Religion

Trends

Statistics Canada collects information on Canadians' religious affiliation every 10 years, on the 1's (1991, 2001, 2011). The information will next be gathered in the 2021 census, and then it will be released a year or two later, once the data have been sorted and analyzed. For now, we will have to make do with details from the 2011 National Household Survey, which give a clear (if somewhat outdated) view of religious representation in this country.

Let's begin with Table 11.2, which compares Canadians' religious affiliation in 2011 and 10 years earlier, in 2001. Trends worth noting are the categories that show the greatest increase and decrease. According to the 2001 census, the categories with the largest increases by percentage from 1991 to 2001 were Pagan (281.2 per cent), Muslim (128.9), "Other Christian" (121.1), Serbian Orthodox (109.5), Hindu (89.3), Sikh (88.8), and Buddhist (83.8). Table 11.2 shows that many of these trends continued from 2001 to 2011.

Several points are worth observing. First, Canada is not "going Pagan." The respondents giving that answer are going from a low number to another low number. That is one reason why a good sociologist—professional or student—does not rely on percentage alone when looking at change. Raw numbers themselves are also important.

Immigration from South Asia is a major factor in the increase of Muslims (primarily from Pakistan), Hindus, and Sikhs shown in Table 11.2. War refugees from Somalia and parts of the Middle East help to account for the increase in Canada's Muslim population. This trend will likely continue in the next census period, reflecting immigration from Syria. The growth of Canada's Tibetan population, owing to China's oppression of Tibet, correlates with the increased number of Buddhists.

The number of "Other Christians not included elsewhere" has risen in part because of West Indians joining local independent churches in relatively large numbers. However, the category also includes people who identify simply as "Christian" without specifying a particular denomination. In other words, they may celebrate Christmas and Easter and haven't given up their belief in God, but they don't

TABLE 11.2 Canadians' Religious Affiliation, 2001–2011

Religion	2001		2011		10-Year Change (%)
	Number	Percentage	Number	Percentage	
Catholic	12,936,905	43.6	12,810,705	40.0	−0.01
Protestant	8,654,850	29.2	7,265,780	22.1	−19.1
Christian Orthodox	479,620	1.6	550,690	1.7	+14.8
Other Christian[1]	780,450	2.6	1,475,575	4.5	+89.0
Muslim	579,640	2.0	1,053,945	3.2	+81.8
Hindu	297,200	1.0	497,960	1.1	+67.6
Sikh	278,410	0.9	454,965	1.4	+63.4
Buddhist	300,345	1.0	366,830	1.1	+22.1
Jewish	329,995	1.1	329,500	1.0	−0.002
Eastern Religions[2]	37,550	0.1	35,185	0.1	−6.7
Other religions[3]	63,975	0.2	160,590	0.5	+51.0
No religious affiliation[4]	4,900,090	16.2	7,850,605	24.0	+60.2

Notes

1. Includes those who indicated just "Christian" and those who indicated Christian religions not included elsewhere, including Born-Again Christian, Apostolic, Messianic Jew, Hutterite, etc.
2. Includes Baha'i, Eckankar, Jains, Shinto, Taoist, Zoroastrian, and Eastern religions not identified elsewhere.
3. Includes Aboriginal spirituality, Pagan, Wicca, Unity, New Thought, Pantheist, Scientology, Rastafarian, New Age, Gnostic, Satanist, etc.
4. Includes Agnostic, Atheist, Humanist, and No religion, and other responses, such as Darwinism, etc.

Source: Statistics Canada, 2011 National Household Survey, cat. no. 99-010-X2011032; Statistics Canada, 2001 Census of Population, cat. no. 95F0450XCB2001005.

identify with or attend a particular church outside of weddings and funerals. People who don't accept the supernatural premise of Christianity but who have a nostalgia for Christian traditions and ceremonies are sometimes known as "secular Christians." It's fair to assume that secular Christians make up a good share of the "Other Christians" category.

The second-largest group in Table 11.2, accounting for close to one-quarter of all Canadians, belongs to those claiming no religious affiliation at all. We can speculate on the reasons why this category grew by over 60 per cent between 2001 and 2011.

One explanation is that the demands of work and family life have left many people without the time to participate in organized religion. The emergence of social media has played a role as well. Have you ever lost four hours of your day turning on your laptop to quickly check your Facebook account? I have. Facebook didn't exist in 2001. This, though, would explain only why attendance at churches, synagogues, mosques, and other places of worship has decreased. It does not explain why people in greater numbers are denying any religious affiliation.

We could speculate that Canadians have become disillusioned with religion because of its central role in many wars and conflicts; it is hard to view religion as a force for peace when it is used as a pretext for attacks on others. In recent years, organized religion in North America has been linked to child sexual abuse and, in Canada, to the residential school system where so many young Indigenous people suffered. These affairs have a high media profile and could play a role in turning people off of religion.

It is possible, too, that organized religion, conservative by nature and steeped in centuries of tradition, has lost followers because it has trouble keeping up with the pace of change in a socially progressive country such as Canada. Some churches are still wrestling with same-sex marriage and equal employment opportunities for women long after gay marriage and the ability of women to lead the world's largest companies and most powerful governments have ceased to be topics of controversy in mainstream society.

Finally, in Canada today it is more socially acceptable than it was even a generation ago to admit to having no religious affiliation. Many Canadians of your grandparents' age, regardless of how deep their faith ran, would have been reluctant to identify as atheists for fear of the social backlash that such a bold declaration of non-faith might attract.

Figure 11.1 shows the percentage of Canadians declaring no religious affiliation by province. What may strike you—as it struck me—is that the percentage is greatest in BC and declines as we move east, province by province, in almost perfect geographic sequence. Notice, too, that Quebec has the second-lowest level of "No Religious Affiliation" among the provinces. This is surprising in the context of Quebec's official policy of secularism, which came up last chapter in the context of the Quiet Revolution and which will come up later this chapter, when we consider the province's attempts to ban religious symbols. My sense is that religiosity generally and Catholicism in particular remains a big part of identity in Quebec, even though the Church's involvement in secular affairs has been minimized, and actual participation in the church is low. Perhaps you have another explanation, particularly if you live or have lived in Quebec. Is there something else at play here?

Returning to Table 11.2, let's take a moment to consider the sociological significance of the decreases shown. Over the 10-year period, the proportion of Canadians identifying as Catholic fell by 3.6 per cent, from 43.6 per cent to 40.0 per cent. The share of Protestants in Canada fell even further, from 29.2 per cent in 2001 to 22.1 per cent in 2011. One correlation to observe is religious affiliation and age (Table 11.3). While over 8 out of 10 Canadians aged 65 and over identified as Christian in 2011, just 6 out of 10 Canadians aged 24 and under did so. We see Muslims and those without religious affiliation concentrated primarily in the younger age groups, offering a possible look at what the future holds. Lack of immigration is also a factor in the decreases. In 2001, the Presbyterian population had the highest median age (46.0) and the largest 10-year decrease in percentage (35.6 per cent). Presbyterianism has a long history in Canada, but it is connected with Scotland, no longer a major source of Canadian immigration. The decrease would be even sharper were it not for immigration from Korea, which was long a major Presbyterian mission. Several other Protestant denominations—the Anglican Church chief among them—have connections to other parts of Britain that, like Scotland, have declined as sources of immigration to this country.

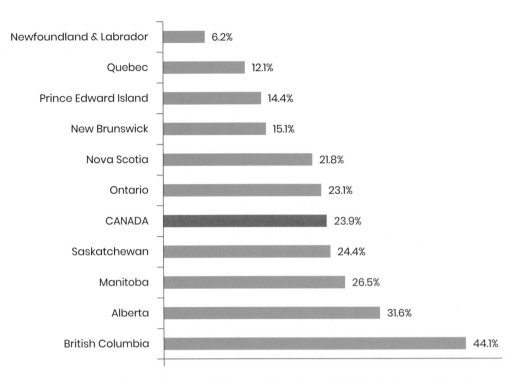

FIGURE 11.1 Canadians Indicating "No Religious Affiliation," by Canada and Provinces

Source: Statistics Canada, 2011 National Household Survey.

TABLE 11.3 Canadians' Religious Affiliation by Age Group, 2011

	Under 15	15–24	25–54	55–64	Over 64
Religion	*n* = 5,592,800	*n* = 4,324,065	*n* = 14,044,940	*n* = 4,338,980	*n* = 4,551,535
Christian	60.3	61.8	64.3	75.4	82.5
Muslim	5.2	3.8	3.4	1.6	1.0
Jewish	1.0	1.0	0.8	1.2	1.3
Buddhist	0.8	1.1	1.3	1.2	0.9
Hindu	1.9	1.6	1.7	1.1	0.8
Sikh	1.8	1.4	1.4	1.0	1.0
Other religions	0.6	0.6	0.7	0.6	0.4
No religious affiliation	28.3	28.7	26.4	17.9	11.9

Note: Figures for 2011 are estimates based on the results of the 2011 National Household Survey, which was distributed to approximately 4.5 million Canadian households.

Source: Statistics Canada, 2011 National Household Survey, cat. no. 99-010-X2011032.

What Do YOU Think?

1. Which religions do you think will continue to show significant increases or declines? Are there any religions you think may show a reversal of the 2001–2011 trend? Why?

2. Why do you think the percentage of Canadians claiming no religious affiliation jumped by over 60 per cent between 2001 and 2011? Do you think the share of Canadians claiming no religious affiliation will level off or continue to grow?

Quick Hits

Comparing the Jewish Communities in Canada and the United States

Canada's Jewish population showed the least amount of change between 2001 and 2011, but according to the authors of a recent survey, Canada will soon be home to the second-largest population of Jews outside of Israel, behind only the United States (Brym, Neuman, & Lenton, 2018). Moreover, the authors of the survey, which was conducted by the Environics Institute in conjunction with the University of Toronto and York University, found that on a number of indicators, Canada's Jewish community is far more cohesive than the community of Jews living in the United States. The table below presents some of these indicators, with percentages from the *2018 Survey of Jews in Canada* (Brym, Neuman, & Lenton, 2018) and a recent Pew Research Center survey of American Jews.

When looking at these results, it is important to know that the majority of practising North American Jews belong to one of three denominations. *Orthodox Judaism* involves strict adherence to a traditional interpretation of Jewish law and observances. How strict? During Orthodox worship, men and women are normally separated. *Conservative Judaism* values tradition and ritual but features a more flexible interpretation of Jewish law. *Reform Judaism*, sometimes called Progressive Judaism, highlights the ethical aspects of faith over ceremony, and abandons aspects of Orthodox worship and ritual in an effort to adapt to modern changes in social, cultural, and political life. Of the Canadian Jews surveyed, 43 per cent were affiliated with either Orthodox or Conservative Judaism, compared

Trevor Brine/CBC

Founded in 1937 in Winnipeg's North End, Gunn's Bakery is a testament to the city's long history of Jewish settlement. Winnipeg, Toronto, Montreal, and Vancouver account for 82 per cent of Canada's highly urbanized Jewish population, and while the Jewish population is declining in Winnipeg and Montreal, it is growing in Toronto and Vancouver, as well as in Ottawa and Calgary (Brym, Neuman, & Lenton, 2018, p. 5).

Continued

Indicator	Canadian Jews surveyed (%)	American Jews surveyed (%)
Being Jewish is a very important part of my life.	64	46
Being part of a Jewish community is essential to being Jewish.	40	28
A member of the household belongs to a synagogue or temple.	58	31
A member of the household belongs to another Jewish organization.	47	18
All or most close friends are Jewish.	57	32
Both parents are Jewish.	90	71
Can carry on a conversation in Hebrew.	40	12
Currently married to/living common-law with a Jewish partner.	77	50

Source: Brym, Neuwman, & Lenton, 2018.

with just 28 per cent of Americans interviewed in the Pew survey. Meanwhile, just 16 per cent of the Canadian group identified with the much more liberal Reform branch, compared with 35 per cent of American respondents (Brym, Neuman, & Lenton, 2018, p. 23). It stands to reason that members of the two more conservative branches of Judaism will score highest on the indicators presented above in the table.

What Do YOU Think?

In 2017, Jews were targeted in 43 per cent of all reported hate crimes in Canada. This is striking when you consider how small Canada's Jewish population is (review Table 11.2). They do not have the traits that often draw the anger of prejudiced people: they are well educated, unlikely to be on welfare, and seldom involved in serious crime. Their financial success is sometimes held against them, despite the fact that Western society reveres the wealthy. And as a population they have frequently been viewed with suspicion by outsiders, who make them the subjects of preposterous conspiracy theories. Why do you think that is?

Age Group versus Cohort

Statistical studies consistently demonstrate that teens and those in their early twenties are less religious than older people are. The danger with looking at such studies in isolation is that they may be taken to mean that overall levels of participation in religion are falling, that as these young people age, there will be significantly fewer religious people in Canada. The mistake is in automatically seeing an **age group** difference (i.e. a consistent difference between old and young) and assuming it is a **cohort** difference (i.e. a difference between people born in two different periods). Young people may not attend church because they are too busy. They may reject religion if they feel it has been forced upon them by their parents. However, they may take up religion later in life—for instance, when they reach marrying age and want a church wedding, or when they become older and turn to a local church as a way to become more involved in the community, through charity work or through a church-based organization. When they are old, they might sense their mortality and need religious answers.

Having said that, it is worth looking at Table 11.3 to see which religions are strongest in different age groups. We can predict that the religious groups with higher concentrations in the lowest age groups are the ones that are likely to grow. The populations that stand out in this regard are Muslim, Hindu, and Sikh. At the other end of the spectrum are the Christian churches: they still have the highest overall numbers, but those numbers are highest in the oldest age categories, and much smaller in the youngest age categories. Still, for every Muslim in Canada today, there are roughly 21 people who identify as Christian. How much do you think that ratio will change over the next 10 years?

Religion and the Family

Religion and the Marginalized Family

Religion is often applauded for promoting "family values." Usually it does. Revisiting Robert Merton's three kinds of function from Chapter 1, we could reasonably identify "strengthening the family" as a manifest (i.e. intended and recognized) or latent (largely unintended and unrecognized) function of religion. Yet there have been times when family and religion have stood in opposition, particularly when a certain kind of family situation has been negatively valued by state officials armed with religion.

In nineteenth-century Ireland, the Catholic Church established institutions to "rehabilitate" prostitutes and unmarried mothers. They were called "Magdalene asylums" (referencing Mary Magdalene, the classic "fallen woman" of the Bible) or sometimes "Magdalene laundries," since the women were often forced into hard labour laundering clothes to earn money for the institution. Many unwed mothers had their children taken away and put up for adoption. Magdalene asylums were established throughout Ireland and Britain, and Canada, some surviving until the late twentieth century (see J.M. Smith, 2007).

In Canada, thousands of Indigenous children were sent to church-run residential schools throughout most of the twentieth century. Consider the conditions:

Children were taken from their parents and extended families for periods of time that often lasted the entire school year, even when the residential schools were located in the students' own communities. Parental visits, when they were permitted, were typically closely monitored in a special "visiting room." Brothers and sisters were often kept apart in strict sexual separation, meaning

that siblings in many cases could communicate with each other only by waving from one building to another or through secretly arranged meetings. (Steckley & Cummins, 2008, p. 194)

Residential schools had a strong detrimental effect on parenting skills in First Nations communities. Raised under the strict and often abusive authority of underpaid, underqualified, and poorly screened teachers and administrators, described by historian J.R. Miller as the "devoted and the deviant" (1996, p. 321), three generations of Indigenous parents had only these harsh role models on which to base their own parenting.

Imports from Britain

In *Empty Cradles*, British social worker **Margaret Humphreys** describes how thousands of British children—the vast majority born to parents who were either poor or socially marginalized as single parents—were shipped to Australia to live in church-run orphanages. Certainly, some of these children benefited from their change in circumstances. Yet as Humphreys relates, many of the children were told that their parents were dead, and were subjected to the same hard labour and abuse that Indigenous children experienced in Canadian residential schools. The following questions come from a woman who was shipped out to Australia when she was eight:

Do you think I've got any family? Cousins, anybody. I'm not fussy. Anybody. They told me that my parents were dead. Do you think that's true? . . . I don't know anything about myself. Until I married, I didn't even have a birth certificate. I felt ashamed . . . Can you find out why they sent me? What did I do wrong? . . . (Humphreys, 1995, p. 14)

Humphreys collected a story of a five-year-old girl who had long, curly, blonde hair when she entered the Catholic orphanage named Goodwood:

After being at Goodwood a few days, she packed all her possessions in a bag and ran down the drive in her nightie. The nuns followed her and dragged her back. The next morning, all the girls were made to line up in the yard and watch her being punished. . . . Two of the nuns held the little girl down, while another started cutting off her hair with garden shears. . . .

When they had finished, there was just an inch or two of hair left on her head. "God wants her punished more than that," one of the nuns said, and she produced a pair of secateurs [small pruning shears]. She started cutting again and didn't stop until the young girl's hair was gone completely and her scalp was bloody with cuts. (Humphreys, 1995, p. 125)

In looking at the treatment of British and Irish orphans and Canadian Indigenous children, we can see common themes that characterize this conflict between religion and family:

- the marginalized (in terms of "race," class, and sexual behaviour) backgrounds of the families from which the children were taken
- the statistically deviant choice made by religious workers such as missionaries, priests, and nuns to opt for "religious life" over "normal" family life in their own society
- the strict hierarchical nature of religion operating in institutions such as religious orders, residential schools, and church-run orphanages
- the strict codes of discipline associated with religious-based institutions
- the ease with which religious concepts such as "sin" can be associated with negative judgement and used to justify harsh punishment.

Hutterites: Religion and Family

The preceding sections illustrate situations in which religion and family come into conflict, with damaging results. In contrast is the strong positive connection between religion and family found in Canada's Hutterite communities. In 2001, the last year for which we have such detailed census data, the Hutterites were the Canadian religious group with the

youngest median age (22.2). Children aged 0 to 14 made up 37 per cent of their population, while young people aged 0 to 24 made up 54 per cent—well over half—of their total population. The Hutterites' fertility rate, despite declining somewhat in recent decades, approaches the maximum fertility rate possible for a single community and is famous in the sociological literature (see Nonaka, Miura, & Peter, 1993). The high fertility rate is attributed to several sociological factors, including

- cultural/religious norms opposing contraception;
- farming as the main industry, requiring a large population of strong, young farmhands; and
- the practice of communal living, which ensures that childcare, a shared responsibility, is always available.

The Hutterites are named after Jacob Hutter, the leader of a radical Christian movement started during the 1520s and 1530s. Along with Mennonites, they were part of the Anabaptist religious movement, which advocated that baptism should be administered only to believing adults. What made them radicals? They opposed the class linkages between the established church, the state, and the rich. They were also pacifists, adhering strictly to the commandment *Thou shalt not kill*. Their belief that people should be baptized as adults, when they're old enough to make a mature choice, ran counter to the rules of the Catholic Church and the law in Austria, where the Hutterites first formed. Hutter was tortured and killed for his ideas.

The Hutterites were driven from one European country after another until they immigrated to the United States during the 1870s. In 1889, the Canadian government, wanting sturdy farmers to exploit the agricultural potential of the Prairies, offered them exemption from military service if they moved to Canada. During the First World War, many Hutterite communities, fearing persecution in the United States, moved to Canada.

The social organization of the Canadian Hutterites involves three communal groups (called "Leuts," meaning "people"): Lehrerleut, Dariusleut, and Schmiedeleut. Each forms a moral community in Durkheim's sense. The Lehrerleut and Dariusleut

Telling It Like It Is

A Historian's POV

The Minister's Role in a Hutterite Community

The following passage comes from a study of the Hutterite community of Pincher Creek, Alberta, published by historian David Flint in 1975.

[The] minister . . . is the single most important member of the community. Not only does he attend to the spiritual needs of the colony, but his advice is often asked on everything from when the pigs should be marketed to the price that should be charged for eggs. He is the colony leader, and his election is the most vital decision the colony makes in affecting its future nature. . . .

Hutterites expect the minister . . . to set standards and demand conformity, and to guard the traditions and values of their religion, and they readily obey him. If the minister is easy-going about slight deviations in dress, the colony will reflect his attitude. On one new colony there was not yet a minister in residence. Dress became sloppy—women went around in summer without kerchiefs and shoes and socks. When asked about this, one embarrassed man replied, "When the cat's away, the mice will play." He admitted that there was laxity and confessed that this would change when the minister arrived. . . .

In the week-by-week, year-by-year operation of the colony, group consensus and Sunday-evening meetings play a vital role in maintaining solidarity and discipline. It is an accepted practice to bring pressure to bear on those adults who do not conform to the will of the community. It is considered ethical and necessary to report an individual's misdoings to the colony meeting, and this is accepted for the common good and in recognition of the weakness of human nature. Usually the minister will first caution any person who is stretching the colony regulations too far—for instance by showing too much interest in photographs or pictures (considered to be vain), by being overly concerned with one's flower garden (over-watering taxes the limited water supply), or by frequent outbursts of anger. If change is not evident in the person's behaviour, then the preacher and the elders will decide on a punishment. The commonly accepted practice is to have the guilty party stand during church service, or kneel in front of the entire congregation and confess guilt, or sit with the children. . . . In cases of minor transgressions against colony rules, the minister, as the elected official responsible for maintaining colony discipline, needs deep human understanding to know when and where to draw the line.

—David Flint (1975)

are found mainly in Alberta, Saskatchewan, and BC, while the Schmiedeleut are in Manitoba. The differences between them are slight, a measure of how conservative or liberal each is.

The three groups exist among roughly 300 farming colonies in Canada, each comprising 60 to 150 people who share a "community of goods," except for small personal possessions. They have frequently encountered opposition to their communal farming practices from other farmers and, in the past, also from provincial governments. The Hutterite system gave them several advantages over single-family farms. By pooling their resources, they could amass greater funds for equipment and supplies, and secure large contracts for their agricultural products, supplied by a large, well-trained, and comparatively cheap workforce.

Hutterite children sit on the front porch of their home in a colony near Moose Jaw, Saskatchewan. More than a third of Canadian Hutterites are below the age of 15. Do you think this means their population is on the rise?

Other characteristics separate the Hutterites from the general population. The primary language of the community is an Austrian dialect of German, which is taught in schools along with a more widely used German dialect and English. They live an austere and conservative lifestyle. They wear dark clothing—black headscarves with white polka dots, long-sleeved blouses and dresses, and long skirts (never pants) for the women. They are not permitted televisions, radios, snowmobiles (for recreational rather than work use), jewellery, makeup, dancing, or swimming (nakedness is an issue). They have a strong sense of spiritual superiority over the mainstream that appears in such phrases as the following, posted on churches: "Whoever cannot give up his private property as well as his own self-will cannot become a disciple and follower of Christ. The ungodly go each their own egotistical way of greed and profit. To such we should not be conformed" (Kirkby, 2007, p. 5).

Religion and Gender

Organized world religions are generally characterized by patriarchal power structures. Women tend to have subordinate roles that marginalize their participation. During the second wave of feminism in the 1960s and early 1970s, women in North America and western Europe became increasingly critical of Christian practices. They viewed Christianity's embedded patriarchy as an influential cultural factor in the reproduction of gender inequality. Consider, they said, just a few examples from the Bible:

- "Man" was created in God's image, while "woman" was created from spare parts (a rib, we are told) to be his companion. (Male and female humans have the same number of ribs.)
- The first woman, Eve, is blamed for having all humans banished from the paradise Eden after she succumbed to temptation by eating an apple supplied to her by the devil.

- The most memorable female characters in the Bible are associated with sin and destruction; among them are Mary Magdalene, who is commonly identified as a prostitute; Delilah, who brought about Samson's downfall; and Jezebel, who was denounced for introducing the worship of rival gods into Israel, and whose name is synonymous with immorality.

Add to these points the Christian tradition of a wife's obedience, subservience, and even belonging to her husband, and you have some powerful examples that inform, transmit, and reproduce patriarchal structures of inequality, including **androcentrism** (from *andro* meaning "man") and sexism. This same patriarchal inequality is blamed for numerous instances of women's oppression in society, from the denial of voting privileges and work opportunities to sexual objectification and male violence. In this sense, Christianity—in fact, all **Abrahamic religions** (including Islam and Judaism)—has much to answer for from a feminist perspective.

Women Priests in the Anglican Church

The Church of England, otherwise known as the Anglican Church (in Canada) or the Episcopal Church (in the United States), is the largest Protestant denomination in the world, with an estimated membership of between 76 and 84 million. Over the past half-century, the battle for women to take on the orders of deacons, priests, and bishops has been long, hard, and accompanied by very emotional dialogue that has at times seriously divided the Church. Of the 38 individual provinces that make up the Anglican Church, the first two to be permitted to ordain female priests were the United States and Canada, in 1976. In Canada, on 30 November 1976, six women were ordained almost simultaneously (so that no one would be considered the first), in four different dioceses.

The situation in the United States is not as clear. While the General Convention passed a resolution stating that "no one shall be denied access" to ordination into the three orders (deacons, priests, bishops) on the basis of their sex, another resolution protects bishops who oppose women priests in their dioceses. As late as 2004, there were still three (of one hundred) dioceses whose bishops would not allow the ordination of women. Bishop Jack Iker, of Fort Worth, Texas, expressed his resistance:

> Are we a culturally conditioned church, trying to keep up with the times, and changing practices and teachings to conform with the times, or are we a part of the historic biblical church of the ages? (2003)

The bishop's rhetorical question raises a conundrum that is central to organized religion today: how to preserve time-honoured values that are central to the church while remaining relevant to a society with changing values and practices.

It wasn't until 1998, when the Japanese province voted to ordain women priests, that most Anglican provinces accepted female clergy. The "mother church" in England began permitting ordination of women only in 1993, four years after the first female bishop was ordained, in the United States. The first female Anglican bishop in Canada was Victoria Matthews, who was consecrated in 1994; at the time, Canada was only the third Anglican province to have a woman bishop. As of 2019, Canada and the United States have had more women bishops (8) than any other province. England itself did not have a woman bishop until 2015, and currently just half of the 44 Anglican provinces allow the consecration of women bishops.

The resistance to women holding positions of authority within the Church is not restricted to Anglicans. It remains the official position of the Roman Catholic Church and of some fundamentalist Christian groups in Canada and the United States (e.g. the Southern Baptists) that women should not be ordained.

Why is there such opposition? Much of it comes back to Christianity's embedded patriarchy, which is extremely difficult to overcome in an institution that derives much of its meaning from its history and traditions. Many Church leaders still justify their opposition to the ordination of women on the grounds that Jesus had no female disciples. Of course, in the patriarchal culture in which Jesus lived, there would have been strong social opposition to his having female disciples. He was revolutionary enough in his respectful treatment of women. And he had women followers who dedicated their lives to learning from him, with his approval (see his attitude toward Mary, sister of Martha, in Luke 10:38–42). The negative attitude of the disciple Paul, as expressed in his letters to the Corinthians, reflects the cultural attitude toward women at that time:

> As in all the churches of the saints, the women should keep silence in the churches. For they are not permitted to speak, but should be subordinate, as even the law says. If there is anything they desire to know, let them ask their husbands at home. For it is shameful for a woman to speak in church. (1 Cor. 14:33–35)

A similar attitude is expressed in Paul's correspondence with Timothy:

> Let a woman learn in silence with all submissiveness. I permit no woman to teach or to have authority over men; she is to keep silent. For Adam was formed first, then Eve; and Adam was not deceived, but the woman was deceived and became a transgressor. Yet woman will be saved through bearing children, if she continues in faith and love and holiness, with modesty. (1 Tim. 2:11–15)

Paul's historical role was to take the ideas of Jesus and organize them into a structure. That the role itself was patriarchal reflects the culture of his upbringing and experience.

What Do YOU Think?

1. Do you think that Paul's statements were (to use Bishop Iker's phrase) "culturally conditioned"?
2. Why do you think that the "innovations" of female priests and bishops came not from the centre of the Anglican Church in England (where the church head, the Archbishop of Canterbury, is housed) but from the fringe or periphery areas of New Zealand, Africa, and North America?

TROY FLEECE / REGINA LEADER-POST

In July 2018, Jane Kryzanowski, of Regina, became the Canadian bishop for the Roman Catholic Women Priests (RCWP). The international organization asserts a connection to the Roman Catholic Church, even though it is not recognized by the Catholic Church, which bars the ordination of women. Can a religion that bars women from positions of authority represent all of its members equally?

Banning Burkini, Headscarves, and Other Conspicuous Religious Symbols

In 1905, the government of France passed a law separating church and state. It stated that the government would not officially recognize or fund any religion. The law was invoked in the 1980s, during debates about French children wearing signs of their religion: Christian students wearing crosses, Jewish boys wearing yarmulkes (kippahs), Sikh boys wearing turbans, and Muslim girls wearing headscarves. The debate centred on two competing principles: freedom of expression and *laïcité*, or secularism of the French state. When, in 1989, three girls were expelled from a school near Paris for refusing to remove their headscarves, the official government opinion was that the school's punishment was too extreme, violating the students' freedom of expression. Supporters of the school's actions argued the opposite, claiming that allowing the girls to wear their headscarves was in essence upholding the oppressive demands of a patriarchal religious culture that prohibits women from revealing more than the face in public.

In the three decades since then, the same debate has played out numerous times, in France and elsewhere, pitting secularists on one side against defenders of religious freedom on the other. Those who oppose any ban on veils, yarmulkes, and turbans insist that these symbols are indispensable elements of their religious observance and should be protected in societies that value freedom of expression and of religion. Proponents of laïcité claim to find the public display of "conspicuous" religious symbols offensive and inappropriate in a secular society. Of all the religious symbols that secularists find objectionable, it is the Muslim headscarf that seems to make them most uncomfortable. In 2016, controversy erupted when several towns on the French Riviera imposed bans on the "burkini," a full body-covering swimsuit worn especially by Muslim women. The mayor of Cannes, the first town to pass the ban, characterized the burkini as "a symbol of Islamist extremism" (Poirier, 2016). A French court that upheld the ban adopted a similar view. In its ruling, the court invoked high-profile terrorist attacks that had happened recently in the country, stating,

> In the context of a state of emergency and after recent Islamist attacks in France, the conspicuous display of religious signs, in this instance in the shape beachwear, is susceptible to create or increase tensions and risk affecting public order. (quoted in Poirier, 2016)

The burkini is a form of dress that allows beach-going Muslim women to comply with Islamic code regarding modesty of appearance. However, in the eyes of the court, it was a frightening symbol of violent religious extremism.

Canada has had its own debates around the display of conspicuous religious symbols. Sikh officers in the Royal Canadian Mounted Police were prohibited from wearing turbans on duty until 1990, and Sikhs have frequently gone to court to defend their right to carry the kirpan, a small ceremonial knife, in schools, in government buildings, and on flights. However, the Muslim headscarf remains the flashpoint in debates. In 2007, a nine-year-old girl was kicked out of a soccer tournament in Quebec

Yasuyoshi Chiba/AFP/Getty Images

During the beach volleyball competition at the 2016 Summer Olympics in Rio de Janeiro, some Muslim women donned body-covering burkinis, challenging the norms of a sport where women are expected to put their bodies on full display. Are both of these athletes conforming to the patriarchal gender expectations of their respective cultures? Is either one really free to dress as she pleases?

for wearing a headscarf. The soccer association cited FIFA, the Fédération Internationale de Football Association, in defending its decision. In December 2011, the federal government banned the wearing of the face-covering *niqab* for new citizens taking the oath of Canadian citizenship; the law was eventually overturned, but not before sparking bitter debates about the right to religious freedom versus the expectation that newcomers to Canada should renounce the traditions of their homeland if they clash with Canadian mainstream cultural values such as a woman's right to reveal her face in public.

In 2013, Quebec's Parti Québécois (PQ) government proposed a law to ban the wearing of all conspicuous religious symbols in public-sector workplaces, including not just government offices but hospitals, government-run daycares, and public schools. The bill failed to pass before the PQ was defeated by the Liberals in the 2014 provincial election. Five years later, in June 2019, the ruling Coalition Avenir Québec (CAQ) passed Bill 21, which prohibits the province's public-sector employees (e.g., teachers, police officers, Crown prosecutors, and judges) from wearing religious symbols while carrying out their civic duties. While the law applies to all visible religious symbols, including Christian crosses and Jewish kippah (plural *kippot*), it will disproportionately affect hijab-wearing Muslim teachers.

Why is this happening in Quebec? In part it is a legacy of the Quiet Revolution that began in the 1960s. If you read Chapter 10, you may remember that the Quiet Revolution refers to a set of province-wide social reforms aimed at curtailing the authority of the Catholic Church in matters relating to education, labour unions, politics, and the delivery

What Do YOU Think?

1. What is your position on Bill 21? Where should we draw the line between defending the freedom of religious expression and promoting secularism, or the separation of church and state?
2. Do you expect other provinces to follow Quebec's lead in passing legislation like Bill 21?

"Conspicuous symbols of religion" include turbans and yarmulkes—head coverings for men—and yet the debate always seems to centre on clothing worn by Muslim women. Why do you think that is the case?

Quick Hits

The Myth about Islam and Women

While it can be argued that there is a tendency in all countries where organized religion is strong for women to be oppressed, the countries of the Middle East, where Islam is the dominant religion, have been singled out as especially oppressive and misogynistic. It is part of a generalized and uncritical targeting of Islam by the conservative Western media, a targeting that is related to deeper Euro-centric cultural beliefs that reproduce **Orientalism** and **Islamophobia**. When examining Islam and the rights of women, it is important to separate those anti-female practices that are specifically Muslim from those practices that happen to occur in Muslim countries but are not supported by the faith. The following list draws on Haroon Siddiqui's book *Being Muslim* (2006):

- The practice of honour killings (killing female relatives for alleged sexual misconduct that brings dishonour upon the family) in countries such as Pakistan, Turkey, and Jordan is *not* an Islamic tradition.
- The practice of female genital cutting (FGC) in North and Central Africa is *not* condoned by Islam. (At the First Islamic Ministerial Conference on the Child, held in Morocco in 2005, FGC was condemned as un-Islamic.)
- The number of cases of polygyny (one man having more than one wife) in Muslim families in Western and Muslim countries is greatly exaggerated. Most Muslim marriages involve couples.
- Most Muslim women around the world do not wear a hijab or head-covering. (Siddiqui, 2006, pp. 96-125)

What Do YOU Think?

What do you think contributes to the distorted view that prevails in the West of the way women are treated under Islamic law and tradition?

---

of social services. The secularization has continued steadily since then.

Quebec nationalism is also a factor. The CAQ was born out of the ashes of the PQ, the party that campaigned persistently for Quebec to separate from Canada. Quebec's premier, François Legault, was first elected to the National Assembly as a member of the PQ before becoming a co-founder of the CAQ.

Nationalism often comes with a dark side. The French term *"pure laine"* (literally "pure wool") is used in Quebec to denote a kind of French racial purity going back to the seventeenth century. Given that the francophone population includes a high percentage of Indigenous genes, this is somewhat ironic. Quebec nationalism may have taken its darkest turn in January 2017, when a young white nationalist murdered six people at a mosque in Quebec City. The killer's name was one of several inscribed on the rifle used to kill 51 Muslims in Christchurch, New Zealand, in March 2019, testifying to how acts of extremism beget others.

Religion and Social Change

Religion has been a primary agent of change throughout history. Both the emergence and spread of new religions—like Islam—and the loss of native religions have brought about and reflected significant social and cultural change. Examples already touched on include the Protestant ethic, which influenced cultural normative structures, and the European missionary movement, which was used to convert and subjugate populations as part of the broader aims of colonialism. And while religion has been used to submit populations to the will of authority, it has been used to emancipate populations as well. Take figures such as Mahatma Gandhi, Mother Teresa, Martin Luther King, Malcolm X, Desmond Tutu, and the aforementioned Canadians Stanley Knowles, J.S. Woodsworth, and Tommy Douglas. All of them were instrumental in using religion as a point of social change for the purposes of social justice. Marx, you will recall, claimed that religion stifles movements for change by pacifying people and persuading them to focus not on their worldly hardships but on the promise of a better life in heaven. However, religion was a driving force behind anti-colonial liberation movements, anti-racism and anti-discrimination movements, struggles against poverty, and democratic reform throughout the nineteenth and twentieth centuries.

Christian Religious Colonialism and Its Impact among Indigenous People in Canada

When missionaries brought Christianity to Indigenous people in Canada, their actions were an integral part of colonization, designed to make the people more like Europeans, not just in beliefs but in other social areas such as gender roles (see Karen Anderson's *Chain Her by One Foot*) and in their obedience to political authority. But the people also had **agency**. They were not merely victims of colonially imposed religions. As Indigenous prophets reacted to the new world of Christian beliefs and ensuing political turmoil, they began to promote innovative religious beliefs. The early nineteenth-century Seneca prophet Handsome Lake (c. 1735–1815) combined elements of traditional belief with what his people had learned from Quakers who had spent time among the Seneca. The Code of Handsome Lake combined traditional aspects of the Great Law of Peace, which had brought the initially five nations (Mohawk, Oneida, Onondaga, Cayuga, and Seneca) of the Iroquois together into one confederacy, with Quaker elements such as a strong opposition to witchcraft, sexual promiscuity, and gambling.

Indigenous people developed new forms of Christianity by integrating European-based religion into their own belief system and practices. In many instances, these adapted forms of Christianity enabled the people to preserve or return to the cohesiveness of Durkheim's moral community that had existed in pre-contact times. In *"Ta'n Teliktlamsitasit* ('Ways of Believing'): Mi'kmaw Religion in Eskasoni, Nova Scotia," Angela Robinson uses the term **Catholic-Traditionalists** to refer to Mi'kmaq who adopted Catholicism but incorporated traditional elements into their religious practices (2002, p. 143). Mi'kmaq scholar **Marie Battiste** offers the following description of how her people claimed Catholicism as their own to give strength to their community:

> In 1610 the Mi'kmaq people entered into a compact with the Holy Roman Empire when our Chief Membertou and 140 others were first baptized. While our alliance with the Church was more political than spiritual, it was solidified in daily rituals when the French priest Father Antoine Maillard learned Mi'kmaq and began addressing the spiritual questions of the people. . . . Following the expulsion of the French priests [by the English] . . . [the] Mi'kmaq people held to their strong spiritual rituals in the Catholic Church by conducting their own services. They had prayer leaders who led Sunday prayers, baptized children, accepted promises of marriage, and provided last rites for the dying. . . . These Catholic rituals continue today in many communities, and elders still play an important role in them, although a priest in the community offers the primary services. (1997, pp. 157–8)

During the late nineteenth and early twentieth centuries, Christian missionaries, along with federal officials in Canada and the United States, took aim at important Indigenous ceremonies that were conducted, in part, to nourish a strong, cohesive sense of community. These ceremonies were the heart and soul of "religious competition" for missionaries, and a form of resistance to political domination for the government officials. The Sun Dance, the main ceremony for Indigenous groups living on the Prairies, is one example. "Sun Dance" is an English term. The Blackfoot, who live in southern Alberta, termed the ceremony *Okan*, after the pole at the centre of the ceremony. The Okan was initiated, sponsored, and presided over by a woman:

> The decision to hold a Sun Dance was made by a pure woman . . . who had a male relative in danger of losing his life. A husband might be ill or a son may not have returned from a raid. The woman made a public vow that if the person's life was spared, she would sponsor a Sun Dance. Then, if her prayer was answered, she began preparations for the summer festival. (Dempsey, 1995, p. 392)

Montana governor John Rickard, speaking in 1894, captured the essence of Christian culture's attitude toward non-Christian religious practices:

> Investigation . . . convinces me that it is not only inhuman and brutalizing, unnatural and indecent, and therefore abhorrent to Christian civilization, but that its aims and purposes are a menace to the peace and welfare of communities. My information . . . leads me to regard the proposed exhibition as wholly inconsistent with Christian civilization. (Quoted in Dusenberry, 1998, p. 219)

One aspect of the ceremony gave Canadian government officials an excuse for issuing a complete ban on the Sun Dance in 1895. Sometimes, as a spiritual offering, young men inserted leather thongs through their chest or back muscles, attaching the other end either to a pole or to the skull of a buffalo. They would then dance until the thongs ripped free—a painful process. Section 114 of the Indian Act was amended to include a provision making it an indictable offence to take part in any ceremony "of which the wounding or mutilation of the dead or living body of any human being or animal forms a part or is a feature." Technically, this would have made the "mortification of the flesh" (selfflagellation, or whipping oneself) illegal, even though it was associated with Christian religious dedication and was practised throughout most of Christianity's history (and is still practised in parts of Latin America and the Philippines). Little Bear, a Cree leader who had moved with his band to Montana, is reported to have

stated that he was willing to remove that part of the ceremony in the spirit of getting along with colonial authorities (Dusenberry, 1998, p. 220). However, the entire ceremony was deemed "uncivilized," prompting this response by one Blackfoot:

> We know that there is nothing injurious to our people in the Sun-dance. . . . It has been our custom, during many years, to assemble once every summer for this festival. . . . We fast and pray that we may be able to lead good lives and to act more kindly towards each other.

> I do not understand why the white men desire to put an end to our religious ceremonials. What harm can they do our people? If they deprive us of our religion, we will have nothing left, for we know of no other that can take its place. (Quoted in McClintock, 1910, p. 378)

The ceremony continued to be held in secret. Participants who were discovered were arrested. The Sun Dance did not return publicly in Canada until 1951. However, the damage to traditional religious beliefs had already taken its toll. The ceremony never recovered its former prominence.

More recently, religious revival among Indigenous people has gained popularity. Termed **neo-traditionalism**, it involves the reinterpretation of traditional beliefs and practices in ways that incorporate elements unique to one's own culture and others borrowed from Indigenous cultures elsewhere. The sweat lodge, the drum, and the medicine wheel are examples of elements used in neo-traditionalist practice. The recovery of traditional customs has been very important in helping Indigenous people find and strengthen their identity. Neo-traditionalist practices are often used in the rehabilitation of people in prison or in treatment for substance abuse.

The Missionary Position

The primary role of missionaries is to change people, to make them leave the religious path they are on and walk a new one, one that often bears the mark of

The Point Is . . .

Jihad Is a Misunderstood Term

A religious practice wrongly connected with terrorism in the Arabic world is jihad. Movies, websites, 24-hour news channels, radio call-in shows, and even dictionaries and encyclopedias often lead us to believe that *jihad* means "holy war." Yet if you look in English copies of the Qu'ran, the Muslim holy book, you will find the Arabic word translated as "struggle, striving, endeavour." The following is a description of jihad taken from the Qu'ran:

> Those who believe, and emigrate
> And strive with might
> And main, in Allah's cause
> With their goods and their persons,
> Have the highest rank
> In the sight of Allah:
> They are the people
> Who will achieve (salvation). (9:20)

There are three types of jihad: personal, community, and martial. In his insightful book *Global Islamic Politics*, **Mir Zohair Husain** explains them in the following way:

> The personal jihad or **jihad-i-akbar**, is the greatest jihad. It represents the perpetual struggle required of all Muslims to purge their baser instincts. Greed, racism, hedonism, jealousy, revenge, hypocrisy, lying, cheating, and calumny [false and malicious accusation] must each be driven from the soul by waging jihad-i-akbar, warring against one's lower nature and leading a virtuous life. . . .

> Likewise, **ummaic jihad** addresses wrongs within the community of Muslims, whether by the written word or by the spoken word. Ummaic jihad represents the nonviolent struggle for freedom, justice and truth within the dar-al-Islam [Muslim world]. . . .
>
> Martial or violent jihad is referred to in Islam as **jihad-i-asghar** (lit., the smaller, lower, or lesser jihad). Martial jihad ideally represents a struggle against aggressors who are not practicing Muslims. . . . Martial jihad should be used to protect and to promote the integrity of Islam and to defend the umma [community] against hostile unbelievers, whether they are invading armies or un-Islamic internal despots. (Husain, 1995, pp. 37–8)

Muslim college students asked for examples of jihad in their lives have answered with the following:

- donating money to a charity rather than spending it on yourself
- studying for an exam rather than watching television
- working hard at a job you don't like because your family needs the money
- avoiding temptation in all forms (similar to Christian avoidance of the seven deadly sins).

What Do YOU Think?

Describe in your own words how the three types of jihad differ. Why do you think non-martial forms of jihad are not well known outside the Muslim world?

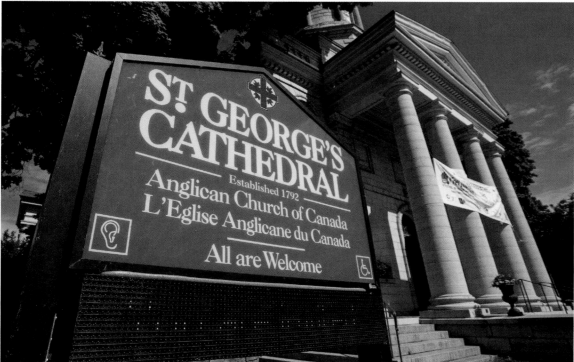

THE CANADIAN PRESS/Lars Hagberg

At the Anglican Church of Canada's 42nd General Synod, in July 2019, a vote on a motion that would have allowed its clergy to solemnize same-sex marriages failed to pass by a few percentage points. You will recall that same-sex marriage has been legal in Canada since 2005. Should religious organizations in Canada preserve traditional practices or adapt to changing social and cultural circumstances?

a different culture. But it is also important that missionaries exemplify the values that are at the core of the religion they represent, particularly the principle of charity. Here the sociologist asks whether the two aims clash. Can there be role strain between conversion and charity?

The practice of sending missionaries into developing countries in need of financial assistance is sometimes called **aid evangelism**. The financial assistance is a kind of **tied aid**—money that comes with strings attached. Often when countries in the developed world (including Canada) spend money on aid, it is given with the condition that the people receiving the assistance must spend at least some of the money on products and services that come from the donor country. Another term for this is **phantom aid**, which captures the idea that the aid is not real but rather a form of investment.

So, do religious-based aid workers and the religious communities that sponsor them sometimes see aid as a form of investment in conversion? Aid evangelism has taken various forms over the last few decades. Some American fundamentalist groups delivered thousands of 70-pound food packages to starving people in Iraq. The packages were covered with biblical verses written in Arabic. Following the disastrous tsunami that hit southern Asia in December 2004, the 2000-member Antioch Community Church, based in Waco, Texas, sent "aid workers" to Sri Lanka to stage children's plays about Jesus and hold Christian prayer services for those suffering from the devastating effects of the flood. Sri Lanka is primarily a Buddhist country, though Hinduism and Islam are also practised; the Christian element is small. Backlash to perceived aid evangelism caused vandalism and threats to local Christian groups, even to the point of attacking the

What Do YOU Think?

What do you think is the motivation behind attacks on Christian aid agencies and government intervention against Christian charity?

offices of the Christian aid agency World Vision, which had no connection with the questionable missionary practices. In Indonesia, the world's largest Muslim country, the government blocked the move of American religious-based aid agency World Help to settle 50 Muslim children from the flooded Aceh province to a Christian orphanage, as they suspected that conversion was the cost of the aid.

Liberation Theology

Liberation theology is a progressive school of Catholic thought that advocates social justice for the poor. It takes as its model the life of Jesus as being politically opposed to privilege. It resembles the **social gospel** movement put forward by Protestant ministers of the late nineteenth and early twentieth centuries, except that it is rooted almost exclusively in the Catholic Church, particularly in Latin America, and especially among members of the Jesuit and Maryknoll religious orders. Liberation theology opposes the oppression of the poor by the corrupt, ruling class in developing and underdeveloped countries. Its proponents emphasize social practices that improve the situation for the poor. These practices are devised based on input received from the poor, not from the rich who, historically, have supported the "monarchic and pyramidic" system of hierarchical authority of the Catholic Church (Russell, 2001). There has been strong opposition from conservatives within the hierarchy of the Catholic Church, particularly those bishops in Latin American countries who had been appointed from the elite class. Marxist advocates for the poor argue that these bishops are conscious of their own class interests, and act upon these interests over those of the poor.

The Sandinista National Liberation Front (known by its Spanish initials FSLN) was a Marxist revolutionary group in Nicaragua that began in the 1960s and overthrew the US-backed right-wing dictator Anastasio Samoza Debayle in 1979. The Sandinistas stayed in political power until 1990 despite an ongoing battle with the counter-insurgency Contras, who were backed by the American Central Intelligence Agency. The Sandinistas supported priests who worked to benefit the poor. The Catholic hierarchy in Nicaragua had supported the dictatorship of Samosa. In an official statement made in 1950, Nicaragua's conservative bishops said,

> [A]ll authority comes from God. God is the Author of all that exists, and from the Author comes Authority; [faithful Catholics] should remember that when they obey the Political Authority, they do not dishonor themselves, but rather they act in a way that basically constitutes obeisance to God. (Quoted in Gilbert, 1988, p. 131)

Priests working with the poor and who believed in liberation theology became members of the FSLN. When the Sandinistas came to power, some priests took political office but were quickly reprimanded by Pope John Paul II and the Vatican hierarchy. One such priest was Father Miguel D'Escoto, who became the foreign minister for the Nicaraguan government. In 2008, he was elected president of the General Assembly of the United Nations.

Brazil is the largest Catholic country in the world, with well over 130 million people, yet it has a chronic shortage of priests. It has been estimated that in Latin America, there is one priest for every 7000 Catholics, versus one for every 880 in the United States (Russell, 2001). One strategy to overcome this shortage supported and implemented by liberation theologians is the establishment of "base communities," numbering as many as about 75,000 in Brazil alone (Russell, 2001). Within the base communities, which average 10 to 30 members each, the focus is on shared religious instruction and prayer as well as communal self-help. Though local priests provide guidance to community leaders, the principal focus of the groups is on relating the lessons of the Bible to the day-to-day activities of their members, whether they are urbanites, slum-dwellers, or rural *campesinos*.

At a typical base community in the town of Campos Eliseos, 14 miles northwest of Rio de Janeiro, 30 local residents meet every Friday night in a cinderblock home to read the Bible and discuss their problems. Antonio Joinhas, a 44-year-old railroad signalman, relates how one study session inspired a local public health centre:

> After reading how one biblical community helped another to overcome a problem, we decided to work together too. We all supplied the manpower and raised money for materials from the community. Now we've got a health center, and it came from the Bible. (Quoted in Russell, 2001)

Wrap it Up

Summary

Religions touch the spiritual and address human needs that are universal. These aspects of religion are, for the most part, outside the critical eye of sociology. However, religions have social organizations and practices that are well within the domain of the sociologist. They are intimately linked with other aspects of society—hierarchy, gender roles, and colonialism, to name just a few—that sociologists regularly analyze. From that link comes the very critical approach that I have brought to this chapter.

Some readers might think that I have gone too far in praising and defending Islam while criticizing Christianity. That is a legitimate impression, but it is not what I set out to do. What I have tried to do is to highlight the social benefits of organized religion while casting a light on some of areas of sociological concern, such as religious intolerance and the abuse of power. In Canada, Islam is often a target of ignorant and intolerant views, while Christian values and practices that are socially beneficial in most contexts have been used on some occasions as instruments of power by government and religious officials (even well-meaning ones). A critical sociology textbook written in a country where Islam, Buddhism, Judaism, or Hinduism are abused as tools of power (and that happens) would offer a different perspective by taking a closer critical look at the abuse of power within those religions.

Think Back

Questions for Critical Review

1. How would you—in your own words—define *religion*? What characteristics do the largest established religious traditions (Judaism, Christianity, Islam) share?
2. Could that workout group in my local park be considered a cult? What ingredients would it need to have to be considered a new religious movement?
3. What are some manifest and latent functions of organized religion? What are religion's latent dysfunction? (Flip back to Table 1.4 if you need some inspiration.) On balance, would you say that religion is a force for good in Canada today?
4. How could you critique organized religion from a feminist standpoint?
5. What is the relationship between religion and colonialism?
6. Which of the religions listed in Table 11.2 do you think will show the most change (increase or decrease) when the 2021 census data on religious affiliation are released? Explain your answer.
7. Is it possible to reconcile freedom of religious expression with a policy of secularism? Why or why not?
8. Would you say that in your own life, religion plays a large, small, or negligible role in your everyday life? Why do you think that is? What would make religion more relevant to you?

Read On

Recommended Print and Online Resources

Casefile, Case 60: Jonestown, https://casefile-podcast.com/case-60-jonestown-part-1/

- This three-part podcast examines one of the cults that gave new religious movements a bad name, the Peoples Temple Agricultural Project, otherwise known as Jonestown. The series traces the movement from the childhood of its charismatic leader, Jim Jones, all the way to the group's mass suicide in 1978, and offers insights into Jones's motivations and his appeal to those who followed him.

Haroon Siddiqui, *Being Muslim* (Toronto: Groundwood Books, 2006).

- This well-written work is designed to inform non-Muslim readers on what Islam is and is not about.

Isabelle Knockwood, *Out of the Depths: The Experiences of Mi'kmaw Children at the Indian Residential School in Shubenacadie, Nova Scotia* (Halifax: Fernwood Publishing, 2001).

- This classic work by a First Nations writer examines life at a residential school for Mi'kmaq children.

Margaret Humphreys, *Empty Cradles: A Shameful Secret, a Miscarriage of Justice, and a Woman Who Wouldn't Give Up* (London: Corgi Books, 1995).

- This book introduces the reader to the story of over 150,000 English children from marginalized families, who were deported to Australian orphanages and similar institutions.

Marx, Weber and Durkheim on Religion, www.jeramyt.org/papers/sociology-of-religion.html

- Jeramy Townsley's very useful (and often plagiarized) article compares the three main sociological theorists of religion.

The Immanent Frame: Secularism, Religion, and the Public Sphere, http://blogs.ssrc.org/tif/category/sociology-of-religion

- Founded in conjunction with the Social Science Research Council's program on religion and the public sphere, this site provides intelligently written blogs and useful articles on the sociology of religion, contributed by specialists representing a range of disciplines.

The Sociological Study of Religion, http://hirr.hartsem.edu/sociology/about_the_field.html

- Maintained by the Hartford Institute for Religion Research, this site presents a good overview of topics and current researchers in the sociological study of religion.

Timothy J. Gianotti, Jr, *In the Light of a Blessed Tree: Illuminations of Islamic Belief, Practice, and History* (Eugene, OR: Wipf & Stock, 2011).

- This is an excellent, readable work explaining the basic beliefs and practices of Islam.

Education

Reading this chapter will help you to ...

- Discuss the history of public education in Canada from the mid-nineteenth century to the present.

- Explain how Foucault's concept of the docile body applies to education.

- Look critically at education through the lens of cultural reproduction theory.

- Outline the advantages and disadvantages of "streaming" (or "tracking") in elementary and secondary education.

- Discuss the positive and negative effects on postsecondary education of becoming reliant on (a) adjunct instructors, (b) online education, and (c) corporate sponsorship of research and infrastructure.

- State your view, from a sociologist's standpoint, of plagiarism occurring today in postsecondary institutions.

- Assess the social value of having schools run by and for marginalized groups such as Indigenous and black Canadian students.

▲ © Photograph by Della Rollins

For Starters

The Academic Underclass: Take a Good Look at Your Professor

Take a good look at your sociology professor or TA—right now, while they're not looking. Are they relatively young? Do they always seem to be running late, to be hurrying in or out, to be distracted before and after class? Does your prof also teach at another school? Does the department secretary know who you're speaking about when you say your instructor's name?

If your instructor is teaching an intro soc course, chances are they've been hired only for a session, a semester, or a year. They probably aren't a full-time, tenured member of the department. They likely fall into the category of "contract faculty" or "sessional staff." Or maybe they're an "adjunct professor," which sounds a bit loftier but still means that they're teaching courses and students—particularly intro courses—that permanent staff members don't want to teach. My *Canadian Oxford Dictionary* defines *adjunct* as "an assistant or a subordinate person, esp. one with a temporary appointment only."

In other words, the person teaching you may be fully qualified but an academic nomad, part of a growing postsecondary underclass that get paid less for teaching you than full-timers do. Their growing presence is an important change taking place in education today. In this chapter, we'll look at what else is changing, and why—and, most important, how it's affecting students and society today.

What Do YOU think?

Do you think you can tell the difference between a full-time professor and an adjunct? Do you know what percentage of your instructors fit the latter category?

Introduction: Education as a Social Institution

To a sociologist, the social institution of education is important because of the multiple influences it has on everything from socialization and status formation to social order and economic productivity. When we refer to the *institution* of education, we're referring to an enduring set of ideas about education and how it can be used to accomplish goals that are deemed important to society. Education is an extremely powerful tool for promoting ideas among impressionable young people. Children spend more time at school than they do with their parents.

Education has a significant impact on the socialization of children and young adults. At school, behaviours are modified, skills for future employment are taught, social interaction and conflict are negotiated, and notions of social reality are defined. Structures of inequality such as classism, sexism, heterosexism, and racism are usually verbally discouraged even as they may be reproduced in actions taken by school boards, school officials, and teachers. Schools prepare children to be productive and obedient citizens. How children do in school plays a large role in determining their potential social acceptability and mobility.

The Rise of Public Education in Canada

Before the Industrial Revolution in Europe and North America there was little interest in educating the masses. But beginning with the rise of industrial capitalism, companies started to demand more from their labour force. Specifically, as industry became more complex, it required a more disciplined, trainable, and literate workforce that would be more economically productive. Industrialization and public education, then, became interdependent in the same way that labour is dependent on **capital** and capital on labour.

In Canada, education was seen as an important means of achieving economic modernization as early as 1846. That's when education reformer Egerton Ryerson (after whom Ryerson University is named) began promoting the idea of a school system that would be universal, free, and compulsory. According to Canadian sociologist **Stephen Schecter** (1977), Ryerson's public education model was not just a method of producing social *order*: it was also a way to ensure social *control* by subverting potential conflict among immigrants, particularly the incoming Irish labourers forced to leave their country during the potato famine of the 1840s. The Irish were poor, and their reputation for rowdy hooliganism preceded them to North America. Speaking of the unskilled Catholic migrants, Ryerson warned, "the physical disease and death which have accompanied their influx among us may be the precursor of the worst pestilence of social insubordination and disorder" (Schecter, 1977, p. 373). Education could avert the threat of discontent from these "alien" labourers by assimilating them into the dominant Protestant culture.

Schecter (1977) argues that compulsory, state-run education legitimized and acted to support social inequality, as it was premised on centralization and uniformity—instruments of social control to be used on the emerging working class. To ensure the uniformity of education—from textbooks to teachers—provincial boards were established to act as executive bodies to set up and maintain large systems of "normal schools" (the old and sociologically significant name for teacher's colleges). School boards were able to enforce codes of discipline and enact hierarchical authority relations that placed both students and parents in positions subordinate to school officials, including the teachers. Such practices served to a significant extent to subordinate the working class and to punish those who were "other than normal" (i.e. deviant).

How was compulsory education used as an instrument of social subordination? Consider the way education was used to rank and sort children in ways that were extremely destructive to those deemed "inferior." University of Lethbridge sociology professor Claudia Malacrida studied Alberta's Michener Institute, where many children were forcibly detained after being labelled "feeble-minded," a technical term based on questionable science of the time. In her study *A Special Hell: Institutional Life in Alberta's Eugenic Years* (2015), she identifies three ways in which children of different intellectual abilities were sorted out of the mainstream:

1. through truancy laws punishing those who did not come to class;
2. through tests and curriculums that standardized expectations of educational success; and
3. through "health" testing conducted via medical and psychological examinations (Malacrida, 2015, pp. 11–12).

Once sorted out of the regular system, these children were institutionalized in places such as the Michener Institute. There, most of their freedoms or rights (including their reproductive rights) were taken away. Their education (deemed "vocational") consisted mainly of forced labour that often served the financial needs of the institutions, a situation very similar to that of the residential schools that housed Indigenous children.

It may sound cynical to suggest that the state-run school system was born of a need to discipline the growing labour force and legitimize the social order. Bear in mind, though, that in the latter half of the

nineteenth century, when public education systems were established, social reformers were warning of the civil disorder that might result from an unhappy working class. The public education system put a check on social conflict by reinforcing class divisions.

Post-War Expansion and the Human Capital Thesis

The Canadian economy after World War II required a workforce that was better educated than before, fuelling an expansion of colleges and universities across Canada to match the economic boom that peaked during the 1960s. Government officials may have loudly championed the expansion of postsecondary institutions as increasing access to education to all classes, but historians Newson and Buchbinder (1988) have argued that economic considerations were the driving force.

The perceived relationship between the expansion of education and economic growth is part of the **human capital thesis**, which asserts that just as industrial societies invest in factories and equipment to attain greater efficiency, so they invest in schools to enhance the knowledge and skills of their workers. When applied to social inequality, the human

The Point Is . . .

Corporate Sponsorship Poses a Double-Threat to Academic Research

Universities and colleges facing government funding challenges (in other words, all universities and colleges) often seek out corporate sponsorships, particularly in the area of research. While, under the best circumstances, these relationships can bring benefits to both the corporate donor and the postsecondary institution, they can also bring a double threat to the credibility of research. The first threat is infringement on the academic freedom of academic researchers. The second is conflict of interest on the part of senior academic administrators who may be on the payroll of the corporate sponsor, typically in a position on the board of directors.

Both of these threats came to pass in the case of the University of Calgary and the Enbridge Centre for Corporate Sustainability

(ECCS), established 2011–12 and sponsored (not surprisingly) by Enbridge, the Alberta-based multinational fuel distributor. The situation has been well documented in a report commissioned by the Canadian Association of University Teachers (CAUT) in 2017 (Hearn & Van Harten, 2017), an "explainer" in the investigative journalism magazine *The Narwhal* (Wilt, 2017), and a 2018 article in the *Canadian Journal of Sociology*, examining the sharp difference in corporate and non-corporate media coverage of the report (McCartney & Gray, 2018).

Under the sponsorship agreement, Enbridge was to give $225,00 per year for 10 years to the University of Calgary to fund a research institute within the university's school of business. The trouble was that the president of the university at the time held a position on a corporate board at Enbridge, a part-time job for which she was compensated $130,500 annually, a little more than one-third of her salary with the university (Wilt, 2017). This might not have been a problem had the president kept out of any business involving the proposed ECCS. However, the CAUT found evidence that she not only involved herself in the sponsorship negotiations but invoked her position on the Enbridge board to pressure university colleagues to support the deal.

Once the Enbridge sponsorship was in place, the university appointed a faculty member to head up the newly minted ECCS. He was subsequently removed from the position after publicly opposing the Enbridge Northern Gateway Pipeline. The individual later spoke of having received pressure from university administrators to toe the Enbridge line. To his thinking (and mine; there goes *my* corporate sponsorship), he was being asked to step out of his role as an independent, objective researcher to publicly defend the corporate interests of Enbridge. The CAUT report concludes that the faculty member's academic freedom was compromised, "due to a desire on the part of senior U of C leadership to please a significant donor" (Hearn & Van Harten, 2017, p. 4).

One of the recommendations of the CAUT report was that senior university administrators should not hold corporate board positions outside of the university, as doing so might compromise the academic freedom of the university. At the very least, the president of the university should have recused herself from the sponsorship negotiations, refusing to participate because of her conflict of interest.

What Do YOU Think?

1. Should colleges and universities court and accept corporate sponsorship? (Remember: those sponsorships help to pay for new buildings and equipment you might benefit from.) If you say no, then what other avenues should academic institutions pursue to make up the shortfall in funding? If yes, then what ground rules should be in place to govern these kinds of relationships?
2. Should university faculty be allowed to hold positions on corporate boards? If so, under what circumstances? Remember, postsecondary educators have a wealth of learning and research experience to bring to a board that may be dominated by representatives of the business community. And shouldn't everyone be allowed to earn a little extra on the side?

---

capital thesis is used to argue that marginalized groups earn less money than dominant groups because they possess less human capital in the form of education, skill, and experience.

Since the early 1970s, decreases in the taxes charged to corporations (but not to individuals) have contributed to cuts in governmental funding for postsecondary institutions. This has allowed the corporate sector to form stronger ties with cash-hungry colleges and universities that, in return for corporate finance, have made concessions to corporate capital. We see this most in increased advertising on campus, visible everywhere but in the classrooms (coming soon?). Academic research has become more closely tied to corporate agendas and control, especially in such areas as medical/pharmaceutical and agricultural product research. How long, I wonder, before your nutrition science class is brought to you by Gatorade?

Models of Public Education in Canada

The Assimilation Model

Education in Canada has historically been based on a monocultural model that emphasizes **assimilation into the dominant culture**. English Canada was viewed as a white Protestant nation. It was seen as natural that people arriving from outside this dominant culture would need to assimilate in order to fit in. The flaw in the assimilation model is that it failed to recognize that racial bias and discrimination—both inside and outside the school system—make the level playing field on which the assimilation model is premised virtually impossible. According to Henry and Tator (2006), the emphasis on **monoculturalism** (the promotion of just one culture) as opposed to **multiculturalism** formed a pervasive ideology that "influenced the training of educators, the practices of teaching, the content and context of learning, the hiring and promotion practices of boards, and the cultural values and norms underpinning all areas of school life" (Henry & Tator, 2006, p. 213). Students were expected to simply leave their cultural, religious, and ethnic identities at the door.

The assimilationist approach continues to influence Canadian public education, as sociologists George Dei and Agnes Calliste observe (Dei, 1996; Dei & Calliste, 2000). The experience begins in primary school and continues throughout secondary and postsecondary education, where literature courses are often really courses in *English* literature, which typically does not include works translated from other languages. Under these circumstances, English literature is really English cultural studies, representing the only 10 to 15 per cent of Canada's population that is of British ancestry. Implicit in this is the notion that British culture is superior, the only one worth learning.

A product of our monocultural education is the **Great White Male** story of history, which celebrates the accomplishments of men of British descent—our "Founding Fathers"—over the contributions of women, Indigenous people, and immigrants from outside of Britain. A recent example of this narrative came in the form of a flyer I received from a local Conservative member of Parliament. In keeping with how Canadian history is often taught, the flyer describes the Canadian Pacific Railway, which joined Eastern Canada to British Columbia, as "Sir John A.'s Railway," drawing a link between our first prime minister (a white male Conservative) and the origin of the transnational railroad. A more multicultural approach would have mentioned the roughly 17,000 Chinese immigrants who helped build the mountainous stretch of the railway through British Columbia. They worked for $1.00 a day and had to pay for their own food and camping/cooking gear. Their white co-workers did not have to pay for their equipment and were paid between $1.50 and $2.50 per day. The Chinese labourers were tasked with the more difficult and dangerous work of blasting the tunnels and clearing and grading the roadbed. Many died. I would say they made greater contributions and sacrifices than the Great White Man who was prime minister at the time. It was not just one (Great White) man's creation.

What Do YOU Think?

What would you say are the biggest obstacles (e.g. gaps in teacher training, lack of source materials, lack of political will) to designing and implementing a public school curriculum that reflects the diversity of Canadian students while tackling racism in a meaningful way? How might these obstacles be overcome?

Multicultural Education

Canada's federal government implemented its official policy of multiculturalism in 1971 to preserve and promote cultural diversity, while removing the barriers that had denied certain groups full participation within Canadian society. With a new objective of creating a learning environment that would respect all learners, school boards launched initiatives to study and celebrate the lifestyles, traditions, and histories of diverse cultures (Henry & Tator,

2006). These initiatives were based on three fundamental assumptions drawn from a study of multicultural education in six countries:

1. Learning about one's culture would improve educational achievement.
2. Learning about one's culture would promote quality of opportunity.
3. Learning about other cultures would reduce prejudice and discrimination.

How do images like this support the Great White Male version of history? Who is left out of this image?

Problems developed. Teachers often had little knowledge of the cultures they were presenting. Classroom focus tended to favour a museum approach that overlooked the complexity and vitality of these different cultures (Dei, 1996). Educators would focus on historical material and the "exotic" aspects of different cultures—food, festivals, and folklore. They would omit the values and beliefs that were fundamental to shaping a particular cultural identity (Dei, 1996).

Anti-Racism and Anti-Oppression Education

Henry and Tator (2006, pp. 213–14) argue that a glaring weakness of multicultural education is its failure to acknowledge that racism is systemic in Canadian society. While the superficial aspects of "other" cultures were being studied, the problem of racial inequality was being ignored.

Anti-racism and anti-oppression education is meant to eliminate institutional and individual barriers to equity. It is intended to create a classroom environment where

- stereotypes and racist ideas can be exposed;
- sources of information can be critically examined;
- alternative and missing information can be provided;
- students can become equipped to look critically at the accuracy of the information they receive; and
- the reasons for the continued unequal social status of different group can be explored.

The aim of this model is to change institutional policies and practices, as well as individual attitudes and behaviours that reproduce social inequality.

Anti-racism and anti-oppression education first appeared in Canada in the 1980s, when some school boards introduced new policies, including changes to teacher education, new criteria for reviewing and evaluating the practices of educators, greater

Randy Risling/Toronto Star via Getty Images

Toronto's Africentric school opened in September 2009 to students of all ethnic backgrounds, but with a curriculum highlighting the perspectives and experiences of people of African descent. The only school of its kind in Canada has seen enrolment decline slightly over its 10-year history, despite producing decent student outcomes. Is it realistic to expect schools to cover all cultures in equal depth, or are schools centred on race and ethnicity the only answer for students who feel left out of the mainstream curriculum?

analysis of teacher placement procedures, employment equity strategies, and resource and curriculum development (Henry & Tator, 2006). The policy has seen gains and setbacks. As Henry and Tator explain,

> While lip service is paid to . . . ensure equality of opportunity for all students in the classroom, in reality, individuals, organizations, and institutions are far more committed to maintaining the status quo, that is, the cultural hegemony of the dominant culture with which most educators identify. (2006, p. 223)

Topics in the Sociology of Education

The Hidden Curriculum

The **hidden curriculum** is a hot topic in the sociology of education, though its definition varies depending upon the issue being discussed and the vantage point of the sociologist doing the discussing. Essentially, the hidden curriculum consists of the unstated or unofficial goals of the education system. We can look at the hidden curriculum in terms of Robert Merton's concepts of latent functions and latent dysfunctions, defined in Chapter 1.

Eurocentric Curriculum and the University

Despite Canada's multicultural character and state-legislated multicultural policy, a **Eurocentric** curriculum still dominates our institutions of "higher learning." Such a curriculum offers a narrow view of the world even though there is a wealth of literature about non-European cultures by non-European academics. These works are not inferior to those of Europeans. They are integral to the attainment of a fuller, more encompassing education in which knowledge and ideas are derived from a wider, culturally diverse range of sources and perspectives. They are particularly useful in dispelling the racist assumptions and myths placed upon "others" by Western society.

In their inadequate attempts to be more inclusive, many of the professors I have encountered take a "just add and stir" approach to the inclusion of Native people, women, and "otherized" groups, which simply does not work. Just as they are treated as asides or special interest groups in society at large, women, Native people, and ethnic groups are often merely added on to Week 13 readings—if they are included at all. It was not until I experienced a course taught by a progressive, culturally sensitive anthropology professor who incorporated a multitude of perspectives that I became aware of the partial and limited view of the world to which I had previously been subjected. Those who perpetuate the mainstream academic curriculum seem to have fallen into a state of historical amnesia, whereby the contributions and, indeed, the very presence of non-Europeans have been omitted from Canadian history. Though Chinese, Japanese, and Indian immigrants arrived in Canada at the same time as most European immigrants, one could pass through the entire school system from kindergarten to university without being aware of the fact. Many students emerge from the school system rightfully well versed in the works of Shakespeare, Plato, and Marx, but how many learned about the cultural genocide of Native peoples, or slavery in Canada?

I am concerned that the exclusion from postsecondary curricula of minority groups, their perspectives, and their writings perpetuates a view of the world taken through a Eurocentric lens. This exclusion is also dangerous because it may lead some students to believe that since little is studied from "other" cultures, then perhaps those cultures have nothing of benefit to offer, or else they are inferior to European thought.

The courses I found the most valuable and educational were those that, though not designated as courses specifically about multiculturalism, or Native people, still managed to incorporate a variety of cultural perspectives into the readings, films, and seminars. A culturally diverse curriculum and alternative critical forms of pedagogy can also have a positive effect on the academic achievement of minority students, whose experiences and interests are not validated but are typically marginalized or excluded from the existing curriculum.

—A.R. Aujla, 1996

What Do YOU Think?

This narrative was written in 1996, roughly 25 years ago. In your experience, how much has changed?

A sociologist adopting a **structural-functionalist** view might say that the hidden curriculum performs a latent function by teaching the norms of society—the value of work, or the need to respect authority and to use one's time efficiently. A conflict sociologist might argue that the hidden curriculum reproduces the class system, hindering class mobility and therefore performing a latent *dys*function.

Discipline, Punishment, and Evaluation

Discipline is a key part of the hidden curriculum. *Discipline* here refers to controlled behaviour, not to the punishment administered for, say, speaking out of turn or passing notes in class. In primary school, discipline is focused on the body, restricting movement, impeding interaction, and normalizing confinement. Children are encouraged to use their "inside voices," to raise their hands before they speak or ask permission to go to the bathroom, to sit quietly in their seats, to keep their hands to themselves, to line up, and to be punctual. Secondary school continues to encourage physical discipline, and stressing a disciplining of the mind.

Common at all levels of education is the external and internal "routinization" of the individual. Punishment is enacted if the rules are not followed: a "time-out," a trip to the principal's office, a detention, or a poor mark on a report card. Grades are sanctions, designed to either negatively or positively reinforce norms.

While discipline can be enabling as well as inhibiting—many young students require and indeed thrive on a formalized structure of rules and routines—much of the discipline within the public school system can be considered repressive. This involves the mind as well as body. Children are naturally curious. Curiosity is the basis for asking questions, which is essential in the process of learning. Educators may learn at teacher's college that there are no "stupid questions," but when they have to stick to a strict schedule and a state-mandated curriculum, and when they are under pressure to see their students succeed on province-wide standardized tests that are used to measure the achievements of individual schools and teachers, they may respond negatively to student questions that deviate from the prescribed lesson plan. By the time they

reach college and university, students have often lost much of their curiosity. Postsecondary students, too, rarely ask questions with respect to ideas (other than *Is this going to be on the exam?*).

In many respects, public education creates what **Michel Foucault** termed the **docile body**, a group of individuals that has been conditioned, through a specific set of procedures and practices, to behave precisely the way administrators want it to (Foucault, 1977). Docile bodies are conditioned through three forms of disciplinary control:

1. hierarchical observation
2. normalizing judgment
3. the examination.

With **hierarchical observation** people are controlled through observation and surveillance. While Foucault used prisons as an example, the principle applies as well to schools and offices—places where our movements and activities are under constant surveillance within a setting based on hierarchical configurations. Educational institutions are based on a hierarchical structure in which authority figures observe and scrutinize the behaviour of students. For Foucault, hierarchical observation works on the psychology of observed individuals as much as it governs their specific movements. When people feel that they are always being watched, it induces in them an awareness of their permanent visibility, enhancing the power of the authority (Foucault, 1977, p. 172).

Normalizing judgment is another instrument of disciplinary control producing docile bodies. Individuals are judged not on the intrinsic rightness or wrongness of their actions but on how their actions rank when compared with the performance of others. Children are ranked at school, schools are ranked against one another, provincial education is ranked, and the level of education among countries is ranked. Ranking is a cultural artifact that we in Western society take for granted. Normalizing judgment is a pervasive means of control because regardless of how one succeeds, a higher level of achievement is always deemed possible.

The **examination** combines hierarchical observation with normalizing judgment. Foucault described it as "a normalizing gaze [that] establishes over individuals a visibility through which one differentiates them and judges them" (1977, p. 184). It is, for him, the locus of power and knowledge, because it combines both "the deployment of force and the establishment of truth" (Foucault, 1977, p. 184). Test scores are documented and recorded, and provide detailed information about the individuals examined. Based on these records, various categories, averages, and norms are formulated by those in control, and these become the basis of knowledge. Power remains invisible, while those constructed as deviant become highly visible: those students with the thickest files are scrutinized by scores of anonymous, invisible functionaries (Foucault, 1977, p. 189). Deviance reflects difference from the norm. Both Lisa and Bart Simpson have the thickest files at school, but for different reasons.

Cultural Reproduction Theory

Jeannie Oakes and the Hidden Curriculum of Tracking

Does the education system, as part of its hidden curriculum, really reproduce class divisions, as our conflict sociologist might argue? Jeannie Oakes (2005) put this idea, known as **cultural reproduction theory**, to the test in an influential study of tracking (or "streaming") in junior and senior high schools in the United States. Oakes defined **tracking** as "the process whereby students are divided into categories so that they can be assigned in groups to various kinds of classes" (2005, p. 3). Both classes and students are ranked according to different levels of aptitude and projected outcomes, such as whether or not students are expected to pursue a postsecondary degree. Oakes studied 297 classrooms in 25 schools in the late 1970s and early 1980s. Her work demonstrated that perceived ability is reflected through a lens of class, race, and ethnicity. She also showed that lower tracks often offer lower quality of education than the higher tracks do. As a consequence, the American tracking system reproduces inequality.

Oakes argued that the disproportionate representation of lower-class and non-white students in the lower track reflects the cultural biases of testing and the prejudices of counsellors and teachers. The inferior quality of lower-track education came partly from the reduced expectations for students in the lower track. Lower-track English courses emphasized basic punctuation and form-filling as opposed to creating writing and studying great works of literature. Lower-track math courses emphasized basic computational skills rather than problem solving, critical thinking, and abstract logic. Lower-track vocational courses focused on clerical skills, not the managerial and financial skills taught in the higher-track courses.

Another important finding relates to differences in classroom time spent on instruction and learning activities versus administrative routines and discipline. The average amounts of classroom time spent on instruction in English and math courses in the higher track were 82 per cent and 77 per cent, respectively; the comparable figures for lower-track time were 71 per cent and 63 per cent.

From a cultural reproduction standpoint, it is also important to look at differences in the relationships among students, between students and teachers, and between students and the institution generally. Samuel Bowles and Harold Gintis point to the "close correspondence between the social relationships which govern personal interaction in the workplace and the social relationships of the educational system" (1976, p. 12). In other words, the education system fosters social relationships that train students in the lower track to become lower-class workers. Oakes summarized this position as follows:

> These [lower-class] workers will be subordinate to external control and alienated from the institutions but willing to conform to the needs of the workplace, to a large extent because of the way they were treated in school. . . . Bowles and Gintis suggest that the absence of close interpersonal relationships is characteristic of both lower-class work environments and classroom environments for lower-class children. In contrast, upper- and middle-class students, destined for upper-status and middle-level positions in the economic hierarchy, are more likely to experience social relationships and interactions that promote active involvement, affiliation with others, and the internalization of rules and behavioral standards. Self-regulation is the goal here rather than the coercive authority and control seen as appropriate for the lower class. (2005, pp. 119–20)

Oakes found that teachers were more punitive in lower-track classes, while higher-track classes cultivated more trusting teacher–student relationships. She wrote, "trust, cooperation, and even good will among students were far less characteristic of low-track classes than of high. More student time and energy were spent in hostile and disruptive interchanges in these classes" (Oakes, 2005, p. 132).

Key to cultural reproduction theory is the **legitimization of inequality**. If students accept that their differential tracking placement is fair, this legitimizes the inequality reproduced by the education system. Oakes found that "students in low-track classes tended to be saying that school's all right, but I'm not so good. In contrast, students in high-track classes were feeling pretty good about both their schools *and* themselves" (2005, pp. 143–4).

Overall, Oakes believes that with the deep class, ethnic, and racial distinctions existing in mainstream American society, a tracking system can only reproduce inequality. She argues for more of a common curriculum shared by all students, and for more mixing of students of different ability levels.

Jean Anyon: Cultural Reproduction Theory in Five New Jersey Schools

An important aspect of cultural reproduction theory is the idea that the education system, as well as other social institutions, help to reproduce the prevailing social structure. In other words, schools help upper-class children grow up to become upper-class adults, middle-class children become middle-class adults, and so on. A landmark study of this is Jean Anyon's "Social Class and the Hidden Curriculum of Work" (1980), based on an ethnographic study of five elementary schools in New Jersey she carried out in 1978–9. Two of the schools she studied could be described as predominantly working-class. Here, most of the fathers had semi-skilled or unskilled jobs (assembly line work, auto repair or assembly, maintenance work); 15 per cent of the fathers were unemployed, and less than 30 per cent of the mothers worked. According to Anyon, schoolwork in these schools consisted of

> following the steps of a procedure. The procedure is usually mechanical, involving rote behavior [i.e. drilled memorization] and very little decision making or choice. The teachers rarely explain why the work is being assigned, how it might connect to other assignments, or what the idea is that lies behind the procedure or gives it coherence and perhaps meaning or significance. . . . Most of the rules regarding work are designations of what the children are to do; the rules are steps to follow. . . . The children are usually told to copy the steps as notes. These notes are to be studied. Work is often evaluated not according to whether it is right or wrong but according to whether the children followed the right steps. (Anyon, 1980)

Students at a third school, which Anyon identified as middle-class, had parents working in skilled, well-paid trades (such as carpentry, plumbing, or electrical work), working as professionals (firefighting, teaching, accounting, etc.), or owning small businesses. Schoolwork here focused on "getting the right answer":

> One must follow the directions in order to get the right answers, but the directions often call for some figuring, some choice, some decision making. For example, the children must figure out by themselves what the directions ask them to do and how to get

Quick Hits

Student Examples from Oakes's Study

What is the most important thing you have learned or done so far in the class (in terms of subject matter)?

Answers from the High Track

- "We've talked about stocks/bonds and the stock market and about business in the USA." – student in junior high vocational education
- "Learned to analyze famous writings by famous people, and we have learned to understand people's different viewpoints on general ideas." – student in junior high English
- "The most important thing is the way other countries and places govern themselves economically, socially, and politically. Also different philosophers and their theories on government and man and how their theories relate to us and now." – student in junior high social studies

Answers from the Low Track

- "Learns to fill out checks and other banking business." – student in junior high English
- "to spell words you don't know, to fill out things where you get a job." – student in junior high English
- "I learned that English is boring." – student in senior high school English

Source: Oakes, 2005, pp. 68–71.

the answer: what do you do first, second, and perhaps third? Answers are usually found in books or by listening to the teacher. Answers are usually words, sentences, numbers, or facts and dates; one writes them on paper, and one should be neat. Answers must be given in the right order, and one cannot make them up. (Anyon, 1980)

très peu est fini

très peu de compréhension

quelques idées très simples

très peu clair

plusieurs erreurs ou omissions graves

avec beaucoup d'aide

Notre salle de classe doit être

Vince Talotta/Toronto Star via Getty Images

School boards across Canada have seen rising registration for public school French immersion programs. In some jurisdictions, competition has parents lining up overnight to claim spots for their children. French language instruction is part of the curriculum for all English-speaking students in Canada—so what do you think is the appeal of immersion programs? Is it all about learning French? A potential ticket to a job in government? Or is it just another high track available within the public school system?

Quick Hits

Social Mobility: Meritocracy versus Cultural Reproduction

During the 1960s, John Porter wrote,

No society in the modern period can afford to ignore the ability which lies in the lower social strata. Whatever may be said about average intelligence and social class, the fact remains that in absolute numbers there is more of the highly intelligent in lower classes than in the higher. If the principles of efficiency and equality are to be upheld, Canada must be prepared to put a great deal more money into education and educational research than it has.... Without such policies, intergenerational continuity of class will remain [and] mobility

deprivation will continue. (in Helmes-Hayes, 2010, pp. 137–8)

There are two fundamentally opposing positions concerning education and **social mobility**. One is that education is **meritocratic**: academic performance reflects natural ability (i.e. merit), and the system provides mobility for those lower-class and minoritized students who work hard to succeed. Cultural reproduction theory, by contrast, argues that the education system reproduces and reinforces the inequality of the surrounding society. Which one do you think presents the more accurate statement about education in Canada as you have experienced it?

A fourth school, identified as "affluent professional," had students whose parents were employed as corporate lawyers, engineers, and advertising executives. At this school, the work involved

creative activity carried out independently. The students are continually asked to express and apply ideas and concepts. Work involves individual thought and expressiveness, expansion and illustration of ideas, and choice of appropriate method and material. . . . The products of work in this class are often written stories, editorials, and essays, or representations of ideas in mural, graph, or craft form. The products of work should not be like anybody else's and should show individuality. . . . One's product is usually evaluated for the quality of its expression and for the appropriateness of its conception to the task. (Anyon, 1980)

The fifth school Anyon called "executive elite," as most of the students' fathers held positions as presidents and vice-presidents of major corporations (it was 1979, so many mothers would not have been working). In this school, work involved

developing one's analytical intellectual powers. Children are continually asked to reason through a problem, to produce intellectual products that are both logically sound and of top academic quality. A primary goal of thought is to conceptualize rules by which elements may fit together in systems and then to apply these rules in solving a problem. (Anyon, 1980)

If there were a sociology class offered at this school level, daily activities in each category might look like this:

working-class school	copying down and memorizing the instructor's notes from the board
middle-class school	reading the textbook and finding the right answer
affluent professional school	finding information on an assigned topic and writing it up in one's own words
executive elite school	analyzing social systems and looking for strengths and weaknesses

Homework and Its Sociological Effects

Sociologists study homework to gauge the extent to which homework helps to reproduce class structure. Children raised by educated middle- and upper-middle-class parents have a number of advantages with respect to homework. Their parents are typically better able to understand teacher instructions and so are in a better position to help their children (sometimes doing the entire project themselves). Parents who work in an office setting are more likely than parents who don't have the software skills needed to support children expected to turn in polished assignments prepared in the latest presentation, image, and design editing software. The children of better-off parents tend to live in larger homes, where they have a quiet, dedicated space for doing homework, high-speed internet access and a newer computer, a colour printer, and other aids to completing their work. As a result, the more a course depends on homework as opposed to class work, the more it favours children from middle- and upper-middle-class households.

The amount of homework a child receives can also have a profound effect on family life. In 2008, Linda Cameron and Lee Bartel (2008) published the findings of a study on the impact of homework on Canadian households. Their research was based on an online questionnaire completed by over 1,000 parents, the vast majority of them in Ontario. Of the 10 main conclusions drawn from the qualitative part of the questionnaire, two related to family life. The first was that homework "reduces family time":

> Homework is often seen as an incursion on what should be discretionary family time.... One parent stated it this way: "My children are in the educational institution for 6.5 hours per day. I feel this should be sufficient time to complete any school-related tasks. I am with them for significantly less time and would prefer to use this time engaging in activities to promote our relationship and increase bonding in order to reduce their stress levels." Consequently, parents often expressed feelings of resentment toward homework and the effect it has on family balance. (Cameron & Bartel, 2008, p. 53)

What Do YOU Think?

If you were the principal of an elementary school, what reasons might you give for "banning homework"? What reasons would you give for taking the opposite position?

The second finding related to family life was that homework "affects family relationships." According to the authors, homework was found to be "a primary source of arguments, power struggles, and disruptive to building a strong family." In the words of one respondent cited by the report's authors, "Fights over homework with my children are common and very upsetting" (Cameron & Bartel, 2008, p. 54). Education administrators have taken steps to limit the homework burden, but in an environment of increasing competition for the good grades required to gain admission to the most coveted universities and postsecondary programs, putting in the time outside of normal working hours is the surest way to get ahead—a lesson students will take with them into their professional lives.

Issues in Indigenous Education
The Politics of Representation in Textbooks

Textbooks, whether online or in print, form an important and influential part of education, and yet they remain an understudied topic in the sociology of education. For my doctoral dissertation, I examined the representation of Indigenous people in 77 Canadian introductory sociology textbooks. What I discovered was a serious and progressive lack of Indigenous voice. Indigenous writers were not represented as a significant source of information on their own people. In Michel Foucault's terminology, theirs were *disqualified knowledges*—"knowledges that have been disqualified as inadequate to their task" (1980, p. 82). Foucault might have argued that Indigenous writers were not included because they were not scientific or objective enough for the writers of sociology textbooks. Yet their viewpoints offer a legitimate alternative to standard sociology knowledge.

Early Canadian introductory sociology textbooks entailed collections of readings. As sociologists were rarely studying Indigenous people then (that was generally left to anthropologists), contributions written about Indigenous people were typically authored by people who were not professional sociologists, including Inuit leader Abraham Okpik, Ojibwa author Wilfred Pelletier, and Cree politician and scholar Harold Cardinal (although he studied sociology for a while at Carleton University). When sociologists began studying Indigenous people in urban settings in the early 1970s, the Indigenous voice was lost from sociology textbooks: the only coverage of Indigenous people came from non-Indigenous sociology writers. It is coming back, but slowly.

Credentialism

Credentialism often blocks Indigenous people's attempts to improve education. It is the practice of valuing credentials—degrees, diplomas, certificates—over actual knowledge and ability in the hiring and promotion of staff. In many Indigenous communities, Elders are deeply involved in educating children and young adults. However, Elders do not typically carry paper credentials; their qualification comes primarily from community recognition and valuing of their knowledge. Elders are recognized in Indigenous communities as being experts in traditional knowledge, such as hunting, fishing, spirituality, healing, childcare, and crafts. Most teachers coming from non-Indigenous communities are not familiar with Elders because the role of Elder is not assigned significant status in mainstream Canadian society.

Assessing Indigenous Education in Canada

Jo-ann Archibald is eminently qualified to speak of the past, present, and future of Indigenous education in Canada. A member of the Stó:lō people of British Columbia (often known in the past as Salish), she has a doctorate in education and taught for 45 years, first at the elementary school level and later at the postsecondary level, where she specialized in training Indigenous teachers. Her book *Indigenous Storywork: Educating the Heart, Mind, Body, and Spirit* (2008) is a classic in explaining Indigenous modes of education for non-Indigenous readers.

In a recent opinion piece in *The Tyee* (Archibald, 2019) she assesses enduring problems and also advances made in Indigenous education (which covers education of both Indigenous and non-Indigenous students). One of the main problems she identifies is what she calls "the racism of low expectations":

> Some teachers will say, "I can't do anything about the Indigenous kids; they come from poor homes," and feel hopeless. I would hope this feeling shifts to excitement and confidence in working with Indigenous students and parents, rather than feeling it's a dismal situation. (Archibald, 2019)

I would extend the definition of "the racism of low expectations" to the minimal standards and extent of Indigenous content required for something to be called "Indigenous education."

In spite of this, Archibald is optimistic. She is especially encouraged by the increasing number of Indigenous people serving as resource educators in the school system. Still, she hopes for a much higher number of Indigenous full-time classroom teachers. Including Indigenous modes of teaching and learning, not just in courses in Indigenous studies but in all subject areas, is something that is beginning to happen in the school system in British Columbia, necessarily so, in her view. It must be more, she says, than just a thoughtful "trip in the woods" but learning experiences that are connected to Elders and their stories.

Archibald also expresses her hope that non-Indigenous teachers will begin to feel "confident" in teaching an Indigenous curriculum. The lack of confidence is a problem that exists at all levels of education. I have seen it directly. I once wrote a piece on the Haudenosaunee (Iroquois) Great Law of Peace, which, among other things, is a traditional story statement of Haudenosaunee political philosophy. I wrote it for what we were then calling the Humanities course, a compulsory elective at the college where I taught. As the article itself was not compulsory reading, many teachers did not discuss it, and those who did often communicated to me their discomfort in teaching it based on their lack of knowledge on the subject. Non-Indigenous teachers at all levels of education are generally ignorant of Indigenous language, culture, and history, because they have been trained in an

Winnipeg Free Press

If there were 10 points that everyone in the Canadian education system should learn about Indigenous people what would they be? Examples could include the fact that more than 95 per cent of the human history of the land that is now Canada is Indigenous history alone. Another point could be the source language and meaning of such place names as Canada, Quebec, Ontario, Manitoba, Saskatchewan, Yukon, Nunavut, Ottawa, Toronto, Winnipeg, Saskatoon, and Kootenay. What else?

environment that did not prioritize this knowledge. That is beginning to change, as it must if our education system is to reflect the true history and diversity of this country.

Best Practices in British Columbia

Sociological discussions of Indigenous people's education tend to focus on the horrific stories of the residential schools, and the poor academic performance of Indigenous students since. An alternative perspective comes from a report published by the C.D. Howe Institute (Richards, Hove, & Afolabi, 2008). Summarizing the results of a study that examined Indigenous student performance in non-Indigenous public schools, the authors identified five "best practices" that are key to the success of Indigenous students:

1. collaboration between school district personnel at all levels and local Indigenous communities
2. commitment by administrators and teachers to incorporating Indigenous content into the curriculum
3. creation of influential positions (such as full-time teachers and school trustees) dedicated to Indigenous education
4. relationship building between Indigenous and non-Indigenous communities in the district
5. willingness of school district authorities to share responsibility for making decisions with Indigenous communities.

Interviews revealed that non-Indigenous teachers often presented obstacles to Indigenous involvement in their classrooms. While it is easy to say that personal racism is involved, sociologists look primarily for institutional barriers. The Canadian education system teaches very little about Indigenous people. Most Canadian teachers are ill prepared to work with an Indigenous curriculum—they are poorly acquainted with Indigenous history, language, and culture generally because they are products of a school system that has failed to adequately cover these subjects. For example, a 2015 report by the advocacy group People for Education found that only 29 per cent of elementary schools in Ontario and 47 per cent of the province's secondary schools offered training on Indigenous issues to teachers (Casey, 2015). The result is a self-perpetuating form of **institutional racism**.

What Do YOU Think?

What obstacles might there be to adopting the best practices referred to in this study?

Issues in Postsecondary Education

Long-Term Adjunct Instructors: An Educational Underclass

The growing ranks of long-term adjunct instructors in postsecondary institutions is the product of several economic and social factors, including the increasing number of postsecondary students, the

Quick Hits

Gay–Straight Alliances: The Politics of the Schoolhouse

In 2015, the Progressive Conservative government of Alberta passed a law making it illegal for school boards or administrators to prevent students from setting up **gay–straight alliances (GSAs)** on school property. The move was applauded by anti-bullying activists and students, who had, prior to the law, been forced to hold GSA meetings outside of their schools. A recent study of Grade 8–12 students in BC suggests that GSAs help reduce "suicidal ideation" (i.e. thinking about suicide) and suicide attempts, as well as the experience of discrimination not only among sexual minority youth but among heterosexual youth who do not conform to normative gender-based behaviour (Saewyc, Konishi, Rose, & Homma, 2014). Nevertheless, the legislation faced stiff opposition from some parents and administrators of faith-based schools, particularly officials in the publicly funded Catholic school system who believe GSAs are too political and promote a lifestyle that is inconsistent with Catholic teachings. After the NDP government updated the legislation in 2017, a group of 24 private religious schools, eight parents, and two non-profit groups launched a constitutional challenge of a part of the law protecting the privacy of students joining GSAs in the province. In 2019, the province's United Conservative Party replaced the legislation with a new act that removed the privacy protections for students, permitting school staff to inform parents of children joining a GSA. The new law also erased a provision compelling a school to set up a gay–straight alliance "immediately" if students request one, meaning that schools could agree to set up a GSA but delay doing so.

The debate in some ways mirrored the controversy sparked when Ontario's provincial government introduced its new sex ed curriculum in 2015. Designed to teach students about diversity in sexual orientation and gender expression at an earlier age, the curriculum was initially opposed by some Catholic school educators who believed that parts of the curriculum did not align with Catholic values. In 2018, the incoming Conservative government put the curriculum on hold, having campaigned on a pledge to do so.

reduction of government investment in postsecondary education, the increasing levels of private corporate funding, and the rising influence of a corporate culture that regards education just like any other business. The trend of turning full-time teaching positions into long-term adjunct posts is not unlike contracting out skilled jobs to avoid having to grant the benefits or long-term commitment that come with full-time work.

Names for this class of education workers differ. They are commonly referred to as **adjunct professors**, but they may also be called "sessionals," "contract staff," or "part-time instructors" (a misleading term, since many put in more hours than full-time instructors do). In Canada, the term *adjunct* is used to refer specifically to an experienced instructor who, because of seniority, is the first in line to take the courses full-timer instructors can't or don't want to take on. Contract teaching used to be a first step on the path toward a full-time job or a tenure-track position. Now that path is narrower and longer.

Ghosts in the Classroom: Stories of College Adjunct Faculty—and the Price We All Pay, edited by Michael Dubson, is a collection of narratives written by adjunct professors at American colleges and universities. Almost all of the contributors are English instructors—not surprising, given that many of them teach writing for a living, and English departments are large, with lots of temporary work for adjuncts. There is a lot of competition for jobs in this area, illustrated in the writers' frequent

Photo by Denin Lawley on Unsplash

Should school staff have the right, under exceptional circumstances, to inform parents that their child belongs to the school's gay–straight alliance?

Catholic schools in Alberta and Ontario are part of the separate school system that exists in some provinces to protect religious minorities from discrimination by allowing them to direct their taxes to supporting faith-based elementary and secondary schools.

What Do YOU Think?

1. Should a Catholic school be forced to allow its students to set up a gay–straight alliance on school property when opposition to homosexuality is a key tenet of the Catholic Church?
2. What role can sociologists play in a controversy such as the one described here?

use of the phrase "dime a dozen" to refer to their competitive position. One of the topics raised repeatedly is the low pay, which is especially tough to swallow given that salaries for full-time staff are well over double what adjunct instructors are paid. One of the collection's contributors speaks eloquently of the sense of **relative deprivation** felt by many adjuncts:

> If I teach eight courses in an academic year, I make approximately $16,000. They [full-time instructors] teach eight to ten courses during an academic year and make, on the average, $40,000. I must horde my money and pinch my pennies for I must live on it during the semester breaks. Full-time teachers get paid all year long, whether they work or not.
>
> Because the pay is so poor, . . . I must string together collections of adjunct course assignments from several different schools. I have taught six, seven, eight classes a semester at three or four different schools. . . . I have worked other jobs and taught on the side. I have split my time between teaching four or five courses, a full-time load, and another job. (M. Theodore Swift, cited in Dubson, 2001, pp. 2–3)

Many contributors to the collection comment on their working conditions, which might involve sharing a desk (or not even having a desk) and having restricted use of facilities and equipment such as the departmental photocopiers. Jody Lannen Brady's description is typical:

> I shared a dingy office with twenty other instructors, and some semesters I was lucky to find a chair to perch on during my office hours. I often met with students in the hallway because it was quieter than the office. I had one file cabinet drawer I could call my own, but I hauled all my papers and books back and forth from home to office and back each day because I couldn't work in the office, never knowing how many times I would have to jump up and answer the

phone, and if I would have a desk to sit at. (in Dubson, 2001, p. 147)

What might surprise full-time professors is the extent to which the adjunct instructors feel they are engaged in a "class war" with full-timers. Two excerpts illustrate the point:

> At one college, I share office space one day a week with one of the full-time instructors. He put a sign with my name by the door as a sort of welcoming gesture. The next week, the secretary of the English Department wrote me a note. Two of the full-time teachers were in a fury at the arrogance of my putting up a nameplate. (Gale, in Dubson, 2001, p. 13)
>
> Once, in a heated personal discussion with a full-time colleague, she blurted out, "Who the hell do you think you are? You're only an adjunct here!" (Werner, in Dubson, 2001, p. 37)

Strained relations with colleagues are compounded by trying relationships with the students. Student evaluations are more important to the employment status of adjuncts than they are to the positions of full-time staff members. A poor evaluation won't get a full-timer fired, but it could cause an adjunct not to be hired back once the contract has ended. One writer explains,

> If I have poor course evaluations, I will be out. . . . If my students complain about me, legitimately or otherwise, I will be out. If a full-time faculty member faces any of this, he or she will be supported, worked with, helped. Full-time tenured faculty may not even be evaluated, and . . . if their students complain about them, nothing affecting their employment or job security will be done. (Swift, in Dubson, 2001, p. 3)

It should not be surprising that adjunct professors have been organizing. The kinds of conditions described above were a flashpoint in the strike by graduate student teaching assistants at York University in 2018.

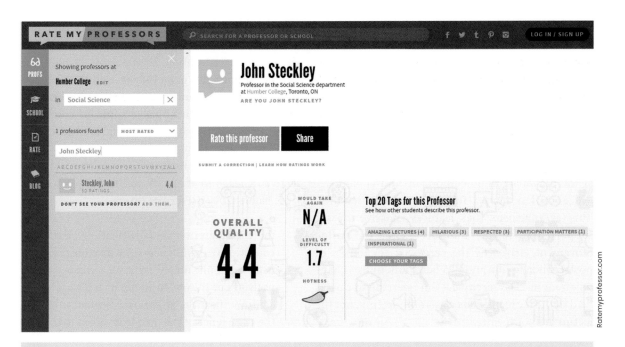

Have you been to this site? What do you think are some of the consequences of rating your instructors online? How are these consequences different for adjuncts and full-time professors?

Online Teaching: A Critical Sociological Approach

During the late 1990s and early 2000s, there was a push throughout North American colleges and universities to offer dramatically more online courses, even to the point of offering online diplomas and degrees, in some cases through "virtual" colleges based entirely online. This was driven by technological improvements, certainly, and by a desire to make education more accessible. But it was also spurred by cuts to postsecondary education funding. The online movement was hyped with the allure of change as progress, and played well to the susceptibility of educators to changes in intellectual fashion. It was also driven by private organizations specializing in delivering educational packages over the internet, who coined or co-opted sexy terms like "advanced learning" and "open learning," in spite of their yet unproven ability to provide education that is either more advanced or more open. They invest heavily in hosting or attending "educational" conferences (popular perks among postsecondary instructors), where they offer product demonstrations, aided by their "pet" instructors.

The financial success of online education providers has come at a time when many colleges and universities, feeling the financial pinch, have turned to the private sector as a partial solution to an underfunded public system. The boosters of online education are more often administrators and education companies looking for the government dollars that flow to public institutions rather than actual instructors, though the latter group does include believers. Student demand for these courses is more unsupported myth than documented fact. The main motivation is political and financial. Ontario Premier Doug Ford's introduction of the idea of mandatory online high school courses in 2019 is a case in point.

In postsecondary education, a magic word is *access*. Online courses promise access to education for those who would find it difficult to attend college or university otherwise, the so-called "non-traditional students" (a group that supposedly includes working parents, who have traditionally made good use of night-school courses). As we have seen, **access without mobility** can readily reproduce the class system, while seeming to improve the lot of the more marginalized social groups.

From a sociological standpoint, how do online courses differ from in-class courses? Before addressing this question, it's worth noting that another flawed feature of many a North American university is the large lecture hall, which shares some weaknesses with online courses. The teacher–student relationship that is possible in smaller classes is replaced by a student's relationship with a teaching assistant (or TA), someone who may be at the university only temporarily and is paid significantly less than a full-time, tenured lecturer. This arrangement that features massive classes supported by smaller tutorials is, like the online movement, driven by the perceived economics of postsecondary education. When I talk in this chapter about in-class teaching, I am referring to classes held in the more intimate classroom setting, not the lecture hall or theatre.

Critics of the online movement (including me) fear that it is driven mainly by economics rather than access to education. Interestingly, though, the savings supposedly achieved by online education may be more apparent than real: acquiring and upgrading expensive technical equipment combined with hiring additional technical and administrative staff can drastically reduce the profit margin.

When boosting revenue becomes the main objective, it leads to the **commodification** of education. Noble (2002) describes this as

the disintegration and distillation of the educational experience into discrete, reified, and ultimately saleable things or packages of things. In the first step toward commodification, attention is shifted from the experience of the people involved in the

The Point Is...

Online Education Is a New Spin on an Old Idea

Historian David Noble (2002) reminds us that a movement similar to the online education movement happened from the 1880s to the 1930s, when correspondence courses, which enabled students to receive lessons and submit their work by mail (yes, mail!), became popular. The movement began with independent, privately run schools, before the universities, fearing competition and eager to benefit from a relatively easy source of profit, got involved. People marketing the correspondence courses used a language familiar to educators today: they promoted the ability to reach "non-traditional students" with the promise of "working on your own time." However, postsecondary administrators saw correspondence courses primarily as a good source of profit with relatively low overhead costs. Tuition was paid up front and was non-refundable, yet the dropout rate was high, the majority of students never completing their courses. Noble refers to this as "drop-out money." At the same time, the faculty involved were underpaid, receiving between 25 and 35 cents a lesson. By the 1930s,

the institutions involved were sharply criticized for being "diploma mills" that served up an inferior education.

The factors that sparked the establishment of correspondence courses in the late nineteenth century are similar to the ones that have created a favourable environment for the growth of online education today:

- the rise of *credentialism* (setting value on credentials such as certificates and diplomas)
- funding cuts, which prompt universities and colleges to seek out new sources of revenue
- the development of private training companies
- the rapid development of information technology (then, of course, advances in mail delivery services).

Noble sees online courses as suffering from the same flaws that plagued correspondence courses: profit considered over education, poorly paid staff with very little job security, and, on average, an inferior education when measured against its in-class equivalent.

educational process to the production and inventorying of an assortment of "course materials"; syllabi, lectures, lessons, exams. . . . [T]hese common instruments of instruction barely reflect what actually takes place in the educational experience, and lend an illusion of order and predictability to what is, at its best, an essentially unscripted and undetermined process. Second, these fragments are removed or "alienated" from their original context, the actual educational process itself, and from their producers, the teachers, and are assembled as "courses," which take on an existence independent of and apart from those who created and gave flesh to them. (2002, p. 3)

Important here is the Marxist concept of **alienation**, which entails the separation between people and the work that they are paid to do. People working on assembly lines are disconnected from what they do. The workers have no say in what they do or how they do it. Chefs with signature dishes are closely connected with their work; people working the chip fryer at McDonald's are not. In a similar way, instructors can become disconnected from their **intellectual property** when it is used as part of an online course. Noble elaborates,

Once faculty put their course material online, . . . the knowledge and course design skill embodied in that material is taken out of their possession. . . . The administration is now in a position to hire . . . cheaper workers to deliver the technologically prepackaged course. It also allows the administration . . . to peddle the course elsewhere without the original designer's involvement or even knowledge, much less financial interest. The buyers of this packaged commodity, meanwhile, . . . are able thereby to contract out . . . the work of their own employees and thus reduce their reliance upon their in-house teaching staff. (1998)

Alienation involves the hierarchical control of a product, in which the boss has ultimate say in how it is developed, used, and distributed. With online courses, the potential for administrative monitoring and control increases. Instructors can be more closely supervised through the educational products they have supplied for the course's website. Online courses also allow administrators to measure instructor interactions with students: How often are instructors logging on? How responsive are they to students' online questions? This kind of supervision is also possible with course components offered by means of packaged web products such as Blackboard.

Online universities are staffed with relatively few full-time instructors and many "tutors." Professors fear that this is the face of the future: part-time and limited-time contract staff dominating over full-time teachers. The following statement from Meritus University, which opened its virtual doors in September 2008, shows that they indeed have something to fear:

While others established academic programs around tradition and tenure, Apollo has built programs in conjunction with the needs of business and industry—effectively translating those needs into clear and transparent learning objectives.

In its first semester, Meritus University had just four full-time teaching staff. In 2011, it closed its virtual doors.

The online delivery of education depends, like many exploitative systems, on getting workers to do more than they are paid for, relying on dedicated teachers who improve a bad situation with their talent and their labour. But some teachers "work to rule," calculating exactly how much work they have to do to get paid and do no more.

So what about the students? These courses suffer from significant dropout rates. Students who succeed are typically highly motivated, disciplined people, who get through despite the flaws inherent in the method of delivery. Their good marks represent triumphs of individuals over systems.

Online education lends itself more to **instrumental education**, where courses are narrowly directed to a limited set of tasks, than to **critical education**, which involves analysis of ideas and, ideally, classroom discussion. With online courses, as the information flow is more one-directional than in the classroom, more controlled by the curriculum than by student–teacher interaction, students have less input into how the course proceeds. Their instructors have less input as well, since they are typically part-timers, vulnerable to administrative control.

Some worry that a two-tiered, two-class system will develop, with the middle and upper classes attending in-class institutions ("bricks and mortar" universities), preparing for jobs that will maintain their family's class standing, while those "attending" the digital institutions ("click universities") will be lower-class students and others for whom regular college or university attendance is financially impossible (including, for instance, single mothers and other working parents). They will receive lower-cost virtual vocational training that will lead them to lower-level, lower-paying service jobs. These are the people most likely to suffer, academically as well as socially, from the isolation that comes with online courses, the ones who would most benefit from in-class discussions. The system would then reproduce rather than challenge the class system.

Do You Want Fries with that Degree?

Students joke about the McJob—the low-paying, unskilled service job—they might get with their degree once they've graduated. The term refers to underemployment, which can have two meanings relevant to this discussion:

- involuntary part-time work for people seeking full-time employment

- low-wage, low-skill employment for people with valuable skills, experience, or academic credentials.

Statistics Canada defines underemployed as "seeking full-time work but finding only part-time work." The category does not include those who have been unable to work full-time for health or other personal reasons, nor does it acknowledge the problem of an overskilled workforce. Underemployment is the result of several factors, including

- the rate of unemployment;
- regional disparity (lack of employment opportunities and resources like training and childcare in economically depressed communities); and
- discrimination based on ethnicity, gender, disability, or lack of "appropriate" credentials.

How does this apply to postsecondary students? Those who hold high-quality skills and academic credentials become underemployed when there is low marketplace demand. The demographic bulge caused by the baby boomers means that access to employment is cut off for those newly entering the workforce, many of whom may be better qualified than their predecessors. For example, I received my college job with an MA. My replacement when I retired required a PhD.

During the 1990s, universities produced 1.2 million graduates, but only 600,000 jobs requiring university-level credentials were created during that same period. Currently, there are about one million students in the postsecondary system. If job creation remains the same as it did in the 1990s, then several hundred thousand graduates each year will be pursuing fewer than 100,000 job openings. This could effectively increase the structural underemployment rate from the 50 per cent level found in the 1980s and 1990s to 75 per cent.

In a 2017 study of labour demand and supply, Statistics Canada researcher Marie Drolet (2017) looked at the relationship between job vacancies and unemployment data for 2015 and 2016. She found that during that two-year period, there were 3.4 unemployed people for every job vacancy in Canada, and roughly half (49 per cent) of all unemployed people had at least

THE CANADIAN PRESS/Andrew Vaughan

A university graduate takes his job search to the streets of Halifax. Should governments be allowed to cap enrolment in disciplines with low labour market demand? Or is up to the student to find the educational path most likely to lead to meaningful employment? What's your plan to avoid underemployment after graduation?

some college or university education. However, a disproportionately high number of the job vacancies (37 per cent) were positions in sales and services, and overall, approximately two-thirds of the job vacancies required no more than a high school education. In other words, the population of unemployed Canadians was largely overqualified for the job vacancies.

In the case of new college and university graduates, underemployment can result from a lack of practical experience, even for those who have technical training in a specific field. As a result, recent graduates may be forced to work in low-paying or part-time jobs until they find work in their field. Canadian studies conducted between 1982 and 2004 suggest that while postsecondary education attainment has increased for various occupational classes,

so too has the underemployment rate for those same occupational classes. The same research also shows that the rate of underemployment is greater than the underqualified rate. In 2004, 45 per cent of those aged 18 to 24 saw themselves as being overqualified for their jobs as opposed to 22 per cent of those 40 and over (Livingstone, 2004).

Among the solutions proposed to reduce underemployment are government-imposed restrictions on enrolment in postsecondary courses and programs with low labour market demand, although they often produce people who could make a significant contribution to the economy of the country. However, the university system would be unable to support such a proposal, as it would reduce student enrolment and, therefore, revenues.

The Sociology of Plagiarism

Ask any professor about the problems of teaching at a postsecondary institution, and **plagiarism** will be mentioned. This is particularly true of instructors teaching courses in the social sciences and the humanities—courses with a heavy grade component based on essay writing.

Plagiarism is the act of copying another person's work or of piecing together work from several sources into an academic pastiche. Basically, it involves passing off someone else's ideas or work as your own. The ideas and words aren't yours, and the sources of those ideas and words aren't properly identified or even mentioned. In pre-internet times, plagiarism was difficult to do by accident: you had to copy, in long hand, from a print source, such as a journal article or book that you found in the library. Today, you can plagiarize with the click of a mouse, and once a piece of information has been copied into your working document, it can be all too easy to forget where it came from. Students will sometimes copy and paste from anonymous websites, believing these are fair game because there is no attributed author. Make no mistake: it is still plagiarism.

Carol Thompson (2006) adopts a sociological approach to address why plagiarism has become such a common phenomenon. She emphasizes the influence of **role models**, asserting that students have the very patterns of behaviour they're warned not to fall into modelled for them by professors, school administrators, famous writers and academics, and politicians. More influential could be parents, who have often helped students in writing and assembling their projects in high school, and who may get involved in their children's postsecondary work as well. The idea that the work submitted does not have to have been prepared entirely on one's own could stem from that experience of having received help from parents.

Plagiarism has spawned two booming industries. One is the essay industry, selling students ready-composed or, for a higher fee, customized papers. These companies are not engaged in anything that is technically against the law, although the means they sometimes use to obtain papers do involve theft of academic property. Copyright laws are fuzzy about academic work. The fact that there are numerous companies of this kind out there, set up to accept your credit card number or payment via PayPal, might make the practice seem legitimate.

The industry can benefit graduate students, who are often desperate for money. They are trained to write academic papers. By selling their services to web-based essay providers, they are capitalizing on their hard-earned skills in an industry in which these skills are valued.

Another group that profits from plagiarism are businesses such as Turnitin and iThenticate, which sell their services to colleges and universities with the claim that they can catch the plagiarizers. They expand their database with every postsecondary institution that pays for their services. You have to wonder how many people working on this side of the business once worked on the other side, like hackers who become computer security specialists.

A potential social factor in the willingness to plagiarize is **social distance**. If you know your instructors and they recognize you by name or by sight, then you are less likely to submit a plagiarized essay, since it would be like cheating a friend. However, if your professor is just a blurry face at the front of a crowded lecture theatre, or an even more anonymous presence online, the social distance is far greater. Plagiarism might be like stealing from a large corporation. It appears to be a "victimless crime," since there is no identifiable injured party. This would make for interesting sociological research: Is there more plagiarism in lower-level courses than in upper-level courses (where the classes are smaller and less likely to be offered online)? Is it more common in larger institutions than in smaller ones?

Cultures of Education

It is also worth considering plagiarism in terms of cultures of education. In mainstream Western culture there is a tendency to emphasize the individual's competition with others. This emphasis is made stronger when, for instance, a large first-year course is known to allow a fixed number of students to graduate with A's, or is marked on a bell curve. This makes these precious marks more valuable by artificially putting them in limited supply.

Other cultures put a greater emphasis on the group. Indigenous students, for example, have traditionally not wanted to be singled out in class. They whisper answers to peers who have been asked to reply to teacher questions, so that there will be no embarrassment for a classmate who doesn't know the answer. Research has shown that they are typically more likely to share answers on tests, the same way they would help their family members and friends. The cultural value of sharing is higher than in mainstream Canadian culture.

The Western culture of education emphasizes putting what you say "in your own words." There are cultural traditions in which "repeating the words of the master" is more valued than personalizing an answer. When international students come to Canada, they are unlikely to have been told about how education in Canada follows a model that may differ from the model used in their country of origin.

Another influential aspect of the Western culture of education is the increasingly corporate nature of postsecondary institutions, where students are viewed as customers (or "stakeholders"—a hideous term). Students may feel that it is their right as consumers to appeal grades or to sue over disappointing marks. As long as school administrators feel that their institutions are competing for students, they may be reluctant to cultivate an unfavourable reputation by aggressively pursuing plagiarizers, risking bad publicity. And with the increased level of credentialism—the emphasis on "getting the piece of paper"—rather than on learning, students may act more like customers than like learners.

The corporate culture of the postsecondary institution is also expressed and experienced internally, within the institution, and can have an influence on how plagiarism is treated and judged. Departments where students write a lot of essays (sociology, anthropology, history, literature, philosophy, and so on) are more involved in providing electives to students who are studying in different programs than in training majors in their fields of study. Pressure can be brought to bear on a department's administrator by administrators of the students' programs to "just let my student pass," rather than doggedly pursuing cases of plagiarism. The competition for students goes on within colleges and universities, as different departments attempt to draw students to take their electives. A popular course gains status for the department and can be used to justify new hires and a higher budget. A course with a high rate of catching plagiarism offenders is not popular. The increased use

What Do YOU Think?

1. Why do you think that plagiarism is on the rise at postsecondary institutions in Canada?
2. Do you accept the idea that students should always be encouraged to put things "in their own words"?

of temporary, sessional, or adjunct professors, who don't want to "rock the boat," also weakens the impulse to take a firm stand against plagiarism. They want to be seen as "team players" so that they will get rehired. Finally, as Thompson (2006) notes, when it comes to plagiarism, word gets around. Those schools that have a clear policy of dealing strictly with plagiarism have fewer instances of the offence. Where people often "get away" with it, student culture might simply become supportive of plagiarism.

Social Inequality and Education

Participation Rates

Postsecondary education can be a major avenue of social mobility, offering people from lower-class families the opportunity to secure jobs paying middle- or upper-class salaries. But if postsecondary education becomes so expensive that low-income students either cannot attend college or university or leave because of crippling student debt, then this avenue for mobility is blocked.

Figure 12.1 shows the results of a recent study of the postsecondary enrolment rate of 19-year-old Canadians (Frenette, 2017). Students in this sample are separated into quintiles (five equal groups), based on the after-tax income of their parents. You can see that 19-year-olds in the highest income quintile have the highest rate of college and university enrolment at close to 80 per cent. This is over 30 per cent higher than the enrolment rate of 19-year-olds in the lowest quintile: only 47 per cent of 19-year-olds in this income quintile attended college or university in 2014. The encouraging news is that while there is a clear correlation between parents' income and the likelihood that their children

Ever been tempted by an ad like this? What about the advertising makes the service seem morally legitimate and socially acceptable?

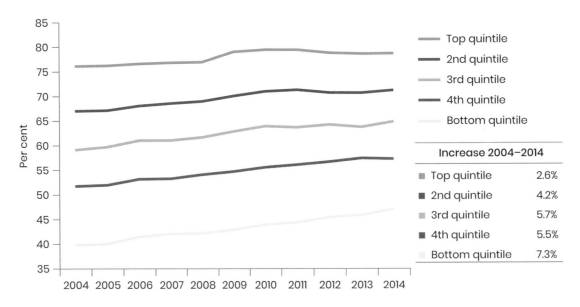

FIGURE 12.1 Postsecondary Attendance Rate by Parents' Income, 2004–2014

1.   Note: The sample consists of 19-year-old youth matched with a parent who lives in one of the 10 provinces.

Source: Frenette, 2017, Chart 1.

will attend college or university, the enrolment rate grew for each quintile, but grew the most among 19-year-olds in the lowest income groups. Here is a question for you: Do you think that tuition became more affordable over that 10-year period? If not, how do you account for the fact that the percentage of 19-year-olds in college and university rose by 7.65 per cent during that span?

In Canada, college tuition costs less and is therefore more accessible than university education. Look at Figure 12.2: Do you think the data point to something of a class system in postsecondary education? Now look at Figure 12.3, which shows the median income of Canadians who graduated from college or university between 2010 and 2014. Together, Figures 12.1, 12.2, and 12.3 show a correlation between the amount of money your parents earn, the likelihood you will participate in postsecondary education, the kind of credential you are most likely to earn, and the amount of money you will garner with that credential.

Tuition Fees and University Education

Tuition fees for university education rose significantly during the 1990s, and have continued to climb, albeit less dramatically, since the start of the twenty-first century. Consider that the average undergraduate tuition fee in Canada has risen from $4400 in the 2006–7 academic year to $6838 in 2018–19, an increase of 55 per cent (Statistics Canada Table 37-10-0045-01). Students in Ontario (71.4 per cent), Saskatchewan (57.6 per cent), and Quebec (53.2 per cent) have faced the steepest tuition increase over that period, although Quebec's tuitions remain among the lowest in Canada. A drop in federal and provincial funding for postsecondary education has been a major factor contributing to the increase.

There are significant regional differences in tuition costs for both undergraduate and graduate students (see Figure 12.4). Ontario has the highest average tuition costs, at $8838 for undergraduate students and $10,028 for graduate students. This should not be surprising as Ontario's provincial government spends less per postsecondary student than any other province. Nova Scotia, Saskatchewan, and New Brunswick are other provinces with undergraduate tuition fees above the Canadian average, while higher-than-average graduate fees are charged in Nova Scotia and British Columbia. The lowest tuitions, for both graduate and undergraduate students, are found in Newfoundland and Labrador and in Quebec, where the fees are below the average by several thousand (see Figure 12.4).

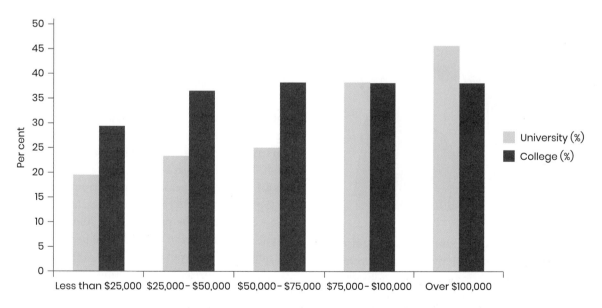

FIGURE 12.2 University and College Participation among 18- to 24-year-olds in Canada, by Parents' Income (2001)

Source: Drolet, 2005.

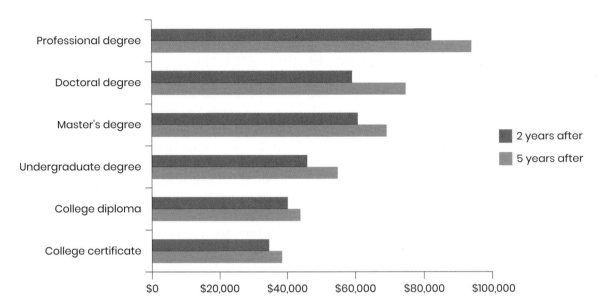

FIGURE 12.3 Median Employment Income of Postsecondary Graduates 2 and 5 Years after Graduation, by Educational Qualification, 2011 Longitudinal Cohort

Source: Statistics Canada, 2018.

In March 2019, US federal prosecutors laid charges in connection with a scheme that enabled students to gain admission to American colleges through bribes and fraudulently inflated entrance exam scores. Could the same thing happen (or be happening) in Canada?

Of course, what you pay depends on not just *where* you're studying but *what* you're studying. The so-called professional schools of dentistry, medicine, law, and pharmacy have the highest average fees across the country, at $23,474, $14,780, $13,332, and $10,746, respectively in 2018–19 (Statistics Canada Table 37-10-0003-01). Needless to say, this has affected who goes to the professional schools. The situation at professional schools changed dramatically after 1997, when tuition fees were deregulated (i.e. government controls on what the universities could charge were withdrawn). A study undertaken in 2004 by the five law schools in Ontario (where the tuition is highest) looked at how the demographics of their students changed in the years following deregulation (King, Warren, & Miklas, 2004). They found that between 1997 and 2004, there was a 4.7 per cent increase in students from families in the top 40 per cent in terms of total household income, and a decrease in the proportion of students whose parents earn incomes in the middle 20 per cent of the distribution (King, Warren, & Miklas, 2004).

As with postsecondary tuition fees generally, there is a regional disparity in the cost of attending a professional school. Table 12.1 shows the average cost of undergraduate programs in dentistry, medicine, law, and pharmacy in the nine provinces where

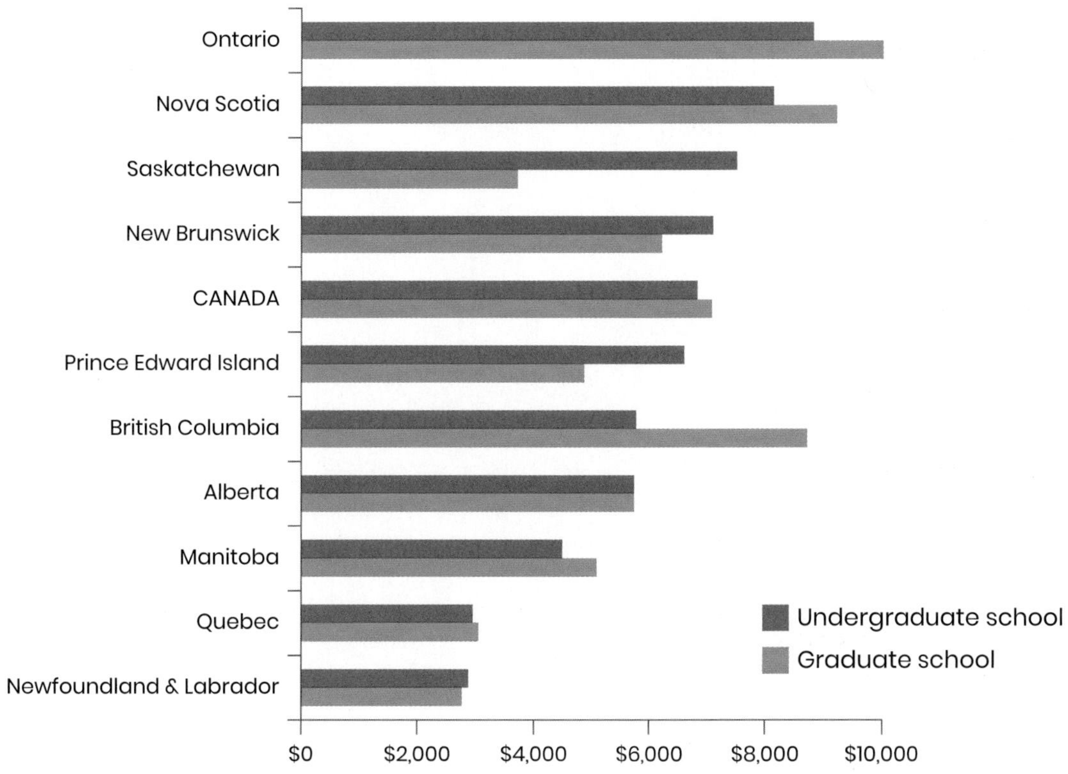

FIGURE 12.4 Average Undergraduate and Graduate Tuition Fees for Canadian Full-Time Students, by Province, 2018–2019

Source: Statistics Canada Table 37-10-0045-01.

these programs were available in 2018–19, presented in order of most to least expensive.

We can see, then, that postsecondary education and class (that is, parental income) relate to one another, particularly when it comes to university, especially with the professional schools. The province in which the student lives is a factor, again especially with the professional schools, with Ontario being the most expensive and Quebec the least expensive province for university education.

TABLE 12.1 Average Tuition Fees ($) for Full-Time Canadian Students in Dentistry, Medicine, and Law, 2018–2019

	Dentistry	Medicine	Law	Pharmacy
Ontario	40,463	26,838	21,614	19,927
Saskatchewan	34,628	17,474	13,653	10,025
Nova Scotia	24,850	20,067	15,045	11,479
Alberta	20,184	13,300	11,025	10,611
Manitoba	21,673	8,834	10,359	8,488
BC	28,770	18,110	13,152	12,751
New Brunswick	N/A	N/A	9,366	N/A
Newfoundland	N/A	10,250	N/A	2,805
Quebec	3,962	3,265	2,881	2,620
Canada	**23,474**	**14,780**	**13,332**	**10,746**

Note

The averages presented for Quebec and Nova Scotia take into account the different fees charged in these provinces to "in province" and "out of province" Canadian students.

Source: Statistics Canada CANSIM Table 37-10-0003-01.

ROGERIO BARBOSA/AFP/GettyImages

In 2012, the province with one of the lowest average tuitions (by a large margin), Quebec, saw massive student unrest concerning a proposed tuition increase, yet the province with the highest tuition, Ontario, had no student response to this strike. Why do you think that is?

Wrap It Up

Summary

We live in a time in which there are a number of important choices to make concerning the future of our education system. The sociology of education can help make those choices truly informed and democratic. At base, the most important issue is whether the Canadian education system—from primary school all the way up to our postsecondary institutions—is fundamentally meritocratic or whether it serves more to reproduce the class system and cultural privileges of the culturally dominant. At the elementary and secondary level, we need to ensure the suitability of the curriculum so that marginalized peoples get to read and hear about people like themselves. The effects of "streaming" (or "tracking") must be seriously studied. At the postsecondary level, we need to look critically at such practices as the increasing dependence on adjuncts, on corporate sponsorship, and on online education, in order to uncover the potential harm as well as benefits that they may bring.

Think Back

Questions for Critical Review

1. What was public education designed to accomplish when it was first established in the mid-nineteenth century? How much would you say the goals of public education have changed since then?

2. How well does Foucault's concept of the docile body apply to the education you have received so far? In the time you have spent at school, have you experienced hierarchical observation, normalizing judgment, and examination?

3. Is education—primary, secondary, postsecondary—an avenue for social mobility? Or does education do more to reinforce existing social differences? Define *cultural reproduction theory*, and explain how much you think it applies to education in the twenty-first century.

4. What evidence of corporate sponsorship exists on your college or university campus? What buildings are named after recognizable companies? What businesses have been granted the right to set up shop on the premises? What do you think are the drawbacks to corporate sponsorship of postsecondary education (including research grants)? Do they outweigh the benefits, including lower tuition costs?

5. Summarize the factors that contribute to the growing problem of plagiarism. Which factors make plagiarism possible? Which ones encourage it? Are there any factors that legitimize it? Is it really the problem we think it is? If so, how would you address it? Consider factors outside of education, such as online music sharing and music sampling: Do we live in a society where originality and authorship are less valued than they once were?

6. What do you see as the connection between the rise of online education and the growing reliance on adjunct professors? Are they both symptoms of the same factors? Which ones?

7. Have you experienced being "overqualified" for a job? Was it possible for you to "take the job seriously," as a less qualified worker might be able to do?

8. Have another look at Figures 12.1, 12.2, and 12.3. In your own words, explain what the data shown in these figures suggest.

9. Postsecondary education offers many things: training for a future career, intellectual stimulation, an avenue to well-paying employment, a chance to break free from parental controls, social networking within your peer group, and numerous opportunities for personal growth. In what three or four ways do you hope to benefit most from your postsecondary education? Do you think these fall within the stated goals of your college or university? Is your college or university set up to help you achieve the things that are most important to you?

Read On

Recommended Print and Online Resources

George Dei & Agnes Calliste, *Power, Knowledge and Anti-Racism Education: A Critical Reader* (Halifax: Fernwood Publishing, 2000).

- An informative collection of readings on what anti-racism education entails.

James Côté & Anton Allahar, *Lowering Higher Education: The Rise of Corporate Universities and the Fall of Liberal Education* (Toronto: University of Toronto Press, 2011).

- This work, from two University of Western Ontario sociologists, looks at the effects on education of universities forming closer ties with large corporations.

Jamie Brownlee, *Academia, Inc.: How Corporatization is Transforming Canadian Universities* (Black Point, NS: Fernwood Publishing, 2015).
- This is the first comprehensive look at corporatization as it affects Canadian universities.

Jeannie Oakes, *Keeping Track: How Schools Structure Inequality*, 2nd edn. (New Haven, CT: Yale University Press, 2005).
- A classic critique of the cultural reproduction function of tracking or streaming students.

Jo-ann Archibald, *Indigenous Storywork: Educating the Heart, Mind, Body and Spirit* (Vancouver, BC: UBC Press, 2008).
- Archibald's exploration of Indigenous storytelling explains, for a non-Indigenous audience, the value of Indigenous modes of education.

John Richards, Jennifer Hove, & Kemi Afolabi, *Understanding the Aboriginal/Non-Aboriginal Gap in Student Performance: Lessons from British Columbia* (Toronto: C.D. Howe Institute, 2008).
- A useful guide to strategies used to improve Aboriginal education.

Michael Dubson, ed., *Ghosts in the Classroom: Stories of College Adjunct Faculty—and the Price We All Pay* (Boston: Camel's Back Books, 2001).
- This book uses the first-hand accounts of adjunct professors to present the experiences and perspectives of the educational underclass.

Nicole Smith, "In Defense of the Traditional Classroom: An Argument Against the Move to Online Classes," www.articlemyriad.com/argument-traditional-classroom-online/
- This online article defends the value of the traditional classroom. To better understand the other side of the argument, have a look at university webpages defending the move to Coursera, like the following, from UBC: http://ctlt.ubc.ca/2012/09/27/ubc-to-offer-free-online-courses-through-coursera/

Pasi Sahlberg & William Doyle, *Let the Children Play: How More Play Will Save Our Schools and Help Our Children Thrive* (New York, NY: Oxford University Press, 2019).
- Research on schools around the world informed this study of how bringing more opportunities for physical and intellectual play into the classroom will help students develop greater creativity, teamwork, focus, resilience, empathy, concentration, and executive function.

People for Education, www.peopleforeducation.ca
- This parent-led and parent-focused guide to educational issues in Ontario offers news and views, as well as research reports and survey findings. It includes a separate tab devoted to Indigenous education.

13

Health and Ability

Reading this chapter will help you to . . .

- Explain how health and ability are socially constructed.

- Define the terms *sick role* and *social course of disease.*

- Outline the principles of biomedicine and contrast them with alternative medical practices.

- Discuss how the process of medicalization takes place.

- Talk about the relationship between medicine and social factors such as race, gender, and class.

- Explain the difference between impairment and disability.

- Differentiate between medical models, economic models, and social constructionist models of disability.

◄ Alleles

For Starters

Gordon Dias, 1985–2001

When a person gets sick, we look for causes. Did you wash your hands? Maybe it wasn't such a good idea to use that gas station washroom. Could you have caught it from Gene? I had a feeling that sushi might have been off—I mean, it's been in the fridge since Friday. We don't imagine the illness originated with the individual: we look for contributing factors outside the person.

In Canada, we are coming to view mental sickness the same way we view other kinds of more obviously physical illness. However, there is still a tendency to look for its causes within the individual while ignoring the external factors that played a role. As you read the following story, think about what may have been happening outside the individual and how it contributed to what turned out to be a fatal illness.

It has been almost 20 years since my nephew Gordon committed suicide. He was 16. He hanged himself from a tree in front of a local high school. As a sociologist, and as his uncle, I struggle to understand why he did this. The causes are social.

Gordon was a young, single man. This made him part of the social group most prone to suicide. He was on the margins of society in several ways. He was the youngest of three children, a child whose brother and sister demanded attention with their achievements. His older brother was the first-born grandchild and nephew on both sides of the family, a position that brought ready attention. His older sister is simply brilliant, a very hard act to follow. Both now have graduate degrees. In my earliest memory of Gordon talking, he is straining to be heard above his siblings.

John Steckley

He was a person of colour, the product of a mixed South Asian and Caucasian marriage, living in the very white city of London, Ontario. He was very close to his South Asian grandmother—so much so that when he left home for a while, he moved in with her. It could not have been easy in that city to have made that choice.

Gordon was artistic. It is not easy for a young man to express himself artistically in our culture, not without presenting some counterbalancing signs of macho behaviour. Perhaps that's one reason why he sought the social company he did. According to my sister and brother-in-law, he had been spending time with guys who regularly got into trouble. This eventually got him suspended from school. Zero-tolerance policies aren't very forgiving of even temporary allegiances with groups of kids who act out. At some level, zero-tolerance is simply intolerance. For Gordon, I guess, that was the final piece of the puzzle. The picture he was left with led him to suicide.

Introduction: Is There a Sociologist in the House?

Sociology students new to the discipline are sometimes surprised when they arrive for the lecture on medical sociology. Medicine? Sociology? Where's the connection? After all, when the restaurant diner starts choking on a fishbone, no one yells, *Is there a sociologist in the house?*

But sociology and health are closely connected, beginning with the view that medical practices and beliefs are intensely social. Like other topics we have considered in earlier chapters—**deviance**, for example—health and ability are socially constructed: how they are defined and viewed varies from culture to culture and changes over time. Consider dyslexia. Sometimes called "reading disorder," it is a general term for difficulties in spelling, learning to read or read quickly, and being able to understand and sound out words that are written as opposed to spoken. While humans may always have been affected by dyslexia, I believe that it would only be viewed as a disability in a literate culture: our preliterate ancestors were likely unaware of it. And, yet, in our deep, dark, not-so-distant past, people with dyslexia were considered stupid or—to use an archaic clinic term—"feeble-minded," when other measures of intelligence, if checked, would show conclusively that this was not true. To take another example, there is a condition unique to Chinese and South Asian cultures called *koro*, which is a profound belief that one's external genitals or nipples are shrinking (Welsch & Vivanco, 2019, p. 283). Symptoms include acute panic attacks that can last from hours to days.

Sociology can help to understand why this very real psychological disorder exists in some cultures but not in others.

A large part of medical sociology involves **policy sociology**, which is about generating sociological data to help governments and health professionals develop the policies that drive health care in this country. Thus, we can say that one of the principal aims of medical sociology is to improve the delivery of health services through sociologically informed research. **Critical sociology** contributes significantly as well, especially when the focus shifts to the practices of multinational pharmaceutical companies, medical schools (particularly when they raise their fees), and privately run, for-profit clinics and hospitals.

Healing is achieved through social means, so it's natural that sociology has a lot to contribute to our understanding of the field of medicine. Race, gender, ethnicity, age, and class—all social factors—can greatly affect an individual's experience of the medical professions. How? Let's say you're a middle-aged woman living outside the city, suffering from intensely sore feet. You go to your family doctor. She was born in Sri Lanka and educated in Britain, having moved to Canada just five years ago. She can't find a cause for your ailment, so she recommends a number of specialists. Which specialists she recommends will depend on her professional social network, the circle of people she knows and trusts. This network depends on such social factors as the location of her practice (outside the city) and the level of status she has as a doctor (itself possibly determined by how long she has been practising and the degree to which she has been politically active in medical associations). Religion can be a factor, since certain hospitals are governed by specific religious groups. Her sex might be a factor, as men are still more prominent in medicine than women are.

Compare this scenario with that of a very successful businessperson with a prominent white male doctor who has hospital privileges at one of the best hospitals in a large city. Your doctor has been head of the provincial medical association and is often asked to present papers at medical conferences. Imagine how his professional social network might differ from that of the doctor discussed in the preceding paragraph, and how your treatment might differ as a result.

This is just one illustration of why sociology cannot be ignored when it comes to health, an idea I hope to reinforce over the course of this chapter with many more examples. Now you can just sit back and say, "Ah!"

The Sick Role

American sociologist **Talcott Parsons** (1902–1979) came up with perhaps the first medical sociology term when, in *The Social System* (1951), he developed the concept of the **sick role** (or **patient role**). Like other sociological roles, he argued, being sick came with certain expectations—four, to be exact. In his thinking, two relate to what the sick person can expect from society, two to what society should expect of the sick person:

1. The person engaged in the sick role should expect to be granted "exemption from normal social responsibilities." In other words, patients should be excused from regular duties, either at home or in the workplace, while they recover.
2. Patients should expect to be "taken care of" rather than having to take care of themselves.
3. Patients are socially obligated to try to "get well" rather than remain in the undesirable state of being ill.
4. The sick person is socially obligated to "seek technically competent help" (in other words, the help of a qualified health professional).

The sick role, according to Parsons, gives the individual licence to be temporarily "deviant" with

regards to the first two expectations, provided they act in accordance with the second two.

Parsons was a **structural-functionalist**. Structural functionalism presumes a social uniformity of experience that conflict or critical sociologists would challenge. Ask yourself this: Is the sick role the same for everybody? The first challenge to the uniformity of the structural-functionalist model came quickly. In 1954, Earl Koos wrote *The Health of Regionville: What the People Thought and Did About It*. It was based on research he had carried out between 1946 and 1950 on differences in what people thought and did about their health depending on their class. He learned that people in higher occupational groups were better able to afford to play the sick role, a privilege less available to those of lower occupational groups.

Similar arguments against the uniformity of the sick role can be made based on gender, race, and age. Society has different expectations for a mother than for a father. When children are sick, the mother is typically expected to take time off work to look after them. And who is *least* likely to be allowed to play

BartCo/iStockphoto

This worker has just been injured on the job. According to the sick role, what actions is he expected to perform? Now assume he has a family dependent on his income, and his job is part-time (meaning he is only paid for the hours he works). Why might he opt out of the social contract that goes along with the sick role?

the sick role if the whole family gets sick? We can also look at people with chronic illnesses or disabilities. Are they to be considered permanently "deviant" according to Parsons's model?

It is hard to defend the universal applicability of Parsons's model of the sick role. In part, this is because the model changes over time. At the turn of the twenty-first century, Ivan Emke (2002) proposed five new expectations for Canadians in the sick role. Two of these are central. First, "patients in the New Economy are responsible for their own illnesses" (Emke, 2002, p. 85). Emke's point is that instead of looking at social and environmental causes of sickness (pollution, unsafe working and living conditions, stress through overworking, economic insecurity, and social disruption), we've become inclined to blame individual "choices" (smoking, drinking, not belonging to a health club, not making time for exercise, eating the wrong foods). Emke notes that the bulk of cancer information provided in ads and public health materials focused on individual risk factors rather than those presented by society, such as polluting industries and weak anti-pollution laws. This lowers society's sense that everyone is equally entitled to free health care. Do we feel less sympathy for smokers with lung cancer? You can see how those who buy into this expectation might use the underlying argument to justify charging user fees for some medical services.

The second of Emke's new expectations is really a conflation of two: "the patient in the New Economy is instructed to tread lightly on the system," and "patients in the New Economy are not to be trusted" (Emke, 2002, pp. 87, 89). We could recast it, a little less subtly, as "patients are assumed to be abusing the system." Emke raises this belief in connection with a public education campaign to encourage people to use as few medical services as they can. He cites a 1994 pilot project by the Conservative Ontario government designed to encourage residents of London to stop going to their family doctor for relatively minor complaints. No research had been done to see whether people were actually "abusing" the system. The assumption underlying the project was that escalating healthcare costs can be attributed to too many "unnecessary" visits to family doctors. Perhaps rising healthcare costs are more the result of building huge technology-intensive hospitals that are less cost-effective than having a greater number

of small-town and community-based medical centres. Perhaps nurses, who make less than doctors do, should be permitted to perform basic medical procedures (stitching wounds, for example) that doctors are normally responsible for, so that the same work can be done at lower cost.

KatarzynaBialasiewicz/iStockphoto

Do you believe that people who smoke are fully entitled to free health care? What about people who eat too much junk food? People who engage in dangerous recreational activities? People who play video games all day?

What Do YOU Think?

1. How do you think factors such as sex and ethnicity affect the universality of Parsons's sick role?
2. Who do you think abuses our healthcare system most: Patients? Doctors? Hospital administrators? Governments? Pharmaceutical companies? Industries that cause pollution?

The Social Course of Disease

A medical breakthrough of the nineteenth century was the realization that every disease has a natural course it goes through, a kind of lifespan during which you catch the disease, suffer through it, and gradually get well (or sicker, in some cases). It depends on the virus or bacterium, and the way the human body reacts to it. Think of a cold. Doctors can prescribe medicine to help alleviate the symptoms and speed up recovery, but they can't fundamentally change the natural course of a cold.

Likewise, we can speak of the **social course** that diseases and disorders go through, a course affected by sociological factors such as the ethnic background, culture, class, age, and sex of the people affected. The following example traces the social course of an injury and illustrates how that course is affected by class.

I once injured myself while running when I should have walked, and I ruptured my Achilles tendon. During my initial trip to the hospital, my left leg was put in a cast, so that I could move only through the use of crutches. I was billed for both the fiberglass cast and the crutches, but because I was then a full-time salaried employee with benefits, my workplace health insurance covered the cost of both. My middle-class job did not require heavy lifting or great physical exertion, so I continued to work, despite having to hobble around the college on crutches for nine weeks. I could have decided not to work during that period, and a good disability allowance would have ensured that I lost no significant income. The injury caused a deadly blood clot to develop, so my doctor proscribed a blood thinner. Fortunately, my drug plan covered almost the entire cost of this expensive drug.

My wife suffers from a disability that makes it very difficult for her to work full-time. Because I was well paid, we could afford to live on one income. My wife was able to be at home to take care of me during my recovery period. It would have been much worse for my emotional state and physical health if she had not been so diligent in helping me. I owe her a lot.

Once the cast was removed, I began physiotherapy. The cost was covered almost completely by my insurance plan at work. It helped immeasurably. My recovery proceeded much more quickly than I had hoped.

I dread to think what the social course of my healing would have been if I had been an unskilled worker in a factory or warehouse. Other sociological factors that influenced the social course of my recovery include my marital status and the fact that I lived and worked near a large urban centre with abundant medical resources and facilities. What would the social course of my recovery have been like had I been living alone, or in a rural area without access to transportation? What other factors might have changed the course?

The feature below provides a good example of factors that affect the social course of a disease. It is important to remember that the sociological factors surrounding a patient, just like physical factors such as medicine, clean living conditions, and rest, can influence the social course of recovery in either a positive or a negative way.

The Point Is...

Ethnicity Affects the Social Course of Tuberculosis among the Inuit

Ethnicity is a sociological factor that can affect the social course of disease. Witness the treatment of Inuit with tuberculosis. By 1949, new antibiotics, combined with improved sanitation, screening, and treatment, had helped reduce the tuberculosis rate in Canada from about 165 deaths per 100,000 in 1908 down to 33. But at the same time, the tuberculosis rate among Inuit in Canada was rising dramatically, peaking in 1952 at 569 per 100,000 (the highest rate among any international population). In that year, there were 54 deaths in an Inuit population of roughly 10,000.

The high rate had a number of causes. First, the severe cold of the Arctic—though not cold enough to kill the *tuberculosis bacillus*—made the Inuit especially susceptible to respiratory problems. The intimate closeness

Inuit Tapiriit Kanatami

Tuberculosis is still a problem among Canada's Inuit. The federal government recently unveiled a plan to eliminate tuberculosis in the North by 2030. Why do you think ethnicity has, for so long, been a factor in the social course of this disease?

of Inuit families living in igloos facilitated the spread of the bacteria. More consequential was the increasing contact with people from southern Canada. Pat Grygier explains that

> as the Inuit adapted to accommodate the desires of the newcomers, trapping to exchange furs for store goods or working for the RCMP or on military construction sites for cash, their highly nutritious fresh meat or fish diet and their warm caribou-skin clothing were gradually exchanged for a diet largely of white flour, lard, tea, jam, and canned goods, and for much less warm southern clothing. When the caribou declined or the pattern of migration changed, . . . malnutrition occurred. (1994, p. 55)

Inuit tuberculosis patients were treated differently from other Canadians. At the time, TB patients would be confined for six months to two years in a hospital or sanatorium. These were not built in the Arctic, so Inuit TB patients were brought (forcibly, in many cases) to southern Canada. Grygier eloquently describes what happened after health professionals brought north by ship had conducted their patient examinations:

> When the doctors had made their final decision on whether an individual should go to hospital for treatment or stay in the North, the evacuees were sent down to the Inuit quarters in the prow of the ship and the rest were sent ashore. The evacuees were not allowed to go ashore to collect belongings, to say goodbye, or to make arrangements for their families or goods. If a mother was judged sick but her children were not infected, the children (sometimes including unweaned babies) were given to an Inuk woman going ashore. Fathers had no chance to arrange for someone to hunt for food for their families or to look after their dogs and equipment. Mothers had no chance to arrange for someone to care for their children or to sew and process the skins needed to keep the family warm. . . . Those needing hospital treatment were kept on board, the rest sent ashore, and on sailed the ship to the next settlement. (1994, p. 96)

The tuberculosis rate among the Inuit dropped during the 1950s to a low of 53 per 100,000 in 1959, but the effects of the separation lasted. Many families were never reunited, often because of death but even in cases where the TB-suffering family member recovered.

Biomedicine

Biomedicine is the application or use of Western scientific principles in the diagnosis and treatment of illness and disease. It uses physical tests to find defined, purely physical entities (such as bacteria, viruses, and trauma) and then applies purely physical medicines and therapies to counteract them. It is the dominant practice in Western society.

Let's say you suffer from migraine headaches. You visit your family doctor, who prescribes medication to reduce the severity of your symptoms. That is biomedicine. If you grew up in Canada, this is probably what you expected when you booked your appointment.

Alternative (or **complementary**) **medicine** is the term for approaches to treatment that fall outside of conventional biomedical practice. For instance, your doctor might have recommended acupuncture for your migraines, or massage therapy or yoga to reduce the stress contributing to your headaches. Your doctor might even have tried to discover environmental causes of your condition—bright lights in the area where you read or study, for example. These would all be considered alternative approaches.

A good example of divergent biomedical and alternative approaches to health is childbirth. Most North American women choose to give birth to their infants in a hospital, under the care of a team of medical professionals including an obstetrician, an anaesthesiologist, and several nurses. Increasingly, however, women are choosing to stay at home to give birth under the care of a midwife or doula. There are good reasons to recommend the latter approach. Many people find hospitals uncomfortable. Some women do not want to be separated from their families, especially if they have other young children. Knowing they will remain at home reduces stress once contractions begin. Unlike most obstetricians, a midwife or doula is available to provide continuous care before and after, as well as during, the delivery. And, it's important to point out, for thousands of years and in many parts of the world today, giving birth at home was and is the only option. Of course, there are many advantages to having a hospital birth, including ready access to doctors and medical equipment in the event that either the mother or the infant requires immediate care for life-threatening complications. Some women choose to combine these approaches by having a hospital birth attended by the midwife who has guided them through their pregnancy. In cases such as this, the term "complementary medicine" is really more apt: biomedicine and alternative medicine do not need to be mutually exclusive.

Biomedicine remains the norm in North America, but it is increasingly called into question by those who endorse a more holistic approach to diagnosis and treatment. Biomedicine has been criticized for looking at health from a **reductionist** perspective that attributes medical conditions to single factors treatable with single remedies. It may fail to take into account the broader set of circumstances surrounding a person's health or illness. Those involved in biomedicine are sometimes accused of being **absolutist**, of not recognizing that just as there are different cultures in business, policing, or fashion, there are **cultures of medicine**, each with a unique approach to interpreting health and sickness. Every patient, critics argue, should be treated in the context of their culture. No single treatment should be applied universally across all cultures.

In Chapter 3, I noted Anne Fadiman's (1997) study of the Hmong people living in the United States. Originally from China, the Hmong were forced to flee their homeland after opposing the Chinese government during the 1960s and 1970s. Fadiman shows how Western biomedical practices were at odds with Hmong cultural beliefs. She cites, as just one example, the how North American doctors failed to take into account the fear—widespread among the Hmong—of soul loss. Hmong adults, children, and even infants wear neck-rings and cotton-string spirit bracelets to combat their fear of soul loss. But Hmong patients arriving at a refugee camp in Thailand had their spirit strings cut by American health workers, who claimed the rings were unsanitary. Which do you think posed a greater threat to the physical and mental health of the Hmong: the spirit strings or the fear of losing their soul?

Medicalization

An offshoot of biomedicine is a practice known as **medicalization**, defined by sociologists Chang and Christakis as the process by which certain behaviours or conditions are defined as medical problems (rather than, for example, as moral or legal problems), and medical intervention becomes the focus of remedy and social control. (2002, p. 152)

Medicalization has been criticized as a form of reductionism that reduces complex medical conditions to biomedical causes without examining possible sociocultural or political factors. A related criticism is that Western health professionals are too quick to situate the problem exclusively or primarily in the individual human body, rather than, say, in an oppressive social or political system. Medicalization, by ascribing conditions like alcoholism to genetic factors, does excuse the sufferer by removing individual blame, but at the same time it portrays the sufferer as a genetic "victim" who can be saved only by an intervention engineered by the medical profession. It takes away the individual's ability to make empowering choices that could affect the outcome of the condition. This leads to a further criticism: that medicalization promotes the **commodification** of health care by identifying certain normal conditions as diseases that may be treated with "commodity cures" (e.g., drugs or procedures). In sociological terms, this makes the normal seem deviant. Examples for the aging male include obesity, male pattern baldness, increasingly frequent nighttime trips to the bathroom, and erectile dysfunction. These are not diseases. They are relatively normal aspects of the aging process that do not need to be medicalized.

Government agencies sometimes medicalize disorders traceable more to social or environmental factors than to purely medical ones. Medical journalist Lynn Payer offers an example in *Disease-Mongers:*

TODD KOROL/THE GLOBE AND MAIL

A social determinist might argue that the upward trend in obesity rates is a societal problem having to do with the prevalence of fast food advertising and the ready availability of cheap, unhealthy food (not to denigrate doughnuts—I can't resist a fresh, well-made doughnut). So if our streets were lined with healthier options, would obesity rates decline? Is obesity a societal problem or an individual one (asks the sociologist with the doughnut problem)?

How Doctors, Drug Companies, and Insurers Are Making You Feel Sick (1992):

> When . . . a child died of lead poisoning in Michigan, there was a call for screening for lead poisoning. But when you read the circumstances, you found that the child was homeless, living in an abandoned building. Calling for blood testing was obviously easier than calling for a policy of providing safe and low-cost shelter for the poor. (1992, p. 39)

Posttraumatic stress disorder (PTSD) is often medicalized (see Kleinman, 1995). Suffered especially by those who have experienced the extreme violence of warfare (as soldiers or civilians), violent political oppression, or crime, PTSD was first diagnosed by Western psychiatrists who traced its origins to bleak, unstable environments in countries such as Cambodia, El Salvador, Tibet, and the former Republic of Yugoslavia. Gradually, though, the focus of treatment has shifted from the pathology of the environment to the pathology of the individual. Patients are often treated as though their psychobiological reactions to these harrowing circumstances are not normal, as if a psychologically healthy person would not react that way. To be clear, it is not wrong to help people by recognizing that they have suffered psychological trauma, but it is misleading to remove from an individual's story the sickness of the social situation endured.

Ivan Illich: Pioneering Critic of Medicalization

Ivan Illich (1927–2002) introduced the notion of medicalization to sociology. Although Illich was trained as a medieval historian, theologian, and philosopher, sociologists stake claim to him as a public sociologist.

Illich developed the concept of medicalization as part of a critique of **radical monopolies** in industrial societies:

> A radical monopoly goes deeper than that of any one corporation or any one government. It can take many forms. . . . Ordinary monopolies corner the market; radical monopolies disable people from doing or making things on their own. . . . They impose a society-wide substitution of commodities for use-values by reshaping the milieu and by "appropriating" those of its general characteristics which have enabled people so far to cope on their own. Intensive education turns autodidacts [people who teach themselves] into unemployables, intensive agriculture destroys the subsistence farmer, and the deployment of police undermines the community's self-control. The malignant spread of medicine has comparable results: it turns mutual care and self-medication into misdemeanors or felonies. (1976, p. 42)

This passage comes from *Medical Nemesis: The Limits of Medicine*, which opens with the claim that "The medical establishment has become a major threat to health" (1976, p. 1). In the book, Illich describes a "doctor-generated epidemic" that is harming the health of citizens in industrialized society by taking away people's freedom to heal themselves and prevent illness, as well as their freedom to criticize industrial society for the ills of stress, pollution, and general danger that make people sick. Illich's term for this is **iatrogenesis**. He distinguished three different kinds:

- clinical iatrogenesis
- social iatrogenesis
- cultural iatrogenesis.

Clinical iatrogenesis refers to the various ways in which diagnosis and cure cause problems that are as bad as or worse than the health problems they are meant to resolve. This occurs when a patient enters hospital for treatment of one ailment and becomes infected with a virus originating in the hospital. **Social iatrogenesis** occurs when political conditions that "render society unhealthy" are hidden or obscured (Illich, 1976, p. 9). In Canada, this includes lax monitoring by government agencies of laws concerning workplace safety, for example. **Cultural iatrogenesis** takes place when the knowledge and abilities of the medical community are extolled or mythologized to the point where the authority of the health profession "tends to mystify and to expropriate the

Quick Hits

Illich on Medicalization

In every society, medicine, like law and religion, defines what is normal, proper, or desirable. Medicine has the authority to label one man's complaint a legitimate illness, to declare a second man sick though he himself does not complain, and to refuse a third social recognition of his pain, his disability, and even his death. It is medicine which stamps some pain as "merely subjective," some impairment as malingering, and some deaths—though not others—as suicide. (Illich, 1976, p. 45)

power of the individual to heal himself and to shape his or her environment" (Illich, 1976, p. 9). In other words, patients are given no credit for their role in recovery: it's all the result of the doctor's work.

Big Pharma: The Role of Drug Companies in Medicalization

The term "**Big Pharma**" is used to refer to the world's large pharmaceutical companies, which reap enormous annual profits from developing, manufacturing, and marketing the drugs used to fight and manage a range of medical conditions, some of them serious (such as HIV), some of them less so (such as insomnia, when this can often be cured through lifestyle changes).

Drug companies invest heavily in research and development. They recover those R&D costs by charging prices well beyond what it costs to manufacture a particular drug product. They can do this when they have a patent on the drug that prevents other companies from copying the product and selling a generic form at lower prices.

Consider the case of Roche, the owners of the patent for Tamiflu. Tamiflu is the proprietary term for oseltamivir, the main vaccine used against some strains of flu. In 2005, there was an international panic around a new strain of flu, officially known as H5N1 but more commonly known as avian flu or bird flu, because it was first found in birds. Soon after several cases were found in humans, Canada, the United States, Britain, Israel, and Australia bought billions of dollars worth of Tamiflu to stockpile just in case of a serious outbreak. The money was mostly wasted on a pandemic that never emerged (or, if you

prefer, that never lived up to the hype). Meanwhile, countries that couldn't afford the expensive patented vaccine, and companies that wanted to provide generic versions of oseltamivir, had to fight to make those cheaper versions of the vaccine available. In 2009, an Indian company (Cipla Ltd) won the right to produce an alternative version of Tamiflu, called Antiflu, for the world's second most populous country. Canadians were not so fortunate.

Consider another product: the EpiPen device. If you know someone with a serious allergy, or if you have one yourself, you have probably seen an EpiPen. It is used to administer a potentially life-saving dose of the drug epinephrine to someone experiencing a serious allergic reaction. In this case it is not the drug itself that is patented but the delivery method: an autoinjector, consisting of a spring-loaded syringe designed to inject the sufferer with the proper dosage of the drug. In the United States, Mylan Pharmaceuticals, which owns the patent, has raised the price of the EpiPen by over 400 per cent since 2009, despite the fact there have been no significant changes to the product to warrant such an increase ("EpiPen Price Furor," 2016). In this case, Canadians *are* lucky: Pfizer, the company with the licence to distribute the product in Canada, has kept the price consistent, partly because it must operate under the oversight of this country's Patent Medicine Prices Review Board.

Big Pharma lobbies hard against generic drugs, which cut into their massive profits, and fiercely defend their patents. But over time, a drug can go off-patent, meaning that the company that developed it no longer holds the right to produce it exclusively. Competition brings the price down—good news for patients—but if the price falls too much, drug companies may decide it is no longer profitable to produce—bad news for patients. This situation is playing out currently in Canada, where there is a shortage of three vital cancer drugs that have recently gone off-patent (Haig, 2019).

Big Pharma's lobby in Canada is strong enough that it affects policy. The flu shot sold in Canada in 2009 had not been through a complete set of clinical trials when it was distributed in the fight against a strain of H1N1 known as swine flu. Possible side effects were not completely known when the vaccine began to be used. Yet the Canadian government granted GlaxoSmithKline (GSK, a manufacturer of the anti–swine flu vaccine) indemnity, meaning that the government (that is, you, the taxpayer) would cover the cost of any lawsuit filed against the drug maker in the event the drug failed to work or produced fatal complications. GSK might have invested heavily in developing the vaccine, but the government gave the company a deal that carried no financial risk and the promise of huge profits for a company that currently earns an estimated $1.66 billion (US) a year on sales of vaccine.

Medicalization and Deaf Culture

One group that has been particularly opposed to medicalization is the Deaf community. Some background here is necessary. Deaf people regard themselves as part of a vibrant cultural group, with their own language, traditions, and history. They embrace the term Deaf (capitalized) and do not consider themselves disabled.

Medicalization, as we have seen, is the tendency to define a particular condition as a medical problem requiring intervention. In this context, it is the view

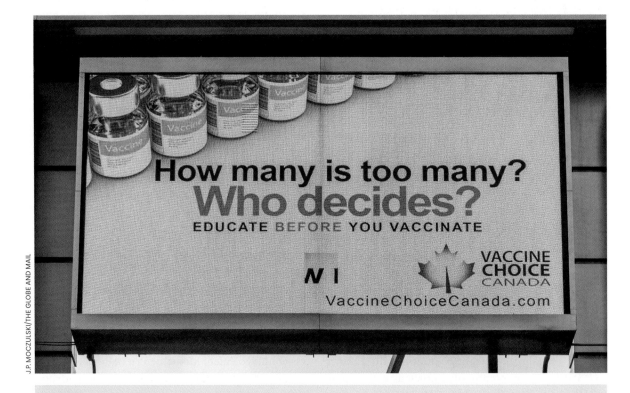

J.P. MOCZULSKI/THE GLOBE AND MAIL

For about one week in February 2019, billboards such as this one popped up in Toronto. They were quickly removed after a public outcry over the anti-vaccine campaign, which critics described as dangerous (Weeks, 2019). A rise in cases of measles in North America has been linked to falling vaccination rates. What are the causes for vaccine hesitancy in Canada? And when it comes to getting vaccinated, who should decide—the government or the individual?

that deafness is an undesirable physical defect that must be "fixed." As Marcel Broesterhuizen (2008) explains, the medicalized approach views Deaf people "as people who lack something, incapable of being fully fledged members of society, less human than others" (p. 108).

Deaf culture's anti-medicalization stance entails an opposition (in certain but not all circumstances) to hearing aids and cochlear implants. A cochlear implant is an electronic device that is surgically implanted in the ear to provide a sense of sound to a Deaf person. Opponents in the Deaf community argue that from a medical standpoint, the surgery is risky and not always completely successful. From a social standpoint, it can interfere with the identity formation of a Deaf person (especially a young Deaf person), depriving the person of membership in the cultural community into which he or she was born (Lane, 1992, 1993). Other medicalized approaches to deafness include the imposition of therapies designed to teach Deaf people to communicate using spoken languages and the promotion of sign systems modelled on spoken languages (English, French, etc.) in terms of their structure and vocabulary (CAD, 2012).

What Do YOU Think?

1. Is deafness primarily a medical problem to be dealt with in a purely medical way? What role should the Deaf community play in dealing with deafness? Do you think that your position might be different if you were deaf or had a family member or friend who was deaf?

2. Some research shows that deaf children fitted with cochlear implants before the age of two develop spoken language skills much more quickly than children older than two who have had the surgery (Kral & O'Donoghue, 2010). Do you think it is appropriate to have this surgery performed on children before they are old enough to be consulted? How do you think your answer might differ if you were a deaf (or Deaf) parent weighing the options?

Medical Sociology, Race, and Ethnicity

Unemployed Immigrant Doctors: A Problem with Many Standpoints

The Canadian healthcare system faces a shortage of doctors in communities outside of large urban centres. At the same time, the country is welcoming immigrants with medical degrees and general credentials that are considered insufficient to qualify them to practise medicine in Canada. It is a perplexing issue, one that must be considered from a number of *standpoints*. The sections that follow outline four of these differing standpoints.

1. Immigrant Doctors

As an immigrant doctor, you came to a country that offered greater financial opportunities for you and your family. On the strength of skills and experience gained in your home country, you scored well in the "point system" used to judge the suitability of candidates for immigration. The Canadian government seemed to welcome your arrival.

As soon as you arrived, problems hit you in the face. If you chose to settle in Toronto—as many do—you encountered a two-step problem. First, your skills and knowledge were assessed through a training program. The Ontario International Medical Graduate Program takes 48 weeks—close to a year—to complete and has limited space. You managed to gain admission to the program and did well, but then you faced a second, even higher hurdle: a residency program of several years in which you would essentially relearn everything you needed to know to earn your medical qualifications in the first place. And then there was the largest problem: the small number of residency positions available. Until recently, you would have been one of more than 1100 immigrant doctors in Ontario competing for just 36 spots open each year in the residency program. The number of spots has recently increased to 250. Still, the odds are not in your favour.

In the meantime, your family must eat. You might get a job in a medical field, possibly (with training) as a lab assistant. But it is more likely you will end up working as a telemarketer, driving an Uber, delivering meals-to-go, or doing manual labour in factories. Your dream of practising your chosen profession in this country has proven elusive.

2. Rural Communities

You live in a community that is home to fewer and fewer doctors. The older ones retire; the young graduates opt to take up medical work in the big city. Your family doctor has retired and closed her practice, and you, like her other patients, are scrambling to find another doctor to take you on. But most family doctors are already seeing more patients than they can handle. The trouble is that you're older and therefore more likely to have complicated and time-consuming medical problems. You are more

Quick Hits

Where Do You Go When You Don't Have a Family Doctor?

According to the Canadian Community Health Survey, in 2018, 5.6 million Canadians over the age of 12 were without a regular family doctor (Figure 13.1). That is up from 4.8 million Canadians without a healthcare provider in 2016 (Statistics Canada, 2017). In all age groups, men were more likely than women to report not having a regular family doctor.

An earlier Statistics Canada report (2013) found that not everyone without a family doctor was looking for one, and 80.6 per cent reported they had a place to go if they needed of health advice; these included:

- walk-in clinics (58.9 per cent)
- hospital emergency rooms (13.0 per cent)
- community health centres (8.7 per cent)

- other facilities, including hospital out-patient clinics and telephone health lines (19.3 per cent)

Among those who had looked for family doctor,

- 36.7 per cent said that doctors in their area were not taking new patients
- 29.7 per cent said their doctor had retired or left the area
- 25.2 per cent said that no doctors were available in their area
- 21.2 per cent gave other reasons

(These add up to more than 100 per cent because respondents were permitted to choose more than one option.)

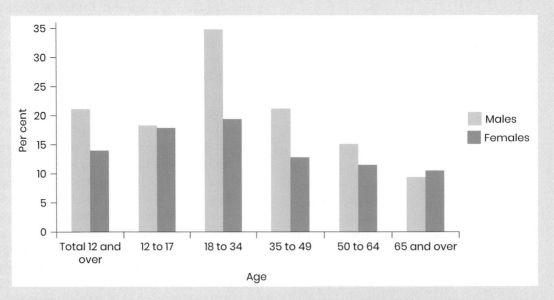

FIGURE 13.1 Percentage of Canadians without a Regular Healthcare Provider, by Age Category and Sex (2018)

Source: Based on Statistics Canada Table 13-10-0096-01, Health characteristics: Annual estimates.

work for a new doctor, who can choose not to take you on as a patient. So you put up with minor complaints, knowing that anything more serious will require a trip to the big city, where the bigger research hospitals and more lucrative practices are.

Occasionally, you wonder whether there's something your town should be doing to attract doctors. You don't care where they come from. In Ontario, 214 communities have been designated as "underserved" by the provincial ministry of health. Saskatchewan and Newfoundland and Labrador have higher percentages of foreign-trained doctors than other provinces. The reason: not as many obstacles for immigrant doctors.

3. Countries of Origin of Internationally Trained Doctors

You live in a developing country, where, especially in rural areas, there are even fewer doctors per population than there are in Canada's rural communities. The cost of educating medical professionals in your country is prohibitively high. It is much more likely that you will lose trained doctors to emigration than benefit from an influx of health professionals.

In post-apartheid South Africa, the government decided to block doctors from immigrating to other African nations to halt the **brain drain**—the exodus of educated professionals—eroding the healthcare systems of those countries. Canada experiences a bit of that brain drain when some of its medical specialists go to the United States, but it's nothing compared to the brain drain of doctors leaving developing countries for North America.

4. Doctors' Associations

Placing restrictions on internationally trained medical graduates gives Canadian-trained doctors more bargaining power as a group. As Linda McQuaig explained in a commentary on the New Brunswick doctors' strike in 2004,

> Doctors have managed to maintain enormous bargaining power in Canada by threatening, from time to time, to abandon us for more prosperous climes. But these threats only have teeth because doctors can rely on the fact that there is no one here to replace them if they go—even when potential replacements are already here and desperate to get to work. (2004)

On the other side, consider the Ontario Medical Association's (OMA) "Position Paper on Physician Workforce Policy and Planning," dated April 2002. It addresses the OMA's concerns about "the problem of inadequate physician human resources, and the related consequences for public access to medical treatment." One of the 18 recommendations in the report was to "Temporarily increase the number of fully qualified international medical graduate (IMG) positions." In a 2004 speech, OMA president Dr Larry Erlick, addressing the same problems, noted,

> We . . . need more foreign-trained physicians to practise in Ontario. The fact that we have relied on foreign-trained physicians in the past should come as no surprise, as 25 per cent of physicians practising today in this province are in fact international medical graduates! Some of the red tape has to be cut.

Still, in both documents, helping foreign-trained physicians gain accreditation to practise in Canada was clearly viewed as a secondary solution. The words "temporarily" and "fully qualified" in the first statement leave holes in that support, and Dr Erlick's recommendation was one of a number of "short-term recommendations," given less priority than bringing back Ontario medical graduates who are now practising elsewhere.

The Racialization of Disease: The 2003 SARS Outbreak

A disease becomes **racialized** when it is strongly associated with people of a particular racial or ethnic background, so that people of this background are treated negatively. An example occurred in 2003, when an outbreak of severe acute respiratory syndrome, or SARS, affected Canadians of all races but became primarily associated with Asians.

Telling It Like It Is

A Student POV

An Account of Systemic Racism from a Black First-Year Nursing Student

I have had my first clinical experience in the nursing profession, and I feel I have already been subjected to systemic racism. Examples of this include disciplinary actions that are different from other student nurses such as when myself and a non-Black student returned late from break. I was pulled aside, and it was stated that the teacher felt sorry for the other student. When I asked "why," it was implied that I coerced her into returning late against her will. Also, vague work appraisals are given, and no specific areas of improvement are suggested. Comments such as, "You seem like a very angry person," and "I have a hard time approaching you and can only imagine how the residents feel," or "Any monkey can be trained to take a blood pressure" are an everyday occurrence. There are many cases where my mistakes are far more noted and exaggerated than those of other students. When defending myself (as I feel I am performing equally well to everyone else), I am labelled as not being "self-aware" and not accepting feedback. Yet, when feedback is taken and changes are made, I am told I take things too literally. As a result, I can do no right.

Events like these are commonplace. As a result, promotions as well as workload may not be fairly distributed.

—Nadine Smith

Canadians began hearing about SARS in March 2003. They quickly learned that the highly contagious respiratory ailment with flu-like symptoms was serious, and in about 10 per cent of cases fatal. This made it the focus of widespread media attention throughout the spring and early summer. Over this period, the disease became racialized: because it originated in China, and because members of a Catholic Filipino community were among those who had contracted it, the disease took on a racial identity. Once cases of the disease began to appear in Canada, Chinese and Filipino Canadians became targets of discrimination.

Researchers Carrianne Leung and Jian Guan (2004) studied how the mainstream media racialized SARS by portraying Asians as carriers of disease in a way that spread fear among non-Asian Canadians. Table 13.1 summarizes their findings about the content of pictures accompanying news stories in four national newspapers and periodicals (Leung & Guan, 2004, pp. 9, 10).

Leung and Guan found that photographs accompanying stories about SARS tended to feature Asians, particularly Asians wearing masks to reduce the spread of the disease. The researchers noted that the use of frightening words and

TABLE 13.1 Photographic Treatment of SARS in the National Media, 2003

Newspaper / Magazine	Number of SARS Photos	Showing People		Showing Asians		Showing Asians with Masks	
		#	%	#	%	#	%
National Post	120	95	82.0	65	54.2	60	50.0
The Globe and Mail	119	68	57.1	52	43.9	41	34.5
Maclean's	27	17	63.0	8	29.6	6	22.2
Time (Canada)	17	15	88.2	8	47.0	6	35.3

Source: Leung & Guan, 2004.

THURSDAY, APRIL 3, 2003 ★ TORONTO STAR ★ B3

SARS Outbreak

China admits wider spread of SARS

12 more deaths reported among inland provinces

First cases found in Latin America and Israel

ANN PERRY
STAFF REPORTER

The global death toll from Severe Acute Respiratory Syndrome jumped yesterday as China broke its silence and admitted it had more cases in more provinces than it had previously revealed.

The South China Morning Post reported today that the first victims of the deadly illness were people in China's southern province of Guangdong who ate or handled wild game, confirming earlier reports linking the disease to ducks.

China said it had 1,190 suspected cases through the end of March, and 46 deaths instead of the 34 it had admitted. Cases were reported in Guangxi, Hunan and Sichuan provinces as well as Guangdong for the first time.

In total, the World Health Organization estimated that SARS has infected more than 2,200 people worldwide and killed an estimated 78.

Brazil reported its first suspected case, which, if confirmed, would be the first in Latin America. Israel also reported its first suspected case.

China agreed yesterday to let a team of WHO investigators visit the southern province of Guangdong, where the disease is believed to have started.

The four-member international team, which will leave Beijing today, will take samples from suspected patients to help identify a culprit virus and assess how infectious and virulent it is.

And, for the first time in its 55-

REUTERS

With Hong Kong being the global centre of the SARS outbreak, face masks are common on the city's streets. Some residents strive for their own style amid the crisis. Chinese officials are reporting there are more cases and more deaths than they previously admitted.

year-history, WHO recommended that travellers avoid part of the world because of an infectious disease: Hong Kong and adjoining Guangdong province.

In the first public statement by a senior leader, Chinese Health Minister Zhang Wenkang said the outbreak was "under effective control."

He said 80 per cent of those diagnosed with SARS have recovered.

For weeks, U.N. agency officials have appealed for more cooperation from China.

"Because the mainland is not sharing information . . . the outbreak has been lengthened," Taiwan's Mainland Affairs Council said in a recent report.

Laboratories around the world are racing to come up with a test for SARS.

The U.S. Centers for Disease Control has issued two tests that health officials can give to patients with suspected SARS. Dr. Julie Gerberding, the director of the Atlanta-based centre, said until a large number of people are tested, no one can say whether the disease is caused by the main suspect — a coronavi-

rus.

But she said so far 400 healthy people had been tested for the virus, a previously unknown relative of one of the common cold viruses, and all had tested negative.

Several patients with SARS have tested positive.

"It is not yet proof. There are other viruses still under investigation," she said. In Toronto, Dr. Raymond Tellier of the Hospital for Sick Children, has developed a test that detects this new species of coronavirus. It is currently being used here.

A top health expert in China told a newspaper the earliest SARS patients in Guangdong had close and continuous contact with chickens, ducks, pigeons and owls.

"We will explore further if the disease was passed to human beings from wild animals. You know, Guangdong people like eating exotic animals and I don't find it a healthy practice," said Bi Shengli, a vice-director at the Chinese Centre for Disease Control and Prevention.

The earliest cases of the disease were traced to either chefs or bird vendors, Bi said.

In Thailand yesterday, the government said it would turn back foreigners suspected of having SARS and would force those allowed in from affected countries to wear masks in public.

In the Philippines, which has no confirmed cases, President Gloria Macapagal Arroyo put in place a contingency plan — including air and seaport checks — to prevent an outbreak. Health officials in New Zealand urged indigenous Maori tribesmen to forgo their traditional "hongi" nose-rubbing greeting for visiting Chinese at a convention.

In Hong Kong, the Roman Catholic Church ordered priests to wear masks during Communion and put wafers in the hands of the faithful rather than on the tongue.

FROM STAR WIRE SERVICES

Toronto Star

Telling It Like It Is

A Student POV

SARS and Being Chinese

Around the time of the SARS crisis, being Chinese made people look at me in a different way, whether it was at school, at work, or in public places such as the subway and buses. It did not bother me at first, but as more and more individuals died due to SARS, the more I kept my eyes open for tainted looks darting in my direction.

Around that time in school, it wasn't so much the looks but comments made in class about the situation. What I have learned and understood in this game we call life is that everyone is entitled to his or her opinion. I have also learned and understood that not all opinions are necessarily right or wrong. Unfortunately, not all people feel that their opinions are wrong, hurtful, disrespectful, condescending, and rude.

One incident happened in my math class at college. Our class got off topic, and our focus was turned from present and future value to SARS. Our teacher was reminding us that proper hand washing helps in preventing the spread of infection. One obnoxious fellow who felt he was the class clown replied to our teacher's comment and stated that to prevent the spread of infection, we need to stay away from all those darn Chinese people. His language use and vocabulary was a little cruder. Being the only Asian person in the class, everyone turned and looked in my direction as if they were expecting me to curse him. I decided to let the one and only authority figure take care of his biased opinion. However, our teacher said absolutely nothing, except to get on with the lesson. His comments offended me, and our teacher not correcting him hurt my feelings. It made me pay more attention to the things that were being said in all the rest of my classes. The impact it had on my school life made me more defensive toward what my peers had to say about those of Asian descent. . . .

Ethnicity is a sociological factor that made an impact on my life within that year. Because I have been on the end of a biased opinion at school and indirect discrimination at work, I have further learned another aspect of the game of life: the value and meaning of equality and fairness and that even though there are different ethnicities and races, we are all part of one race called the human race.

—Karin Koo

unreasonable links to the Spanish influenza pandemic of 1918–19 (in which at least 20 million people died over an 18-month period) were also part of media hysteria. Fear surrounding the disease had a devastating economic impact on parts of Canada where the outbreak was prevalent, notably Toronto and, in particular, its various Chinatowns. Media commentators noted that many of the patrons suddenly avoiding Chinese businesses were themselves Chinese, as though this somehow justified similar acts of discrimination by non-Asian Canadians. Regardless, the loss of business occurred because the disease was racialized to the point where many Canadians changed their purchasing habits as a precaution against contracting the virus in communities where it was thought to be prevalent.

Medical Sociology and Gender

Female Doctors and the Feminization of the Medical Profession

We can say that the medical profession is becoming "feminized." This means that the percentage of women becoming and being doctors in Canada is growing. As recently as 1959 (it was recent for me—I was a child then), women accounted for about 6 per cent of medical school graduates in Canada. They remained a distinct minority over the next two decades, even while their numbers rose. In her preface to an edited collection of articles on female doctors in Canada, Shelley Ross, an associate professor in the Department of Family Medicine at the University of Alberta, explains what has happened since:

> Until the early 1980s, women made up less than one-third of the annual enrolment in Canadian faculties of medicine. Since 1982, however, the number of women enrolling in Canadian medical schools has consistently increased. By 1995, women made up half of those entering medical classes across the country. Since that year, women have been the majority in medical school classes in Canada. Although the high of a 59.1 per cent female incoming cohort across Canada in 2004 has not recurred, the ratio of 55:45 female-to-male has now become the new normal, with some provinces and territories consistently showing even higher proportions of female students in their intake. (Waugh et al. 2019, p. ix)

Male physicians still dominate the profession numerically, and in terms of influence in provincial and territorial medical associations. In 2007, there were roughly twice as many male as female doctors in Canada (Canadian Institute for Health Information, 2007). But there is an age group difference: the older the age group, the greater the percentage of male doctors. As older doctors retire, the profession will become more feminized.

Gender matters in an individual's experience of being a doctor. Women and men tend to differ in the types of medicine they practise. Women are more likely to be family physicians than specialists, particularly surgical specialists. And it was noted in 2007 that women who specialized went into predictable areas: 71 per cent went into obstetrics and gynecology, and 67 per cent into pediatrics (Malicki, 2007). Women enter areas considered "appropriate" for women, and may be sanctioned by the medical community for venturing into other areas. Women entering the profession follow their role model predecessors into these same fields of practice.

There are certain stresses felt more by female doctors than by male doctors. One is the struggle to achieve a work–life balance. Women are more likely to experience role conflict in this regard, especially regarding family life. As a result, they may see fewer patients and work fewer hours. These stresses make

What Do YOU Think?

1. Ross (2019, p. 8) comments that there is social resistance to claims that women and men experience medical education and practice differently. Why do you think that is?
2. Why might female physicians be less likely to become surgeons? Consider several reasons.
3. Do you think that the feminization of the medical professional might significantly lessen the power differential between doctors and nurses?

them more likely than their male counterparts to take short periods of time off or to retire prematurely (Hedden et al., 2017).

Medical Marginality: The Intersectionality of Gender and Race

In 1866, two First Nations men became the first Indigenous people in Canada to earn medical degrees. Both were more westernized than most Indigenous people of the time and yet were leaders of their people. Peter Edmund Jones, or Sacred Feathers, was a member of the Mississauga (Anishinaabe) Nation and was educated at the University of Toronto and Queen's University. Peter Martin, or Oronhyatekha ("Burning Sky"), was Mohawk and attended Oxford University (through contacts with Prince Edward) before completing his degree at the Toronto School of Medicine, later incorporated into the University of Toronto.

The first Canadian women to become doctors were Jennie Trout and Emily Stowe. Both attended the Toronto School of Medicine, where they were regularly harassed by their male colleagues with the encouragement of their male professors. Scottish-born Jennie Trout left Canada to complete her medical degree at the Women's Medical College of Pennsylvania in 1875, before returning to practise in Canada, becoming the first woman licensed to do so. She helped establish a women's medical college at Queen's University in 1883.

Emily Stowe was a woman of firsts, being the first female principal of a public school in Upper

Canada (later Ontario). In 1865, she applied to the Toronto School of Medicine but was rejected because she was a woman. She then went to the United States, where she received a degree in homeopathic medicine at the New York Medical College in 1867. She practised homeopathic medicine in Toronto until 1870, when she and Jennie Trout were accepted by special permission into the Toronto School of Medicine. Frustrated by the persistent harassment she received and the unwillingness of administrators to intervene, Emily Stowe refused to take her exams. She was officially licensed in 1880. Her daughter, Ann Augusta Stowe-Gullen, was the first woman in Canada to be awarded a medical degree, in 1883 at the University of Toronto.

Elizabeth Steinhauer, who is Cree, became the first Indigenous woman to be licensed as a doctor in Canada, in 1980, more than 100 years after Peter Jones and Peter Martin became the first licensed Indigenous doctors and Jennie Trout became Canada's first woman doctor. Why did it take so long? The residential school system crushed the desire of many Indigenous people to pursue higher education. As well, the Indian Act forbade Indigenous people to go to university unless they became enfranchised: status Indians would have to surrender Indigenous and treaty rights, and perhaps be forced to leave their home reserve. For most Indigenous people, this was too much to ask. Both Jones and Martin became doctors before the Indian Act was passed.

While the first formal nursing school in Canada was established in St Catharines, Ontario, in 1874, it wasn't until 40 years later that Canada had its first Indigenous nurse. Charlotte Edith Anderson Monture, a Mohawk of the Six Nations, graduated with a degree in nursing in 1914, but not from any school in Canada. After being turned down by Canadian nursing schools, she was forced to pursue her degree at the New Rochelle Nursing School in New York, where she began her career as a public school nurse. During World War I, she served in France in the US Army Nurse Corps. Upon her return, she worked as a nurse at a hospital in Six Nations.

Canadian schools trained no black nurses until 1950, after a ban on black nursing students was lifted. Toronto-born Bernice Redmon, who was educated at St Phillip Hospital Medical College in Virginia, having been refused entry at Canadian schools, was the first black woman licensed as a nurse in Canada.

After graduating in 1945, she got a job with the Nova Scotia Department of Public Health, and later became the first black woman to become a member of the Victorian Order of Nurses.

Although I have been engaged in Indigenous studies for over 40 years, I was unaware of the history of Indigenous women doctors until January 2015, when an Indigenous woman, Sally Simpson, who entered university in her forties, compiled a list of "Indigenous Women's Firsts" as a university project. You can find a link to the list at the end of this chapter.

Medical Sociology and Class

The Inverse Care Law

Dr Julian Tudor Hart (1927–2018) studied medicine at Cambridge and interned at the equally prestigious St George's Hospital in London. The natural career move for a British doctor on that path would have been to serve the needs of the wealthier classes in London or some other big city. Instead, he dedicated his life to helping the citizens of a working-class mining village in Wales. Dr Hart became famous among medical sociologists for an article he wrote in 1971. In it, he introduced the idea of the **inverse care law**:

> The availability of good medical care tends to vary inversely with the need for it in the population served. This inverse care law operates more completely where medical care is most exposed to market forces, and less so where such exposure is reduced. (Hart, 1971, p. 405)

Hart was describing a system that had, for almost 20 years, experienced socialized health care similar to Canada's—a system markedly different from the private or market-force system found in the United States. In the British context, the inverse care law was evident in statistics concerning infant mortality from 1949 to 1953. According to Hart, these statistics

> showed combined social classes I and II (wholly non-manual) with a standardised mortality from all causes 18 per cent below

the mean, and combined social classes IV and V (wholly manual) 5 per cent above it. Infant mortality was 37% below the mean for social class I (professional) and 38 per cent above it for social class V (unskilled manual). (1971, p. 405)

In other words, the death of an infant in its first year of life was far more likely to occur among the lower classes (those engaged in manual labour). This was a product of differences both in the working and living conditions of the different classes and in the medical care available in different areas defined by class. Regarding doctors, Hart observed the following trends:

In areas with most sickness and death, general practitioners have more work, larger lists [of patients], less hospital support, and inherit more clinically ineffective traditions of consultation [e.g. short visits with little listening to patients' problems] than in the healthiest areas; and hospital doctors shoulder heavier case-loads with less staff and equipment, more obsolete buildings, and suffer recurrent crises in the availability of beds and replacement staff. (1971, p. 412)

What Do YOU Think?

1. Do you think the inverse care law holds in Canada? How would you, as a sociologist, go about trying to prove or disprove it?

2. We know that even in Canada, people in certain positions are routinely allowed to "jump the queue" to receive medical procedures faster than most Canadians are normally be able to. (When was the last time you heard of an NHL player having to wait four to six months for an MRI?) Who, in your opinion, is entitled to priority care? Professional athletes? High-ranking politicians? People who have donated to the hospital? Emergency services professionals (paramedics, police officers, fire fighters)? Hospital workers? Spouses and families of any of the above?

The Sociology of Dis/Ability

What Is a Disability? The Challenge of Operational Definition

Like poverty and pollution, **disability** is hard to define precisely. We can probably find consensus on some types of disability, such as paralysis or blindness; as with the homeless poor and oil-contaminated water, the extreme cases are easy to identify. But devising an **operational definition**—a working definition that we can use for statistical purposes—forces us to consider less obvious cases.

The *Oxford English Dictionary* provides us with a starting point. It defines *disability* as "a physical or mental condition that limits a person's movements, senses, or activities" (www.oed.com). But does that mean that a person who cannot drive without glasses is disabled? What about someone with a speech impairment, such as a stutter, or an invisible condition, such as dyslexia? Is disability necessarily a chronic condition, or could we consider someone who is for a few months in a cast with a broken ankle disabled?

An editorial that appeared in a 1999 issue of the eminent medical journal *The Lancet* captures the challenge of establishing an operational definition for disability. The writer reasons that because we all have different degrees of physical and intellectual aptitude, we can all be said to experience disability—in the broadest sense—when it comes to everyday tasks we don't manage as well as our peers do. For me, that includes keeping my shoelaces tied, re-sealing Ziploc bags, and doing anything new with a computer.

All of us could be considered as disabled to some extent. Individuals differ in many ways in the manners in which they cope with the activities of daily living, or have a real but common handicap to which society has adjusted well. Deciding how far ability has to be impaired to constitute a disability is no easy matter—too vague, and abuse of special opportunities and services may follow; too rigid, and people who may benefit are excluded. ("The Spectrum of Disability," 1999, p. 693)

Postmodernist sociological theory teaches us to be suspicious of **binaries**, those either/or distinctions that are used to separate people into supposedly discrete categories such as male/female, heterosexual/homosexual, black/white. It was postmodernist theorists who argued, compellingly, that gender was better viewed as a continuum, with "male" and "female" at the extremes and a lot of territory in between. We could approach the condition of dis/ability the same way. But that won't help us with our operational definition, and as *The Lancet*'s editorial writer points out, disability is an identity with some social and political weight, one that may gain a person access to special resources and services set aside for people with disabilities, as difficult as those often may be to access.

Measuring and Defining Disability

In 2018, Statistics Canada revealed that 6.25 million Canadians aged 15 and over—more than 22 per cent of the population—had one or more disabilities that limited their daily activities, based on the 2017 Canadian Survey on Disability (Statistics Canada, 2018). So how does Canada's official data collection bureau define *disability*? Rather broadly, according to its analysts Elisabeth Cloutier, Chantal Grondin, and Amélie Lévesque (2018). The agency uses a social constructionist model of disability that views disability as "the result of the interaction between an person's functional limitation and barriers in the environment, including social and physical barriers that make it harder to function day-to-day" (Cloutier, Grondin, & Lévesque, 2018, p. 6). I will have more to say about the social constructionist model shortly, but the key point here is the distinction between an *impairment*, which describes a person's physical or intellectual limitation, and a *disability*, which is the limitation a person experiences because of barriers in the environment. Or, as Statistics Canada puts it, "disability is a social disadvantage that an unsupportive environment imposes on top of an individual's impairment" (Cloutier et al., 2018, p. 6). You may require a wheelchair because of a physical impairment; you experience disability when you have to access an office building with stairs to the front door and no ramp.

Quick Hits

Disability Categories Used by Statistics Canada

In its research on Canadians with disabilities, Statistics Canada recognizes ten different types of disability, described as follows:

- *hearing*: limitations in the ability to hear, even with a hearing aid or cochlear implant
- *seeing*: limitations in the ability to see, even when wearing eyeglasses or contact lenses
- *mobility*: difficulty in walking on flat surfaces for 15 minutes without rest, or in walking up or down a flight of 12 stairs
- *flexibility*: difficulty bending down or reaching for an object
- *dexterity*: difficulty using the fingers to grasp small objects
- *pain*: limitations because of pain that is constant or recurrent
- *learning*: difficulty learning because of a condition such as dyslexia, hyperactivity, or attention deficit disorder, whether the condition is self-identified or diagnosed by a teacher or health professional
- *memory*: ongoing memory problems or periods of confusion (not including occasional moments of forgetfulness)
- *developmental disabilities*: limitations due to a diagnosed developmental disorder, such as Down syndrome, autism, or Asperger syndrome, or an intellectual impairment caused by a lack of oxygen at birth
- *mental health*: limitations due to an emotional, psychological, or mental health condition, such as anxiety disorder, depression, bipolar disorder, substance abuse, anorexia as well as other conditions

Source: Cloutier, Grondin, & Lévesque, 2018, Appendix B.

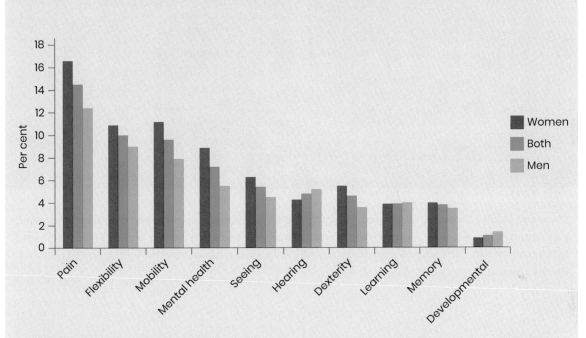

FIGURE 13.2 Percentage of Canadians 15 Years of Age and Over with a Disability, by Disability Type and Sex (2017)

Source: Morris, Fawcett, Brisebois, & Hughes, 2018, Table 3.

Irving Zola: A Pioneer in the Sociological Study of Disability

Irving K. Zola (1935–1994) has been called the "father" of the sociology of disability, with good reason. He helped establish the Society for Disability Studies, an organization that promotes the study of disability as a bona fide academic discipline, and was the founding editor of the society's journal, *Disabilities Studies Quarterly*. As well as being a professor of medical sociology at Brandeis University in Massachusetts, he was an activist for disability rights and a prolific writer on the subject.

Zola's best-known work, *Missing Pieces* (1982), is essentially a sociological diary of a week he spent in Het Dorp ("The Village"), an institutionalized community of 400 people—almost all of them disabled—in the Netherlands. Zola's study combines **participant observation**—he lived among the people in one of the special apartments provided for

Jo-Mei Games

Released in 2019, Sea of Solitude is an adventure game in which players help a character named Kay emerge from a dark, submerged world by coming to terms with a series of traumas she has experienced. Can games such as this really help young people better understand their own mental health?

residents with disabilities—and **institutional ethnography**, since he was writing from the viewpoint of the village's residents, not its administrators. This is not to say that Zola was unremittingly critical of Het Dorp, which was very progressive in a number of ways, or entirely uncritical of its patients, who themselves held some of the anti-disability prejudices Zola observed among the "normals."

Zola's approach shows parallels with the work of postmodernist feminist theorists such as **Dorothy Smith** (b. 1927), who were, at around the same time, establishing **standpoint theory** to promote the authority of women's unique and subjective interpretations of their experiences. As a sociologist with a physical disability (he wore a heavy leg brace as a result of childhood polio and a car accident when he was 20), Zola could readily see the need for an academic discipline devoted to the

study of disability. As a researcher, he had insider insights as to what questions to ask and what answers might be trusted.

Models of Disability

Like other areas of concern for the sociologist, disability can be examined from a number of vantage points. In this section we will look at different models used to understand disability.

Medical Models

The **medical model** is a framework for presenting and interpreting disability that is determined and directed by doctors, specialists, and other medical practitioners. It is a **positivist** model in that it reflects

Young, Disabled, and Wanting to Transit

As someone with an unsteady gait, no single transit ride is ever the same. I was born with a yet-to-be-diagnosed physical disability characterized by weak legs and poor balance, which is most prominent in my walking, but not so much when I'm sitting. This causes strangers to provide one of the following options when they see me getting onto a bus or SkyTrain: (a) asking if I would like their seat; (b) standing up immediately and walking away from their seat; or, most commonly, (c) looking the other way.

This experience was one that was unique, which happened one summer when my cousin was visiting Canada a few years back. We were en route to the PNE, the seasonal amusement park in Vancouver. As we boarded the bus, we made our way toward the back of the bus, away from the priority and courtesy seats, and sat down. A few stops later, two women, one in her thirties and another who was seemingly her mother, also made their way down to the end. Out of the full bus of everyone sitting, the lady directed my cousin and me to get up and provide our seats to them. I can only assume they selected us because we looked the youngest. Not wanting to start any conflict, we stood up in obedience while everyone stared in glimpses and through the window reflection. It was only when I moved away from my seat that the lady saw how I walked. She developed a pink tinge in her face but was apparently determined to refrain from telling me to sit back down. For the remaining fifteen minutes of our ride, the mother sat, my cousin and I stood, and the lady also stood in front of the empty seat. We got off the bus without looking back. Out of all the rides my cousin and I enjoyed on that day, that bus ride was surely the most memorable.

Visible disability, invisible disability, or no disability at all, appearances do not work as the telltale of a person. As easy as it is to judge someone as "fragile" for having a disability, or "impolite" for not offering the elderly their seat, it is just as easy to not judge someone at all, and to simply ask if you require help.

—Anonymous student, University of British Columbia

the belief that it takes an "expert," using science, to determine the treatments, policies, and programs required to help people living with disabilities.

The medical model guides research that has led to important, life-altering advances in the way disabilities are diagnosed and treated, and its benefits are undeniable. It has been criticized, though, when used without the insights available from people outside the medical community. York University sociologist Karen Anderson outlines some potential weaknesses of research on people with disabilities carried out according to this approach:

> [B]esides being difficult for the uninitiated to understand, . . . it usually leaves out the perspective of the individual person who is being studied, and the meaning of his or her life in any discussion of the design, methods, or results of the research. . . . Medical practitioners often focus on the presenting problem and its treatment without taking into account all aspects of the patient's life or considering if the treatment proposed, and its hoped-for results, will improve the person's life. (1996, p. 386)

Again, this is not to say that this approach has no or little legitimacy. Rather, it is one of several paths of knowledge and causes of action that have legitimacy, and all of them need to be considered.

Economic Models

Economic models of disability are those that view people with disabilities in terms of their contributions to, or drain on, the economy. They can be either sympathetic or unsympathetic toward people with disabilities.

Favourable Economic Models

A sympathetic economic model is one that views people with disabilities in terms of their ability to perform meaningful labour. It looks for ways to maximize the skills of people with disabilities to enable them to become "productive" (i.e. wealth-creating) members of society. Organizations that arrange training and employment opportunities for people with disabilities, and those that fight to remove barriers to employment by promoting accessibility in the workplace, fall into this category.

The economic model has also produced some well-meaning but paternalistic approaches that reflect a limited view of how productive people with disabilities can be. A notorious case involves a program initiated in 1984 by fast-food giant McDonald's to train people with disabilities to work in its restaurants. The McJOBS program was like an internship, with prospective employees undergoing both classroom and on-site training under the supervision of a mentor. In television commercials that you can view for yourself on YouTube, McDonald's boasted of its success in integrating people with mental and physical disabilities into the workforce.

The program was launched at a time when the kind of employment that McDonald's had come to represent—unchallenging, highly structured, low-paying work with few prospects for career advancement—was coming under scrutiny. Sociologist **Amitai Etzioni** (b. 1929) argued that "McJobs are bad for kids" in an article in which he attacked fast-food restaurants as "breeding grounds for robots working for yesterday's assembly lines, not tomorrow's high-tech posts" (Etzioni, 1986). By 1991, when Canadian author Douglas Coupland popularized the term "McJob" as a "low-pay, low-prestige, low-dignity, low-benefit, no-future job in the service sector" (Coupland, 1991, p. 5), McDonald's had abandoned the McJOBS program.

While there may be a tendency to underestimate the skills and potential productivity of people with disabilities, there is also a danger in setting the bar too high. In *Missing Pieces*, Irving Zola comments on how Americans' attitudes toward people with disabilities have been shaped by a version of the economic model that reflects the **American dream** (2003, p. 95). This is the idea that people can overcome adverse circumstances to achieve success through hard work. According to Zola (2003, p. 121), a number of American movies offer a depiction of disability in which the hero with a disability "makes it" in the end, triumphing over the limitations of the disability to become successful. (He cites *The Miracle Worker* and *The Monty Stratton Story*; you can consider Marvel's Professor X, the paraplegic with superhuman abilities, as a more recent example.) Zola argues that this kind of portrayal creates unrealistic expectations and reflects negatively on people whose disabilities are not as easily managed. People in mainstream society may be left with the impression that anyone who does not live up to the Hollywood image has essentially failed to realize their full potential and is therefore less deserving of respectful treatment.

Unfavourable Economic Models

Realistic or unrealistic, the economic models described above have one thing in common: they view people with disabilities in terms of the meaningful work they can contribute to society. In contrast to these are economic models that view people with disabilities as a drain on the state. Perhaps the most extreme, and certainly the most cruel, of these involved eugenics, a now discredited approach that we examined in Chapter 6.

A quick recap: **eugenics** (which means "good genes") is the science of improving the population through controlled breeding to limit the incidence of undesirable heritable characteristics. It is chiefly associated with Francis Galton (pioneer of statistical analysis), Henry Goddard (American psychologist), and the Nazis. As promoted by Goddard especially, eugenics was premised on two mistaken beliefs: that intelligence could be precisely measured, and that intelligence was a heritable characteristic, passed directly from parent to child. Goddard believed he could accurately test a person for "feeble-mindedness" (then an accepted clinical term), which he was convinced was a hereditary trait. He failed, however, to take into account social conditions of the person he was testing. Poverty and a lack of formal schooling are no reflection of a person's intellectual capabilities, and yet these could leave a

Blinded as a young boy, Matt Murdock, a.k.a. Daredevil, is a lawyer and vigilante who uses his extraordinarily heightened senses to fight crime on the mean streets of New York. Is this an inspiring representation of disability on screen, or does it set unrealistic expectations about what people with visual impairments are capable of?

Everett Collection Inc / Alamy Stock Photo

person without the worldly knowledge to succeed on Goddard's vaunted intelligence test.

Despite its now obvious flaws, Goddard's work on eugenics was very influential in the early twentieth century. In Canada, the hype surrounding eugenics inspired two provinces—Alberta in 1928 and British Columbia in 1933—to enact legislation making it legal to have mentally ill people sexually sterilized. Identifying "mental defectives" for sterilization remained an inexact and controversial process, and the legislation victimized not only those with legitimate mental health conditions but also those who were marginalized by race, ethnicity (especially new immigrants), and sex (many young women were sterilized because they were "sexually promiscuous" or involved in prostitution—two immoral tendencies that were taken as signs of mental defectiveness). The legislation was not repealed until 1972 in Alberta and 1973 in BC.

Despite the repeal of this legislation in Alberta and BC, the issue of whether individuals with mental disabilities could be sterilized without their consent remained a grey area until a 1986 Supreme Court of Canada ruling involving a girl known as Eve (not her real name). Eve had a mental disability that prevented her from communicating and understanding complex thoughts. When she was in her early twenties, her mother tried to get a court order to have Eve sexually sterilized. She was concerned that Eve, who had developed a close relationship with a male student at the boarding school they both attended, might accidentally become pregnant.

The case was first heard in 1978 in the Supreme Court of Prince Edward Island, where the judge felt that he could not permit an individual to undergo sterilization via hysterectomy—a major surgical procedure—without her consent. The PEI Court of Appeal overturned the decision but did not act on it because the ruling was challenged by Eve and the Canadian Association for the Mentally Retarded (it isn't called that anymore). The association was motivated to get involved by another incident at the time, in which a 10-year-old with an intellectual disability (legally referred to as "Infant K") had been secretly sterilized because, her parents explained, she reacted hysterically to the sight of blood and was therefore likely to find menstruation emotionally difficult (Hubert, 1985). The association wanted to ensure that the reproductive rights of people with mental disabilities were preserved. In the case of *E. (Mrs) v. Eve* [1986], the Supreme Court of Canada denied Eve's mother's petition, ruling against the sexual sterilization of a mentally disabled person for non-therapeutic reasons (i.e. for reasons other than the treatment of disease) without the individual's consent.

Social Constructionist Models

A **social constructionist model** begins with the idea that any human social category—race, gender, ability, and so on—is not a totally natural category, but has an important social component. **Critical disability theory** (or CDT) is a social constructionist theory that makes a distinction between a *natural impairment*, on the one hand, and *disability*, which can be understood as the barriers set up by society in dealing with that impairment. (We saw this distinction earlier in the definition of disability used by Statistics Canada.) A medical condition that causes paralysis in the legs is a natural impairment until the

person born with the condition is denied access to public transit because the nearest subway station has no elevator: then it's a socially constructed disability. For this reason, critical disability theorists place the emphasis on changing society rather than on "curing" the individual.

Activism based on critical disability theory aims for *substantive equality* rather than *formal equality*. A goal of **substantive equality** would be building modifications that guarantee people with natural impairments equal accessibility to and within buildings (e.g. with ramps, automatic doors, and sidewalks with no sudden drops to the road). Under the **formal equality** model, everyone faces and must adapt to the same socially driven architecture that gives advantages to non-disabled people. Full inclusion and participation are the goals of CDT ideas and practices.

Another tenet of social constructionist theory is that every culture constructs its own version of social categories such as "disabled." Nora Groce is a medical anthropologist who looks at how different societies treat and theorize about people with disabilities. She argues that "the lives of individuals with disability around the world are usually far more limited by prevailing social, cultural, and economic constraints than by specific physical, sensory, psychological, or intellectual impairments" (Groce, 1999, p. 756). Groce identifies three main areas in which cultures differ in how they view disability:

1. causality
2. valued and devalued attributes
3. anticipated adult status.

Causality is "the cultural reason for why a disability occurs" (Groce, 1999). Early Europeans, for example, attributed some disabilities (especially those involving epileptic seizures) to demon possession or witchcraft; as you can imagine, they treated people with disabilities with great suspicion and fear. Other cultures have viewed disability as the result of divine judgment, as God's punishment for some act committed by the community, or for "sins" of the parents being visited upon the children. This is an idea that seems to cross cultures and persist over time. But Groce also cites studies by medical

What Do YOU Think?

1. Are there any circumstances that would justify having a person sexually sterilized without their consent? What if the individual were a convicted sex offender? What if the individual came from a family with a history of a disabling disorder?
2. Should economic concerns (i.e. the potential to save taxpayers' money) ever be a consideration in deciding who has or does not have the right to have children?

anthropologists Benedicte Ingstad (1988) and M. Madiros (1989) showing that among the Tswana people of Botswana (in southern Africa) and among the peasant people of northern Mexico, "the birth of a disabled child is viewed as evidence of God's trust in specific parents' ability to care well for a delicate child" (Groce, 1999, p. 756).

Groce's second point has to do with the "qualities a society finds important." In societies that value physical strength, people with physical disabilities are at a greater disadvantage than they are in a society that values intellectual accomplishments.

How a society regards people with disabilities also depends on what role people with disabilities are expected to occupy (Groce, 1999). If they are expected to participate fully in society, contributing meaningful labour and having families, then society will be willing to provide the resources to make this possible. A society that views its citizens with disabilities as a financial burden, as people in need of looking after and not in a position to contribute meaningfully, will likely be stingy about the resources it allocates to help individuals overcome disability.

Quick Hits

Master Status and Labelling Theory

In Chapter 5 we considered the statuses that people have at any given time. Remember that a **status** is a position one holds that is recognized by society. Some of the statuses I hold right now are retired professor, writer, husband, stepfather, brother, grandfather, and parrot owner. A person's **master status** is the one that leads the way in terms of how a person's identity is defined and how others see and interact with that person. **Labelling theory**, also presented in Chapter 5, explains that society can sometimes turn a negative label into a master status that defines a person. Zola, who wore a leg brace and walked with a cane, gives an example of how the label "disabled" was applied to him and became, for many people he met, his master status:

> [F]or years I have had the experience of being mistaken for someone else. Usually I was in a new place and a stranger would greet me as Tom, Dick, or Harry. After I explained that I was not he, they would usually apologize, saying "You look just like him." Inevitably I would meet this Tom, Dick, or Harry, and he would be several inches shorter or taller, forty pounds heavier or lighter, a double amputee on crutches or a paraplegic in a wheelchair. I was

annoyed and even puzzled how anyone could mistake him for the "unique me." (Zola, 2003, p. 199)

David Morrison is a blogger and college student who has cerebral palsy. In one of his blog posts directed at people without disabilities, he provides four tips to avoid making a person's disability into a master status:

1. Speak to the person, not the wheelchair or the person's assistant.
2. Make eye contact as often as possible.
3. Treat a wheelchair as part of personal space
4. Assist the person only after asking. (Morrison, 2010)

A final tip: avoid labels that emphasize limitation. Referring to someone as a "disabled person" or "an epileptic" is like labelling the whole person with the disability, turning it into a master status. Instead, use descriptive phrases that put the person before the disability, and reserve labels for achievements: "A good friend of mine who has epilepsy," "A brilliant student who uses a wheelchair." Avoid pitying phrases such as "who suffers from" or "who is stricken with," and mention the disability only when it is relevant.

Photo by Natalie Behring/Getty Images

What do you see? A disabled athlete? An athlete with a disability? Or just an athlete?

Wrap it Up

Summary

Congratulations: you're now a doctor! Well, no, that's not quite true. But it's no surprise that a knowledge of sociology is now required to pass the latest (2015) version of the Medical College Admission Test that is used to screen applicants for medical schools in North America. Sociology has a vitally important role to play in the way health care is taught and delivered. Medical sociologists look carefully at the relationships between standard social factors such as class, gender, race and ethnicity, and location, and document inconsistencies in the way patients are treated. They study the social course of disease and record how different illnesses are portrayed in the media.

Canada has a public healthcare system, but make no mistake about it: it's a big business heavily influenced by big business interests. Hospitals grappling with barely adequate budgets make business decisions every day,

deciding where best to allocate their funding, while companies ranging in size from huge multinationals selling pharmaceutical products to private clinics offering cosmetic procedures like tummy tucks have a vested interest in making us feel less healthy and less able than we are, and incapable of improving our health without costly medical interventions.

Like health, ability is a concept that is too often defined without considering all relevant perspectives. The point to keep in mind is that while *people have impairments*, it is *society that constructs disability* as a social category. This is the underlying principle of critical disability theory, where the standpoint of the individual with the limitation is key. Medical professionals approach disability as a condition to be reversed or repaired; that is their job, and health professionals and researchers have made astonishing advances in treating impairments ranging form vision and hearing loss to limited mobility and chronic pain. But if we fail to consider other, non-medicalizing standpoints, we will be missing something critical. Think of Canada's Deaf community, many of whom are fiercely proud of the culture. Who is in the best position to decide if a deaf person is disabled?

Think Back

Questions for Critical Review

1. Take a particular disease or injury that you have experienced and discuss the social course that you went through to have it diagnosed and treated. Where did you go? Who healed you? How were you socially processed?

2. Identify what biomedicine is and talk about its weaknesses and strengths. In what situations is biomedicine most successful? In what situations does it fail to serve the needs of patients as well as alternative medical approaches?

3. How and why are certain physical conditions medicalized? When is medicalization more harmful than helpful?

4. Describe the situation that faces immigrant doctors upon arriving in Canada. What barriers do they face to practising medicine in this country? Why do these barriers exist? What would happen if they did not exist?

5. How would you say that class affects the social course of disease? Is the relationship between class and the experience of disease different in Canada than it in the United States? Why or why not?

6. Explain the concepts of impairment and disability in terms of Deaf culture.

7. Have you ever experienced, or do you currently experience, an impairment of some kind? Consider anything from a mobility-limiting injury (broken arm, ankle sprain) or congenital condition (muscular dystrophy) to a learning disability (dyslexia, attention-deficit disorder). How does your experience connect with what was written in this chapter? Under what circumstances did the impairment become a disability?

8. In "The Country of the Blind" (1904), a short story by H.G. Wells, a mountaineer in Ecuador stumbles upon an isolated village of people who have never known sight and cannot even imagine what it is like to see. The title comes from the saying, "In the country of the blind, the one-eyed man is king," but the sighted mountaineer soon discovers that the blind villagers have come to survive quite well without the sense of sight—in fact, they interpret his own ability to see as a form of madness, a disability. What lesson does this hold about the social construction of disability?

Read On

Recommended Print and Online Resources

Canadian Association of the Deaf (CAD), http://cad.ca/issues-positions/terminology/

- When it comes to disability, like other social conditions, labelling is a thorny issue. This page, from the CAD's website, gives the organization's position on a variety of terms relating to hearing impairment.

Canadian Centre on Disability Studies (CCDS), http://disabilitystudies.ca

- The CCDS is dedicated to studying and developing programs with and for people with disabilities. The website has news about current projects and events, as well as published reports on research and completed community projects.

Earle Waugh, Shelley Ross, & Shirley Schipper (eds), *Female Doctors in Canada: Experience and Culture* **(Toronto: University of Toronto Press, 2019).**

- This comprehensive, up-to-date collection of articles looks at how the medical profession is becoming feminized, and what that means to the emerging generation of women doctors in Canada.

Eugene Raikhel, "50 Years of Medical Sociology," *Somatosphere* **(2010), http://somatosphere. net/2010/12/50-years-of-medical-sociology-html**

- In 2010, Eugene Raikhel looked back at some of the key issues that had been tackled in the 50-year history of the *Journal of Health and Social Behavior*. It is effectively an overview of issues in the history of American medical sociology.

Irving K. Zola, *Missing Pieces: A Chronicle of Living with a Disability*, **2nd edn (Philadelphia, PA: Temple University Press, 2003).**

- A first-person narrative, by a sociologist with a disability, of living in a planned community for people living with disabilities in the Netherlands.

L. Hedden, M.R. Lavergne, K.M. McGrail, M.R. Law, L. Cheng, M.A. Ahuja, & M.L. Barer, "Patterns of Physician Retirement and Pre-Retirement Activity: A Population-Based Cohort Study," *Canadian Medical Association Journal* **189, 49 (2017), pp. 1517–23.**

- Focusing on doctors in British Columbia, the researchers looked at patterns and timing of physician retirement by age, sex, specialty, and location, in order to see what indicators can help predict when and how physicians will retire.

Nursing Education in Nova Scotia: Male Nurses, http://forms.msvu.ca/library/tutorial/ nhdp/history/malenurses.htm

- Mount Saint Vincent University is home to a fascinating archive of Nova Scotia's nursing history. This link features a 21-minute recording by Frank Graham, who shares his experiences as a male nursing student in the 1930s.

Pat Grygier, *A Long Way from Home: The Tuberculosis Epidemic among the Inuit* **(Montreal, QC: McGill-Queen's University Press, 1994).**

- Grygier provides an enlightening (and alarming) examination of how Inuit with tuberculosis were treated in Canada during the 1950s.

Sally Simpson, Female Indigenous Firsts, https://www.canadianwomen.org/ wp-content/uploads/2018/06/Female-Indigenous-Born-in-Northern-Turtle-Island-Did-it-First-List.pdf

- Sally Simpson's list of Indigenous firsts is proof that a sociology assignment can inspire important scholarship that will broaden the knowledge of others.

Society for Disability Studies, http:// disstudies.org/

- Established in part by Irving Zola, the SDS is committed to establishing disability studies as a bona fide academic discipline. The website provides information on the organization's mission and current work.

Tania Das Gupta, *Real Nurses and Others: Racism in Nursing* **(Halifax, NS: Fernwood, 2009).**

- Tania Das Gupta is a professor in the Department of Equity Studies at York University. This book is her study of the racism experienced by visible-minority nurses in Canada.

The Environment

14

Reading this chapter will help you to ...

- Describe how race and environmental practices intersect.
- Understand the vested interests that come into play when "scientific judgments" are made about the health of the environment.
- Explain the social ecology position and its relationship to issues of class and race.
- Critically assess the theory that environmental disasters can produce positive social change.
- Identify the environmental effects of the China price.
- Be aware of the sociological implications of proposals to combat climate change.

For Starters

Not in My Country: Rich Countries Dumping Waste in Poor Countries

AP Photo/Aaron Favila, File

You may be familiar with the acronym NIMBY. It stands for "not in my backyard," and it comes up in the news whenever a community group is attempting to stop an undesirable outsider from setting up shop in the neighbourhood. Group homes, halfway houses, and safe-injection sites are among the "social pariahs" that tend to find opposition from NIMBYism. The term is often applied derisively to self-interested residents concerned that their comfortable way of life may be threatened by a project that serves the greater good of the community. In the international context, it describes the very real victimization of vulnerable nations by well-developed countries, including Canada, that are looking for dumping grounds for toxic garbage.

The African coastline, especially the waters of some of the poorer and least powerful countries, has for some time experienced environmental damage resulting from the actions of more powerful countries of the developed North. One reason for the rise of modern piracy off the Somali coast is the decline in ocean food resources—once a staple of the Somali economy—due to the offshore dumping of toxic waste. In 2006, the small West African country of Côte d'Ivoire had a health crisis on its hands owing to massive amounts of toxic waste dumped by a local contractor in some 12 sites in the port city of Abidjan, the country's capital. The culprit was the Netherlands-based oil and commodity shipping company Trafigura Beheer BV, using a ship licensed in Panama.

The Canadian story involves the illegal dumping of 103 forty-foot shipping containers filled with what was labelled "heterogeneous plastic scrap materials"—in other words, assorted plastic meant to be recycled. Upon inspection, Philippine customs officials found that about two-thirds of the materials were actually mixed household waste that included rotting food and used diapers (Gutierrez, 2016). The made-in-Canada waste was shipped from Vancouver to the Philippines by a private firm based in Ontario between 2013 and 2014. The leaking containers presented a significant environmental health hazard to the local Philippine community, but despite international petitions (I signed one) and political pressure from environmental groups and the United Nations, the Canadian government did nothing to remedy the situation or prosecute the offending Canadian company, which argues it was acting in compliance with Canadian (if not international) law. The Philippines, which has received millions of Canadian dollars in tourism grants and disaster relief (following a typhoon that devastated Southeast Asia in 2013), was understandably reluctant to press the matter in international courts (Gutierrez, 2016). Not until president of the Philippines Rodrigo Duterte made a series of public threats ("I will declare war against them. I will advise Canada that your garbage is on the way. Prepare a grand reception. Eat it if you want to. Your garbage is coming home." [quoted in Canadian Press, 2019]) did Canada's government finally take responsibility for the mess. In May 2019, Canada hired a ship to return 69 of the containers, destined for a waste disposal facility in Burnaby, BC.

The diversion of Canadian waste to the Philippines is a case of **environmental racism**, which sets a double standard for managing the environment depending on the part of the world affected and the ethnicity of the people harmed. It cannot be blamed on corporate and political actors alone. After all, who's in the best position to keep that wax-lined coffee cup out of the blue bin—and the backyard of people living halfway around the world?

Environmental Sociology: Science or *Social* Science?

Environmental sociology is a fast-growing subdiscipline that examines our relationship with the environment, focusing especially on where we have gone wrong and looking for ways to reverse our mistakes in the future. There is a lot of science involved in environmental studies—in proving climate change, in tracking carbon emissions and weather patterns, in testing the safety of drinking water—but sociology teaches us that the science of the environment is deeply embedded in a social context. The scientific world is political. Scientific facts cannot "speak for themselves"—they have interpreters who are part of the social world and who cannot always be trusted to report "the facts" without a distorting bias based on their place in that world, their **standpoint**.

In the 1970s and 1980s, Canadian investigative journalist Lloyd Tataryn researched and wrote on environmental dangers ranging from the formaldehyde in our home insulation (1983) to the uranium mined at Elliot Lake (1976). His investigations often featured places where environmental science and politics collide. In his best-known work, *Dying for a Living*, he wrote,

> The scientific truth must first run a political gauntlet. For after the authorities give their advice, and all the technical data is in, the decision arrived at is ultimately a political verdict and merely masquerades as a purely scientific ruling.
>
> Politicians, corporations, and unions are aware of this environmental fact of life. And since in the long run they must rely upon the combined political and scientific judgement of their technical advisors, they tend to choose as advisors scientists whose biases are similar to their own—scientists who are prone to ask the type of questions that produce answers which most often serve the interests of their employers. . . .

Unfortunately, the public is seldom informed of the political, economic, and scientific biases which scientists in environmental health conflicts bring to their investigations. Most of us have been led to believe that "science" and "scientists" are above such considerations. (1979, p. 90)

This book, now 40 years old, was written well before climate change became a topic of mainstream concern (and fierce political denial), and before the debates around tar sands and pipelines and single-use plastic straws. Do you think the general situation Tataryn described has changed?

Assessing Environmental Arguments: Two Keys for Social Scientists

Operational Definitions

In Chapter 2, we looked at the importance of establishing clear **operational definitions** for variables in social research. Operational definitions are essential to creating policies on social issues. But it can be difficult to take abstract concepts such as poverty and abuse and turn them into concrete, countable entities. All operational definitions "leak": they are imperfect, and sociologists, as scientists, often disagree on the best way to define a term.

Disagreement among academic researchers, provided it is conducted in a civil manner, is healthy for any discipline. Scholarly debate can bring clarity to the issue or issues at hand, especially during the **peer-review process**, when the draft of a research article, report, or book undergoes rigorous assessment by other experts in the field to ensure that it is suitable for publication. The author must take into account any and all criticisms before the work can be published. Eventually, through this scientific social process, issues are brought into sharper focus and, in terms of operational definitions, the best leaky term wins out.

Peer review and follow-up are steps in the social process that helps to advance any scientific discipline as a whole. Unfortunately, while the process is familiar to most scientists, it is not always

well understood outside the scientific community. Among the outsiders are journalists, politicians, and corporate interest groups, who are often guided by non-scientific social processes and ideas, like the notion that there are two valid sides to every story, and that presenting a "balance of views" is necessary. A classic example is the persistent attempt by American Christian groups to provide "balance" to the discussion of evolution by bringing forward non-scientific arguments in support of creationism and intelligent design (only evolution is scientific). Remember the lesson from Chapter 2: when assessing arguments of this kind, never be afraid to ask *How do you know that?*

In the study of the environment, the same difficulties are involved, with critical arguments hinging on abstract terms that are difficult to define. How would you begin to devise an operational definition for *pollution*? Where do you set the limits on "safe" versus "dangerous" or "acceptable" versus "unacceptable" levels of exposure to a particular toxin? The stakes are high when millions of dollars and people's lives are involved. Consider the following statement from uranium miner Gus Frobel, who later died from the cancer that he rightfully believed was caused by his working conditions:

When you read the scientific papers you find the really knowledgeable scientists, the experts in the field, don't use the term "safe" level of exposure. They know they can't defend it scientifically. They say that to their knowledge there is no "safe" level. Some use the term "acceptable level." Now what's an "acceptable level?" That means some men have to die—but how many? How many deaths are acceptable? (quoted in Tataryn, 1979, p. 100)

Pollution is like poverty. Just as you can tell when someone is very poor (a person sleeping on the street is definitely poor), so you can tell when water or air is extremely polluted: it smells bad, looks horrible, and makes you sick. Extremes are easy to identify. Finding the line that separates "polluted" from "not polluted" is not so easy—it takes a scientific approach to get there. It is especially difficult when the damaging effects of pollution may not become apparent for many years. If it takes 20 years for an asbestos mine worker to die from exposure to an unsafe level of asbestos in the air, it could take 20 years for a hypothesis of what constitutes an "unsafe level of exposure" to be proven true, although reasonably sound predictions can be made earlier.

Operational definition thus becomes a key aspect of environmental debates. In any discussion of the environment, look closely for abstract terms. Are they carefully defined? Do the definitions look sound? How were the definitions arrived at? Do the people presenting the information use the words *significant* or *serious* without explaining what they mean by them? The answers to these questions will tell you a lot about whether a particular argument is being fought more on scientific grounds or political ones.

Vested Interests

Even when operational definitions of an environmental argument have been assessed, important sociological questions remain. Who paid for any research studies cited in the argument? Who stands to benefit or lose from a particular test result? Politics are involved in environmental research, especially when some social policy is being proposed, implemented, attacked, or defended. That's why it is important to identify the **vested interests** surrounding any argument about the environment.

A vested interest is any social or financial interest a party may have in the results of a scientific study and the way those results are interpreted, particularly if the interest is strong enough to override the interest of ensuring those results are accurate, or "truthful." Although scientific measurement can be precise, the interpretation of data can be highly subjective. Give two scientists the same numbers, and they may come up with two very different interpretations.

The way operational definitions are derived may be influenced by the vested interests of the person designing the study or interpreting the results. It is statistically predictable that if one scientist is paid by a mining company, that scientist is likely to have a lower threshold for what constitutes a safe level of exposure to the material being mined, and will be more likely than an impartial scientist to give

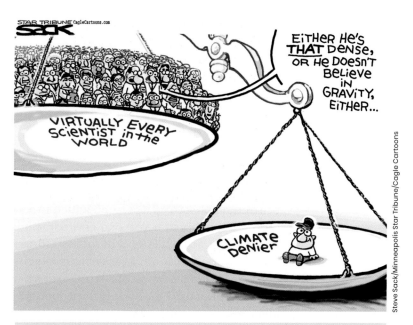

The climate change denier will sometimes pose as a devil's advocate, feigning detachment from a dubious or unpopular position under the pretense of bringing balance to the conversation. When it comes to debating climate change, should both sides be given equal weight?

workers a clean bill of health. A scientist paid by the miners' union or one who is an independent researcher at a local university or hospital will have a different view.

A 2018 study by researchers at the University of British Columbia sheds some light on how vested interests can affect operational definitions. The team examined 10 recent environmental impact assessments conducted in BC (Murray et al., 2018). Environmental impact assessments, or EIAs, are commissioned and paid for by a company that is applying for government approval to start or expand a project (e.g. a mine or a pipeline) that could have environmental, social, economic, or health-related consequences for the local community. The EIA is normally carried out by independent professional geoscientists or engineers, who are paid by the company behind the proposal to see if any risks to the environment are "significant." Can you see where operational definition and vested interests are about to collide?

The UBC researchers found that in the 10 EIAs they examined, "findings of significant impacts

The Point Is . . .

Scientists with Vested Interests Developed the "Tobacco Strategy"

An important work on the subject of vested interests is Naomi Oreskes and Erik Conway's *Merchants of Doubt: How a Handful of Scientist Obscured the Truth on Issues from Tobacco Smoke to Global Warming* (2010). They assert that multinational corporations in different industries use a common set of tactics to manufacture and market doubt about health and environmental concerns raised by scientific researchers. These tactics involve the use of paid scientific researchers to fight "good" science with "bad" science in the name of industry. We can call these "bad science" researchers *scientific mercenaries*.

Many of today's scientific mercenaries follow the blueprint drafted in the 1960s by scientists employed to undermine critics of the tobacco industry. By the mid-twentieth century, medical researchers were beginning to understand how damaging cigarette smoking could be to one's health. By the 1960s, the community of scholars knew it, but the tobacco industry successfully combatted the growing evidence by hiring teams of scientists to offer their own evidence that minimized the harmful effects of tobacco and, in some cases, pointed to the health benefit of smoking.

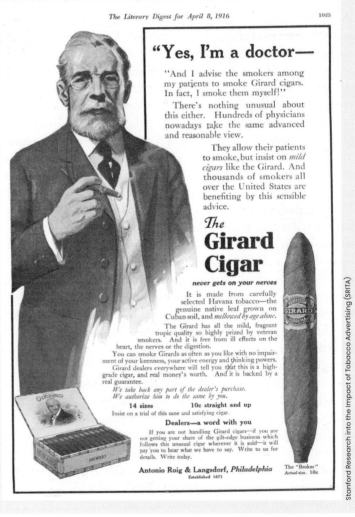

Frederick Seitz and Siegfried Singer were scientists who had produced legitimate research in physics before their connections with conservative American government administrations and industry interests seriously affected the scientific credibility of their work. In the following passage from *Merchants of Doubt*, Oreskes and Conway describe their work on behalf of the tobacco industry:

> From 1979 to 1985, Fred Seitz directed a program for R.J. Reynolds Tobacco Company that distributed $45 million to scientists around the country for biomedical research that could generate evidence and cultivate experts to be used in court to defend the "product." In the mid-1990s, Fred Singer co-authored a major report attacking the US Environmental Protection Agency [EPA] over the health risks of second-hand smoke. Several years earlier, the US surgeon general had declared that second-hand smoke was hazardous not only to smokers' health, but to anyone exposed to it. Singer attacked this finding, claiming the work was rigged, and that the EPA review of the science—done by leading experts from around the country—was distorted by a political agenda to expand government control over all aspects of our lives. Singer's anti-EPA report was funded by the Tobacco Institute, channeled through a think tank, the [conservative, climate change-denying] Alexis de Tocqueville Institution. (2010, pp. 5–6)

What came to be known as the **tobacco strategy** essentially forestalled the onslaught of successful lawsuits against the industry until the 1990s. The tobacco strategy has since been used by other deniers of science to dispute legitimate scientific findings concerning acid rain, ozone layer depletion, and, most recently, human-produced climate change.

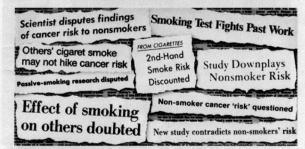

Stanford Research into the Impact of Tobacco Advertising (SRITA)

(on facing page) Having grown up in an age where the dangers of tobacco use are well established, you might find it easy to scoff at the naiveté of magazine readers in the first half of the twentieth century who found this kind of advertising compelling. But be honest: how often do you find yourself picking up the skincare product, toothpaste, or pain-relief medication that is advertised as "doctor-recommended" or "clinically proven"? (left) The Scientific Division of the US Tobacco Institute put out this ad encouraging readers to get the whole story on second-hand smoke. Look at how the argument is crafted. Is it effective?

were exceedingly rare" (Murray et al., 2018). Part of the reason for this is that quantitative (i.e. measurable) thresholds of "significance determination" were seldom used in the assessment of health or environmental risks, and when they were, "practitioners used a variety of rationales to demote negative impacts to non-significance" (Murray et al., 2018). In other words, as Judith Lavoie (2018) explains in her account of the research, "when impacts are likely to exceed established criteria—push past those accepted thresholds—experts find a variety of innovative ways to minimize potential problems."

Those innovative ways of downplaying concerns include referencing less-strict guidelines in use in other jurisdictions and expanding the scale of the impacted area from a small, local community to a much larger area. This would be like arguing that the impact of an increase in pollutants on the nearest town is not so significant if you look at how that increase will affect the much larger region the town is situated in. To take another example, in Bolton, the town of 26,000 where I live, late-winter flooding of the Humber River caused great damage to homes of people living in the valley; up on the south hill, where I live, there was no damage. Imagine a study of the impact of the flood on people living in all of Bolton (or the GBA—the Greater Bolton Area—as I like to call it). The percentage of Bolton residents affected would be small, but the impact those valley residents experienced was enormous.

Paid experts are not unbiased: they have a vested interest in pleasing the company that is paying for the report by overlooking or downplaying problems that might call for expensive changes to the proposal or an outright rejection of the application. Expanding the scale of the area impacted by the development and playing fast and loose with the term *significant* are examples of how operational definitions can be manipulated to minimize concerns over dangerous risks to the local community.

When searching for vested interests, it is always important to trace the science back to its social location. Many of the think tanks, institutes, and other organizations that publish reports are funded by large companies, and they tend to be conservative. For example, the climate change–attacking Friends

of Science is an organization founded by oil industry geologists and funded by oil companies. They generally take positions that support the big business agenda while downplaying or dismissing potential harm to the environment or industry-related health risks. University researchers are generally more reliable when it comes to environmental issues, but always check first to see who is funding the work. As we saw in Chapter 12 in the case of Enbridge and the University of Calgary, universities often receive funding from deep-pocketed donors with vested interests.

The Big Business behind the UFFI Disaster: A Case of Vested Interests

Citizens depend on their governments to protect them from the harmful effects of industrial pollution. Government agencies study the health impacts of different manufacturing materials, approving the ones that are safe and recommending bans on the ones that are not. The system fails when government has a vested interest in promoting an unsafe product. A Canadian case in point surrounds the widespread use of urea formaldehyde foam insulation (UFFI) during the late 1970s and 1980s.

Formaldehyde is a chemical with many uses. It is an ingredient of a glue used to bind wood fibres together in products such as particle board, chipboard, and plywood. In Canada in the 1960s, it was introduced as foam insulation.

Complaints about the formaldehyde-based insulation began to surface in the 1970s, primarily in northern European countries such as Denmark, Sweden, and the Netherlands, where governments were generally quick to respond to concerns around industrial pollution. There were reports that the foam encouraged harmful fungal growth. Also, the formaldehyde-based glue used in composite wood products was causing allergic reactions and respiratory problems among people living in mobile homes, where particleboard and plywood were among the principal building materials. What's more, UFFI was not proving effective as an insulation material. Canada's own National Research Council (NRC) had tested the foam and found it liable to shrink, crack, and crumble, greatly decreasing its value as an insulator.

Why then, in the light of these ominous findings, did Canada's government continue to endorse the use of formaldehyde-based products?

A pivotal event occurred in the mid-1970s, when the Organization of the Petroleum Exporting Countries (OPEC), representing the world's major oil-producing countries, declared an embargo against the West, creating an oil shortage that led to a sharp rise in North American and European gas and oil prices. The industry solution was to promote greater use of insulation to improve the efficiency of heating in homes and workplaces. Formaldehyde-based insulation was a key part of this proposal, which required the approval of various federal agencies, including the Canadian General Standards Board (CGSB) and the Canada Mortgage and Housing Corporation (CMHC). These government regulatory bodies were ill prepared to counter the strong-arm tactics of the chemical companies. Moreover, the government itself was in a conflict of interest, as the federally financed Canadian Development Corporation owned 40 per cent of one of the foam-producing chemical companies.

In 1977, the federal government announced the Canadian Home Insulation Program (CHIP), which provided financial incentives to homeowners to upgrade their insulation. Some 80,000 Canadian homeowners registered for CHIP. The government set standards on the percentage of formaldehyde that could be used in UFFI products, but these limits were voluntary, not enforceable, and therefore largely ignored. No consideration was given to the health of contractors installing the insulation.

By 1978, homeowners began to complain about the deteriorating quality of foam insulation and its effects on health. In 1979, Massachusetts became the first jurisdiction to ban UFFI, a move influenced by a scientific study that had found a link between formaldehyde and cancer. Chemical companies responded with an industry-funded conference in 1980, in which 22 of the 26 papers delivered were by industry "experts" who defended the safety and reliability of the product. They argued against any form of regulation.

In December 1980, urea formaldehyde foam insulation was banned in Canada. Homeowners and contractors installing the product were left stranded.

By permission of Harold Orr

In 1977, the same year the Canadian Home Insulation Program was announced, an energy-efficient, solar-paneled model home with superior insulation was built in Regina. Funded by the Saskatchewan Research Council, it required so little energy input to heat that it did not even have a furnace. The design became a model for home building in Europe but was never replicated in Canada. Why do you think the UFFI insulation took off instead of energy-efficient houses? How much of our purchasing decisions are influenced by corporations in ways we don't even realize?

Social Ecology

The late twentieth century brought a growing awareness of the human role in environmental issues, from the importance of household recycling to the dangers of our carbon emissions. As is written in many self-help books, the first and hardest step is acknowledging you have a problem. This is a key tenet of **social ecology**, a school of thought founded by American thinker and ecologist **Murray Bookchin** (1921–2006). He explained social ecology as follows:

> What literally defines social ecology as "social" is its recognition of the often overlooked fact that nearly all our present ecological problems arise from deep-seated social problems. Conversely, present ecological problems cannot be clearly understood, much less resolved, without resolutely dealing with problems within society. To make this point more concrete: economic, ethnic, cultural, and gender conflicts, among many others, lie at the core of the most serious ecological dislocations we face today. . . . (Bookchin, 1996)

To get a better sense of how a social ecologist might view the relationship between social conflict and environmental issues, we will look at the role of class conflict in the context of industrial pollution.

Industrial Pollution and Social Ecology

We can adopt a social ecology approach to better understand how the exposure of workers to unsafe environmental conditions reflects larger trends in the issue of industrial pollution. First, in order for workers to be placed in this situation, it requires the complicity of the employer—the company that requires the work—and sometimes the government, which is ultimately responsible for overseeing environmental protection as well as workplace safety. As Lloyd Tataryn notes,

> Today, people who work and live in contaminated environments serve as early warning systems for toxic substances, much like the ancient royal food tasters and the canaries the coal miners once trundled underground to test the air. Workers and those who live in the shadow of polluting industries are the first people to encounter intense and prolonged exposure to toxic wastes. Much of what is known about environmental health and the consequences of exposure to poisonous and cancer-causing materials has been learned from examining disease patterns among workers and exposed populations. Exposure standards are usually established once an unusual pattern of disease has been detected. In this way workers and people living in industrially contaminated environments act as guinea pigs for the rest of society. (1979, p. 1)

There appear to be two different ways of interpreting workplace-related illness and injury. The first is the social ecology view, which sees these as essentially *social* in their origin and in the way that they are dealt with. Working conditions are set in place by a company and monitored in varying degrees by the political authorities in an area. This reflects C. Wright Mills's notion of the **sociological imagination**, in which individual problems and situations readily connect with the broader social structure and its processes. The workers are not in a position to oppose the company's unsafe environmental practices. This is essentially a class conflict. What does that say about industrial pollution on a larger scale?

A sociologically *uninformed* way of interpreting workplace illness is to keep it individual and personal, reflecting the individual choices and physical constitution of the person afflicted. Far from being symptomatic of broader social processes, a worker's disease is viewed as a result of personal choices taken by the individual worker: smoking, drinking, lack of exercise, and poor lifestyle choices in general. With this view, injuries happen at job sites because workers are careless (a viewpoint reflected in early commercials promoting workplace safety as an individual responsibility). It would be wrong to say that individuals are powerless to play a role in workplace safety; however, this second view leans too far in the direction of William Ryan's notion of **blaming the victim**. It's a recurring theme—watch for it in sections that follow.

The Asbestos Industry: Dying for a Living

It has long been known that asbestos is hazardous to human health. Roman writers in the second century CE noted that those who spun its threads into valuable robes often became sick. By the early twentieth century, some North American insurance companies were refusing to insure asbestos workers, recognizing that these employees had relatively low chances of long-term survival at the job. In 2012, a consortium of **epidemiology** organizations from around the world issued a position statement on asbestos, declaring their opinion that "all types of asbestos fibre are causally implicated in the development of various diseases and premature death" (JPC-SE, 2012, p. 2). These diseases include lung cancer, mesothelioma, and asbestosis.

Canada became a major producer of asbestos in 1879, when the fibrous mineral was first mined in Thetford Mines, Quebec. In the early twentieth century, other jurisdictions began to observe standards of what was considered "acceptable" risk of exposure, a figure first set at 35 fibres per cubic centimetre in 1938, before falling, with

further study, to 12, then 5, then 2. By contrast, Thetford Mines, the world's largest producer of asbestos, observed no such standard until 1978, when it finally bowed to media and public pressure by adopting limits of "acceptable" exposure. In the mid-1970s, a worker at another Canadian mine, Paul Formby, discovered levels ranging from 30 to 50 fibres per cubic centimetre where he was working.

It is not just the miners who have been exposed to the environmental hazards of asbestos:

> Towering over the town of Thetford Mines are massive grey piles of asbestos tailings. These tailings poke their way like giant fingers into sections of the town, spilling asbestos waste into the yards of many of the homes. Positioned on top of the tailings are machines called swivel pilers, constantly spraying out clouds of asbestos waste, a practice that Mount Sinai's doctors say would be illegal in the United States. Thetford's tailings daily grow higher and higher, leaving the town covered in grey dust. (Tataryn, 1979, p. 23)

The prevailing attitude in a one-industry town like Thetford Mines is often one that defends the business that brings food to the table, even in the face of environmental health studies with grave conclusions about the health risks to the town's citizens. In a 2007 article, one retired miner, who had worked in the mines for 38 years, articulated this view:

> Those people who had their houses tested [for asbestos] are just whiners, looking for compensation. . . . We made a very good living in the mines, and I don't regret it for a minute. . . . It's paranoia. It's just like smoking. I know lots of people who smoke and live to be 80 or 90 years old. (cited in Lalonde, 2007)

Although some of his colleagues had died of asbestos-caused illnesses, the miner, according to the article, believed the deaths were owing to "a vulnerability on their part" (Lalonde, 2007).

While studies of the health risks of asbestos exposure were being carried out and debated, the provincial government of Quebec and Canada's federal government continued to promote the use of asbestos products, particularly in developing countries, the destination for 90 per cent of the 150,000 tonnes of asbestos produced in Canada. It was not until September 2012, shortly after the last Canadian asbestos mine closed, that the federal Conservative government announced it would no longer oppose global rules restricting the use and shipment of asbestos (CBC News, 2012).

The Canadian government lagged behind other countries in banning asbestos. Finally, in July 2015, Health Canada revised its long-held position that asbestos was dangerous only when inhaled "in significant quantities"; the agency now states plainly that "breathing in asbestos fibres can cause cancer and other diseases" (Grant, 2015). In 2018, the federal government introduced new regulations that would ban the import, sale, or use of asbestos and asbestos-containing products, beginning in 2019.

What Do YOU Think?

Why do you think Canada's government promoted asbestos use primarily in developing countries? Can Canada's policy be characterized as an instance of environmental racism?

However, the new regulations do not prohibit companies from sifting through the 800 million tonnes of mining residues near the towns of Thetford Mines and Asbestos to extract magnesium and other minerals from the tailings (Rabson, 2018).

A comparable situation surrounds coal mining, which has an ugly history in Canada of unhealthy working conditions (see, for example, the Westray disaster of 1992, in which 26 miners in Nova Scotia died owing to a methane explosion). The burning of coal for electricity contributes significantly to the conditions promoting climate change. There are still major coal mines in British Columbia, Alberta,

Francis Vachon/TCPI/The Canadian Press

Rising majestically behind this row of houses in Thetford Mines is a large tailings pile from the town's asbestos quarry. How comfortable would you feel living in one of these houses? Describe the social profile of the typical resident of this street.

and Saskatchewan, and 90 per cent of the millions of tonnes mined are burned for electricity across Canada. Coal mining contributes billions of dollars to the Canadian economy and provides thousands of jobs. Do you think that all of the mines will be shut down during the next 20 years? What about the next 40?

Paul Formby: Environmental Hero in the Fight Against Asbestos

After graduating in philosophy from the University of British Columbia, Paul Formby felt the call of the Canadian north. In the early 1970s he travelled to Clinton Creek, Yukon, where he started work in the asbestos mine. He soon wound up in charge of the health and safety committee of the miner's union—an often thankless task—where he encountered significant resistance from the mining company. He explains,

> As far as the company was concerned, . . . asbestos dust levels were a taboo subject. From the company's point of view the most important safety measure was safety glasses. As long as we all wore safety glasses everything was supposed to be OK. It was almost as if it was more important to keep the stuff out of our eyes than out of our lungs. By arguing in this way, the company was trying to shift the responsibility for health and safety off of its shoulders and onto ours. The company refused to admit that the work environment it created could possibly be hazardous to its workers. (cited in Tataryn, 1979, p. 20)

At issue was the union's right to test the air for asbestos contamination, as well as the company's questionable claim that the white asbestos (chrysotile) that they were mining was far safer than the dangerous blue asbestos (crocidolite) found in the mines of South Africa and Australia. This is a **red herring**: a logical fallacy in which an irrelevant topic is introduced in an argument in order to divert attention from the original and more important issue (in this case, the hazards of chrysotile). Company management and physicians may have believed in the safety of white asbestos, but

their lives were never endangered the way that those of the miners were:

> During contract negotiations the company absolutely refused to discuss the union's right to test the air. . . . The management stated emphatically that asbestos dust levels were not an issue in Clinton Creek. Furthermore, they assured me that the white asbestos found in Canada was so safe I could pour it on my breakfast cereal every morning and suffer no ill effects. The bad stuff, they said, was the blue asbestos that is mined only in South Africa. (Formby, in Tataryn, 1979, p. 21)

Formby remained unconvinced, and decided to take his inquires further afield. In early 1974, he expressed his concerns in a letter to Dr Irving Selikoff, the head of the environmental sciences laboratory at New York's Mount Sinai Medical School and a leading authority on asbestos-related lung cancer and asbestosis (the scarring of the lung by the body's reaction to the indestructible fibres of asbestos entering the lungs). Selikoff wrote back, confirming that Formby's concerns were valid, and taking issue with the supposed "safety" of the white asbestos.

Formby then asked for and received a leave of absence from work. He travelled across the continent to New York, and walked into Mount Sinai Hospital asking to be trained in taking air samples to test for asbestos fibres. Hospital officials were surprisingly sympathetic and accommodating. Rather than treating him like a fanatic, they agreed to train him.

Formby next went to Montreal to contact the union that represented the workers in Thetford Mines, home to Canada's largest asbestos mine. There he spoke with the union's health and safety representative about testing for asbestos particles in the air. Formby was well received, and was assisted in carrying out tests on the air quality at the mine.

For Formby, it was then back to Clinton Creek, where he secretly tested the air there—and then quit. After then he went south to conduct air quality tests at the mine in Cassiar, British Columbia (closed, since 1992, after 40 years in existence). Living out of a suitcase, and occasionally sleeping in his old car, Formby went back to Thetford Mines, where he trained the miners to collect air samples. They had to do this in secret, as the company considered their actions grounds for suspension or dismissal.

Formby had samples from the three mines sent to Mount Sinai Hospital for testing. The union at Thetford Mines arranged to have a team of doctors and technical experts, Canadian and American, visit the mine to examine the workers for signs of asbestosis and cancer. Although the miners had previously received class "A" health ratings from the doctors who worked for the mining company, the independent experts found many sick, some dying.

Paul Formby significantly raised the profile of the dangers of asbestos, both for miners and for other workers (such as builders) exposed to the deadly material. His work spawned awareness-raising documentaries and government actions that have reduced (but not eliminated) the risks of human exposure to asbestos.

In July 2015, Health Canada finally changed the information on its website, which had long maintained that chrysotile was "less potent" and less dangerous than other forms of asbestos (Grant, 2015).

Industrial Communities and the Disposable People of Pollution

The story of Thetford Mines and Asbestos, Quebec—towns whose names are synonymous with the industry they revolve around—underline the fact that it is not just workers who are exposed to the hazardous pollutants produced by environmentally unfriendly companies. Also affected are the communities surrounding these dangerous enterprises. Again, we find the social ecology approach useful in examining how the poor and marginalized communities are usually the ones most powerfully affected. An illustrative case is that of the chemical giant Monsanto and the tiny city of Anniston, Alabama.

The Industrial Contamination of Anniston, Alabama

The following is a classic case of environmental racism. A little background information is necessary. Monsanto, from its founding in 1901, manufactured and distributed some of the most toxic

chemicals ever produced. Specifically, the company was involved in the production and sale of polychlorinated biphenyls, or PCBS, from 1929 until the early 1980s, when the substance was effectively banned through a series of regulations. What are PCBS? In the words of journalist Marie-Monique Robin, "for half a century they colonized the planet; they were used as coolants in electric transformers and industrial hydraulic machines, but also as lubricants in applications as varied as plastics, paint, ink, and paper" (2010, p. 11).

Monsanto also produced the deadly compound dioxin. It was used as an ingredient in Agent Orange, the notorious broad-based plant killer and defoliant that was dumped in massive quantities on the jungles and people of Vietnam by the United States during the Vietnam War to deprive the enemy fighters of cover. So powerful was Agent Orange that plants still do not grow around an airport in western Newfoundland where the chemical was tested during the 1970s (personal observation, 2013). Then there are the other deadly D's, including 2-4-D (a component of Agent Orange, used for a time in household weed killers) and the environmentally toxic insecticide DDT.

During the 1980s and 1990s, Monsanto shifted its focus from chemical manufacture to agricultural biotechnology, and became a pioneer in the development of genetically modified (GMO) plant crops. In 2018, Monsanto was purchased by German multinational drug producer Bayer AG. Bayer soon found itself on the hook for over $2 billion in damages awarded in May 2019 to a California couple who successfully argued in court that their non-Hodgkins lymphoma was caused by long-term exposure to glyphosate, a chief ingredient of the Monsanto weed killer Roundup they used on their property between 1975 and 2011. Bayer successfully petitioned to have the damages reduced, but this will likely not be the last lawsuit the company faces in relation to Roundup, which remains the market-leading herbicide in the United States.

And now I will tell the story of the small city of Anniston.

Situated in Calhoun County, Alabama, Anniston was home to a Monsanto production facility for PCBs beginning in 1929. Most of the workers at Monsanto's plant in Anniston were black. Many of them lived in the neighbourhoods surrounding the

The Point Is...

It Takes Courage to Blow the Whistle

John O'Connor started his career as a physician in northern Alberta in 1993, spending much of this time in the oil sands boomtown of Fort McMurray. In 2001, he started working with the Indigenous community of Fort Chipewyan, population 1200, located a little way downriver from the sands. Shortly after beginning to work with the Fort Chipewyan community, whose Elders told O'Connor about new deformities they were seeing in fish—a staple of their diet—along with a peculiar oily taste, the doctor began to notice evidence of health problems he hadn't seen in Fort McMurray. Specifically, he observed new cases of cholangiocarcinoma, a rare bile duct cancer that had killed his father, and that often showed up in bile ducts of fish swimming in oil-infested water. He also found a high incidence of liver cancers.

When Dr O'Connor began voicing his concerns, Canada's federal agency, Health Canada, approached the community for its medical files. One government representative even made a very public visit to declare the water fit for consumption. He demonstrated this with a rather unscientific gesture: at the local nursing station, he filled his mouth with water from a tap and announced to an attending *Globe and Mail* reporter: "There's nothing wrong with the water in Fort Chip."

Health Canada presented the findings of their report to the Alberta Energy and Utilities Board in Fort McMurray one week *before* they spoke with members of the Fort Chipewyan community about their experience. After a quick analysis of the data set, which mysteriously omitted statistics from 2004 and 2005, the agency gave the community a clean bill of health.

The agency's work didn't end there, as O'Connor, in a statement given in the House of Commons in June 2009, explained,

In 2007 I got a large envelope in the mail from the College of Physicians and Surgeons in Edmonton.... It was a list of complaints that Health Canada had laid about my activities in Fort Chip. They accused me of blocking access to files, billing irregularities, engendering a sense of mistrust in government in Fort Chip, and causing undue alarm in the community. (Canada, 2009)

It was the first time that a Canadian government agency had ever used a patient complaint process to attack a physician in this way. The charges were serious and could have led to the suspension—temporary or permanent—of O'Connor's licence to practise medicine. The first three charges were dismissed relatively quickly. The people of Fort Chipewyan, who hadn't been consulted concerning whether they felt "undue alarm," supported him, and in fact requested the dismissal of Health Canada's senior physician. Members of the Alberta Medical Association were unanimous in their support.

In 2008, the Alberta Cancer Board engaged in a more comprehensive study of the community, releasing their findings in February 2009. In their report, the board stated that while the number of cases of cholangiocarcinoma and colon cancer were "within the expected range" during the period of investigation,

[t]he number of cancer cases overall was higher than expected. In particular, increases of observed over expected were found for biliary tract cancers as a group and cancers of the blood and lymphatic system. These increases were based on a

Continued

small number of cases and could be due to chance or increased detection. The possibility that the increased rate is due to increased risk in the community, however, cannot be ruled out. (Alberta Cancer Board, 2009, p. 10)

The board concluded that further study was warranted to see if there was any risk associated with living in Fort Chipewyan. In November 2009, the charge against O'Connor of "causing due alarm" was dropped. In 2015, he was fired from the Nunee Health Board in Fort Chipewyan with no explanation.

plant, which were likewise predominantly black. During the 1930s, Monsanto was already receiving and documenting warnings about the deadly risks of PCBs to anyone in close contact with the toxic compound, and the company continued to acquire and file away such information until they stopped producing PCBs over 30 years later, in 1971. During that 30 plus–year interval, they did nothing to warn or protect either their workers or their Anniston neighbours.

The truth of Anniston's PCB contamination began to leak out in a series of news items in 2002. By 2005, the US Environmental Protection Agency was reporting that 60 million pounds of PCBs had been emitted into the atmosphere surrounding Anniston. A nearly equivalent amount—68 million pounds—of PCB-contaminated waste had been dumped at a disposal site in Anniston, while 1.8 million pounds of PCBs had been poured into local streams, where the locals sometimes fished for food. The reported effects on the health of Anniston's residents included rare cancers, brain tumours, miscarriages, and brain damage to infants and children caused by contaminated breast milk.

Monsanto had taken steps to limit the legal damage it knew could result from any discovery of the extent of contamination. They had begun to buy up homes surrounding the disposal site, offering "good money" in exchange for a written promise from any seller not to sue the company. In 1997, Monsanto sold its industrial chemical division, which included the factory in Anniston, to another company, Solutia Inc., in a move widely seen as an attempt to evade financial liability in lawsuits the company was anticipating.

Nevertheless, in 2002, Monsanto and Solutia were successfully sued in a class action suit by former employees and the citizens of Anniston. Money was awarded to the individual plaintiffs based on the quantities of PCB in their blood, with the cut-off being 20 parts per million (ppm)—10 times the acceptable rate. Under these conditions, only 15 per cent of the plaintiffs qualified for compensation, up to a maximum of US$500,000. One of the leaders of the lawsuit, David Barker, whose brother had died of cancer at 17, had a bloodstream PCB level of 341 ppm—170 times the acceptable level—and was awarded $33,000.

As Marie-Monique Robin reports, the jury's decision was unequivocally condemning:

The legal grounds for the verdict were "negligence, wantonness, fraud, trespass, nuisance, and outrage," and it included a harsh judgment of Monsanto's conduct, which was "so outrageous in character and extreme in degree as to go beyond all possible bounds of decency, so as to be regarded as atrocious and utterly intolerable in civilized society." (2010, p. 27)

How could a company conduct business in this way? Is it arrogance, cynicism, or plain greed? Sociologists might look at the **organizational culture** of such a huge corporate entity, whereby the company and the work it does become a part of the individual identity of the employees working there, especially those at the upper level. They might draw on Durkheim's study of religions, drawing on his notion of a **moral community**, where individuals have shared mutual identities and a commitment to a common purpose. It's a situation that fosters group loyalty—the kind that is strengthened when the group with which you identify is threatened by outsiders. In war your first loyalty is to those beside you in the trenches. But the situation can also be viewed as a reflection of prevailing class and "race" relations, where the majority of those in positions of power—the scientists and administrators

AP Photo/Francois Mori

In March 2019, French activists demonstrate in front of the Paris headquarters of Bayer AG to protest its production of chemical pesticides. Two months later, French demonstrators joined protesters in other countries in what has become an annual march calling for an end to the use of pesticides and other "agrochemicals." Bayer–Monsanto has been a lightening rod for a resistance to pesticides that is generally much fiercer in Europe than it is in North America. Why do you think that is?

who directed company policy—were white, while the non-corporate members, the "Other," were predominantly black and without power, and therefore more disposable.

Monsanto Again: A Canadian Connection

Consider for a moment the different ways of owning the environment. You can own a piece of property. You might own the rights to the resources beneath the surface, and to the plants growing on top. But what about owning an entire biological entity, patenting a life form? The following case involves a Canadian farmer and the chemical giant Monsanto. It's a David and Goliath story, only in this instance, Goliath wins.

Born in Bruno, Saskatchewan, in 1930, Percy Schmeiser grows canola, the oily seed plant formerly known as rapeseed. He has been mayor of his small town and a local member of Saskatchewan's legislative assembly. He has worked his 1500 acre farm for over 50 years.

In 1997, Schmeiser sprayed the ditches bordering his land with Roundup, Monsanto's market-leading (and trademarked) weed killer. Unfortunately, he found that it was ineffective in killing the plants that were threatening to encroach on his canola fields. After consulting with a Monsanto representative, Schmeiser learned the source of his problem: the encroaching plants were a Monsanto-patented "Roundup-Ready Canola," meaning that they were grown from a Monsanto-engineered seed made to be resistant to a Monsanto-engineered weed killer.

The following year, Schmeiser replanted his fields using seeds from the previous year's crops, as is common practice. In August, around harvest time, he was contacted by a Monsanto representative who informed him that inspectors had, without notifying him (much less asking for permission), trespassed on Schmeiser's property and taken a sample of his crops. Laboratory analysis provided evidence that the canola crops were of the patented Monsanto variety. The representative proposed that Schmeiser agree to a settlement for compensation or else be sued by the multinational company.

Schmeiser opted not to settle, and a court battle followed. "Experts" disagreed over the percentage of plants affected. Schmeiser lost the first case, with the judge ruling as follows:

> [A] farmer whose field contains seed or plants originating from seed spilled into them, or blown as seed, in swaths from a neighbor's land, or even growing from germination by pollen carried into his field from elsewhere by insects, birds, or by the wind, may own the seed or plants on his land even if he did not set about to plant them. He does not, however, own the right to the use of the patented gene or cell [since] growth of the seed, reproducing the patented gene and cell, and sale of the harvested crop constitutes taking the essence of the plaintiff's invention and using it without permission. (cited in Robin, 2010, p. 215)

Schmeiser's "crime," in other words, was not harvesting the Monsanto-patented canola plants that happened to be growing in his field, but inadvertently using seeds from those plants to plant his next year's crops. The company was awarded damages of $15,450 ($15 per harvested acre), plus the cost of their legal fees. Schmeiser's own legal fees were nearly $200,000. Schmeiser appealed his case to the Supreme Court of Canada, which supported the lower court's decision (by a 5–4 margin) but did not make Schmeiser pay the damages or Monsanto's legal fees.

What this means is that genetically modified plants, which have the capacity to spread like weeds

> **What Do YOU Think?**
> Genetically modified plants may be stronger than traditional crops, being more resistant to drought, disease, and damage caused by insects. Farmers stand to gain from such improvements. Should the company that invents these tougher varieties be allowed to profit from their use, even if the plants grow by chance, winning out over inferior varieties? More generally, should companies hold patents on living things?

and may have localized evolutionary advantages over traditional organic crops, are working for their masters (usually Monsanto, which owns about 90 per cent of the patents) by taking over the farmlands. The damage to the environment in this case is social and economic, although we haven't yet learned if genetically modified organisms pose significant biological dangers.

It is worth noting that Schmeiser has become something of a folk hero among anti-Monsanto farmers and anti-GMO activists. He has already been the subject of a 2009 documentary, *David versus Monsanto*, and his story is the focus of a 2019 film, *Percy* (in post-production, at time of writing), starring Christopher Walken as Schmeiser.

The Environment and Race

So far in this chapter, we have seen that pollution is racialized. Rich, predominantly white nations dump waste in poorer black and brown nations. For many years, Canada shipped most of its asbestos to developing nations, where the lethal health risks of the substance were not as widely understood or where safer alternatives were prohibitively expensive. Monsanto employed a large percentage of black workers to produce PCBs in a predominantly black neighbourhood of Anniston, Alabama. To this list we add the story of Africville, a black neighbourhood outside of Halifax, Nova Scotia, that was forced to share space with a series of polluting companies and an open-pit dump.

This genetically modified pig, developed at the University of Guelph, provides a distinct advantage over regular pigs: its pig poo is environmentally friendly! If you're a bacon lover, would you have any reservations about eating meat from a genetically modified pig? If you're a vegetarian, how do you feel about the fact that many soy products are made with genetically modified soybeans? Overall, what are the benefits and dangers of consuming food with genetically modified ingredients?

Africville: An Environmental Racism Disaster

Situated a little north of Halifax, Africville was a Canadian black village with origins in the eighteenth century. At its peak, it had a population of roughly 400. It was a thriving community that became a haven for those wanting to escape the racism of mainstream society, and during the first half of the twentieth century it became a home for black culture that attracted visits from internationally prominent black athletes and musicians come to visit. In 1996, it was declared a National Historic Site.

Despite it social and cultural importance, Africville was constantly dumped upon by mainstream society. It became a place for governments and businesses to locate the most environmentally gruesome operations and substances: a fertilizer plant, a slaughterhouse, a garbage dump, a deposit site for "night soil" (a polite term for human excrement), and an infectious diseases hospital. Basic municipal services including running water, street lighting, garbage removal, and waste disposal were never provided to the residents of Africville.

During the 1960s, Africville's citizens were forcibly removed from their community, their homes expropriated and demolished. Government officials reasoned that the area was an environmental disaster. Of course, it was, though not through neglect on the part of the community's residents. Displaced Africvillians were given meagre payouts to help them relocate to other parts of Halifax, but many left the region for good. Private homes and a municipal park were built on the former site of the village of Africville.

Bob Brooks/Nova Scotia Archives

Young boys play by a CN railcar, along the railway that ran through the heart of Africville. What do you think might have happened to the community had the city of Halifax decided to provide the village with basic services—clean water, waste removal—rather than demolishing it? Do you think it might still be a black neighbourhood today? Why or why not?

For those who are interested, there is a rich literature on Africville, both sociological (e.g. Clairmont & Magill, 1999) and more personal accounts by former inhabitants and their descendants (e.g. Grant, 2018).

The Case of Grassy Narrows

In *A Poison Stronger Than Love: The Destruction of an Ojibwa Community* (1985), Anastasia Shkilnyk presents an often cited case study of how pollution is racialized. It is a sympathetic study of the plight of the Anishinaabe, or Ojibwa, people of Grassy Narrows, a First Nations community in northwestern Ontario, near the city of Kenora. However, Shkilnyk's study is flawed in being entrenched in **victimology**: it portrays the people as hapless victims of an industrial attack on the environment, rather than as agents and leaders in the fight against such an attack. For this reason, the incident and Shkilnyk's role in reporting

on it are worth studying together as an example both of how environmental issues intersect with race and of how knowledge is produced.

In the mid-twentieth century, fishing was vital to the community of Grassy Narrows, both as a source of food and as a source of income (largely through tourism). Between 1962 and 1970, Reed Paper Company, a British-owned multinational, began dumping huge amounts of mercury—about 20,000 pounds—into the English–Wabigoon river system, about 170 kilometres upstream from Grassy Narrows. In 1970, significantly high amounts of the deadly element were detected in the local fish. Two years later came the first human casualty, a 42-year-old fishing guide.

The people of Grassy Narrows knew that mercury was making the fish and the people who depended on them sick, but the provincial government, with significant financial interests at stake, downplayed the problem. The pulp and paper industry, which was the source of the mercury pollution, was a major employer in northwestern Ontario—so much so, in fact, that the government was supporting Reed Paper with tax rebates. Local tourism, another important industry, stood to suffer if concerns about mercury contamination of the river system became public. There, again, the Ontario government was a stakeholder, having invested large sums in Minaki Lodge, just 45 kilometres west of Grassy Narrows. In 1977, it was revealed that the government had spent about $7.5 million in its acquisition and renovation of the lodge.

The people of Grassy Narrows, led by Chief Andy Keewatin, were not afraid to pursue their case against the company and the government's negligence. In 1975, they contacted the people of Minamata, Japan, a fishing community whose name is now synonymous with a motor and nervous disorder resulting from mercury poisoning (Minamata disease). They paid to have experts from Japan come to assess their situation, and armed with evidence of the river's contamination, they took their fight to the courts. In December of that year, the Chiefs and Councillors of Grassy Narrows, along with those of neighbouring Whitedog, threatened to deliver poisoned fish to the homes of Ontario's premier, the ministers of natural resources and of health, the attorney general, the leaders of the opposition parties, and the president of Reed. In a letter sent to these individuals, the representatives of Grassy Narrows clearly articulated their determination not to be victims:

> We know that the fish are poisonous. We know that eating the fish can destroy the mind and health and take the life of Indians and whites. This cannot fail to be known by anybody who, for five long years, has watched the growing violence, the deteriorating health, and the declining morale of our people. . . .
>
> For five years, we have fought the bias, indifference and hostility of your minister of natural resources.
>
> It is long enough. Enough have died. Enough people have died. Enough of our people have been destroyed. Enough lack of

understanding. Enough pro-polluter bias. Enough indifference. (cited in Hutchison & Wallace, 1977, p. 140)

In 1976, Anastasia Shkilnyk was hired by the Department of Indian Affairs and Northern Development (DIAND) to study the community of Grassy Narrows, which she did over the next two years, returning for follow-up research in 1981 and 1983. She had a genuine interest in helping the people, and her work produced some valuable insights. However, she failed to question seriously the destructive role of the multinational company then fighting the community in the courts and the weak response and motives of both the federal government (her employer) and the provincial government. Further, she failed to accurately represent the active role taken by the people in their effort to resolve the crisis. In her work, the people neither understand their situation nor mount any resistance to the large corporate and governmental players. They are merely victims. There is little Indigenous voice in this book.

Sociology textbooks addressing the circumstances of Grassy Narrows typically give equal weight to two other factors: abuse and alcoholism. They do not mention that the people eventually were able to win $8.7 million in an out-of-court settlement from Reed Pulp and Paper in 1985. They do not talk about the community's fight since 1993 against the environmental impact of the logging practices of Abitibi Consolidated Inc. They are locked into a time zone of perpetual environmental victimhood.

In 2011, Grassy Narrows First Nation won an Ontario Supreme Court victory stating that the province could not authorize logging operations that would infringe on federal Indigenous rights to hunting and trapping. In spite of the ruling, the provincial government in 2014 denied the community's request to conduct an environmental assessment of Abitibi's commercial timber extraction, even though the people's concerns were supported by locally knowledgeable biologists working for the province.

Meanwhile, the fight over contaminated water is not over. An Ontario government report released in June 2015 revealed that waterways in and around the Grassy Narrows community continue to show

Jody Porter/CBC

For over 40 years, the community of Grassy Narrows First Nation has been pushing for governments of all parties (Conservative, Liberal, and New Democratic) at both the provincial and federal levels to do something about the deadly mercury poisoning in the water. To date, nothing substantial has been accomplished. Why do you think it has taken so long?

high levels of mercury. One year later, another government-funded report acknowledged that there was "an ongoing, yet unknown, source of mercury in the water," rumoured to be a mercury disposal site where dozens of barrels of the poisonous substance are thought to have been dumped (Porter, 2016). In June 2019, the federal minister of Indigenous Services presented the First Nation with a proposal to start construction on a local health-care facility specializing in the detection and treatment of mercury poisoning; however, the Grassy Narrows leadership rejected it because it did not contain sufficient guarantees of ongoing funding to operate the facility once construction is complete (Prokopchuk, 2019).

Simon Fobister was a young man when he became Chief of the Grassy Narrows First Nation, a position he held for 10 years. He was also a leading figure in the fight for remediation for the contamination of his community's traditional lands. He died as a result of mercury poisoning in August 2019, at the age of 63.

The Environment and Class

As we have seen already in this chapter, there is a fairly clear relationship between **class** and the environment. People from the lower classes are more likely than those of the upper classes to live and work in conditions characterized by high levels of pollution or environmental hazards. People from the higher socioeconomic classes can also better afford to eat foods that are healthier and less affected by pollution. The following sections provide two illustrations of the way that environmental issues intersect with class.

Walkerton and the Social Politics of Water

In May 2000, the town of Walkerton, Ontario, was hit by an epidemic of the bacterium *Escherichia coli*, commonly known as *E. coli*, which came from their main water supply. In total, an estimated 2300 people

The Point Is...

Disaster Brings Social Change, but Not Always for the Better

Central to the social ecology viewpoint is the idea that environmental problems reproduce—and even arise from—existing social inequalities. We can consider this idea in the context of "natural" environmental disasters. But can they produce positive social change?

Samuel Henry Prince (1886–1962) was an influential Canadian sociologist who taught in Halifax at King's University (now part of Dalhousie University) from 1924 until 1955. An ordained Anglican minister, Prince received his PhD in sociology in 1919 from Columbia University, where his doctoral dissertation involved pioneering work on "disaster" as a sociological context for social change. His study dealt with the Halifax Explosion of 1917, in which a docked naval vessel carrying explosives caught fire and blew up in Halifax Harbour, rocking the city of some 50,000 with blast, fire, and floods that killed nearly 2000 people. Prince's hypothesis was that a disaster can lead to significant social change. In Halifax, he explained,

> the shock resulted in disintegration of social institutions, dislocation of the usual methods of social control and dissolution of the customary; that through the catastrophe the community was thrown into the state of flux which . . . is the logical and natural prerequisite for social change. . . . [T]he shock was of a character such as "to affect all individuals alike at the same time," and to induce that degree of fluidity most favorable to social change. (Prince, 1920)

Prince demonstrated how this disaster led to a broad variety of changes, including the improvement of public transportation and a building code that would gradually replace the previous wood-dominated housing with building using materials less likely to burn. His argument that catastrophe can lead to positive social change is an important and contentious sociological point, and we will take it up in a moment in the context of Hurricane Katrina, which hit New Orleans in 2005. The Halifax Explosion was nothing like the natural event that Hurricane Katrina was, but it caused environmental devastation on a comparable scale, and Prince's work has great relevance in an investigation of the aftermath of Hurricane Katrina.

First, though, we should point out that Prince's work reflects a greater sense of **positivism** than one finds in current work taking the social ecology approach. Contemporary studies tend to support the hypothesis that there is a direct connection between social and environmental problems. So-called natural disasters occur in a social context. They have different impacts on groups of people occupying different social locations within the same basic geographical location. The effects of gender, race, ethnicity, class, age, and ability are all felt by the victims of natural disasters. The greatest number of victims of Hurricane Katrina were black, female, poor, and disabled. The greater the number of those social features you possessed (remember the concept of **intersectionality**), the more likely you were to suffer, or even die, from the natural effects of the storm and the social response to the storm. It illustrates the concept of environmental racism introduced at the start of the chapter as well.

So what of Prince's hypothesis that disaster brings positive social change? Rebuilding in New Orleans tended to benefit large, well-connected companies that were able to obtain government reconstruction contracts. A 10-year-long project to reinforce the city's levees was completed in May 2018, but less than a year later, a US Army Corp report warned that the system could become obsolete as early as 2023, thanks to rising sea levels (Kaufman, 2019). The city faced its biggest threat since Katrina in July 2019, when a major Gulf Coast

Continued

weather system swept inland. Fortunately for the city's residents, "Barry" was downgraded to a tropical depression by the time it made landfall, and New Orleans escaped with relatively minor flooding, with no serious property damage or human injuries. Even though the city is now better protected and prepared for the natural aspects of a future hurricane (the damage from Hurricane Isaac in August 2012 was considerably less), it would be inaccurate to say that Hurricane Katrina has brought significant positive social change to New Orleans, or that the city—particularly the parts of it where the majority of the residents are African American—is better off than it was before the storms of 2005.

Residents of New Orleans wade through floodwaters from tropical storms in July 2019.

were affected by the outbreak; just over half of them were residents of the town itself, meaning that roughly one-quarter of Walkerton's population became ill. Seven people died as a consequence of the infection.

The tragedy raised questions about whom to trust when it comes to the social management of pollution. The province's Conservative government had been pursuing a policy of privatizing public-sector government departments, including the one responsible for inspecting the water supply. As a result of granting contracts for testing the water to private companies, the province had drastically reduced its funding to the Ministry of the Environment. Journalist Colin Perkel, in his thorough investigation into the Walkerton tragedy, cites this as evidence of a lack of social responsibility, both on the part of the government and on the part of the American firm, A & L Canada Laboratories East, that filled the government-created vacuum:

> Although A & L Canada Laboratories East, a US-based franchise operation, had never tested for bacteria and was not accredited to do so, it nevertheless accepted water samples from Walkerton. In the absence of updated guidelines or regulations the provincial government felt no need to implement, A & L followed private industry practice in deeming test results to be confidential, to be shared only with the client [i.e. the town workers responsible for monitoring the pollution levels of the water]. (Perkel, 2002: p. 35)

One social product of having a private company do this work was a breakdown in the chain of communication and responsibility between the town and Ministry of the Environment.

When the story hit the news, the media followed two main storylines. One focused on the personal incompetence and lack of responsibility shown by the Walkerton employee who was primarily responsible for monitoring the water and notifying the Ministry of the Environment of any problems. We can call this the **rotten apple approach**, which aims to argue that the fault lies not with the system but with the individuals who make it up. This non-sociological line of inquiry, which is typical of tabloid-style reporting, dominated certain parts of the media coverage. A bumbling rural official is an easy target for big-city reporters.

Sociologists tend to believe that there are no rotten apples, just a bad orchard—the social system surrounding the situation. The second main storyline, exhibited in the work of journalists such as Perkel, took this view, arguing that the *E. coli* epidemic was an inevitable result of the Ministry of the Environment's loss of influence over water testing. The less oversight shown by a large and authoritative social body, the greater the chance that something

important will go unnoticed—with tragic consequences, in the case of Walkerton.

The China Price: The True Cost of Chinese Competitive Advantage

Does it seem like everything you buy is made in China?

According to the US Central Intelligence Agency's World Factbook (CIA, n.d.), China is the world's leading exporter of goods, ahead of the European Union, the United States, and Germany. How did China become the "workshop of the world"? Much of it has to do with what is often called the **China price**. China has a huge competitive advantage in the manufacture and assembly of just about any kind of goods, as it is incredibly cheap to have work done in China. This cheapness comes at the expense of exploited Chinese workers and the environment. Alexandra Harney (2009) looked at the China price and, in turn, the price paid by China for its manufacturing success—a price too dear, in Harney's view.

The mechanism of China's global competitive advantage has been called the "survival of the cheapest" (Harney, 2009, p. 40). Less than 20 years ago,

it was estimated that the average wage for Chinese manufacturing workers was just 57 cents an hour. That has risen recently to $3.60 per hour (in US dollars; Yan, 2017). But despite this recent jump, there are literally millions of migrant workers competing for manufacturing jobs. Tens of millions of them are **environmental refugees** from farming areas and smaller villages now considered "cancer villages" or "widow towns." The few health benefits that workers can draw on are administered by the household registration system, or *hukou*, which typically favours those from cities over those from villages.

The importance of health benefits to Chinese workers cannot be overstated, since the workplace in China is a major source of pollution. Work-related lung diseases such as silicosis (producing scar tissue in the lungs, and often leading to tuberculosis) claim as many as one million new cases every year (Harney, 2009, p. 57), many of them in industries relating to jewellery manufacture. Perhaps the greatest environmental villain is coal, used to provide power to the ever-growing number of Chinese industries, as well as supplying fuel for household heat and cooking. China is the world's largest producer and consumer of coal, and because of that it emits more carbon dioxide and sulphur dioxide than any other country (Harney, 2009, p. 89). Corrosive acid rain soaks the ground in nearly all parts of the country.

It is not just the burning of coal but the extraction of coal that makes it an environmental hazard. In 2006, according to official statistics, 4746 people died in Chinese coal mines (Harney, 2009, p. 90). However, since much of the coal is produced in relatively small, private, often "illegal" mines, the actual number is probably higher. Owning a coal mine is a lucrative enterprise in China. While China still retains some of the political mechanisms of its earlier communist period, it is now very much a free-wheeling capitalist economy, with the free exploitative hand of the market wielding more power in some ways than in most countries of the West.

Officially, China takes strong measures to control the pollution, and it does not lack the resources to improve its air quality when it is sufficiently motivated to do so. Too often, though, this is not the case, as there are huge financial benefits tied to the lack of effective supervision, both in terms of corporate profits and in personal gain for environmental regulators who take bribes to look the other way. It is easy to blame the Chinese government, but the truth is that Western companies that invest in profitable Chinese businesses regardless of their environmental records make it easy to justify lax oversight of environmental policies.

The Sociology of Climate Change

In the run-up to the 2019 federal election, Elections Canada issued a warning to charitable organizations dedicated environmental causes: Don't talk about climate change unless you register with us first (McCarthy & Walsh, 2019). Climate change was emerging as a partisan issue, and charitable organizations, unlike political parties and special interest groups registered with Elections Canada, are not allowed to air partisan advertising. Partisan, in this context, refers to any material that could be seen as telling people which party or candidate to vote for or not to vote for.

It is common for organizations that promote environmental causes to encourage voters to speak with local candidates about the environment before marking their ballots. This is not new and has nothing to do with telling people how to vote; it is about asking them to keep the environment in mind when making their ballot decision. So what changed? How did climate change become a partisan issue?

In the months before the 2019 election, all of Canada's major federal parties started announcing their plans to tackle climate change, recognizing that the environment had, for the first time, become the most important issue for a segment of the electorate too large to ignore. Enter Maxime Bernier and his fledgling People's Party of Canada (PPC), which disputes the notion that climate change is influenced by humans and requires urgent action on the part of Canadian voters. Suddenly, a social media campaign about what humans must do to avoid an environmental catastrophe entered the realm of partisan advertising because it could be seen to discredit the official platform of the PPC. Elections Canada later clarified their position—somewhat—but not before creating a lot of confusion about the line between political statement and scientific fact.

Fortunately, aspiring and practising sociologists need not abide by Election Canada rules and their fuzzy distinction between scientific reality and politics. This is a good thing, because climate change has some serious sociological implications. From activists to entrepreneurs, everybody today has a quick fix for global warming, but there's a need for sociologists of today and the future to point to the social impacts of the ideas being proposed. We close out our discussion of the environment by considering just a few of these, some more serious than others.

Have Fewer Children

In an article published in *Environmental Research Letters*, Seth Wynes (a researcher at the University of British Columbia) and Kimberly Nicholas show that among a broad range of individual actions with the potential to substantially reduce personal carbon emissions, having one fewer child has the potential to save 58.6 tonnes of CO_2-equivalent (tCO_2e) emissions per year per person (Wynes & Nicholas, 2017). To put that awkward metric in perspective, consider that number 2 on their list of high-impact options, living car-free, is likely to save only 2.4 tCO_2e emissions per year, and reducing air travel is likely to save no more annually than 1.6 tCO_2e.

Wynes and Nicholas are not the first to suggest having fewer children as a way to reduce carbon emissions, but what are the sociological implications of such an action? Canada's birth rate at present is just 1.6, well below the replacement level of 2.1 required to keep the population at present levels. What would happen if Canadian families pledged to have just one child rather than two or three? Would the government allow the national population to drop? Or would it open the doors to more immigration, since a dramatic population reduction could have dramatic negative consequences on the country's economy? What would be the social impacts of higher levels of immigration? We could also consider the history of one-child policies in countries like China. Some have argued that the one-child policy in place in China between 1979 and 2015 distorted the natural balance of men and women (because of the preference for boys). According to a CBC report, "Even the government acknowledges the problem and has expressed concern about the tens of millions of young men who won't be able to find brides and

may turn to kidnapping women, sex trafficking, other forms of crime or social unrest" (CBC News, 2015).

Travel Less

This may have occurred to you already. But what would happen if Canadians dramatically reduced their use of cars? This could be achieved, for instance, if more people worked remotely online or adopted a shorter work week (reducing the number of commuting days). How might this affect the way we work? Would we become less social beings, living much more locally? Or would this effectively strengthen neighbourhoods?

To extend the thought, what if we dramatically reduced our flying time? It is not unreasonable to think there might soon be a significant social stigma attached to non-essential air travel. The notion exists already in Sweden, where Greta Thunberg (see Chapter 6) has brought attention to *flygskam*, or flight shame. One day soon, jetting off to Europe may be something you would not wish to admit to. Will this make us less worldly people, less aware of and sympathetic toward people living in parts of the world we never experience? Or will advances in augmented reality allow us to immerse ourselves in other cultures without having to leave our homes? A technological alternative would be to devote serious research to finding alternative fuels and means of propelling airplanes. Personally, I am hoping for *Star Trek* transporters.

Educate More Girls

This is a sociological solution with benefits to the environment, rather than an environmental solution with social impacts. According to Project Drawdown, a multidisciplinary organization researching climate change solutions, increasing the education rate of girls in the developing world is sixth in a list of the 80 solutions with the greatest potential to reduce climate change between now and 2050 (Basij-Rasikh, 2018). As Shabana Basij-Rasikh (2018) explains,

> an educated girl marries later and has fewer and healthier children. She lives longer and enjoys greater economic prosperity. She can be expected to direct a significant amount of her income back to her family. Perhaps most important in the context of global

GLENN LOWSON/THE GLOBE AND MAIL

Coming soon to a campus near you: the dockless scooter, seen here in a trial run at the University of Waterloo. Touted as an eco-friendly alternative to driving, the latest mode of micro-transportation may not be as environmentally friendly as its promoters suggest. A 2019 study (Hollingsworth, Copeland, & Johnson, 2019) suggests their benefits may be outweighed by the environmental impact of building, repairing, and picking up the fragile scooters, which passengers are not required to return to the point of departure. While a scooter trip produces fewer carbon emissions than a comparable trip by car, it is as likely to be used as an alternative to walking as it is to driving. If you used a scooter, what mode of transportation would it be replacing?

warming, an educated girl is equipped with the skills to withstand and overcome the shocks of extreme weather events and changing weather cycles.

Could there be any downsides to this proposal? What social outcomes would result from raising education levels among girls and women in the developing world?

Final Thoughts

Smaller people apparently have a smaller carbon footprint. This is not a joke: if humans were smaller, our metabolic needs would be reduced, which means we would have smaller diets, which means less global food production; we would require smaller articles of clothing and could live in smaller, more fuel-efficient homes and drive smaller, more fuel-efficient vehicles, according to Matthew Liao, Anders Sandberg, and Rebecca Roache (2012). They propose a series of "human engineering" solutions that would involve genetic modifications to the species. Personally, I find that very scary. Maybe we should just ban pizza delivery and offer discounts to people who walk home with their order.

It is easy to be flippant about some of the proposals for fighting global warming, but climate change is serious, affecting not just our physical environment and well-being but also our mental health, according to Elizabeth Wiley (2019) of the Environmental Health Committee of British Columbia. "Specifically," writes Dr Wiley, "climate change has been associated with numerous mental health conditions including **posttraumatic stress disorder** (PTSD), depression, anxiety, grief, substance use disorders, and suicidal ideation among many others" (2019). These are grave threats to human health. In that context, no solution is too strange to consider, and sociologists have a role to play in helping understand the implications of all ideas, no matter how far-fetched they may seem.

Wrap It Up

Summary

It is easy to find discouraging evidence concerning the state of the environment, but in this chapter I have tried to find some hope to balance any feelings of despair you might be experiencing. Human action is the main cause of environmental degradation, but human action can play the most important role in reversing the process. Natural disasters typically bring about uneven results to different social groups, but they can, in theory, provide opportunities for development that will benefit different social groups equally.

It would take an entire book to provide a comprehensive account of the environmental issues of concern to sociologists today. "The environment" is a hot-button topic, with daily news items about the food we eat and where it comes from, about climate change, about environmental disasters and cleanup, all backed by the latest research and statistics. What I hope I have provided you with here are some sociological tools with which you can assess the issues surrounding the interaction between groups in society and the fate of the environment. These tools include the concepts of social ecology, environmental racism, vested interests, the tobacco strategy, the China price and, as well, the example of people like Paul Formby and Percy Schmeiser, demonstrating what individuals can do in the fight against socially powerful opponents.

Think Back

Questions for Critical Review

1. In your own words, define *environmental racism*. Provide two or three examples noted in the chapter, and discuss the extent to which they have been resolved. Are the solutions satisfactory? As our awareness of threats to the environment grows, do you think we will see fewer cases of environmental racism or more?

2. Imagine that a large petroleum-exporting company wanted to run a natural gas pipeline through your community. Who would you trust to give you reliable information on its safety: An engineer employed by the company? An environmental regulator working for the federal government (whose job status might be affected by a negative report)? A university professor whose research is funded by a grant? An activist working for a charitable organization dedicated to saving the environment? What are the vested interests of each party?

3. You are geological engineer who has been hired by a mining company to perform an environmental impact assessment of a proposed mining project in northern BC. What vested interests might you face? What kinds of concepts would you need to operationalize to provide an accurate assessment of environmental risks associated with the project?

4. What is the tobacco strategy, and how does it affect social policy concerning the environment?

5. What is meant by the claim that there is no such thing as a (purely) natural disaster?

6. Pioneering social ecologist Murray Bookchin (1996) wrote that "present ecological problems

cannot be clearly understood, much less resolved, without resolutely dealing with problems within society." Apply this statement to
the case of Grassy Narrows First Nation.

7. What is wrong with the "rotten apple approach" to dealing with issues of pollution?
Why does it not make for good sociology?

8. Consider the following proposals for fighting

global warming and assess them from a sociological perspective:

a. axing meat products to encourage Canadians
to adopt a more plant-based diet

b. adopting a three-day work week

c. banning online shopping to encourage more
local spending while reducing overall purchases of non-essential consumer goods

Read On

Recommended Print and Online Resources

Alexandra Harney, *The China Price: The True
Cost of Chinese Competitive Advantage* (New
York: Penguin Books, 2009).

- This is an important work outlining the social and environmental cost of the China
price. Read it together with her 20-minute
TEDx talk, found at www.youtube.com/
watch?v=xMFp8feQbvc

Colin N. Perkel, *Well of Lies: The Walkerton
Water Tragedy* (Toronto: McClelland & Stewart,
2002).

- This book describes in great detail how the
Walkerton tragedy was allowed to occur, and
how the drama played out.

David vs. Monsanto, www.youtube.com/
watch?v=rf0BBDYl6bo

- This is a one-hour documentary film about
Saskatchewan farmer Percy Schmeiser's battle with agrichemical company Monsanto.

Lloyd Tataryn, *Dying for a Living* (Ottawa, ON:
Deneau and Greenberg, 1979); *Formaldehyde
on Trial: The Politics of Health in a Chemical
Society* (Toronto: Latimer, 1983).

- Two older but still very relevant works show
how corporate greed and a lack of government oversight create dangerous situations
for Canadians.

Mathieu Asselin, *Monsanto: A Photographic
Investigation* (Verlag Kettler, 2017).

- Asselin's work includes his own photographs,
taken over a seven-year period, as well as archival material and some of Monsanto's own
marketing materials. There are many photos
of Anniston, Alabama, which was home to
one of the company's chemical production.

Murray Bookchin, *The Philosophy of Social
Ecology Essays on Dialectical Naturalism*
(Montreal: Black Rose Books, 1996).

- This work contains the essential ideas of
Bookchin's social ecology.

Naomi Oreskes & Erik M. Conway, *Merchants of
Doubt: How a Handful of Scientists Obscured
the Truth on Issues from Tobacco Smoke to
Global Warming* (New York: Bloomsbury, 2010).

- The authors outline how a few politically
well-connected scientists assist polluting
companies in resisting environmental policies.

Project Drawdown, www.drawdown.org

- Visit this site to view a list of proposed climate
solutions, including the suggestion of educating more girls and women.

Stanford Research into the Impact of Tobacco
Advertising (SRITA), http://tobacco.stanford.
edu/tobacco_main/index.php

- This interdisciplinary research project draws
contributions from Stanford faculty and students in the departments of medicine, history,
and anthropology, all looking at the effects
of advertising. If you've grown up in the age
where tobacco advertising is absent from
Canadian magazines and television, you'll
likely be astonished by this site's gallery of
print and TV ads—particularly those featuring
doctor endorsements and those unabashed-
ly targeting teens.

The Story of Grassy Narrows (2016), www.
youtube.com/watch?v=9E06pWtCHIg

- A seven-minute video tells the story of mercury contamination in the Grassy Narrows
community.

Social Change and the Future

15

Reading this chapter will help you to . . .

- Outline and contrast five different models of social change.
- Apply the cycle of civilization to the United States and comment on its applicability.
- Summarize the social changes to which the Luddites were reacting and draw connections to contemporary society.
- Outline Arthur Kroker's idea of the virtual class and discuss its relevance today.

For Starters

Raging against the Machine

The burning of Factorys or setting fire to the property of People we know is not right but Starvation forces Nature to do that which he would not, nor would it reach his Thoughts had he sufficient Employ. We have tried every Effort to live by Pawning our Cloaths and Chattles so we are now on the brink for the last struggle. (cited in Sale, 1996, p. 71)

These words were used in 1802 by an English "cropper" (an independent producer of woollen cloth) to characterize the desperate condition of people who lived by this trade and to describe what he wanted to do to the machines that were so dramatically changing the cropper's way of life. People sharing his view would later be known as Luddites, a term that has become synonymous with a resistance to industrialization or new technology. But the Luddites were not really raging against technology as much as they were raging against the social and political machinery of their time—the "system," in other words. To use an expression we will return to later, they knew that technology was not *socially neutral*, that it produces winners and losers.

In this sense, the Luddites have much in common with those fighting to change the system today, from anti-racism groups like Idle No More and Black Lives Matter to those joining the School Strike for Climate or marching in solidarity with the citizens of Hong Kong. These are the people bringing about social change in our time; maybe you're one of them.

Introduction: Why Predicting the Future Is a Fool's Game

A 2019 poll commissioned by the CBC produced some interesting findings on Canadians' attitudes toward social change (Grenier, 2019). It seems that while a majority of those surveyed considered themselves LGBTQ2-friendly (85 per cent) and were proud of our country's history of tolerance (77 per cent), a sizable majority of respondents (65 per cent) agreed that "we have gone too far in accommodating every group in society," and 56 per cent felt "worried that accepting too many immigrants would change Canada" (Grenier, 2019). It is as though when it comes to social change, Canadians are pleased with how far we have come but worried about going further.

So what exactly do we mean by **social change**? When I use the term, I mean that a group of people has experienced dramatic change in at least one part of their lives and must make adjustments in other areas of their lives in order to adapt. The central fact about society today is that it is changing—quickly. Things are not what they used to be, even just a few years ago. Think of personal technology change: we only have to look back a few years to remember a time before touchscreens and streaming services, Fitbits and Bluetooth headphones—and any of a number of items and apps that first seemed gimmicky and are now indispensable to most people (not me). Some of us can even remember unfolding a map or dialing a phone.

Throughout much of this textbook I have presented trends and events that triggered, exemplified, or proceeded from social change. I have tried to show that these trends and events are subject to different and often equally valid interpretations by groups examining them from different standpoints, depending on such factors as gender, race, class, and so on. In other words, examining social change in the past is no straightforward exercise. Imagine, then, the difficulty of predicting social change in the future.

Ultimately, it's a fool's game. In 1987, no one could have predicted that the divorce rate would peak that year and then decline over the next 25 years. (For that matter, 30 years ago, I could not have predicted that I would get married for a third time—and have that marriage last!) At the start of the twenty-first century, no "futurist" (a consultant who is paid a lot of money to study trends and make predictions that generally don't come true) predicted that within 10 years there would be a black president of the United States, that General Motors would crash, that the Canadian and American governments would bail out and impose tight conditions on the automotive industry (once thought to be the ultimate capitalist industry), and that Ontario would become one of Canada's "have-not" provinces. Of course, no one on New Year's Day 2001 could have foreseen the extraordinary set of social changes that would be set in motion by the events of that now infamous date just eight months and eleven days later.

Another cautionary note concerning any discussion of social change: It is important to recognize that as rapid as change is today, it is wrong to think that earlier society was primarily static, sitting still. Think, for instance, of the Austronesian-speaking people, perhaps as far back as 2000 years ago, who travelled from mainland Southeast Asia to the far-flung islands of Taiwan, Malaysia, Indonesia, Hawaii, Easter Island, New Zealand, and even Madagascar, hundreds of years before the era of modern travel— all in relatively small outrigger canoes. Think, too, of fourteenth-century China, Africa, and Europe, whose populations, recovering from the devastating effects of the Black Plague, saw their cultures change on a large scale. In Europe, surviving labourers of the plague-ravished workforce were able to charge more for their work. Dramatic social change, certainly a defining feature of our present age, is nevertheless not unique to it.

Five Interpretations of Social Change

Any one instance of social change may be interpreted in a number of different ways. No single model of interpretation is the "right" one all the time. The five I will invite you to consider here have varying degrees of applicability to different situations. They are

1. modernism
2. conservatism
3. postmodernism
4. evolution
5. fashion.

As I present each one, I will point out situations where it is and is not likely to apply. First, though, I offer a disclaimer concerning sociological models based on analogy. It comes from American sociologist Robert A. Nisbet (1913–1996), in *Social Change and History: Aspects of the Western Theory of Development*:

> No one has ever seen a civilization die, and it is unimaginable, short of cosmic disaster or thermonuclear holocaust, that anyone ever will. Nor has anyone ever seen a civilization—or culture or institution—in literal process of decay and degeneration, though there is a rich profusion of these words and their synonyms in Western thought. . . . Nor, finally, has anyone ever seen—actually, empirically seen, as we see these things in the world of plants and animals—growth and development in civilizations and societies and cultures, with all that is clearly implied by these words: change proceeding gradually, cumulatively, and irreversibly, through a kind of unfolding of internal potentiality, the whole moving toward some end that is presumably contained in the process from the start. We see none of these in culture: death, degeneration, development, birth. (1969, p. 3)

1. Modernism

Modernism holds that change equals progress, that what is modern or new will automatically be better than the older thing it replaces. It views society as advancing along a straight path from primitive to more sophisticated, from out-of-date to up-to-date, from worse to better. This change is usually portrayed as a single, straight line, one that is not open to different paths of development.

Seen in its best light, the modernist view is the view of the future long envisioned by Gene Roddenberry, creator of *Star Trek*, and captured in the fictional space crew's stated mission "to boldly go where no [hu]man has gone before." Seen in a more sinister light, modernism reduces progress to a formula that equates "new" with "better" and simultaneously "more expensive." Education technology has co-opted the term "advanced learning" without even having to demonstrate that it is in any way more "advanced" or "better" than traditional methods of instruction. Teachers using older methods are portrayed as educational dinosaurs. (My name is John, but you can call me Professor T. Rex. I believe that blackboards and chalk are more reliable than any high tech form of teaching . . .)

The Origins of Modernism

French thinker **Auguste Comte** (1798–1857), often called the modern founder of sociology, was a cheerleader for modernism:

> The true general spirit of social dynamics [i.e. sociology] then consists of each . . . social [state] as the necessary result of the preceding, and the indispensable mover of the following. . . . [T]he present is big [i.e. pregnant] with the future. In this view the object of science is to discover the laws which govern that continuity. (Comte, 1853)

Positivism, which characterized Comte's view and dominated much of the early history of sociology, is an aspect of modernism. Positivism, as defined in Chapter 2, involves a belief that the rules, methods, and presumed objectivity of the natural sciences can be applied to the social sciences with no accommodation made for the biases, or subjectivity, of the social scientist. This is why Comte, in the passage quoted above, feels it's within the sociologist's abilities to examine the course of social history to find the secrets behind the seemingly "inevitable" progress from one period to the next.

Along with Charles Darwin's theory of evolution came the idea, often referred to as **social Darwinism**, that societies naturally proceed from simple (and inferior) to complex (and superior), and that only the strongest societies triumph. This notion of progress was articulated by **Herbert Spencer** (1820–1903), who coined the phrase **survival of the fittest** to refer not to species (as is widely believed) but to societies. The idea that society progresses through distinct stages was developed and put forward by anthropologist **Lewis Henry Morgan** (1818–1881), who identified the three stages of **savagery, barbarism**, and **civilization** (Morgan, [1877]/1964, p. 12).

The following passage from his study of human society lays the groundwork for his argument:

> The latest investigations respecting the early condition of the human race are tending to the conclusion that mankind commenced their career at the bottom of the scale and slowly worked their way up from savagery to civilization through the slow accumulations of experimental knowledge.
>
> As it is undeniable that portions of the human family have existed in a state of savagery, other portions in a state of barbarism, and still other portions in a state of civilization, it seems equally so that these three distinct conditions are connected with each other in a natural as well as necessary sequence of progress. . . .
>
> An attempt will be made in the following pages to bring forward additional evidence of the rudeness of the early condition of mankind, of the gradual evolution of their mental and moral powers through experience, and of their protracted struggle with obstacles while winning their way to civilization. It will be drawn, in part, from the great sequence of inventions and discoveries which stretches along the entire pathway of human progress; but chiefly from domestic institutions, which express the growth of certain ideas and passions. (Morgan, [1877]/1964, p. 11)

The influence of Morgan's three-tiered view of human development lasted well into the twentieth century. Vestiges of it can be seen in **Durkheim**'s *Elementary Forms of Religious Life* (1912) and in the writings of **Talcott Parsons**. In *Societies: Evolutionary and Comparative Perspectives* (1966), Parsons divided societies into the supposedly less judgmental but nevertheless still misleading "primitive," "intermediate," and "modern."

Up until the mid-twentieth century, a key aspect of modernism was the belief that science

They may have dreamt it, but your grandparents likely never believed we would one day be receiving packages delivered by autonomous vehicles. Assess package delivery by drone or autonomous robot from a modernist perspective: What problems does this development solve? What concerns might you have if you didn't believe the modernist credo that technology moves us inexorably to a better world?

and technology would combine to create a material heaven on Earth. Science would become a rational, hard evidence–based religion to supersede the traditional religions built on faith. Technology would free people from having to perform hard physical labour on the job and at home. Thus liberated from drudgery and tedious labour, humans would have abundant leisure time for more worthwhile pursuits. It's easy to smirk at the idealism of the 1950s and early 1960s, but how different is that from the message we hear in TV and radio ads today about the newest form of techie toys? Alexa, can you pass me the remote?

Modernism and Politics

Modernist theories of politics incorporate the idea that societies are constantly improving *politically*. According to this view, societies are becoming more democratic, with respect for human rights on the rise and barriers between societies falling, all of which will help to eradicate the threat of war. Indeed, this was the optimistic premise behind the founding of the United Nations after World War II. A glimpse into that postwar feeling comes from the general introduction to a series of philosophical and religious works put together by liberal, religious-minded Oxford scholars during the 1950s:

> [These readings] will help men and women to find "fullness of life," and peoples to live together in greater understanding and harmony. Today the earth is beautiful, but men are disillusioned and afraid. But there may come a day, perhaps not a distant day, when there will be a renaissance of man's spirit: when men will be innocent and happy amid the beauty of the world, or their eyes will be opened to see that egoism and strife are folly, that the universe is fundamentally spiritual, and that men are the sons of God. (The Editors, "Introduction," cited in Kaizuka, [1956]/2002, p. 8)

It is easy for the leaders of developing empires to use modernist principles to justify their decisions on the grounds that their latest achievement represents the culmination of progress and that whatever is in the best interests of their country is in the best interests of humankind. American public intellectual **Noam Chomsky** (b. 1928) has expressed his concern that American presidents and policymakers have taken this approach, wrapping American policy in the flag of modernism. In *Hegemony or Survival: America's Quest for Global Dominance*, he describes the modernist thinking of the American power elite:

> [T]here is a guiding principle that "defines the parameters within which the policy debate occurs," a consensus so broad as to exclude only "tattered remains" on the right and left and "so authoritative as to be virtually immune to challenge." The principle is *"America as historical vanguard"*: "History has a discernible direction and destination. Uniquely among all the nations of the world, the United States comprehends and manifests history's purpose." Accordingly, US hegemony is the realization of history's purpose, and what it achieves is for common good, the merest truism, so that empirical evaluation is unnecessary, if not faintly ridiculous. (Chomsky, 2004, pp. 42–3)

Chomsky here identifies one of the flaws of the modernist model, namely its **narrow vision**, roughly cast as "Whatever innovation benefits the dominant class is justifiable on the grounds of progress." Today, many are skeptical of modernism. Science, technology, and industry have created problems of pollution that we need to solve more by how we live than by adding more technology. Commercials for SUVs promise personal freedom, yet if we in North America did not manufacture vehicles with such poor fuel efficiency, if we depended less on automobiles and more on bikes and public transit to commute to work and to school, our demand for oil and the consequent damage to our environment would be less.

Meanwhile, human leisure time is not increasing. People with jobs seem to be working longer hours than in decades past in spite of labour-saving technology. The office is now a virtual space, as advances in telecommunications make it more difficult for people to leave their work at the office. Business associates, no matter where they are in the world, are just a Skype call way, day or night, evenings and weekends.

And then there's politics. In 2015, Canadians elected Justin Trudeau as prime minister on his promise of bringing "sunny ways" to Ottawa and a more worldly, empathetic approach to governing. At the time, the United States was still led by its first black president, and it was easy to believe that, in North America at least, we were enjoying a modernist moment of political optimism. But two ethics controversies, including a very public dispute with Jody Wilson-Raybould, his Indigenous attorney general, have made Canadians cynical about Trudeau's ability to deliver a better kind of government that respects Indigenous viewpoints and the voices of women. And then in 2017, Donald Trump took office as president of the United States on a promise to "make America great again"—a pledge that runs counter to the modernist straight-line view of continuous improvement. If, as Chomsky argued, past American presidents have invoked modernist ideals to defend their agenda, Trump has taken that idea and trampled on it. His America-first policy makes no pretense of achieving a "common good" for the rest of the world; in fact, he appears content to operate impetuously and unilaterally without the broad consensus Chomsky describes, much less the support of the "'tattered remains' on the right and left" (Chomsky, 2004, p. 42). His time in office has been marked by growing isolationism, parochialism, and suspicion of others, be they immigrants, racial minorities, political elites, members of the party other than the one I support, or the much maligned (for no good reason) millennials.

Does all of this invalidate political modernism? Not necessarily. A defect in the modernist viewpoint is the notion that improvement occurs *continuously*. It is more realistic to believe that in whatever area of life we apply the modernist lens to—politics, technology, culture—progress takes two steps forward and one step back. It may feel as though we are in the middle of a very large step back, but it does not mean there hasn't been, or won't be, progress.

Where might the modernist view be most valid? When asked this question in the classroom, students typically point to medical technology. Certainly diagnostic and life-saving technology has become more sophisticated, and in this sense it validates a modernist view of progress. At the same time, in some senses reliance on this technology as an alternative to adopting preventative social practices is

> **What Do YOU Think?**
>
> 1. From the seventeenth century into the early 1920s in Canada, European explorers, trading companies, missionaries, and governments brought many changes they thought would improve the lives of people living here. From an Indigenous perspective, which "improvements" might in fact have seemed like the exact opposite?
> 2. Is there an example of social change that does not come at a cost? Consider the answer in terms of social institutions (family, religion, education, health) presented earlier in the book.

not a social improvement. The old saying "an ounce of prevention is worth a pound of cure" seems valid, even if it isn't metric.

2. Conservatism

Conservative thinkers see social change as potentially more *de*structive than *con*structive, especially in emotionally charged areas of life such as family, gender roles, sexuality, and the environment.

It would be easy to dismiss conservatism as an "unrealistic" interpretation of social change held by old-timers or religious fanatics romanticizing the past, by red-necked reactionaries gazing down the gun barrel at anyone attempting to interfere with their rights, or by anti-business, tree-hugging nature "freaks." It would be wrong to do so. Some values and customs, such as community and "neighbourliness," need to be preserved. Their loss is neither inevitable nor desirable.

Conservatism as it relates to social change should not be confused with the political principles of right-wing, large-C Conservative parties in Canada, Britain, Australia, and New Zealand. An excellent example of small-c conservatism is found in the nationalist sentiment of **George Grant** (1918–1988), one of Canada's foremost conservative public intellectuals. Grant taught philosophy at McMaster, Dalhousie, and Queen's. His *Lament for a Nation* (1965) is recognized as a landmark of Canadian writing. His concern, as expressed in

Everett Collection Inc /Alamy Stock Photo

The modernist view of society's continued improvement is countered in popular culture by the popularity of post-apocalyptic dystopias presenting a future world that is much worse than the one we currently inhabit. (Think, for example, of *Black Mirror*, *The Handmaid's Tale*, or recent book and movie franchises such as *The Hunger Games* and *Divergent*.) Why do you think we spend so much time contemplating society's inevitable demise?

Lament and in *Technology and Empire* (1969), was that the technology, culture, and sense of progress emanating from the United States would lead to the destruction of Canada as a place that cultivated and cherished an alternative to the American vision. A man of deep religious convictions, he inspired Canadian nationalists across the political spectrum.

I mentioned earlier the modernist belief that science will ultimately replace traditional religion. So far this has not happened, and I bet on the side of it won't happen. Humans, it would appear, have spiritual needs, however defined, that science cannot completely address. We see, in the enduring strength of conservative religion in the United States and in the battles that proponents of non-scientific "intelligent design" or "scientific creationism" are mounting against the scientific fact of evolution, that the modernist vision of the new religion of science has not overcome the old religions of faith.

One of the ideas closely associated with conservatism is that of the **cycle of civilization**. This is

the belief that civilizations rise and fall in a predictable cycle. It was early articulated by Greek historian Polybius (*c.* 200–*c.* 118 BCE) in explaining to his fellow Greeks how the Roman Empire came to have dominance over them, while warning the Romans about the potential for their collapse:

[T]he destruction of the human race, as tradition tells us, has more than once happened, and as we must believe will often happen again, all arts and crafts perishing at the same time, then in the course of time, when springing from the survivors as from seeds men have again increased in numbers. (cited in Nisbet, 1969, p. 34)

Historian Oswald Spengler, in *The Decline of the West* (1918–22), took a similar view when he wrote that civilization was passing "through the age-phases of the individual man. It has its childhood, youth, manhood, and old age" (cited in Nisbet, 1969, p. 8). Adherents of conservatism are sometimes guilty of the logical fallacy known as **slippery-slope** reasoning. This occurs when they cite one instance of social change—say, for example, gay marriage—as evidence of the imminent collapse of the entire social order (including, to keep with this particular example, polygamy and bestiality). It is an overreaction.

Another pitfall of the conservative position is a tendency to project backwards an idealized picture of social life from which the modern world is said to have fallen. For instance, people who bemoan what they consider the rampant sexual promiscuity occurring today speak in idealized terms of a time when couples would not engage in sex before marriage. They are misinformed. British social historian Peter Laslett (1971) wrote about how it was common in the late sixteenth century for couples to contract marriage (like our engagement) and then immediately live together for months, with full sexual benefits. In his conclusion to a discussion of the county of Leicester, Laslett observes that "brides in Leicestershire at this time must normally have gone to their weddings in the early, and sometimes in the late, stages of pregnancy" (1971, p. 150). Donald Trump's vow to "make American great again" is meant to arouse nostalgia for an unspecified, idealized past that was never as great as his conservative followers remember or imagine it.

Sometimes modernism and conservatism combine in theories that view signs of decline as indications that progress is on the horizon. In **Marx**'s thinking, the worse capitalism got, with the shrinking of the bourgeoisie and the growth of the proletariat to include a falling middle class, the more likely capitalism would collapse altogether, leading to the ultimate social change, the communist revolution. With a similar perspective, albeit from a very different position, conservative Americans who believe in fundamentalist Christianity often look upon environmental, economic, political, and social (i.e. moral) decline in their country as a sign that the world is on the verge of the apocalypse. American movies and TV shows often reflect an apocalyptic or dystopic view (the negative opposite of utopian view). American writer Kirkpatrick Sale (2005) cites a survey, commissioned by conservative media *Time* and CNN, that indicates 59 per cent of Americans polled believed the apocalypse was just around the corner.

Photo by Jon Kopaloff/FilmMagic

Joy Villa (Princess Joy Villa to some) is an American-born singer-songwriter whose mother's ancestry is African American and Choctaw, and whose father's ancestry is Argentinian. And, as the dress she wore to the 2017 Grammys makes clear, she is an ardent supporter of Donald Trump. Do you think she fits the typical profile of those who support Donald Trump's pledge to "make America great again"?

A Case Study in Social Change and Conservatism: The Luddites

From 1811 to 1813, beginning in the English industrializing area of Nottinghamshire and spreading to Yorkshire and Manchester, a group of independent textile workers took desperate measures into their hands by destroying what would today amount to millions of dollars' worth of property. In the words of Kirkpatrick Sale, they were "rebels against the future" (1996). Part of a larger movement occurring at the time in Britain, France, Germany, and the United States, they made nighttime raids to destroy

Quick Hits

The Impending Collapse of the American Empire?

A good example of modern conservatist thinking is an argument Kirkpatrick Sale makes in his essay "Imperial Entropy: Collapse of the American Empire" (2005). Sale regards the United States as an empire, and therefore subject to what he believes is the inevitable fate of all empires: collapse.

Sale points to four things that have toppled empires of the past and could bring about the collapse of the American empire:

- environmental degradation

- economic meltdown (through excessive resource exploitation)
- military overstretch
- domestic dissent and upheaval.

I would add "decline in creativity" to this list, as evidenced in American television, movies, and music. Think of how many recent Hollywood movies are remakes and spinoffs of successful franchises like Marvel Studios' Infinity Saga. Think of the endless mill of procedural crime shows on Netflix.

What Do YOU Think?

1. Do you think that the United States can be considered an empire like the Greek, Roman, Mongol, Ottoman, British, and Soviet empires?
2. Do you agree with Sale that the decline or collapse of the United States is inevitable? Given the divisiveness of the country's current political climate, could it be occurring right now?

machinery, sent anonymous threatening letters to known industrialists, stockpiled weapons, and participated in food riots in the marketplace.

They were called **Luddites**, after a mythical, Robin Hood–like figure, Edward (Ned) Ludd, whose precise origin is unknown. They were skilled tradesmen—croppers (finishers of wool cloth), wool combers, handloom wool weavers—who in the late eighteenth century worked out of their homes and made good wages. They had leisure time probably similar to that of most Canadians today, and were part of strongly linked small communities.

But the work of the Luddites was becoming obsolete. While in 1812, in Yorkshire, there were about 5000 croppers, within a generation there were virtually none. Huge steam-driven machines owned by the rising class of factory owners, combined with new business practices, were changing the working and social world. Even with the earliest generation of machines, one person could do the work of five or six. Contrary to the tradition surrounding the old-fashioned machine-hating Luddites, the social practices accompanying the machines were just as

much the enemy. A typical workday in the new factories averaged 12 to 14 hours in length, sometimes as many as 16 to 18, and people worked six days a week. Children as young as four and women were hired in preference to men, and they made up a great majority of the workforce (80 per cent, according to Sale). They received about a third of a man's wages, and were thought to be less likely than men to resist owner oppression.

Desperate poverty for millions of people resulted. Life expectancy dropped drastically. In the rough statistics for 1830, it was reckoned that 57 per cent of the people of Manchester died before the age of five. While the life expectancy at birth for people throughout England and Wales was 40, for labourers in the textile manufacturing cities of Manchester and Leeds, it was thought to be about 18 (Sale, 1996, p. 48).

Working conditions were not the only social change the Luddites rebelled against. They also opposed the **manufacturing of need**. One of the most profound social changes accompanying the Industrial Revolution and the manufacture of consumer goods was the sudden creation of a need where people had once been mostly self-sufficient. Food and clothing now had to be purchased rather than produced at home. The social change this brought about was neatly summed up by nineteenth-century British writer Thomas Carlyle in *The Gospel of Mammonism* (1843): "We have profoundly forgotten everywhere that *Cash-payment* is not the sole relation of human beings" (quoted in Sale, 1996, p. 39). This trend, described by French historian Fernand Braudel as "a revolution in demand," extended from Britain to the colonies—particularly India, where millions of consumers were created by the dumping of manufactured cloth from Britain. It was not until the 1930s and 1940s, with the peaceful intervention of Gandhi and the lesser-known Muslim Pathan Badshah Khan (leader of the Khudai Khidmatgar), that the people of India began to boycott British cloth and make their own, as had been their tradition.

A remarkable aspect of the Luddite social movement was its solidarity. Despite the rich rewards paid to those who would snitch on their neighbours, despite the torture alleged to have been used on those who were caught, there were few informers. In all, 24 Luddites were hanged, and about an equal number died in the raids; a similar number were put in prison, while at least 37 were sent to the prison colony of Australia.

What did they achieve? There were a few short-term gains for the Luddites. Wages were raised slightly in areas where the Luddites had been the most active. Social reform got on the political agenda, although it would be a long time before significant changes were made. And the "poor laws," which administered what we might today call social welfare, received more attention and greater funding, although charities continued to carry the greater part of the welfare load.

Perhaps the main accomplishment of the Luddites lies in what they can teach us today about social change and what Sale calls the "machine question." We need to realize that technology is not socially neutral. It creates certain kinds of jobs but destroys others. The Luddites were not backward-looking "loonies" refusing to face the inevitability of technological "progress." They wanted an alternative future, an alternative modern. That progress can take many forms is perhaps the most important lesson of the

What Do YOU Think?

1. Why can it be said that technology is not neutral in terms of social change?
2. The term *Luddite* today is most often applied to someone considered too small-minded to embrace change. Is this a fair way to characterize the original Luddites? Were they unable to understand "progress," or did they understand progress too well?
3. Forty years ago you could not pull your car into any gas station and fill it up yourself: you required an attendant to do this for you. Banking transactions were most commonly conducted in person, not through a machine. Today, self-serve checkout lines have replaced many drugstore and grocery store cashiers. If you have been through an airport recently, think of all the technology you were forced to interact with there. I am thinking particularly of kiosk-crazy Pearson Airport in Toronto. What are the benefits of these changes? Are there any other than profit for big corporations? Do they have negative impacts on society? Whom does this kind of change benefit the most? Whom does it harm?

Luddite movement. It's why I never bristle when my tech-addicted colleagues call me a Luddite.

Opposing Globalization: A Conservatist Stance

There are fundamentally two kinds of opposition to globalization: particularist and universalist. **Particularist protectionist** opponents of globalization focus on the socioeconomic, political, and cultural problems caused in their home territory by increasing processes of globalization. In Manfred Steger's words,

> Fearing the loss of national self-determination and the destruction of their cultures, they pledge to protect their traditional ways of life from those "foreign elements" they

In August 2019, the Russian space agency sent its life-sized humanoid robot Fedor up to the International Space Station to learn to work like an astronaut. Advances in AI—artificial intelligence—bring us face to face with what Kirkpatrick Sale calls "the machine question." Would you go to a humanoid dentist, lawyer, realtor, or teacher? What would be lost other than good jobs for humans with such humanoids?

consider responsible for unleashing the forces of globalization. (2003, p. 114)

Particularist protectionists are a mixed group. They include **Islamists** who oppose globalization with narrow-minded and very distorted fundamentalist notions of Islam (al-Qaeda and ISIS are examples). They also include European ethnic entrepreneurs, who use principles of particularist protectionism to defend their campaign for "racial/national purity." They include British citizens who voted in 2016 to leave the European Union in order to safeguard British jobs for "British" workers.

Particular protectionists also include Americans who argue that skilled and unskilled trade workers are losing their jobs to citizens of the developing world, and are not benefitting from economic globalization the way the power elite are. While they

sometimes identify "big business" as the culprit, it is often easier to blame Japanese-owned firms, outsourced workers in India, or immigrants, legal or otherwise. British sociologist Roland Robertson, who taught for a time in the United States at the University of Pittsburgh, wrote the following for a Japanese publication in 1997:

I can assure you that the *anti*-global sentiment is very, very strong in the United States of America. It is playing a key part in the current campaign to decide which candidate should run for president from the Republican Party; the phrase "anti-globalism" is a significant one in American politics; there are numerous movements which are directed in opposition to the teaching of the subject of globalization, to so-called "international education"; there have been people protesting at school boards all over America about American children learning about other countries; they fear that if they learn about ancient Greek philosophy or about Japanese religion or French philosophy, that their minds will be destroyed, in other words, that their views will be relativized.

That was in 1997. Much more recently, the same anti-globalism sentiment (except in the military sense) was central to both the Republican and the Democratic races. Opposition to free trade, and to foreigners generally, helped push Donald Trump to victory in the campaign for the Republican Party nomination. On the Democratic side, the particular-protectionist ideas of Bernie Sanders kept him in the race against Hillary Clinton long after pundits thought he would disappear.

Is particular protectionism a bad policy? From a Canadian perspective, a certain amount of particularist protection would seem necessary. Only about

The Point Is...

A Modernist Might Argue that Political Globalization Spreads Democracy

Political globalization, as defined by **Manfred Steger** (b. 1961), is "the intensification and expansion of political interrelations across the globe" (Steger, 2003, p. 56). It is manifest in the United Nations and its affiliated organizations, as well as regional coalitions such as the European Union and NATO (the North Atlantic Treaty Organization). Political globalization also involves NGOs (non-government organizations) such as Amnesty International and Greenpeace.

Champions of globalization, taking a modernist view of change, argue that it benefits many countries by spreading democracy (Steger, 2003, p. 110). The validity of this claim depends on how broadly **democracy** is defined. At the foundation of a democracy is a government elected by its citizens. But this is a rather thin definition. Merely holding a vote for a leader does not guarantee democracy. In the former Soviet Union, citizens would go through the exercise of voting for the one name on the ballot. And how many people must be allowed to vote in order for there to be a true democracy? A broader definition of democracy might include features such as

- an electorate that is broad-based in terms of gender, class, ethnicity, and race
- freedom of the press and freedom of speech

- freedom of association and of travel (within and between countries)
- the presence of a viable opposition (and one that does not literally fear for its life)
- a system of education in which people can teach and take courses critical of society's institutions
- protection of the rights of minorities
- equality of men and women.

Thin democracy might be spreading, but broad democracy really is not.

Around the time of the US-led invasion of Iraq in 2003, there was a joke going around that George W. Bush was trying to bring democracy to Iraq—and if it worked there, he was going to try to bring it to Florida (the deciding state in the 2000 presidential election, which became the focus of allegations of voter fraud). The joke raises an interesting question: When *do* we have democracy? A typical definition of democracy involves some notion of government by citizens. Note the Greek root of the word, *demos*–, meaning "the people." But the ancient Greeks, who coined the term, can hardly be said to have had democracy themselves. Women and the large class of slaves were excluded from having a voice.

What are the analytical alternatives to "democracy" when describing a society? In

Continued

A Preface to Democratic Theory (1956), American political scientist and sociologist **Robert A. Dahl** (1915–2014) suggested that modern industrial states were governed by **polyarchies**, shifting coalitions of powerful interest groups. In *Power Elite*, published that same year, **C. Wright Mills** disagreed, arguing that the power elite, who ran the big companies and had the most significant say in government, was not a shifting group but one that was relatively stable. In essence, he claimed that there was an **oligarchy**, rule by a few powerful individuals or groups. Russia is often said to be governed by oligarchs today. Kirkpatrick Sale (1980) has argued that democracy cannot exist in a population over 10,000, so that we can have only relative degrees of democracy in state-level societies. While the actual number can be debated, the basic premise seems sound.

What Do YOU Think?

What features would have to be in place in any society for it to be considered relatively "democratic"? In what ways would you consider Canada "democratic" and "undemocratic"?

AP Photo/Frank Augstein

In 2016, the people of Britain voted to withdraw from the European Union, an economic association of countries promoting open borders and the free movement of goods and of people. Three years later (at time of writing), "Brexit" has yet to occur. What view of social change best characterizes the sentiment of those who voted to leave the EU and "put the Great back in Britain?"

2 per cent of the movies we watch are Canadian, despite the fact that there is a relatively successful movie production business in Toronto, Vancouver, and Montreal. Think of how often you have seen someone play the part of an American president in a movie. Can you ever remember seeing a movie with someone cast as the Canadian prime minister? Our stories are not being told on film, except in Quebec, where French-language films are being produced for the domestic market. Canadian content rules and specially funded programs have helped many of our musicians begin careers in the face of the competition from the loud voices to the south.

While particularist protectionists argue that globalization causes social, cultural, and political problems in their own countries, **universalist protectionists**, as Steger describes them, promote the interests of the poor and marginalized groups worldwide (Steger, 2003, p. 115). Amnesty International, Doctors Without Borders, and similar organizations can be seen as universalist protectionist, taking up the cause of those hurt by globalization worldwide.

3. Postmodernism

Postmodernism, as a social theory, relates largely to voice. It challenges the notion that researchers can speak for peoples that they study without letting the people studied themselves have a voice. Postmodernism disputes the argument that anyone can, with any authority, talk of progress or decline broadly across all society. Instead, a sociologist with a postmodernist perspective might ask, *Progress for which group(s)? Decline for which group(s)?* The same sociologist, hearing conservatives complain about how Canadian values are eroding, might wonder if what they really mean is that *their* ethnic group with *its* set of values is no longer dominating as it once did.

Think of how modernist media present advances in technology as bringing about benefits to everyone. But how often do you hear or read the opinions of those, even within Canada, who cannot afford high-speed internet access or a computer that is less than five years old? There continues to be, both globally and locally, a **digital divide** that separates those with the technology to learn, work, and compete in the modern world from those without. One person known for thinking this way is Arthur Kroker.

Arthur Kroker and the Virtual Class

Arthur Kroker, of the University of Victoria's political science department, is a Canadian futurist who advanced the notion of the **virtual class** in the mid-1990s as part of his conservatist position. His writing combines Marxist views on class with a lot of postmodernist wordplay (which can make him hard to read). His work is difficult to summarize in an introductory textbook because it depends on a great deal of jargon. However, I can give you a taste of what Kroker has to say.

The virtual class, according to Kroker, is a class of visionary capitalists or, as he calls them,

> visionless-cynical-business capitalists, and theperhapsvisionary,perhapsskill-oriented, perhaps indifferent techno-intelligentsia of cognitive scientists, engineers, computer scientists, video-game developers, and all the other communication specialists, ranged in hierarchies, but all dependent for their economic support on the drive to virtualization. (Kroker & Weinstein, 1995, pp. 15–16)

We will briefly outline three ways in which this diverse group acts like a **class**.

First, says Kroker, this class is responsible for the loss of jobs by those who do not belong to the class. This group supports the goals of a **neoliberalism** that promotes the interests of big business. This is how Kroker accounts for the corporate downsizing that became a widespread cost-saving strategy among North American businesses during the early 1990s:

> Against economic justice, the virtual class practices a mixture of predatory capitalism and gung-ho technical rationalizations for laying waste to social concerns for employment, with insistent demands for "restructuring economies," "public policies of labor adjustment," and "deficit cutting," all aimed at maximal profitability. (Kroker & Weinstein, 1995, p. 5)

Another example of the virtual class's move for power has to do with its role in the way the internet,

The Point Is...

Those Left Behind by Globalization May Turn to Nihilism

In an editorial for a January 2015 issue of *The New York Times*' Sunday Review, political philosopher Kenan Malik characterized Islamist attacks such as the one on the editorial offices of *Charlie Hebdo*, the Taliban attacks on schools in Pakistan, and the Boko Haram kidnapping of schoolgirls in Nigeria as examples of nihilism. Central to this brand of **nihilism** is the rejection of traditional moral principles, including those articulated in the Qur'an.

Malik points out that nihilism was not always a feature of the radical politics of Africa and Asia. For most of the twentieth century the radical politics of the region embodied a Marxist stand against imperialism and a desire to bring the non-Western world into modernity. However, when that failed, modernity itself became the target of hatred and anger. The result, as Malik contends, is "the transformation of anti-Western sentiment from a political challenge to imperialist policy to an inchoate [i.e., just begun, not fully formed] rage against modernity" (2015).

Many people in the West would agree that anti-West radicalism is to be expected given the way North American and European powers have exploited the people of these areas. As a radical ideology, Islamic extremism presents a significant challenge to Western ideals and globalization generally. Recently, though, nihilism has been taking on a different appearance in the form of domestic terrorism. Examples include the Quebec City mosque shooting, in which 6 people were shot and killed (January 2017); the Norway attacks that killed 77 people (July 2011); the Tree of Life Synagogue shooting that killed 11 people in Pittsburgh, Pennsylvania (October 2018); the Christchurch, New Zealand, mosque shootings, in which 51 people were killed (March 2019); and the mass shooting at a Walmart store in El Paso, Texas, that claimed the lives of 22 people (August 2019). All of these crimes were carried out by young, white men motivated by their hatred of racial and ethnic minorities and vehemently opposed to immigration. They are white supremacists who act violently and with disregard for human life on their believe that certain ideals of globalization, notably the loosening of borders to allow the freer movement of people and goods, threatens the purity of the white "race." They lack a unifying claim for Christian purity, but, since his election, all seem to quote Donald Trump.

What Do YOU Think?

1. How would you interpret nihilist movements from a modernist, conservativist, and post-modernist perspective?
2. Some would argue that Islamic terrorists are united, at least ostensibly, in their devotion to religious ideals (even though violence is not part of the Muslim faith); white supremacists, while they may find encouragement for their ideas online, tend to act alone, and in their rejection of traditional moral and religious ideals may be better examples of nihilists. Would you agree?

once democratic and freely accessible, became restricted by the authoritarian "digital superhighway" ever more controlled by what Kroker calls "privileged corporate codes." To use an example close to my own heart, online access to sociology journals is being more and more limited to those who possess expensive memberships and those who are affiliated with universities and not community colleges. Now retired, I don't have such access to those journals.

What Do YOU Think?

1. How does Kroker portray the virtual class as a class in the Marxist sense?
2. Do you think that Kroker leans a little too far toward conspiracy theory in his worldview?

The third defining characteristic of the virtual class is the way this group, according to Kroker, restricts the freedom of creativity, promoting instead "the value of pattern-maintenance (of its own choosing)" (Kroker & Weinstein, 1995, p. 5). Have you ever noticed how computer-generated zombies, ghosts, and aliens all look remarkably alike? How often have you seen black smoke issuing from people possessed by demons? This is an example of "pattern maintenance": the tools of the trade are controlled by a few companies.

4. Evolution

Evolution is perhaps the most misused of all scientific concepts. The biological term does not refer to general progress or improvement of a species. What it means is adapting well to particular circumstances. Darwin's use of Spencer's phrase "survival of the fittest" is best interpreted as "survival of the *best fit*"—the one best suited to the environment. It was not about the biggest, the meanest, the fastest, and so on.

Jonathan Weiner, in *The Beak of the Finch: A Story of Evolution in Our Time* (1995), provides an example of evolution when he explains that guppies swimming in the rivers of Venezuela come in two basic colour patterns. High in the hills, where the rivers are little more than streams, the guppies are brightly coloured. They compete in terms of sexual selection, with the most colourful having the greatest chance of attracting a mate. The bright colours are the result of the competition. In the waters down in the valleys, the guppies swim where deep-water predators feed upon those guppies that are easily seen. Not surprisingly, the guppies there are less brightly coloured. The competition has less to do with attracting a mate and more to do with not being seen by predators. Neither colour pattern represents an improvement in the species. Each is a better fit in the local environment.

How does this apply to social change? We can look at the history of the family structure in Canada as an example. At different times, the number of children born to parents has varied. In times and places where agriculture was the primary source of income, the number of children was relatively high, since children grow up to be good unpaid help to work the land. During the 1950s and early 1960s, the number of children went up, going against the trend of previous decades, because it was a time of prosperity. People could afford to have more children. Today, with increasing urbanization, Canadian families are less likely to require children as labour; well-paying jobs require more postsecondary education, delaying the point at which young families are in a comfortable position to start having children, and it is generally more expensive to raise children today. Couples today may choose to have just one child or no children at all out of environmental considerations. Hence, the birth rate has declined. The "ideal" number of children changes with the circumstances—just like the colours of the Venezuelan guppies.

5. Fashion

Sometimes a change is just change for its own sake. Our tastes change, we seek novelty, and the result is neither an improvement nor a turn for the worse. And it does not reflect some deeper meaning, or a value shift. In this case, we have the **fashion** model of change. Fashion here does not refer strictly to physical appearances, such as changing tastes in clothing or décor. In fact, it could be argued that trends in clothing and design are driven primarily by commercial interests; they certainly stand to gain from people's desire for the new. Stanley Lieberson (2000) has argued that the change in North American baby names falls into the category of fashion. Certain names cycle in and out of popularity with the main cause being our search for novelty. Emulating the baby-naming practices of celebrities is another cause.

An example of a changing social fashion is the recent growth in popularity of board games. Tabletop games have been commercially produced in North America since the mid-nineteenth century, when they were designed for the moral instruction of children. From the 1960s to the 1980s, board games were a popular way for families to spend leisure time together, and for adults to socialize with friends at home. Board games fell out of fashion during the late twentieth century, owing largely to the booming popularity of video games; they were the last resort of children stuck inside on a rainy day at a home or cottage without access to better (typically, electronic) forms of entertainment. Yet the tabletop game is enjoying a renaissance among young adults, fuelling (and in turn fuelled by) the spread of bars and cafés where people can meet to play their favourite board games, both classic and new. The nostalgia for pre-internet '80s culture among millennials and the digital natives of Generation Z is part of a broader course correction against the pervasiveness of digital technology; however, it would be wrong to suggest it represents an outright rejection of digital culture—many board game players still carry iPhones and are actively involved in social media. The growth in popularity of board games has interesting social consequences, since it encourages in-person, face-to-face patterns of interaction that online gaming, and social media generally, does not allow. The board game café has also emerged as an important social alternative to clubs and house parties for young people who don't drink or who are more introverted.

Education involves fashion changes, too. Catchy phrases such as "whole language," "collaborative learning," and "adaptive learning" are used to promote new styles in education, but they often reflect people's need to feel they have a fresh approach to an age-old problem. Education fashions come and go, but real improvement or decline is hard to measure. The culture around education changes and has an impact on the scores that quantify educational "excellence." Declining marks in North American literacy tests may reflect educational changes, but they might also reflect an increase in the number of students whose first language is not English, and a decrease in reading as a leisure activity when video games are ever-present. Declining performance in math tests have sparked a "back to basics" approach that emphasizes memorization in favour of experiential learning, discovery math, and other in vogue pedagogical techniques. Repeat after me: two times one is two; two times two is four; two times three is six . . .

What Do YOU Think?

1. A millennial suggested to me that the popularity of board game cafés is partly a product of an indebted, frugal culture that borrows rather than buys. Would you agree?
2. Vaping and juuling have become popular among students at Canadian high schools, colleges, and universities, much to the consternation of parents, educators, and healthcare professionals. Can this be described as a fashion trend—change for the sake of novelty—or is there something more significant to it?

Tattoos

The American poet T.S. Eliot (1888–1965) once wrote, "Art never improves, but . . . the material of art is never quite the same."

The number of people who have tattoos has increased greatly over the last two decades. Estimates have it that one in five adults in the West has at least one, whether it is boldly presented on an arm or neck or tucked away secretly in a place far from public view. How would a sociologist look at that aspect of social change? Here are several ways.

First, there is a traditional association of tattoos with marginalized people: prisoners, sailors, prostitutes, and people in circus side-shows (also sometimes called freak shows). Second, it is generational: people in their twenties and thirties (and increasingly their forties and fifties) are the most likely to have tattoo in the highest numbers. Third, it is gender-related: more women than men sport body art.

What happens when the tattoo, a traditional demonstration of **deviance**, comes into conflict with mainstream values and attitudes? It becomes a social issue, as we have seen in the hiring practices of many employers, particularly those in retail. Andrew Timming, a sociologist teaching in the School of Management at the University of St Andrews, Scotland, presented a paper at a 2013 conference of the British Sociological Association. He had interviewed 15 managers (aged 30 to 60+) with responsibility for

Across the Board Game Café, Winnipeg. Picture by Michael Linton

Viewed through the lens of conservatism, the popularity of board games today is not just the result of a search for novelty, but an expression of conservative values manifested in a rejection of digital culture. Do you view board game culture through the lens of conservatism or fashion? Do you think this bustling board game café in Winnipeg will still be there in five years? In ten?

hiring about how they reacted to job candidates with visible tattoos. His findings:

"Most respondents agreed that visible tattoos are a stigma," Dr Timming told the conference. One woman manager told him that "they make a person look dirty." Another male manager told him "subconsciously that would stop me from employing them." Another male manager said "tattoos are the first thing they [fellow recruiters] talk about when the person has gone out of the door."

The managers were concerned about what their organisations' customers might think, said Dr Timming. "Hiring managers realise that, ultimately, it does not matter what they think of tattoos—what really

matters, instead, is how customers might perceive employees with visible tattoos.

"Respondents expressed concern that visibly tattooed workers may be perceived by customers to be 'abhorrent', 'repugnant', 'unsavoury' and 'untidy'. It was surmised that customers might project a negative service experience based on stereotypes that tattooed people are thugs and druggies."

One woman manager told him: "We all judge people on first impressions and what we sum up is quite quick. When they [customers] walk in the door and see that there's a receptionist with guns or knives tattooed, or 'hate' tattooed, I think that is something that would be uncomfortable." (Sage, 2013)

There are a few things I can add to this. One, as we can see from the last sentence, responses are based at least partly on the nature of the tattoos. The more aggressive the tattoo, the less acceptable it is. This can give a hiring advantage to women, who *typically* sport more modest decorations. Second, there are cases where having a tattoo would be an advantage, something Timming also noted. He mentioned people who work with prisoners as an example. Third—and this is a question closely tied to our interpretations of social change—as time passes, a tattoo in the workplace has become more and more acceptable and will continue to do so. Imagine a student with a tattoo working part-time at Canadian Tire today and regarded with suspicion by some customers: she will likely finish school, graduate, enter a profession, and then return to the same store as a customer to be waited on by a young person with a tattoo. Will she give it even a second glance? Knowing about how tattoos are driven by fashion, I am often tempted to say to multi-tattooed men, "Your grandchildren will mock you." I don't, however, as some of those guys look pretty tough. I do feel comfortable talking to men following the trend for long beards.

Primeop76/iStockphoto

This woman's tattoo is likely not a barrier to her being employed as a restaurant server. Is that because she is benefitting from a gender double-standard or because her body art is situated somewhere where it can be concealed? Or have we, as a society, simply stopped caring about people's tattoos?

What Do YOU Think?

1. A similar **stigma** was once attached to men with long hair (personal experience). In what ways would this be similar to having a tattoo? In what ways different?

2. In what other workplaces might there be an advantage to having visible tattoos? What workplaces would show the greatest resistance to tattooed employees?

3. Do you agree that women are more likely than men to have tattoos, but that their tattoos are likely to be more modest? If so, why do you think this is?

4. Some people have argued that we have reached "peak tattoo"—that it's a fad that is nearing its end now that the novelty, and perhaps the stigma, of having a tattoo is fading. Can you see a time where tattoos are once again viewed more negatively than positively?

Social Change in Canada: Two Case Studies

Canadians have been and are experiencing social change in many forms. In earlier chapters, we have looked at how social change is playing out in all aspects of life, from the family and education to health and culture. The following sections present two striking, and very different, examples of recent social change in Canada.

Social Change and the Decline of the Cod Fishery in Newfoundland and Labrador

One of the most devastating social changes to hit any part of Canada in recent decades is the loss of the cod fishery in Newfoundland and Labrador. Sociologists Lawrence Hamilton and Cynthia Duncan and biologist Richard Haedrich (2004) have described how that change has affected communities along the province's Northern Peninsula.

As the three researchers explain, the most fisheries-dependent part of the province, the Northern Peninsula, was hardest hit by the closure of the cod fishery, which had sustained the region for centuries. The first signs of trouble appeared in the 1970s, when it became apparent that cod stocks were diminishing, owing largely to overfishing by foreign vessels and mismanagement of the resource. When, in 1976, the 200-mile economic exclusion zone was declared, reserving waters within 200 nautical miles of the shore for Canadian fishers, many in the province thought that the troubles were over. People who had left returned, and the fishing population grew.

Sociologically and technologically, there were two different cod fisheries in Newfoundland: the dragger, or long-liner, fishery, and the in-shore fishery. The first made use of larger boats, more technology, and longer trips. Traditionally, both were profitable, and the fishing community overall was very egalitarian. And in the "glory years" following the establishment of the 200-mile line, the dragger fleet increased, as did the catch, which reached unprecedented levels. Dragger captains made huge profits, some as much as $350,000 to $600,000 a year, and even sharemen (often the teenage sons of dragger boat owners) could earn $50,000 a year. But the in-shore fishery started to suffer. In the words of one fisher, "Guys were makin' big bucks and the other guys were just survivin'. Just livin' from day to day, where the other guys were drivin' fancy skidoos and two vehicles" (cited in Hamilton, Duncan, & Haedrich, 2004). The community was more financially divided than ever before.

Eventually, the cod fishery crashed. In 1992, the federal government declared a two-year moratorium on the fishery from the Labrador coast to the southeastern tip of Newfoundland, temporarily suspending cod fishing in this part of the province;

the following year, the closure area was expanded to include the southern shore of the island. Although it was supposed to be in effect for just two years, the moratorium has yet to be lifted.

It was not just fishers and their families who were hit by the moratorium but others along the chain of the fishing industry. At a local fish-processing plant on the Northern Peninsula, 400 workers were laid off.

Different adaptations occurred among the people in the area. For instance, the birth rate went down, from one of the highest in Canada to just slightly above the national average. Some of the dragger captains were well placed to shift their prey species from fish to invertebrates, such as snow crab, northern shrimp, and the more traditional lobster. Fortunately for them, government money was available to make the transition easier. This new fishery brought revenues comparable to those of the glory days of the cod fishery, but these were distributed across a much smaller segment of the local population.

Many, forced out of their livelihoods, had to leave the province to look for a new line of work. Young people especially travelled west to find work on Alberta's oil fields, and you can see the oil field money in some parts of the province, where earnings made outside of the province have been returned to family members left behind.

Others who remained could not afford to become involved in the new fishery, yet refused to move off the island because they didn't feel they could leave their home. The province invested heavily in its own offshore oil industry, but a growing percentage of the local income came from government transfer payments in the form of employment insurance and welfare. The most recent hope, at least for the provincial government, lies with Muskrat Falls, a huge energy project to harvest hydroelectric power in the lower Churchill River in Labrador.

Beginning in 2012, twenty years after the moratorium was imposed, northern cod stocks finally began to show signs of a noticeable, albeit modest, recovery, and by 2014, the total biomass of cod off the northeastern Newfoundland had climbed to 238,000 tons, roughly half of what it was at its peak in 1990 (450,000 [Thornhill Verma, 2019]). In 2019, a federal report

Telling It Like It Is

Four-Letter Words and Social Change, or How I Learned to Love the F-Bomb

I don't remember the first time I heard the "f-word" used, but I do recall that in the suburban, middle-class junior high school that I attended in the early 1960s, there was one really tough guy, feared by everyone, who seemed to use it in every sentence he spoke. He was eventually expelled for hitting a teacher.

The first movie I heard the f-word uttered in was the 1970 film *Joe*. It was carefully and deliberately used for shock effect by the character played by Peter Boyle, a working-class guy who stuns his polite upper-middle-class companions by shouting, "Fucking right!"

The one and only time I heard the word spoken in a university classroom was when a very well-spoken classmate of mine used it (with implied quotation marks around it) after the word "mind," to refer to someone trying to psyche someone out. Her male classmates were dumbstruck.

As far as I can remember, the mores, or customs, surrounding the use of the word as I was growing up in my middle-class neighbourhood were these: I could, as a teenage boy, use the word (but not too frequently) with my buddies, but never with my parents or teachers (no matter how tempted I was on occasion to tell them all to f— off). I would not use the word in front of a girl or woman, ever. Generally, use of the f-word in front of a woman was considered a vile offence committed by a man too drunk, too stoned, or too angry to realize what he was doing. Use of the word *by* a woman would normally illicit shock and disgust.

That was a different time. Now, and in the Toronto college where I used to teach, use of the word seems to depend on location. It was in the general concourse that I first started hearing the word regularly, between 15 and 20 years ago, and it is where I used to hear it most often. True, it is on the premises of the college, but it isn't really a site of education; it is more of a public place. Then I started to hear the f-word in the halls between classrooms. About 10 years ago I heard the word spoken for the first time in my classroom. It wasn't spoken in anger, but it

announced that the biomass of cod's spawning stock was higher than the 2018 forecast (McKenzie-Sutter, 2019), which was good news for the hard-luck province. But cod stocks overall remain in the critical zone, and it is not known if or when the fish population will recover enough to allow the people to resume their traditional way of life.

Religious Change: Islam as a Canadian Religion

As we saw in Chapter 11, Islam is Canada's fastest-growing organized religion. From 1991 to 2001, the number of Canadian Muslims rose by 128.9 per cent—more than twice the increase for the period 1981–91. In 2001, Canada's 579,640 Muslims made up 2 per cent of the country's total population. Most of them (352,525) were living in Ontario, where the province's Muslim population had grown by 142.2 per cent over the same 10-year period. Islam was the sixth largest religion in the country, just a little behind the Baptist and Lutheran churches, and way behind the "big three"—the Catholic Church, the United Church, and the Anglican Church. But in contrast to these, Islam was the religion with the youngest median age: its followers averaged just 28.1 years. Muslims come from a broad variety of ethnic backgrounds and countries, including Iran, Iraq, Pakistan, India, Afghanistan, Turkey, Somalia, Bosnia, and Indonesia.

By 2011, Muslims had surpassed Baptists and Lutherans to become the fourth largest religious denomination in Canada, according to the National Household Survey. Between 2001 and 2011, their numbers nearly doubled, from 579,640

ugurhan/iStockphoto

was used for effect by someone with a reputation for brash attention-seeking behaviour.

In my final years of teaching, the f-word had become relatively commonplace in the concourse and still not infrequent in the halls, used with no apparent concern that a teacher walking past might hear. I heard it in the classroom in general conversation during breaks and used about as often by women as by men.

What Do YOU Think?

1. How have the rules, or mores, surrounding use of the f-word changed, according to this narrative? What changes have you noticed where you go to school?
2. What would it take for these mores to change back? Could they change back?
3. Could this kind of language use be considered a verbal "fashion statement"?

to 1,053,945, and from 2.0 per cent of all Canadians to 3.2 per cent.

While there isn't what could be called a "Muslim tradition" in Canada, the faith is not entirely new to the country. In 1871, according to that year's census, there were 13 Muslims living in Canada. The first mosque in Canada—in all of North America, in fact—was Al Rashid, built in Edmonton in 1938, funded by local Muslims, Arab Christians, and Jews.

What Do YOU Think?

What adaptations did the people of Newfoundland and Labrador make with the loss of the cod fishery? What kinds of social change did these adaptations bring about? Which of the five models of social change described earlier best characterizes the changes?

What Do YOU Think?

1. Canada's Muslim population represents a variety of ethnic backgrounds. Do you think this will lead to the development of "Canadianized" multicultural mosques?
2. Canadian introductory sociology textbooks often present Muslims, even those living in Canada, as "them," or an "Other." What do you think is the effect among non-Muslim Canadians of reading this treatment of Muslim Canadians?

Asif Rehman Photography

Mombasa is an amateur boxer and PhD candidate. Does she fit your idea of a young Canadian Muslim woman? What do you think it will take for Canada to be considered, at least in part, a "Muslim country"?

Telling It Like It Is   An Expert's POV

Irshad Manji on the Gender Challenge for Canadian Muslim Women

A few years ago, the Ontario government considered allowing Islamic *sharia* law to be applied in family law cases involving Muslims. It was strongly opposed by most Muslim women as well as by more liberal Muslim groups. The Canadianization of Islam poses a considerable gender challenge, as the Muslim writer of the excerpt below, Irshad Manji, explains. Born in Uganda in 1972, Manji and her family emigrated to Canada when she was four, during the expulsion of Uganda's South Asian population under Idi Amin. As an activist and a lesbian, Manji has faced considerable opposition from within her Muslim community. In her provocative book *The Trouble with Islam: A Wake-Up Call for Honesty and Change* (2003), Manji describes how she discovered, at the madressa (the Muslim school she attended on

weekends), that the separation and inequality of the genders found in strict Muslim countries were being reproduced in Canada. That this situation was not being challenged but obeyed without question conflicted with what she was learning about the importance of individuality and equality taught to her in the regular school system. In the following, she describes the conflict that led her to leave the madressa:

The trouble began with *Know Your Islam*, the primer that I packed in my madressa bag every week. After reading it, I needed to know more about "my" Islam. Why must girls observe the essentials, such as praying five times a day, at an earlier age than boys? Because, Mr Khaki [her nickname for her teacher] told me, girls mature sooner. They reach the "obliga-tory age" of practice at nine compared to thirteen for boys.

"Then why not reward girls for our matu-rity by letting us lead prayer?" I asked.
"Girls can't lead prayer."
"What do you mean?"
"Girls aren't permitted."
"Why not?"
"Allah says so."
"What's His reason?"
"Read the Koran." (Manji, 2003, pp. 13–14)

Manji did not find an answer there that satisfied her Western-trained (and somewhat Western-biased) mind. Still, she remains a Muslim. Later in the book, she writes the following:

Had I grown up in a Muslim country, I'd probably be an atheist in my heart. It's because I live in this corner of the world, where I can think, dispute, and delve fur-ther into any topic, that I've learned why I shouldn't give up on Islam just yet. (Manji, 2003, p. 228)

Social Change and Sociology in Canada

Like all academic disciplines, sociology must change, and it must do so in a way that involves all five of the models of change discussed above. It needs to im-prove, to get better, in a modernist sense. Perhaps some of this improvement will come in the way sociology is presented to students of the discipline, just as I've tried to fashion something a little dif-ferent with this textbook. But sociology also needs a touch of conservatism to ensure that it does not stray too far from the early vision that gave it percep-tion; otherwise, it will diminish. It must constantly have postmodern eyes, using fly-like, multidimen-sional perception to look at who has benefitted and who hasn't from sociology as it has been tradition-ally practised and written about. And it must adapt, evolve.

Concerning this last point, sociology in Canada is facing some serious challenges. In 2003, in the *Canadian Journal of Sociology*, Robert Brym re-marked on the fact that while the Canadian Sociol-ogy and Anthropology Association was the official organization of Anglo-Canadian sociology, it was losing members, even while the number of faculty members in sociology and anthropology was grow-ing. Membership had peaked at 1165 in 1993 and within 10 years had dropped by 39 per cent. Brym has his explanations for this phenomenon, including

(1) external competition from American sociologi-cal organizations, (2) internal competition from the *Canadian Journal of Sociology*, (3) a changing orga-nizational environment, and (4) unprofessionalism. On the second-to-last point, he notes reform move-ments that are "left-leaning" and "feminist." Those he names might argue that they left or never even joined because the organization had become an old boys' club that failed to represent their interests. Whichever way you interpret it, Canadian sociology needs to change. In the personal narrative that ends this introduction to the discipline, I suggest one way I would like to see sociology change.

Concluding Narrative: Where Does Sociology Go from Here?

In a book that emphasizes the importance of per-sonal narratives that highlight unique perspectives on our social world, it is only fitting that we should end with a narrative.

In the conclusion to my doctoral dissertation on how Canadian introductory sociology textbooks present information about Indigenous people, I argued that in order for textbook writers to present the information in a way that is worthy of the best aims and works of the discipline, they must engage in what can be called "Aboriginal sociology." We could generalize this approach to a broader category of "minorities sociology," but here I will speak in terms of the minority I know best.

This Aboriginal sociology, as I envisioned it, must begin by recognizing the inadequacy of traditional methods of producing sociological knowledge concerning Indigenous people. The voices of the people need to be heard. I warned that if the writers of these textbooks continued to ignore Indigenous voices in their knowledge production, they would continue to be complicit in the colonialist practices of governments. They were not being neutral, objective, or distanced. They were taking a side.

Equally important is the related recognition that the non-Indigenous cultural background of the writers of introductory sociology textbooks permits them but a limited perspective, one that, as **Dorothy Smith** (1990) informs us, will miss core concepts that are intrinsically important to understanding Indigenous people from an Indigenous standpoint. The important place of Elders in Indigenous society is one of these core concepts. Elders are involved in all the social institutions of Indigenous life—education, justice, religion, and politics, for example—and anyone in any way involved in Indigenous society is aware of their significance. But people coming from other cultures that diminish the role of the elderly could easily miss this important point. Indeed, they *have* missed it. Spirituality is another core concept, one that tends to be erased in sociology textbooks. The reserve is a spiritual centre, often (one can probably say *usually*) the location of a number of sacred sites of significance, and yet in sociology textbooks it is only a site for sorry statistics and horror stories.

More generally, the development of an Aboriginal sociology entails the recognition that non-sociologists have authority in talking about Indigenous life. There are very few Indigenous professional sociologists, something that the discipline should note and rectify. For the Indigenous standpoint to be represented, the knowledge production of Indigenous journalists, educators, filmmakers, Elders, and literary writers should be sought out and respected. All of them have voices that are valued in Aboriginal

Gabriela Campos for VICE.com

society. That alone should guarantee their inclusion in introductory sociology textbooks.

In my first year of university, sociology opened my eyes to a world of understanding that changed my perception forever. Every semester that I have taught introductory sociology, I have told my students that my goal in teaching the course is to change how they think. I quote, with pride, a former sociology student of mine—a Brazilian nun—who said that my course had "ruined her" by forcing her (enabling her?) to question her previous perceptions of society.

I am a believer in the discipline. But I strongly believe that it needs to change its textual presentation of Indigenous people, as well as its presentation of other groups that do not belong to the dominant culture, in ways as radical as how the discipline itself altered my viewpoint. It requires more voices to thrive in Canada in the twenty-first century.

Think Back

Questions for Critical Review

1. Compare and contrast the five different models of social change presented in this chapter.
2. Outline the features of the cycle of civilization, and discuss the degree to which it might apply to the United States.
3. Explain who the Luddites were, and outline the social changes to which they were reacting. Do you see parallels between history's Luddites and today's proponents of food-related trends such as urban farming, craft beer (three cheers!), and free-range and other anti-industrial farming movements?
4. How can sociology be made to appeal to Indigenous students, to encourage the growth of Indigenous sociology in Canada?
5. In North America we have cultivated a workplace culture that encourages people to work longer hours in the name of "greater productivity." Smartphones keep us tethered to the office during the supposed off hours from work. Meanwhile, some social reformers, including author and historian Rutger Bregman, are advocating a 15-hour work week. Provided the pay remains roughly the same, is a shorter work week the way of the future?

6. Change happens fast in today's digital world. Snapchat erases photos from our social media accounts within minutes and from our memories in barely more time than that. Memes that go viral can fall out of currency within days of being posted. Buzzfeed announces that such-and-such a photo or tweet has broken the internet, but when I check the next day, it appears to be working again, full of new ideas and content. Do digital ideas have significance in terms of long-term social change? Can something trending today have relevance a month or a year from now? Do trending issues ever have long-term significance?
7. As English becomes the world's global language, we are losing other languages at an alarming rate. Do you think that attempts by Indigenous people to preserve their languages is an impractical conservatism or an important measure for maintaining a strong sense of their Indigenous identity? I am biased in that regard in that I am the Tribal Linguist of the Wyandotte Nation of Oklahoma, a part-time job that I love.
8. In Chapter 1, I said that by the time you reached the end of this book, you should have a better sense of what sociology is. So, here we are: What is sociology?

Read On

Recommended Print and Online Resources

Arthur Kroker & Michael A. Weinstein (1995), *Data Trash: Theory of the Virtual Class* **(Montreal: New World Perspectives).**

- It is in this now classic work that the Canadian technology and cultural theorist Arthur Kroker expounds his theory of the virtual class.

Canadian Centre for Policy Alternatives: Commentary and Fact Sheets, www.policy-alternatives.ca/publications/commentary

- The CCPA is a liberal think tank headquartered in Ottawa. This page provides commentaries on a range of current issues that reflect the centre's approach to influencing social policy in an attempt to make Canada more democratic.

George Grant (1965), *Lament for a Nation* **(Toronto: McClelland & Stewart).**

- A classic Canadian work "lamenting" the changes taking place in mid-twentieth-century Canadian society.

Interview—Kirkpatrick Sale, www.primitivism.com/sale.htm

- This online interview with Kirkpatrick Sale examines the author's views on Luddites, industrialism, and the dangers of new technology.

Irshad Manji, *Don't Label Me: An Incredible Conversation for Divided Times* **(New York: St Martin's Press, 2019).**

- The most recent book by Canadian educator Irshad Manji, cited in the feature on page 488, argues that diversity without labels is key to achieving social justice.

John Steckley (2003), *Aboriginal Voices and the Politics of Representation in Canadian Sociology Textbooks* **(Toronto: Canadian Scholars' Press).**

- This is my doctoral dissertation made readable. It argues for the need to develop a stronger Aboriginal sociology in Canada.

Kirkpatrick Sale (1996), *Rebels Against the Future: The Luddites and Their War on the Industrial Revolution-Lessons for the Computer Age* **(Cambridge, MA: Perseus).**

- An elegant case study of an epic fight against the destruction of a social class by technology.

Kwame Anthony Appiah, *The Lies That Bind: Rethinking Identity* **(New York: Liveright, 2018).**

- A good companion to Manji's work is this exploration of identity by American professor of philosophy and law Kwame Anthony Appiah, which looks at how humans came to acquire the labels that define us.

Rutger Bregman, "Why We Should Give Everyone a Basic Income" (2014), www.youtube.com/watch?v=aIL_Y9g7Tg0

- In this TEDx talk, Dutch historian and author Rutger Bregman discusses the ideas behind his book *Utopia for Realists*, which makes the case for a universal basic income and a 15-hour work week.

Glossary

Abell, Helen C. (1917–2005) Canadian sociologist considered a founding figure of rural sociology in Canada, particularly regarding the roles women played on the farm.

Abrahamic religions The three major religions—Judaism, Christianity, and Islam—that trace their origin to the biblical patriarch Abraham.

absolute poverty Poverty calculated in absolute material terms. To exist in absolute poverty is to be without sufficient nutritious food, clean and safe shelter, access to education, etc. *Compare* **relative poverty**.

absolutist Holding or having to do with the view that certain things are always right, good, moral, modern, or beautiful. Ethnocentrism is a negative example of an absolutist position.

access without mobility A buzzword in postsecondary education referring to the availability of online courses to those who would not otherwise be able to attend a college or university because of factors such as cost and family situation. The "without mobility" part is my own addition to the buzzword.

achieved Denoting a **status** that a person has earned but was not born into. Professional titles are an example. *Compare* **ascribed**.

actual culture Social life and institutions as they actually exist. *Compare* **ideal culture**.

Addams, Jane (1860–1935) American social reformer, activist, and sociologist, who in 1889 founded Hull House, a centre for the care and education of the poor in Chicago.

adjunct professor A college or university professor who is employed on a contract basis and who does not enjoy the benefits and job security of a full-time member of staff.

age group A group composed of people of a particular age (e.g. teenagers, "tweens," twenty-somethings), studied over time.

agency The capacity to influence what happens in one's life. *Compare* **victimology**.

agents of socialization The groups that have a significant influence on a person's socialization. Examples include family, **peer group**, community, school, mass media, the legal system, and culture generally.

aid evangelism The practice of sending religious missionaries into developing countries in need of financial assistance, and using their need as a tool for trying to convert them.

Algonquian The largest family of Indigenous languages in Canada, including Abenaki, Algonquin, Blackfoot, Cree, Delaware, Maliseet, Mi'kmaq, and Ojibwa.

alienation In Marxist theory, a condition experienced by workers in a capitalist economy when they feel a lack of identity with the products of their labour and a sense of being controlled or exploited.

alternative medicine Any medical treatment or remedy that falls outside of conventional Western medical practices. Examples include traditional Chinese medicine, healing techniques such as acupuncture and massage therapy, and herbal remedies. *See* **biomedicine**, **complementary medicine**.

American dream The mostly unrealistic belief that one can become rich and successful through hard work and determination alone. A naive belief in the American dream is sometimes used to justify punishing others for being poor (the "American nightmare").

androcentrism From *andro*, meaning "man," a form of sexism that views men as central and more important than women.

anomie **Durkheim's** term for a societal state of breakdown or confusion, or a more personal one based on an individual's lack of connection or contact with society.

anti-colonialism *Another term for* **postcolonialism**.

archaeology of knowledge **Foucault's** term for the process of "digging down" to find out how a piece of information was constructed, typically in order to discover or expose flaws in the way supposed facts or truths were established.

aristocrats In Marxist theory, the landowner class of feudal times, who owned the land worked on by the class of **peasants**.

ascribed Denoting a **status** that a person is born into (female, daughter, older sister) or has entered involuntarily (adult, diabetic). *Compare* **achieved**.

assimilation The process by which minorities, Indigenous Peoples, and immigrants lose their distinctive cultural characteristics to become like members of the dominant culture. It is a key principle of **melting pot** societies.

authenticity The quality of being true to the traditions of a people. Authenticity is often **contested** by the modern representatives of the people themselves and "experts" from outside the community.

autism spectrum disorder A broad range of neurodevelopment disorders that involve a relative lack of ability to communicate and generally interact with others. It is also associated with restricted repetitive behaviours, interests, and activities. While it was once attributed to socialization (*see* **refrigerator mothers**), it is now believed to be primarily genetic.

average A statistical figure determined by adding up the numbers for a given phenomenon and dividing the sum by the number of individuals in the statistical population. Five squirrels picked up 24 peanuts from my front porch. The average number of peanuts per squirrel is $24 \div 5 = 4.8$.

back stage As described by **Goffman**, the site of private, personal, or intimate encounters between individuals. *See* **dramaturgical approach**, **front stage**, **impression management**.

bakla In Tagalog (the national language of the Philippines), a word referring to the cultural configuration of someone who is assigned male gender at birth but is usually attracted to other males and typically engages in cross-dressing and behaviour deemed more "feminine" than "masculine."

Bales, Robert F. (1916–2004) American social psychologist who taught at Harvard and developed **interaction process analysis**, a framework for studying social interaction in small groups.

barbarism As described by **Morgan** in the nineteenth century, the second stage of social evolution on the way to modern civilization. It was identified as one of a series of stages all societies were thought to pass through in their natural development. *Compare* **civilization**, **savagery**.

bar mitzvah A Jewish **rite of passage** in which a boy becomes a man.

bat mitzvah A Jewish **rite of passage** in which a girl becomes a woman.

Battiste, Marie (b. 1949) Canadian Mi'kmaq educator who specializes in the sociology of anti-colonialism and decolonization in education and knowledge.

Baudrillard, Jean (1929–2007) French sociologist, political commentator and postmodernist cultural theorist, associated with the term *simulacrum*.

Beaujot, Rod (b. 1946) Canadian demographer specializing in the sociology of the family.

Becker, Howard (b. 1928) American sociologist specializing in the sociology of deviance, particularly with regard to **labelling theory**.

Becker, Howard (b. 1928) American sociologist specializing in the sociology of deviance, particularly with regard to **labelling theory**.

behaviourism A school of thought in psychology that emphasizes that behaviour can be studied and explained scientifically not in terms of internal mental states (unlike **psychoanalysis**) but through observing how people's actions are supposedly conditioned by earlier actions and reactions.

behaviour modification An approach to changing someone's behaviour by giving rewards for behaviour that one wishes to encourage and, sometimes, issuing sanctions for behaviour one wishes to discourage. *See* **law of effect**.

best practices Strategies with a demonstrated history of achieving desired results more effectively or more consistently than similar methods used either in the past by a particular organization or currently by other organizations in the same industry.

Bettelheim, Bruno (1903–1990). Australian-born American child psychologist who, before both his credentials and his work were discredited, became famous for his work with autistic children. See refrigerator mothers.

binaries Either/or distinctions used to separate people into supposedly discrete categories, such as male/female or able-bodied/disabled, typically when applied to social factors (gender, ability) that are better viewed in terms of a spectrum of possibilities.

biological sex The socially constructed category to which people are assigned at birth based on certain biological criteria, such as the reproductive organs they possess. Western society typically recognizes the biological sexes male, female, and intersex.

biomedicine The application of standard principles of Western scientific disciplines (particularly biology) in the diagnosis and treatment of symptoms of illness. *Compare* **alternative medicine**.

bisexual A person who is sexually attracted to men and women.

blaming the victim **William Ryan**'s term for the process of assigning responsibility to individuals for events or circumstances that have broader social or genetic causes. Example: ascribing unemployment to laziness on the part of unemployed people while failing to consider that job creation is not keeping pace with population increases.

Blumer, Herbert (1900–1987) American sociologist who was a pioneer in **social interactionism**, as well as a critic of positivist sociological research.

bodily stigmata *See* **stigma**.

Bookchin, Murray (1921–2006) American thinker prominent in the ecology and anarchism movements.

Bott, Elizabeth (1924–2016) Canadian-born anthropologist and social psychologist who specialized in the study of family networks. She is best known for formulating the theory that came to be known as the Bott hypothesis.

Bott hypothesis The theory that when a husband's and wife's separate social networks are dense and closely connected, the husband and wife are likely to take on segregated, rather than joint, conjugal roles in the household; joint conjugal roles are more likely to exist where husband and wife do not have close social networks outside of the household.

Bourdieu, Pierre (1930–2002) French sociologist and social critic who introduced the concepts of **cultural capital** and **habitus** to sociology.

bourgeoisie *See* **capitalists**.

boyah (plural *boyat*) A woman living in an Arab country of the Middle East who adopts a masculine style of dress and appearance (e.g. by cutting her hair short) as a way of defying gender norms.

brain drain The exodus of scientists, doctors, and other skilled professionals from a country.

branding The corporate use of marketing as an instrument of socialization to encourage teens and younger children to covet brand-name products linked, via advertising, to the cool or fashionable identity of the day.

broad socialization Socialization in which individualism and independence are promoted. *Compare* **narrow socialization**.

Butler, Judith (b. 1956) American feminist theorist who examined the way people perform gender roles in an effort to meet society's expectations of what it means to be "male" or "female."

capital **Marx**'s term for the funds and properties necessary for the large-scale manufacture and trade of goods.

capitalists **Marx**'s term for the owners of the means of production (or capital, as these were known during the industrial era). *Also called* **bourgeoisie**.

case study approach A research design that explores a social entity or phenomenon by examining a single representative case or a few selected examples.

Catholic–Traditionalist Angela Robinson's term for Mi'kmaq who adopted Catholicism but incorporated non-Christian elements into their religious practices.

causation The relationship between cause and effect.

China price The true cost of China's competitive advantage in manufacturing, which takes into account the harm done to exploited workers and damage caused to the environment.

Chomsky, Noam (b. 1928) American theoretical linguist, social critic, and activist who demonstrated that language is innate, not learned.

cisgender A term used for people who identify with the gender corresponding to their biological sex. *Compare* **transgender**.

civilization As described by **Morgan** in the nineteenth century, the third and final stage of social evolution of all societies, viewed by European and North American thinkers as best exemplified by European and North American culture. *Compare* **barbarism**, **savagery**.

Clark, Samuel Delbert (1910–2003) Canadian sociologist whose writings about Canada's social development helped sociology gain respectability in Canada. He founded the sociology department at the University of Toronto.

class **Marx**'s term for a socioeconomic group defined either relationally—that is, in Marxist terms, with respect to their relationship to the **means of production** (e.g. owner, worker)—or absolutely, in terms of access to socially valued goods such as money, education, and respect.

class consciousness The intellectual fallacy that all forms of oppression are just about class and class differences, a view that wrongly downplays the role of factors such as "race," ethnicity, gender, and age.

class reductionism the intellectual fallacy that all forms of oppression are just about class and class differences, a view that wrongly downplays the role of factors such as race, ethnicity, gender, and age.

clinical iatrogenesis **Illich**'s term for the ways in which diagnosis and cure cause problems that are equal to or greater than the health problems they are meant to resolve. An example would be catching a virus while in hospital for minor surgery.

cluttered nest A situation in which adult children continue to live at home with their parents. *Compare* **empty nest**.

cohabiting union (**or couple**) *See* **common-law union**.

Cohen, Albert (1918–2014) American sociologist specializing in criminology. He is most famous for his **subcultural theory** of delinquents (or **delinquent subculture**).

cohort A group of people with a common statistical characteristic. Examples include baby boomers, who were born during the same period, and the frosh of 2017, who entered college or university in the same year.

collective consciousness Durkheim's term for shared feeling and understanding among people belonging to a particular religion, fostered by group experiences and rituals.

collectives *another term for* **small group**.

Collins, Patricia Hill (b. 1948) American critical sociologist who is best known for her work on feminist standpoint theory and **intersectionality**.

colonialism The policy or practice of acquiring full or partial control over another country, occupying it with settlers, and exploiting it economically or culturally.

colourism Prejudice or discrimination against individuals with a dark skin tone, particularly among people of the same ethnic or racial background.

commodification The tendency to treat something as though it were an object to be bought or sold. For example, the commodification of medicine involves identifying certain conditions that might be normal (though slightly regrettable) as diseases that may be treated with "commodity cures" (such as drugs or surgical procedures).

common-law union (or **couple**) Two people of the same or opposite sex who are living together as a couple but who are not legally married to each other. *Also called* **cohabiting union**.

companionate conjugal roles The overlapping **conjugal roles** of partners in a marriage who both work outside the home and do work around the house. *Compare* **complementary roles**.

complementary conjugal roles The **conjugal roles** of partners in a marriage when one (traditionally the husband) does paid work, while the other (traditionally the wife) does the unpaid work of childcare and housework. *Compare* **companionate roles**.

complementary medicine Alternative medicine practised in conjunction with conventional medicine. *See* **alternative medicine**, **biomedicine**.

complex household A household in which there are two or more adults who are related but not married to each other.

complicit masculinity Forms of masculinity that do not contribute to or embody male hegemony yet still benefit from it.

Comte, August (1798–1857) French proponent of **positivism** who aimed to develop a truly scientific social science that could be used for social reconstruction.

confirmation A Christian **rite of passage** in which an adult who was baptized as a child or an infant affirms Christian belief and is admitted as a full member of the church.

conflict deviance Behaviour that is subject to debate over whether or not it is deviant. Examples: marijuana use; "creative accounting" on tax returns.

conflict theory A sociological perspective espousing the view that complex societies are made up of groups in conflict, with one or more groups dominating or oppressing the others.

Confucius (c. 551–479 BCE) Chinese philosopher whose ideas on the importance of practical moral values contain some early sociological insights into topics such as role modelling.

conjugal roles The distinctive roles of spouses that result from the division of labour within the family.

conservatism A view of social change as potentially more destructive than constructive, especially in emotionally charged areas of life such as family, gender roles, sexuality, and the environment.

content analysis A study of a set of **cultural artifacts** (e.g. children's books, newspaper articles, internet memes) or events by systematically counting them and interpreting the themes they reflect.

contested Describing a practice whose moral goodness or badness, normalcy or deviance, or general predominance is disputed by some members of society.

control One of four main elements of **Weber's** model of **formal rationalization**, having to do with the use of rules, regulations, and a hierarchical structure to keep workers in line. *See* **efficiency**, **predictability**, **quantification**.

Cooley, Charles (1864–1929) American sociologist who was an early proponent of **symbolic interactionism**, reflected in his introduction of the concept of the **looking-glass self**.

corporate (**or** **organic**) **identity** The shared sense of common membership and common purpose that a social group can have.

corporate crimes As described by Clinard & Quinney, (1) offences committed by corporate officials on behalf of the corporation they represent, or (2) the offences of the corporation itself. *Compare* **occupational crimes**.

correlation A mutual relationship or interdependence among **variables**. *See* **direct correlation**, **inverse correlation**.

cosmology An account or theory of the origin of the universe.

countercultures Groups that reject selected elements of the dominant culture, such as clothing styles or sexual norms. *Compare* **subculture**.

counter-ideology A set of beliefs that challenges or contests the **dominant ideology** put forward by the dominant culture and the ruling classes.

covert characteristics (**of deviance**) The unstated qualities that might make a particular group a target for sanctions. *Compare* **overt characteristics** (**of deviance**).

credentialism A bias in favour of job candidates with academic degrees, diplomas, or certificates over those without, regardless of their demonstrated knowledge, ability, and experience.

Crenshaw, Kimberlé (b. 1959) American legal theorist who helped develop critical race theory and who introduced the term intersectionality to refer to the linking forms of prejudice based on "race" and gender.

criminology The study of crime in terms of such key sociological elements as causation, prevention, management, or control, and the statistical patterning among certain groups and geographical areas.

critical disability theory (**or CDT**) A social constructionist theory that distinguishes between natural impairment (e.g. paralysis of the legs) and disability, which occurs when society sets up barriers to dealing with impairment (e.g. building stairs without wheelchair-accessible ramps).

critical education An education model that involves the analysis and discussion of ideas. *Compare* **instrumental education**.

critical management studies Research that challenges traditional theories of management by examining previously neglected factors such as the effects of gender, "race," and class on groups and organizations.

critical sociology Sociology that challenges both established sociological theories and the research that sociologists do.

crude marriage rate The number of marriages per 1000 people in a population.

cultural artifacts Items produced for mass cultural consumption, with value to a researcher engaged in content analysis. Cultural artifacts can include books, articles, websites, advertisements, and other items created to be seen but not specifically to be studied.

cultural capital As described by **Bourdieu**, the knowledge and skills required to develop the sophisticated taste that mark someone as a person of high culture and upper class.

cultural iatrogenesis As described by **Illich**, a situation in which the knowledge and abilities of health professionals have become so mythologized that individuals lose the capacity to heal themselves.

cultural mosaic A metaphor for any society in which individual ethnic groups are able to maintain distinctive identities. *Compare* **melting pot**.

cultural relativism The view that any aspect of a culture, including its practices and beliefs, is best explained within the context of the culture itself, not by the standard or ways of the researcher's own culture.

cultural reproduction theory The theory that the education system reproduces and reinforces the inequality of the surrounding society.

cultural studies A field of study drawing on both the social sciences (primarily sociology) and the humanities (primarily literature and media studies) to cast academic light on the meanings expressed in popular culture and their significance.

culture A social system (sometimes **contested**) comprising behaviour, beliefs, knowledge, practices, values, and material such as buildings, tools, and sacred items.

culture and personality As described by R. Benedict, a now discredited school of thought that argued that every culture has a distinct personality that is encouraged by its cultural practices and beliefs.

cultures of medicine The recognition that different cultures have different ways of practising medicine, including different **social courses of disease**, different techniques, and different physical remedies.

cycle of civilization The supposed rise and fall of **civilizations** in somewhat predictable cycles. The term has been applied to the Roman empire, the

Mongol empire, the Ottoman (Turkish) empire, and the American empire.

Dahl, Robert A. (1915–2014) American political scientist who specialized in looking at types of power or influence. He discussed this in terms of **oligarchy** and **polyarchy**.

Dawson, Carl Addington (1887–1964) Canadian sociologist trained at the University of Chicago, formed Canada's first postsecondary department of sociology, at McGill University.

decipherment The process of examining a text to discover its true meaning, which often involves looking beyond the explicit message to discover the intent (conscious or unconscious) of the individual or organization that produced it.

definition of the situation In symbolic-interactionist thinking, the notion that different individuals will define a given situation differently, possibly in contradictory ways, based on their own subjective experiences. As a result, understanding how an individual defines a situation is crucial to understanding the individual's actions and responses to it.

degradation ceremony A **rite of passage** designed to strip a person of his or her individuality. Hazing is an example of a degradation ceremony.

delinquent subculture As described by A. **Cohen**, the **subordinate culture** of teenage gangs. *See* **subcultural theory**.

democracy A political system that involves a broad-based voting electorate, an opposition that is free to criticize the group in power without fear, freedom of the press and of speech, protection of the rights of minorities, and relative equality of men and women.

dependent variable A **variable** that is assumed to be affected by an **independent variable**.

desensitization theory The idea that increased exposure to media violence (e.g. from television, movies, and video games) blunts, or desensitizes, natural feelings of revulsion at the sight or thought of violence.

determinism The belief that personal characteristics, including behaviour and attitudes, are shaped by forces beyond the control, or **agency**, of the individual.

deviance Straying from or different to what is considered usual or normal.

dialect A version of a language, usually with a unique set of features (in terms of vocabulary, grammar, and pronunciation) and a socially identifiable group of speakers. Newfoundland English is an example of a dialect (even though technically there are several Newfoundland dialects).

digital divide The situation in which citizens of the world's wealthier nations, as well as richer citizens of the poorer nations, have an access to computers and related technology that gives them an enormous social, economic, and political advantage over the poorer citizens of the richer nations and most people in the poorer countries.

direct correlation A relationship between two **variables** in which an increase (or decrease) in one causes a corresponding increase (or decrease) in the other. *Compare* **inverse correlation**.

disability Any condition—physical or mental, permanent or temporary—that limits a person's ability to participate in regular activities in the home, at work, at school, or in recreational pursuits.

discourse A conceptual framework with its own internal logic and underlying assumptions. Different disciplines, such as sociology and psychology, have their own discourses.

discourse analysis An approach to analyzing a conversation, a speech, or a written text. The scope of discourse analysis has broadened recently to encompass entire academic disciplines, such as sociology and political philosophy.

discrimination Acts by which individuals are differentially rewarded or punished based on their membership in a social group defined by class, sexual orientation, ethnicity, and so on.

disenchanted Lacking in magic, fantasy, or mystery. **Weber** used the term to characterize the secular, rationalized West.

disjuncture A gap between knowledges produced from two or more different perspectives (e.g. those of management and employees).

disproportionate representation A situation that occurs when an atypically high or low number of a particular social group is associated with a specific situation. South Asian men are overrepresented in the population of cricket players in Canada but are underrepresented in the population of professional hockey players: in both cases, disproportionate representation exits.

docile body **Foucault**'s term for a group that has been conditioned, through a specific set of procedures and practices, to behave in a particular, preprogrammed way.

dominant capitalist class The social class composed primarily of those who own or control the **means of production**.

dominant culture The culture that through its political and economic power is able to impose its values, language, interpretations of events, and ways of behaving on a given society.

dominant ideology A set of beliefs put forward by and in support of the dominant culture and/or ruling classes within a society, to help them justify their dominant position and dominating practices.

dominants The group within a society that has the most political and social power, whose culture or subculture is seen as "the" culture of a country. They make up the **dominant culture**.

double burden (**or ghetto**) A term used to characterize the imbalance in gender roles in situations where a married woman works a paid job during the day and is expected to perform the unpaid domestic work (cleaning house, preparing meals, looking after children, etc.) traditionally associated with women when she comes home. *See* **second shift**.

double ghetto See **double burden**.

Dragon Lady As described by Tajima & Das Gupta, a stereotype of East Asian women as tough, ruthless, and mercenary. The stereotype is seen in film and TV portrayals of hardened prostitutes and madams, and women who fight with nasty, angry facial expressions. *Compare* **Lotus Blossom Baby**.

dramaturgical approach As described by **Goffman**, a way of approaching sociological research as if everyday life were taking place on the stage of a theatre. *See* **backstage**, **front stage**, **impression management**.

Du Bois, W.E.B. (1868–1963) African American social philosopher who was among the first to document the experience of American blacks from a sociological perspective.

Duffy, Ann Canadian sociologist who works from a feminist political economy perspective, and who has a long history of studying the sociology of families.

Durkheim, Émile (1858-1917) French founding figure of sociology, who studied society in terms of social facts such as ethics, occupations, religion, and suicide.

Ebaugh, Helen Rose Fuchs (b. 1942) American sociologist who specializes in organizational sociology and the sociology of religion. She has studied and written about **role exit**.

economic model (**of disability**) A way of understanding and representing disabled people in terms of their contribution to or drain on the economy. Compare **medical model** (**of disability**).

efficiency One of four main elements of **Weber**'s model of **formal rationalization**, having to do with the streamlined movement of people and things. *See* **control**, **predictability**, **quantification**.

egalitarianism (*adj.* **egalitarian**) The principle that all people are equal and deserve equal rights and opportunities.

ego As described by **Freud**, the conscious aspect of the individual personality. *Compare* **id**, **superego**.

Elkind, David (b. 1931) American child psychologist, who has studied culture as an agent of child socialization. He developed the concept of **hurried child syndrome**.

empty nest A situation in which the children of an older couple have grown up and moved out of the family home. *Compare* **cluttered nest**.

endogamy The practice of marrying within one's class, "race," or ethnic group. *Compare* **exogamy**.

Engels, Friedrich (1820–1895) German economist, who co-wrote, with **Marx**, *The Communist Manifesto* (1848).

environmental racism A double standard in attitudes around environmental protection, depending on which "race" or ethnicity prevails in the threatened region. "White" places generally attract a high level of concern and care, while places associated with racial minorities are often neglected.

environmental refugees People forced to leave their home region owing to sudden changes to the local environment (e.g., drought, melting land ice, polluted water) that pose a threat to their livelihood or survival.

epidemiology The study of public health, specifically the incidence and spread of diseases in a population.

Erikson, Erik (1902–1994) German-born American psychoanalyst who believed that human identity develops through a series of stages lasting from infancy to old age.

eros As described by **Freud**, the "sexual" or "life" instinct within the **id**.

essentialism The view that every ethnic group is made up of a set of readily identifiable traits that have been passed down from the past to the present with little or no change. *Also called* **primordialism**.

essentialist feminism A feminist approach that involves looking at differences between the way women and men think while arguing for the equality—and sometimes female superiority—in that difference.

ethics The honourable moral principles that govern sociological research, including respect for the privacy and the rights and concerns of the research subjects.

ethnic entrepreneurs Individuals who manipulate symbols with strong meaning to their ethnic group in order to gain and wield personal power. Examples include Adolf Hitler and Slobodan Milošević.

ethnicity Membership in a social group that shares a common national or cultural tradition.

ethnocentrism The belief that one culture (often one's own, occasionally another considered more powerful or respectworthy) is the absolute standard by which other cultures should be judged.

ethnography A research method, shared by sociology and social anthropology, in which communities or groups are studied through extensive fieldwork. Ethnography requires the researcher to participate daily in the lives of the subjects, observing their actions and asking questions. *See* **institutional ethnography**.

Etzioni, Amitai (b. 1929) German-born American sociologist and proponent of communitarianism (a belief in the social value of communities) as a response to the individualist mindset encouraged by capitalism..

eugenics The science of improving a population by controlled breeding. The idea was especially popular in the early twentieth century, when people believed that "good traits" and "bad traits" were inherited, and that the poor, the colonized, and other marginalized people should be sterilized to prevent them from reproducing.

Eurocentric (*n.* **Eurocentrism**) Generally, the belief that "European" (i.e. western and northern European, plus North American) culture is superior to other cultures; more specifically in sociology, the use of a European viewpoint to address others, often with the assumption that the audience shares (or would like to share) that viewpoint.

Eurocentrism (*adj.* **Eurocentric**) Generally, the belief that "European" (i.e. western and northern European, plus North American) culture is superior to other cultures; more specifically in sociology, the use of a European viewpoint to address others, often with the assumption that the audience shares (or would like to share) that viewpoint.

evolution A model of **social change** in which change is seen as an adaptation to a set of particular circumstances, an idea captured by the expression **survival of the fittest**. *See* **social Darwinism**.

examination A form of disciplinary control that combines the methods of **hierarchical observation** and **normalizing judgment** to condition group behaviour; it is part of a set of tactics used to produce what **Foucault** called a **docile body**.

exogamy The practice of marrying outside of one's class, "race," or ethnic group. *Compare* **endogamy**.

experiential Based on or acquired through one's own experience.

extended family The family beyond mother, father, and children. Use of this term reflects the user's belief that the **nuclear family** is the model of a "normal" family.

fact Something that has been observed, and that as far as can be proven is believed to be true.

false consciousness As described by **Marx**, the belief that something (e.g. capitalism, religion) is in the best interests of one's class when it is not.

Fanon, Franz (1925–1961) Afro-Caribbean thinker from Martinique, who engaged in pioneering work in **anti-colonialism**.

fashion A model of **social change** that promotes change for its own sake, not for better (**modernism**), not for worse (**conservatism**), nor even for adaptation (**evolution**). Fashion change may occur because a manufacturer wants consumers to believe a product has been improved (though it hasn't), or it may occur because people desire something different.

fecundity A woman's ability to conceive, which changes with age.

feminization The process whereby an occupational sphere becomes dominated by and associated with women (e.g. secretarial work, clerical work). Feminized occupations are usually rewarded with lower salaries and fewer benefits.

folk society As described by R. Redfield, a rural, small-scale, homogeneous society imbued with a strong sense of the sacred and the personal, usually in contrast to an urban society.

folkways As described by **Sumner**, **norms** that in the usual course of events one *should* not (rather than *must* not) violate. They are the least respected and most weakly sanctioned norms.

food bank A central clearing house run by a non-profit organization to collect, store, and distribute food free of charge to the poor.

formal equality (in critical disability theory) a model according to which everyone faces and must adapt to the same socially driven architecture that gives advantages to people without disabilities. The term is also used in studies of gender and ethnicity, where it refers to the criteria set for job application when these criteria give advantage to applicants who are male and white. This situation existed with the RCMP, where minimum height and weight requirements favoured white, male applicants before minimum strength requirements were put into place. *Compare* **substantive equality**.

formal rationalization (or rationality) As described by **Weber**, a model of improving the effectiveness of an organization or process based on four elements: (1) efficiency, (2) quantification, (3) predictability, and (4) control. Weber was critical of the concept, believing that it led to **disenchantment** and alienation of the individuals involved in the rationalized process or organization.

formal social movement organizations As described by Carol Mueller, a type of **feminist organization** characterized as professionalized, bureaucratic, and inclusive.

Foucault, Michel (1926–1984) French social theorist who studied and wrote about the relationship between power and the acceptability of different socially placed knowledges. His methodology, known as **archaeology of knowledge**, is a valuable sociological tool.

Frazier, E. Franklin (1894–1962) African American sociologist who is best known for his research on the subject of the "Negro family" in the United States.

friendly racism As described by H. Codjoe, a form of racism that is subtle and seemingly (to the perpetrator) harmless.

Front stage As described by **Goffman**, the site of social interactions designed for public display. *See* **back stage**, **dramaturgical approach**, **impression management**.

Galton, Francis (1822–1911) English statistician who coined the terms **eugenics** and **correlation**, as well as the phrase "nature vs nurture" (with reference to the two influences of genetics and society).

game stage As described by **Mead**, the third stage of intellectual development, in which the child considers simultaneously the perspective of several roles. *Compare* **play stage**, **role-taking**.

gay An informal term for someone (male or female) who is sexually attracted to people of the same sex.

gay–straight alliance A student-led club established at a school to provide a safe, supportive environment for LGBTQ2 youth.

gender As described by Ann Oakley, the socially constructed and socially unequal division of masculinity and femininity, as opposed to the biological division of **sex**.

gendered Denoting occupations or postsecondary programs dominated either by men or by women. Examples include early childhood education and interior design for women, firefighting and industrial design for men.

gender role The role that a culture or society assigns as "normal" for boys/men and girls/women.

gender strategy As described by Arlie Hochschild, a way of dealing with situations in different areas of life (work, family, etc.) based on culturally defined **gender roles**. For example, in a dual-income household, the typical gender strategy for caring for infants is for the mother to take time off of work.

genealogy A form of **discourse analysis** that involves tracing the origin and history of modern **discourses** (e.g. the importance of light-coloured skin in South Asian culture). The term is sometimes considered interchangeable with the **archaeology of knowledge**.

general intelligence The mistaken idea that people have a single intelligence level that applies to many areas of life, skills, and abilities. Belief in general intelligence would lead one to conclude that a boy or girl who does not earn high marks at school but has other skills is stupid.

generalized other As described by **Mead**, the attitudes, viewpoints, and general expectations of the society that a child is socialized into.

genocide A set of social practices designed to eliminate or exterminate a people. These practices include warfare, displacement from a homeland, enforced sexual sterilization, separation of family members, and banning languages and other culturally identifiable features, all of which were committed against Indigenous people in Canada.

Gilligan, Carol (b. 1936) American educational psychologist and feminist theorist, who identified stages of moral development in girls and women.

Goffman, Erving (1922–1982) Alberta-born sociologist, best known for his work on **total institutions**, **stigma**, social roles, and **impression management**.

Gramsci, Antonio (1891–1937) Radical Italian Marxist thinker and politician, best known for his concept of **hegemony**.

Grant, George (1918–1988) Canadian philosopher and nationalist who warned against cultural absorption by the United States and the excesses of technologically driven modernity.

Great White Male A biased portrayal of history that records and values almost exclusively the lives and historical contributions of white men in positions of leadership (e.g. prime ministers, governors, missionaries, traders, and explorers).

habitus **Bourdieu**'s term for a set of class-affected or culturally affected and socially acquired characteristics (e.g. opinions, definitions of "manners" and "good taste," leisure pursuits).

haram Forbidden or proscribed under Islamic law.

Hart, Julian Tudor (1927–2018) British doctor who served the working classes and introduced the **inverse care law**.

hegemonic masculinity As described by R. Connell, practices and beliefs that normalize and naturalize men's dominance and women's subordination.

hegemony As described by **Gramsci**, a set of relatively non-coercive methods of maintaining power used by the dominant class (e.g. through the various media and the legal system). Often the terms *hegemony* and *hegemonic* are used to refer just to the possession and exercise of power (see, for instance, **hegemonic masculinity**).

heteronormativity Denoting or relating to the norms, mores, rules, and laws that uphold heterosexual standards of identity and behaviour and heterosexuality as natural and universal.

heterosexual A person who is sexually attracted to people of the opposite sex.

hidden curriculum The unstated, unofficial agenda of school system authorities, including elements such as obedience and ranking.

hierarchical observation A form of disciplinary control in which group behaviour is conditioned through observation and surveillance; it is one of three tactics used to produce what **Foucault** called a **docile body**. *Compare* **examination**, **normalizing judgment**.

high culture The culture within a society that is deemed to be sophisticated, civilized, and possessing great taste.

Highland Clearances The eviction by land-owning aristocrats of tenant farmers in Scotland in the late eighteenth and early nineteenth centuries. The clearances, which were carried out to make room for sheep, helped aristocrats capitalize on the rapidly growing textile industry while sending many peasant farmers abroad to find work.

Hill, Daniel G. (1923–2003) American-born Canadian sociologist who specialized in human rights and black Canadian history, later becoming ombudsman of Ontario.

Hirschi, Travis W. (1935–2017) American criminologist whose social control theory suggests that young people engage in antisocial or delinquent behaviour if their bonds to social institutions—family, religion, school, etc.—are weak or broken.

Hitchcock, John T. (1917–2001) American anthropologist who specialized in South Asian studies. His classic work is of the family **socialization** of the Rajput of Khalapur.

homosexual A person (male or female) who is sexually attracted to people of the same sex.

Hughes, Everett C. (1897–1983) American sociologist, trained at the University of Chicago, who while working at McGill University explored the ethnic division of labour between French and English in Quebec.

human capital thesis The theory that marginalized groups earn less money than dominant groups because they possess less human capital in the form of education, skill, and experience.

Humphreys, Margaret (b. 1944) English social worker and social activist who drew public attention to the British government's program of forcibly relocating the children of poor families to Australia, Canada, and other countries of the British Commonwealth.

hurried child syndrome As described by **Elkind**, a situation in which a child, pushed to high levels of accomplishment in school and in after-school activities (such as extracurricular sports and clubs), experiences adult-like levels of stress, guilt, and inadequacy.

Husain, Mir Zohair American Muslim academic who writes about the politics of Islam worldwide.

hypothesis A statement that is verifiable/falsifiable (i.e. that can be proven true or false) and that proposes a specific relationship between or among **variables**. Example: "Playing violent video games makes a person more violent or anti-social."

iatrogenesis As described by **Illich**, health problems that are supposedly caused by health professionals. *See* **clinical iatrogenesis**, **cultural iatrogenesis**, **social iatrogenesis**.

id As described by **Freud**, the instinctive part of the subconscious. (Remember it by the term *inner demons*.)

ideal culture Social life and institutions as they ought to exist based on our social norms, values, and goals. *Compare* **actual culture**.

ideology (*adj.* **ideological**) A relatively coherent set of interrelated beliefs about society and the people in it. Examples include **dominant ideology**, **counter-ideology**, and **liberal ideology**.

ideology of "fag" As described by George Smith, the use of such labels as "gay" and "lesbian" pejoratively as a way to make people conform to strictly prescribed gender roles (e.g. telling a young man who expresses interest in poetry, "You're so gay.").

Illich, Ivan (1926–2002) Austrian philosopher who was a social critic of the **institutions** of modern Western society, especially those of education and medicine.

impression management As described by **Goffman**, the ways in which people present themselves publicly in specific roles and social circumstances. *See* **back stage**, **dramaturgical approach**, **front stage**.

independent variable A **variable** that is believed to have some effect on another variable. *Compare* **dependent variable**.

Indian princess An Indigenous woman portrayed or seen as beautiful, submissive to white men, and ready to betray her nation for the love of a European man. The classic example is Disney's Pocahontas. *Compare* **squaw**.

indirect rule A colonial policy in which a European nation uses members of a particular ethnic group as its intermediaries in ruling an area. The policy often leads to dual colonialism and internal colonialism.

Indo-European (1) A language family that includes almost every language spoken in Europe, as well as the languages of Iran, Afghanistan, Pakistan, and India. (2) The prehistoric peoples that swept from a presumed location in Ukraine to where these languages are spoken today.

informant A person knowledgeable in his or her own culture who provides his or her views of the culture to an outside researcher (a sociologist, an anthropologist, or another ethnographer).

informed consent The process whereby fully informed research subjects indicate their understanding and acceptance of the research conditions and formally agree to be studied. Informed consent includes the understanding that permission can be revoked at a later time.

Innis, Harold (1894–1952) Canadian pioneer of **political economy**, who examined the influence of staples (e.g. fish, fur, minerals, wheat) on the economic and social development of Canada.

insider perspectives The viewpoint(s) of those who experience the subject being studied or written about. *Compare* **outsider perspective**. *See also* **standpoint theory**, **subjective**.

institution an enduring set of ideas, established by law, customs, or practice, about how to accomplish goals that are deemed important within a society or culture. Marriage is an institution, as are education and religion.

institutional ethnography A form of ethnography that challenges the need for a neutral stance in sociological research, claiming instead that any institution or organization can be seen as having two sides: one representing the **ruling interests** of the organization, one representing the interests of those working for the organization (typically in a non-administrative capacity).

institutional racism *Another term for* **systemic racism**.

instrumental education An education model in which courses are narrowly directed to particular sets of tasks or outcomes, and do not involve challenging or being critical of information received. *Compare* **critical education**.

intellectual property Intangible property items such as ideas or artistic works (e.g. literary products, music, films, videos, photographs, drawings, and sculptures) that are the result of a person's creativity.

intelligences A term that expresses the idea that we have different levels of intelligence in different areas of life (e.g. mathematical, computer-related, literary, musical, artistic, culinary, architectural, etc.).

interaction process analysis (IPA) A method pioneered by **Bales** and used in the experimental study of small groups; it codes observations in terms of task vs relationship orientation, dominant vs submissive approach, acceptance vs rejection of authority, and so on.

interlocking matrix of domination The effect on an individual or group of gender-based stereotypes when combined with other minoritizing social factors, such as class or ethnicity.

intersectionality The way different social factors—"race" and ethnicity, gender, sexual orientation, class, age, and disability—combine to shape the negative experience of a minoritized group. The greater the number of negatively valued social locations you have, the greater the degree of discrimination you are likely to experience.

intersex A person with both male and female sexual characteristics, as a result of a biological condition that produces either an atypical combination of male and female chromosomes or both male and female genitals/secondary sexual characteristics.

inverse care law The theory, articulated by **Hart**, that good medical care is most available in populations where it is needed the least and least available in populations where it is needed the most.

inverse correlation A relationship between two **variables** in which an increase in one variable causes a decrease in the other, or vice versa. *Compare* **direct correlation**.

Islamists People who oppose globalization and Western culture generally with narrow-minded and distorted fundamentalist notions of Islam.

Islamophobia Fear or hatred of Muslims or of Islam, especially when viewed as a political or social force.

jihad-i-akbar The personal **jihad**, which represents the perpetual struggle to purge oneself of baser instincts such as greed, racism, hedonism, jealousy, revenge, hypocrisy, lying, and cheating.

jihad-i-asghar Literally "the smaller, lower, or lesser jihad," it is the struggle against aggressors who are not practising Muslims. Islamists practise a distorted version of this.

joint conjugal roles **Conjugal roles** in which many tasks, interests, and activities are shared. *Compare* **segregated conjugal roles**.

Kachuck, Beatrice (1926–2014) American educational psychologist and feminist researcher who identified four categories of feminism: **liberal, essentialist, socialist,** and **postmodernist**.

Khaldûn, Ibn (1332–1406) Arab scholar who presented early, insightful analyses of Middle Eastern societies.

Kroker, Arthur (b. 1945) Canadian political scientist, whose work explores the relationship between technology and culture.

labelling theory As described by **Becker**, the theory that individuals and groups outside the mainstream internalize the labels applied to them by the dominant class. The label may, in this way, cause labelled people to act in a way consistent with the label.

latent dysfunctions As described by **Merton**, the unintended negative consequence of a social process or institution. Example: the latent dysfunction of religion is that it divides people into violently opposed groups. *Compare* **manifest function**.

latent functions As described by **Merton**, the largely unintended and unrecognized positive consequence of a social process or institution. Example: a latent function of religion is that it provides social opportunities for older people who might otherwise be socially isolated. *Compare* **manifest function**.

law of effect As described by **Thorndike**, the principle that the likelihood of a person's repeating an action increases if the action is rewarded, while the likelihood decreases if the action is punished or ignored. The law of effect is central to **behaviour modification**.

legitimzation of inequality In **cultural reproduction theory**, the validation of streaming that occurs when students accept their categorization as, say, "basic" or "advanced" (a judgment that may reflect that person's class or "race"), thereby reproducing social inequality within the school system.

lesbian A woman who is sexually attracted to other women.

liberal feminism A feminist approach that typically involves working toward **pay equity** for women. This form of feminism is criticized as reflecting the concerns of white middle-class Western women while overlooking the concerns of women of different ethnicities and classes.

liberal ideology A set of beliefs that focuses on the individual as an independent player in society, not as a member of a class or an ethnic group. Components of this set include a strong belief in the potential for **social mobility** in the individual (as seen in the **American dream**).

liberation theology A political movement based on a progressive school of Christian thought, rooted in the Catholic Church in Latin America, which advocates social justice for the poor, especially in the developing world.

linguistic determinism (*or* causation) The theory that the way an individual understands the world is shaped by the language he or she speaks. *See* **Sapir–Whorf hypothesis**.

living wage Generally, a salary sufficient to pay for housing, food, and other basic necessities. Any specific definition of this term will be **contested**.

longitudinal studies a study that continues over time to track changes in the research subjects as they get older.

looking-glass self As described by **Cooley**, the self as defined and reinforced through interactions with others.

Lotus Blossom Baby As described by Tajima and Das Gupta, a stereotype of East Asian women as childlike, sexually available, and respectful of men. Evidence of this stereotype may be found in the China doll and in Western notions of the Japanese geisha. *Compare* **Dragon Lady**.

low income cut-off (LICO) A measure of poverty derived by calculating the percentage of a family's income spent on food, clothing, and shelter.

Luddites British members of an early anti-industrial movement in Europe, in which craftspeople who had lost their work with the introduction of labour-saving machines protested by destroying the new machinery. The term is used today to refer to people who resist new technology.

lumpenproletariat As described by **Marx**, the group of people in capitalist society who neither own capital nor participate in wage labour. For the most part, they get by with casual/occasional labour, scavenging for food and articles to sell, and crime.

MacLean, Annie Marion (1869–1934) Canadian sociologist, the second woman to receive a PhD in sociology, and a pioneering researcher in using **participant observation**.

macrosociology An approach to sociological inquiry that involves looking at the large-scale structure and dynamics of society as a whole.

Magdalene laundries (*or asylums*) A Church-run institution for prostitutes, unwed mothers, and young women deemed, based on their supposed promiscuity or low intelligence, to be at risk of being led into premarital sexual relationships. The term comes from St Mary Magdalene, identified by some Christian scholars as a reformed prostitute.

Malthus, Thomas (1766–1834) English minister whose contribution to the study of **political economy** and demography was his view that population growth would inevitably be checked by the opposing impact of famine and disease.

Mandell, Nancy Canadian sociologist who specializes in the study of family and gender.

manifest functions As described by **Merton**, the intended and widely recognized function of a social process or institution. *Compare* **latent function**.

manufacturing of need The creation of consumer demand for (1) items that were once produced in the home, or (2) products that were once considered inessential.

marginalization The experience of being treated as insignificant or of being moved beyond the margin of mainstream society.

marginalized masculinity As described by R. Connell, those forms of masculinity that, owing to class, "race," sexual orientation, and ethnicity, are accorded less respect than other forms of masculinity.

marital roles *Another term for* **conjugal roles**.

Market Basket Measure (MBM) An estimate of the cost of a specific basket of goods and services for a given year, assuming that all items in the basket were entirely provided for out of the spending of the household. Having an income lower than the MBM constitutes low income or poverty.

Martineau, Harriet (1802–1876) British sociologist who is generally considered to be the first woman in the discipline.

Marx, Karl (1818–1883) Influential German economist and thinker, who viewed society primarily in terms of **class** and **social change** in terms of economic factors; he was the founder of modern communism.

mass culture The **culture** of the majority, when that culture is produced by big companies and powerful governments.

master narrative A story that a nation or a people constructs about itself. A master narrative typically makes one group (the group that produced it) look heroic while casting other peoples, including minorities within the group, as bad or invisible.

master status The **status** of an individual that dominates all of his or her other statuses in most social contexts, and plays the greatest role in defining the individual's social identity.

McDonaldization As described by Ritzer, the application of principles of **formal rationalization** seen in the fast-food industry to other sectors of society.

Mead, George Herbert (1863–1931) American founding figure of **symbolic interactionism**

looked at how the self is constructed through personal exchanges with others.

mean A statistical figure usually calculated in the same way as the **average**, but for some purposes determined by taking the sum of the highest and lowest figures only and dividing by two. If I have six coffees one day, then two coffees another, and three another, the mean is $(6 + 2) \div 2 = 4$.

means of production As described by **Marx**, the social means required for producing wealth (e.g. land in feudal times; capital—wealth, machinery—during the industrial period).

median The number that falls in the middle of a series of figures for a given population or group. I worked 10 hours on Monday, 10 hours again on Tuesday, 5 hours on Wednesday, 2 hours on Thursday, and 1 hour on Friday. The median of the set 10, 10, 5, 2, 1 is 5.

medicalization The process by which certain behaviours or conditions are defined as medical problems (rather than, say, social problems), and medical intervention becomes the focus of remedy and social control.

medical model (of disability) A positivist view of disability, representing the perspective of doctors, researchers, and others who believe that science can and should be used to determine treatments, policies, and programs for people living with disabilities. Compare **economic model (of disability)**.

medical sociology The use of sociological research and data to analyze and improve public health, focusing primarily on how health care is administered and whether the medical system adequately supports both the providers and the recipients of health care and health services.

melting pot A metaphor for a country in which immigrants are believed or expected to lose their cultural distinctiveness and assimilate into the dominant society. *Compare* **cultural mosaic**.

Memmi, Albert (b. 1920) French social philosopher of Tunisian Jewish origin, who is one of the foundational writers on the subject of **anti-colonialism**.

meritocratic Describing the tendency to award power or rewards to people based on their demonstrated ability or achievements.

Merton, Robert K. (1910–2003) American sociologist whose many contributions to the discipline include his work in the sociology of science and his coining of important terms such as **reference group**, **role model**, and **status set**.

Métis People of mixed First Nations and European ethnicity (usually Cree or Saulteaux and French) who took on a sense of nationality as well as a distinct legal status.

microsociology An approach to sociology that focuses not on the grand scale of society but on the plans, motivations, and actions of the individual or a specific group. *Compare* **macrosociology**.

middle class The social class made up primarily of small-scale businesspeople, educated professionals, and salaried employees possessing certifiable credentials.

Mills, C. Wright (1916–1962) Influential American sociologist engaged in issues of class, whose work embraced **public sociology**, and who introduced the important concept of the **sociological imagination**.

Miner, Horace (1912–1993) Chicago school American sociologist and anthropologist whose work put the study of French Canada at the forefront of Canadian sociology.

Minturn, Ann Leigh (1928–1999) American social psychologist involved with cross-cultural studies of family and child-rearing.

mismatch A situation in which a person with postsecondary education is working at a job that requires a high school education or less. *See* **underemployment**.

misogyny (*adj.* **misogynous** *or* **misogynistic**) Practices or beliefs in a patriarchal culture that show contempt for women.

mixed-methods approach A research approach that combines qualitative and quantitative methods.

mobility sports Sports such as soccer and boxing that provide access to socioeconomic mobility for the poorest groups in society. These sports do not require significant funds or access to resources and can be played with little or no equipment.

modernism An optimistic view of **social change** that sees change as producing circumstances better than those that preceded them.

moral community As described by **Durkheim**, a group of individuals sharing a commitment to a common moral (usually religious) worldview. Durkheim differed from his contemporaries in viewing religion as a communal rather than individual experience.

moral entrepreneur Someone who tries to convince others of the existence of a particular social problem that he or she has defined.

moral panic Widespread concern over an issue believed to threaten both society and the individuals in it. It is typically the product of exaggeration on the part of a manipulative **moral entrepreneur** (e.g. Donald Trump) or sensationalistic mass media (e.g. Fox News).

moral stigmata *See* **stigma** norm. *Compare* **covert characteristics**.

mores As described by **Sumner**, rules that one *must not* violate. Some of these are enshrined in the criminal code as laws; violation of mores often results in shock, severe disapproval, or punishment.

Morgan, Lewis Henry (1818–1881) Pioneering American anthropologist best known for his work with the Haudenosaunee (Iroquois) in the areas of kinship and social structure.

multiculturalism The set of policies and practices directed toward the respect for cultural differences in a country.

Nakhaie, M. Reza Arab Canadian sociologist involved with a broad range of study areas, including studies of gender and housework.

narrative Stories that reflect the lives and views of the tellers.

narrow socialization Socialization in which obedience and conformity to the standards and expectations of the community are emphasized, and punishment for deviation is practised. *Compare* **broad socialization**.

narrow vision As described by **Chomsky**, a short-sighted view, held by those who believe in **modernism**, that whatever innovation benefits the dominant class is justifiable on the grounds of progress.

national character A now discredited belief, belonging to the culture and personality school of thought, that people of different countries have distinct personalities unique to their country (e.g. Italians are passionate, Germans are cold).

negative correlation *See* **inverse correlation**.

negative sanction Ways of punishing people who contravene cultural norms. Examples include laughing at, isolating, or shaming an individual.

neoliberalism or neoliberal ideology A set of financial policies designed to free (i.e. *liberate*) big businesses through tax cuts, deregulating the economy, eliminating tariffs and other barriers to free trade, and weakening labour unions. *Also called* **neoconservatism**.

neo-traditionalism Among some Indigenous Peoples, a religious movement that involves the reinterpretation of traditional beliefs and practices in ways that incorporate elements unique to one's own culture and others borrowed from Indigenous cultures elsewhere.

Nietzsche, Friedrich (1844–1900) German philosopher championed the "will to power" of the *Übermensch* ("Superman"), who could rise above the restrictions of ordinary society and its morality.

nihilism The extremely pessimistic position that traditional moral principles and values are unimportant or non-existent. It is often accompanied by actions aimed at destruction for its own sake.

niqab An article of clothing that covers the head and face, with a narrow opening for the eyes, worn by some Muslim women for religious and cultural reasons.

non-utilitarian Denoting actions that are not designed to gain financial rewards or desired possessions.

normalized Made to seem "normal," "right," and "good."

normalizing judgment A form of disciplinary control in which group behaviour is conditioned through a judging system that ranks individual performance in relation to the performance of others, rather than on its intrinsic merits; it is one of three tactics used to produce what **Foucault** called a **docile body**. *Compare* **examination**, **hierarchical observation**.

norms Rules or standards of behaviour that are expected of a group, society, or culture.

nuclear family A family comprising a mother, a father, and children. The term is used to describe what is typically considered a "normal" family in North American society.

Oakley, Ann (b. 1944) British feminist sociologist and novelist, who was among the first to distinguish the concepts of **sex** and **gender** in a sociological context.

objectivity (*adj.* **objective**) A supposed quality of scientific research that is not influenced by emotions, personality, or particular life experiences of the individual scientist. It better applies to the physical sciences—physics, chemistry, biology, etc.—than to the social sciences.

observational learning theory The theory that children acquire "aggressive scripts" for solving social problems through watching violence on television.

occupational crimes As described by Clinard and Quinney, offences committed by individuals for themselves in the course of their occupations, or by employers against their employees. *Compare* **corporate crimes**.

occupational segregation As described by **Beaujot**, the situation in which women choose (or end up in) occupations that afford them some flexibility and greater tolerance of childcare-related **work interruptions**.

oligarchy Rule of a country by a few powerful individuals or groups.

operational definition The definition of an abstract quality (e.g. poverty, pollution) in such a way that it can be counted for statistical purposes.

organizational behaviour The study of organizations in terms of the way the individuals within organizations interact.

organizational culture The dynamics of an organization studied in terms of the ritual and symbolic acts carried out by its members.

organizational theory The study of the way organizations operate.

Orientalism As described by **Said**, a romanticized **discourse** about the Middle East and the Far East constructed by outsider "experts" from the West.

Other, the An exotic, often fearful image of a racialized subordinate culture conjured up by the dominant culture.

outsider perspectives The viewpoint(s) of those outside of the group or culture being studied. The outsider perspective was once considered a privileged position, with the outsider viewed as an expert. *Compare* **insider perspective**.

oversocialized As described by **Wrong**, a misleading conception of humans as passive recipients of socialization.

overt characteristics (of deviance) Actions or qualities taken as explicitly violating the cultural.

Park, Robert (1864–1944) American urban sociologist who was a founding member of the Chicago school of sociology.

Parsons, Talcott (1902–1979) Influential conservative American sociologist linked with **structural functionalism.participant observation** A form of research in sociology and anthropology that entails both observing people as an outsider would and actively participating in the various activities of the studied people's lives. It is often used in **ethnographic** research.

particularist protectionist Describing policies (or those who promote them) designed to protect the culture, politics, and economy of a country from foreign competition and the forces of globalization in general. *Compare* **universalist protectionist**.

passing The practice of downplaying or disowning an ascribed status (typically "race" or sexuality) by claiming a dominant status. Indigenous people, for example, may try to pass for white to avoid discrimination; likewise, gay people may pass for straight for the same reason.

patient role See **sick role**.

patriarchal construct A set of social conditions structured in a way that favours men and boys over women and girls.

patriarchy A social system in which men hold political, cultural, and social power. Patriarchy is visible in societies where only male political leaders are elected and where the media and the arts are dominated by male views.

pay equity Compensation paid to women in traditionally female-dominated industries (e.g. child care, library science, nursing, and secretarial work) where salaries and benefits have been lower than those given to employees in comparable (in terms of educational qualifications, hours worked, and social value) professions dominated by men.

peasants In Marxist thinking, the people who in feudal times worked the land but did not own it.

pecking order A hierarchical arrangement of people or animals within a group.

peer group The social group to which one belongs, or to which one wishes to belong, as a more-or-less equal.

peer pressure The social pressure put on an individual to conform to the ways of a particular group that the individual belongs to or wishes to belong to.

peer-review process The rigorous assessment by academic experts of the draft of a scholarly article or book to ensure that the research findings are sound and the work overall is suitable for publication.

petty (or petite) bourgeoisie As described by **Marx**, the sub-class made up of small-time owners with little capital.

phantom aid *See* **tied aid**.

plagiarism A serious form of academic misconduct in which another person's ideas are presented as one's own, whether knowingly or unknowingly.

play stage As described by **Mead**, the second developmental sequence for child socialization, in which pretending is involved. *See* **game stage**, **role-taking**.

policy sociology The use of sociological research and data to produce social change, especially through government or corporate policy.

polite racism *Another term for* **friendly racism**.

political economy An interdisciplinary discipline that involves sociology, political science, economics, law, anthropology, and history. It looks primarily at the relationship between politics and the economics surrounding the production, distribution, and consumption of goods.

political globalization As described by **Steger**, the intensification and expansion of political connections across the world.

polyarchy Literally, government by many people. As described by **Dahl**, this refers to government by changing coalitions of powerful interest groups.

polygamy The practice of having more than one husband or wife at the same time.

polygyny The situation in which a man has more than one wife at the same time is **polygyny**; the analogous situation in which a woman has more than one husband at the same time is **polyandry**.

popular culture Commercial culture based on popular taste.

Porter, John (1921–1979) Influential Canadian sociologist who engaged in foundational work looking at social stratification as it relates to ethnicity. His *Vertical Mosaic* is a classic work in Canadian sociology.

positive correlation *Another word for* **direct correlation**.

positive sanction Ways of rewarding people for following the norms of a society (e.g. inclusion into a desired group, career success).

positivism The belief that every rational assertion can be verified by scientific proof.

positivist Based on or influenced by the belief that every rational assertion can be verified by scientific proof.

postcolonialism A theoretical framework developed by **Fanon** and **Memmi** to analyze the destructive impact colonialism has on both the colonizer and the colonized. *Also called* **anti-colonialism**.

postmodernism A model of **social change** that recognizes that change can benefit some while harming others (e.g. a **digital divide**).

postmodernist Based on or having to do with the model of social theory that discourages the application of binaries to the interpretation of social categories such as gender, "race," and ability.

postmodernist feminism A feminist approach that involves looking at women more as subjects (i.e. people with **voices** and **standpoints** of interpretation) who guide research, rather than as objects being researched.

posttraumatic stress disorder (PTSD) A condition in which the sufferer experiences serious psychobiological symptoms stemming from his or her experience of harrowing events, such as warfare, political oppression, or crime. The condition is often medicalized, so that treatment focuses on the pathology of the individual rather than the pathology of the social environment that provides the context for the event experienced by the sufferer. *See* **medicalization**.

Potlatch Any of various traditional ceremonies of Indigenous groups of the Northwest Coast. It involves reaffirming traditional values and stories through speaking, acting, dancing, and singing important stories, and reflecting the traditional value of generosity through large-scale giveaway of cherished items.

poverty A state of doing or being without what are considered essentials.

poverty line The arbitrary dividing point, usually based on household income, that separates the poor from the rest of society. It can differ according to the cost of living in the studied environment, and it may differ for urban and rural communities. It can also vary according to the political biases of the person drawing the line.

predictability One of four main elements of **Weber**'s model of **formal rationalization**, having to do with setting clear expectations for both the employee and the consumer. *See* **control**, **efficiency**, **quantification**.

prejudice The pre-judging of people based on their membership in a particular social group.

preparatory stage As described by **Mead**, the first developmental sequence of child socialization, which involves pure imitation.

presentism An uncritical adherence to present-day values, seen especially in a tendency to judge or interpret past events in terms of modern values.

primary socialization The earliest socialization that a child receives.

primordialism (*or primordiality*) *Another term for* **essentialism**.

Prince, Samuel Henry (1886–1962) Early Canadian sociologist involved with research of a practical application. His study of the Halifax

Explosion of 1917 is a classic work on the sociology of disasters.

profane Not sacred or concerned with religion. *Compare* **sacred**.

professional sociology Sociology that involves research typically designed to generate highly specific information, often with the aim of applying it to a particular problem or intellectual question. Its usual audience is the academic world of sociology departments, academic journals, professional associations, and conferences.

professionalization The process of turning work done by volunteers into paid work.

proletariat *See* **workers**.

Protestant (work) ethic As described by **Weber**, a set of values embodied in early Protestantism, believed to have led to the development of modern capitalism.

psychoanalysis As described by **Freud**, an approach to psychological study that involves hypothesized stages of development and components of the self (*see* **ego**, **eros**, **id**, **superego**, and **thanatos**). It is used by sociologists to look at individual relationships to society and at cultural expression.

public sociology As described by H. Gans, sociology that addresses an audience outside of the academy. It is presented in a language that can be understood by the college-educated reader, without the dense style of the academic paper or journal, and expresses concern for a breadth of sociological subjects.

purple-collar Modelled on the analogy of white-collar office work, blue-collar manual work, and pink-collar clerical work, this is Emmanuel David's term to describe the work role of transgender women in the Philippines, which involves lightening the mood of colleagues in an environment where the work can be repetitive, dull, or demoralizing. *See* **queer value**.

qualitative research The close examination of characteristics that cannot be counted or measured.

quantification One of four main elements of **Weber**'s model of **formal rationalization**, having to do with breaking a process down into a number of quantifiable tasks that can be easily measured to gauge success. *See* **control**, **efficiency**, **predictability**.

quantitative research The close examination of social elements that can be counted or measured, and therefore used to generate statistics.

queer An informal term for someone (male or female) who is sexually attracted to people of the same sex.

queer theory As described by **Judith Butler**, an approach that rejects the idea that gender identity is connected to some biological essence, proposing instead that gender reflects social performance on a continuum, with "male" and "female" at opposite poles.

queer value Emmanuel David's term for the benefits **purple-collar** transgender employees bring to an office where dull, repetitive, and sometimes demoralizing work is performed. These benefits include the transwomen's ability to entertain and boost the morale of their co-workers.

Quiet Revolution A period in Quebec during the 1960s characterized by province-wide social, economic, and educational reforms, as well as mounting secularization and separatist sentiment.

quintile Each of five ranked groups making up 20 per cent of a total population, used for statistical analysis of such things as household income.

racial bigotry The open, conscious expression of racist views by an individual.

racial profiling Actions undertaken supposedly for reasons of safety, security, or public protection, based on racial stereotypes, rather than on reasonable suspicion.

racialization (*adj.* **racialized**) A social process in which groups of people are viewed and judged as essentially different in terms of their intellect, morality, values, and innate worth because of differences of physical type or cultural heritage.

racialized Categorized or judged (in terms of intellect, morality, values, and innate worth) according to cultural heritage or visible racial characteristics (especially skin colour).

racializing deviance The creation of a connection, through various media (television, movies, textbooks), between a racialized group and a form of deviance or crime (e.g. Latinos and drug dealing, black people, and prostitution).

radical monopoly As described by **Illich**, a situation in which professional control work is deemed socially important (e.g. teachers in education; doctors/nurses in health care). **reading** The process of analyzing or interpreting narrative texts produced by the culture industry, often in ways not necessarily intended by the creators of the text.

red herring A logical fallacy in which a fundamentally irrelevant topic is presented in an argument in order to divert attention from the original and more important issue. Red herrings also occur in literature, as an apparent villain who isn't really that bad. Snape, in the *Harry Potter* series, is an example—his character diverts the reader's attention from other, real villains.

reductionist Denoting any unrealistic statement or theory that attempts to explain a set of phenomena by referring to a single cause. In sociology, this includes **class reductionism**, or reducing all inequality to gender, "race," or ethnicity.

reference group A group perceived by another group to be equal but better off.

refrigerator mothers Women whose lack of maternal affection was thought to be a cause of autism in their sons. The refrigerator mother was a central component of **Bettelheim**'s outdated and now disproven hypothesis surrounding the causes of autism.

Registered Indian An Indigenous person who bears federal government recognition of his or her legal right to the benefits (and penalties) of being "legally Indian." *Formerly called* **status Indian**.

relational Denoting the relationship between a class and the means of producing wealth.

relative deprivation A situation in which an individual or the members of a group feel deprived compared to a **reference group** that they see as having no greater entitlement to their relatively better situation.

relative poverty A state of poverty based on a comparison with others in the immediate area or country. *Compare* **absolute poverty**.

replacement rate The rate at which children must be born in order to replace the generation before them.

reproduction As described by **Bourdieu** the reproduction of social structure refers to the means by which classes, particularly the upper or dominant class, preserve status differences between classes.

research methodology The system of methods a researcher uses to gather data on a particular question.

residential schools A system of educating Indigenous children that involved removing them from their homes and communities, isolating them from their culture, and often abusing them physically, emotionally, and sexually. Underfunded by the federal government, the schools were run by a number of church groups, primarily the Roman Catholic, Anglican, and Presbyterian churches. The system, which began in the late nineteenth century and was formalized in 1910, ended slowly between the 1960s and the 1990s.

resocialization The process of unlearning old ways and learning new ways upon moving into a significantly different social environment.

risk behaviours The social pressure put on an individual to conform to the ways of a particular group that the individual belongs to or wishes to belong to.

rite of passage A ceremony or ritual that marks the passage from one stage of life to another. A wedding is a rite of passage marking the passage from single to married.

ritualized Describing patterns of actions or behaviour that have been established through repetition.

role The function assumed or the part played by a person holding a particular status.

role conflict A situation that occurs when the demands of two separate roles a person has are incompatible. Example: a father who works as a city bus driver cannot pick his sick daughter up from daycare because the demands of his job prevent him from leaving work early.

role exit The process of disengaging from a role that has been central to one's identity and establishing a new role. Role exit occurs, for example, when a person leaves a long-held job or a marriage.

role model An influential person whose patterns of behaviour are observed and imitated by others.

role models An influential person whose patterns of behaviour are observed and imitated by others.

role-playing game A game that allows players to experiment with roles outside of their usual experience by adopting fictitious statuses.

role set All of the roles attached to a particular **status**. For example, attached to the status of "professor" are the roles of educator, colleague, writer, and employee.

role strain A situation that occurs when two or more roles associated with one **status** come into conflict. A nurse may experience role strain when his duty to his employer (the hospital) may come into conflict with his obligations to a patient.

role-taking As described by **Mead**, the developmental stage at which children assume the perspective of **significant others**, imagining what they are thinking as they act the way they do. *Compare* **game stage**, **play stage**.

Ross, Aileen (1901–1995) First Canadian woman hired as a sociologist at a Canadian university. Her *The Lost and Lonely* is a classic work in employing **narrative** as a sociological tool.

rotten apple approach An attempt to downplay the systemic problems in a process or an organization by placing the blame on individuals.

ruling interests The interests of an organization, particularly its administration, or the interests of those who are dominant in society, particularly when these trump the interests of the individual.

ruling relations The conformity of workers to the rules and practices of the organization they work for; ruling relations are activated when workers fulfill the organization's **ruling interests**.

Ryan, William American psychologist and author of *Blaming the Victim*.

sacred Describing an act or experience that is positively regarded and deemed worthy of respect and veneration, being associated with religion and set apart from ordinary acts and experiences. *Compare* **profane**.

Said, Edward (1935–2003) Palestinian American cultural critic and public intellectual whose classic work *Orientalism* describes the West's romanticized perception of the Middle East.

sanctions *See* **negative sanctions**, **positive sanctions**.

Sapir–Whorf hypothesis the theory that the structure of a language determines a person's perception of experience. A milder version argues for linguistic relativity, the view that language and culture have a unique relationship in each society. *See* **linguistic determinism**.

savagery As described by **Morga**, the supposed first stage of social evolution toward modern civilization. *Compare* **barbarism**, **civilization**.

Schecter, Stephen Canadian sociological theorist, as well as poet and performance artist, who applies systems theory to the study of society, which he sees as functionally differentiated and highly complex.

scientific classism The use of flawed, pseudo-scientific ideas (e.g. **eugenics**) to justify discriminatory actions against poor people.

scientific management (*or* Taylorism) An approach to workplace efficiency that involves studying the least amount of time, methods, and tools required for a proficient worker to complete a specific task in order to determine the single best way of doing that job (typically from a management perspective, not the worker's). Named for American mechanical engineer **Frederick Taylor**.

scientific method A method of scientific study that consists of systematic observation, measurement, and experiment, and the formulation, testing, and modification of hypotheses.

scientific racism The use of flawed, pseudo-scientific ideas (e.g. **eugenics**, measuring brain sizes) to justify discriminatory actions against certain racialized groups.

second shift The household labour a woman is expected to perform in addition to the labour she performs in the workplace. *See* **double burden**.

secondary socialization Any socialization that occurs later than the **primary socialization** in the life of a child.

secularism (*adj.* **secular**) Attitudes and activities with no basis in religion.

segregated conjugal roles **Conjugal roles** in which tasks, interests, and activities are clearly differentiated. *Compare* **joint conjugal roles**.

semi-structured interviews Informal, face-to-face interviews designed to cover specific topics without the rigid structure of a questionnaire but with more structure than an open interview.

service-provider organizations As described by Carol Mueller, a type of **feminist organization** that combines elements of **formal social movement organizations** and **small groups**.

settlement house A building in a low-income, working-class, or immigrant neighbourhood where volunteers offer educational, recreational, and other social services to the community. Hull House, established by Jane Addams in Chicago (1889), was one of the earliest settlement houses in North America. Evangelia House, established in Toronto (1902), was an early Canadian example.

sex The biological differences between boys/men and girls/women, as opposed to the sociological differences (which come under the term **gender**).

sexuality Feelings of sexual desire and attraction and how these are expressed.

sick role As described by **Parsons**, the set of expectations that surround a sick person and the experience of being sick.

Siddiqui, Haroon (b. 1942) Indian-born Canadian journalist whose work *Being Muslim* provides an excellent account of Islam for non-Muslims.

Sigmund Freud (1856–1939) Austrian neurological doctor who founded the psychological methodology of **psychoanalysis**.

significant others As described by **Mead**, those key individuals—primarily parents, to a lesser degree older siblings and close friends—whom young children imitate and model themselves after.

Simmel, Georg (1858–1918) German sociologist and initiator of **microsociology**, which involves studying the way people experience the details of daily life.

simple household A household consisting of unmarried, unrelated adults with or without children.

simulacra As described by **Baudrillard**, cultural images, often in the form of stereotypes, that are produced and reproduced like material goods or commodities by the media and sometimes by academics.

Sixties Scoop The removal, between the 1960s and the early 1980s, of thousands of Indigenous children from their families, their communities, their home provinces (particularly Manitoba), and sometimes their home country, to place them in non-Indigenous homes.

slippery slope The logical fallacy that one small change will automatically snowball into the collapse of the entire social order. Slippery-slope arguments are often voiced by adherents of **conservatism**.

small groups As described by Carol Mueller, a type of **feminist organization** with an informal structure, which typically requires large commitments of time and resources from its members. *Also called* **collective**.

smiling racism *Another term for* **friendly racism**.

Smith, Adam (1723–1790) Scottish founder of modern economics, who advocated minimal state interference in business, making him a pioneer of **neoliberalism**.

Smith, Dorothy (b. 1926) British-born Canadian feminist sociologist, who pioneered **standpoint theory** and **institutional ethnography**.

social change The set of adjustments or adaptations made by a group of people in response to a dramatic change experienced in at least one aspect of their lives.

social constructionism The idea that social identities such as gender, ethnicity, and "race" do not exist naturally but are constructed by individuals or groups for different social purposes; **instrumentalism** is an example of social constructionism.

social constructionist model A sociological framework based on the idea that any human social category—"race," gender, ability, etc.—is

not a strictly natural category but a category with an important social component.

social course (**of disease**) The social interactions that a sick person goes through in the process of being treated.

social Darwinist The application to human groups of the principle of **survival of the fittest** in the late nineteenth and early twentieth centuries; it was used to justify the power wielded by Europeans and the upper classes on the grounds that they were the strongest and the "best fit" to hold power.

social distance A lack of personal familiarity that exists when individuals do not have face-to-face interactions, or any interaction at all. Social distance may exist between students of online courses and their instructors.

social ecology A school of thought, founded by **Bookchin**, that recognizes the link between environmental issues and social problems, including economic, cultural, ethnic, and gender conflicts.

social fact **Durkheim**'s term for a patterned way of acting, thinking, and feeling that exists outside of the individual but that exerts control over all people.

social gospel A movement in the late nineteenth and early twentieth centuries in Canada, the United States, and various European countries to apply the human welfare principles of Christianity to the social, medical, and psychological ills brought on by industrialization and uncontrolled capitalism.

social iatrogenesis As described by **Illich**, the deliberate obscuring of political conditions that render society unhealthy.

social inequality The long-term existence of significant differences in access to goods and services among social groups defined by class, ethnicity, etc.

social location Unique vantage point influenced by the important social characteristics of an individual, including class, "race," age, gender, sexual orientation, and degree of ability, that inform the individual's perspective and shape his or her experience.

social mobility The ability to move from one social class into another (usually higher) class.

social order The network of human relationships within society or, more generally, the way society is structured or organized.

social organization The social and cultural principles around which things are structured, ordered, and categorized.

social resources The knowledge and ability required to get what one needs from the system. In the context of law, for example, social resources include knowledge of the legal system, the ability to pay for legal advice, and the ability to present oneself as respectable in a courtroom.

socialist feminism A feminist approach that involves looking at the intersections of oppression between class and gender, focusing mainly on the struggles faced by lower-class women.

sociolinguistics As described by W. Labov, the study of language (particularly **dialect**) as a social marker of status or general distinctiveness, or the study of how different languages conceptualize the world. *See* **Sapir–Whorf hypothesis**.

sociological imagination As described by **Mills**, the capacity to shift from the perspective of the personal experience to the grander, societal scale that has caused or influenced that personal experience.

sociology The social science that studies the development, structure, and functioning of human society.

Spencer, Herbert (1820–1903) British social thinker who believed that societies evolved like plants and animals do. He coined the term **survival of the fittest** and applied it both within and between societies.

spurious reasoning The perception of a correlation between two factors that are wrongly seen as cause and effect.

squaw an offensive stereotype of the Indigenous woman as lazy, drunken, and available for abuse by Indigenous men. *Compare* Indian Princess.

standpoint The unique perspective of an individual based on a set of sociological characteristics including age, sex, gender, social class, "race" or ethnic background, employment status, family situation, degree of physical ability, etc.

standpoint theory As described by **Dorothy Smith**, the view that knowledge is developed from a particular lived position, or "standpoint," making **objectivity** impossible.

statistics A science that, in sociology, involves the use of numbers to map social behaviour and beliefs.

status A recognized social position that a person occupies, which comes with a set of responsibilities and expectations. People hold more than one status (husband, stepfather, pet owner, sociology professor, ball fan, garage band drummer, small-town resident), and a person's statuses can and do change over time. More generally, status refers to the relative social standing of a person or group, typically when it is highly regarded.

status consistency *See* **status inconsistency**.

status frustration As described by **Cohen**, a feeling of failure to succeed in middle-class terms or institutions, leading to participation in **delinquent subculture**. *See* **subcultural theory**.

status hierarchy The ranking of **statuses** within the categories of ethnicity, class, age, etc., based on the degree to which they are favoured by society generally. Heterosexuality, for example, is generally ranked above homosexuality and bisexuality in the status hierarchy associated with sexual preference.

status inconsistency A situation in which the **statuses** a person holds do not align in terms of how they are generally ranked by society. A successful First Nations businessman may experience status inconsistency because his ethnic status is not favoured the way his professional and economic statuses are. When an individual's statuses do align, the result is **status consistency**.

status Indian *A former term for* registered Indian.

status set The complete set of **statuses** held by an individual.

Steger, Manfred (b. 1961) Austrian-born sociologist who specializes in the study of globalization.

stigma (*plural* **stigmata**) As described by **Goffman**, a human attribute that is seen to discredit an individual's social identity: **bodily stigmata** are any of various physical deformities; **moral stigmata** are perceived flaws in the character of an individual; **tribal stigmata** relate to being of a particular lineage or family that has been stigmatized (e.g. the family of a murderer or gang member).

strain theory As described by **Merton**, the theory that individuals are drawn to crime because of the frustration they feel at being prevented by their real-life circumstances from attaining society's culturally defined goals (expressed as the **American dream**).

strata (*sing.* **stratum**) Social classes in ranked layers, with no specific relationship to the means of producing wealth.

structural functionalism A sociological approach that examines the way social systems operate by viewing those systems in terms of the various parts or structures of which they are made. The structural-functionalist approach views society as being like a human body, made up of different structures, with each having a vital function in ensuring the survival of the whole body.

structural-functionalist Approach that views society as being like a human body, made up of different structures, with each having a vital function in ensuring the survival of the whole body.

subcultural theory As described by **Cohen**, the theory that youths drawn to crime are those who, having failed to succeed in middle-class institutions (specifically school), become socialized into a **delinquent subculture** in which the values of middle-class institutions are inverted. Cohen's theory builds on Merton's **strain theory**.

subculture A group that is organized around occupations or hobbies differing from those of the **dominant culture** but that is not engaged in any significant opposition to the dominant culture. People involved in furry fandom, a fascination with anthropomorphic animal characters and costumes, constitute a subculture.

subjective Denoting theories, beliefs, and opinions influenced by emotions, personality, and particular life experiences of the individual. The term is used in opposing ways: some sociologists discredit observation that is "merely subjective" rather than "objective fact"; others argue that all "facts" are to some degree subjective but hide behind the mask of objectivity.

subordinate masculinity As described by R. Connell, behaviours and presentations of self that can threaten the legitimacy of hegemonic masculinity. The usual examples given are gay or effeminate men, and those whose lives and beliefs challenge traditional definitions of male success.

substantive equality In **critical disability theory**, a model according to which architectural modifications guarantee people with physical limitations equal accessibility to and within buildings. More generally, the term applies to situations in which social disadvantages are reduced or eliminated so that all groups have access to a valued good. Compare **formal equality**.

substantive rationalization (*or* rationality) A model of corporate rationality that emphasizes values and ethical norms, rather than the efficiency of business practices. *Compare* **formal rationality**.

Sumner, William Graham (1840–1910) The first American professor of sociology, who introduced to the discipline such terms as **ethnocentrism** and **folkways**.

superego As described by **Freud**, the human conscience or moral sense.

survival of the fittest As described by **Spencer**, the principle, wrongly attributed to Darwin, that only the biggest and strongest survive, both in nature and in human society.

Sutherland, Edwin (1883–1950) American criminal sociologist and **symbolic interactionist**, who introduced the idea of **white-collar crime**.

swaddling hypothesis As described by Gorer and Richman, a hypothesis that attributed the presumed "moodiness" of Russian citizens to their having been too tightly swaddled or wrapped up as infants.

symbol An aspect of a culture that has many strings of meaning that are unique to that culture. Examples include the flag for Americans, hockey for Canadians, songs of the early fourteenth century for Scots.

symbolic interactionism A view of social behaviour that looks at the meaning of daily social interactions, including the words and gestures we use and how these are interpreted by others.

systemic racism Racist practices, rules, and laws that have become institutionalized or made "part of the system." People who benefit from this type of racism tend to be blind to its existence. *Also called* **institutional racism**.

taboo A **norm** so deeply ingrained that the mere thought or mention of it is enough to arouse disgust or revulsion. Examples include incest and cannibalism.

tabula rasa The idea that every human is born as a "blank slate" upon which the culture writes or inscribes a personality, values, and/or a set of abilities.

Taylor, Frederick W. (1856–1915) American mechanical engineer who developed what is termed **scientific management** or **Taylorism.**

Taylorism An approach to workplace efficiency that involves studying the least amount of time, methods, and tools required for a proficient worker to complete a specific task in order to determine the single best way of doing that job (typically from a management perspective, not the worker's). Named for American mechanical engineer **Frederick Taylor**. *Also called* **scientific management**.

team approach A business approach that encourages workers to feel greater involvement in the operation of the company by inviting their ideas and input.

thanatos As described by **Freud**, the violent death instinct within the **id**.

theocracy A system of government in which the leaders rule in the name of a god or gods.

theory An attempt to explain something that has been observed.

third variable A variable that explains the connection or correlation between two other variables.

Thomas theorem The notion that individuals interpret shared experiences differently, and that an individual's view of a particular situation will influence the way she reacts to it.

Thorndike, Edward (1874–1949) American psychologist involved in the establishment of the psychological school of **behaviourism**, largely through his development of the **law of effect**.

Thrasher, Frederic (1892–1962) American sociologist, part of the University of Chicago school of sociology, involved with studying gangs and juvenile delinquency.

tied aid Financial assistance given to a developing country with conditions attached (e.g. that the developing country must spend a portion of the money on products purchased from the donor country). This is sometimes called **phantom aid**, which captures the idea that the aid is not real but rather a form of investment on which the donor country expects to realize a significant return.

tobacco strategy A marketing strategy in which a medical professional or other scientific "expert" is paid by a company to endorse the company's product on scientific grounds. The tactic was first used by tobacco producers, who hired medical researchers to combat public concerns about the health risks of cigarettes.

total fertility rate An estimate of the average number of children that a woman between the ages of 15 and 49 will have in her lifetime if current age-specific fertility rates remain constant during her reproductive years.

total institution As described by **Goffman**, institutions such as the military, hospitals, and asylums that regulate all aspects of an individual's life.

totalitarian discourse Any **discourse** that makes a universal claim about how all knowledge and understanding can be achieved.

totem From the Ojibwa word *ndotem*, meaning "my clan," an animal or natural object that has spiritual significance for a group and is adopted as the group's emblem. **Durkheim** viewed the totem as symbolic both of a particular society and of its god, leading him to conclude that *god = society*.

transgender A person (male or female) who either (a) does not conform to the gender role associated with their biological sex, or (b) does not self-identify with the biological sex assigned to them at birth.

transgender man (*or* **transman**) A female-body person who identifies as a man.

transgender woman (*or* **transwoman**) A male-body person who feels a greater connection to the gender role associated with being a woman.

transsexual A person who either (a) has the physical characteristics of one sex and a persistent desire to belong to the other, or (b) has had surgery (or is undergoing surgery) to have his or her sex changed surgically.

triangulation The use of at least three narratives, theoretical perspectives, or investigators to examine the same phenomenon.

tribal stigmata *See* **stigma**.

trickle-down theory The misleading notion that if wealthy corporations are permitted to operate unfettered by trade restrictions and high corporate taxes, they will generate greater revenues, some of which will "trickle down" to society's poorer citizens in the form of more jobs and higher wages. It is a central pillar of **neoliberalism**.

Two-Spirit people The umbrella term to describe those who identify with one of the many gender roles beyond male and female recognized by Indigenous groups across North America.

ummaic jihad The non-violent struggle for freedom, justice, and truth within the Muslim community. *Compare* **jihad-i-akbar**, **jihad-i-asghar**.

underemployment a situation in which a person does not have enough paid work or else has paid work that does not make full use of the person's abilities and experience. A person with a medical degree earned outside of North America who earns a living as a dab driver because he or she has not been licensed to practise medicine in Canada may be considered underemployed. (It does make a taxicab a good place to give birth.)

universalist protectionist Describing policies (and those who support them) that shield the domestic culture, politics, and economy of poorer countries from foreign competition and the processes of globalization in general. Universalist protectionists are motivated to promote the interests of poor and other marginalized groups and greater social, economic, environmental, political, and cultural equality worldwide. *Compare* **particularist protectionist**.

values Those features held up by a culture as good, right, desirable, and admirable. Values are typically **contested**.

variable A factor or element that is likely to vary or change according to the circumstances governing it. *See* **dependent variable, independent variable**.

Veblen, Thorstein (1857–1929) American economist and social critic best known for critiquing *conspicuous consumption* in the United States.

vertical mosaic **Porter**'s metaphor to describe a society or nation in which there is a hierarchy of higher and lower ethnic groups. *See* **cultural mosaic**.

vested interests A personal interest in a situation from which an individual or group stands to gain in some way. A vested interest can contribute to bias if it is strong enough to override an individual's interest in learning and presenting the truth.

victimology Generally, the study of victims of crime and the psychological effects on them of their experience; in sociology, it often refers to the way a person is portrayed as the victim of some event or situation in a way that downplays or denies the person's **agency**.

virtual class **Kroker**'s term for a **class** of people who control and are dependent for their jobs and economic well-being on digital technologies and the internet.

visible minorities According to Canadian law, people of non-Caucasian ethnicity, non-white skin colour, and non-Indigenous ancestry. As of the 2011 National Household Survey, the three largest visible-minority groups in Canada are South Asians, Chinese, and blacks.

vision quest In traditional Indigenous cultures, a **rite of passage** in which an adolescent leaves the community for a brief period in the hopes of having a vision that will reveal his or her guardian spirit, personal songs, and other things.

voice The expression of *a* (not *the*) viewpoint that comes from occupying a particular **social location**.

Watson, John B. (1878–1958) American psychologist and researcher was a pioneer in **behaviourism**, which he applied to the study of animal behaviour, the raising of children, and advertising.

Weber, Max (1864–1920) German founding figure in sociology, best known for identifying a set of values, the **Protestant (work) ethic**, which he identified as central to the rise of capitalism.

white-collar crime As described by **Sutherland**, non-violent crime committed by a person of the middle or upper middle class in the course of his or her job. Examples include embezzlement and fraud. *See* **corporate crimes, occupational crimes**.

workers As described by **Marx**, the people who work for wages and do not own capital, the means of production, in an industrial, capitalist society. *Also called* **proletariat**.

work interruptions As described by **Baudrillard**, time taken off work, typically by a woman, to care for an infant (i.e. during maternity or paternity leave) or a child who is sick.

working class The social class made up primarily of those who lack resources or skills apart from their own labour power.

Wrong, Dennis H. (1923–2018) Canadian-born sociologist who has specialized in writing about the nature of power and of socialization.

XYY males Men and boys who differ from the "normal" XY chromosome pattern. They are associated with above-average height, a tendency to have acne, impulsive or anti-social behaviour, and slightly lower intelligence than "normal" men and boys.

Zola, Irving K. (1935–1994) American sociologist, activist, and pioneer of disability studies, whose ethnography *Missing Pieces* (1982) chronicles his time spent living in a Dutch community for people with disabilities.

References

Chapter 1

Addams, Jane (1893). "The Subjective Necessity for Social Settlements." In Henry C. Adams (ed.). *Philanthropy and Social Progress*. New York: Thomas Y. Crowell.

Addams, Jane, ed. (1896). *Hull-House Maps and Papers: A Presentation of Nationalities and Wages in a Congested District of Chicago, together with Comments and Essays on Problems Growing out of the Social Conditions*. New York: Thomas Y. Crowell.

Blumer, Herbert (1969). *Symbolic Interactionism: Perspective and Method*. Englewood Cliffs, NJ: Prentice-Hall.

Burawoy, Michael (2004). "The World Needs Public Sociology." *Sosiologisk tidsskrift* (*Journal of Sociology*) 3. http://burawoy.berkeley.edu/PS/Norway.pdf.

Burgess, Ernest (1928). "Factors Determining Success or Failure on Parole." In Illinois, Committee on Indeterminate-Sentence Law and Parole, *The Workings of the Indeterminate-sentence Law and the Parole System in Illinois*, pp. 203–49. Springfield, IL: Division of Pardons and Paroles.

Clark, S.D. (1962). *The Developing Canadian Community*. Toronto: University of Toronto.

Clark, S.D. (1976). *Canadian Society in Historical Perspective*. Toronto: McGraw-Hill.

Criado-Perez, Caroline (2019, Feb. 23). "The Deadly Truth about a World Built for Men—from Stab Vests to Car Crashes." *The Guardian* (online).

Dawson, Carl A., & Warren E. Getty (1948). *An Introduction to Sociology*, 3rd edn. New York: Ronald.

Durkheim, Émile (1951). *Suicide: A Study in Sociology*. Trans. John A. Spaulding & George Simpson. New York: Free Press of Glencoe. (Original work published 1897)

Eichler, Margrit (2001). "Women Pioneers in Canadian Sociology: The Effects of a Politics of Gender and a Politics of Knowledge." *Canadian Journal of Sociology* 26, no. 3 (Summer), pp. 375–404.

Fleras, Augie, & Jean Elliott (1999). *Unequal Relations: An Introduction to Race, Ethnic, and Aboriginal Dynamics in Canada*, 3rd edn. Scarborough, ON: Prentice-Hall, Allyn & Bacon.

Forum Research Inc. (2018, Oct. 15). "Half Approve of Legalized Cannabis." News release, https://poll.forumresearch.com

Foucault, Michel (1980). "Two Lectures." In Colin Gordon (ed.), *Power/Knowledge*, pp. 78–108. New York: Pantheon.

Gallagher, James E., & Ronald D. Lambert, eds (1971). *Social Process and Institution: The Canadian Case*. Toronto: Holt, Rinehart and Winston.

Gans, Herbert (1989, Feb.). "Sociology in America: The Discipline and the Public." *American Sociological Review* 54, pp. 1–16.

Giroux, Henry (2006). *Beyond the Spectacle of Terrorism: Global Uncertainty and the Challenge of the New Media*. Boulder, CO: Paradigm.

Goffman, Erving (1959). *The Presentation of Self in Everyday Life*. New York: Anchor.

Goffman, Erving (1961). *Asylums: Essays on the Social Situation of Mental Patients and Other Inmates*. New York: Anchor.

Harrison, Deborah (1999). "The Limits of Liberalism in Canadian Sociology: Some Notes on S.D. Clark." In Dennis W. Magill & William Michelson (eds), *Images of Change*. Toronto: Canadian Scholars' Press.

Hiller, Harry H., & Linda Di Luzio (2001). "Text and Context: Another 'Chapter' in the Evolution of Sociology in Canada." *Canadian Journal of Sociology* 26 (3), pp. 487–512.

Hofley, John R. (1992). "Canadianization: A Journey Completed?" In William K. Carroll, et al. (eds), *Fragile Truths: 25 Years of Sociology and Anthropology in Canada*, pp. 102–22. Ottawa: Carleton.

Hughes, Everett C. (1963). *French Canada in Transition*. Chicago: University of Chicago. (Original work published 1943)

Hunter College Women's and Gender Studies Collective, & Simalchik, Joan (2017). *Women's Realities, Women's Choices: An Introduction to Women's and Gender Studies*. Don Mills, ON: Oxford University Press.

Ibn Khaldûn (1981). *The Muqaddimah: An Introduction to History*. Trans. N.J. Dawood. Princeton, NJ: Princeton University Press.

Kaizuka, Shigeki (2002). *Confucius: His Life and Thought*. Mineola, NY: Dover. (Original work published 1956)

Lindner, Rolf (1996). *The Reportage of Urban Culture: Robert Park and the Chicago School*. Trans. Adrian Morris. Cambridge, UK: Cambridge University Press.

Lundy, Katherina, & Barbara Warme (1990). *Sociology: A Window on the World*. Toronto: Methuen. (Original work published 1986)

MacLean, Annie Marion (1910). *Wage-Earning Women*. New York: Macmillan.

Marshall, Gordon (1998). *Oxford Dictionary of Sociology*. New York: Oxford.

Marx, Karl (1967). *Capital: A Critique of Political Economy*. Ed. F. Engels. New York: International. (Original work published 1867)

Marx, Karl, & Friedrich Engels (1967). *The Communist Manifesto*. New York: Pantheon. (Original work published 1848)

Marx, Karl, & Friedrich Engels (1970). *The German Ideology*, part 1. Ed. C.J. Arthur. New York: International. (Original work published 1845–6)

Mead, George Herbert (1934). *Mind, Self, and Society*. Chicago: University of Chicago.

Merton, Robert K. (1938). "Social Structure and Anomie." *American Sociological Review* 3 (5), pp. 672–82.

Merton, Robert K. (1968). *Social Theory and Social Structure*. New York: Free Press. (Original work published 1949)

Mills, C. Wright (1948). *The New Men of Power: America's Labor Leaders*. Harcourt, Brace.

Mills, C. Wright (1951). *White Collar: The American Middle Classes*. New York: Oxford.

Mills, C. Wright (1956). *The Power Elite*. New York: Oxford.

Mills, C. Wright (1959). *The Sociological Imagination*. New York: Oxford.

Mills, C. Wright (2001). *Letters and Writings by C. Wright Mills*. Ed. Kathryn Mills and Pamela Mills. Berkeley: University of California.

Miner, Horace (1963). *St Denis: A French Canadian Parish.* Chicago: University of Chicago. (Original work published 1939)

Park, Robert E., & Ernest W. Burgess (1921). *Introduction to the Science of Sociology.* Chicago: University of Chicago.

Park, Robert E., Ernest W. Burgess, & Roderick Duncan McKenzie (1967). *The City: Suggestions for the Study of Human Nature in the Urban Environment.* Chicago: University of Chicago. (Original work published 1925)

Porter, John (1965). *The Vertical Mosaic: An Analysis of Social Class and Power in Canada.* Toronto: University of Toronto.

Ross, Aileen (1962). *The Hindu Family in Its Urban Setting.* Toronto: University of Toronto.

Ross, Aileen (1982). *The Lost and the Lonely: Homeless Women in Montreal.* Montreal: Canadian Human Rights Commission.

Ryan, Erin Gloria (2013). "Smartphones Are Made for Giant Man-Hands." *Jezebel* (online).

Ryan, William (1976). *Blaming the Victim.* New York: Pantheon. (Original work published 1971)

Smith, Dorothy (1987). *The Everyday World as Problematic: A Feminist Sociology.* Boston: Northeastern University.

Smith, Dorothy (1990). *The Conceptual Practices of Power: A Feminist Sociology of Knowledge.* Toronto: University of Toronto.

Steckley, John L. (2003). *Aboriginal Voices and the Politics of Representation in Canadian Sociology Textbooks.* Toronto: Canadian Scholars' Press.

Vermond, Kira (2016, Jan. 19). "Small Change: Women Can Beat the 'Pink Tax' by Buying Guys' Supplies." *The Globe and Mail* (online).

Weber, Max. (1930). *The Protestant Ethic and the Spirit of Capitalism.* Trans. Talcott Parsons. New York: Charles Scribner's Sons. (Original work published 1904)

Weber, Max. (1958). "Essays in Sociology." In M. Weber, H. Gerth, & C.W. Mills (eds), *From Max Weber.* New York: Oxford. (Original work published 1946)

Zhang, Mona (2017, Sept 30). "The Crimes of Reefer Madness." *High Times,* https://hightimes.com/culture/crimes-reefer-madness

Chapter 2

Aboriginal Policing Directorate (1995, July). "Mentor User Guide Gives Aboriginal Youth and Police a Chance to Build Bridges." *First Nations Policing: Update,* 3. Ottawa, ON: Solicitor General Canada: p. 3. www.publicsafety.gc.ca/lbrr/archives/fnpu%203-1995-eng.pdf

Best, Joel (2001). *Damned Lies and Statistics: Untangling Numbers from the Media, Politicians, and Activists.* Berkeley: University of California.

Campbell, Marie, & Frances Gregor (2002). *Mapping Social Relations: A Primer in Doing Institutional Ethnography.* Aurora, ON: Garamond.

Centers for Disease Control and Prevention (2018, Dec. 19). "Prescription Opioid Data" (online). Atlanta, GA: CDC.

Comte, Auguste (1830–42). *Cours de Philosophie Positive.* Paris: Librairie Larousse.

Comte, Auguste (1851–4). *Système de Politique Positive.*

Comte, Auguste (1853). *The Positive Philosophy of August Comte.* Trans. & ed. Harriet Martineau. Longon: Longmans.

Comte, Auguste (1877). *The System of Positive Polity.* London: Longmans, Green.

Durkheim, Émile (1951). *Suicide: A Study in Sociology.* Trans. John A. Spaulding & George Simpson. New York: The Free Press of Glencoe. (Original work published 1897)

Esar, Evan (1943). *Esar's Comic Dictionary of Wit and Humour.* New York: Horizon.

Foucault, Michel (1961). *Madness and Civilisation: A History of Insanity in the Age of Reason.* New York: Vintage.

Foucault, Michel (1975). *Discipline and Punish: The Birth of the Prison.* New York: Vintage.

Foucault, Michel (1978). *The History of Sexuality. Vol. 1: An Introduction.* New York: Pantheon.

Gephart, Robert (1988). *Ethnostatistics: Qualitative Foundations for Quantitative Research.* London: Sage.

Giles, Philip. 2004. "Low Income Measurement in Canada," cat. no. 75F0002MIE, Statistics Canada. https://www150.statcan.gc.ca/n1/pub/75f0002m/75f0002m2004011-eng.pdf

Goffman, Alice (2014). *On the Run: Fugitive Life in an American City.* Chicago: University of Chicago Press.

Goffman, Erving (1976). *Gender Advertisements.* New York: Harper Torch.

Gomm, Roger, & Patrick McNeil, eds (1982). *Handbook for Sociology Teachers.* London: Heinemann Educational.

Griswold, Wendy (1994). *Cultures and Societies in a Changing World.* London: Sage.

Hall, Elaine J. (1988). "One Week for Women? The Structure of Inclusion of Gender Issues in Introductory Textbooks." *Teaching Sociology* 16 (4), pp. 431–2.

Hughes, Everett C. (1963). *French Canada in Transition.* Chicago: University of Chicago. (Original work published 1943)

Humphreys, R.A. Laud (1970). *Tearoom Trade: A Study of Homosexual Encounters in Public Places.* London, UK: Duckworth.

Jhally, Sut (1990). *The Codes of Advertising: Fetishism and the Political Economy of Meaning in the Consumer Society.* New York: Routledge.

Lammam, Charles, & Hugh MacIntyre (2016, January). *An Introduction to the State of Poverty in Canada.* Toronto, ON: Fraser Institute.

Leung, Pamela T.M., Erin M. Macdonald, Irfan A. Dhalla, & David N. Juurlink (2017, Jun. 1). "A 1980 Letter on the Risk of Opioid Addiction." *New England Journal of Medicine* 376, pp. 2194–5.

Maines, D.R. (1993). "Narrative's Moment and Sociology's Phenomena—Toward a Narrative Sociology." *Sociological Quarterly* 34 (1), pp. 17–37.

Maracle, Brian (1996). *Back on the Rez: Finding The Way Home.* Toronto: Viking Penguin.

Maracle, Lee (1992). *Sundogs.* Penticton, BC: Theytus.

Marshall, Gordon (1998). *Oxford Dictionary of Sociology.* New York: Oxford.

Miner, Horace (1963). *St Denis: A French Canadian Parish.* Chicago: University of Chicago. (Original work published 1939)

Pew Research Center (2016, Aug.). "Opinions on Gun Policy and the 2016 Campaign." Washington, DC: Pew (online).

Porter, Jane, & Hershel Jick (1980). "Addiction Rare in Patients Treated with Narcotics." *New England Journal of Medicine* 302, p. 123.

Reinharz, Shulamit (1992). *Feminist Methods in Social Research.* New York: Oxford.

Road Safety Research Office (2016). Preliminary 2016 Ontario Road Safety Annual Report Selected Statistics. Toronto, ON: Ministry of Transportation. www.mto.gov.on.ca/english/publications/pdfs/preliminary-2016-orsar-selected-statistics.pdf

Ross, Aileen (1961). *Becoming a Nurse.* Toronto: Macmillan.

Ross, Aileen (1982). *The Lost and the Lonely: Homeless Women in Montreal*. Montreal: Canadian Human Rights Commission.

Said, Edward (1979). *Orientalism*. New York: Pantheon.

Sarlo, Christopher (2013, Nov.). "Poverty: Where Do We Draw the Line?" Toronto, ON: Fraser Institute.

Smith, Joanna (2015, Feb. 8). "High-Paid Chiefs are Outliers, Data Shows." *Toronto Star* (online).

Smith, Linda Tuhiwai (1999). *Decolonizing Methodologies: Research and Indigenous Peoples*. London: Zed Books.

Sofalvi, Alan J. (2008). "Male Condom Advertising in United States Magazines and on the World Wide Web from 1997–2007: Implications for Media Literacy and Health Literacy." *International Electronic Journal of Health Education* 11: pp. 81–94.

Special Advisory Committee on the Epidemic of Opioid Overdoes (2019, June). *National Report: Apparent Opioid-Related Deaths in Canada (January 2016 to December 2018)*. Web-based report. Ottawa, ON: Public Health Agency of Canada. https://health-infobase.canada.ca/datalab/national-surveillance-opioid-mortality.html

Statistics Canada (2011). "Low Income Cut-Offs." *Low Income Lines, 2009–2010*. Income Research Paper Series. www.statcan.gc.ca/pub/75f0002m/75f0002m2011002-eng.htm

Statistics Canada (2013). "National Household Survey Dictionary, 2011," cat. no. 99-000-X2011001. Ottawa, ON: Minister of Industry.

Statistics Canada (2017). "Table 4.5: Market Basket Measure (MBM) thresholds for economic families and persons not in economic families, 2015." *Dictionary, Census of Population, 2016*. https://www12.statcan.gc.ca/census-recensement/2016/ref/dict/tab/t4_5-eng.cfm

Weaver, R., C. Ferguson, M. Wilbourn, & Y. Salamonson (2014, April). "Men in Nursing on Television: Exposing and Reinforcing Stereotypes." *Journal of Advanced Nursing* 70 (4), pp. 833–42.

Whyte, William F. (1955). *Street-Corner Society: The Social Structure of an Italian Slum*, 2nd edn. Chicago: University of Chicago.

Chapter 3

Adams, Michael (2003). *Fire and Ice: The United States and the Myth of Converging Values*. Toronto: Penguin Canada.

Adams, Michael (2014). *Fire and Ice Revisited: American and Canadian Social Values in the Age of Obama and Harper*. Speech presented at the Woodrow Wilson Center, Washington, DC, March 14.

Adams, Michael (2017, May 27). "Trump, Trudeau and the Patriarchy." *The Globe and Mail*, p. F7.

Anderson, Karen L. (1996). *Sociology: A Critical Introduction*. Toronto: Nelson.

Baudrillard, Jean (1983). *Simulations*. Trans. Paul Foss, Paul Patton, & Philip Beitchman. New York: Semiotext[e].

Bissell, Tom (2003). *Chasing the Sea: Lost Among the Ghosts of Empire in Central Asia*. New York: Pantheon.

Bohannan, Laura (1966). "Shakespeare in the Bush." *Natural History* (Aug./Sept.). Reprinted in E. Angeloni (ed.), *Annual Editions Anthropology, 1995/1996*, pp. 65–9.

Bourdieu, Pierre (1970). *La reproduction: Eléments pour une théorie d'enseignement*. Paris: Éditions de Minuit.

Brean, Joseph (2014, Jun. 17). "Vancouver School Board's Genderless Pronouns—Xe, Xem, Xyr—Not Likely to Stick, If History Is Any Indication." *National Post* (online).

de Certeau, Michel (1984). *The Practice of Everyday Life*. Trans. S. Rendell. Berkeley, CA: University of California.

Fadiman, Anne (1997). *The Spirit Catches You and You Fall Down. A Hmong Child, Her American Doctors, and the Collision of Two Cultures*. New York: Farrar, Straus and Giroux.

Fikes, Jay (1996). "A Brief History of the Native American Church." In Huston Smith & Reuben Snake, eds (1996), *One Nation Under God: The Triumph of the Native American Church*. Santa Fe, NM: Clear Light Publishers.

Fiske, John (2010). *Understanding Popular Culture*, 2nd edn. London: Routledge.

Gidén, Carl, Patrick Houda, and Jean-Patrice Martel (2014). *On the Origin of Hockey*. Hockey Origin Publishing.

Hodkinson, Paul (2011). "Ageing in a Spectacular Youth Culture: Continuity, Change and Community in the Goth Scene." *British Journal of Sociology* 62, pp. 262–82.

Hodkinson, Paul (2013). "Family and Parenthood in an Ageing 'Youth' Culture: A Collective Embrace of Dominant Adulthood?" *Sociology* 47 (6), pp. 1072–87.

Hoodfar, Homa (2003). "More Than Clothing: Veiling as an Adaptive Strategy." In Sajida Alvi, H. Hoodfar, & Sheila McDonough (eds), *The Muslim Veil in North America: Issues and Debates*, pp. 3–40. Toronto: Women's Press.

James, Jennifer (2009, Oct.). "Peyote & Mescaline: History Lessons." Cat. no. 133. Do It Now Foundation (online).

LaRocque, Emma (1975). *Defeathering the Indian*. Agincourt, ON: Book Society of Canada.

Lutz, John (2012). "Vanishing the Indians: Aboriginal Labourers in Twentieth-Century British Columbia." In Kristen Burnett & Geoff Read, eds, *Aboriginal History: A Reader*, pp. 305–20. Don Mills, ON: Oxford.

MacCannell, Dean (1999). *The Tourist: A New Theory of the Leisure Class*. Berkeley: University of California Press. (Original work published 1976)

McGillivray, Anne & Brenda Comaskey (1999). *Black Eyes All of the Time: Intimate Violence, Aboriginal Women and the Justice System*. Toronto: University of Toronto.

Norton, William (2006). *Cultural Geography: Environments, Landscapes, Identities, Inequalities*, 2nd edn. Don Mills, ON: Oxford.

Plante, Courtney, Stephen Reysen, Sharon E. Roberts, Kathleen C. Gerbasi (2016). "Fur Science! A Summary of Five Years of Research from the International Anthropomorphic Research Project" (online). Retrieved: https://furscience.com/wp-content/uploads/2017/10/Fur-Science-Final-pdf-for-Website_2017_10_18.pdf

Porter, John (1965). *The Vertical Mosaic: An Analysis of Social Class and Power in Canada*. Toronto: University of Toronto.

Said, Edward (1979). *Orientalism*. New York: Pantheon.

Smith, N. (2009). "Beyond the Master Narrative of Youth: Researching Ageing Popular Music Scenes." In D. Scott (ed.), *The Ashgate Research Companion to Popular Musicology*. Farnham, UK: Ashgate.

Steger, Manfred B. (2003). *Globalization: A Very Short Introduction*. Oxford, UK: Oxford.

Sumner, William Graham (1906). *Folkways: A Study of the Sociological Importance of Usages, Manners, Customs, Mores, and Morals*. Boston: Ginn and Co.

Van De Poel, Nana (2018, Sept. 26). "Explainer: 'I Speak Dutch, Not Flemish." *Culture Trip*, https://theculturetrip.com/europe/the-netherlands/articles/explainer-i-speak-dutch-not-flemish

Chapter 4

Aguiar, Luis (2001). "'Whiteness' in White Academia." In Carl James & Adrienne Shadd (eds), *Talking About Identity: Encounters in Race, Ethnicity and Language*, 2nd edn, pp. 177–92. Toronto: Between the Lines.

Armstrong, Karen (2005). *Through the Narrow Gate: A Memoir of Life in and out of the Convent*. Toronto: Vintage Canada. (Original work published 1982)

Arnett, Jeffrey, & Lene Balle-Jensen (1993). "Cultural Bases of Risk Behavior: Danish Adolescents." *Child Development* 64, pp. 1842–55.

Bhanot, Ruchi, & Jasna Jovanovic (2005, May). "Do Parents' Academic Gender Stereotypes Influence Whether They Intrude on Their Children's Homework?" *Sex Roles* 52 (9–10), pp. 597–607.

Bourdieu, Pierre (1996). *On Television*. New York: New.

Brown, W. Michael Court (1968). "Males with an XYY Sex Chromosome Complement." *Journal of Medical Genetics* 5 (4), pp. 341–59.

Bushman, Brad J., & L. Rowell Huesmann (2001). "Effects of Televised Violence on Aggression." In D. Singer & J. Singer (eds), *Handbook of Children and the Media*, pp. 223–54. Thousand Oaks, CA: Sage.

Cooley, Charles Horton (1902). *Human Nature and the Social Order*. New York: Charles Scribner's Sons.

Cooley, Charles Horton (1909). *Social Organization: A Study of the Larger Mind*. New York: Charles Scribner's Sons.

Elkind, David (2001). *The Hurried Child: Growing Up Too Fast Too Soon*, 3rd edn. Cambridge, MA: Perseus. (Original work published 1981)

Elkind, David (2003). "The Reality of Virtual Stress." *CIO* (Fall/Winter). www.cio.com/archive/092203/elkind

Finkel, Michelle A. (2002). "Traumatic Injuries Caused by Hazing Practices." *Journal of Emergency Medicine* 20, pp. 228–33.

Fowles, Jib (1999). *The Case for Television Violence*. London: Sage.

Fowles, Jib (2001, March). "The Whipping Boy: The Hidden Conflicts Underlying the Campaign against TV." *Reason* (online).

Freud, Sigmund (1977). *On Sexuality*, vol. 7. London: Penguin. (Original work published 1916–17)

Gilligan, Carol (1990). *Making Connections: The Relational Worlds of Adolescent Girls at Emma Willard School*. Cambridge, MA: Harvard University Press.

Goffman, Erving (1961). *Asylums: Essays on the Social Situation of Mental Patients and Other Inmates*. New York: Anchor.

Gorer, Geoffrey, & John Rickman (1949). *The People of Great Russia: A Psychological Study*. New York: Norton.

Hersh, Seymour (2004). "The Gray Zone: How a Secret Pentagon Program Came to Abu Ghraib." *The New Yorker* (24 May).

Hitchcock, John T., & Leigh Minturn (1963). "The Rajputs of Khalapur." In B. Whiting (ed.), *Six Cultures: Studies of Child Rearing*, pp. 203–362. New York: John Wiley & Sons.

Huesmann, L. Rowell, & L.D. Eron (1986). *Television and the Aggressive Child: A Cross-national Comparison*. Mahwah, NJ: Lawrence Erlbaum.

Huesmann, L. Rowell, J. Moise, C.P. Podolski, & L.D. Eron (2003). "Longitudinal Relations between Childhood Exposure to Media Violence and Adult Aggression and Violence: 1977–1992." *Developmental Psychology* 39 (2), pp. 201–21.

Jacobs, Patricia A., Muriel Brunton, Marie M. Melville, Robert P. Brittain, & William F. McClemont (1965). "Aggressive Behaviour, Mental Sub-normality and the XYY male." *Nature* 208 (5017), pp. 1351–2.

Kane, P.R., & A.J. Orsini (2003). "The Need for Teachers of Color in Independent Schools." In P.R. Kane & A.J. Orsini (eds), *The Colors of Excellence: Hiring and Keeping Teachers of Color in Independent Schools*, pp. 7–28. New York: Teachers College.

Keilman, John (2013, June 26). "Youth Sports That Don't Keep Score? How Un-American." *Chicago Tribune* (online).

Kirby, Sandra L., & Glen Wintrup (2002). "Running the Gauntlet: An Examination of Initiation/Hazing and Sexual Abuse in Sport." *Journal of Sexual Aggression* 8 (2), pp. 49–68.

Klopfenstein, Kristin (2005). "Beyond Test Scores: The Impact of Black Teacher Role Models on Rigorous Math Taking." *Contemporary Economic Policy* 23, pp. 416–28.

Knockwood, Isabelle (1992). *Out of the Depths: The Experiences of Mi'kmaw Children at the Indian Residential School at Shubenacadie*. Lockeport, NS: Roseway.

Kohn, Melvin L. (1959). "Social Class and Parental Values." *American Journal of Sociology* 64 (4), pp. 337–66.

Kohn, Melvin L. (1977). *Class and Conformity: A Study in Values*, 2nd edn. Chicago: University of Chicago Press.

Marshall, Gordon (1998). *Oxford Dictionary of Sociology*. New York: Oxford.

McInnis, Opal A., Matthew M. Young, & Student Drug Use Surveys Working Group (2015, Sept.). *Urban and Rural Student Substance Abuse: Technical Report*. Ottawa, ON: Canadian Centre on Substance Abuse.

Mead, George Herbert (1934). *Mind, Self, and Society*. Chicago: University of Chicago.

Nicolosi, Joseph, & Linda Ames Nicolosi (2002). *A Parent's Guide to Preventing Homosexuality*. Downers Grove, IL: InterVarsity Press.

Ontario Soccer Association (OSA) (2015). *The Ontario Soccer Association Grassroots Festival Guide*. www.ontariosoccer.net/images/publications/2015/about/employment/Grassroots_Festival_Guide_2015.pdf

Organisation for Economic Co-operation and Development (OECD) (2016). *PISA 2015 Results (Vol. 1): Excellence and Equity in Education*. Paris, France: OECD Publishing.

O'Sullivan, Patrick, with Gare Joyce (2015). *Breaking Away: A Harrowing Story of Resilience, Courage, and Triumph*. Toronto: HarperCollins.

Patai, Raphael (2014). *The Arab Mind*, updated edn. New York: Recovery Resources Press. (Original work published 1973)

Postman, Neil (1982). *The Disappearance of Childhood*. New York: Delacorte Press.

Price, William H., & Peter B. Whatmore (1967). "Behaviour Disorders and Pattern of Crime among XYY Males Identified at a Maximum Security Hospital." *British Medical Journal* 2 (5601), pp. 533–6.

Steckley, John, & Brian Rice (1997). "Lifelong Learning and Cultural Identity: A Lesson from Canada's Native People." In Michael Hatton (ed.), *Lifelong Learning: Policies, Programs & Practices*, pp. 216–29. Toronto: APEC.

Telfer, Mary A. (1968). "Are Some Criminals Born That Way?" *Think* 34 (6), pp. 24–8.

Thorndike, Edward (1999). *Animal Intelligence: Experimental Studies*. Piscataway, NJ: Transaction. (Original work published 1911)

Ungerleider, Charles, Terri Thompson, & Tracy Lavin (2012, Dec. 26). "No Quick Fix for Gender Gap in Education." *Toronto Star* (online).

Voyer, D., & S.D. Voyer (2014, July). "Gender Differences in Scholastic Achievement: A Meta-Analysis." *Psychological Bulletin* 140 (4), pp. 1174–204.

Waldron, J.J., & C.L. Kowalski (2009). "Crossing the Line: Rites of Passage, Team Aspects, and Ambiguity of Hazing." *Research Quarterly for Exercise and Sport* 80 (2), pp. 291–302.

Watson, John B. (1925). *Behaviorism*. New York: Norton.

Watson, John B., & Rosalie Rayner (1920). "Conditioned Emotional Reactions." *Journal of Experimental Psychology* 3 (1), pp. 1–14.

Whiting, Beatrice B. (1963). *Six Cultures: Studies of Child Rearing*. New York: John Wiley.

Willis, Paul E. (1977). *Learning to Labour: How Working Class Kids Get Working Class Jobs*. New York: Columbia University Press.

Wrong, Dennis (1961). "The Oversocialized Conception of Man in Modern Sociology." *American Sociological Review* 26 (2), pp. 183–93.

Chapter 5

APA. (2006). "When the Boss is a Woman." Available at https://www.apa.org/research/action/boss

Bales, Robert F. (1950). *International Process Analysis: A Method for the Study of Small Groups*. Chicago: University of Chicago Press.

Barrowcliffe, Mark (2008). *The Elfish Gene: Dungeons, Dragons and Growing Up Strange—A Memoir*. London, UK: Soho.

Becker, Howard (1963). *Outsiders: Studies in the Sociology of Deviance*. New York: The Free Press.

Ebaugh, Helen Rose Fuchs (1988). *Becoming an EX: The Process of Role Exit*. Chicago: University of Chicago.

Etzioni, Amitai (1964). *Modern Organizations*. Englewood Cliffs, NJ: Prentice-Hall.

Fletcher, Michael A., & Jon Cohen (2011, Feb. 20). "Economy Poll: African Americans, Hispanics Were Hardest Hit but Are Most Optimistic." *The Washington Post* (online).

Frum, David (2017, Oct. 3). "On Gun Control Following the Las Vegas Shooting." Interview by Matt Galloway. *Metro Morning* [Toronto], CBC Radio. www.cbc.ca/news/canada/toronto/programs/metromorning/on-gun-control-following-the-las-vegas-shooting-1.4318401

Hanson, Glen R., Peter J. Hanson, Peter J. Venturelli, & Annette E. Fleckenstein (2009). *Drugs and Society*, 10th edn. New York: Jones and Bartlett.

Hughes, Everett C. (1945). "Dilemmas and Contractions of Status." *American Journal of Sociology* 50 (5), pp. 353–9.

Islam, Gazy, & Michael J. Zyphur (2009). "Rituals in Organizations: A Review and Expansion of Current Theory." *Group Organization Management* 34 (114), pp. 114–39.

Jones, Robert P. (2017, July 4). "Trump Can't Reverse the Decline of White Christian America." *The Atlantic* (online).

Kearney, Melissa S., Brad Hershbein, & Elisa Jácome (2015, April 20). *Profiles of Change: Employment, Earnings, and Occupations from 1990–2013*. The Hamilton Project. Washington, DC: Brookings.

Kushner, David (2009). *Levittown: Two Families, One Tycoon, and the Fight for Civil Rights in America's Legendary Suburb*. New York: Walker & Company.

Ligaya, Armina & Deschamps, Tara (2018). "The Corporate Climb: Stalled Progress for Women in Canada C suites." The Canadian Press (31 July).

Long, Elizabeth (2003). *Women and the Uses of Reading in Everyday Life*. Chicago: University of Chicago Press.

Love, John F. (1995). *McDonald's: Behind the Arches*, rev. edn. Toronto: Bantam.

Merton, Robert K. (1968). *Social Theory and Social Structure*. New York: Free Press. (Original work published 1949)

Mills, Albert J., & Tony Simmons (1995). *Reading Organization Theory: A Critical Approach*. Toronto: Garamond.

Mueller, Carol (1995). "The Organizational Basis of Conflict in Contemporary Feminism." In Myra Marx Ferree & Patricia Yancey Martin (eds), *Feminist Organizations*, pp. 263–75. Philadelphia: Temple University.

Penny, Laura (2005). *Your Call Is Important to Us: The Truth about Bullshit*. Toronto: McClelland & Stewart.

Ritzer, George (2004). *The McDonaldization of Society*, rev. edn. Newbury Park, CA: Pine Forge Press.

Thomas, W.I. (1966). *W.I. Thomas on Social Organization and Social Personality. Selected Papers*. Ed. Morris Janowitz. Chicago: University of Chicago.

Thomas, W.I., & Florian Znaniecki (1996). *The Polish Peasant in Europe and America*. Urbana: University of Illinois. (Original work published 1918–20)

Thompson, Derek (2016, May 13). "Donald Trump and the Twilight of White America." *The Atlantic* (online).

Thrasher, Frederic M. (1927). *The Gang: A Study of 1,313 Gangs in Chicago*. Chicago: University of Chicago.

Totten, Mark, (2014). *Gang Life: 10 of the Toughest Tell Their Stories*. Toronto: James Lorimer.

Totten, Mark, & Daniel Totten (2012). *Nasty Brutish and Short: The Lives of Gang Members in Canada*. Toronto: James Lorimer Press.

Venkatesh, Sudhir (2008). *Gang Leader for a Day: A Rogue Sociologist Takes to the Streets*. New York: Penguin.

Weber, Max (1930). *The Protestant Ethic and the Spirit of Capitalism*. Trans. Talcott Parsons. New York: Charles Scribner's Sons. (Original work published 1904)

Weber, Max (1958). "Essays in Sociology." In M. Weber, H. Gerth, & C.W. Mills (eds), *From Max Weber*. New York: Oxford. (Original work published 1946)

Weber, Max (1968). *Economy and Society: An Outline of Interpretive Sociology*. New York: Bedminster. (Original work published 1914)

Whyte, William F. (1955). *Street-Corner Society: The Social Structure of an Italian Slum*, 2nd edn. Chicago: University of Chicago.

Chapter 6

Allen, M. (2018). Police-Reported Crime Statistics in Canada, 2017. Available at https://www150.statcan.gc.ca/n1/en/pub/85-002-x/2018001/article/54974-eng.pdf?st=-5Rtky5_

Becker, Howard (1963). *Outsiders: Studies in the Sociology of Deviance*. New York: The Free Press.

Clinard, M., & R. Quinney (1973). *Criminal Behavior Systems: A Typology*, 2nd edn. New York: Holt, Rinehart, and Winston.

Cohen, Albert K. (1955). *Delinquent Boys: The Culture of the Gang*. Glencoe, IL: Free Press.

Contenta, Sandro & Jim Rankin (2009, June 6). "Suspended Sentences: Forging a School-to-Prison Pipeline?" *Toronto Star* (online).

Davis, Lennard J. (2006). "Constructing Normalcy: The Bell Curve, the Novel, and the Invention of the Disabled Body in the Nineteenth Century." In Lennard J. Davis (ed.), *The Disability Studies Reader*, 2nd edn, pp. 3–16. New York: Routledge.

Demerson, Velma (2004). *Incorrigible*. Waterloo, ON: Wilfrid Laurier University Press.

EKOS (2017). *National Justice Survey: Canada's Criminal Justice System*. Department of Justice Canada (online).

http://publications.gc.ca/collections/collection_2018/jus/J4-52-2017-eng.pdf

Ford, Matt (2016, April 15). "What Caused the Great Crime Decline in the US?" *The Atlantic* (online).

Gaul, Ashleigh (2014, Sept. 20). "Between the Lines: Tracing the Controversial History and Recent Revival of Inuit Facial Tattoos." *Up Here* (online).

Goddard, Henry H. (1911). "Heredity of Feeble-Mindedness." *American Breeders Magazine* 1 (3).

Goffman, Erving (1963). *Stigma: Notes on the Management of Spoiled Identity.* Englewood Cliffs, NJ: Prentice-Hall.

Gramlich, John (2017, Feb. 21). "5 Facts about Crime in the US." *Factank: News in the Numbers.* Washington, DC: Pew Research Center.

Hanlon, Tegan (2015, Oct. 16). "Inupiaq Woman Joins Movement to Revitalize Traditional Tattooing." *Alaska Dispatch News* (online).

Hayes, Chris (2017). *A Colony in a Nation.* New York: Norton.

Hirschi, Travis W. (1969). *Causes of Delinquency.* Berkeley: University of California Press.

Lieberman, Jay A., Christopher Weiss, Terence J. Furlong, Mati Sicherer, & Scott H. Sicherer (2010, Oct.). "Bullying among Pediatric Patients with Food Allergy." *Annals of Allergy, Asthma & Immunology* 105 (4), pp. 282–6.

Matthews, Dylan (2014, June 5). "How Mid-Century Ireland Dealt with Unwed Mothers and Their Children, and Why We're Talking about It Today." *Vox Media* (online).

Mazón, Mauricio (1984). *The Zoot-Suit Riots: The Psychology of Symbolic Annihilation.* Austin: University of Texas.

Merton, Robert K. (1938). "Social Structure and Anomie." *American Sociological Review* 3 (5), pp. 672–82.

Muir, Leilani (2014). *A Whisper Past—Childless after Eugenic Sterilization in Alberta.* Calgary: Friesen Press.

Murphy, Emily (1973). *The Black Candle.* Toronto: Coles. (Original work published 1922)

Ontario Human Rights Commission (OHRC) (2003). *Paying the Price: The Human Cost of Racial Profiling.* Inquiry Report. Toronto: OHRC. www.ohrc.on.ca/en/paying-price-human-cost-racial-profiling

Quan, Douglas (2015, Feb. 12). "Harper Vows to Appeal Court Ruling Allowing Women to Wear Niqab during Citizenship Oath, Calls It 'Offensive.'" *National Post* (online).

Reiman, Jeffrey (2007). *The Rich Get Richer and the Poor Get Prison: Ideology, Class, and Criminal Justice,* 8th edn. Boston: Allyn & Bacon.

Rotenberg, Cristine (2016, April 12). *Aboriginal Peoples Survey, 2012: Social Determinants of Health for the Off-Reserve First Nations Population, 15 Years of Age and Older, 2012.* Statistics Canada cat. no. 89-653-X2016009. Ottawa, ON: Minister of Industry.

Said, Edward (1979). *Orientalism.* New York: Pantheon.

Scull, Andrew (2009). *Hysteria: The Disturbing History.* Oxford, UK: Oxford University Press.

Smith, James M. (2007). *Ireland's Magdalen Laundries and the Nation's Architecture of Containment.* Notre Dame, IN: University of Notre Dame.

Stote, Karen (2015). *An Act of Genocide: Colonialism and the Sterilization of Aboriginal Women.* Halifax: Fernwood Publishing.

Sutherland, Edwin (1940). "White Collar Criminality." *American Sociological Review* 5 (1), pp. 1–12.

Sutherland, Edwin (1949). *White Collar Crime.* New York: Holt, Rinehart and Winston.

Swift, Art (2016, Oct. 19). "Support for Legal Marijuana Use Up to 60% in U.S." *Social Issues.* Washington, DC: Gallup.

Tepperman, Lorne, & Michael Rosenberg (1998). *Macro/Micro: A Brief Introduction to Sociology,* 3rd edn. Scarborough, ON: Prentice Hall, Allyn & Bacon.

Truman, Jennifer L., & Rachel E. Morgan (2016, Oct.). *Criminal Victimization, 2015.* Bureau of Justice Statistics bulletin NCJ 250180. Washington, DC: U.S. Department of Justice.

Usher, Nikki (2016, July 26). "Interview: Why the Public Perception of Crime Exceeds the Reality." *All Things Considered.* National Public Radio.

Venkatesh, Sudhir (2008). *Gang Leader for a Day: A Rogue Sociologist Takes to the Streets.* New York: Penguin.

York, Geoffrey (1990). *The Dispossessed: Life and Death in Native Canada.* Toronto: Lester & Orpen Dennys.

Zimring, Franklin E. (2007). *The Great American Decline.* New York: Oxford University Press.

Chapter 7

Blatchford, Andy (2015, Feb. 1). "'Middle-Class' Politics: Who Belongs to this Vote-Rich Group?" *CBC News* (online).

Blum, William (2003). *Killing Hope: US Military & CIA Interventions since World War II.* London: Zed Books.

Bouw, Brenda (2018, Oct. 23). "Ontario to Freeze Minimum Wage, Eliminate Mandatory Paid Sick Days." *The Globe and Mail* (online).

Bregman, Rutger (2016). *Utopia for Realists: The Case for a Universal Basic Income, Open Boarders, and a 15-Hour Workweek.* The Correspondent (Kindle edition).

Bruemmer, René, & Kevin Dougherty (2012, May 3). "CLASSE Student Group Presents Counter Proposal to End Boycott." *The Gazette* (online).

"Canada's Top CEOs Leave the 99% in Their Gold Dust" (2012, Jan. 3). *Toronto Star* (online).

Crehan, Kate (2002). *Gramsci, Culture and Anthropology.* Berkeley: University of California.

Cummins, Bryan D. (2003). *Only God Can Own the Land,* Canadian Ethnography Series Vol. 1. Toronto: Pearson.

Curtis, James, Edward Grabb, & Neil Guppy, eds (1999). *Social Inequality in Canada: Patterns, Problems and Policies,* 3rd edn. Scarborough, ON: Prentice-Hall.

Dubrick, James, Brandon Mathews, & Clare Cady (2016). *Hunger on Campus: The Challenge of Food Insecurity for College Students.* http://studentsagainsthunger.org/wp-content/uploads/2016/10/Hunger_On_Campus.pdf

Flavelle, Dana (2012, Jan. 3). "Canada's 0.01%." *Toronto Star,* pp. B1–B3.

Food Banks Canada (2004). *HungerCount 2004: A Comprehensive Report on Hunger and Food Bank Use in Canada, and Recommendations for Change.* Mississauga, ON: Canadian Association of Food Banks.

Food Banks Canada (2015). *HungerCount 2015: A Comprehensive Report on Hunger and Food Bank Use in Canada, and Recommendations for Change.* Mississauga, ON: Food Banks Canada.

Food Banks Canada (2017). *HungerCount 2016.* Mississauga, ON: Food Banks Canada.

Food Banks Canada (2019). *HungerCount 2018.* Mississauga, ON: Food Banks Canada.

Forbes (2018). The World's Highest-Paid Athletes: 2018 Ranking. www.forbes.com/athletes/list/

Forget, Evelyn L. (2011). "The Town with No Poverty: Using Health Administration Data to Revisit Outcomes of a

Canadian Guaranteed Annual Income Field Experiment" (online). University of Manitoba.

Goldrick-Rab, Sara (2016). "Preface." In James Dubrick, Brandon Mathews, & Clare Cady, *Hunger on Campus: The Challenge of Food Insecurity for College Students.* http://studentsagainsthunger.org/wp-content/uploads/2016/10/Hunger_On_Campus.pdf

Gramsci, Antonio (1992). *Prison Notebooks*, vol. 1. Ed. Joseph A. Buttligieg. New York: Columbia University Press.

Grattan, E. (2003). "Social Inequality and Stratification in Canada." In Paul Angelini (ed.), *Our Society: Human Diversity in Canada*, 2nd edn, pp. 61–86. Scarborough, ON: Thompson-Nelson.

Hodges, David, & Mark Brown (2015, Jan. 27). "Are You in the Middle Class?" *Maclean's* magazine (online).

Hopper, Tristin (2016, Apr. 27). "Why Canadian White People Have So Much Trouble Understanding Why Somebody Wouldn't Want to Leave Attawapiskat." *National Post* (online).

Lemieux, Thomas, & W. Craig Riddell (2015, July 9). *Who Are Canada's Top 1 Percent?* (online). Montreal: Institute for Research on Public Policy.

Lowe, Kevin, Stan Fischler, & Shirley Fischler (1988). *Champions: The Making of the Edmonton Oilers.* Scarborough, ON: Prentice-Hall.

Marx, Karl (1967). *Capital: A Critique of Political Economy.* Ed. F. Engels. New York: International. (Original work published 1867)

Marx, Karl, & Friedrich Engels (1967). *The Communist Manifesto.* New York: Pantheon. (Original work published 1848)

McQuaig, Linda, & Neil Brooks (2012). *Billionaire's Ball: Gluttony and Hubris in an Age of Epic Inequality.* Boston: Beacon Press.

Ormsby, Mary (2007). "Why Gear Is Dear." *Toronto Star* (8 Dec.), pp. S1, S6.

Rutherford, Kate (2016, April 9). "Attawapiskat Declares State of Emergency over Spate of Suicide Attempts." *CBC News* (online).

Rutherford, Kristina (2009, Jan. 16). "Is the Cost Keeping Kids out of Minor Hockey? Absolutely, Players and Parents Say." *CBC News* (online).

Ryan, William (1976). *Blaming the Victim.* New York: Pantheon. (Original work published 1971)

Scoffield, Heather (2011, Nov. 29). "Locals Disagree on Who's to Blame for Attawapiskat Crisis." *The Globe and Mail* (online).

Smith, Adam (1976). *The Theory of Our Moral Sentiments.* Ed. D.D. Raphael & A.L. Macfie. Oxford: Oxford University Press. (Original work published 1759)

Snowden, Jonathan (2013, May 3). "Family's History of Violence Has Shaped Money May." *Bleacher Report* (online).

Standing, Guy (2011). *The Precariat: The New Dangerous Class.* London and New York: Bloomsbury Academic.

Statistics Canada. Table 36-10-0586-01, Distributions of household economic accounts, income, consumption, and saving, by characteristic.

Statistics Canada. Table 36-10-0586-01, Distributions of household economic accounts, wealth, Canada, regions, and provinces.

Statistics Canada (2018). *Canadian Megatrends: The Fall and Rise of Canada's Top Income Earners.* www150.statcan.gc.ca/n1/pub/11-630-x/11-630-x2016009-eng.htm

Tencer, Daniel (2019, Feb. 9). "Did Ontario's Minimum Wage Hike Kill Jobs? A Look at the Numbers, 1 Year Later." *Huffington Post* (online).

Weber, Max (1930). *The Protestant Ethic and the Spirit of Capitalism.* Trans. Talcott Parsons. New York: Charles Scribner's Sons. (Original work published 1904)

Weber, Max (1958). "Essays in Sociology." In M. Weber, H. Gerth, & C.W. Mills (eds), *From Max Weber.* New York: Oxford. (Original work published 1946)

Weber, Max (1968). *Economy and Society: An Outline of Interpretive Sociology.* New York: Bedminster. (Original work published 1914)

Chapter 8

Adachi, Ken (1976). *The Enemy That Never Was: A History of Japanese Canadians.* Toronto: McClelland & Stewart.

Armstrong, Amelia (2019, April 30). "Police-Reported Hate Crime in Canada, 2017." *Juristat.* Statistics Canada, cat. no. 85-002-X.

Backhouse, Constance (1999). *Colour-Coded: A Legal History of Racism in Canada, 1900–1950.* Toronto: University of Toronto Press.

Burnet Jean R., & Howard Palmer (1988). *"Coming Canadians": An Introduction to a History of Canada's Peoples.* Ottawa, ON: Ministry of Supply and Services.

Chan, Anthony B. (2019, May 22). Chinese Canadians. *The Canadian Encyclopedia* (online).

Chrétien, Jean-Pierre (1997). *Le défi de l'ethnisme: Rwanda et Burundi, 1990–1996.* Karthala.

Cobb, Russell (2017). "Dreams of a Black Oklahoma: On the Trail of the Forgotten Okies of Alberta." In *Race Reader: A Literary Chronicle of Conflict and Oppression in Middle America*, pp. 15–21. Tulsa, OK: This Land Press.

Codjoe, Henry M. (2001). "Can Blacks Be Racist? Further Reflections on Being 'Too Black and African.'" In Carl James & Adrienne Shadd (eds), *Talking about Identity: Encounters in Race, Ethnicity and Language*, pp. 277–90. Toronto: Between the Lines.

Collins, Patricia Hill (1990). *Black Feminist Thought: Knowledge, Consciousness and the Politics of Empowerment.* Boston: Unwin Hyman.

Dauvergne, Mia, & Shannon Brennan (2011). "Police-Reported Hate Crime in Canada, 2009." *Juristat.* Statistics Canada, cat. no. 85-002-X.

Dick, Lyle (2010). "Sergeant Masumi Mitsui and the Japanese Canadian War Memorial." *The Canadian Historical Review* 91 (3), pp. 435–63.

Du Bois, W.E.B. (1896). *The Suppression of the African Slave Trade in America.* New York: Longmans, Green.

Du Bois, W.E.B. (1903). *The Souls of Black Folk.* Chicago: A.C. McClurg.

Du Bois, W.E.B. (1935). *Black Reconstruction: An Essay toward a History of the Part which Black Folk Played in the Attempt to Re-Construct Democracy in America.* New York: Harcourt Brace.

Du Bois, W.E.B. (1940). *Dusk of Dawn.* New York: Harcourt, Brace & World.

Du Bois, W.E.B. (1967). *The Philadelphia Negro: A Social Study.* New York: Schocken Books. (Original work published 1899)

Fanon, Franz (1965). *The Wretched of the Earth.* New York: Grove. (Original work published 1961)

Fanon, Franz (1967). *Black Skin, White Masks.* New York: Grove. (Original work published 1952)

Foucault, Michel (1980). "Two Lectures." In Colin Gordon (ed.), *Power/Knowledge*, pp. 78–108. New York: Pantheon.

Foucault, Michel (1994). *The Archaeology of Knowledge*. London: Routledge. (Original work published 1972.)

Gonzalez-Barrera, Ana & Mark Hugo Lopez (2015, June 15). "Is Being Hispanic a Matter of Race, Ethnicity or Both?" *Fact Tank: New in the Numbers*. Washington, DC: Pew Research Center.

Hill, Daniel (1960). *Negroes in Toronto: A Sociological Study of a Minority Group*. Unpublished doctoral dissertation.

Hill, Daniel (1981). *The Freedom Seekers: Blacks in Early Canada*. Agincourt, ON: Book Society of Canada.

Isajiw, Wsevolod W. (1999). *Understanding Diversity: Ethnicity and Race in the Canadian Context*. Toronto: Thomson.

Johnston, Hugh (1989). *The Voyage of the* Komagata Maru: *The Sikh Challenge to Canada's Colour Bar*. Vancouver: University of British Columbia Press.

Jolly, Joanna (2019). *Red River Girl: The Life and Death of Tina Fontaine*. New York: Viking.

LaRocque, Emma (1993). "Three Conventional Approaches to Native People." In Brett Balon & Peter Resch (eds), *Survival of the Imagination: The Mary Donaldson Memorial Lectures*, pp. 209–18. Regina: Coteau.

Lewis, Oscar (1998). "The Culture of Poverty." *Society* 35 (2), pp. 7–9.

Matthews, Jason (2011, November 22). "Black Kickers in the NFL 1966 to 2015–16: Final Prejudice or Rarest Athlete?" www.thebigbangauthor.com/2011/11/black-kickers-in-nfl-final-prejudice-or.html

Memmi, Albert (1991). *The Colonizer and the Colonized*. Boston: Beacon. (Original work published 1957)

Milan, Anne, & Kelly Tran (2004, spring). "Blacks in Canada: A Long History." *Canadian Social Trends*, pp. 2–7.

Newbury, Catharine (1993). *The Cohesion of Oppression*. New York: Columbia. (Original work published 1988)

Nightengale, Bob (2016, April 15). "As MLB Celebrates Jackie Robinson, Dearth of Black Pitchers Concerns Many." *USA Today* (online).

Owusu-Bempah, Akwasi, & Scot Wortley (2014). "Race, Crime, and Criminal Justice in Canada." In Sandra Bucerius & Michael Tonry (eds), *The Oxford Handbook of Ethnicity, Crime, and Immigration*. New York: Oxford.

Priest, Lisa (1989), *Conspiracy of Silence: The Riveting Account of the The Pas Murder, Cover-up, and Inquiry*. (Toronto, ON: McClelland & Stewart.)

Sapers, Howard (2015). *Annual Report of the Office of the Correctional Investigator, 2014–15*. Ottawa, ON: Ministry of Public Safety.

Statistics Canada (2015, Dec. 24). *Aboriginal Statistics at a Glance*, 2nd edn, cat. no. 89-645-x2015001. Ottawa, ON: Minister of Industry.

Statistics Canada (2017a, Oct. 25). "Aboriginal Peoples in Canada: Key Results from the 2016 Census." *The Daily* (online). Ottawa, ON: Minister of Industry.

Statistics Canada (2017b). *Canada: Census Profile*. Cat. no. 98-316-X2016001. Ottawa, ON: Minister of Industry.

Statistics Canada (2017c, Oct. 25). *Visible Minority and Population Group Reference Guide, Census of Population, 2016*. Cat. no. 98-500-X2016006. Ottawa, ON: Minister of Industry.

Statistics Canada (2018). *Aboriginal Population Profile, 2016 Census*. Cat. no. 98-510-X2016001. Ottawa, ON: Minister of Industry.

Statistics Canada (2019, Feb. 27). "Diversity of the Black Population in Canada: An Overview." *Ethnicity, Language, and Immigration Thematic Series*. Cat. no. 89-657-X2019002. Ottawa, ON: Minister of Industry.

Steckley, John L. (2003). *Aboriginal Voices and the Politics of Representation in Canadian Sociology Textbooks*. Toronto: Canadian Scholars' Press.

Steckley, John L. (2013). *Learning from the Past: Five Cases of Aboriginal Justice*. Whitby, ON: De Sitter Publications.

Tatum, Beverly Daniel (2003). *"Why Are All the Black Kids Sitting Together in the Cafeteria?" and Other Conversations about Race*, rev. edn. New York: Basic Books.

Taylor, Drew Hayden (1996). *Funny, You Don't Look Like One: Observations from a Blue-Eyed Ojibway*. Penticton, BC: Theytus.

Tuck, Eve, & K. Wayne Yang (2012). "Decolonization Is Not a Metaphor." *Decolonization: Indigeneity, Education & Society* 1 (1), pp. 1–40.

Veenstra, Gerry (2011, Oct.). "Mismatched Racial Identities, Colourism, and Health in Toronto and Vancouver." *Social Science & Medicine* 73 (8), pp. 1152–62.

Venkatesh, Sudhir (2006). *Off the Books: The Underground Economy of the Urban Poor*. Cambridge, MA: Harvard University Press.

Wilson, William Julius (2009). *More than Just Race: Being Black and Poor in the Inner City*. New York: Norton.

Chapter 9

Bauer, Greta R., Ayden I. Scheim, Jake Pyne, Robb Travers, & Rebecca Hammond (2015). "Intervenable Factors Associated with Suicide Risk in Transgender Persons: A Respondent Driven Sampling Study in Ontario, Canada." BMC *Public Health* 15, p. 525.

Bothelo-Urbanski, Jessica (2016, July 11). "Baby Storm Five Years Later: Preschooler on Top of the World." *Toronto Star* (online).

Brightwell, Laura (2016, May 10). "Attack on Canada's Only Surgery Clinic for Trans People Elicits 'Zero Reaction.'" *Rabble.ca*.

Butler, Judith (1990). *Gender Trouble: Feminism and the Subversion of Identity*. London: Routledge.

Cameron, S., 2010, *On the Farm: Robert William Pickton and the tragic story of Vancouver's missing women*, Toronto: Knopf Canada.

Chen, Anita Beltran (1998). *From Sunbelt to Snowbelt: Filipinos in Canada*. Calgary: Canadian Ethnic Studies Association.

Cohoon, J.M. (2006). "Just Get over It or Just Get on with It: Retaining Women in Undergraduate Computing." In J.M. Cohoon & W. Aspray (eds), *Women in Information Technology: Research on Underrepresentation*, pp. 205–37. Cambridge, MA: MIT Press.

Colapinto, John (2000). *As Nature Made Him: The Boy Who Was Raised as a Girl*. New York: HarperCollins.

Connell, R.W. (1995). *Masculinities*. Berkeley: University of California.

"Cross about Cross-Dressing: Is It a Wicked Western Habit that Should Be Stopped?" (2010, Jan. 28). *The Economist* (online).

Dalton, Lync (2017, June 5). "There's a Lot of Talk about 'Toxic Masculinity.' Is There an Equivalent 'Toxic Femininity'?" Quora (online).

Das Gupta, Tania (1996). *Racism and Paid Work*. Toronto: Garamond.

David, Emmanuel (2015). "Purple-Collar Labor Transgender Workers and Queer Value at Global Call Centers in the Philippines." *Gender & Society* 29 (2), pp. 169–94.

"Defying Gender Expectations through Gender Performance: Boyat in the UAE" (2009, Feb. 23). *The Globe and Mail* (online).

Elder, Miriam (2013, Jun. 11). "Russia Passes Law Banning Gay 'Propaganda'." *The Guardian* (online).

Feirstein, Bruce (1982). *Real Men Don't Eat Quiche; A Guidebook to All That Is Truly Masculine.* New York: Pocket Books.

Goulding, W. D., 2001, *Just Another Indian: A Serial Killer and Canada's Indifference*, Markham: Fifth House.

Hango, Darcy (2013, Dec.). "Gender Differences in Science, Technology, Engineering, Mathematics and Computer Science (STEM) Programs at University." *Insights on Canadian Society*, Statistics Canada, cat. no. 75-006-X. Ottawa, ON: Minister of Industry.

Hochschild, Arlie (1983). *The Managed Heart: Commercialization of Human Feeling.* Berkeley: University of California Press.

Hurst, Mike (2009, Sept. 11). "Caster Semenya Has Male Sex Organs and No Womb or Ovaries." *The Daily Telegraph* (London, UK) (online).

Jivani, Jamil (2018). *Why Young Men: Rage, Race, and the Crisis of Identity.* Toronto: HarperCollins.

Kachuck, Beatrice (2003). "Feminist Social Theories: Themes and Variations." In Sharmila Rege (ed.), *Sociology of Gender: The Challenge of Feminist Sociological Knowledge.* New Delhi: Sage. (Original work published 1995)

Kehoe, Alice (1995). "Blackfoot Persons." In L. Klein & L. Ackerman, *Women and Power in Native North America.* Norman: University of Oklahoma Press.

Keleta-Mae, Naila (2016, Feb. 8). "Get What's Mine: 'Formation' Changes the Way We Listen to Beyonce Forever." *Vice.com.*

Kruijver, FP, J.N. Zhou, C.W. Pool, M.A. Hofman, L.J. Gooren, & D.F. Swaab (2000, May). "Male-to-Female Transsexuals Have Female Neuron Numbers in a Limbic Nucleus." *Journal of Clinical Endocrinology and Metabolism* 85 (5), pp. 2034–41.

Leffingwell, William (1925). *Office Management: Principles and Practice.* Chicago: A.W. Shaw.

Lowe, Graham S. (1980). "Women, Work and the Office: The Feminization of Clerical Occupations in Canada, 1901–1931." *The Canadian Journal of Sociology*, 5 (4), pp. 361–81.

Mangis, Kari (2017). "Okay Men, Let's Talk About Toxic Femininity." The Good Men Project. https://goodmenproject.com/featured-content/talk-about-toxic-femininity-chwm/

Moyser, Melissa (2017, March 8). *Women in Canada: A Gender-based Statistical Report. Women and Paid Work.* Statistics Canada, cat. no. 89-503-X. Ottawa, ON: Minister of Industry.

Naidoo, Amelia (2011, April 21). "Shedding Light on the 'Boyat' Phenomenon." *GulfNews.com.*

Oakley, Ann (1972). *Sex, Gender and Society.* London: Temple Smith.

Priest, Lisa, 1989, *Conspiracy of Silence*, Toronto: McClelland & Stewart.

Poisson, Jayme (2013, Nov. 15). "Remember Storm? We Check in on the Baby Being Raised Gender-Neutral." *Toronto Star* (online).

Rosario, M., E. Scrimshaw, J. Hunter, & L. Braun (2006). "Sexual Identity Development among Lesbian, Gay, and Bisexual Youths: Consistency and Change Over Time." *Journal of Sex Research* 43 (1), pp. 46–58.

Ruddick, Sara (1989). *Maternal Thinking: Toward a Politics of Peace.* Boston: Beacon.

Sargent, Paul (2005, Feb.). "The Gendering of Men in Early Childhood Education." *Sex Roles: A Journal of Research* 52 (3/4), pp. 251–59.

Smits, David D. (1982). "The 'Squaw Drudge': A Prime Index of Savagism." *Ethnohistory* 29 (4), pp. 281–306.

Statistics Canada (2016). 2016 Census of Population, Statistics Canada cat. no. 98-400-X2016295 to 98-400-X2016298. Ottawa, ON: Minister of Industry.

Statistics Canada (2018a). Table 14-10-0023-01. Labour force characteristics by industry, annual (x 1,000).

Statistics Canada (2018b). Table 37-10-0012-01. Postsecondary graduates, by program type, credential type, Classification of Instructional Programs, Primary Grouping (CIP_PG) and sex.

Steckley, John L. (1999). *Beyond Their Years: Five Native Women's Stories.* Toronto: Canadian Scholars' Press.

Steckley, John, 2013, "The Helen Betty Osborne Case,", pp. 55-86, *Learning from the Past: Five Cases of Aboriginal Justice*, Whitby: De Sitter.

Tajima, E. Renee (1989). "Lotus Blossoms Don't Bleed: Images of Asian Women." In Asian Women United of California (ed.), *Making Waves: An Anthology of Writings by and About Asian American Women*, pp. 305–9. Boston: Beacon.

Ubelacker, Sheryl (2015, April 17). "Health Care System Can Often Be a Challenge for Transgender Patients." *Global News* (online).

Uppal, Sharanjit, & Sébastien LaRochelle-Côté (2014, April). "Changes in the Occupational Profile of Young Men and Women in Canada." *Insights on Canadian Society*, Statistics Canada, cat. no. 75-006-X. Ottawa, ON: Minister of Industry.

Warner, Jessica (2002). *Craze: Gin and Debauchery in an Age of Reason.* New York: Basic.

West, Candace, & Don H. Zimmerman (1987, June). "Doing Gender." *Gender and Society* 1 (2), pp. 125–51.

York, Geoffrey, & Paul Waldie (2019, May 1). "International Sports Court Upholds Testosterone Testing for Women against Caster Semenya Challenge." *The Globe & Mail.*

Chapter 10

Armstrong, Pat, & Hugh Armstrong (2010). *The Double Ghetto: Canadian Women and Their Segregated Work.* Don Mills, ON: Oxford University Press. (Original work published 1978)

Baudrillard, Jean (1983). *Simulations.* Trans. Paul Foss, Paul Patton, & Philip Beitchman. New York: Semiotext[e].

Baynes, Chris (2017, July 8). "More than 200,000 Children Married in the US over the Last 15 Years." *The Independent* (online).

Beaujot, Rod (2000). *Earning and Caring in Canadian Families.* Peterborough, ON: Broadview.

Beaujot, Rod (2002). "Earning and Caring: Demographic Change and Policy Implications." *Canadian Studies in Population* 29 (2), pp. 195–225.

Beaujot, Rod (2004, June 15). "Delayed Life Transitions: Trends and Implications." *Vanier Institute of the Family.* www.vifamily.ca/library/cft/delayed_life.html

Bibby, Reginald Wayne (1995). *The Bibby Report: Social Trends Canadian Style.* Toronto: Stoddard.

Bolaria, B. Singh, & Peter S. Li (1985). *Racial Oppression in Canada.* Toronto: Garamond.

Bott, Elizabeth (1957). *Family and Social Networks: Roles, Norms, and External Relationships in Ordinary Urban Families.* London: Tavistock.

Budgell, Janet (1999). *Our Way Home: A Report to the Aboriginal Healing and Wellness Strategy: Repatriation of Aboriginal*

People Removed by the Child Welfare System: Final Report. Prepared by Native Child and Family Services of Toronto, Sevenato and Associates. Toronto: Native Child and Family Services of Toronto.

Dasgupta, Sathi (1992). "Conjugal Roles and Social Network in Indian Immigrant Families: Bott Revisited." *The Journal of Comparative Family Studies* 23 (3), p. 465.

Dosman, Edgar J. (1972). *Indians: An Urban Dilemma.* Toronto: McClelland & Stewart.

Fournier, S., & E. Crey (1997). *Stolen from Our Embrace.* Vancouver: Douglas & McIntyre.

Goldscheider, Frances, & Regina Bures (2003). "The Racial Crossover in Family Complexity in the United States." *Demography* 40 (3), pp. 569–87.

Hochschild, Arlie Russell, & Anne Machung (1989). *The Second Shift: Working Parents and the Revolution at Home.* New York: Viking Penguin.

Houle, Patricia, Martin Turcotte, & Michael Wendt (2017, June 1). "Changes in Parents' Participation in Domestic Tasks and Care for Children from 1986 to 2015." *Spotlight on Canadians: Results from the General Social Survey.* Statistics Canada cat. no. 89-652-X. Ottawa, ON: Minister of Industry.

Human Resources and Skills Development Canada (2014). *Indicators of Well-Being in Canada: Family Life—Marriage.* Online.

Kelly, Mary Bess (2012). "Divorce Cases in Civil Court, 2010/2011." *Juristat,* Statistics Canada cat. no. 85-002-X. Ottawa: Minister of Industry.

Kimelman, Edwin C. (1985). *No Quiet Place: Review Committee on Indian and Metis Adoption and Placements.* Manitoba Community Services.

Larkin, Philip (1974). "This Be The Verse." *High Windows.* London: Faber and Faber.

Leah, Ronnie, & Gwen Morgan (1979). "Immigrant Women Fight Back: The Case of the Seven Jamaican Women." *Resources for Feminist Research* 7 (3), pp. 23–4.

Mandell, Nancy, & Ann Duffy (1995). *Canadian Families: Diversity, Conflict and Change.* Toronto: Harcourt Brace.

Milan, Anne (2013, July). "Fertility: Overview, 2009 to 2011." Report on the Demographic Situation in Canada. Statistics Canada cat. No 91-209-X.

Milan, Anne, Hélène Maheux, & Tina Chui (2012). *A Portrait of Couples in Mixed Unions.* Statistics Canada cat. no. 11-008-X. Ottawa, ON: Minister of Industry.

Miller, J.R. (1996). *Shingwauk's Vision: A History of Native Residential Schools.* Toronto: University of Toronto Press.

Nakhaie, M. Reza (1995). "Housework in Canada: The National Picture." *Journal of Comparative Family Studies* 23 (3), pp. 409–25.

"Plural Wife Describes Life in Bountiful Commune" (2011, Jan. 27). *CTV News* (online).

Provencher, Claudine, Anne Milan, Stacey Hallman, & Carol D'Aoust (2018, June 5). "Fertility: Overview 2012 to 2016." *Report on the Demographic Situation in Canada.* Statistics Canada cat. no. 91-209-X. Ottawa, ON: Minister of Industry.

Rajulton, Fernando, T.R. Balakrishnan, & Zenaida R. Ravanera (1990). "Measuring Infertility in Contracepting Populations." Presentation, Canadian Population Society Meetings (Victoria, BC, June 1990).

Reiss, Fraidy (2015, Oct. 13). "America's Child-Marriage Problem." *The New York Times* (online).

Revised Statutes of Canada, c. C-34, s. 43.

Seeley, John, R. Alexander Sim, & E.W. Loosely (1956). *Crestwood Heights: A Study of the Culture of Suburban Life.* Toronto: University of Toronto Press.

Statistics Canada (2009). "Household Size Declining." *Canada Year Book Overview, 2008.* Ottawa, ON: Minister of Industry.

Statistics Canada (2011). *Women in Canada: A Gender-Based Statistical Report,* cat. no. 89-503-X. Ottawa, ON: Minister of Industry.

Statistics Canada (2012). *Portrait of Families and Living Arrangements in Canada: Families, Households, and Marital Status, 2011 Census of Population,* cat. no. 98-312-X2011001. Ottawa, ON: Minister of Industry.

Statistics Canada (2014). "Mixed Unions in Canada." *National Household Survey (NHS), 2011,* cat. no. 99-010-X2011003. Ottawa, ON: Minister of Industry.

Statistics Canada (2016). "Fertility: Fewer Children, Older Moms." *The Daily: Canadian Megatrends,* cat. no. 11-630-X. Ottawa, ON: Minister of Industry.

Statistics Canada (2017a). *2016 Census of Population,* cat. no. 98-400-X2016028. Ottawa, ON: Minister of Industry.

Statistics Canada (2017b, Aug. 2). "Young Adults Living with Their Parents in Canada in 2016." *Census in Brief,* cat. no. 98-200-X2016008. Ottawa, ON: Minister of Industry.

Statistics Canada (2019). Table 17-10-0060-01. Estimate of population as of July 1st, by marital status or legal marital status. Ottawa, ON: Minister of Industry.

Statistics Canada (n.d.). *Canadian Vital Statistics, Birth Database, Survey 3231.* Ottawa, ON: Minister of Industry.

Statistics Canada (n.d.). Table 39-10-0008-01. Vital statistics, divorces. Ottawa, ON: Minister of Industry.

Statistics Canada (n.d.). Table 13-10-0416-01. Live births, by age of mother. Ottawa, ON: Minister of Industry.

Statistics Canada (n.d.). Table 11-10-0017-01. Census families by family type and family composition including before and after-tax median income of the family. Ottawa, ON: Minister of Industry.

Tang, Jackie, Nora Galbraith, & Johnny Truong (2019, Mar. 6). Living alone in Canada. *Insights on Canadian Society.* Statistics Canada cat. no. 75-006-X. Ottawa, ON: Minister of Industry.

TNS Canadian Facts (2003). *Public Divided About Definition of Marriage: Results of a Public Opinion Poll on Same-Sex Marriage.* www.tns-cf.com/news/03.09.05-samesex-charts.pdf

Truth Commission into Genocide in Canada (2001). *The Untold Story of the Genocide of Aboriginal Peoples by Church and State in Canada.* http://canadiangenocide.nativeweb.org/genocide.pdf

Chapter 11

Anderson, Karen L. (1991). *Chain Her by One Foot: The Subjugation of Women in Seventeenth-Century New France.* London: Routledge.

Aristotle (2000). *Politics.* Mineola, NY: Dover Publications.

Battiste, Marie (1997). "Mi'kmaq Socialization Patterns." In L. Choyce & R. Joe (eds), *Anthology of Mi'kmaq Writers.* East Lawrencetown, NS: Pottersfield.

Benton-Banai, Edward (1988). *The Mishomis Book: The Voice of the Ojibway.* St Paul, MN: Red School House, Indian Country Communications.

Brym, Robert, Keith Neuman, & Rhonda Lenton (2018). *2018 Survey of Jews in Canada: Final Report.* Toronto: Environics Institute.

Dawson, Lorne L. (1998), *Comprehending Cults: The Sociology of New Religious Movements*. Don Mills, ON: Oxford University Press.

Dempsey, L. James (1995). "Alberta's Indians in WWII." In Ken Tingley (ed.), *King and Country, Alberta in the Second World War*. Edmonton: Provincial Museum of Alberta.

Durkheim, Émile (1951). *Suicide: A Study in Sociology*. Trans. John A. Spaulding & George Simpson. New York: The Free Press of Glencoe. (Original work published 1897)

Durkheim, Émile (1995). *The Elementary Forms of the Religious Life*. Trans. Karen Fields. New York: Simon & Schuster. (Original work published 1912). Reprinted with permission of Free Press of Simon & Schuster, Inc. Copyright © 1995 by Karen E. Field. All rights reserved.

Dusenberry, Verne (1998). *The Montana Cree: A Study in Religious Persistence*. Norman: University of Oklahoma.

Fields, Karen (1995). Introduction. In Karen Fields (trans.), *The Elementary Forms of the Religious Life*, by Émile Durkheim. New York: Simon & Schuster.

Flint, David (1975). *The Hutterites: A Study in Prejudice*. Don Mills, ON: Oxford University Press.

Gilbert, Dennis (1988). *Sandanistas: The Party and the Revolution*. Oxford: Basil Blackwell.

Humphreys, Margaret (1995). *Empty Cradles*. New York: Doubleday. Reprinted by permission of The Random House Group Ltd..

Husain, Mir Zohair (1995). *Global Islamic Politics*. New York: HarperCollins. © 1995. Reprinted by permission of Pearson Education, Inc., Upper Saddle River, NY.

Iker, Jack (2003, Aug 1). "A Church's Choice." *WCNY Online NewsHour*. www.pbs.org/newshour/bb/religion/july-dec03/episcopalian_8-1.html

Kirkby, Mary-Ann (2007). *I Am Hutterite*. Prince Albert, SK: Polka Dot.

Marx, Karl (1976). *Introduction to A Contribution to the Critique of Hegel's Philosophy of Right*. Trans. Joseph O'Malley. New York: Oxford. (Original work published 1844)

McClintock, Walter (1910). *The Old North Trail. Life, Legends, and Religion of the Blackfeet Indians*. London: Macmillan.

Merton, Robert K. (1968). *Social Theory and Social Structure*. New York: Free Press. (Original work published 1949)

Miller, J.R. (1996). *Shingwauk's Vision: A History of Native Residential Schools*. Toronto: University of Toronto Press.

Nonaka, K., T. Miura, & K. Peter (1993). "Low Twinning Rate and Seasonal Effects on Twinning in a Fertile Population, the Hutterites." *International Journal of Biometeorology* 37 (3), pp. 145–50.

Poirier, Agnes (2016, Aug. 17). "Burkini Beach Row Puts French Values to Test." *BBC News* (online).

Robinson, Angela (2002). "Ta'n Teli-ktlamsitasit ('Ways of Believing'): Mi'kmaw Religion in Eskasoni, Nova Scotia." *Open Access Dissertations and Theses*, Paper 1477. http://digital-commons.mcmaster.ca/opendissertations/1477

Russell, George (2001, June 24). "Cover Stories Taming the Liberation Theologians." *Time Magazine World*. www.time.com/time/magazine/article/0,0171,141037,00.html

Siddiqui, Haroon (2006). *Being Muslim*. Toronto: Groundwood Books.

Smith, James M. (2007). *Ireland's Magdalen Laundries and the Nation's Architecture of Containment*. Notre Dame, IN: University of Notre Dame.

Statistics Canada (2003). *2001 Census of Population – Religions in Canada*, cat. no. 95F0450XCB2001005. Ottawa, ON: Minister of Industry.

Statistics Canada (2013). *2011 National Household Survey*, cat. no. 99-010-X2011032. Ottawa, ON: Minister of Industry.

Steckley, John, & Bryan Cummins (2008). *Full Circle: Canada's First Nations*, 2nd edn. Toronto: Pearson.

Van Poppel, Frans, & Lincoln H. Day (1996). "A Test of Durkheim's Theory of Suicide—Without Committing the 'Ecological Fallacy.'" *American Sociological Review* 61, pp. 500–7.

Van Tubergen, Frank, Manfred te Grotenhuis, & Wout Ultee (2005). "Denominatino, Religious Context, and Suicide: Neo-Durkheimian Multilevel Explanations Tested with Individual and Contextual Data." *American Journal of Sociology* 111 (3), pp. 797–823.

Weber, Max. (1930). *The Protestant Ethic and the Spirit of Capitalism*. Trans. Talcott Parsons. New York: Charles Scribner's Sons. (Original work published 1904)

Chapter 12

Anyon, Jean (1980). "Social Class and the Hidden Curriculum of Work." *Journal of Education* 162 (1), pp. 67–92.

Archibald, Jo-ann (2008). *Indigenous Storywork: Educating the Heart, Mind, Body, and Spirit*. Vancouver: UBC Press.

Archibald, Jo-ann (2019, Jan. 14). "My Dreams for Indigenous Education in Canada." *The Tyee* (online).

Bowles, S., & H. Gintis (1976). *Schooling in Capitalist America: Educational Reform and Contradictions of Economic Life*. New York: Basic.

Cameron, Linda, & Lee Bartel (2008). *Homework Realities: A Canadian Study of Parental Opinions and Attitudes*. Technical Report. Toronto: University of Toronto, Ontario Institute for Studies in Education.

Casey, Liam (2015, June 9). "Ontario Teachers Need More Training on Aboriginal Issues: Report." *CBC News* (online).

Dei, George (1996). *Anti-Racism Education: Theory and Practice*. Halifax: Fernwood.

Dei, George, & Agnes Calliste (2000). *Power Knowledge and Anti-Racism Education: A Critical Reader*. Halifax: Fernwood.

Drolet, Marie (2005, Feb.). "Participation in Post-secondary Education in Canada: Has the Role of Parental Income and Education Changed over the 1990s?" Analytical Studies Branch Research Paper Series. Statistics Canada cat. no. 11F0019MIE. Ottawa, ON: Minister of Industry.

Drolet, Marie (2017, Nov. 1). "Linking Labour Demand and Labour Supply: Job Vacancies and the Unemployed." *Insights on Canadian Society*. Statistics Canada cat. no. 75-006-X. Ottawa, ON: Minister of Industry.

Dubson, Michael, ed. (2001). *Ghosts in the Classroom: Stories of College Adjunct Faculty—and the Price We All Pay*. Boston: Camel's Back.

Foucault, Michel (1977). *Discipline and Punish: The Birth of the Prison*. New York: Pantheon.

Foucault, Michel (1980). "Two Lectures." In Colin Gordon (ed.), *Power/Knowledge*, pp. 78–108. New York: Pantheon.

Frenette, Marc (2017, Apr. 10). "Postsecondary Enrolment by Parental Income: Recent National and Provincial Trends." *Economic Insights*. Statistics Canada cat. no. 11-626-X. Ottawa, ON: Minister of Industry.

Hearn, Alison, & Gus Van Harten (2017, Oct.). Report of the CAUT Ad Hoc Investigatory Committee into the Enbridge Centre for Corporate Sustainability at the University of Calgary. Ottawa, ON: CAUT.

Helmes-Hayes, Rick (2010). *Measuring the Mosaic: An Intellectual Biography of John Porter*. Toronto: University of Toronto Press.

Henry, Frances, & Carol Tator (2006). *The Colour of Democracy: Racism in Canada*. Toronto: Nelson Thomson.

King, Alan, Wendy Warren, & Sharon Miklas (2004). "Study of Accessibility to Ontario Law Schools." Executive Summary of the Report Submitted to Deans of Law at Osgood Hall, York University; University of Ottawa; Queen's University; University of Western Ontario; University of Windsor. Queen's University: Social Program Evaluation Group.

Livingstone, David W. (2004). *The Education–Jobs Gap: Underemployment or Economic Democracy*, 2nd edn. Toronto: Garamond.

Malacrida, Claudia (2015). *A Special Hell: Institutional Life in Alberta's Eugenic Years*. Toronto: University of Toronto Press.

McCartney, Kevin D., & Garry Gray (2018). "Big Oil U: Canadian Media Coverage of Corporate Obstructionism and Institutional Corruption at the University of Calgary." *Canadian Journal of Sociology* 43 (4).

Newson, Janice, & Howard Buchbinder (1988). *The University Means Business: Universities, Corporations and Academic Work*. Toronto: Garamond.

Noble, David (1998). "Digital Diploma Mills: The Automation of Higher Education." *Science as Culture* 7 (3), pp. 355–68.

Noble, David (2002). *Digital Diploma Mills: The Automation of Higher Education*. Toronto: Between the Lines.

Oakes, Jeannie (2005). *Keeping Track: How Schools Structure Inequality*, 2nd edn. New Haven, CT: Yale University Press.

Richards, John, Jennifer Hove, & Kemi Afolabi (2008, Dec.). *Understanding the Aboriginal/Non-Aboriginal Gap in Student Performance: Lessons from British Columbia*. Commentary 276. Toronto: C.D. Howe Institute.

Saewyc, Elizabeth, Chiaki Konishi, Hilary Rose, & Yuko Homma (2014). "School-Based Strategies to Reduce Suicidal Ideation, Suicide Attempts, and Discrimination among Sexual Minority and Heterosexual Adolescents in Western Canada." *International Journal of Child, Youth, and Family Studies* 5 (1).

Schecter, Stephen (1977). "Capitalism, Class, and Educational Reform in Canada." In L. Panitch (ed.), *The Canadian State: Political Economy and Political Power*. Toronto: University of Toronto Press.

Statistics Canada (2018, Dec. 4). "Labour Market Outcomes for College and University Graduates, Class of 2010 to 2014." *The Daily*. Ottawa, ON: Minister of Industry.

Statistics Canada (2019). Table 37-10-0045-01. "Canadian and international tuition fees by level of study." Ottawa, ON: Minister of Industry.

Statistics Canada (2019). Table 37-10-0003-01. "Canadian undergraduate tuition fees by field of study." Ottawa, ON: Minister of Industry.

Thompson, Carol (2006). "Unintended Lessons: Plagiarism and the University." *Teachers College Record* 108 (12), pp. 2439–49.

Wilt, James (2017, Oct. 13). "Five Things We Learned from the Damning Report on the University of Calgary's Connections with Enbridge." *The Narwhal* (online).

Chapter 13

Anderson, Karen (1996). *Sociology: A Critical Introduction*. Toronto: Nelson.

Broesterhuizen, Marcel (2008). "Worlds of Difference: An Ethical Analysis of Choices in the Field of Deafness." *Ethical Perspectives: Journal of the European Centre for Ethics* 15 (1), pp. 103–31.

Canadian Association of the Deaf (CAD) (2012). Issues & Positions: Deaf Culture vs. Medicalization. www.cad.ca/deaf_culture_vs._medicalization.php

Canadian Institute for Health Information (2007). Canada's Health Care Providers, 2007. Ottawa, ON: CIHI.

Chang, Virginia, & Nicholas Christakis (2002). "Medical Modelling of Obesity: A Transition from Action to Experience in a 20th Century American Medical Textbook." *Sociology of Health and Illness* 24 (2), pp. 151–77.

Cloutier, Elisabeth, Chantal Grondin, & Amélie Lévesque (2018, Nov. 28). *Canadian Survey on Disability, 2017: Concepts and Methods Guide*. Statistics Canada cat. no. 89-654-X2018001. Ottawa, ON: Minister of Industry.

Coupland, Douglas (1991). *Generation X: Tales for an Accelerated Culture*. New York: St Martin's Press.

Emke, Ivan (2002). "Patients in the New Economy: The 'Sick Role' in a Time of Economic Discipline." *Animus: A Philosophical Journal for Our Time* 7, pp. 81–93.

"EpiPen Price Furor Heats up in US" (2016, Aug. 24). *CBC News* (online).

Etzioni, Amitai (1986, Aug. 24). "The Fast-Food Factories: McJobs Are Bad for Kids." *The Washington Post*.

Fadiman, Anne (1997). *The Spirit Catches You and You Fall Down. A Hmong Child, Her American Doctors, and the Collision of Two Cultures*. New York: Farrar, Straus and Giroux.

Groce, Nora E. (1999). "Disability in a Cross-Cultural Perspective: Rethinking Disability." *The Lancet* 354 (9180), pp. 756–7.

Grygier, Pat (1994). *A Long Way from Home: The Tuberculosis Epidemic among the Inuit*. Montreal: McGill-Queen's University Press.

Haig, Terry (2019, Aug. 5). "Cancer Professionals Are Worried about Shortage of Some Important Drugs." RCI (Radio Canada International).

Hart, Julian Tudor (1971, Feb.). "The Inverse Care Law." *The Lancet* 27, pp. 405–12.

Hedden, Lindsay, M. Ruth Lavergne, Kimberlyn M. McGrail, Michael R. Law, Lucy Cheng, Megan A. Ahuja, & Morris L. Barer (2017, Dec. 11). "Patterns of Physician Retirement and Pre-retirement Activity: A Population-Based Cohort Study." *Canadian Medical Association Journal* 189 (49), pp. 1517–23.

Hubert, Nadine (1985, Aug. 14). "Sterilization and the Mentally Retarded." *The Interim*. www.theinterim.com/issues/bioethics/sterilization-and-the-mentally-retarded

Illich, Ivan (1976). *Medical Nemesis: The Limits of Medicine*. London: Penguin.

Ingstad, B. (1988). "Coping Behavior of Disabled Persons and Their Families: Cross-Cultural Perspectives from Norway and Botswana." International Journal of Rehabilitation Research 11, pp. 351–9.

Kleinman, Arthur (1995). *Writing at the Margin: Discourse between Anthropology and Medicine*. Berkeley: University of California Press.

Koos, E.L. (1954). *The Health of Regionsville: What the People Thought and Did About It*. New York: Columbia University Press.

Kral, Andrej, & Gerard M. O'Donoghue (2010). "Profound Deafness in Childhood." *New England Journal of Medicine* 363, pp. 1439–50. DOI:10.1056/NEJMra0911225

Lane, Harlan L. (1992). *The Mask of Benevolence: Disabling the Deaf Community*. New York: Alfred A. Knopf.

Lane, Harlan L. (1993). "The Medicalisation of Cultural Deafness in Historical Perspective." In Renate Fischer & Harlan L. Lane (Eds), *Looking Back: A Reader on the History of Deaf Communities and Their Sign Languages*, pp. 479–94. International Studies on Sign Language and Communication of the Deaf. Hamburg: Signum.

Leung, Carrianne, & Jian Guan (2004). "Yellow Peril Revisited: Impact of SARS on the Chinese and Southeast Asian Canadian

Communities." Toronto: Chinese Canadian National Council, www.ccnc.ca

McQuaig, Linda (2004). "Closed Shop Gives Doc the Hammer in New Brunswick Strike." *Straight Goods.* www.straightgoods.com/McQuaig/010122.shtml

Madiros, M. (1989). "Conception of Childhood Disability among Mexican-American Parents." *Medical Anthropology* 12, pp. 55–68.

Malicki, M. (2007). "Code Blue! (Or Pink!): Perceptions of Men and Women Physicians in Specific Gender-Dominated Medical Subfields." *UW-L Journal of Undergraduate Research*, X, 1–3.

Morris, Stuart, Gail Fawcett, Laurent Brisebois, & Jeffrey Hughes (2018, Nov. 28). "A Demographic, Employment, and Income Profile of Canadians with Disabilities Aged 15 Years and Over, 2017." *Canadian Survey on Disability Reports.* Statistics Canada cat. no. 89-654-X. Ottawa, ON: Minister of Industry.

Morrison, David (2010). "Should Disability Be Considered a Master Status?" Blog post (1 February), retrieved: http://disabilities.blogs.starnewsonline.com/10988/should-disability-be-considered-a-master-status

Ontario Medical Association (2002, April). "Position Paper on Physician Workforce Policy and Planning." Toronto, ON: OMA.

Parsons, Talcott (1951). *The Social System.* New York: Free Press.

Payer, Lynn (1992). *Disease-Mongers: How Doctors, Drug Companies, and Insurers Are Making You Feel Sick.* New York: Wiley.

Ross, Shelley (2019). "The Feminization of Medicine: Issues and Implications." In Earle Waugh, Shelley Ross, Shirley Schipper (Eds), *Female Doctors in Canada: Experience and Culture*, pp. 5–23. Toronto: University of Toronto Press.

Waugh, Earle, Shelly Ross, & Shirley Schipper (2019). "Preface: Why a Book about Female Doctors?" In Earle Waugh, Shelley Ross, Shirley Schipper (Eds), *Female Doctors in Canada: Experience and Culture*, pp. ix–x. Toronto: University of Toronto Press.

"The Spectrum of Disability" (1999, Aug. 28). *The Lancet* 354, p. 693.

Statistics Canada (2013). "National Household Survey Dictionary, 2011," cat. no. 99-000-X2011001. Ottawa, ON: Minister of Industry.

Statistics Canada (2017, Sept. 27). "Primary Health Care Providers, 2016." *Health Fact Sheets.* Cat. no. 82-625-X. Ottawa, ON: Minister of Industry.

Statistics Canada (2018, Nov. 28). "Canadian Survey on Disability, 2017." *The Daily.* Ottawa, ON: Minister of Industry.

Statistics Canada (2019). Table 13-10-0096-01. "Health characteristics, annual estimates." Ottawa, ON: Minister of Industry.

Weeks, Carly (2019, Feb. 27). "Anti-vaccine Group Launches Billboard Campaign in Toronto and Surrounding Area." *The Globe and Mail* (online).

Welsch, Robert K., & Luis A. Vivanco (2019). *Asking Questions about Cultural Anthropology: A Concise Introduction.* New York: Oxford University Press.

Zola, Irving K. (2003). *Missing Pieces: A Chronicle of Living with a Disability*, 2nd edn. Philadelphia, PA: Temple University Press.

Chapter 14

Alberta Cancer Board (2009). *Cancer Incidence in Fort Chipewyan, Alberta, 1995–2006.* Alberta Cancer Board: Division of Population Health and Information Surveillance (online).

Basij-Rasikh, Shabana (2018, Oct. 9). "Want to Fight Climate Change? Educate a Girl." Ted.com. https://ideas.ted.com/want-to-fight-climate-change-educate-a-girl

Bookchin, Murray (1996). *The Philosophy of Social Ecology: Essays on Dialectical Naturalism.* Montreal: Black Rose.

Canada, 40th Parliament, 2nd Session (2009, June 11). Standing Committee on Environment and Sustainable Development: Evidence. www.parl.gc.ca/House Publications/Publication.aspx?DocId=3983714&Language=E&Mode=1

Canadian Press (2019, April 23). "'Eat It If You Want To': Filipino President Duterte Lashes Out over Canadian Cargo of Trash." *CBC News* (online)

CBC News (2012, Sept. 14). "Canada Won't Oppose Asbestos Limits: Federal Tories Reverse Course and Won't Veto Substance's Listing in Rotterdam Convention" (online).

CBC News (2015, Oct. 29). "5 Things to Know about China's 1-Child Policy." *CBC News* (online).

Central Intelligence Agency (CIA) (n.d.). "Country Comparison: Exports." World Factbook. www.cia.gov/library/publications/the-world-factbook/rankorder/2078rank.html

Clairmont, Donald H., & Dennis W. Magill (1999). *Africville: The Life and Death of a Canadian Black Community.* Toronto: Canadian Scholars' Press.

Grant, Shantay (2018). *Africville.* Toronto: Groundwood.

Grant, Tavia (2015, July 1). "Ottawa Reverses Stand on Health Risks of Asbestos in 'Landmark Shift.'" *The Globe and Mail* (online).

Gutierrez, Richard (2016, March 2). "Canada's Waste Trade Policy: A Global Concern." *Philippine Daily Inquirer* (online).

Harney, Alexandra (2009). *The China Price: The True Cost of Chinese Competitive Advantage.* New York: Penguin.

Hollingsworth, Joseph, Brenna Copeland, & Jeremiah X. Johnson (2019, Aug. 2). "Are E-Scooters Polluters? The Environmental Impacts of Shared Dockless Electric Scooters." *Environmental Research Letters* 14 (8).

Hutchison, George, & Dick Wallace (1977). *Grassy Narrows.* Toronto: Van Nostrand Rinehold.

Joint Policy Committee of the Societies of Epidemiology (JPC-SE) (2012, June 4). "Position Statement on Asbestos." www.jpc-se.org/documents/01.JPC-SE-Position_Statement_on_Asbestos-June_4_2012-Summary_and_Appendix_A_English.pdf

Kaufman, Alexander C. (2019, July 12). "New Orleans' Levees Face Biggest Test since Hurricane Katrina." *Huffington Post* (online).

Lalonde, Michelle (2007, Nov. 9). "Town Built on Asbestos Downplays Health Risks." Montreal *Gazette.*

Lavoie, Judith (2018, Dec. 21). "Industry-Hired Experts Downplay Impacts of Major Projects: UBC Study." *The Narwhal.* https://thenarwhal.ca/industry-hired-experts-downplay-impacts-of-major-projects-ubc-study

Liao, S. Matthew, Anders Sandberg, & Rebecca Roache (2012). "Human Engineering and Climate Change." *Ethics, Policy, and the Environment* 15 (2), pp. 206–11.

McCarthy, Shawn, & Marieke Walsh (2019, Aug. 20). "Want to Talk about Climate Change during the Federal Election? You'll Have to Register for That." *The Globe and Mail* (online).

Murray, Cathryn Clarke, Janson Wong, Gerald G. Singh, Megan Mach, Jackie Lerner, Bernardo Ranieri, Guillaume Peterson St-Laurent, Alice Guimaraes, & Kai M.A. Chan (2018, June). "The Insignificance of Thresholds in Environmental Impact Assessment: An Illustrative Case Study in Canada." *Environmental Management* 61 (6), pp. 1062–71.

Oreskes, Naomi, & Erik M. Conway (2010). *Merchants of Doubt: How a Handful of Scientists Obscured the Truth on Issues from Tobacco Smoke to Global Warming.* New York: Bloomsbury.

Perkel, Colin N. (2002). *Well of Lies: The Walkerton Tragedy.* Toronto: McClelland & Stewart.

Porter, Jody (2016, June 20). "'Guilt' Drives Former Dryden, Ont. Mill Worker to Reveal His Part in Dumping Toxic Mercury." *CBC News* (online).

Prince, Samuel Henry (1920). *Catastrophe and Social Change: Based upon a Sociological Study of the Halifax Disaster.* New York: Columbia University Press.

Prokopchuk, Matt (2019, June 7). "Grassy Narrows Leadership to Review Ottawa's Latest Mercury Poisoning Care Home Agreement." *CBC News* (online).

Rabson, Mia (2018, Oct. 17). "Canada's Ban on Asbestos to Take Effect but Mining Residues Are Exempt." *Financial Post* (online).

Robin, Marie-Monique (2010). *The World According to Monsanto: Pollution, Politics, and Power; An Investigation into One of the World's Most Controversial Companies.* Melbourne: Spinifex. Copyright © 2008 by Editions La Decouverte/Arte Edition. English translation © 2010 by The New Press. Reprinted by permission of The New Press. www.thenewpress.com

Shkilnyk, Anastasia M. (1985). *A Poison Stronger Than Love: The Destruction of an Ojibwa Community.* New Haven, CT: Yale University Press.

Tataryn, Lloyd. (1976, June). "The Tortured Future of Elliott Lake." *Saturday Night* [magazine].

Tataryn, Lloyd (1979). *Dying for a Living.* Ottawa: Deneau and Greenberg.

Tataryn, Lloyd. (1983) *Formaldehyde on Trial: The Politics of Health in a Chemical Society.* Toronto: Lorimer.

Wiley, Elizabeth (2019, May). "The Unseen Impacts of Climate Change on Mental Health." *BC Medical Journal* 61 (4).

Wynes, Seth, & Kimberly A. Nicholas (2017). "The Climate Change Mitigation Gap: Education and Government Recommendations Miss the Most Effective Individual Actions." *Environmental Research Letters* 12.

Yan, Sophia (2017, Feb. 27). "'Made in China' Isn't So Cheap Anymore, and That Could Spell Headache for Beijing." *CNBC* (online).

Chapter 15

Bregman, Rutger (2016). *Utopia for Realists: The Case for a Universal Basic Income, Open Boarders, and a 15-Hour Workweek.* The Correspondent (Kindle edition).

Brym, Robert J. (2003). "Note on the Discipline: The Decline of the Canadian Sociology and Anthropology Association." *Canadian Journal of Sociology* 28 (3), pp. 411–26.

Chomsky, Noam (2004). *Hegemony or Survival: America's Quest for Global Dominance.* New York: Henry Holt.

Comte, Auguste (1853). *The Positive Philosophy of August Comte.* Trans. & ed. Harriet Martineau. Longon: Longmans.

Dahl, Robert A. (1956, 2006). *A Preface to Democratic Theory.* University of Chicago Press.

Durkheim, Émile (1965). *The Elementary Forms of Religious Life.* New York: Free Press. (Original work published 1912)

Grant, George (1965). *Lament for a Nation: The Defeat of Canadian Nationalism.* Toronto: McClelland & Stewart.

Grant, George (1969). *Technology and Empire: Perspectives on North America.* Toronto: House of Anansi.

Grenier, Éric (2019, June 30). "Conflicted and Worried: CBC News Poll Takes a Snapshot of Canadians ahead of Fall Election." *CBC News* (online).

Hamilton, Lawrence, Cynthia Duncan, & Richard Haedrich (2004). "Social/Ecological Transformation in Northwest Newfoundland." *Population and Environment* 25 (3), pp. 195–215.

Kaizuka, Shigeki (2002). *Confucius: His Life and Thought.* Mineola, NY: Dover. (Original work published 1956)

Kroker, Arthur, & Michael A. Weinstein (1995). *Data Trash: The Theory of the Virtual Class.* Montreal: New World Perspectives.

Laslett, Peter (1971). *The World We Have Lost.* London: Methuen.

Lieberson, Stanley (2000). *A Matter of Taste: How Names, Fashions and Cultures Change.* New Haven, CT: Yale University Press.

Malik, Kenan (2015, Jan. 3). "Radical Islam, Nihilist Rage." *The New York Times* (online).

Manji, Irshad (2003). *The Trouble with Islam: A Wake Up Call for Honesty and Change.* Toronto: Random House. Copyright © 2003, 2005 Irshad Manji. Reprinted by permission of Random House Canada.

McKenzie-Sutter, Holly (2019, April 2). "Small Rebound for Newfoundland's Northern Cod, but Stock Still in Critical Zone." *Toronto Star* (online).

Mills, C. Wright (1956). *The Power Elite.* New York: Oxford.

Morgan, Lewis Henry (1964). *Ancient Society or Researches in the Lines of Human Progress from Savagery through Barbarism to Civilization.* Cambridge, MA: Harvard University Press. (Original work published 1877)

Nisbet, Robert A. (1969). *Social Change and History: Aspects of the Western Theory of Development.* Oxford: Oxford University Press.

Parsons, Talcott (1966). *Societies: Evolutionary and Comparative Perspectives.* Englewood Cliffs, NJ: Prentice-Hall.

Robertson, Roland (1997. *Globalization and Indigenous Culture.* Institute for Japanese Culture and Classics. Kokugakuin University.

SAGE Publications (2013, Sept. 4). "Tattoos Reduce Chances of Getting a Job." *Science Daily* (online).

Sale, Kirkpatrick (1980). *Human Scale.* New York: Coward, McCann & Geoghegan.

Sale, Kirkpatrick (1996). *Rebels against the Future: The Luddites and Their War on the Industrial Revolution—Lessons for the Computer Age.* Cambridge, MA: Perseus.

Sale, Kirkpatrick (2005, Feb.). "Imperial Entropy: Collapse of the American Empire." *CounterPunch* 22.

Smith, Dorothy (1990). *The Conceptual Practices of Power: A Feminist Sociology of Knowledge.* Toronto: University of Toronto Press.

Spengler, Oswald (1918–22). *The Decline of the West.* New York: Alfred A. Knopf.

Steger, Manfred B. (2003). *Globalization: A Very Short Introduction.* Oxford: Oxford University Press.

Thornhill Verma, Jenn (2019, July 2). "Cod and the Fishery: Down, but Not Out." *The Independent* (online).

Weiner, Jonathan (1995). *The Beak of the Finch: A Story of Evolution in Our Time.* New York: Alfred A. Knopf.

Index